Essential Maths
Pure Mathematics Book 2

Lauren Gurney
David Rayner
Paul Williams

El… ion

First published 2018 by
Elmwood Education Ltd
Unit 5 Mallow Park
Watchmead
Welwyn Garden City
Herts AL7 1GX
Tel. 01707 333232

British Library Cataloguing in publication Data

Elmwood Education
The moral rights of the author have been asserted.
Database right Elmwood Education (maker)

ISBN 9781 906 622 701

Typeset and illustrated by Tech-Set Ltd, Gateshead, Tyne & Wear

CONTENTS

Part 10 Differentiation 2

Part 11 Integration

Part 12 Vectors

Part 13 Proof by contradiction

PREFACE

This book is for students working towards A Level Mathematics. Together with Book 1 it covers all the Pure Mathematics necessary for the full A Level. It can be used in the classroom, and also contains sufficient explanations and worked examples for students who are working on their own. The exercises are plentiful, and graded in difficulty, to allow students to build confidence where necessary, and to extend themselves where possible.

The work is collected into sections on Algebra, Coordinate Geometry, Binomial Expansion, Calculus, Trigonometry, Exponentials and Logarithms, Vectors and Proof, in line with the 2017 syllabus, and is suitable for use by students studying under any of the main examination boards.

Mathematics can be a deeply rewarding subject, provided that the level of difficulty is just right. Pupils need to experience plenty of success in order to maintain their enthusiasm, and they also need the opportunity to stretch their understanding. This book provides a good number of straightforward questions aimed at building confidence, as well as plenty of more demanding problems for those pupils who feel ready for the challenge.

In order to prepare students fully, a section of past examination questions has been included at the end of each chapter where available. Teachers will note that the specifications and questions set by all the main boards are very similar. This book can be used with confidence when preparing for the A Level examinations set by all the main boards.

Thanks are due to AQA, EDEXCEL, MEI and OCR for kindly allowing the use of questions from their past mathematics papers. The answers are solely the work of the authors and not ratified by the examining groups.

The authors are indebted to Sam Hartburn and Jonathan Stevens for their invaluable contributions to this book.

L. Gurney
D. Rayner
P. Williams

PART 1

Algebra and functions 1

1.1 Simplifying rational expressions

A rational expression is a fraction. We simplify algebraic fractions using the same rules that we use when simplifying numerical fractions.

Example 1

Simplify

a $\frac{12}{15}$ b $\frac{7a}{5a^2}$ c $\frac{3x+9}{6x}$

d $\frac{x^2+2x}{x+2}$ e $\frac{x^2+2x-3}{x^2+5x+6}$

a $\frac{12}{15}$. Dividing numerator and denominator by 3, we have $\frac{12}{15}=\frac{4}{5}$.

b $\frac{7a}{5a^2}$. Dividing numerator and denominator by a, we have $\frac{7a}{5a^2}=\frac{7}{5a}$

c $\frac{3x+9}{6x}$. A common mistake is often made with fractions like this. Do **not** cancel the xs.

Instead we write $\frac{3x+9}{6x}=\frac{3(x+3)}{6x}=\frac{(x+3)}{2x}$.

d Factorising the numerator, $\frac{x^2+2x}{x+2}=\frac{x(x+2)}{x+2}=x$

e Factorising $\frac{x^2+2x-3}{x^2+5x+6}=\frac{(x-1)(x+3)}{(x+2)(x+3)}=\frac{x-1}{x+2}$

EXERCISE 1A

Simplify as far as possible:

1 $\frac{24}{30}$ 2 $\frac{4a^2}{a}$ 3 $\frac{x}{3x}$ 4 $\frac{8x^2}{2x^2}$

5 $\frac{2a}{4b}$ 6 $\frac{6m}{2m}$ 7 $\frac{5ab}{10b}$ 8 $\frac{8ab^2}{4ab}$

9 $\frac{15y}{20y^2}$ 10 $\frac{11xy}{12x^2}$ 11 $\frac{8ya^2}{12a}$ 12 $\frac{12m^2n^2}{3mn^3}$

13 Sort these into four pairs of equivalent expressions:

A $\dfrac{x^2}{4x}$ B $\dfrac{x(x+1)}{x^2}$ C $\dfrac{x^2+x}{x^2-x}$ D $\dfrac{3x+6}{3x}$

E $\dfrac{x+1}{x}$ F $\dfrac{x+2}{x}$ G $\dfrac{x}{4}$ H $\dfrac{x+1}{x-1}$

In questions **14** to **29** simplify as far as possible:

14 $\dfrac{7a^2b}{35ab^2}$ **15** $\dfrac{(2a)^2}{4a}$ **16** $\dfrac{7yx}{8xy}$ **17** $\dfrac{3x}{4x-x^2}$

18 $\dfrac{5x+2x^2}{3x}$ **19** $\dfrac{9x+3}{3x}$ **20** $\dfrac{4a+5a^2}{5a}$ **21** $\dfrac{5ab}{15a+10a^2}$

22 $\dfrac{3x-x^2}{2x}$ **23** $\dfrac{12x+6}{6y}$ **24** $\dfrac{3(2x^2+5x)}{6x}$ **25** $\dfrac{xy+x^2y}{x}$

26 $\dfrac{5x^3+4x^2}{x(3x^2-2x)}$ **27** $\dfrac{a+4a^2}{ab+ab^2}$ **28** $\dfrac{4+8x+8x^2}{4x}$ **29** $\dfrac{54mn^2-27m^2n}{18(mn)^2}$

30 Look at each of the following and decide if the statement is 'true' or 'false':

a $\dfrac{4x^2+8}{2x}=\dfrac{4x+8}{2}$ **b** $\dfrac{x^2y+xy^2}{xy}=x+y$

c $\dfrac{4ab^2c^3}{a^3b^2c}=\dfrac{4c^2}{a^2}$ **d** $\dfrac{5x+6}{6y}=\dfrac{5x+1}{y}$

31 a Factorise the expression x^2-x-6.

b Hence simplify the expression $\dfrac{x^2-x-6}{(x+2)}$.

32 Simplify as far as possible:

a $\dfrac{x^2-3x-4}{x+1}$ **b** $\dfrac{x^2+x-6}{x^2+2x-3}$ **c** $\dfrac{x^2+3x-10}{x^2-4}$

d $\dfrac{x^2-3x}{x^2-2x-3}$ **e** $\dfrac{x^2+4x}{2x^2-10x}$ **f** $\dfrac{x^2+6x+5}{x^2-x-2}$

g $\dfrac{2x^2+x}{4x^2-1}$ **h** $\dfrac{2x^2-5x-3}{2x^2-3x-9}$ **i** $\dfrac{3x^2+x-4}{9x^2-16}$

33 Write the expression $\dfrac{x+\frac{1}{2}}{x+\frac{1}{3}}$ in a more simple form without fractions on the numerator and denominator.
[Hint: Multiply numerator and denominator by 6.]

34 Write the following in a more simple form without fractions:

a $\dfrac{x+\frac{1}{x}}{x}$ **b** $\dfrac{2x-\frac{1}{x}}{\frac{1}{x}}$ **c** $\dfrac{x-\frac{1}{2}}{\frac{1}{2}}$

d $\dfrac{3x + \frac{1}{4}}{\frac{1}{4}}$ **e** $\dfrac{5x - \frac{1}{3}}{\frac{1}{6}}$ **f** $\dfrac{\frac{1}{4} - x}{\frac{1}{2}}$

g $\dfrac{3x + \frac{1}{x}}{x + \frac{2}{x}}$ **h** $\dfrac{x - \frac{4}{x}}{x - 2}$ **i** $\dfrac{2x - 3}{4x - \frac{9}{x}}$

j $\dfrac{1 - \frac{1}{x^2}}{\frac{1}{x^2}}$ **k** $\dfrac{1 - \frac{4}{x^2}}{1 - \frac{2}{x}}$ **l** $\dfrac{1 + \frac{2}{x} - \frac{3}{x^2}}{1 + \frac{3}{x} - \frac{4}{x^2}}$

Addition and subtraction of algebraic fractions

Example 2

a Write as a single fraction $\dfrac{2}{x} + \dfrac{3}{y}$

The L.C.M. of x and y is xy.

$$\therefore \frac{2}{x} + \frac{3}{y} = \frac{2y}{xy} + \frac{3x}{xy} = \frac{2y + 3x}{xy}$$

b Write as a single fraction $\dfrac{4}{x} + \dfrac{5}{x - 1}$

The L.C.M. of x and $(x - 1)$ is $x(x - 1)$

$$\therefore \frac{4}{x} + \frac{5}{x - 1} = \frac{4(x - 1) + 5x}{x(x - 1)}$$

$$= \frac{9x - 4}{x(x - 1)}$$

EXERCISE 1B

1 Write as a single fraction:

a $\dfrac{2x}{5} + \dfrac{x}{5}$ **b** $\dfrac{2}{x} + \dfrac{1}{x}$ **c** $\dfrac{x}{7} + \dfrac{3x}{7}$ **d** $\dfrac{1}{7x} + \dfrac{3}{7x}$

e $\dfrac{5x}{8} + \dfrac{x}{4}$ **f** $\dfrac{5}{8x} + \dfrac{1}{4x}$ **g** $\dfrac{2x}{3} + \dfrac{x}{6}$ **h** $\dfrac{2}{3x} + \dfrac{1}{6x}$

2 Sort into four pairs of equivalent fractions:

A $\dfrac{x}{2} + \dfrac{x}{4}$ **B** $\dfrac{2}{x} + \dfrac{2}{x}$ **C** $\dfrac{9x}{8} - \dfrac{x}{4}$ **D** $\dfrac{7x}{8}$

E $\dfrac{5x}{x^2} - \dfrac{2}{x}$ **F** $\dfrac{3x}{4}$ **G** $\dfrac{3}{x}$ **H** $\dfrac{4}{x}$

3 Simplify:

a $\dfrac{3x}{4} + \dfrac{2x}{5}$ **b** $\dfrac{3}{4x} + \dfrac{2}{5x}$ **c** $\dfrac{3x}{4} - \dfrac{2x}{3}$

d $\dfrac{3}{4x} - \dfrac{2}{3x}$ **e** $\dfrac{x}{2} + \dfrac{x + 1}{3}$ **f** $\dfrac{x - 1}{3} + \dfrac{x + 2}{4}$

4 Work out these subtractions:

a $\frac{x+1}{3} - \frac{(2x+1)}{4}$ b $\frac{x-3}{3} - \frac{(x-2)}{5}$ c $\frac{(x+2)}{2} - \frac{(2x+1)}{7}$

5 Work out these additions and subtractions:

a $\frac{2x-1}{5} + \frac{x+3}{2}$ b $\frac{1}{x} + \frac{2}{x+1}$ c $\frac{3}{x-2} + \frac{4}{x}$

d $\frac{5}{x-2} + \frac{3}{x+3}$ e $\frac{7}{x+1} - \frac{3}{x+2}$ f $\frac{x}{2} + \frac{x+3}{x+2}$

Multiplication and division

The method is similar to that used when multiplying and dividing ordinary numerical fractions.

Example 3

a $x^2 \div \frac{x}{2} = x^2 \times \frac{2}{x} = 2x$

b $\frac{2a}{3x} \times \frac{2x^2}{5a} = \frac{4\cancel{a}x^{\cancel{2}}}{15\cancel{a}x} = \frac{4x}{15}$

c $\frac{(x-1)}{(x+2)} \div \frac{2(x-1)}{(x+3)} = \frac{\cancel{(x-1)}}{(x+2)} \times \frac{(x+3)}{2\cancel{(x-1)}}$

$$= \frac{(x+3)}{2(x+2)}$$

Exercise 1C

Simplify the following:

1 $\frac{3x}{2} \times \frac{2a}{3x}$ **2** $\frac{5mn}{3} \times \frac{2}{n}$ **3** $\frac{3y^2}{x^2} \times \frac{2x}{9y}$ **4** $\frac{5ab^2}{2} \times \frac{3}{2a^2b}$

5 $\frac{2}{a} \div \frac{a}{2}$ **6** $\frac{4x}{3} \div \frac{x}{2}$ **7** $\frac{x-1}{2} \div \frac{x+2}{2}$ **8** $\frac{x}{5} \times \frac{y^2}{x^2}$

9 $\frac{x-1}{4} \times \frac{x}{2x-2}$ **10** $\frac{x^2-4}{3} \times \frac{9}{x-2}$

Questions **11** onwards involve addition, subtraction, multiplication and division.

11 Copy and complete:

a $\frac{x^2}{3} \times \frac{\square}{x} = 2x$ b $\frac{8}{x} \div \frac{2}{x} = \square$ c $\frac{a}{3} + \frac{a}{3} = \frac{\square}{3}$

12 Sort these into four pairs of equivalent expressions:

A $\frac{x^2}{3x}$ B $\frac{x}{2} \times \frac{x}{2}$ C $\frac{12x+6}{6}$ D $\frac{x}{5} - \frac{2}{5}$

E $\frac{2x^2+x}{x}$ F $\frac{x(x+1)}{3x+3}$ G $\frac{x-2}{5}$ H $\frac{ax^2}{4a}$

13 Write as a single fraction in its simplest form:

a $\frac{5a}{7} \times \frac{14b}{15a}$ **b** $\frac{3pq}{5} \times \frac{10}{p^2}$ **c** $\frac{3y^2}{3} \times \frac{2x}{9y}$

d $\frac{2}{q} \div \frac{a}{2}$ **e** $\frac{5y}{2} \div \frac{y}{10}$ **f** $\frac{x}{4} \times \frac{2y}{x^2}$

g $\frac{a^2}{5} \div \frac{a}{10}$ **h** $\frac{x^2}{x^2 + 2x} \div \frac{x}{x + 2}$

14 Simplify the following:

a $\frac{x}{y} \times \frac{xy}{z} \times \frac{z}{x^2}$ **b** $\frac{ab}{x} \times \frac{xb^2}{a^2} \times \frac{a^2}{x}$

c $\frac{x^2 + 7x}{x^2 - 1} \times \frac{x + 1}{x + 7}$ **d** $\frac{\left(\frac{x}{y}\right)}{z} \times \frac{z^3}{x}$

15 Copy and complete:

a $\frac{x}{5} - \frac{\square}{\square} = \frac{x}{10}$ **b** $\frac{\square}{2} + \frac{x}{4} = \frac{7x}{4}$ **c** $\frac{3}{2x} - \frac{1}{8x} = \frac{\square}{8x}$

16 The perimeter of the rectangle shown is 24 units.
Form an equation and solve it to find x.

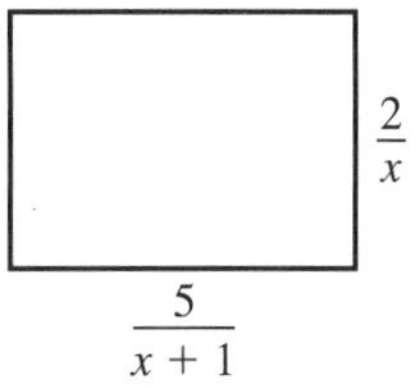

17 A rectangle measuring $\frac{3}{x}$ by $\frac{6}{x + 1}$ has an area of 75 square units.

Find x.

1.2 Functions and mappings

If A and B are non-empty sets then a *mapping* from A to B is a rule which associates an element of B with every element of A.

Here are two types of mappings.

Type 1

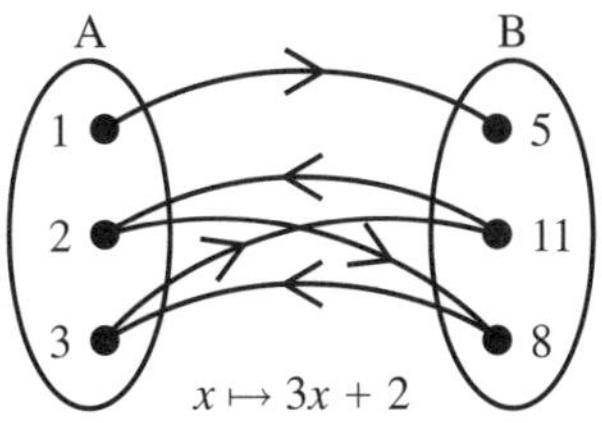

This is called a **one-to-one mapping**.

Type 2

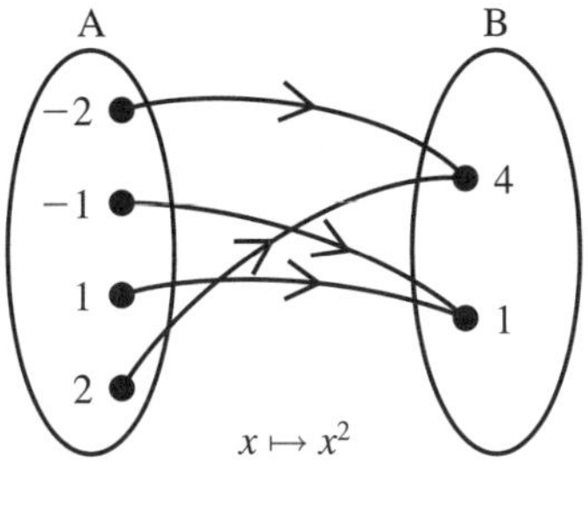

This is called a **two-to-one mapping** or a **many-to-one mapping**.

A *function* is a mapping which associates one and only one element of B with every element of A.
So a function is a one-to-one mapping or a many-to-one mapping.

The mapping below is *not* a function.

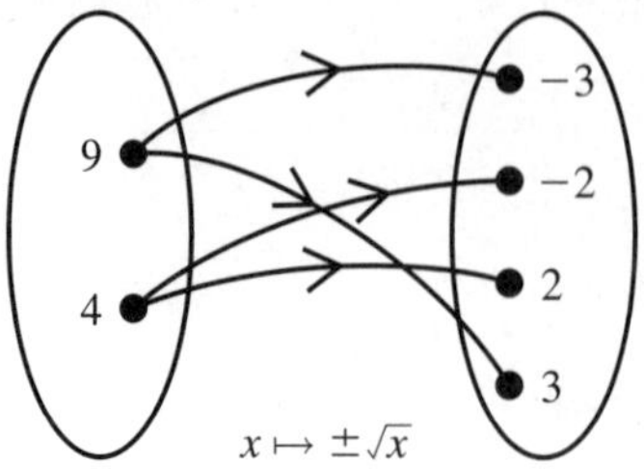

This is a one-to-many mapping.

Our main interest in this section is with *functions*.

The notations used for functions are either **a** $f(x) = x^2$
or **b** $f: x \mapsto x^2$

We use 'an arrow with a tail' $\mapsto$ to avoid confusion with a simple arrow such as '$x \to 0$' which means '*x tends towards 0*'.

The graph of $y = 2x + 1$ is a one-to-one mapping

The graph of $y = \frac{1}{x}$ is a one-to-one mapping

The graph of $y = \sin x$ is a many-to-one mapping.

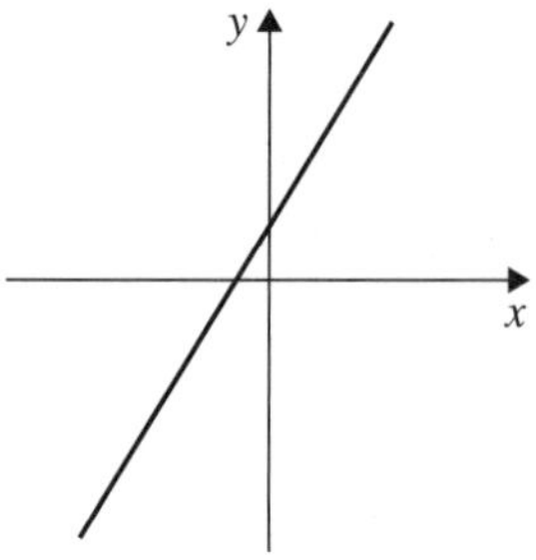

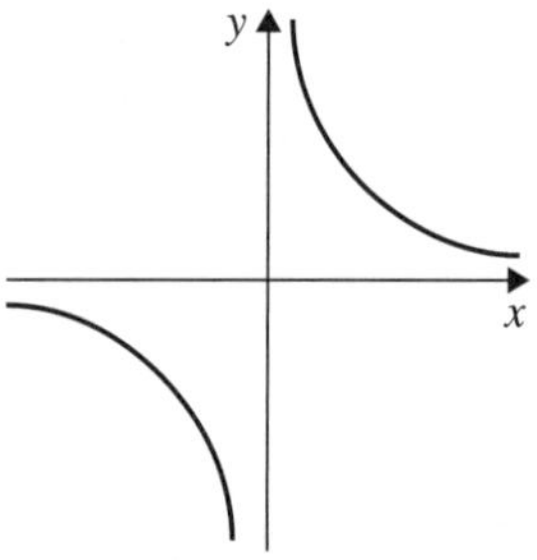

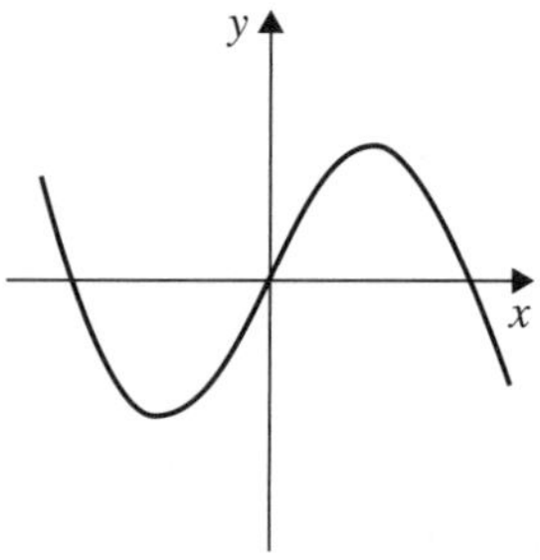

The Domain of a function is the set of all the points on which the function acts. These are the x-values on a graph.

The Range of a function is the set of all the points to which the function maps. These are the y-values on a graph.

In general the best way to find the range of a function is to sketch a graph of the function.

Example 1

Find the range of each function below.

a $f(x) = x^2$, for $x \in \mathbb{R}$

The domain $[x \in \mathbb{R}]$ is the set of all real numbers.
The graph of $f(x) = x^2$ is shown.
The range of the function is $f(x) \geqslant 0$.

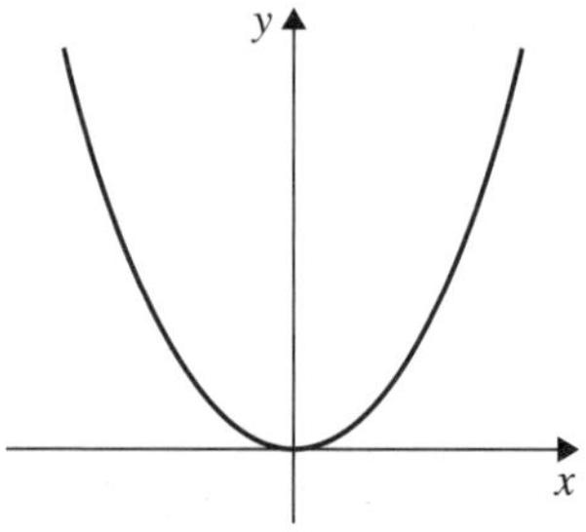

b $f(x) = 2x + 1$, for $x \in \mathbb{R}, x > 0$

The domain is all values of x greater than 0.
From the graph of $f(x) = 2x + 1$, we see that the range is $f(x) > 1$.
Notice that since $x = 0$ is not in the domain, the range is $f(x) > 1$ and *not* $f(x) \geqslant 1$.

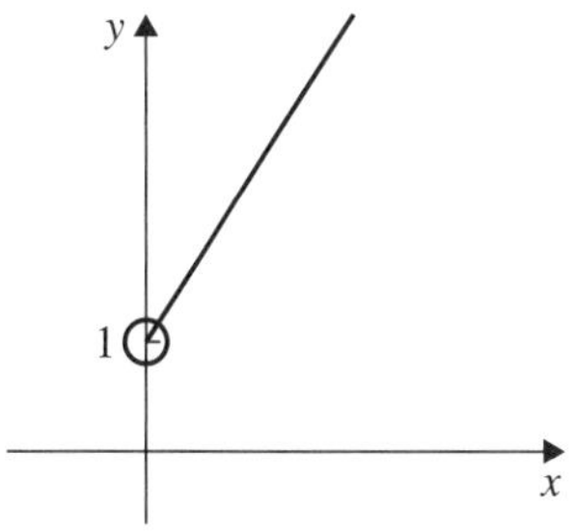

c $f(x) = \sin x$, for $0° \leqslant x \leqslant 360°$

The range of the function is $-1 \leqslant f(x) \leqslant 1$.

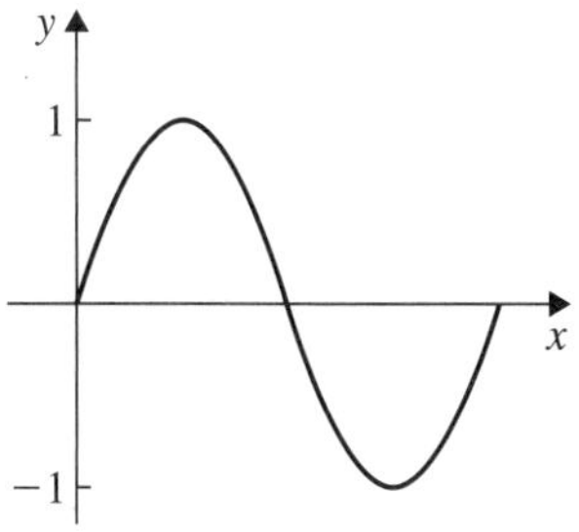

Exercise 1D

1 Decide which of these functions are one-to-one and which are many-to-one:

a $f: x \mapsto 2x - 5, \quad x \in \mathbb{R}$
b $f: x \mapsto x^2 + 2, \quad x \in \mathbb{R}$
c $f: x \mapsto \dfrac{1}{x}, \quad x \in \mathbb{R}, x \neq 0$
d $f: x \mapsto x^3, \quad x \in \mathbb{R}$
e $f: x \mapsto x(x - 1), \quad x \in \mathbb{R}$
f $f: x \mapsto \cos x, \quad 0° \leqslant x \leqslant 360°$
g $f: x \mapsto (x - 1)^2 + 2, \quad x \in \mathbb{R}$
h $f: x \mapsto x(x - 1)(x - 2), \quad x \in \mathbb{R}$
i $f: x \mapsto x^3 + 10, \quad x \in \mathbb{R}$
j $f: x \mapsto \sqrt{x}, \quad x \in \mathbb{R}, x \geqslant 0$

2 Find the range of each function:

a $f(x) = 2x + 1, \quad x \in \mathbb{R}, x \geqslant 0$
b $f(x) = x^2 + 2, \quad x \in \mathbb{R}$
c $f(x) = x + 1, \quad x \in \mathbb{R}, x \geqslant 0$
d $f(x) = x^3, \quad x \in \mathbb{R}, x \geqslant 0$
e $f(x) = \sin x, \quad 0° \leqslant x \leqslant 180°$
f $f(x) = x(x - 3), \quad 0 \leqslant x \leqslant 3$
g $f(x) = 5x - x^2, \quad 0 \leqslant x \leqslant 5$
h $f(x) = \sqrt{x}, \quad 0 \leqslant x \leqslant 25$
i $f(x) = \dfrac{1}{x}, x \geqslant 1$
j $f(x) = \dfrac{1}{1 + x^2}, \quad x \in \mathbb{R}$

3 **a** By completing the square, write $f(x) = x^2 + 6x + 4$ in the form $(x + a)^2 + b$.
b Sketch the graph of $y = f(x)$ and state its range for $x \in \mathbb{R}$.

4 Find the range for each of these functions for $x \in \mathbb{R}$:

a $x^2 - 6x + 12$
b $x^2 + 20x + 50$
c $\dfrac{1}{x^2 + 2}$
d $\dfrac{1}{x^2 + 4x + 5}$

Composite functions

The function $f: x \mapsto 3x + 2$ is itself a composite function, consisting of two simpler functions: 'multiply by 3' and 'add 2'.

If $f: x \mapsto 3x + 2$ and $g: x \mapsto x^2$ then fg is a composite function where g is performed first and then f is performed on the result of g.

The function fg may be found using a flow diagram.

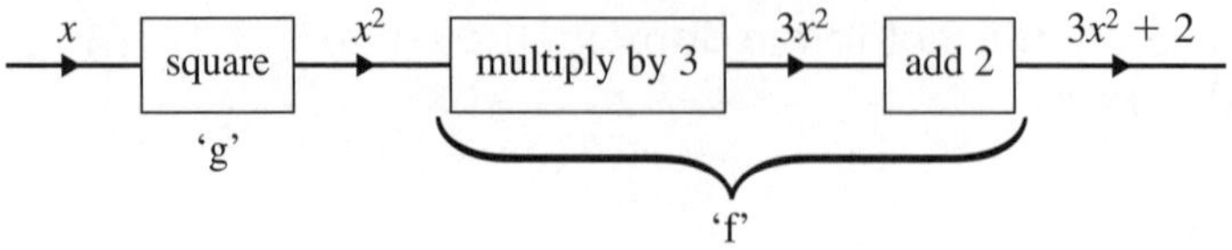

Thus $fg: x \mapsto 3x^2 + 2$.

A composite function can also be found algebraically.

$$\begin{aligned} fg(x) &= f(g(x)) \\ &= 3(g(x)) + 2 \\ &= 3x^2 + 2 \end{aligned}$$

Example 2

Given $f(x) = x^2$, $g(x) = x - 3$, $h(x) = 3x + 2$.

Find **a** $fg(x)$
b $gf(x)$
c $hf(x)$
d $gfh(x)$

a $$\begin{aligned} fg(x) &= f(g(x)) \\ &= (g(x))^2 \\ &= (x - 3)^2 \end{aligned}$$

b $$\begin{aligned} gf(x) &= g(f(x)) \\ &= f(x) - 3 \\ &= x^2 - 3 \end{aligned}$$

c $$\begin{aligned} hf(x) &= h(f(x)) \\ &= 3(f(x)) + 2 \\ &= 3x^2 + 2 \end{aligned}$$

d $$\begin{aligned} gfh(x) &= g(f(h(x))) \\ &= g((h(x))^2) \\ &= g((3x + 2)^2) \\ &= (3x + 2)^2 - 3 \end{aligned}$$

Inverse functions

If $f(x)$ is a **one-to-one function** then it has an **inverse function** denoted by $f^{-1}(x)$ such that $f^{-1}[f(x)] = x$ for all values of x [and also $f[f^{-1}(x)] = x$]. You can think of an inverse function as 'undoing' the original function.

The inverse of a given function can be found by two different methods:

Method A using a flow diagram or
Method B by letting $y = f(x)$ and rearranging to make x the subject.

The two methods are illustrated below.

Example 3 (Method A)

Find the inverse of f where $f(x) = \dfrac{5x - 2}{3}$.

a Draw a flow diagram for f

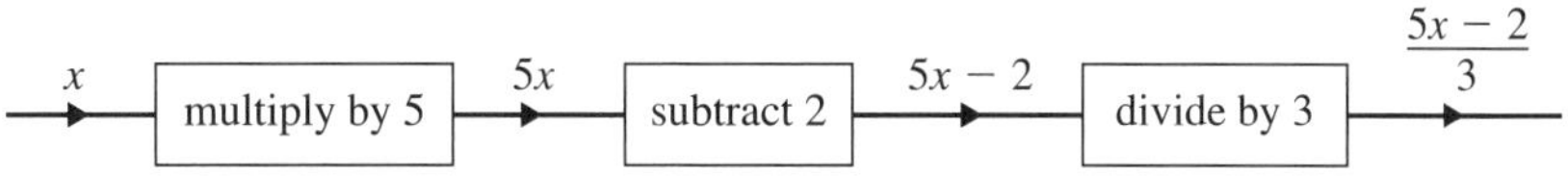

b Draw a new flow diagram with each operation replaced by its inverse. Start with x on the right.

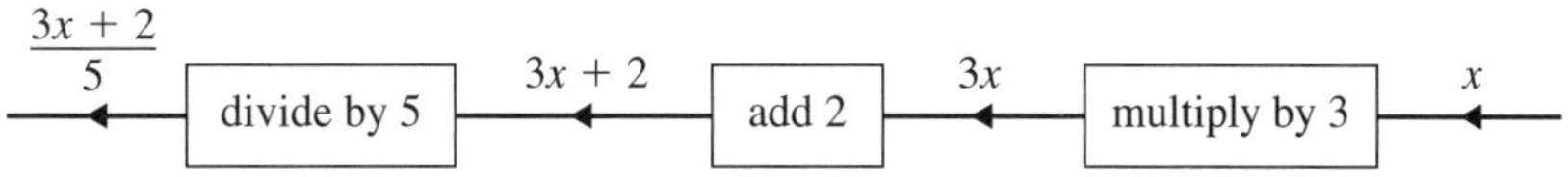

Thus the inverse of f is given by

$$f^{-1}(x) = \frac{3x + 2}{5}$$

It is worth noting that this method is only suitable for relatively simple functions.

Example 4 (Method B)

Find the inverse of the function $f(x) = \dfrac{5x - 2}{3}$.

Let $y = \dfrac{5x - 2}{3}$.

Rearrange to make x the subject.

$$5x - 2 = 3y$$

$$x = \frac{3y + 2}{5}$$

So the inverse function is $f^{-1}(x) = \dfrac{3x + 2}{5}$.

Why does this method work?

In the example above given x we can find $y = f(x) = \dfrac{5x - 2}{3}$.

Now if we are given y, the value of x can be found using $x = \dfrac{3y + 2}{5}$.

So the inverse function is given by $f^{-1}(x) = \dfrac{3x + 2}{5}$.

Example 5

The function f is defined by $f(x) = \dfrac{x + 1}{x}$ for $x \in \mathbb{R}, x \neq 0$.

Find an expression for f^{-1}.

$$f(x) = \frac{x + 1}{x}$$

Let $y = \frac{x+1}{x}$ and rearrange to make x the subject.

$$xy = x + 1$$
$$xy - x = 1$$
$$x(y - 1) = 1$$
$$x = \frac{1}{y-1}$$

So $f^{-1}(x) = \frac{1}{x-1}$

We can check the answer by substituting any value for x, say 3.

$$f(3) = \frac{3+1}{3} = \frac{4}{3}$$

$$f^{-1}\left(\frac{4}{3}\right) = \frac{1}{\frac{4}{3} - 1} = \frac{1}{\frac{1}{3}} = 3 \text{ (as expected)}$$

EXERCISE 1E

In this exercise the domain for each function is the set of real numbers unless otherwise stated.

For questions **1** and **2**, the functions f, g and h are as follows:

$f(x) = 4x$ $\quad$ $g(x) = x + 5$ $\quad$ $h(x) = x^2$

1 Find the following:

a $fg(x)$ **b** $gf(x)$ **c** $hf(x)$ **d** $fh(x)$
e $gh(x)$ **f** $gg(x)$ **g** $fgh(x)$ **h** $hfg(x)$

2 Find

a x if $hg(x) = h(x)$ **b** x if $fh(x) = gh(x)$

For questions **3**, **4** and **5**, the functions f, g and h are as follows:

$f: x \mapsto 2x$ $\quad$ $g: x \mapsto x - 3$ $\quad$ $h: x \mapsto x^2$

3 Find the following in the form '$x \mapsto \ldots$'

a fg **b** gf **c** gh **d** hf
e ff **f** ghf **g** hgf

4 Evaluate:

a fg(4) **b** gf(7) **c** gh(−3)
d fgf(2) **e** ggg(10) **f** hfh(−2)

5 Find:

a x if $f(x) = g(x)$ **b** x if $hg(x) = gh(x)$
c x if $gf(x) = 0$ **d** x if $fg(x) = 4$

For questions **6**, **7** and **8**, the functions l, m and n are as follows:

$l(x) = 2x + 1 \qquad m(x) = 3x - 1 \qquad n(x) = x^2$

6 Find the following

a lm(x) **b** ml(x) **c** ln(x)

d nm(x) **e** lnm(x) **f** mln(x)

7 Find

a lm(2) **b** nl(1) **c** mn(−2)

d mm(2) **e** nln(2) **f** llm(0)

8 Find

a x if $l(x) = m(x)$

b two values of x if $nl(x) = nm(x)$

c x if $ln(x) = mn(x)$

In questions **9** to **14**, find the inverse of each function $f^{-1}(x)$:

9 $f(x) = 5x - 2$ **10** $f(x) = 5(x - 2)$ **11** $f(x) = 3(2x + 4)$

12 $g(x) = \dfrac{2x + 1}{3}$ **13** $f(x) = \dfrac{3(x - 1)}{4}$ **14** $f(x) = 2(3x + 4) - 6$

In questions **15** to **20**, find the inverse of each function in the form '$x \mapsto \ldots$'

15 $h : x \mapsto \frac{1}{2}(4 + 5x) + 10$ **16** $k : x \mapsto \dfrac{-7x + 3}{2}$ **17** $j : x \mapsto \dfrac{12 - 5x}{3x}$

18 $l : x \mapsto \dfrac{4 - x}{3} + 2x$ **19** $m : x \mapsto \dfrac{\left[\dfrac{(2x - 1)}{4} - 3\right]}{5}$ **20** $n : x \mapsto \dfrac{12}{x}, x \neq 0$

For questions **21** to **24**, the functions f, g and h are defined as follows:

$f : x \mapsto 3x \qquad g : x \mapsto x - 5 \qquad h : x \mapsto 2x + 1$

21 Find in the form '$x \mapsto \ldots$'

a f^{-1} **b** g^{-1} **c** h^{-1}

d fg **e** $(fg)^{-1}$ **f** $g^{-1}f^{-1}$

22 Find in the form '$x \mapsto \ldots$'

a hf **b** hf^{-1} **c** $f^{-1}h^{-1}$

d hg **e** $(hg)^{-1}$ **f** $g^{-1}h^{-1}$

23 Find:

a $g^{-1}(2)$ **b** $fg^{-1}(2)$ **c** $(gf)^{-1}(10)$

d $f^{-1}g^{-1}(10)$ **e** $f^{-1}f^{-1}ff(2)$

24 Find:

a x if $h(x) = f(x)$

b the set of values of x for which
  i $f(x) > g(x)$
  ii $fg(x) > 0$

25 The function f is defined by $f : x = \dfrac{2x + 5}{3}$

a Find f^{-1} in the form '$x \mapsto \ldots$'

b Find $f^{-1}(3)$

c Show that $f^{-1}(3)$ is the solution of the equation $f(x) = 3$.

Inverse functions and their graphs

Consider $f(x) = x + 2$ and its inverse $f^{-1}(x) = x - 2$ and $g(x) = 2x + 1$ and its inverse $g^{-1}(x) = \dfrac{x - 1}{2}$

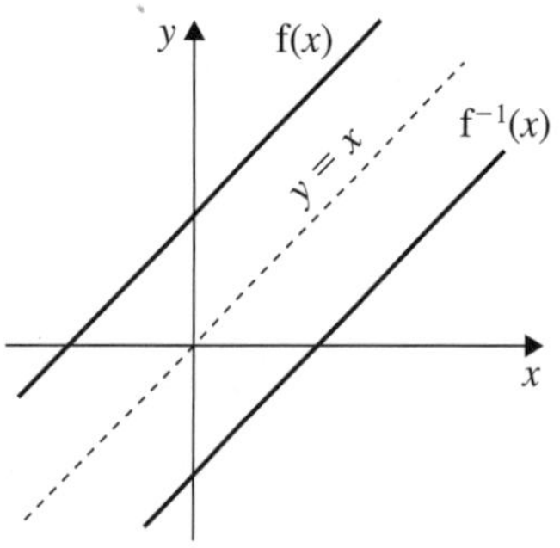

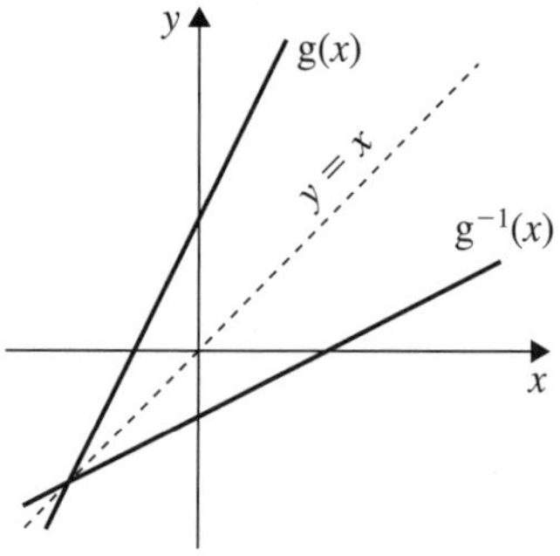

You see that:

$f^{-1}(x)$ is the reflection of $f(x)$ in the line $y = x$
$g^{-1}(x)$ is the reflection of $g(x)$ in the line $y = x$

This is a general result for any function and its inverse.

For every point (x, y) on the graph of the function f there is a point (y, x) on the graph of f^{-1}. Also the range of f is the domain of f^{-1} and the domain of f^{-1} is the range of f.

Example 6

Find the inverse of the function $f(x) = x^2, x \geqslant 0$

Note that $f(x)$ is a one-to-one mapping as the domain is $x \geqslant 0$.

To find the inverse, let $y = x^2$

Rearranging $x = \pm\sqrt{y}$

We require the positive square root, $x = \sqrt{y}$, as the domain is $x \geqslant 0$.

So $f^{-1}(x) = \sqrt{x}$.

Here are the graphs of f(x) and $f^{-1}(x)$. Notice that $f^{-1}(x)$ is the reflection of f(x) in the line $y = x$.

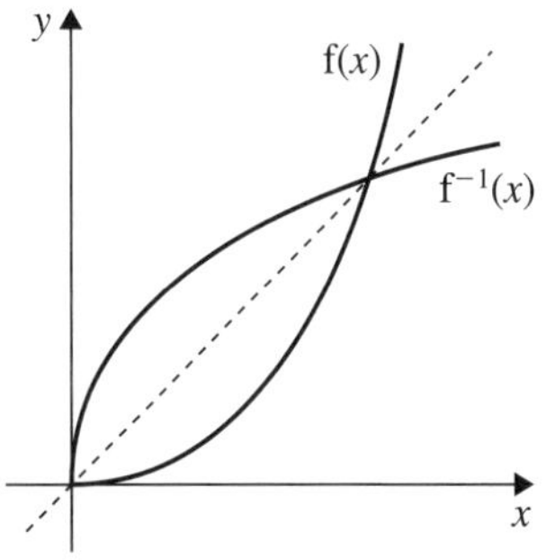

Example 7

Given $f(x) = (x - 1)^2 + 3, x \geqslant p$ is a one-to-one function,

a Find the minimum value of p.

b Find $f^{-1}(x)$ and state its domain.

a Sketch the curve $y = (x - 1)^2 + 3$

We see that f(x) is a one-to-one function for $x \geqslant 1$

$\therefore \quad p = 1$

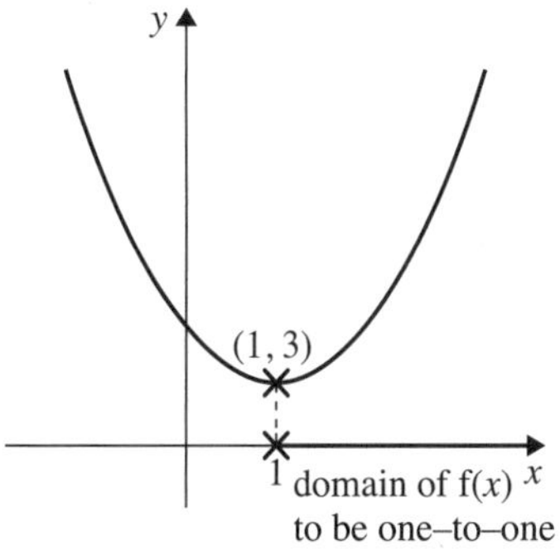

b $y = (x - 1)^2 + 3$

Rearrange to make x the subject,

$$(x - 1)^2 = y - 3$$
$$x - 1 = \pm\sqrt{y - 3}$$
$$x = 1 \pm \sqrt{y - 3}$$

We require the positive square root, $x = 1 + \sqrt{y - 3}$, since it is specified that $x \geqslant p$

$$\therefore \quad f^{-1}(x) = 1 + \sqrt{x - 3}$$

The domain of $f^{-1}(x)$ is $x \geqslant 3$

Notice that the *range* of f(x) is $f(x) \geqslant 3$. Sometimes it is easier to work out the range of f(x) than the domain of $f^{-1}(x)$, and vice versa.

Exercise 1F

1 Find the inverse of the following functions:

a $f(x) = 2 - x, \quad x \in \mathbb{R}$

b $f(x) = \dfrac{13}{2x}, \quad x \in \mathbb{R}, x \neq 0$

c $f(x) = 3 - 5x, \quad x \in \mathbb{R}$

d $f(x) = \dfrac{2x + 5}{x - 7}, \quad x \in \mathbb{R}, x \neq 7$

e $f(x) = \dfrac{3x - 5}{2x + 7}, \quad x \in \mathbb{R}, x \neq -\dfrac{7}{2}$

2 The function f(x) is defined by $f(x) = x^2 + 1, x \geqslant 0$. On the same diagram draw a sketch of $y = f(x)$ and $y = f^{-1}(x)$.

3 **a** If $f(x) = 3x - 1$ and $g(x) = x + 7$, calculate $f^{-1}g(x)$ and $gf^{-1}(x)$.

b Find the values of $f^{-1}g(4)$ and $gf^{-1}(2)$.

4 A function is defined by $f(x) = 3x - 1$ for all x.

a Find ff(x) and $f^{-1}(x)$.

b Show that $(ff)^{-1}(x)$ is identically equal to $f^{-1}f^{-1}(x)$.

5 A function is defined by $f(x) = \dfrac{x + 10}{x - 8}, x \neq 8$.

a Find $f^{-1}(x)$.

b Find $f^{-1}(5)$.

c Find a positive integer p such that $f(p) = p$.

d Find also $f^{-1}(p)$ for the positive integer found in part **c**.

6 **a** Sketch the curve of $y = x^2 - 2x - 3$ showing where the curve cuts the x-axis.

b You are given the function $f(x) = x^2 - 2x - 3, x \geqslant 1$.

i Find the range of f.

ii State the range and domain of f^{-1}.

iii Sketch the graph of f^{-1}, showing where the graph meets the coordinate axes.

7 A function f is defined by $f: x \mapsto 2 - \dfrac{1}{x}, x \neq 0$.

a Find f^{-1} and state the value of x for which f^{-1} is not defined.

b Find the value of x for which $f(x) = f^{-1}(x)$.

8 The function f is defined by $f: x \mapsto (x - 2)^2, x \geqslant 2$.

a State the domain and range of the inverse function f^{-1}.

b Find an expression for $f^{-1}(x)$.

c Find a solution to the equation $f(x) = f^{-1}(x)$.

9 The one-to-one functions f and g are defined by $f(x) = \sqrt{x - 2}$ for $x \geqslant a$ and $g(x) = \dfrac{1}{x^2}$ for $x > b$.

a Find the smallest possible values of a and b.

b Find $f^{-1}(x)$ and $g^{-1}(x)$ and state the restrictions, if any, on the domains of these inverse functions.

10 The functions f and g are defined by $f(x) = 2x + 1$ for all x and $g(x) = \dfrac{5}{x - 3}$, $x \neq 3$. Find $f^{-1}(x)$ and $g^{-1}(x)$ and state the restrictions, if any, on the domains of these inverse functions.

11 Copy and complete the domains for the following functions so that the domains are as large as possible for the functions to be one-to-one:

a $f(x) = 3x - 1$ $\quad \ldots \leqslant x \leqslant \ldots$

b $f(x) = 2x^2$ $\quad x \geqslant \ldots$

c $f(x) = \sin x$ $\quad -90° < x \leqslant \ldots$

d $f(x) = (x - 1)^2 + 3$ $\quad x \geqslant \ldots$

e $f(x) = x^2 + 2x - 3$ $\quad x \leqslant \ldots$

f $f(x) = x^2 + 8x + 13$ $\quad x \geqslant \ldots$

1.3 The modulus function

The **modulus** of x is written $|x|$ and means 'the positive value of x'.
For example, $|-2| = 2$, $|7| = 7$

Example 1

Sketch the graph of $y = |x - 2|$

a Sketch $y = x - 2$

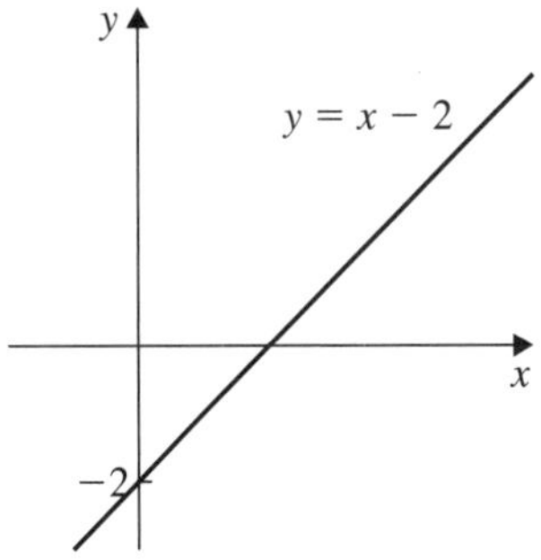

b Where y is negative, draw the reflection of $y = x - 2$ in the x-axis.

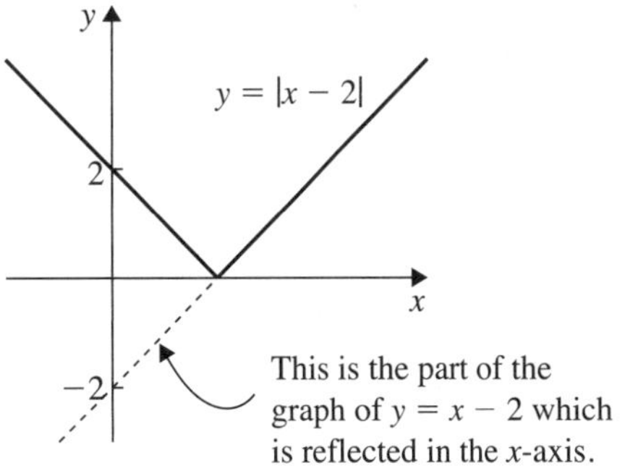

Example 2

Sketch the graph of $y = |\sin x|$ for $-360° \leqslant x \leqslant 360°$

a Sketch $y = \sin x$

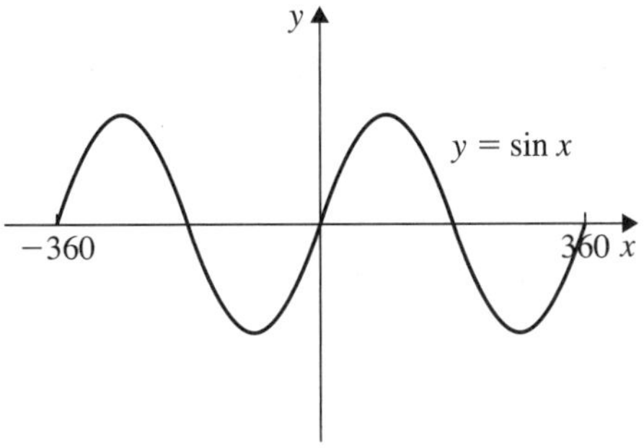

b Where y is negative, reflect the curve in the x-axis.

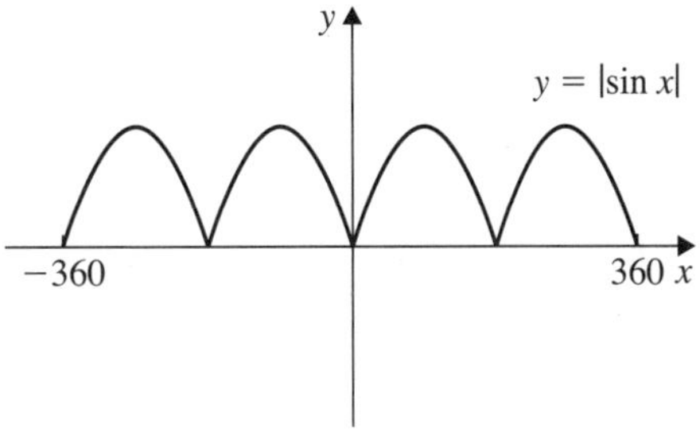

Example 3

Solve the equation $|x - 2| = 3$

Method A

We have either $x - 2 = 3 \Rightarrow x = 5$

or $-(x - 2) = 3$

$-x + 2 = 3 \Rightarrow x = -1$

Method B

Sketch the graphs of $y = |x - 2|$ and $y = 3$

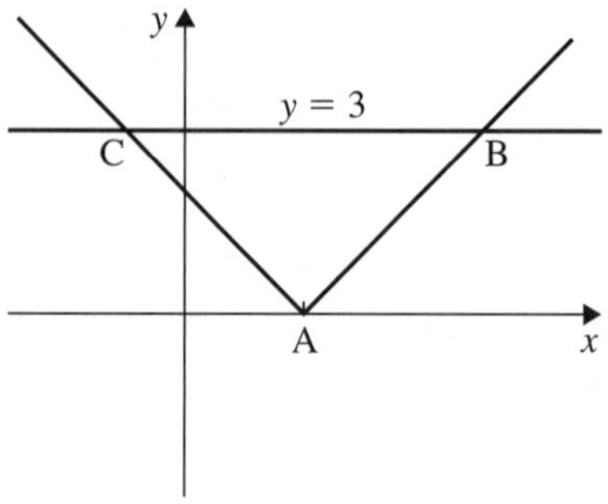

Line AB has equation $y = x - 2$

At B, $x - 2 = 3$

$x = 5$

Line AC has equation $y = -(x - 2)$

At C, $-(x - 2) = 3$

$x = -1$

You can use whichever method you prefer.

Example 4

Solve the inequality $|2x - 1| < 5$

Sketch the graph of $y = |2x - 1|$

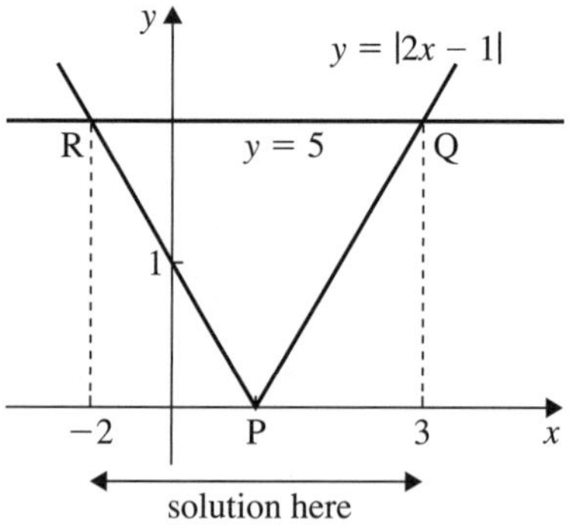

The inequality is satisfied where the graph of $y = |2x - 1|$ is below $y = 5$.

At Q $2x - 1 = 5 \Rightarrow x = 3$

At R, $-(2x - 1) = 5$

$-2x + 1 = 5 \Rightarrow x = -2$

The solution is $-2 < x < 3$

Example 5

Solve the inequality $|x + 2| > |2x - 1|$

This question could be done like Example 4 by sketching the graphs of $y = |x + 2|$ and $y = |2x - 1|$.

Alternatively we can adopt an algebraic approach.

Since **both** sides of the inequality are positive, we can square both sides

$$|x + 2|^2 > |2x - 1|^2$$
$$(x + 2)^2 > (2x - 1)^2$$
$$x^2 + 4x + 4 > 4x^2 - 4x + 1$$
$$3x^2 - 8x - 3 < 0$$
$$(3x + 1)(x - 3) < 0$$

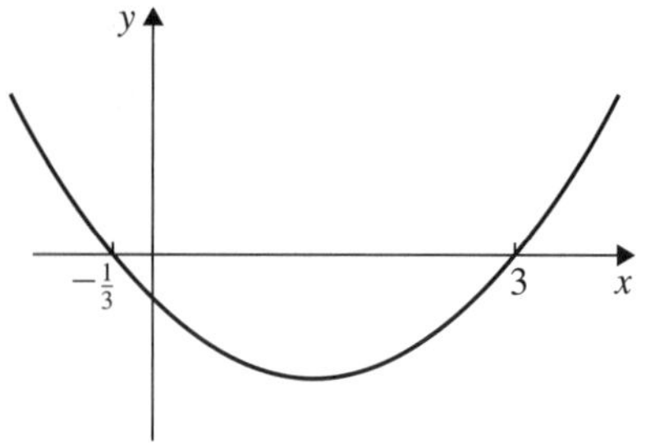

Sketch the curve $y = (3x + 1)(x - 3)$

The solution is $-\frac{1}{3} < x < 3$.

The graph of $y = f(|x|)$

We sketch the graph of $y = f(x)$ for $x \geqslant 0$ and then reflect this graph in the y-axis.

Example 6

Sketch the graph of $y = |x| - 1$.

a Sketch $y = x - 1$ for $x \geqslant 0$

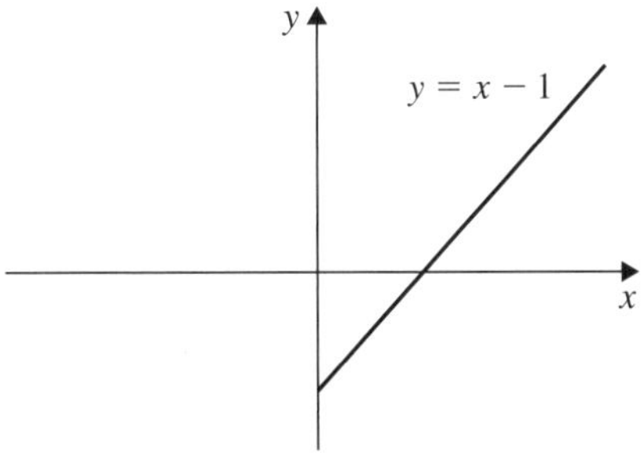

b Reflect in the y-axis

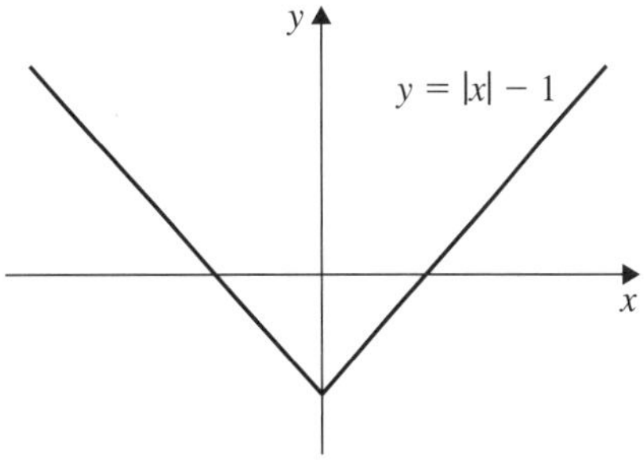

Example 7

Sketch the graph of $y = |x|^2 - |x|$.

a Sketch $y = x^2 - x$ for $x \geqslant 0$

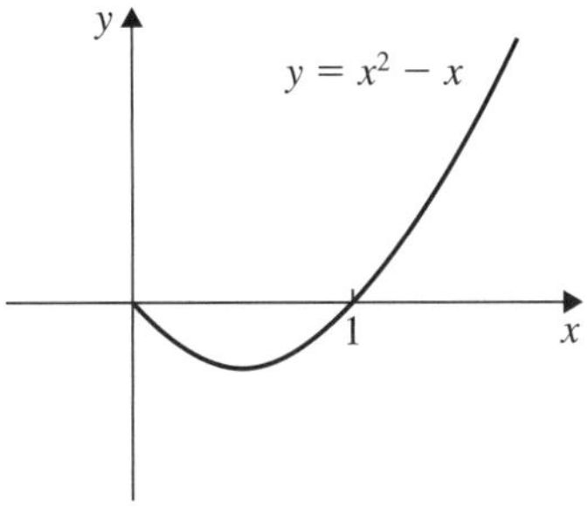

b Reflect in the y-axis

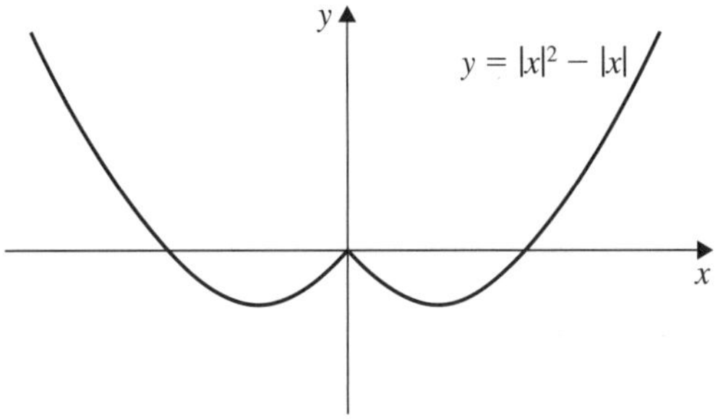

Exercise 1G

1 Sketch the graphs of the following, marking where the graphs cross the axes:

a $y = |x - 4|$ **b** $y = |x + 2|$ **c** $y = |3x - 1|$

d $y = |x^2 - 2x|$ **e** $y = |x^2 - 9|$ **f** $y = |x^2 - 5x + 4|$

g $y = \left|\frac{1}{x}\right|$ **h** $y = |x^3 - x^2 - 6x|$

2 Solve the following equations:

a $|x - 2| = 5$ **b** $|2x - 3| = 3$ **c** $|1 - 2x| = 5$

d $|x^2 - 5| = 4$ **e** $|x^2 - 37| = 12$ **f** $2|x + 3| = 8$

g $3|2x - 1| = 9$ **h** $\left|\frac{1}{x}\right| = 2$

3 Solve the following inequalities:

a $|x - 4| > 5$ **b** $|x + 1| < 3$ **c** $|2x + 3| > 7$

d $|3x - 1| > -1$ **e** $|x + 2| < \frac{1}{2}x + 5$ **f** $|3x - 2| < 6 - x$

g $|x| > |2x - 1|$ **h** $|x + 4| > |x - 2|$ **i** $2|x - 1| < |x - 2|$

4 Sketch the graphs of $y = |3x - 1|$ and $y = |x^2 - 5x + 4|$ and hence solve the equation $|3x - 1| = |x^2 - 5x + 4|$.

5 Sketch the graphs of the following, marking where the graph crosses the axes.

a $y = |x| - 2$ **b** $y = |x| + 3$ **c** $y = 2|x| - 1$

d $y = |x|^2 - 2|x|$ **e** $y = \cos|x|$ **f** $y = \dfrac{1}{|x|}$

6 The graphs of $y = f(x)$ and $y = g(x)$ are shown below.

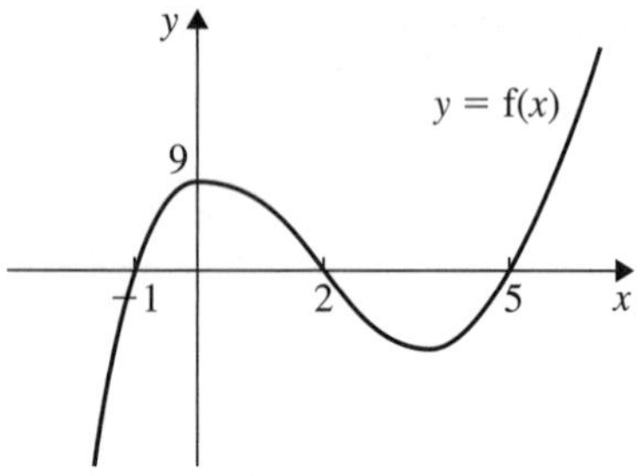

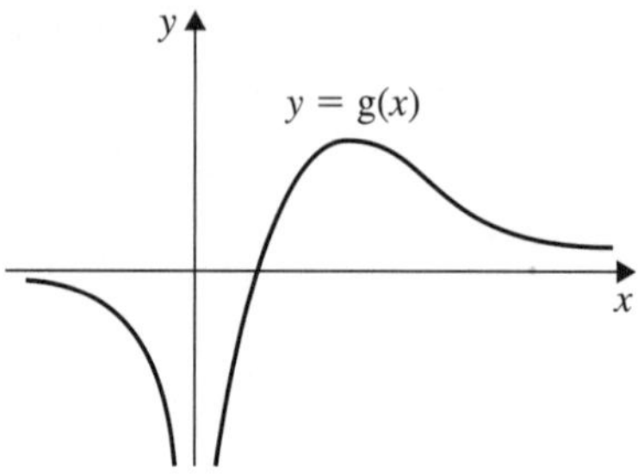

Sketch the graphs of

a $y = |f(x)|$ **b** $y = f(|x|)$ **c** $y = |g(x)|$ **d** $y = g(|x|)$

7 a Sketch the graph of $y = \sin|x|$.

b How many solutions are there to the equation

$$\sin|x| = \tfrac{1}{2}, \text{ for } -180° \leqslant x \leqslant 180°?$$

8 a Sketch the graphs of $f(x) = |x| - 3$ and $g(x) = \frac{1}{3}x$.

b Hence solve the inequality $|x| - 3 > \frac{1}{3}x$.

9 a On the same diagram, sketch the graphs of

$$y = \frac{1}{x - 1} \text{ and } y = 9|x - 1|.$$

b Hence find the set of values of x for which

$$\frac{1}{x - 1} < 9|x - 1|.$$

10 a Sketch the graphs of the following, marking where the graphs cut the axes:

i $y = 2 - |x + 1|$

ii $y = 5 - |x - 1|$

b State the range of each function.

11 Given that $f(x) = x^2 - 3x$, $x \in \mathbb{R}$, sketch in separate diagrams the graphs of:

a $y = f(x)$ **b** $y = |f(x)|$ **c** $y = f(|x|)$

1.4 Transformations of the graph of a function

In 'Pure Mathematics Book 1' we discussed the important single transformations of the graph of a function.
Here is a summary:

$y = f(x) + a$	Translation by a units parallel to the y-axis.
$y = f(x - a)$	Translation by a units parallel to the x-axis (note the negative sign).
$y = af(x)$	Stretch parallel to the y-axis by a scale factor a.
$y = f(ax)$	Stretch parallel to the x-axis by a scale factor $\frac{1}{a}$. (note the reciprocal of a).
$y = -f(x)$	Reflect $f(x)$ in the x-axis.
$y = f(-x)$	Reflect $f(x)$ in the y-axis.

Example 1

The diagram shows a graph of $y = f(x)$.
Sketch the graphs of

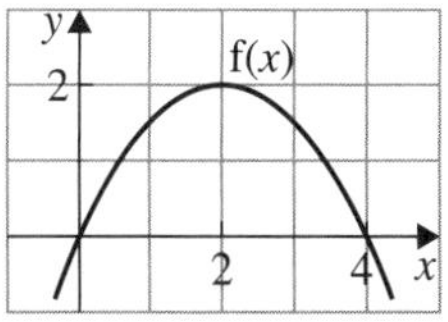

a $y = f(x) + 1$ **b** $y = f(x + 1)$ **c** $y = 2f(x)$
d $y = f(2x)$ **e** $y = -f(x)$ **f** $y = f(-x)$

a Translation 1 unit ↑

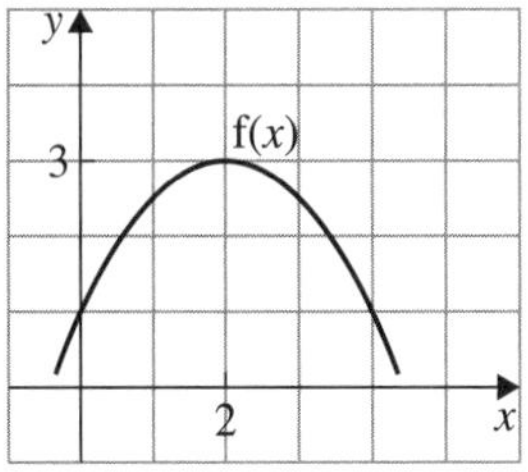

b Translation 1 unit ←

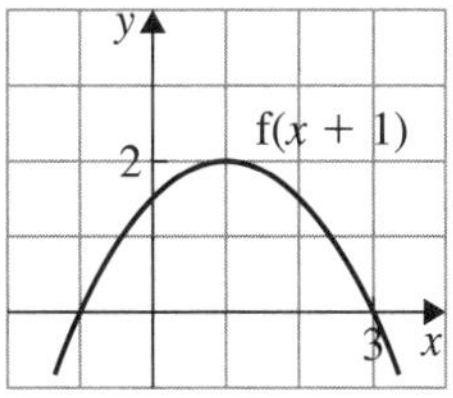

c Stretch ↕, scale factor 2

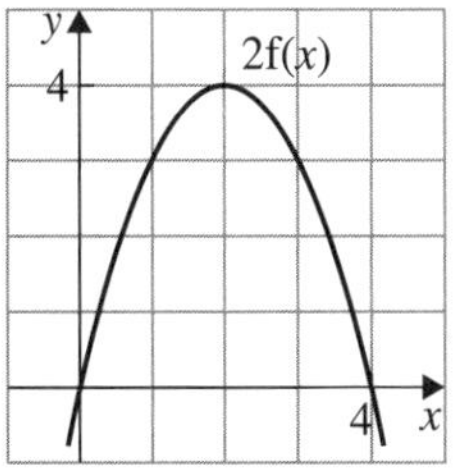

d Stretch ↔, scale factor $\frac{1}{2}$

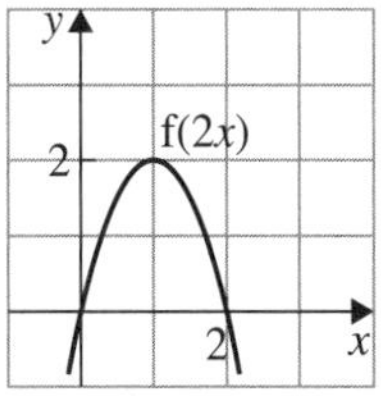

e Reflection in x-axis

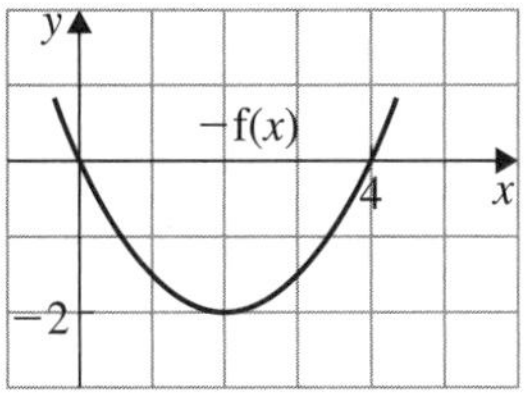

f Reflection in y-axis

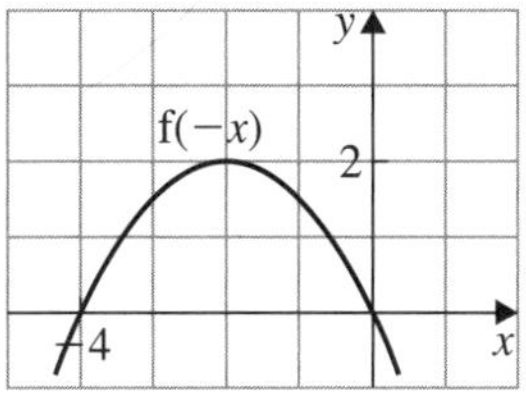

Combination of transformations

We now consider a combination of transformations.

a Suppose we begin with $y = x^2$ (i.e. $f(x) = x^2$)

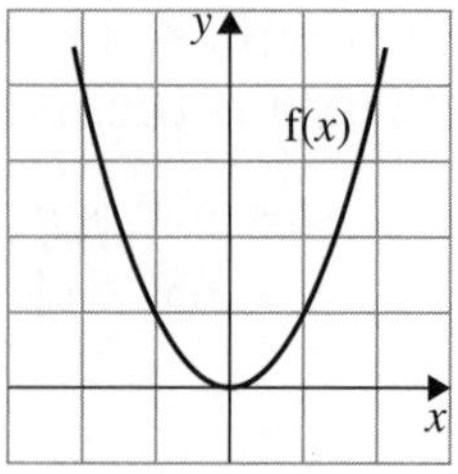

b We now translate the curve by 3 units in the positive x-direction.
This graph has equation $y = (x - 3)^2$

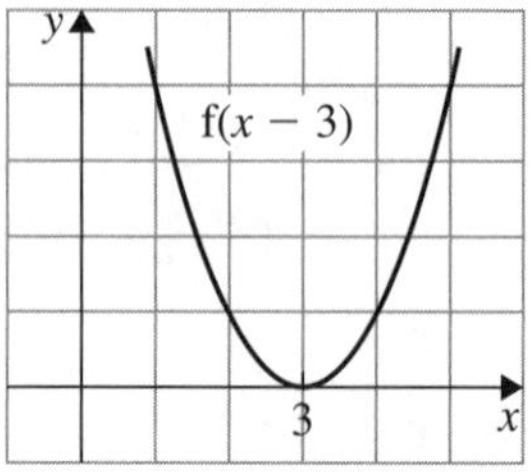

c We now translate this new graph by 2 units in the positive y-direction.
This graph has equation $y = (x - 3)^2 + 2$

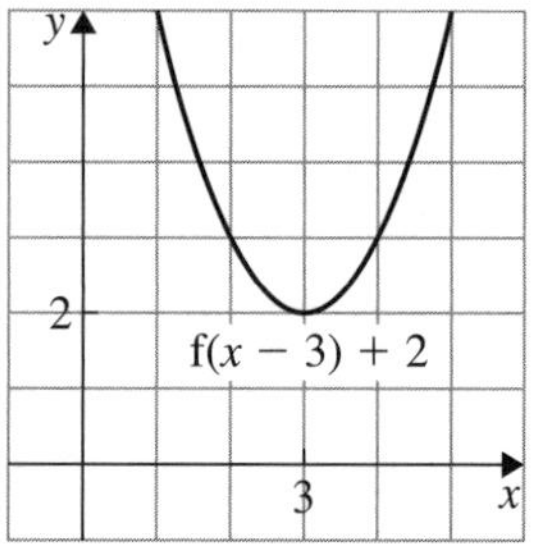

Example 2

A sketch of the curve $y = \sin x$ is shown.
Sketch the graphs of

a $y = \sin\frac{1}{2}x$

b $y = \sin\frac{1}{2}x + 1$

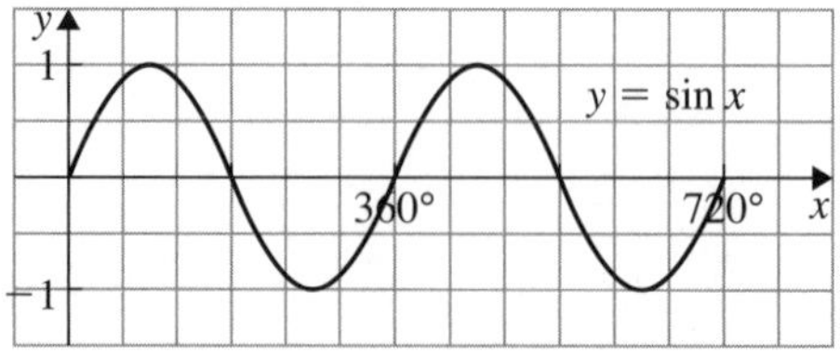

a $y = \sin\frac{1}{2}x$: Stretch ↔, scale factor 2

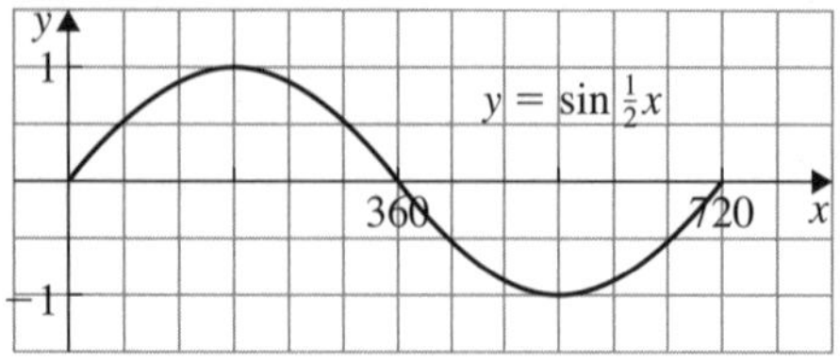

b $y = \sin\frac{1}{2}x + 1$: Translation 1 unit ↑

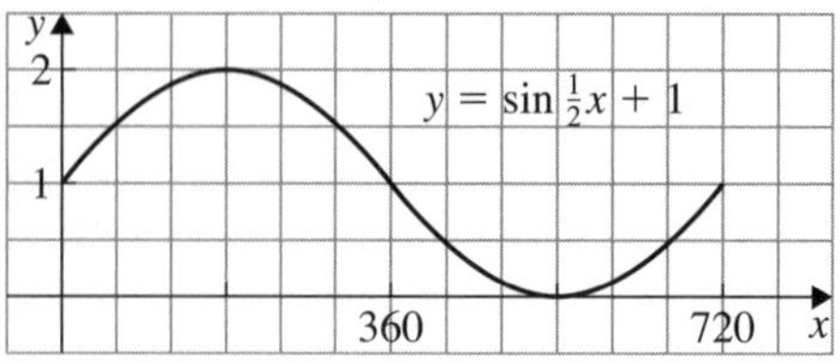

Example 3

This is a sketch of the curve $y = f(x)$.
The only vertex of the curve is at A(2, −4).
The curve $y = x^2$ has been translated to give the curve $y = f(x)$.
Find f(x) in terms of x.

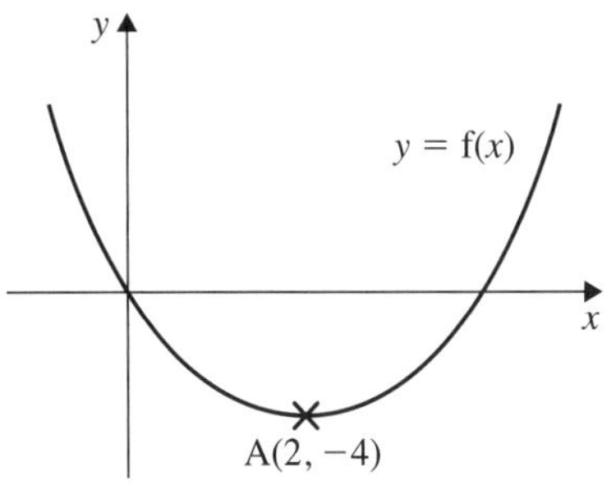

Answer:
The curve $y = x^2$ has been translated 2 units in the positive x direction and 4 units in the negative y direction.

$$\therefore \quad f(x) = (x - 2)^2 - 4$$
$$= x^2 - 4x + 4 - 4$$
$$f(x) = x^2 - 4x$$

EXERCISE 1H

1 The graph of $y = f(x)$ is shown.
Sketch the graphs of

a $y = f(x + 2)$

b $y = -f(x)$

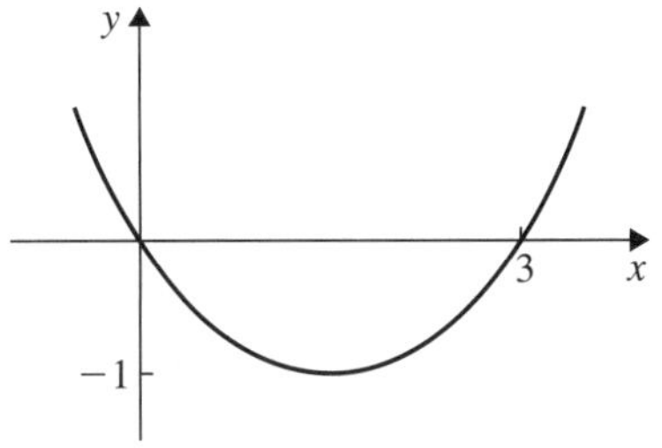

2 This is the sketch graph of $y = f(x)$.

a Sketch the graph of $y = f(x) + 2$

b Sketch the graph of $y = f(x - 1)$

c Sketch the graph of $y = -f(x)$

d Sketch the graph of $y = f(-x)$.

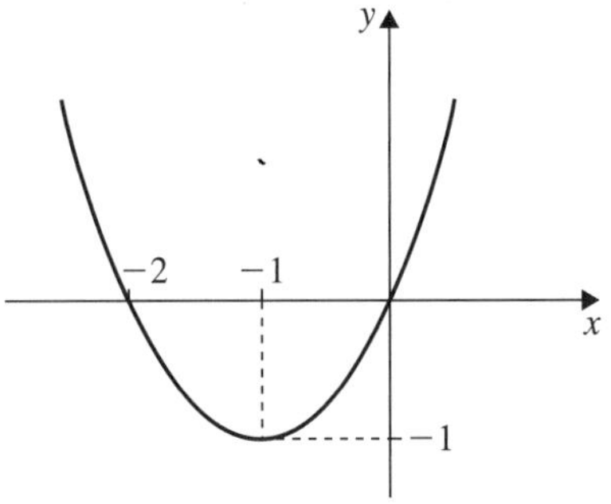

3 This is the sketch of $y = f(x)$ which passes through A, B, C.
Sketch the following curves, giving the new coordinates of A, B, C in each case.

a $y = 2f(x)$

b $y = f(x - 2)$

c $y = f(\frac{1}{2}x)$.

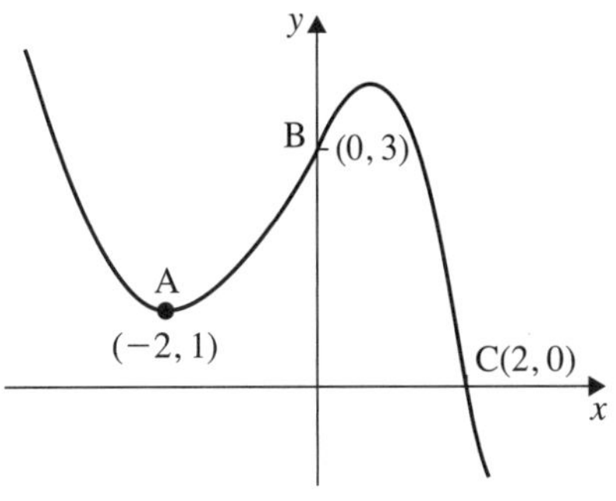

In questions **4** to **9** each graph shows a different function f(x). On squared paper draw a sketch to show the given transformation. The scales are 1 square = 1 unit on both axes.

4

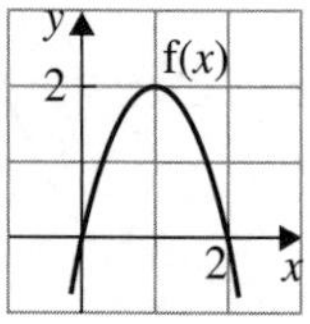

Sketch f(x + 2)

5

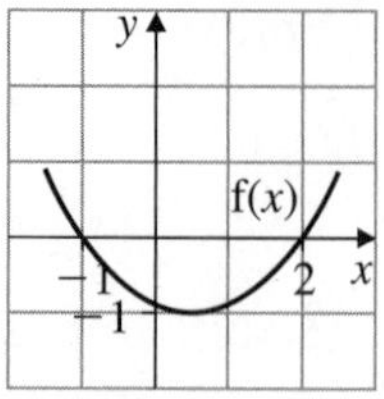

Sketch f($-x$)

6

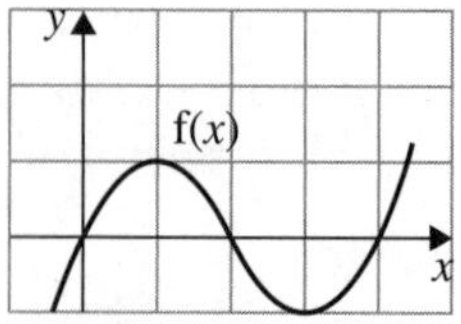

Sketch f($\frac{1}{2}x$)

7

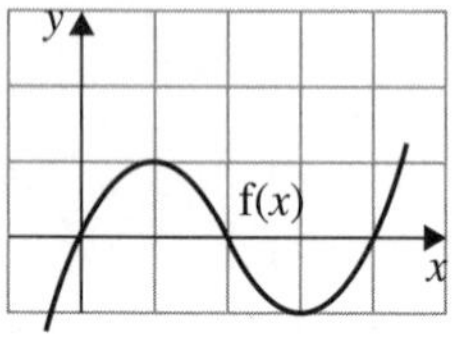

Sketch 2f(x)

8

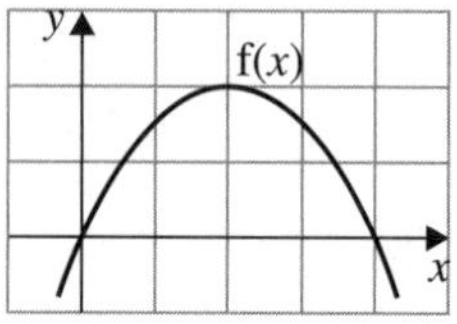

Sketch f(2x)

9

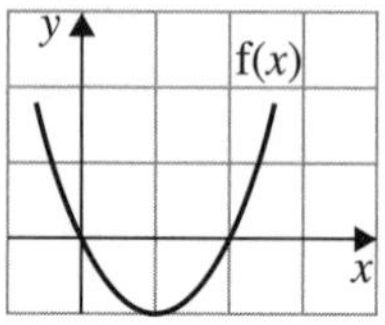

Sketch −f(x)

10 This is the sketch graph of y = f(x).

a Sketch y = f(x − 3)

b Sketch y = f(x − 3) + 4

Give the new coordinates of the point A on the two sketches.

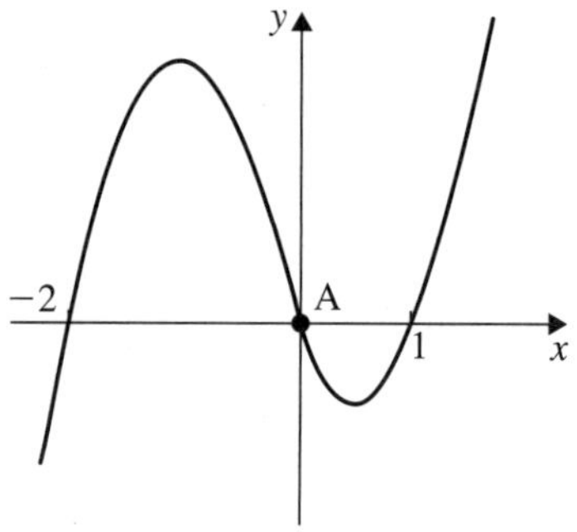

11 On the same axes, sketch and label:

a $y = x^2$

b $y = (x - 2)^2$

c $y = (x - 2)^2 + 4$

12 **a** Sketch and label y = f(x), where f(x) = $x(x - 4)$.

b On the same axes, sketch and label:

i y = f(2x) **ii** y = −f(2x)

13 This is a sketch of y = f(x).

a Sketch y = f(x + 1) + 5

b Sketch y = f(x − 3) − 4

c Sketch y = 1 + f(2x)

Show the new coordinates of the point A on each sketch.

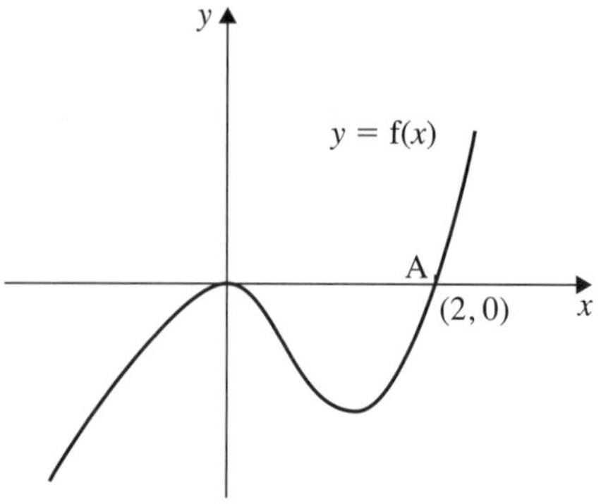

14 **a** Find the equation of the curve when $y = x^3$ is translated 5 units in the direction $\uparrow$.

b Find the equation of the curve when $y = x^3$ is translated 2 units in the direction $\rightarrow$.

c Find the equation of the curve when $y = x^3$ is translated by the vector $\begin{pmatrix} 2 \\ 5 \end{pmatrix}$.

15 **a** Sketch the graph of $y = \sin x$, for $0 \leqslant x \leqslant 360°$

b Sketch the graph of $y = \sin \frac{1}{2}x$, for $0 \leqslant x \leqslant 360°$

16 **a** Sketch the graph of $y = \tan x$, for $0 \leqslant x \leqslant 2\pi$.

b Sketch the graph of $y = \tan\left(x - \frac{\pi}{2}\right)$, for $0 \leqslant x \leqslant 2\pi$.

17 You are given $f(x) = 2x + 1$ and $g(x) = 6x - 1$.
Find a pair of successive transformations which, applied to $f(x)$, will give $g(x)$.

18 You are given $f(x) = \frac{1}{2}x - 2$ and $g(x) = 2x + 1$.
Find a pair of successive transformations which, applied to $f(x)$, will give $g(x)$.

19 $f(x) = x^2$ and $g(x) = x^2 - 4x + 7$.

a If $g(x) = f(x - a) + b$, find the values of a and b.

b Hence sketch the graphs of $y = f(x)$ and $y = g(x)$ showing the transformations from f to g.

20 $f(x) = x^2$ and $g(x) = x^2 + 8x + 17$.

a If $g(x) = f(x + a) + b$, find the values of a and b.

b Hence sketch the graphs of $y = f(x)$ and $y = g(x)$ showing the transformation from f to g.

Questions **21** and **22** involve the graphs of $y = e^x$ and $y = \log_e x$ which are discussed in Part 3 of this book.

21 This is the graph of $y = e^x$.

Sketch $y = e^{2x} - 1$.

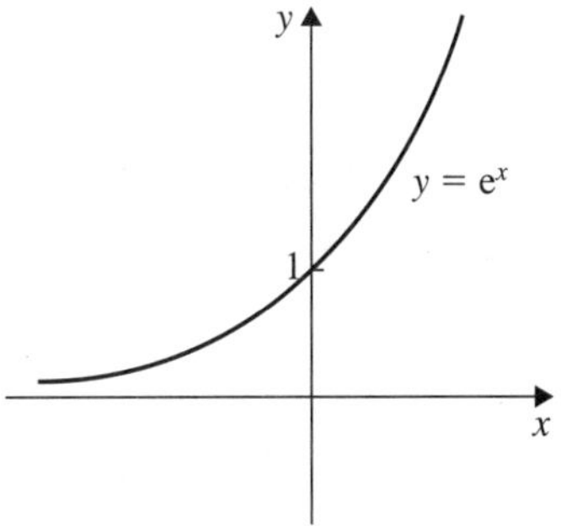

22 This is the graph of $y = \log_e x$.

a Sketch $y = \log_e (x - 2)$

b Sketch $y = 2\log_e (x - 2)$.

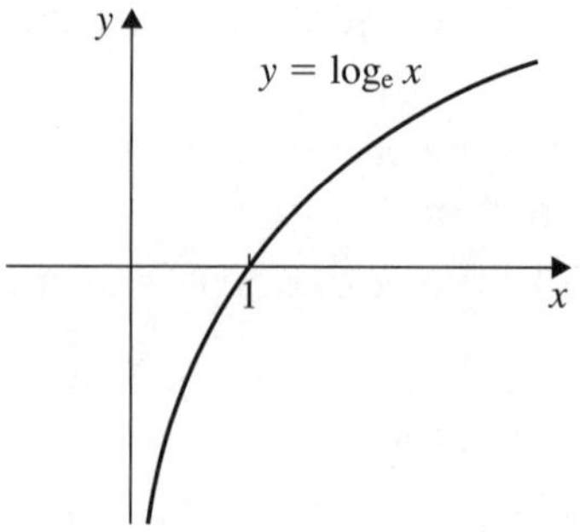

Review Exercise 1I

1 Simplify as far as possible:

a $\dfrac{5x}{3x - x^2}$ **b** $\dfrac{5x^2y}{10y}$ **c** $\dfrac{9x + 6}{3x}$

d $\dfrac{1 - x^2}{1 - x}$ **e** $\dfrac{x + 4x^2}{xy + xy^2}$ **f** $\dfrac{(3x)^2}{6x}$

2 Factorise completely $4x^2 - 4$ and hence simplify $\dfrac{x^2 - 5x + 4}{4x^2 - 4}$.

3 Simplify as far as possible.

a $\dfrac{x^2 + x - 2}{x^2 - x}$ **b** $\dfrac{x^2 - 5x + 6}{x^2 - x - 2}$ **c** $\dfrac{2x^2 + 7x - 4}{x^2 - 16}$

d $\dfrac{2x + \frac{1}{x}}{x}$ **e** $\dfrac{3x - \frac{1}{x}}{\frac{1}{x}}$ **f** $\dfrac{4 - \frac{1}{x^2}}{\frac{1}{x}}$

4 Write as a single fraction:

a $\dfrac{x + 1}{3} + \dfrac{2x + 1}{2}$ **b** $\dfrac{1}{x} + \dfrac{3}{x + 1}$ **c** $\dfrac{2}{x + 1} + \dfrac{x}{x - 1}$

d $\dfrac{x + 1}{3} - \dfrac{x}{4}$ **e** $\dfrac{x}{5} - \dfrac{x + 1}{2}$ **f** $\dfrac{x - 1}{3} \div \dfrac{x + 3}{6}$

5 You are given $f(x) = 6x^2 - x - 1$ and $g(x) = 4x^3 - x$.

a By finding $f(\frac{1}{2})$ and $g(\frac{1}{2})$, or otherwise, show that $f(x)$ and $g(x)$ have a common linear factor.

b Hence write $\dfrac{f(x)}{g(x)}$ in its simplest form.

6 The function f is defined by $f: x \mapsto 1 - x^2, x \in \mathbb{R}$.

a State the range of f.

b Find the values of x for which $ff(x) = 0$.

7 The function f is defined by f: $x \mapsto \dfrac{2x + 1}{x}$, $x \in \mathbb{R}$, $x \neq 0$.

Find, in a similar form, the functions

a ff **b** f^{-1}

8 A function f is defined by

$$f: x \mapsto 4 - \frac{3}{x}, x \neq 0$$

a Find f^{-1} and state the value of x for which f^{-1} is not defined.

b Find the values of x for which $f(x) = f^{-1}(x)$.

9 The function f is defined by f: $x \mapsto \sqrt{\left(1 - \dfrac{9}{x^2}\right)}$ with domain $x \in \mathbb{R}$ and $x \geqslant 3$.

a Find the range of f.

b Find an expression for $f^{-1}(x)$ and state the range and domain of f^{-1}.

10 The functions f and g are defined with their respective domains by

$$f: x \mapsto \frac{3}{2x - 1}, x \in \mathbb{R}, x \neq \tfrac{1}{2}$$

$$g: x \mapsto x^2 + 3, x \in \mathbb{R}$$

a State the range of g.

b Find fg(x), giving your answer in its simplest form.

c Find an expression for $f^{-1}(x)$.

d Solve the equation $f(x) = f^{-1}(x)$.

11 The functions f and g are defined by

$$f(x) = \frac{2}{x + 1}, x > 0 \qquad g(x) = 1 - x^2, x \in \mathbb{R}$$

a Find fg(x), giving your answer in its simplest form.

b Find $f^{-1}(x)$.

c Solve the equation $f(x) = f^{-1}(x)$.

12 The function f is defined by $f(x) = x^2 - 4x - 5$, $x \in \mathbb{R}$, $x \geqslant 2$.

a Find the range of f.

b Write down the domain and range of f^{-1}.

c Sketch the graph of f^{-1}, showing any points where the graph intersects the coordinate axes.

13 Sketch the graphs of the following, marking where the graphs cross the axes:

a $y = |x - 3|$ **b** $y = |3x + 1|$

c $y = |x^2 - 1|$ **d** $y = |\sin x|$ for $0 \leqslant x \leqslant 2\pi$

14 The graphs of $y = f(x)$ and $y = g(x)$ are shown.

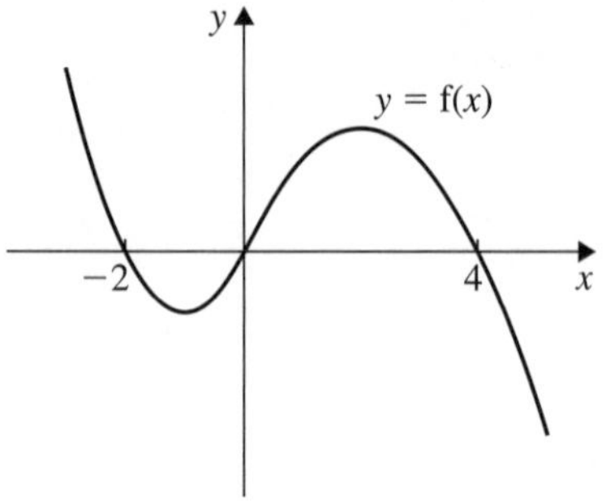

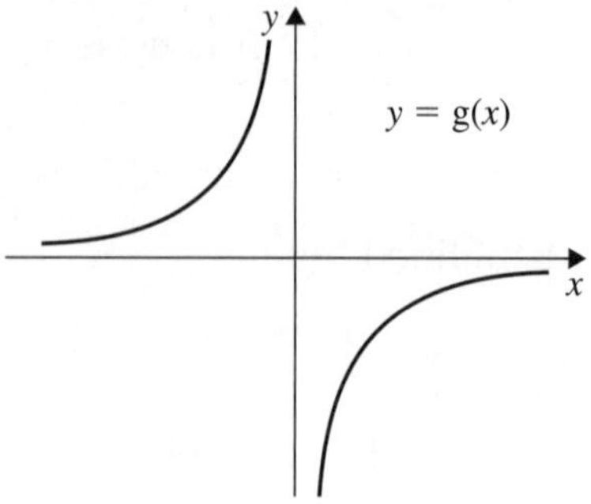

Sketch the graphs of

a $y = |f(x)|$ **b** $y = |g(x)|$ **c** $y = f(|x|)$ **d** $y = g(|x|)$

15 Solve the inequalities:

a $|x - 1| < |x + 2|$

b $|2x + 1| > |x - 1|$

16 Solve the inequalities:

a $|x - 1| < 5$

b $|2x - 3| > 1$

17 a Sketch the graph of $y = |x^2 - 4|$.

b Solve the inequality $|x^2 - 4| > 5$.

18 a On the same axes, sketch the graphs of $y = |2x + 1|$ and $y = \frac{2}{x}$.

b How many solutions are there to the equation $|2x + 1| = \frac{2}{x}$?

19 Sketch the graphs of:

a $y = |x| - 2$

b $y = 2|x| - 3$

c $y = |x|^2 - |x|$

20 a Sketch the graphs of $f(x) = |x| - 5$ and $g(x) = \frac{1}{2}x$.

b Hence solve the inequality $|x| - 5 > \frac{1}{2}x$.

21 The function f is defined for all real values of x by

$$f(x) = |x - 3| + 2$$

a Sketch the graph of $y = f(x)$ and state the range of f.

b Solve the equation $f(x) = 5$.

c Evaluate ff(1).

22 a Sketch the graph of $y = 4 - |x + 1|$, showing where the graph crosses the axes.

b State the range of the function $f(x) = 4 - |x + 1|$.

23 **a** Sketch the graph of $y = 5 - |2x + 1|$.

b How many roots are there to the equation $5 - |2x + 1| = 3$?

c State the range of the function $g(x) = 5 - |2x + 1|$.

24 The diagram shows part of the graph of $y = f(x)$.

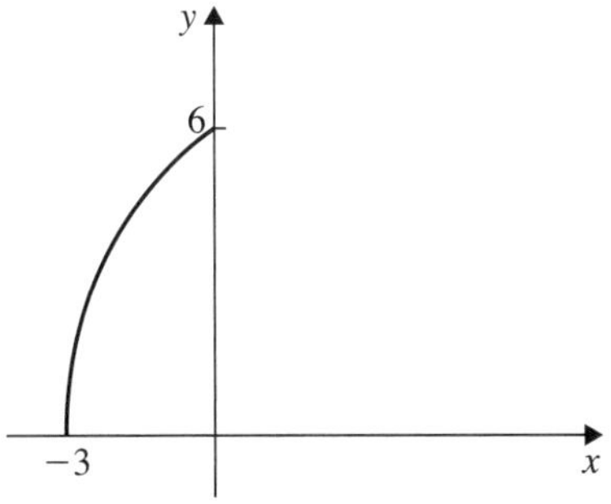

On separate diagrams, sketch the curve with equation:

a $y = \frac{1}{2}f(x)$ **b** $y = f(2x)$

c $y = f(x - 5)$ **d** $y = f(-x)$

Indicate clearly the new positions of the points $(-3, 0)$ and $(0, 6)$ for each function.

25 The sketch shows the curve with equation $y = f(x)$. It passes through the origin O.

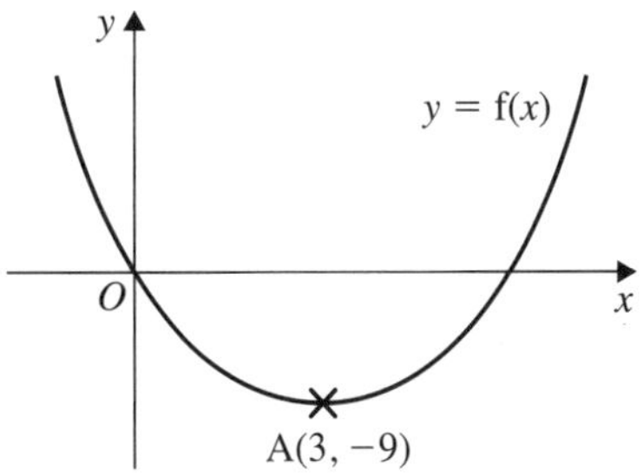

The only vertex of the curve is at A(3, −9).

a Write down the coordinates of the vertex of the curve with equation

i $y = f(x + 1)$

ii $y = f(x) + 5$

iii $y = -f(x)$

iv $y = f(3x)$

v $y = f(-x)$

The curve with equation $y = x^2$ has been translated to give the curve $y = f(x)$ shown in the diagram.

b Find $f(x)$ in terms of x.

26 The sketch shows the curve with equation $y = f(x)$.

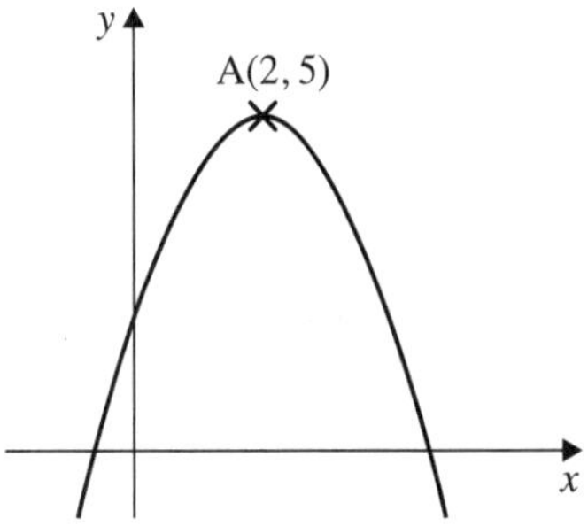

The only maximum point of the curve $y = f(x)$ is A(2, 5).

a Write down the coordinates of the maximum point for the curves with each of the following equations:

i $y = f(x + 3)$

ii $y = f(x) - 6$

iii $y = f(-x)$

The curve with equation $y = -x^2$ has been translated to give the curve $y = f(x)$.

b Find $f(x)$ in terms of x.

27 Describe a series of geometrical transformations that maps the graph of $y = x^2$ onto the graph of $y = 2(x - 3)^2 - 4$.

28 Describe a series of geometrical transformations that maps the graph of $y = \cos x$ onto the graph of $y = -1 + \cos 2x$.

29 The functions $\mathrm{f}(x)$ and $\mathrm{g}(x)$ are such that

$$\mathrm{g}(x) = \mathrm{f}\left(\tfrac{1}{2}x\right) + 3$$

Describe a sequence of two transformations that maps the graph of $y = \mathrm{f}(x)$ onto the graph of $y = \mathrm{g}(x)$.

30

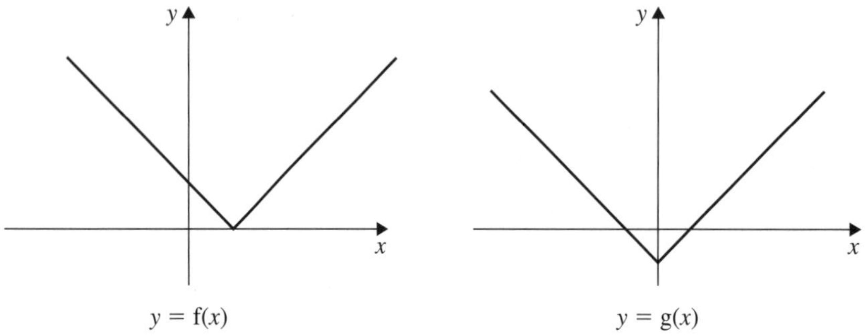

The diagrams show the graphs of $y = \mathrm{f}(x)$ and $y = \mathrm{g}(x)$, where

$$\mathrm{f}(x) = |x - 4| \text{ and } \mathrm{g}(x) = |x| - 3,\ x \in \mathbb{R}$$

Describe the geometrical transformations by which each of the above graphs can be obtained from the graph of $y = |x|$.

Examination Exercise 1

1 Express:

$$\frac{3x + 5}{x^2 + x - 12} - \frac{2}{x - 3}$$

as a single fraction in its simplest form.

[EDEXCEL, GCE Mathematics, C3 1R, June 2013]

2 Simplify:

i $\dfrac{1 - x}{x^2 - 3x + 2}$,

ii $\dfrac{(x + 1)}{(x - 1)(x - 3)} - \dfrac{(x - 5)}{(x - 3)(x - 4)}$

[OCR, GCE Mathematics, C4, June 2012]

3 **i** Express $\dfrac{2}{3 - x} + \dfrac{3}{1 + x}$ as a single fraction in its simplest form.

ii Hence express $\left(\dfrac{2}{3 - x} + \dfrac{3}{1 + x}\right) \times \dfrac{x^2 + 8x - 33}{121 - x^2}$ as a single fraction in its lowest terms.

[OCR, GCE Mathematics, C4, June 2015]

4

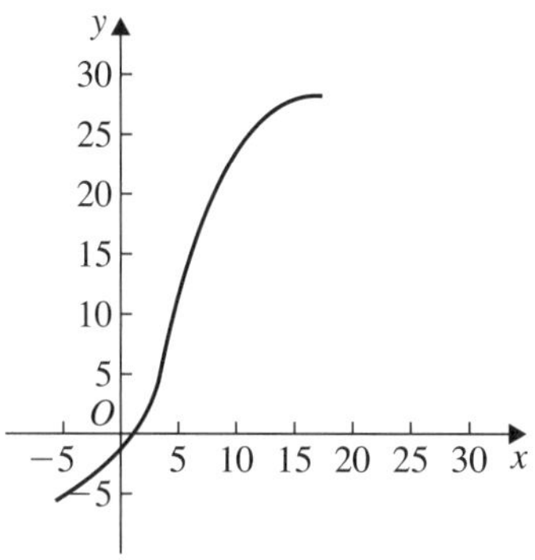

It is given that f is a one-to-one function defined for all real values. The diagram shows the curve with equation $y = f(x)$. The coordinates of certain points on the curve are shown in the following table.

x	2	4	6	8	10	12	14
y	1	8	14	19	23	25	26

i State the value of $ff(6)$ and the value of $f^{-1}(8)$.

ii Sketch the curve $y = f^{-1}(x)$, indicating how the curves $y = f(x)$ and $y = f^{-1}(x)$ are related. [OCR, GCE Mathematics, C3, Jan 2012]

5 The functions f and g are defined for all real values of x by

$$f(x) = 2x^3 + 4 \quad \text{and} \quad g(x) = \sqrt[3]{x - 10}.$$

i Evaluate $f^{-1}(-50)$

ii Show that $fg(x) = 2x - 16$. [OCR, GCE Mathematics, C3, June 2014]

6 The functions f and g are defined by

$$f : x \rightarrow 7x - 1, \quad x \in \mathbb{R}$$

$$g : x \rightarrow \frac{4}{x - 2}, \quad x \neq 2, x \in \mathbb{R}$$

a Solve the equation $fg(x) = x$

b Hence, or otherwise, find the largest value of a such that $g(a) = f^{-1}(a)$

[EDEXCEL, GCE Mathematics, C3, June 2016]

7 The functions f and g are defined by

$$f(x) = 5 - e^{3x}, \quad \text{for all real values of } x$$

$$g(x) = \frac{1}{2x - 3}, \quad \text{for } x \neq 1.5$$

a Find the range of f.

b The inverse of f is f^{-1}.

i Find $f^{-1}(x)$.

ii Solve the equation $f^{-1}(x) = 0$.

c Find an expression for $gg(x)$, giving your answer in the form $\frac{ax + b}{cx + d}$, where a, b, c and d are integers. [AQA, GCE Mathematics, C3, June 2015]

8 The function f has domain $-2 \leqslant x \leqslant 6$ and is linear from $(-2, 10)$ to $(2, 0)$ and from $(2, 0)$ to $(6, 4)$. A sketch of the graph of $y = \mathrm{f}(x)$ is shown:

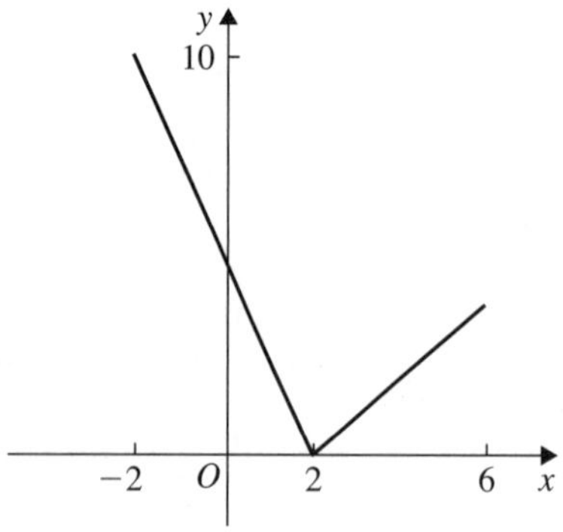

a Write down the range of f.

b Find ff(0).

The function g is defined by

$$\mathrm{g}: x \rightarrow \frac{4 + 3x}{5 - x}, \quad x \in \mathbb{R}, \quad x \neq 5$$

c Find $\mathrm{g}^{-1}(x)$

d Solve the equation $\mathrm{gf}(x) = 16$ [EDEXCEL, GCE Mathematics, C3, June 2013]

9 The functions f and g are defined with their respective domains by

$\mathrm{f}(x) = x^2 - 6x + 5$, for $x \geqslant 3$

$\mathrm{g}(x) = |x - 6|$, for all real values of x

a Find the range of f.

b The inverse of f is f^{-1}.
Find $\mathrm{f}^{-1}(x)$. Give your answer in its simplest form.

c **i** Find $\mathrm{gf}(x)$.

ii Solve the equation $\mathrm{gf}(x) = 6$. [AQA, GCE Mathematics, C3, June 2014]

10 Solve

$x^2 \geqslant |5x - 6|$ [AQA, GCE Mathematics, C3, June 2016]

11 It is given that $|x + 3a| = 5a$, where a is a positive constant. Find, in terms of a, the possible values of

$|x + 7a| - |x - 7a|$ [OCR, GCE Mathematics, C3, June 2015]

12 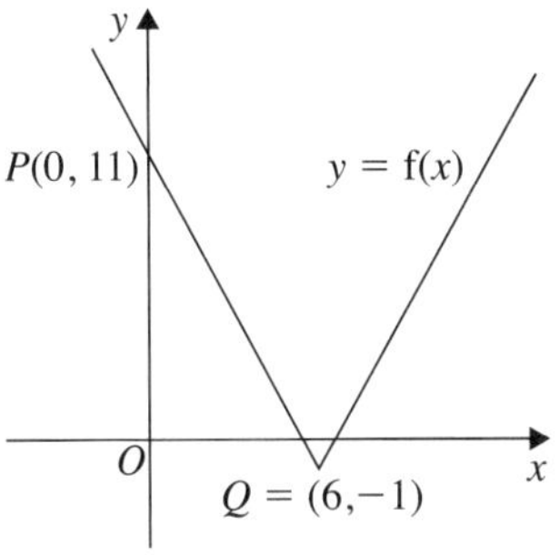

The diagram shows part of the graph with equation $y = \mathrm{f}(x)$, $x \in \mathbb{R}$.

The graph consists of two line segments that meet at the point $Q(6, -1)$.

The graph crosses the y-axis at the point $P(0, 11)$.

Sketch, on separate diagrams, the graphs of

a $y = |\mathrm{f}(x)|$

b $y = 2\mathrm{f}(-x) + 3$

On each diagram, show the coordinates of the points corresponding to P and Q.

Given that $\mathrm{f}(x) = a|x - b| - 1$, where a and b are constants,

c state the value of a and the value of b.

[EDEXCEL, GCE Mathematics, C3, June 2014]

13 **i** Give full details of a sequence of two transformations needed to transform the graph of $y = |x|$ to the graph of $y = |2(x + 3)|$.

ii Solve the inequality $|x| > |2(x + 3)|$, showing all your working.

[OCR, GCE Mathematics, C3, June 2013]

PART 2

Trigonometry 1

2.1 Radians

When you begin to study mathematics, angles are given in degrees. At a more advanced level it is convenient to measure angles in **radians**. When we differentiate or integrate with trigonometric expressions like $\sin\theta$, we *must* work with angles in radians.

Definition
An arc of length r subtends an angle of one radian at the centre of a circle of radius r.

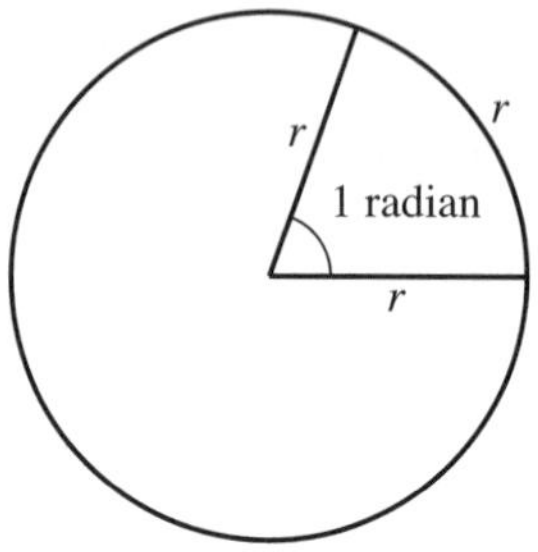

From this definition it follows that there are 2π radians in 360°.

So $\boxed{\pi \text{ radians} = 180°}$ Remember this.

To convert radians to degrees we multiply by $\frac{180}{\pi}$ and to convert degrees to radians we multiply by $\frac{\pi}{180}$. The abbreviation for radian is **rad**.

Sometimes angles in radians are written with a small 'c' (for circular measure). So '2^c' means 2 radians.

Example 1

Convert the following angles into radians:

a 90° **b** 140°

a $90° = 90 \times \frac{\pi}{180}$ radians

$= \frac{\pi}{2}$ radians

b $140° = 140 \times \frac{\pi}{180}$ radians

$= \frac{7\pi}{9}$ radians

Example 2

Convert the following angles into degrees:

a $\frac{2\pi^c}{3}$ **b** 3.5^c

a $\frac{2\pi^c}{3} = \frac{2\pi}{3} \times \frac{180}{\pi}$ degrees

$= 120°$

b $3.5^c = 3.5 \times \frac{180}{\pi}$ degrees

$= 201°$ (3 sf)

Most people find that it is worth learning the following important angles:

$30° = \frac{\pi}{6}$ radians	$60° = \frac{\pi}{3}$ radians	$180° = \pi$ radians
$45° = \frac{\pi}{4}$ radians	$90° = \frac{\pi}{2}$ radians	$360° = 2\pi$ radians

Example 3

Calculate $\sin\left(\frac{3\pi}{4}\right)$

We could first convert $\frac{3\pi}{4}$ into degrees, but it is simpler to switch your calculator into radian mode.

$$\sin\left(\frac{3\pi}{4}\right) = \frac{\sqrt{2}}{2}$$

Check: $\frac{3\pi}{4}$ radians $= \frac{3\pi}{4} \times \frac{180}{\pi} = 135°$

$$\sin(135°) = \frac{\sqrt{2}}{2}$$

Note: be careful always to have your calculator in the appropriate mode!

Example 4

Sketch the graph of $y = \cos x$ for $-\pi \leqslant x \leqslant \pi$

Remember: $-\pi^c = -180°$ and $\pi^c = 180°$

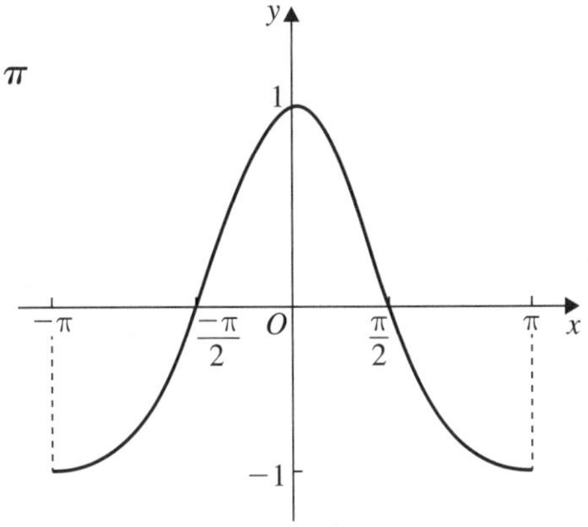

Example 5

Sketch the graph of $y = \sin\left(x - \frac{\pi}{6}\right)$ for $0 \leqslant x \leqslant 2\pi$

This graph is a translation of $y = \sin x$, $\frac{\pi}{6}^c$ in the positive x direction.

Sometimes you willl find it easier to keep in mind the equivalent angles in degrees, other times you will find it easier to work entirely in radians.

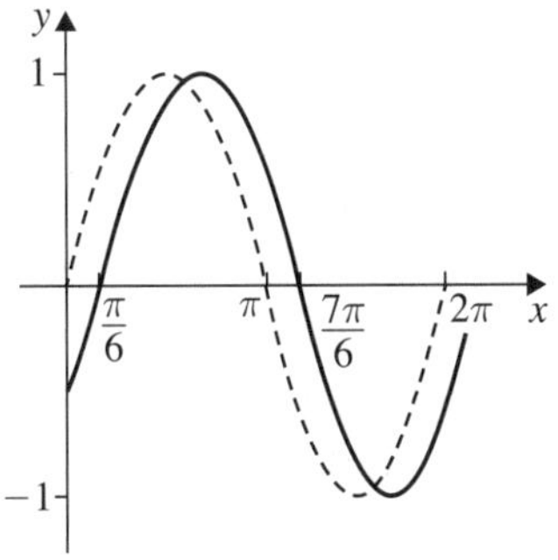

EXERCISE 2A

1 Convert the following angles into radians, leaving your answers in terms of π:

a 120° **b** 270° **c** 135° **d** 330° **e** 315° **f** 720°

2 Convert the following angles into radians, giving your answers to 3 significant figures:

a 40° **b** 100° **c** 50° **d** 218° **e** 87° **f** 1°

3 Convert the following angles into degrees, giving your answers to 3 significant figures where necessary:

a $\frac{5\pi}{4}^{c}$ **b** $\frac{3\pi}{2}^{c}$ **c** $\frac{7\pi}{8}^{c}$ **d** 2^{c} **e** 1.3^{c} **f** $\frac{1}{2}^{c}$

4 Calculate the following:

a $\sin\left(\frac{2\pi}{3}\right)$ **b** $\tan\left(\frac{\pi}{4}\right)$ **c** $\cos\left(-\frac{\pi}{6}\right)$

d $\sin(-0.7^{c})$ **e** $\cos(2.8^{c})$ **f** $\tan(1.2^{c})$

5 Sketch the following graphs for $-2\pi \leqslant x \leqslant 2\pi$:

a $y = \sin x$ **b** $y = \cos x$ **c** $y = \tan x$

6 Sketch the following graphs:

a $y = \sin x + 1$ for $0 \leqslant x \leqslant 2\pi$

b $y = 2\cos x$ for $-\pi \leqslant x \leqslant \pi$

c $y = \cos\left(x + \frac{\pi}{2}\right)$ for $0 \leqslant x \leqslant 2\pi$

d $y = \tan(2x)$ for $0 \leqslant x \leqslant \pi$

e $y = \tan\left(x - \frac{\pi}{3}\right)$ for $-\pi \leqslant x \leqslant \pi$

2.2 Arc length and area of a sector

Consider the sector shown on the right. If we were working in degrees we would say

$$\text{Arc length} = \frac{\theta}{360} \times 2\pi r$$

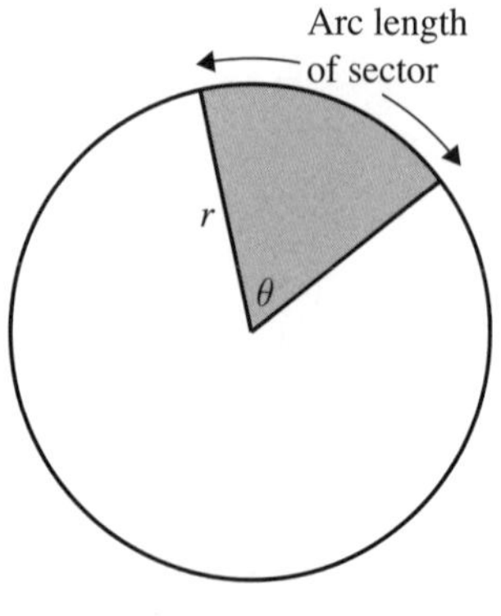

But when we are working in radians we use the fact that $360° = 2\pi^{c}$, so

$$\text{Arc length} = \frac{\theta}{2\pi} \times 2\pi r$$

$$l = r\theta$$

Similarly, to calculate the area of the sector using degrees we would use

$$\text{Area of sector} = \frac{\theta}{360} \times \pi r^2$$

Working in radians, we now use the formula

$$\text{Area of sector} = \frac{\theta}{2\pi} \times \pi r^2$$

$$A = \tfrac{1}{2} r^2 \theta$$

You should learn these two results.

Example 1

In the diagram arc AB subtends an angle of 1.2 radians at the centre of a circle of radius 10 cm. Find

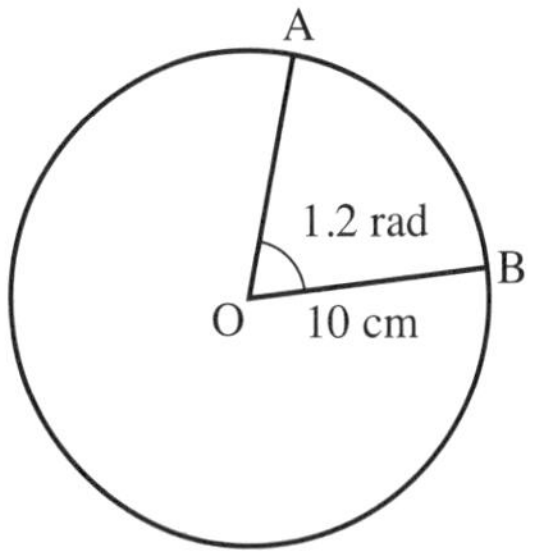

a the length of minor arc AB

b the area of sector AOB

a length of arc AB $= 10 \times 1.2$ $\quad (l = r\theta)$

$= 12$ cm

b area of sector AOB $= \frac{1}{2} \times 10^2 \times 1.2$ $\quad (A = \frac{1}{2}r^2\theta)$

$= 60\,\text{cm}^2$

Example 2

The arc of a sector of a circle, radius 5 cm, is of length 7 cm. Calculate the area of the sector.

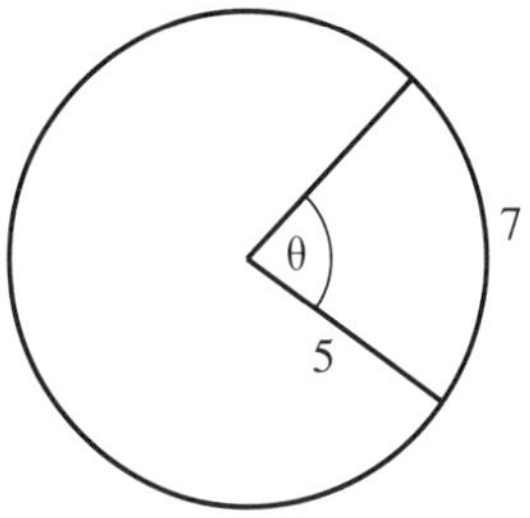

Let the angle at the centre of the circle be θ radians.

We have $\quad 7 = 5\theta \qquad (l = r\theta)$

$\theta = \frac{7}{5}$ radians

$\therefore$ Area of sector $= \frac{1}{2} \times 5^2 \times \frac{7}{5}$

$= 17\frac{1}{2}\,\text{cm}^2$

Example 3

The length of an arc of a circle is 9 cm.

The corresponding sector area is 27 cm².

Find:

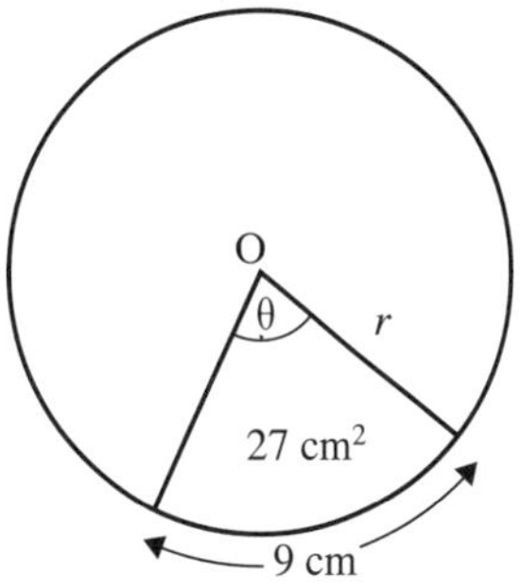

a the radius of the circle

b the angle subtended at the centre of the circle by the arc.

a Using r and θ, as shown in the diagram,

we have $\quad r\theta = 9 \qquad \ldots$ ①

and $\quad \frac{1}{2}r^2\theta = 27 \qquad \ldots$ ②

Write equation ② as $\frac{1}{2}r.r\theta = 27$

Substitute from equation ① for $r\theta$,

We have $\quad \frac{1}{2}r \times 9 = 27$

$r = \frac{27}{9} \times 2$

$r = 6\,\text{cm}$

b From ① $\quad \theta = \frac{9}{6} = 1.5$ radians

We can also solve geometrical problems by using the sine rule and cosine rule as we have done previously, we just need to ensure our calculator is in radian mode.

Example 4

Find x (to 3 significant figures).

$x^2 = 12^2 + 9^2 - 2 \times 12 \times 9 \times \cos\left(\frac{3\pi}{5}\right)$

$= 291.7\ldots$

$x = 17.1\,\text{cm}$

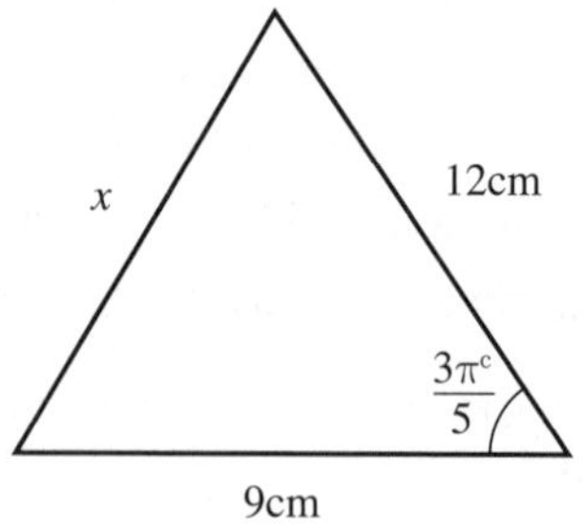

Example 5

Find the area of $\triangle$ABC, where AC = 3 cm
BC = 5 cm
$A\hat{C}B = 0.9$ radians

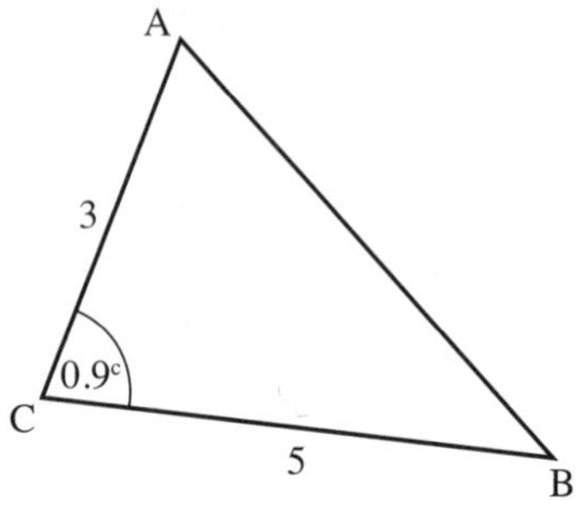

We have two sides and the included angle of triangle ABC.

Use the formula 'Area $= \frac{1}{2}ab\sin C$'.

Area of $\triangle ABC = \frac{1}{2} \times 3 \times 5 \times \sin 0.9$.

Area $= 5.87\,\text{cm}^2$ (2 dp)

Exercise 2B

1

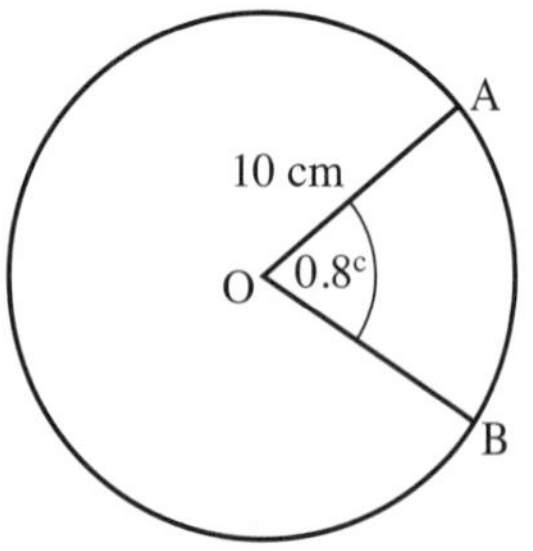

O is the centre of the circle of radius 10 cm and $A\hat{O}B = 0.8$ radians.
Find:

a the arc length AB

b the area of sector AOB

2 In the diagram shown,

r = radius of circle
l = arc length
θ = angle at centre in radians
A = area of sector

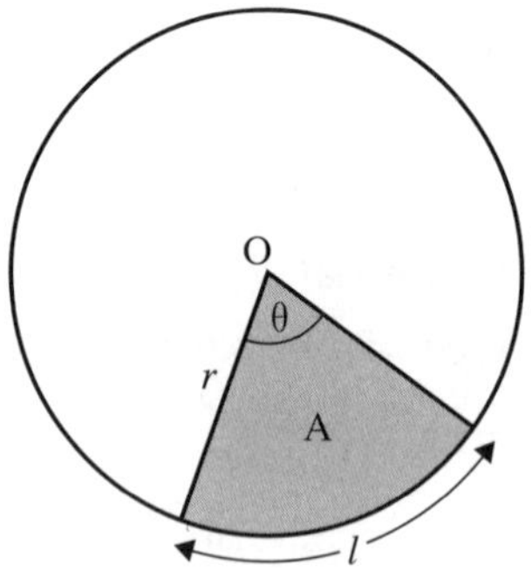

a If $r = 5$ cm and $\theta = 0.8$, find l.

b If $r = 10$ cm and $\theta = 1.2$, find A.

c If $l = 0.8$ cm and $r = 2$ cm, find θ.

d If A $= 4\frac{1}{2}\,\text{cm}^2$ and $\theta = 0.25$, find r.

e If $r = 1.2$ m and $\theta = 0.1$, find A.

3 In the diagram, BC = 15 m and AD = 8 m

a Find angle $B\hat{D}C$

b Find DC

c Find angle $D\hat{A}C$

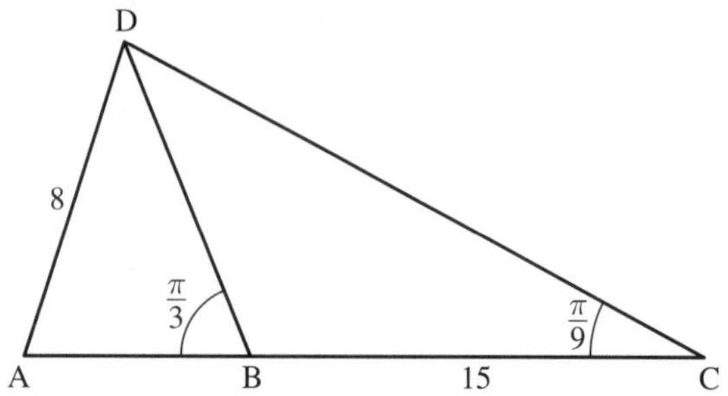

4 Find the labelled angle:

a

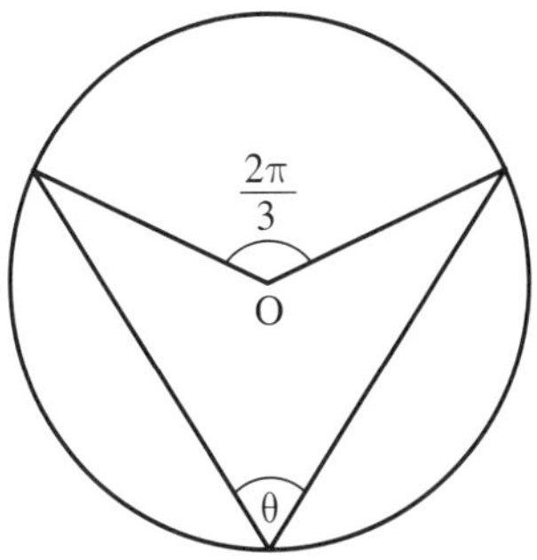

b

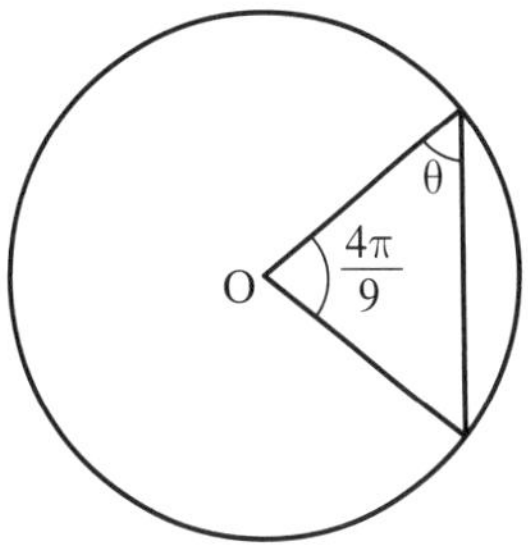

5 O is the centre of a circle and A and B are two points on the circumference. Find the following:

a The angle AOB (in radians), if OA = 3 cm and the arc length AB is 2.4 cm.

b The length OA (to 3 sf), if $\angle AOB = \frac{\pi}{6}$ radians and the area of sector AOB is 30 cm^2.

c The angle AOB (in radians), if OA = 5 cm and the area of sector AOB is 10 cm^2.

d The length OA (to 3 sf), if $\angle AOB = \frac{\pi}{4}$ radians and the area of sector AOB is 25 cm^2.

e The length OA, if the area of sector AOB is 150 cm^2 and the arc length AB is 75 cm.

6 The length of an arc of a circle is 6 cm. The corresponding sector area is 27 cm^2. Find:

a the radius of the circle

b the angle subtended at the centre of the circle by the arc.

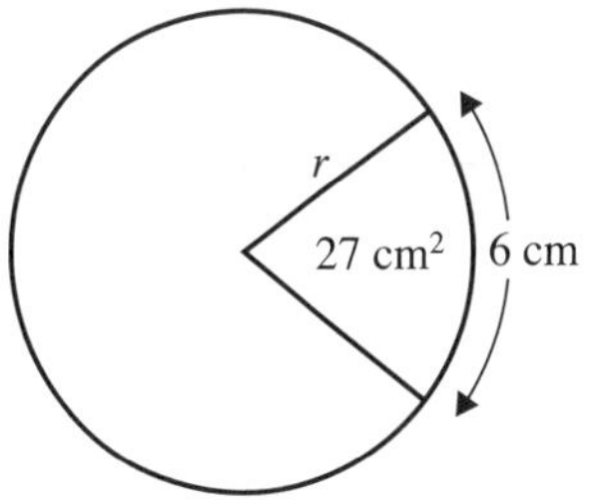

7 The length of an arc of a circle is 15 cm. The corresponding sector area is 150 cm^2. Find:

a the radius of the circle

b the angle subtended at the centre of the circle by the arc.

8 Find the length of an arc of a circle, which subtends an angle of 47° at the centre, if the radius of the circle is 8 cm. You may either work entirely in degrees, or you may convert to radians.

9 The radius of the circle shown is 10 cm and $A\hat{C}B = 45°$.
Find the length of the arc AB.

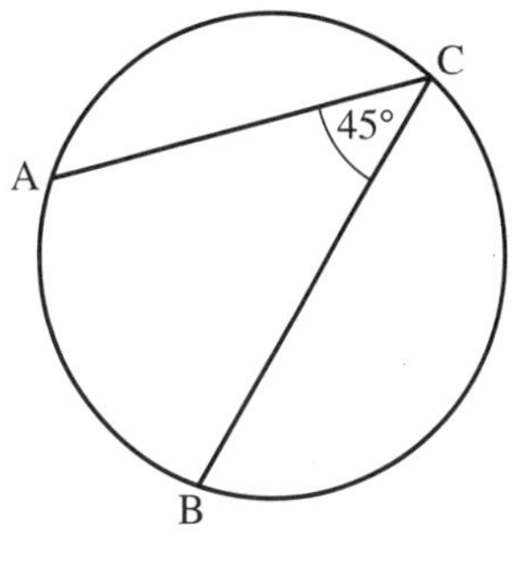

10 O is the centre of a circle of radius 8 cm and A and B are two points on the circumference such that $\angle AOB = \frac{\pi}{3}$ radians. The tangents at A and B meet at the point C (remember that the angles OAC and OBC are both right angles).

a Draw a diagram to represent this information.

b Find an expression for the area of the sector AOB (in terms of π).

c Show that the length AC is 4.62 cm (to 3 significant figures) by trigonometry on the triangle OAC.

d Use this to find (to 3 significant figures) the area of the triangle OAC and the quadrilateral AOBC.

e Hence find (to 3 significant figures) the area enclosed between the lines AC, BC and the arc AB.

11

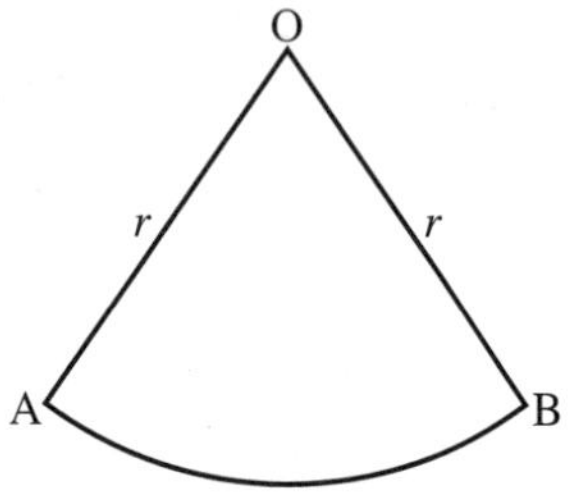

The diagram shows a sector of a circle with centre O and radius r. The length of the arc is equal to one quarter of the perimeter of the sector. Find the angle AOB in radians.

12

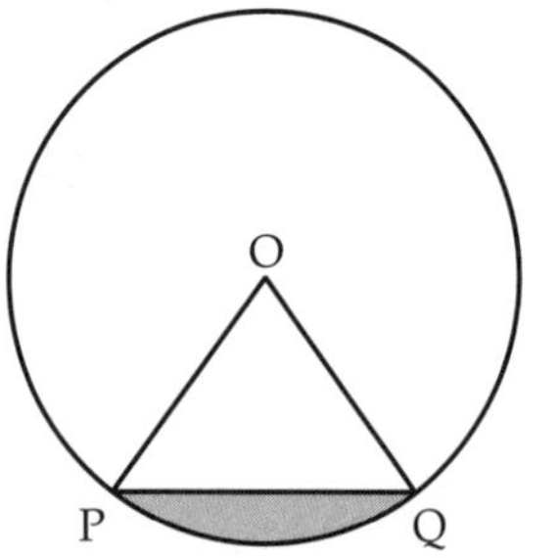

In the diagram, radius OP = 7 cm and $P\hat{O}Q = 1.4$ radians.
Calculate:

a the area of sector POQ

b the area of triangle POQ

c the shaded area.

13 O is the centre of a circle of radius 10 cm and A and B are two points on the circumference such that $\angle AOB = \theta$ radians.

a Find expressions, in terms of θ, for:

i the area of the sector AOB

ii the area of the triangle AOB

iii the area enclosed between the chord AB and the arc AB.

b If the area in **a iii** is one quarter of the area of the sector then show that $3\theta - 4\sin\theta = 0$.

14 A chord AB divides a circle with centre O into 2 regions whose areas are in the ratio 2 : 1.
If angle AOB = θ radians, show that

$$3\theta - 3\sin\theta = 2\pi$$

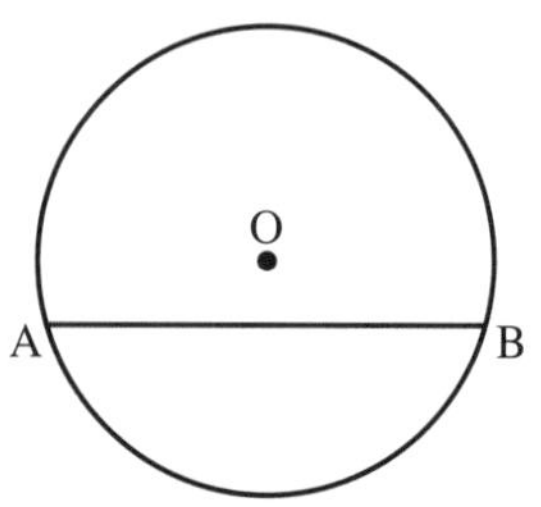

15 In the diagram, AB is a tangent to the circle at A. Straight lines BCD and ACE pass through the centre of the circle C.
Angle ACB $= x$ radians and the radius of the circle is 1 unit.

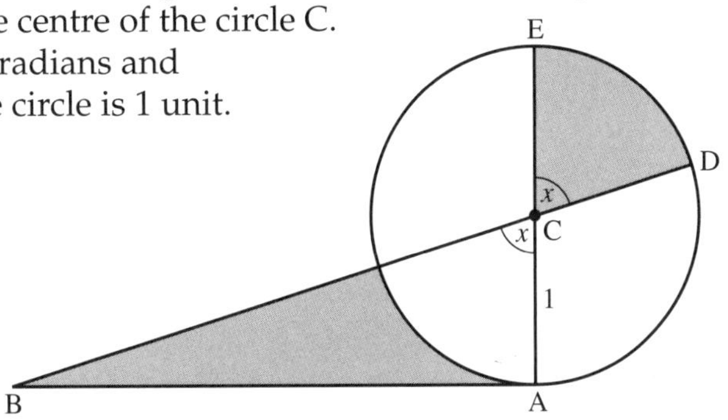

The two shaded areas are equal.

a Show that x satisfies the equation $x = \frac{1}{2}\tan x$.

b Use trial and improvement to find a solution for x correct to 2 dp.

16 A slice is taken out of a cylindrical cake of height 6 cm such that the angle of the slice is $\frac{\pi}{3}$.

a If the radius of the cake is r cm find an expression for the total surface area of the slice.

b If the total surface area of the slice is 200 cm^2 then write down a quadratic equation involving r.

c Use trial and improvement, or the quadratic formula, to find r (to 1 decimal place).

17 O is the centre of a circle of radius 4 cm and A and B are two points on the circumference.

a If $\angle AOB$ is θ, then find an expression for:

i the area of the sector AOB

ii the area of the triangle AOB

iii the area enclosed between the chord AB and the arc AB.

b If the area between the chord AB and the arc AB is 1.5 cm^2 then find, by trial and improvement, θ to 1 dp.

18 O is the centre of a circle of radius 6 cm and A and B are two points on the circumference such that $\angle AOB = \theta$ radians.

a Show that the length AB is equal to $\sqrt{72(1 - \cos\theta)}$.

b Hence write down the perimeter, in terms of θ, of the shape enclosed by the chord AB and the arc AB.

c If the perimeter is 18 cm then write down an equation involving θ.

d Find, by trial and error, the value of θ to 1 decimal place.

19 The two circles shown both have radius 4 cm. The centre of each circle lies on the circumference of the other. Find the *exact* area which is common to both circles.

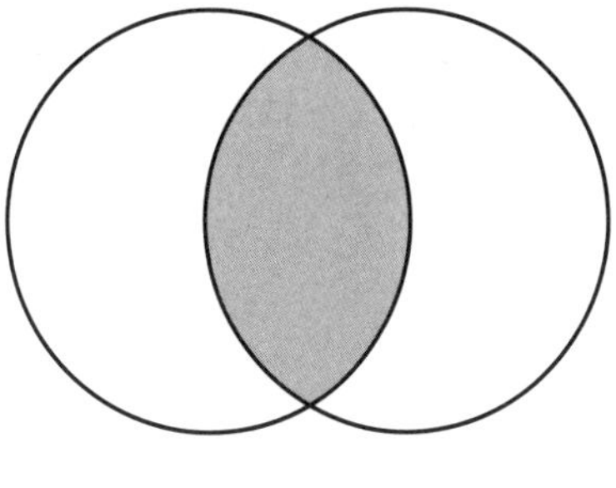

2.3 Solving equations using radians

Example 1

Solve the equation $\cos x = \frac{1}{2}$ for $0 \leqslant x \leqslant 2\pi$.

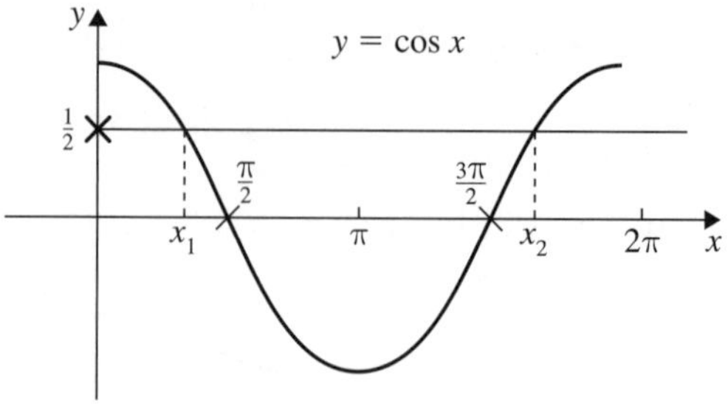

Method A

Sketch the curve $y = \cos x$ and draw the line $y = \frac{1}{2}$.

With our calculator in radian mode,

$$\cos^{-1}\left(\frac{1}{2}\right) = \frac{\pi}{3}$$

So solution x_1 is $\frac{\pi}{3}$ and, by symmetry, solution x_2 is $2\pi - \frac{\pi}{3}$.

$\therefore$ Solutions are $x = \frac{\pi}{3}$ or $\frac{5\pi}{3}$.

Method B

Many people find it quicker and easier to use a 'CAST diagram' instead of sketching the whole graph each time. Remember: angles are measured anti-clockwise from the positive x-axis.

We still use our calculator to find our principal value:

$$\cos^{-1}\left(\frac{1}{2}\right) = \frac{\pi}{3}$$

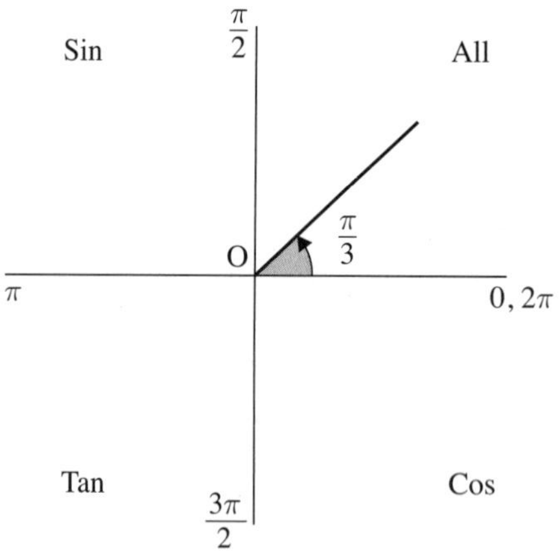

The other place that cosine is positive is in the 'C quadrant'.

$x_1 = \frac{\pi}{3}$ and $x_2 = 2\pi - \frac{\pi}{3} = \frac{5\pi}{3}$

$\therefore$ Solutions are $x = \frac{\pi}{3}$ or $\frac{5\pi}{3}$

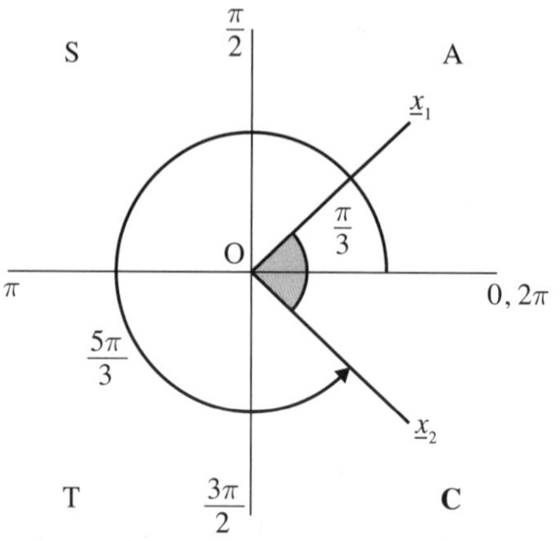

Example 2

Solve the equation $\sin x = 0.71$ for $0 \leqslant x \leqslant 2\pi$.

Method A

Sketch the curve $y = \sin x$ and draw the line $y = 0.71$.

Using a calculator in radian mode,

$\sin^{-1}(0.71) = 0.78950$ (5 dp)

So $x_1 = 0.790$ (3 dp)

and $x_2 = \pi - 0.78950$

$x_2 = 2.352$ (3 dp)

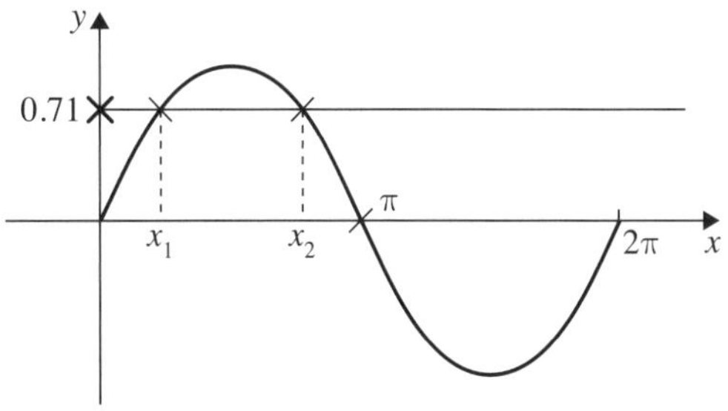

N.B. It is better to 'keep the working on the calculator'.
We have written working correct to 5 dp to indicate the method.

Method B

$\sin^{-1}(0.71) = 0.78950$

So $x_1 = 0.790$ (3 dp)

and $x_2 = \pi - 0.78950$

$= 2.352$ (3 dp)

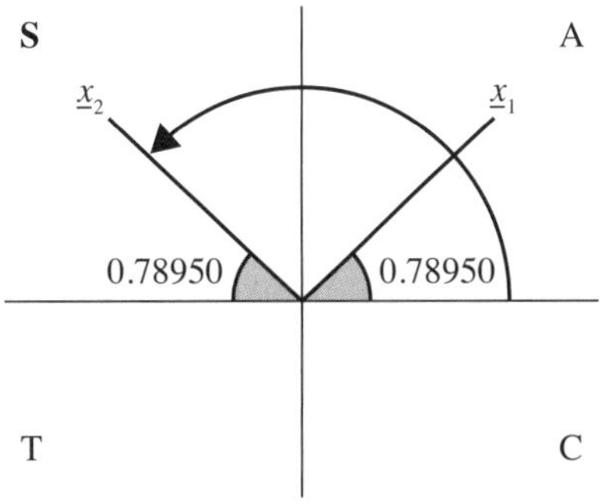

Example 3

Solve the equation $\sin 2\theta = 0.45$ for $0 \leqslant x \leqslant 2\pi$.

Method A

Sketch the curve $y = \sin x$ and draw the line $y = 0.45$.

Notice that we sketch the curve for $0 \leqslant x \leqslant 4\pi$ because the equation to be solved involves '2θ'.

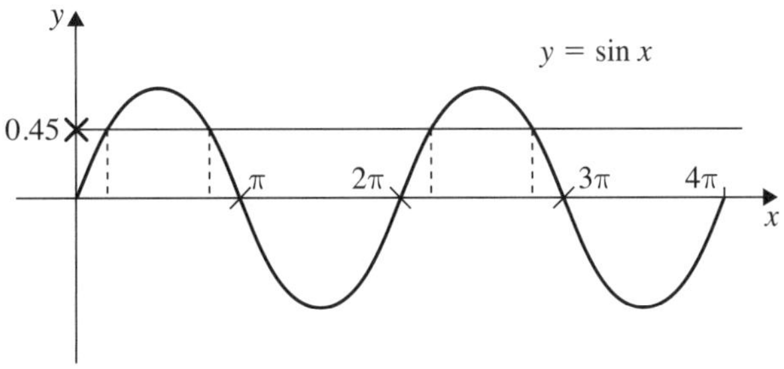

Using a calculator in radian mode, $\sin^{-1} 0.45 = 0.46677$ (5 dp).

So $2\theta = 0.46677, \pi - 0.46677, 2\pi + 0.46677, 3\pi - 0.46677$ (5 dp).

$2\theta = 0.46677, 2.67483, 6.74995, 8.95801$ (5 dp)

$\theta = 0.233, 1.337, 3.375, 4.479$ (3 dp)

[Once again it is better to 'keep the working on the calculator' if possible.]

Method B

$\sin^{-1}(0.45) = 0.46677$

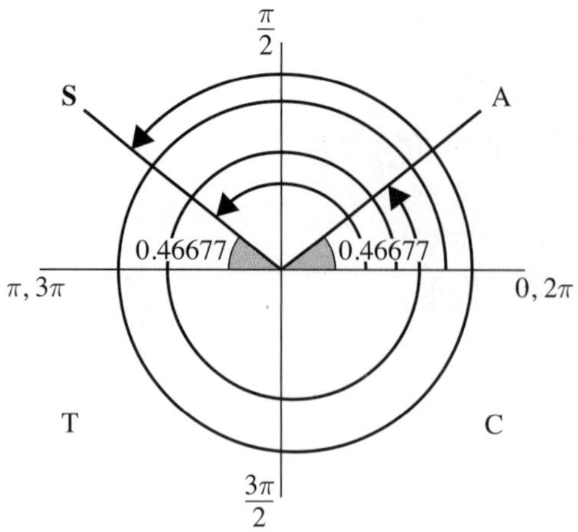

So $2\theta = 0.46677, \pi - 0.46677, 2\pi + 0.46677, 3\pi - 0.46677$

$2\theta = 0.46677, 2.67483, 6.74995, 8.95801$

$\theta = 0.233, 1.337, 3.375, 4.479$ (3 dp)

Example 4

Solve the equation $\sin\theta + \cos\theta = 0$ for $-\pi \leqslant \theta \leqslant \pi$.

Sometimes we will need to use the identities covered in Book 1:

$$\frac{\sin\theta}{\cos\theta} \equiv \tan\theta$$

$$\sin^2\theta + \cos^2\theta \equiv 1$$

$$\sin\theta + \cos\theta = 0$$

$$\frac{\sin\theta}{\cos\theta} + \frac{\cos\theta}{\cos\theta} = 0$$

$$\tan\theta + 1 = 0$$

$$\tan\theta = -1$$

Method A

Sketch the curve $y = \tan\theta$ and the line $y = -1$

Using a calculator in radian mode,

$$\tan^{-1}(-1) = -\frac{\pi}{4}$$

$$\theta_1 = -\frac{\pi}{4}$$

and $\theta_2 = \pi - \frac{\pi}{4} = \frac{3\pi}{4}$

so $\theta = -\frac{\pi}{4}, \frac{3\pi}{4}$

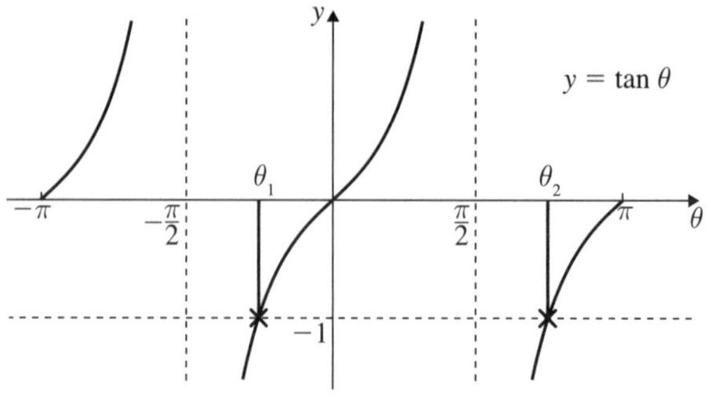

Method B

$\tan^{-1}(-1) = -\dfrac{\pi}{4}$

The principal angle is **negative** in this case, hence we draw it **clockwise** from the positive x-axis.

The other place tan is **negative** is in the 'S quadrant', because only sine is positive in this quadrant.

So $\theta_1 = -\dfrac{\pi}{4}$ and $\theta_2 = \pi - \dfrac{\pi}{4} = \dfrac{3\pi}{4}$

So $\theta = -\dfrac{\pi}{4}, \dfrac{3\pi}{4}$

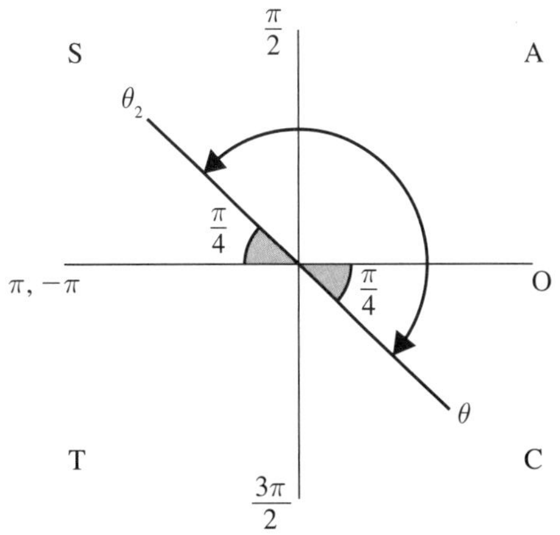

Example 5

Solve the equation $11\sin x - 2\cos^2 x + 7 = 0$ for $0 \leqslant x \leqslant 2\pi$

$$11\sin x - 2(1 - \sin^2 x) + 7 = 0$$
$$11\sin x - 2 + 2\sin^2 x + 7 = 0$$
$$2\sin^2 x + 11\sin x + 5 = 0$$
$$(2\sin x + 1)(\sin x + 5) = 0$$

$\sin x = -\frac{1}{2}$ or $\sin x = -5$ (no real solutions)

Method A

$\sin^{-1}\left(-\dfrac{1}{2}\right) = -\dfrac{\pi}{6}$

$x_1 = -\dfrac{\pi}{6}$ out of range

$x_2 = \pi + \dfrac{\pi}{6} = \dfrac{7\pi}{6}$

$x_3 = 2\pi - \dfrac{\pi}{6} = \dfrac{11\pi}{6}$

So $x = \dfrac{7\pi}{6}, \dfrac{11\pi}{6}$

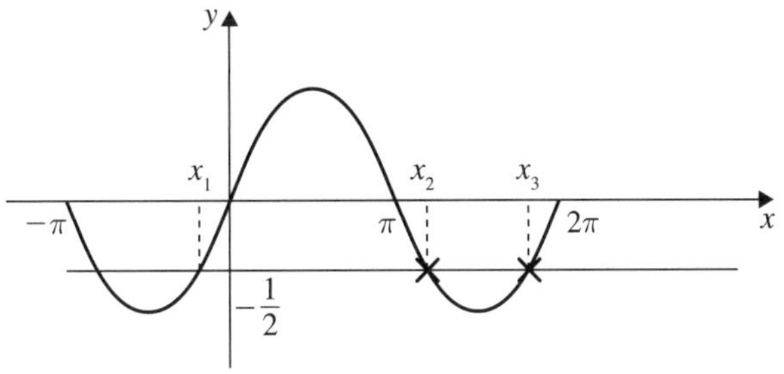

Method B

$\sin^{-1}\left(-\dfrac{1}{2}\right) = -\dfrac{\pi}{6}$

Note: sine is negative in the 'C quadrant' and the 'T quadrant'.

$x_1 = \pi + \dfrac{\pi}{6} = \dfrac{7\pi}{6}$

$x_2 = 2\pi - \dfrac{\pi}{6} = \dfrac{11\pi}{6}$

So $x = \dfrac{7\pi}{6}, \dfrac{11\pi}{6}$

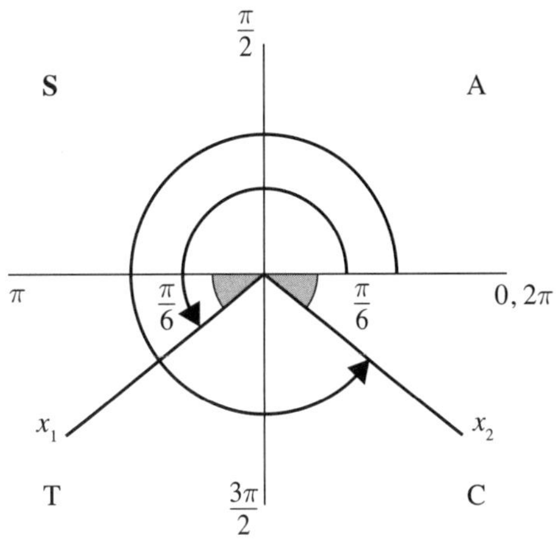

EXERCISE 2C

1 Write down the value of the following. The angles are in radians:

a $\sin \pi$ **b** $\cos \frac{\pi}{2}$ **c** $\tan 2\pi$ **d** $\sin 2\pi$

e $\tan \pi$ **f** $\cos(-\pi)$ **g** $\sin\left(-\frac{\pi}{2}\right)$ **h** $\cos 4\pi$

2 Look at the triangles shown.
Copy and complete the table.

	0	$\frac{\pi}{6}$	$\frac{\pi}{4}$	$\frac{\pi}{3}$	$\frac{\pi}{2}$
sin					
cos					
tan					

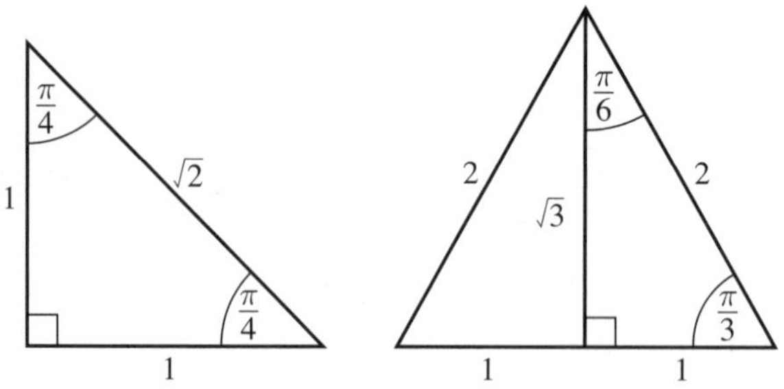

3 Use your table from the last question to write down:

a $\sin \frac{2\pi}{3}$ **b** $\cos \frac{3\pi}{4}$ **c** $\tan\left(-\frac{\pi}{4}\right)$ **d** $\sin \frac{5\pi}{6}$

4 Use a calculator in radian mode to find the following.
Give answers correct to 3 significant figures.

a $\sin 0.63^c$ **b** $\tan 3.4^c$ **c** $\cos 2^c$

d $\tan^{-1} 1.4$ **e** $\cos^{-1} 0.9$ **f** $\sin^{-1} 0.278$

In Questions **5**, **6**, **7** give your answers in terms of π.

5 Solve the equation $\sin x = \frac{1}{2}$ for $0 \leqslant x \leqslant 2\pi$.

6 Solve the equation $\tan x = \sqrt{3}$ for $0 \leqslant x \leqslant 2\pi$.

7 Solve the following equations for $0 \leqslant x \leqslant 2\pi$.

a $\cos \theta = \frac{1}{\sqrt{2}}$ **b** $\sin \theta = 1$ **c** $\tan \theta = \frac{1}{\sqrt{3}}$

8 Solve the following, giving your answers in radians correct to 3 dp:

a $\sin \theta = 0.4$ for $0 \leqslant x \leqslant 2\pi$

b $\sin \theta = 0.65$ for $0 \leqslant x \leqslant \pi$

c $\cos \theta = 0.21$ for $0 \leqslant x \leqslant 2\pi$

d $\tan \theta = 2$ for $0 \leqslant x \leqslant 2\pi$

9 Solve the following equations. Give your answers in terms of π where possible or otherwise correct to 3 dp:

a $\cos \theta = \frac{\sqrt{3}}{2}$ for $-\pi \leqslant \theta \leqslant \pi$

b $\sin \theta = -0.7$ for $0 \leqslant \theta \leqslant 2\pi$

c $\tan \theta = 1.7$ for $-\pi \leqslant \theta \leqslant \pi$

d $\cos \theta = -\frac{1}{2}$ for $0 \leqslant \theta \leqslant 4\pi$

10 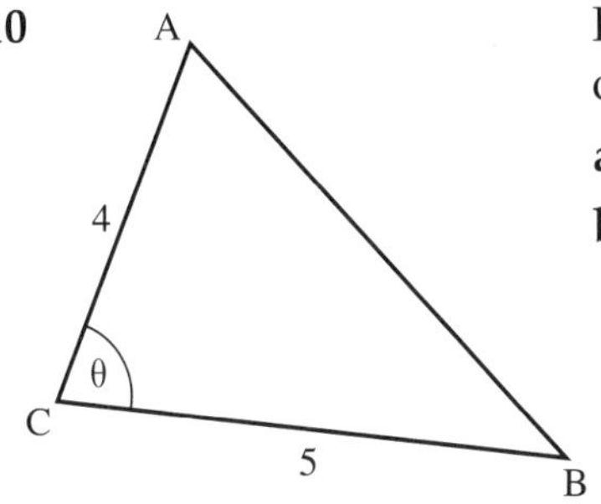

In $\triangle ABC$, AC = 4 cm, BC = 5 cm and the area of the triangle is $7\,\text{cm}^2$.

a Find angle ACB in radians.

b Is there more than one possible answer? If so, find it.

11 O is the centre of a circle of radius r cm and angle AOB = $\theta = 2$ radians. Given that the shaded area is $20\,\text{cm}^2$, find the value of r.

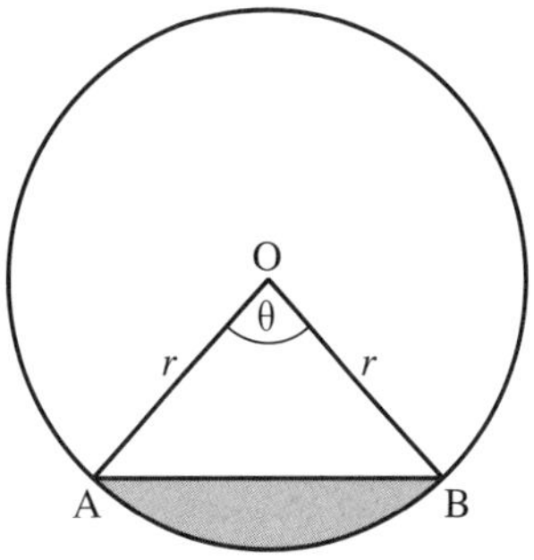

12 Solve the equations for $0 \leqslant \theta \leqslant 2\pi$:

a $\sin 2\theta = 1$ **b** $\cos 2\theta = 0$

c $\tan 2\theta = 1.5$ **d** $\cos\dfrac{\theta}{2} = 0.4$

13 Solve the equations for $0 \leqslant \theta \leqslant 2\pi$:

a $\cos\left(\theta - \dfrac{\pi}{4}\right) = \dfrac{1}{2}$ **b** $\sin\left(\theta - \dfrac{\pi}{6}\right) = \dfrac{1}{\sqrt{2}}$

c $\tan\left(\theta - \dfrac{\pi}{6}\right) = \sqrt{3}$ **d** $\sin(\theta - 0.5^c) = 0.9$

Solve the following equations for $0 \leqslant x \leqslant \pi$. Give your solutions in terms of π or as decimals correct to 3 dp:

14 $\cos^2 x = \frac{1}{4}$ **15** $2\sin x = 3\cos x$

16 $\tan^2 x = 1$ **17** $\sin^2 x = 2\sin x\cos x$

18 $3\tan x = \cos x$ **19** $\tan x = 2\sin x$

20 $\sin^2 x + \sin x = 2$ **21** $\tan^2 x = \tan x + 2$

22 $\sin 2x = \cos 2x$ **23** $1 + \sin x = 2\cos^2 x$

24 $\tan\left(x - \dfrac{\pi}{4}\right) = 1$ **25** $\cos\left(x - \dfrac{\pi}{6}\right) = \dfrac{1}{2}$

2.4 Small angle approximations

Trigonometric functions are very difficult to evaluate without the use of a calculator. It can be useful, therefore, to find **approximations** for $\sin\theta$, $\cos\theta$ and $\tan\theta$.

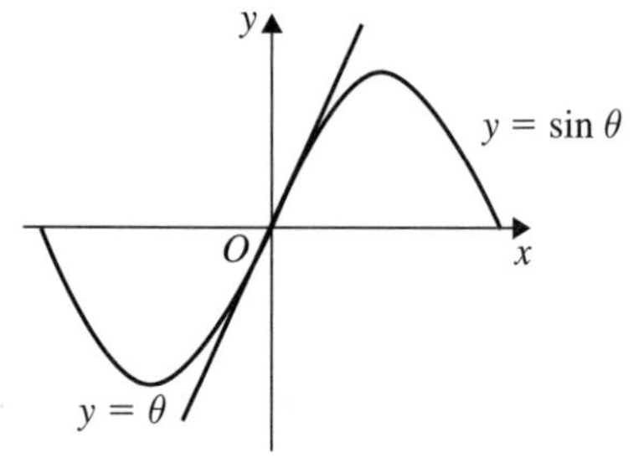

$y = \theta$ is a very simple approximation for $y = \sin\theta$, but it is a good approximation for small values of θ.

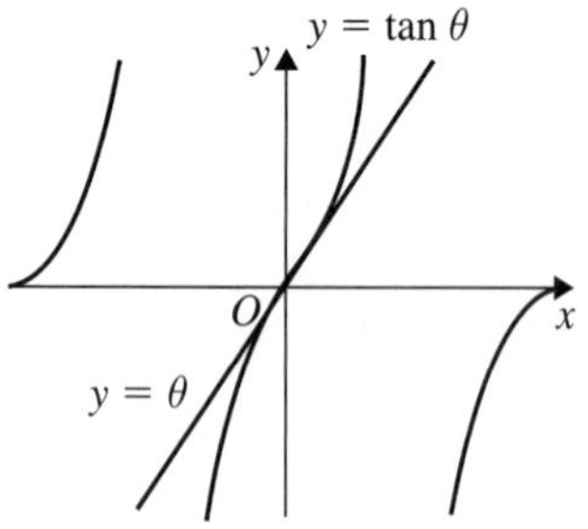

We can see that $y = \theta$ is also a good approximation for $y = \tan\theta$, for small values of θ only.

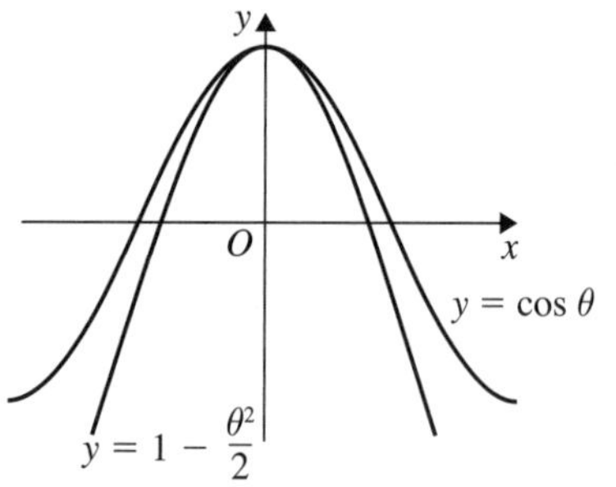

The graph of $y = \cos\theta$ requires a more complicated approximation for small values of θ. We use the graph of $y = 1 - \frac{\theta^2}{2}$.

$\sin\theta \approx \theta$
$\tan\theta \approx \theta$
$\cos\theta \approx 1 - \frac{\theta^2}{2}$

You should learn these.

Note: these approximations are only valid for **small values** of θ, and θ must be measured in **radians**.

Example 1

Show that, when θ is small,

$$5\sin 2\theta + 4\cos\theta - 2\tan 3\theta \approx 4\theta - 2\theta^2 + 4$$

$$\begin{aligned} 5\sin 2\theta + 4\cos\theta - 2\tan 3\theta &\approx 5(2\theta) + 4\left(1 - \frac{\theta^2}{2}\right) - 2(3\theta) \\ &= 10\theta + 4 - 2\theta^2 - 6\theta \\ &= 4\theta - 2\theta^2 + 4 \end{aligned}$$

Example 2

When x is small, find the approximate value of $\dfrac{3\sin^2 5x}{1 - \cos 4x}$

$$\frac{3\sin^2 5x}{1-\cos 4x} \approx \frac{3(5x)^2}{1-\left(1-\dfrac{(4x)^2}{2}\right)}$$

$$= \frac{3(25x^2)}{1-1+\dfrac{16x^2}{2}}$$

$$= \frac{75x^2}{8x^2}$$

$$= \frac{75}{8}$$

Does this approximation hold true when $x = 0$?

Example 3

When θ is small, find the approximate value of $\dfrac{2\tan 3\theta + \sin^2 2\theta}{7\theta - \sin 5\theta}$

$$\frac{2\tan 3\theta + \sin^2 2\theta}{7\theta - \sin 5\theta} \approx \frac{2(3\theta) + (2\theta)^2}{7\theta - 5\theta}$$

$$= \frac{6\theta + 4\theta^2}{2\theta}$$

$$= 3 + 2\theta$$

Now, when θ is small, 2θ will also be small, so we can disregard it. Hence

$$3 + 2\theta \approx 3$$

So, for small values of θ

$$\frac{2\tan 3\theta + \sin^2 2\theta}{7\theta - \sin 5\theta} \approx 3$$

EXERCISE 2D

1 **a** Calculate the value of $\sin(0.25^c)$ correct to 5 dp.

b Use the approximation for $\sin\theta$ to find an approximate value for $\sin(0.25^c)$.

c Find the percentage error in the approximation for $\sin(0.25^c)$.

2 Calculate the percentage error in the approximation for sin(0.85).

3 Calculate the percentage error in the approximation for cos(0.5).

4 When θ is small, show that:

a $\tan 3\theta - 3\cos 2\theta + 2\sin\theta \approx 6\theta^2 + 5\theta - 3$

b $3\sin^2 2\theta + 2\cos 3\theta \approx 3\theta^2 + 2$

c $\dfrac{\cos 2\theta + \tan\theta - 1}{2\theta + \sin 3\theta} \approx \dfrac{1}{5}(1 - 2\theta)$

d $\dfrac{(\sin\theta + \tan 2\theta)^2}{1 - \cos 3\theta} \approx 2$

5 **a** When θ is small, show that $\cos 3\theta - 2(\tan 2\theta + \sin\theta) \approx 1 - \frac{9}{2}\theta^2 - 6\theta$

b Hence write down the approximate value of $\cos 3\theta - 2(\tan 2\theta + \sin\theta)$ when θ is small.

6 For small values of θ, find the approximate values of

a $\dfrac{\theta^2 + \sin 3\theta}{3\theta - \tan 2\theta}$ **b** $\dfrac{\cos 4\theta + 3\sin\theta - 1}{\tan\theta}$

c $\dfrac{3\tan\theta}{\sin\theta} + 4\cos 3\theta$ **d** $\cos^2 3\theta + \sin 4\theta + 5$

7 Find the approximate values of x and y.

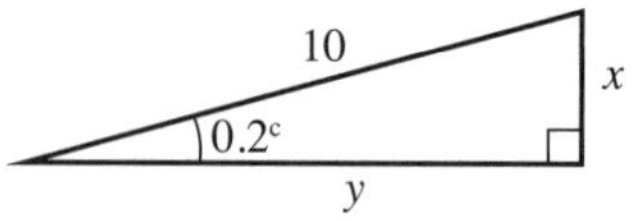

8 Find the approximate values of a and b, giving your answer correct to 1 dp.

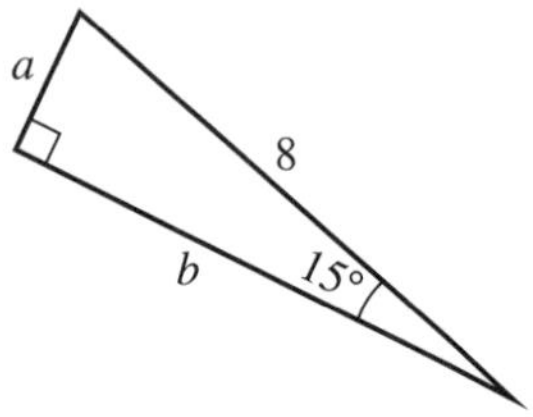

Review Exercise 2E

1 Calculate the length of the side marked with a letter. All lengths are in cm.

a

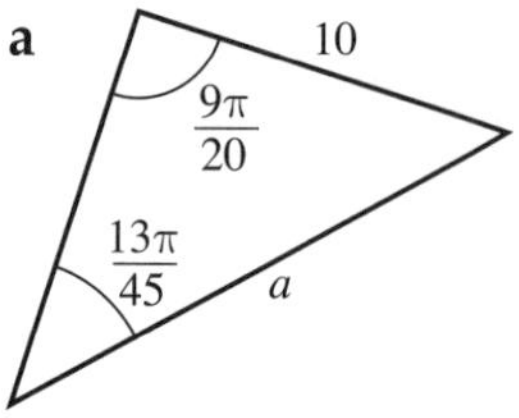

b

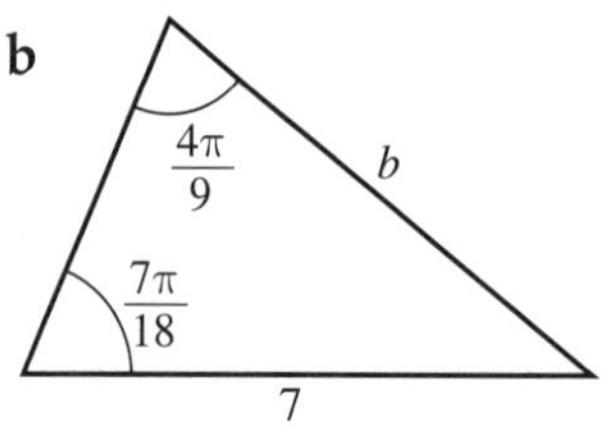

c

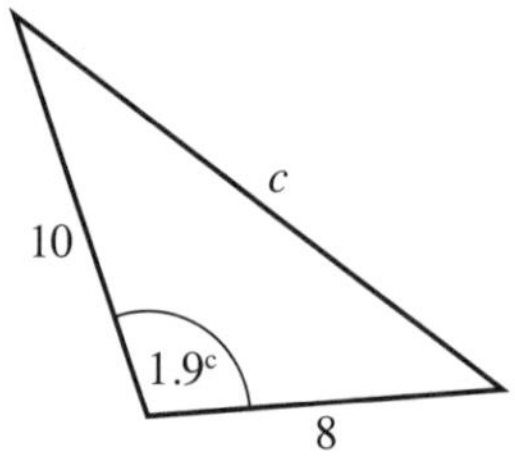

2 In triangle ABC, $a = 4.3$, $b = 7.2$, $c = 9$. Find $\hat{C}$, giving your answer in radians.

3 In triangle DEF, $\hat{D} = \dfrac{3\pi}{10}$, EF = 7.2, DE = 5.4. Find $\hat{F}$.

4 In triangle PQR, $p = 8$, $q = 14$, $r = 7$. Find $\hat{Q}$, giving your answer in radians.

5 In triangle XYZ, $\hat{Y} = 1.7^c$, XZ = 22, XY = 14. Find $\hat{Z}$.

6 Find the area of each triangle. All lengths are in cm.

a

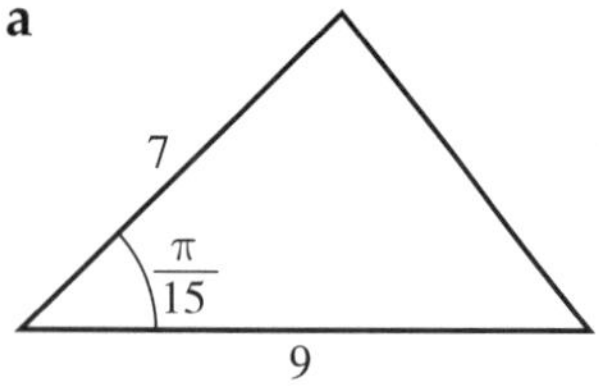

b

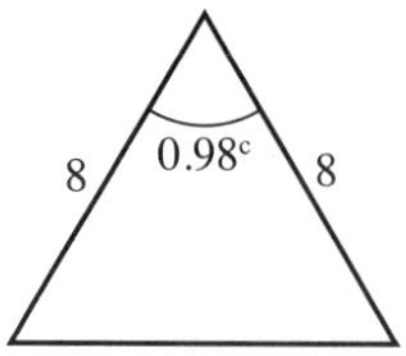

7 If $\sin\dfrac{3\pi}{5} = 0.951$, give another angle whose sine is 0.951.

8 Sort the following into pairs of equal value.

$\sin\frac{\pi}{4}$	$-\sin\left(-\frac{\pi}{3}\right)$	$\sin\frac{5\pi}{6}$	$\tan\left(-\frac{\pi}{6}\right)$
$\sin\frac{\pi}{6}$	$\tan\frac{\pi}{6}$	$\cos\frac{\pi}{4}$	$\cos\frac{\pi}{6}$
$\tan\frac{5\pi}{6}$	$\cos\frac{11\pi}{6}$	$\sin\frac{2\pi}{3}$	$\tan\left(-\frac{5\pi}{6}\right)$

9 Sketch the following curves for $0 \leqslant x \leqslant 2\pi$:

a $y = 3\sin x$ **b** $y = \cos\left(x - \frac{\pi}{2}\right)$ **c** $y = \sin 2x$

d $y = 1 + \cos x$ **e** $y = 4\cos 2x$

10 **a** Sketch the curve $y = 2\tan 2x$ for $0 \leqslant x \leqslant \pi$.

b **i** In the range $0 \leqslant x \leqslant \pi$, how many solutions are there to the equation $2\tan 2x = 11$?

ii How many solutions will there be in the range $0 \leqslant x \leqslant 2\pi$?

11 In the diagram shown,
r = radius of circle
l = arc length
θ = angle at centre in radians
A = area of sector

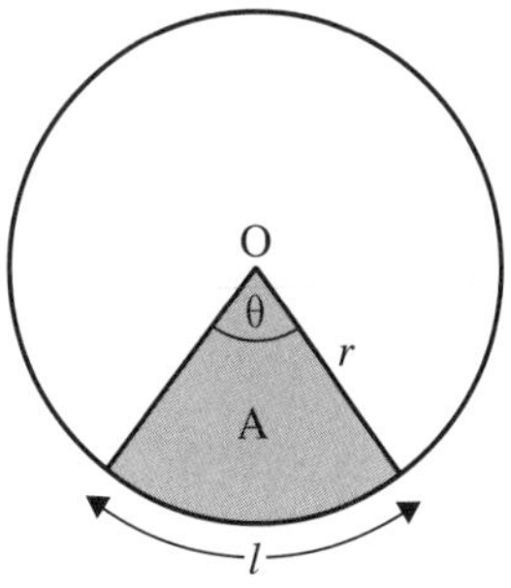

a If $r = 8\,\text{cm}$ and $\theta = 1.5$, find l.

b If $r = 6\,\text{cm}$ and $\theta = 0.8$, find A.

c If $l = 12\,\text{cm}$ and $\theta = 1$, find r.

d If A $= 20\,\text{cm}^2$ and $r = 2\,\text{cm}$, find θ.

e If $l = 50\,\text{cm}$ and $r = 20\,\text{cm}$, find θ.

f If A $= 3\,\text{cm}^2$ and $l = 3\,\text{cm}$, find r and θ.

g If A $= 8\,\text{cm}^2$ and $l = 4\,\text{cm}$, find r.

12 A chord PQ of a circle of radius 10 cm subtends an angle of $\frac{\pi}{2}$ radians at the centre O. Calculate the exact areas of the two parts into which the chord PQ divides the sector POQ.

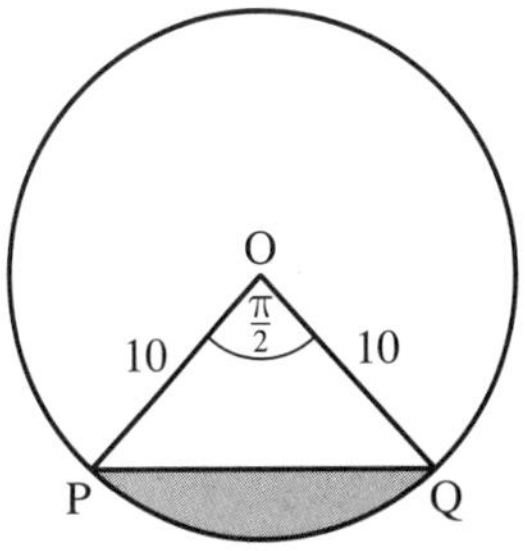

13

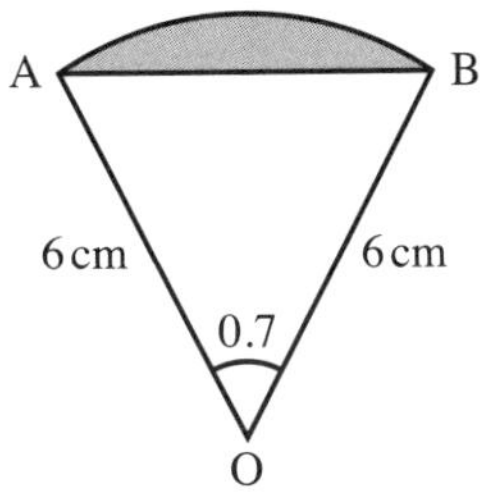

The diagram shows a sector of a circle with centre O and radius 6 cm. The angle AOB is 0.7 radians. Find

a the length of the arc AB

b the area of the shaded segment

14 The diagram shows a sector ABC of a circle with centre A and radius AB. The triangle ABC is equilateral, with a perpendicular height of 30 cm.

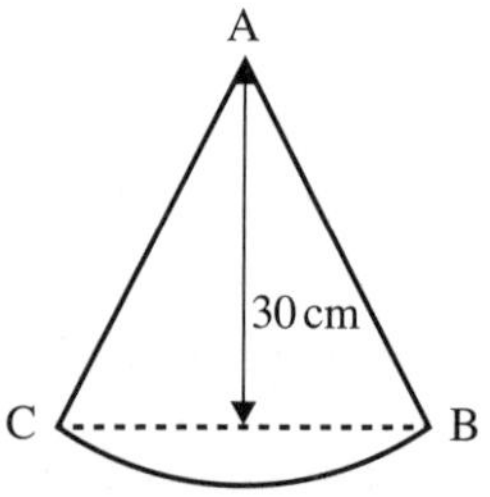

a Find the exact length of AB.

b Find the exact area of the sector ABC.

c Find the exact perimeter of the sector ABC.

15 In the diagram, the circle has centre O and radius r. Angle AOB is θ radians and C is the mid-point of OB. The length of AC is l.

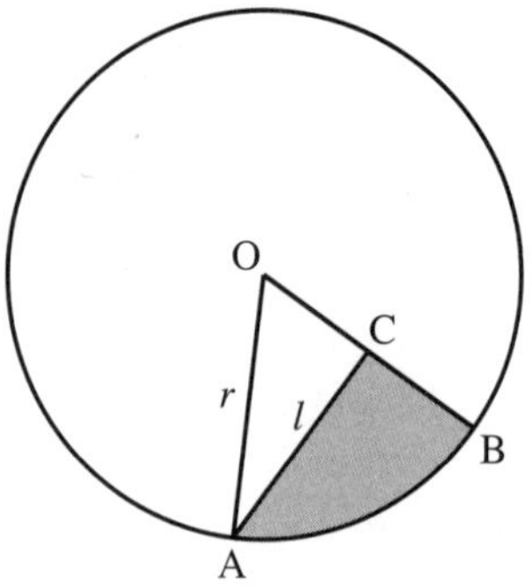

a Express l^2 in terms of r and θ.

b Given that $l = \frac{2}{3}r$, calculate the value of θ, correct to 3 dp.

c Given that $r = 2$ cm, calculate the area of the shaded region, giving your answer correct to 2 dp.

16 A circle, centre A and radius 5 cm, intersects a triangle ABC as shown. Calculate:

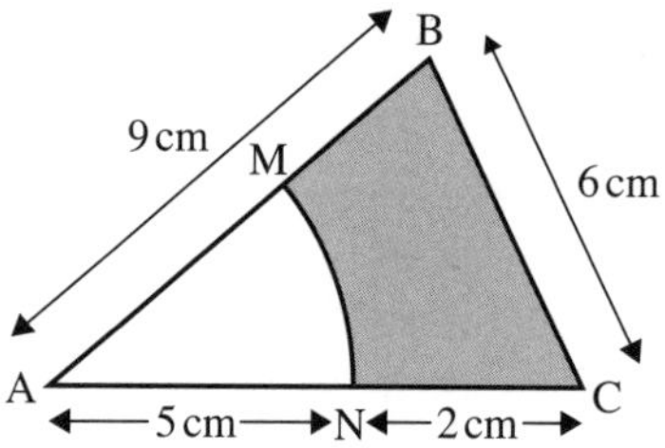

a the angle $B\hat{A}C$, giving your answer in radians

b the area of the sector AMN

c the shaded area MNCB

d the perimeter of the shaded region MNCB

17 Solve the following trigonometric equations in the given intervals (to 1 dp where necessary):

a $\cos x = \frac{1}{2}$ for $0 \leqslant x \leqslant 2\pi$

b $\tan x = 1$ for $-\pi \leqslant x \leqslant \pi$

c $\cos x = \dfrac{1}{\sqrt{2}}$ for $0 \leqslant x \leqslant 2\pi$

d $\sin x = \dfrac{\sqrt{3}}{2}$ for $-\pi \leqslant x \leqslant \pi$

e $\sin x = -\frac{2}{3}$ for $0 \leqslant x \leqslant 2\pi$

f $\cos x = -\frac{3}{4}$ for $0 \leqslant x \leqslant 2\pi$

g $\tan x = -0.7$ for $-\pi \leqslant x \leqslant \pi$

h $\sin x = -\frac{1}{2}$ for $-\pi \leqslant x \leqslant \pi$

18 Solve the following trigonometric equations in the given intervals:

a $\sin\left(x - \dfrac{\pi}{2}\right) = -\dfrac{\sqrt{3}}{2}$ for $0 < x < 2\pi$

b $\sin\left(x - \dfrac{\pi}{3}\right) = \dfrac{1}{2}$ for $0 < x < 2\pi$

c $\cos\left(x + \dfrac{\pi}{4}\right) = -\dfrac{1}{2}$ for $0 < x < 2\pi$

d $\tan\left(x - \dfrac{\pi}{4}\right) = 1$ for $-\pi < x < \pi$

19 Find all values of θ between 0^c and $2\pi^c$ for which $2\sin\theta + 8\cos^2\theta = 5$.

20 Solve the following trigonometric equations in the given intervals:

a $\cos^2 x + 2\sin x - 2 = 0$ for $0 \leqslant x \leqslant 2\pi$ (1 exact value)

b $2\sin^2 x - \cos x - 1 = 0$ for $0 \leqslant x \leqslant 2\pi$ (3 exact values)

c $6\cos^2 x + \sin x - 5 = 0$ for $-\pi \leqslant x \leqslant \pi$ (2 exact values and 2 values to 1 dp)

d $6\sin^2 x + \cos x - 4 = 0$ for $-\pi \leqslant x \leqslant \pi$ (2 exact values and 2 values to 1 dp)

e $4\cos^2 x - 4\sin x - 5 = 0$ for $-\pi \leqslant x \leqslant \pi$ (2 exact values)

21 Find the *exact solutions* to the following trigonometric equations in the given intervals:

a $\sin^2\left(x + \frac{\pi}{6}\right) = \frac{1}{2}$ for $-\pi \leqslant x < \pi$

b $\cos^2\left(x - \frac{\pi}{3}\right) = \frac{1}{4}$ for $0 < x < 2\pi$

c $\sin^2\left(x + \frac{\pi}{2}\right) = \frac{3}{4}$ for $0 \leqslant x < 2\pi$

22 Solve the following trigonometric equations in the given intervals:

a $\sin^2\left(x - \frac{\pi}{4}\right) = \frac{3}{4}$ for $0 \leqslant x \leqslant 2\pi$ (exact values)

b $\cos 2x = \frac{1}{2}$ for $0 \leqslant x \leqslant 2\pi$ (exact values)

c $8\cos^2 x + 2\sin x - 5 = 0$ for $0 \leqslant x \leqslant 2\pi$ (to 1 dp)

d $\sin x = 3\cos x$ for $0 \leqslant x \leqslant 2\pi$ (to 2 dp)

e $2\sin^2 x = \sin x \cos x$ for $0 \leqslant x \leqslant 2\pi$

23 When θ is small, show that:

a $\sin 2\theta + \cos^2 2\theta - \tan 3\theta \approx 1 - 4\theta^2 - \theta$

b $\dfrac{\tan\theta - \cos 2\theta}{2\sin 3\theta} \approx \dfrac{2\theta^2 + \theta - 1}{6\theta}$

24 For small values of x, find the approximate values of

a $\tan 4x - 3(\cos 2x - \sin 5x)$

b $\dfrac{(\sin 2x + \tan 3x)^2}{\tan x}$

Examination Exercise 2

1 The diagram shows a sector AOB of a circle with centre O and radius r cm. The angle AOB is 54°. The perimeter of the sector is 60 cm.

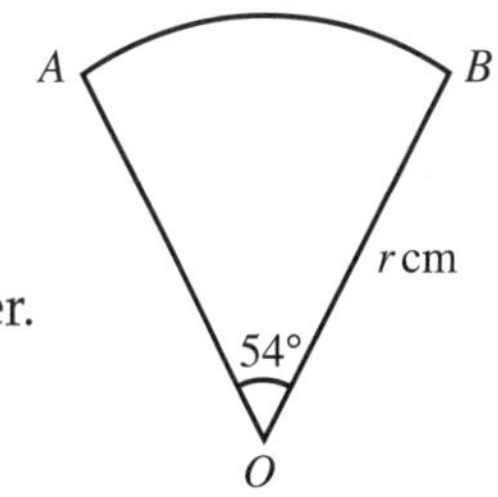

i Express 54° exactly in radians, simplifying your answer.

ii Find the value of r, giving your answer correct to 3 significant figures.

[OCR, GCE Mathematics, C2, June 2016]

2

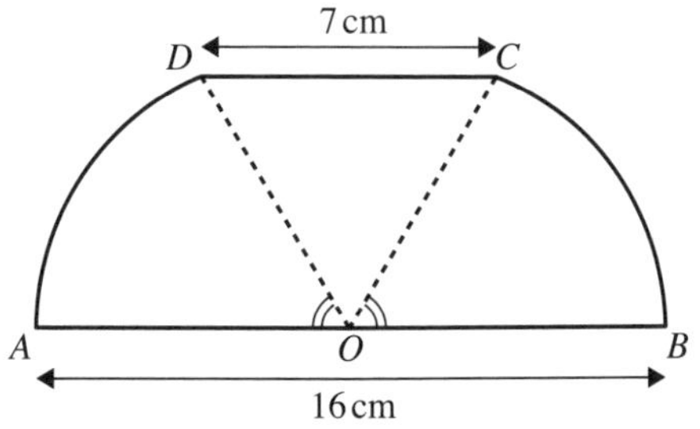

The diagram shows a sketch of a design for a scraper blade. The blade $AOBCDA$ consists of an isosceles triangle COD joined along its equal sides to sectors OBC and ODA of a circle with centre O and radius 8 cm. Angles AOD and BOC are equal. AOB is a straight line and is parallel to the line DC. DC has length 7 cm.

a Show that the angle COD is 0.906 radians, correct to 3 significant figures.

b Find the perimeter of $AOBCDA$, giving your answer to 3 significant figures.

c Find the area of $AOBCDA$, giving your answer to 3 significant figures.

[EDEXCEL, GCE Mathematics, C2, June 2015]

3

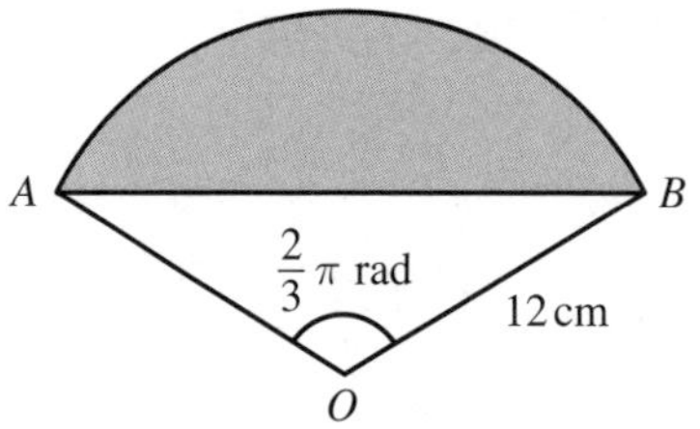

The diagram shows a sector OAB of a circle, centre O and radius 12 cm.

The angle AOB is $\frac{2}{3}\pi$ radians.

i Find the exact length of the arc AB.

ii Find the exact area of the shaded segment enclosed by the arc AB and the chord AB. [OCR, GCE Mathematics, C2, June 2014]

4 The diagram shows a sector OAB of a circle with centre O and radius r cm.

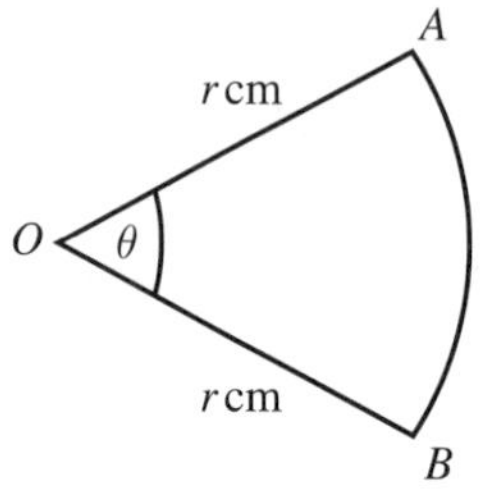

The angle AOB is θ radians.

The area of the sector is 12 cm^2.

The perimeter of the sector is four times the length of the arc AB.

Find the value of r. [AQA, GCE Mathematics, C2, June 2014]

5

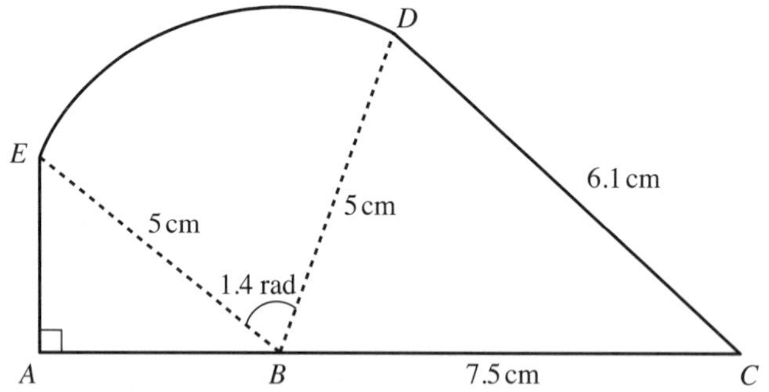

The shape $ABCDEA$, as shown in the diagram, consists of a right-angled triangle EAB and a triangle DBC joined to a sector BDE of a circle with radius 5 cm and centre B.

The points A, B and C lie on a straight line with $BC = 7.5$ cm.

Angle $EAB = \frac{\pi}{2}$ radians, angle $EBD = 1.4$ radians and $CD = 6.1$ cm.

a Find, in cm^2, the area of the sector BDE.

b Find the size of the angle DBC, giving your answer in radians to 3 dp.

c Find, in cm^2, the area of the shape $ABCDEA$, giving your answer to 3 significant figures. [EDEXCEL, GCE Mathematics, C2, June 2014]

6

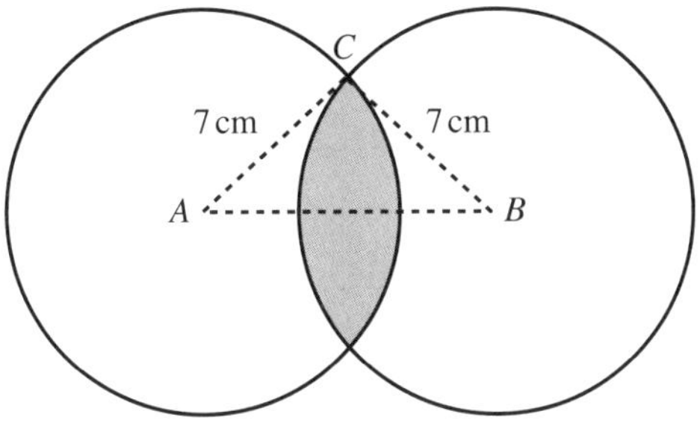

The diagram shows two circles of radius 7 cm with centres A and B. The distance AB is 12 cm and the point C lies on both circles. The region common to both circles is shaded.

i Show that angle CAB is 0.5411 radians, correct to 4 significant figures.

ii Find the perimeter of the shaded region.

iii Find the area of the shaded region. [OCR, GCE Mathematics, C2, Jan 2013]

7

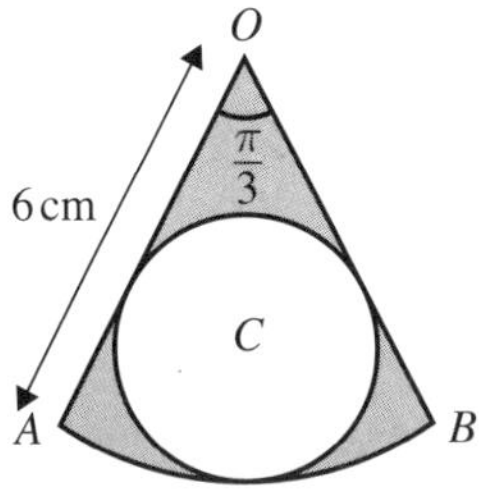

The shape shown is a pattern for a pendant. It consists of a sector OAB of a circle centre O, of radius 6 cm, and angle $AOB = \frac{\pi}{3}$. The circle C, inside the sector, touches the two straight edges, OA and OB, and the arc AB as shown.

Find

a the area of the sector OAB,

b the radius of the circle C,

The region outside the circle C and inside the sector OAB is shown shaded.

c Find the area of the shaded region.

[EDEXCEL, GCE Mathematics, C2, June 2011]

8 The diagram shows a triangle ABC.

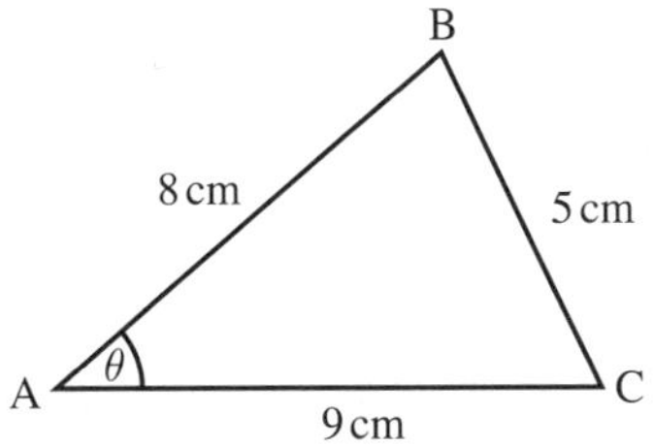

The lengths of AB, BC and AC are 8 cm, 5 cm and 9 cm respectively.

Angle BAC is θ **radians**.

a Show that $\theta = 0.586$, correct to three significant figures.

b Find the area of triangle ABC, giving your answer, in cm^2, to three significant figures.

c A circular sector, centre A and radius r cm, is removed from triangle ABC. The remaining shape is shown shaded in the diagram below.

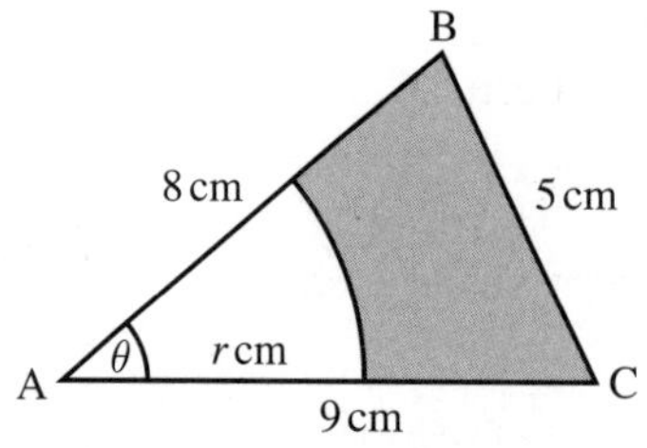

Given that the area of the sector removed is equal to the area of the shaded shape, find the perimeter of the shaded shape. Give your answer in cm to three significant figures. [AQA, GCE Mathematics, C2, June 2016]

9 Solve, for $-\pi < \theta \leqslant \pi$,

$$1 - 2\cos\left(\theta - \frac{\pi}{5}\right) = 0$$

giving your answers in terms of π.

[EDEXCEL, GCE Mathematics, C2, June 2016]

10 The cubic polynomial f(x) is defined by $f(x) = 4x^3 - 7x - 3$.

i Find the remainder when f(x) is divided by $(x - 2)$.

ii Show that $(2x + 1)$ is a factor of f(x) and hence factorise f(x) completely.

iii Solve the equation

$$4\cos^3\theta - 7\cos\theta - 3 = 0$$

for $0 \leqslant \theta \leqslant 2\pi$. Give each solution for θ in an exact form.

[OCR, GCE Mathematics, C2, June 2013]

11 Solve, for $-\pi \leqslant x < \pi$, the equation

$$2\tan x - 3\sin x = 0$$

giving your answers to 2 dp where appropriate.

[EDEXCEL, GCE Mathematics, C2, June 2014]

12 Solve the equation

$$4\cos^2 x + 7\sin x - 7 = 0,$$

giving all values of x between 0 and 2π.

[OCR, GCE Mathematics, C2, June 2012]

13 **a** Solve the equation $\sin(x + 0.7) = 0.6$ in the interval $-\pi < x < \pi$, giving your answers in radians to two significant figures.

b It is given that $5\cos^2\theta - \cos\theta = \sin^2\theta$.

i By forming and solving a suitable quadratic equation, find the possible values of $\cos\theta$.

ii **Hence** show that a possible value of $\tan\theta$ is $2\sqrt{2}$.

[AQA, GCE Mathematics, C2, June 2015]

14 i Show that the equation

$$\sin x - \cos x = \frac{6\cos x}{\tan x}$$

can be expressed in the form

$$\tan^2 x - \tan x - 6 = 0.$$

ii Hence solve the equation $\sin x - \cos x = \dfrac{6\cos x}{\tan x}$ for $0 \leqslant x \leqslant 2\pi$.

[OCR, GCE Mathematics, C2, June 2014]

15 By first showing that $\dfrac{16 + 9\sin^2\theta}{5 - 3\cos\theta}$ can be expressed in the form $p + q\cos\theta$, where p and q are integers, find the least possible value of $\dfrac{16 + 9\sin^2\theta}{5 - 3\cos\theta}$.

State the exact value of θ, in radians in the interval $0 \leqslant \theta < 2\pi$, at which this least value occurs. [AQA, GCE Mathematics, C2, June 2016]

16 i Sketch the graph of $y = \tan\left(\frac{1}{2}x\right)$ for $-2\pi \leqslant x \leqslant 2\pi$.
On the same axes, sketch the graph of $y = 3\cos\left(\frac{1}{2}x\right)$ for $-2\pi \leqslant x \leqslant 2\pi$, indicating the point of intersection with the y-axis.

ii Show that the equation $\tan\left(\frac{1}{2}x\right) = 3\cos\left(\frac{1}{2}x\right)$ can be expressed in the form

$$3\sin^2\left(\tfrac{1}{2}x\right) + \sin\left(\tfrac{1}{2}x\right) - 3 = 0.$$

Hence solve the equation $\tan\left(\frac{1}{2}x\right) = 3\cos\left(\frac{1}{2}x\right)$ for $-2\pi \leqslant x \leqslant 2\pi$.

[OCR, GCE Mathematics, C2, January 2012]

Part 3

Partial fractions

We have already looked at how to add two fractions together. We saw in Part 1 that if we want to write $\frac{4}{x} + \frac{5}{x-1}$ as a single fraction we first need to write both fractions over a common denominator.

So in this example our common denominator would be $x(x-1)$.

We see that
$$\begin{aligned}\frac{4}{x} + \frac{5}{x-1} &= \frac{4(x-1)+5x}{x(x-1)} \\ &= \frac{4x-4+5x}{x(x-1)} \\ &= \frac{9x-4}{x(x-1)}\end{aligned}$$

3.1 Partial fractions

We now want to perform the reverse process, that is we want to go from $\frac{9x-4}{x(x-1)}$ to $\frac{4}{x} + \frac{5}{x-1}$.

This will be particularly useful when we come to integrate expressions containing algebraic fractions.

When we do this we are said to be expressing $\frac{9x-4}{x(x-1)}$ in partial fractions.

In order to do this we first of all see that we can write $\frac{9x-4}{x(x-1)}$ in the form $\frac{A}{x} + \frac{B}{x-1}$ where A and B are numbers that we need to find.

So we have $\frac{9x-4}{x(x-1)} = \frac{A}{x} + \frac{B}{x-1}$.

We now rewrite the right hand side of the equation, by adding the fractions.

$$\frac{A}{x} + \frac{B}{x-1} = \frac{A(x-1)+Bx}{x(x-1)}$$

and so we see that $\frac{9x-4}{x(x-1)} = \frac{A(x-1)+Bx}{x(x-1)}$

In fact, because this is true for all values of x, we should write

$$\frac{9x-4}{x(x-1)} \equiv \frac{A(x-1)+Bx}{x(x-1)}$$

We see that $9x-4 \equiv A(x-1)+Bx$.

There are two methods we can use to find A and B.

Method 1

We multiply out the RHS of the equation to get $9x - 4 \equiv Ax - A + Bx$
$\equiv (A + B)x - A.$

It follows from this that $A = 4$ and $A + B = 9$.

Hence we have $A = 4$ and $B = 5$.

Method 2

To solve $9x - 4 \equiv A(x - 1) + Bx$, we substitute certain values of x.

Substituting $x = 0$, we get $9 \times 0 - 4 \equiv A(0 - 1) + B \times 0$,

and so $A = \dfrac{9 \times 0 - 4}{(0 - 1)} = 4$.

Substituting $x = 1$, we get $9 \times 1 - 4 \equiv A(1 - 1) + B \times 1$,

and so $B = \dfrac{9 \times 1 - 4}{1} = 5$.

Example 1

Express $\dfrac{7 + 5x}{(x + 1)(x + 2)}$ in the form $\dfrac{A}{(x + 1)} + \dfrac{B}{(x + 2)}$.

We write $\dfrac{7 + 5x}{(x + 1)(x + 2)} \equiv \dfrac{A}{(x + 1)} + \dfrac{B}{(x + 2)} \equiv \dfrac{A(x + 2) + B(x + 1)}{(x + 1)(x + 2)}$

So we have $7 + 5x \equiv A(x + 2) + B(x + 1)$.

Method 1

We multiply out the RHS of the equation to get $7 + 5x \equiv (A + B)x + (2A + B)$

So we see that $A + B = 5$ and $2A + B = 7$

Solving these gives $A = 2$, $B = 3$.

Method 2

To solve $7 + 5x \equiv A(x + 2) + B(x + 1)$ we substitute certain values of x.

Substituting $x = -1$, we get $7 + 5 \times -1 \equiv A(-1 + 2)$, and so $A = \dfrac{7 + 5 \times -1}{(-1 + 2)} = 2$.

The quickest way to get B is to compare x coefficients, seeing that $A + B = 5$ and so $B = 3$.

We could, however, substitute $x = -2$ and we get

$7 + 5 \times -2 \equiv A(-2 + 2) + B(-2 + 1)$, and so $B = \dfrac{7 + 5 \times -2}{(-2 + 1)} = 3$.

Example 2

Express $\dfrac{3x + 1}{(x + 1)(2x + 1)}$ in the form $\dfrac{A}{(x + 1)} + \dfrac{B}{(2x + 1)}$.

We write $\dfrac{3x + 1}{(x + 1)(2x + 1)} \equiv \dfrac{A}{(x + 1)} + \dfrac{B}{(2x + 1)} \equiv \dfrac{A(2x + 1) + B(x + 1)}{(x + 1)(2x + 1)}$

So we have $3x + 1 \equiv A(2x + 1) + B(x + 1)$.

Method 1

Multiply out the numerator on the RHS of the equation to get
$3x + 1 \equiv (2A + B)x + (A + B)$

So we see that $2A + B = 3$
$A + B = 1$

Solving these gives $A = 2, B - 1$.

Method 2

To solve $3x + 1 \equiv A(2x + 1) + B(x + 1)$ we substitute certain values of x.

Substituting $x = -1$, we get $3 \times (-1) + 1 \equiv A(2 \times (-1) + 1) + B(-1 + 1)$, and so

$$\text{A} = \frac{3 \times (-1) + 1}{(2 \times (-1) + 1)} = 2.$$

The quickest way to get B is to compare x coefficients, seeing that $2A + B = 3$ and so $B = -1$.

We could, however, substitute $x = -\frac{1}{2}$ and we get

$3 \times -\frac{1}{2} + 1 \equiv A(2 \times -\frac{1}{2} + 1) + B(-\frac{1}{2} + 1)$, and so $B = \dfrac{3 \times -\frac{1}{2} + 1}{(-\frac{1}{2} + 1)} = -1.$

Note: If we had to express $\dfrac{3x - 2}{x^2 - 4}$ in partial fractions then we would first factorise

the denominator as $(x + 2)(x - 2)$ and then write $\dfrac{3x - 2}{x^2 - 4} \equiv \dfrac{A}{(x + 2)} + \dfrac{B}{(x - 2)}$.

The 'cover up rule'

- Consider how we could express $\dfrac{5x + 7}{(x + 1)(x + 2)}$ in partial fractions.

  We need to find A and B where $\dfrac{5x + 7}{(x + 1)(x + 2)} \equiv \dfrac{A}{(x + 1)} + \dfrac{B}{(x + 2)}$.

  Method 2 can be shortened to what is called the 'cover up rule'. The cover up rule says that to find the numerator (e.g. A) above a particular denominator (e.g. $x + 1$) when written as partial fractions, we 'cover up' that factor

  (i.e. $x + 1$) in the original expression to get $\dfrac{5x + 7}{(x + 2)}$. We then substitute the value

  of x that makes the 'covered up' factor equal to zero (i.e. $x = -1$) to get

  $$A = \frac{5 \times -1 + 7}{-1 + 2} = 2.$$

To find B we look at the denominator of the fraction B. In this case it is $x + 2$. We then substitute $x = -2$ (the solution to $x + 2 = 0$) into the left hand side with $x + 2$ 'covered up'. That is $B = \dfrac{5 \times -2 + 7}{-2 + 1} = 3$.

So $\dfrac{5x + 7}{(x + 1)(x + 2)} \equiv \dfrac{2}{(x + 1)} + \dfrac{3}{(x + 2)}$

- If we go right back to the initial question, that is, $\dfrac{9x - 4}{x(x - 1)} \equiv \dfrac{A}{x} + \dfrac{B}{x - 1}$ we can again use the 'cover up rule'.

To find A we look at what the denominator of the fraction under A is on the right hand side. In this case it is x. We then substitute $x = 0$ into the left hand side with x 'covered up'. That is $A = \dfrac{9 \times 0 - 4}{(0 - 1)} = 4$.

To find B we substitute $x = 1$ into the left hand side with $(x - 1)$ covered up. So $B = \dfrac{9 \times 1 - 4}{1} = 5$.

We can only use the cover up method to find the numerator of a fraction whose denominator is a single linear expression.

Exercise 3A

1 Find A and B in the following:

a $\dfrac{3x - 5}{(x - 1)(x - 3)} \equiv \dfrac{A}{(x - 1)} + \dfrac{B}{(x - 3)}$

b $\dfrac{5x - 19}{(x - 2)(x - 5)} \equiv \dfrac{A}{(x - 2)} + \dfrac{B}{(x - 5)}$

c $\dfrac{5x + 11}{(x + 1)(x + 4)} \equiv \dfrac{A}{(x + 1)} + \dfrac{B}{(x + 4)}$

d $\dfrac{7x + 17}{(x + 1)(x + 3)} \equiv \dfrac{A}{(x + 1)} + \dfrac{B}{(x + 3)}$

e $\dfrac{5x + 31}{(x + 2)(x + 5)} \equiv \dfrac{A}{(x + 2)} + \dfrac{B}{(x + 5)}$

f $\dfrac{x - 19}{(x + 1)(x - 4)} \equiv \dfrac{A}{(x + 1)} + \dfrac{B}{(x - 4)}$

2 Express the following as partial fractions:

a $\dfrac{9x - 26}{(x - 3)(x - 2)}$

b $\dfrac{3x - 4}{(x - 1)(x - 2)}$

c $\dfrac{8x + 11}{(x + 1)(x + 2)}$

d $\dfrac{7x + 15}{(x + 2)(x + 3)}$

e $\dfrac{3x}{(x - 1)(x + 2)}$

f $\dfrac{x + 7}{(x - 1)(x + 3)}$

g $\dfrac{x + 8}{x(x - 2)}$

h $\dfrac{5x + 2}{x(x + 1)}$

3 Find A and B in the following:

a $\dfrac{5x+2}{(2x-1)(x+1)} \equiv \dfrac{A}{(2x-1)} + \dfrac{B}{(x+1)}$ **b** $\dfrac{9x+7}{(x-1)(3x+1)} \equiv \dfrac{A}{(x-1)} + \dfrac{B}{(3x+1)}$

c $\dfrac{7x-1}{(2x-1)(x+2)} \equiv \dfrac{A}{(2x-1)} + \dfrac{B}{(x+2)}$ **d** $\dfrac{5x-4}{(3x-2)(x-1)} \equiv \dfrac{A}{(3x-2)} + \dfrac{B}{(x-1)}$

e $\dfrac{x+10}{x(2x-5)} \equiv \dfrac{A}{x} + \dfrac{B}{(2x-5)}$ **f** $\dfrac{4x-23}{(3x+2)(x-3)} \equiv \dfrac{A}{(3x+2)} + \dfrac{B}{(x-3)}$

4 Express the following as partial fractions:

a $\dfrac{11x-21}{(2x-3)(x-3)}$ **b** $\dfrac{5x-2}{(2x+1)(x-1)}$

c $\dfrac{21x+16}{(3x-2)(3x+4)}$ **d** $\dfrac{7x-2}{(2x-1)(5x-1)}$

e $\dfrac{11x+5}{(2x-1)(x+3)}$ **f** $\dfrac{13x+9}{(2x-3)(3x+5)}$

g $\dfrac{12x+8}{4x^2-1}$ **h** $\dfrac{55x-14}{25x^2-4}$

Example 3

Express $\dfrac{27x^2+14x+4}{(3x-1)(x+2)(2x+1)}$ as partial fractions. The denominator is the product of three different linear factors.

Let $\dfrac{27x^2+14x+4}{(3x-1)(x+2)(2x+1)} \equiv \dfrac{A}{(3x-1)} + \dfrac{B}{(x+2)} + \dfrac{C}{(2x+1)}$

$27x^2 + 14x + 4 = A(x+2)(2x+1) + B(3x-1)(2x+1) + C(x+2)(3x-1)$

Substitute $x = -2$ to give $21B = 84$ and so $B = 4$

$x = \dfrac{1}{3}$ gives $\dfrac{35}{9}A = \dfrac{35}{3}$ and so $A = 3$

$x = -\dfrac{1}{2}$ gives $-\dfrac{15}{4}C = \dfrac{15}{4}$ and so $C = -1$

Hence we have $\dfrac{27x^2+14x+4}{(3x-1)(x+2)(2x+1)} \equiv \dfrac{3}{(3x-1)} + \dfrac{4}{(x+2)} - \dfrac{1}{(2x+1)}$

3.2 Repeated factor

We need to be able to deal with a denominator in which there is one linear expression repeated, for example in $\dfrac{12x^2-13x+2}{(2x-1)^2(x-1)}$.

The procedure here is slightly different. We do not try to express $\frac{12x^2 - 13x + 2}{(2x-1)^2(x-1)}$

in the form $\frac{A}{(2x-1)} + \frac{B}{(2x-1)} + \frac{C}{(x-1)}$ but instead we write it in the form

$\frac{A}{(2x-1)} + \frac{B}{(2x-1)^2} + \frac{C}{(x-1)}$.

Example 4

Express $\frac{12x^2 - 13x + 2}{(2x-1)^2(x-1)}$ as partial fractions.

Let $\frac{12x^2 - 13x + 2}{(2x-1)^2(x-1)} \equiv \frac{A}{(2x-1)} + \frac{B}{(2x-1)^2} + \frac{C}{(x-1)}$

So we have:

$$12x^2 - 13x + 2 = A(2x-1)(x-1) + B(x-1) + C(2x-1)^2$$

Substitute $x = 1$ to find $C = 1$

Substitute $x = \frac{1}{2}$ to find $B = 3$

Now we could substitute $x = 0$ to give $2 = A - B + C$ and so $A = 4$.

Alternatively we could compare x^2 coefficients to see that $12 = 2A + 4C$ and so $A = 4$.

Hence we have $\frac{12x^2 - 13x + 2}{(2x-1)^2(x-1)} \equiv \frac{4}{(2x-1)} + \frac{3}{(2x-1)^2} + \frac{1}{(x-1)}$

EXERCISE 3B

1 Find A, B and C in the following:

a $\frac{6x^2 + 23x + 19}{(x+1)(x+2)(x+3)} \equiv \frac{A}{(x+1)} + \frac{B}{(x+2)} + \frac{C}{(x+3)}$

b $\frac{2x^2 + 5x + 5}{(x+2)(x+1)(x-1)} \equiv \frac{A}{(x+2)} + \frac{B}{(x+1)} + \frac{C}{(x-1)}$

c $\frac{11x^2 + 31x + 2}{(x+1)(x+4)(x-2)} \equiv \frac{A}{(x+1)} + \frac{B}{(x+4)} + \frac{C}{(x-2)}$

d $\frac{8x^2 - 31x + 31}{(x-1)(x-2)(x-3)} \equiv \frac{A}{(x-1)} + \frac{B}{(x-2)} + \frac{C}{(x-3)}$

e $\frac{6x^2 - 5x - 34}{(x-4)(x-2)(x+3)} \equiv \frac{A}{(x-4)} + \frac{B}{(x-2)} + \frac{C}{(x+3)}$

2 Express the following as partial fractions:

a $\dfrac{7x^2 + 2x - 12}{(x - 2)(2x + 1)(x + 2)}$ b $\dfrac{11x^2 + 24x + 9}{(x - 3)(x + 1)(2x + 3)}$

c $\dfrac{-5x^2 + 19x - 16}{x(x - 1)(3x - 4)}$ d $\dfrac{91x^2 - 75x + 14}{(5x - 2)(4x - 1)(3x - 2)}$

e $\dfrac{7x^2 + 4x - 21}{(x^2 - 1)(x - 2)}$ f $\dfrac{116x^2 + 63x + 4}{(5x + 1)(4x + 3)(4x - 1)}$

3 Express the following as partial fractions:

a $\dfrac{7x^2 - 2x - 19}{(x + 3)(x - 2)^2}$ b $\dfrac{x^2 + 4x + 13}{(x - 1)(x + 2)^2}$

c $\dfrac{21x^2 + 5x + 11}{(2x - 1)(3x + 1)^2}$ d $\dfrac{32x^2 - 33x + 8}{(3x - 2)(2x - 1)^2}$

4 Express the following as partial fractions:

a $\dfrac{x}{(x - 2)^2}$ b $\dfrac{2x - 3}{(2x - 1)^2}$

c $\dfrac{5x^2 - 6x + 9}{(x + 1)(x - 1)^2}$ d $\dfrac{3x^2 + 17x + 28}{(x - 1)(x + 3)^2}$

e $\dfrac{4x^2 + 55x + 90}{(3x - 2)(x + 5)^2}$ f $\dfrac{x^2 - 10x - 5}{x^3 - x}$

g $\dfrac{8x + 3}{4x^3 - x}$ h $\dfrac{x^2 - 6x + 10}{(x + 4)(x - 1)^2}$

3.3 Improper fractions

If the highest power of x in a polynomial is x^n then n is said to be the degree of that polynomial.

So, for example, the highest power of x in the expression $(3x - 2)(2x - 1)^2$ is x^3 and so the expression has degree 3.

In all the examples we have covered so far the degree of the numerator has been less than the degree of the denominator.

We are now going to deal with examples where the degree of the numerator is equal to, or greater than the degree of the denominator. These are called improper fractions.

In order to express an improper fraction in partial fractions we can first use algebraic division to decrease the degree of the numerator.

Example 1

Express $\dfrac{x^2 + 4x - 7}{(x-2)(x-1)}$ in partial fractions.

In order to divide the numerator by the denominator, we must first multiply it out:

$$(x-2)(x-1) \equiv x^2 - 3x + 2$$

Now we can perform the division:

$$\begin{array}{r|l} & \quad 1 \\ x^2 - 3x + 2 & x^2 + 4x - 7 \\ & \underline{x^2 - 3x + 2} \\ & \qquad 7x - 9 \end{array}$$

- x^2 'into' x^2 'goes' 1 time (written on top)
- multiply $(x^2 - 3x + 2)$ by 1 and write under $x^2 + 4x - 7$
- subtract
- repeat if necessary (in this case, $x^2 - 3x + 2$ has a higher degree than $7x - 9$, so we are finished)

So $\dfrac{x^2 + 4x - 7}{(x-2)(x-1)} \equiv 1 + \dfrac{7x - 9}{(x-2)(x-1)}$

Now we need to express $\dfrac{7x-9}{(x-2)(x-1)}$ in partial fractions.

$$\frac{7x-9}{(x-2)(x-1)} \equiv \frac{A}{x-2} + \frac{B}{x-1} \equiv \frac{A(x-1) + B(x-2)}{(x-2)(x-1)}$$

So we have $7x - 9 \equiv A(x-1) + B(x-2)$

Substitute $x = 1$ to find $B = 2$

Substitute $x = 2$ to find $A = 5$

Hence we have $\dfrac{x^2 + 4x - 7}{(x-2)(x-1)} \equiv 1 + \dfrac{5}{(x-2)} + \dfrac{2}{(x-1)}$

Example 2

Express $\dfrac{x^3 + 10x^2 + 35x + 39}{(x+3)(x+2)}$ in partial fractions.

Firstly $(x+3)(x+2) \equiv x^2 + 5x + 6$.

Now

$$\begin{array}{r|l} & \quad x + 5 \\ x^2 - 5x + 6 & x^3 + 10x^2 + 35x + 39 \\ & \underline{x^3 + 5x^2 + 6x} \quad \downarrow \\ & \qquad 5x^2 + 29x + 39 \\ & \qquad \underline{5x^2 + 25x + 30} \\ & \qquad\qquad 4x + 9 \end{array}$$

So $\dfrac{x^3 + 10x^2 + 35x + 39}{(x + 3)(x + 2)} \equiv x + 5 + \dfrac{4x + 9}{(x + 3)(x + 2)}$

Now $\dfrac{4x + 9}{(x + 3)(x + 2)} \equiv \dfrac{A}{x + 3} + \dfrac{B}{x + 2} \equiv \dfrac{A(x + 2) + B(x + 3)}{(x + 3)(x + 2)}$

so we now have $4x + 9 \equiv A(x + 2) + B(x + 3)$

Substitute $x = -2$ to find $B = 1$

Substitute $x = -3$ to find $A = 3$

Hence we have $\dfrac{x^3 + 10x^2 + 35x + 39}{(x + 3)(x + 2)} \equiv x + 5 + \dfrac{3}{x + 3} + \dfrac{1}{x + 2}$

Example 3

Express $\dfrac{9x^4 - 27x^3 - 2x^2 + 26x + 35}{(x - 2)^2(3x + 1)}$ in partial fractions.

Firstly $(x - 2)^2(3x + 1) \equiv (x^2 - 4x + 4)(3x + 1) \equiv 3x^3 - 11x^2 + 8x + 4$

Now

$$
\begin{array}{r|l}
 & 3x + 2 \\
\hline
3x^3 - 11x^2 + 8x + 4 & 9x^4 - 27x^3 - 2x^2 + 26x + 35 \\
 & 9x^4 - 33x^3 + 24x^2 + 26x \quad \downarrow \\
\hline
 & 6x^3 - 26x^2 + 14x + 35 \\
 & 6x^3 - 22x^2 + 16x + 8 \\
\hline
 & -4x^2 - 2x + 27
\end{array}
$$

So $\dfrac{9x^4 - 27x^3 - 2x^2 + 26x + 35}{(x - 2)^2(3x + 1)} \equiv 3x + 2 + \dfrac{-4x^2 - 2x + 27}{(x - 2)^2(3x + 1)}$

Now $\dfrac{-4x^2 - 2x + 27}{(x - 2)^2(3x + 1)} \equiv \dfrac{A}{x - 2} + \dfrac{B}{(x - 2)^2} + \dfrac{C}{3x + 1}$

so $-4x^2 - 2x + 27 \equiv A(x - 2)(3x + 1) + B(3x + 1) + C(x - 2)^2$

Substitute $x = 2$: $-4(2)^2 - 2(2) + 27 = B(6 + 1)$

$$-16 - 4 + 27 = 7B$$

$$1 = B$$

Substitute $x = -\frac{1}{3}$: $-4\left(-\frac{1}{3}\right)^2 - 2\left(-\frac{1}{3}\right) + 27 = C\left(-\frac{1}{3} - 2\right)^2$

$$-\tfrac{4}{9} + \tfrac{2}{3} + 27 = \tfrac{49}{9}C$$

$$5 = C$$

Substitute $x = 0$: $27 = -2A + B + 4C$

$$27 = -2A + 1 + 20$$

$$6 = -2A$$

$$-3 = A$$

Hence finally we have

$$\frac{9x^4 - 27x^3 - 2x^2 + 26x + 35}{(x-2)^2(3x+1)} \equiv 3x + 2 - \frac{3}{x-2} + \frac{1}{(x-2)^2} + \frac{5}{3x+1}$$

Note: You may find it quicker to do these questions involving improper fractions if you are able to recognise in advance what form the final answer will take.

In Example 5 $\frac{x^2 + 4x - 7}{(x-2)(x-1)}$ the numerator has the same degree as the denominator. We therefore know that

$$\frac{x^2 + 4x - 7}{(x-2)(x-1)} \equiv A + \frac{B}{x-2} + \frac{C}{x-1}$$

and hence $x^2 + 4x - 7 \equiv A(x+2)(x-1) + B(x-1) + C(x-2)$

We can then substitute values for x, or equate coefficients, to find A, B and C.

In Example 6 $\frac{x^3 + 10x^2 + 35x + 39}{(x+3)(x+2)}$ the degree of the numerator is 3, whilst the degree of the denominator is only 2, therefore

$$\frac{x^3 + 10x^2 + 35x + 39}{(x+3)(x+2)} \equiv Ax + B + \frac{C}{x+3} + \frac{D}{x+2}$$

and hence $x^3 + 10x^2 + 35x + 39 \equiv (Ax + B)(x+3)(x+2) + C(x+2) + D(x+3)$

This approach can save time by eliminating the need to perform a lengthy long division, but it relies on your being able to correctly identify the form of the final answer. It can also lead to more cumbersome substitution and equating of coefficients. You may wish to experiment with both methods to find which works better for you.

Exercise 3C

1 Express the following as partial fractions:

a $\frac{x^2 + 3x - 5}{(x+3)(x-2)}$

b $\frac{30x^2 - x}{(5x+1)(2x-1)}$

c $\frac{x^3 - 4x^2 + 5x - 4}{(x-3)(x-1)}$

d $\frac{2x^3 - 6x^2 + 9x - 8}{(x-2)(x-1)}$

e $\frac{x^3 + 5x^2 + 14x + 18}{(x+3)(x+1)}$

f $\frac{2x^3 + 5x^2 - 18x - 59}{(x-3)(x+4)}$

g $\frac{6x^3 + 7x^2 + 2x - 5}{(x+1)(2x-1)}$

h $\frac{12x^3 - 44x^2 + 55x - 26}{(2x-3)(3x-5)}$

2 Express the following as partial fractions:

a $\dfrac{3x^3 - 2x^2 - 3x + 6}{(x-1)^2(x+1)}$

b $\dfrac{36x^3 - 69x^2 + 38x - 7}{(3x-2)^2(2x-1)}$

c $\dfrac{x^4 - 4x^3 + 7x^2 - 5x - 1}{(x-1)^2(x-2)}$

d $\dfrac{x^4 - 3x^3 + 5x^2 - 3x + 6}{(x-2)^2(x+1)}$

3 Write $\dfrac{1 - x - x^2}{(1-x)^2(1-2x)}$ in partial fractions.

Examination Exercise 3

1 Express $\dfrac{19x - 3}{(1+2x)(3-4x)}$ in the form $\dfrac{A}{1+2x} + \dfrac{B}{3-4x}$.

[AQA, GCE Mathematics, C4, June 2016]

2 It is given that $f(x) = \dfrac{19x - 2}{(5-x)(1+6x)}$ can be expressed as $\dfrac{A}{5-x} + \dfrac{B}{1+6x}$, where A and B are integers.

Find the values of A and B.

[AQA, GCE Mathematics, C4, June 2015]

3 $\dfrac{9x^2}{(x-1)^2(2x+1)} = \dfrac{A}{(x-1)} + \dfrac{B}{(x-1)^2} + \dfrac{C}{(2x+1)}$.

Find the values of the constants A, B and C.

[EDEXCEL, GCE Mathematics, C4, June 2011]

4 Express $\dfrac{7 - 2x}{(x-2)^2}$ in the form $\dfrac{A}{x-2} + \dfrac{B}{(x-2)^2}$, where A and B are constants.

[OCR, GCE Mathematics, C4, Jan 2011]

5 Express $\dfrac{x^2 - x - 11}{(x+1)(x-2)^2}$ in partial fractions.

[OCR, GCE Mathematics, C4, June 2012]

6 Express $\dfrac{(x-7)(x-2)}{(x+2)(x-1)^2}$ in partial fractions.

[OCR, GCE Mathematics, C4, June 2013]

7 Express $\dfrac{25}{x^2(2x+1)}$ in partial fractions.

[EDEXCEL, GCE Mathematics, C4 1R, June 2014]

PART 4

Sequences and series

4.1 Sequences, the nth term

A sequence is a set of numbers formed by following a particular rule.

The numbers in a sequence are called *terms*.

Consider the sequence $5, 9, 13, 17, \ldots$

The first term is 5, the second term is 9, the nth term is $4n + 1$.

The *general term* or the nth term is often written as u_n.

In this example, $u_n = 4n + 1 \quad \text{for} \quad n \geqslant 1$.

For any sequence you find the first, second, third terms and so on by substituting $n = 1, n = 2, n = 3 \ldots$ into the expression for the nth term.

Example 1

Write down the first three terms and the 10th term of the sequence whose nth term is given by

$$u_n = 3n - 2 \quad \text{for} \quad n \geqslant 1$$

Let $n = 1, 2, 3, 10$: $u_1 = 1$

$u_2 = 4$

$u_3 = 7$

$u_{10} = 28$

Example 2

Find an expression for the nth term of the sequence

$$8, 14, 20, 26, \ldots$$

The difference between terms is 6, so consider $u_n = 6n$.

This generates the sequence $6, 12, 18, 24, \ldots$

We see that the general term of the sequence required is $u_n = 6n + 2$.

Example 3

Find an expression for the nth term of the sequence

$$1, 4, 9, 16, \ldots$$

The sequence may be written $1^2, 2^2, 3^2, 4^2, \ldots$

The nth term is given by $u_n = n^2$.

4.2 Recurrence relations, convergent, divergent and periodic sequences

Some sequences can be defined using a recurrence relation (or an iterative formula). Each successive term is found from the previous term.

Example 4

A sequence $u_1, u_2, u_3, \ldots$ is such that $u_1 = 5$ and $u_{n+1} = u_n + 3$.
Find the first four terms of the sequence.

Let $n = 1$,
$$u_2 = u_1 + 3$$
$$= 5 + 3$$
$$= 8$$

Let $n = 2$,
$$u_3 = u_2 + 3$$
$$= 11$$

Let $n = 3$,
$$u_4 = u_3 + 3$$
$$= 14$$

The first four terms of the sequence are 5, 8, 11, 14.

Example 5

A sequence $u_1, u_2, u_3, \ldots$ is such that $u_1 = 2$, $u_2 = 5$ and $u_{n+1} = u_n + u_{n-1}$.
Find the first four terms of the sequence.

Let $n = 2$,
$$u_3 = u_2 + u_1$$
$$u_3 = 5 + 2$$
$$u_3 = 7$$

Let $n = 3$,
$$u_4 = u_3 + u_2$$
$$u_4 = 7 + 5$$
$$u_4 = 12$$

The first four terms of the sequence are 2, 5, 7, 12.

Example 6

Find a recurrence relation to describe the sequence generated by the formula $u_n = 5 - 2n$.

Let $n = 1, 2, 3, 4$
$$u_1 = 3$$
$$u_2 = 1$$
$$u_3 = -1$$
$$u_4 = -3$$

The first term is 3. Each term is found by subtracting 2 from the previous term.

Hence, $u_1 = 3$ and $u_{n+1} = u_n - 2$.

Example 7

Find the nth term of the sequence given by the recurrence relation $u_{n+1} = u_n + 4$ where $u_1 = -3$.

Let $n = 1$,
$$\begin{aligned} u_2 &= u_1 + 4 \\ &= -3 + 4 \\ &= 1 \end{aligned}$$

Let $n = 2$,
$$\begin{aligned} u_3 &= u_2 + 4 \\ &= 1 + 4 \\ &= 5 \end{aligned}$$

Let $n = 3$,
$$\begin{aligned} u_4 &= u_3 + 4 \\ &= 5 + 4 \\ &= 9 \end{aligned}$$

The first three terms of the sequence are 1, 5, 9, …
The nth term is given by $u_n = 4n - 3$.

Example 8

Comment on the sequences whose nth terms are given. ($n \geqslant 1$)

a 2^{-n} **b** $3n + 1$ **c** $5 + (-1)^n$

a The first four terms of the sequence are $2^{-1}, 2^{-2}, 2^{-3}, 2^{-4}$.
As fractions the terms are $\frac{1}{2}, \frac{1}{4}, \frac{1}{8}, \frac{1}{16}$.
This is a *convergent* sequence as the nth term gets closer and closer to a number as n increases. This number is the *limit*.
In this case the limit is 0.

b $u_n = 3n + 1$
The first four terms are 4, 7, 10, 13.
This sequence does not converge to a limit.
It is a *divergent* sequence.

c $u_n = 5 + (-1)^n$
The first five terms of the sequence are 4, 6, 4, 6, 4.
The only two terms are 4 and 6.
This is a *periodic* sequence.
The period is the number of terms before the sequence repeats.
Here the period is 2.
As a further example, the period of the sequence 1, 3, 5, 7, 1, 3, 5, 7, 1, 3, 5, 7, … is 4.

Exercise 4A

1 Write down the first four terms of the sequences whose nth terms are given for $n \geqslant 1$:

a $3n + 1$ b $4n - 1$ c n^2 d $\frac{1}{n}$

e 2^n f $n(n + 1)$ g $\frac{n}{n+2}$ h $(-1)^n$

2 Find an expression for the nth term of each sequence:

a 5, 10, 15, 20, 25, … b 3, 5, 7, 9, 11, … c 1, 5, 9, 13, 17, …

d $1^2, 2^2, 3^2, 4^2, \ldots$ e $3^1, 3^2, 3^3, 3^4, \ldots$ f 10, 100, 1000, 10 000

g $\frac{1}{2}, \frac{2}{3}, \frac{3}{4}, \frac{4}{5}, \ldots$ h 1, 8, 27, 64, 125, … i $\frac{1}{2}, \frac{1}{3}, \frac{1}{4}, \frac{1}{5}$

3 Write down the first five terms of the following sequences:

a $u_{n+1} = u_n + 5, u_1 = 2$ b $u_{n+1} = 10 + u_n, u_1 = -1$

c $u_{n+1} = 8 - u_n, u_1 = 1$ d $u_{n+1} = u_n^2, u_1 = 2$

e $u_{n+1} = \frac{1}{u_n}, u_1 = 2$ f $u_{n+1} = 3u_n - 2, u_1 = 0$

g $u_{n+1} = \frac{u_n}{10}, u_1 = 1000$ h $u_{n+1} = u_n + \frac{1}{u_n}, u_1 = 1$

4 Find the nth term, u_n, of the sequences generated by the following recurrence relations:

a $u_{n+1} = u_n + 2, u_1 = 5$ b $u_{n+1} = u_n - 4, u_1 = 10$

c $u_{n+1} = u_n + 7, u_1 = -8$ d $u_{n+1} = u_n - 3, u_2 = 6$

5 Use a recurrence relation to describe the sequence whose nth term is given by:

a $u_n = 5n + 2$ b $u_n = 3n - 5$

c $u_n = 4 - 2n$ d $u_n = 10 + \frac{n}{2}$

6 The nth term of a sequence is $\frac{1}{n}$ $(n \geqslant 1)$.

a Write down the first six terms of the sequence.

b Decide whether the sequence is convergent or not.

c If it is convergent, write down the limiting value to which it is converging.

7 Consider the sequence whose nth term is $\frac{n-1}{n+1}$ for $n \geqslant 1$.

a Write down the first four terms of the sequence and decide whether or not the sequence is convergent.

b If it is convergent, write down the limiting value to which it is converging.

8 Write down the first four terms, for $n \geqslant 1$, of each sequence to determine whether the sequence is convergent, divergent or periodic. State the limiting value of the convergent sequences:

a $u_n = \dfrac{1}{3^{n-1}}$

b $u_n = 4n + 1$

c $u_n = n^2 + 1$

d $u_n = \dfrac{n}{n+1}$

e $u_n = 5 \times (-1)^n$

f $u_{n+1} = 6 - u_n, u_1 = 1$

g $u_{n+1} = \dfrac{1}{u_n}, u_1 = 5$

h $u_{n+1} = \dfrac{100}{u_n^2}, u_1 = 1$

i $u_{n+1} = \dfrac{24}{u_n}, u_1 = 2$

j $u_n = (-2)^n$

9 Here is a famous recurrence relation involving two previous terms:

$$u_{n+1} = u_n + u_{n-1}, \text{ where } u_1 = 1, u_2 = 2$$

Write down the first six terms of the sequence.

10 Find the first five terms of the sequence

$$u_{n+1} = u_n + 3u_{n-1}, \text{ where } u_1 = 1, u_2 = 2$$

11 Work out the first eight terms of the sequence

$$u_{n+1} = \frac{7}{u_n} + 3, \text{ where } u_1 = 3$$

a The sequence converges to a limit, u. Find the value of u correct to 2 dp.

b Explain why u satisfies the equation $x^2 - 3x - 7 = 0$.
[Hint: As $n \to \infty$, $u_{n+1} \to u_n$. Put $u_{n+1} = u_n$.]

12 Work out the first six terms of the sequence

$$u_{n+1} = \frac{1}{2}\left(\frac{1}{u_n} + 5\right), u_1 = 1$$

a The sequence converges to a limit, u. Find the value of u correct to 2 dp.

b Show why u satisfies the equation $2x^2 - 5x - 1 = 0$.

13 a Show that the sequence $u_{n+1} = \dfrac{5}{u_n} - 1$ converges to a limit, u, and find the value of u correct to 2 dp.

b Show that u is one solution of the equation $x^2 + x - 5 = 0$.

14 a Show that the sequence $u_{n+1} = \dfrac{1}{u_n} + 3$ converges to a limit, u, and find the value of u correct to 2 dp.

b Find the equation of which u is one solution.

4.3 The sigma notation, Σ

The sequence $u_1, u_2, u_3, u_4, \dots u_n$ is a set of terms.

To find the sum of the first n terms, we work out

$$u_1 + u_2 + u_3 + u_4 + \dots + u_n$$

This is called a finite *series*.

It can be written more simply using the sigma notation (Σ).

$$u_1 + u_2 + u_3 + \dots + u_n = \sum_{r=1}^{n} u_r$$

We substitute 1, 2, 3, … n for r in u_r.

The sign Σ is a Greek capital S to represent sum.

We obtain an *infinite* series if we continue adding terms without stopping.

The infinite series $2^1 + 2^2 + 2^3 + 2^4 + \dots + 2^n + \dots$ can be written

$$\sum_{r=1}^{\infty} 2^r$$

Example 1

Write down the first four terms of the sequence defined by $u_r = 3r - 1$ for $r \geqslant 1$.

Hence find $\sum_{r=1}^{4} 3r - 1$.

Solution:

$$\begin{aligned} r = 1, &\quad u_1 = 3 \times 1 - 1 = 2 \\ r = 2, &\quad u_2 = 3 \times 2 - 1 = 5 \\ r = 3, &\quad u_3 = 3 \times 3 - 1 = 8 \\ r = 4, &\quad u_4 = 3 \times 4 - 1 = 11 \end{aligned}$$

$$\sum_{r=1}^{4} 3r - 1 = 2 + 5 + 8 + 11 = 26$$

Example 2

Work out **a** $\sum_{r=3}^{6} r^2$ **b** $\sum_{r=1}^{4} (-1)^r 3r$ **c** $\sum_{r=1}^{5} 2$

a $\sum_{r=3}^{6} r^2 = 3^2 + 4^2 + 5^2 + 6^2$ [Notice that we start with $r = 3$.]

$= 86$

b $\sum_{r=1}^{4} (-1)^r 3r = (-1)^1 \times 3 + (-1)^2 \times 6 + (-1)^3 \times 9 + (-1)^4 \times 12$

$= -3 + 6 - 9 + 12$

$= 6$

c $\sum_{r=1}^{5} 2 = 2 + 2 + 2 + 2 + 2$

$= 10$

N.B. Summations where there is no 'r' term often cause problems.
Here is another example:

$$\sum_{r=1}^{3} 5 = 5 + 5 + 5 = 15$$

EXERCISE 4B

1 Write down the terms in each series and then find the sum:

a $\sum_{r=1}^{4} 2r + 1$ **b** $\sum_{r=1}^{3} r^2$ **c** $\sum_{r=1}^{5} r - 1$ **d** $\sum_{r=2}^{4} r(r + 1)$

e $\sum_{r=2}^{5} (r - 1)^2$ **f** $\sum_{r=1}^{4} \frac{1}{r}$ **g** $\sum_{r=1}^{6} (-1)^r r^2$ **h** $\sum_{r=1}^{7} 4$

i $\sum_{r=0}^{5} 2^r$ **j** $\sum_{r=2}^{5} (-1)^r 3r$ **k** $\sum_{r=1}^{5} 7$ **l** $\sum_{r=1}^{3} \frac{r}{r + 1}$

2 Write each series using the Σ notation:

a $1^2 + 2^2 + 3^2 + 4^2$

b $3^1 + 3^2 + 3^3 + 3^4$

c $\frac{1}{1} + \frac{1}{2} + \frac{1}{3} + \frac{1}{4} + \frac{1}{5}$

d $2 + 4 + 6 + 8$

e $1 + 2 + 3 + 4 + \ldots + 100$

f $(1 \times 2) + (2 \times 3) + (3 \times 4) \ldots n(n + 1)$

g $\frac{1}{2} + \frac{2}{3} + \frac{3}{4} + \ldots \frac{100}{101}$

h $-1 + 1 - 1 + 1 - 1 + 1$

i $5 + 9 + 13 + 17 + 21$

j $4 + 9 + 14 + 19 + 24$

k $1^3 + 2^3 + 3^3 + \ldots$

l $2 - 4 + 6 - 8 + 10 - \ldots$

3 Work out $\sum_{r=1}^{5} 2r - \sum_{r=1}^{4} 2r$

4 Work out $\sum_{r=1}^{100} r^2 - \sum_{r=1}^{99} r^2$

5 Work out $\sum_{r=10}^{1000} \frac{1}{r} - \sum_{r=10}^{999} \frac{1}{r}$

4.4 Arithmetic sequences and series

Consider the *sequence* 3, 8, 13, 18, …

If the terms of the sequence are added,

$$3 + 8 + 13 + 18$$

the expression is called a *series*.

In an arithmetic series the difference between consecutive terms is constant and is called the *common difference*.

Here are three different arithmetic series.

$$1 + 4 + 7 + 10 + \dots + 58$$
$$4 + 14 + 24 + 34 + \dots + 214$$
$$10 + 8 + 6 + \dots - 20$$

The arithmetic series with first term a and common difference d is:

$$a + (a + d) + (a + 2d) + (a + 3d) + \dots$$

You can see that the **nth term is $a + (n - 1)d$**

Example 1

a Find the nth term of the arithmetic series $3 + 8 + 13 + 18 + \dots$

The first term, a, is 3 and the common difference, d, is 5.

$$\begin{aligned}\text{The } n\text{th term} &= a + (n - 1)d \\ &= 3 + (n - 1) \times 5 \\ &= 3 + 5n - 5 \\ &= 5n - 2\end{aligned}$$

b Similarly the nth term of the arithmetic series $7 + 10 + 13 + 16 + \dots$ is

$$\begin{aligned}&7 + (n - 1) \times 3 \\ &= 7 + 3n - 3 \\ &= 3n + 4\end{aligned}$$

4.5 The sum of an arithmetic series

Consider the arithmetic series $3 + 8 + 13 + \dots + 98$

Let the sum of the terms be S.

$$S = 3 + 8 + 13 + \dots + 98$$

Writing the terms in reverse order, we get

$$S = 98 + 93 + 88 + \dots + 3$$

Adding up in columns,

$$S + S = 101 + 101 + 101 + \dots + 101$$

There are 20 terms on the right hand side,

so $2S = 101 \times 20$

$$S = 1010$$

Now suppose we wish to derive a formula to calculate the sum of the first n terms of a general arithmetic series with first term a, and common difference d. You must understand and be able to reproduce the proof of this formula.

The sum of the first n terms, S_n, of a general arithmetic series is given by

$$S_n = a + (a + d) + (a + 2d) + \dots + (a + (n - 2)d) + (a + (n - 1)d)$$

Writing this series in reverse order,

$$S_n = (a + (n - 1)d) + (a + (n - 2)d) + (a + (n - 3)d) + \dots + (a + d) + a$$

Adding these two series in columns,

$$S_n + S_n = (2a + (n - 1)d) + (2a + (n - 1)d) + \dots + (2a + (n - 1)d)$$

As there were n terms in the series, we have

$$2S_n = n[2a + (n - 1)d]$$

$$\boxed{S_n = \frac{n}{2}[2a + (n - 1)d]}$$

Note: as the last term of the series L is given by $L = a + (n - 1)d$, it can sometimes be more convenient to use the formula in the form

$$S_n = \frac{n}{2}[a + L]$$

Example 1

Find the sum of the first 30 terms of the arithmetic series

$$3 + 9 + 15 + \dots$$

We have $a = 3, d = 6, n = 30$

The sum of the first 30 terms, $S_{30} = \frac{n}{2}[2a + (n - 1)d]$

$$S_{30} = \frac{30}{2}[(2 \times 3) + (30 - 1) \times 6]$$

$$= 2700$$

Example 2

In an arithmetic series the second term is 8 and the eighth term is 38. Find the first term and the common difference.

The nth term, $u_n = a + (n - 1)d$

We have $a + d = 8$ ①

$a + 7d = 38$ ②

Subtracting, $6d = 30$

$d = 5$

From ① $a = 3$

Example 3

a Find the nth term of the arithmetic series $7 + 11 + 15 + \dots$

b Which term of the series $7 + 11 + 15 + \dots$ is equal to 51?

c Hence find $7 + 11 + 15 + \dots + 51$.

a The first term, a, is 7 and the common difference, d, is 4.

So the nth term $= 7 + (n - 1) \times 4$

$= 4n + 3$

b For what value of n is $4n + 3$ equal to 51?

$$4n + 3 = 51$$
$$4n = 48$$
$$n = 12$$

The twelfth term is 51.

c We use $S_n = \frac{n}{2}[2a + (n - 1)d]$, with $a = 7, d = 4, n = 12$.

So $S_{12} = \frac{12}{2}[(2 \times 7) + (12 - 1) \times 4]$

$= 6 \times 58$

$= 348$

Exercise 4C

1 Decide which of these sequences are arithmetic sequences. Write down the common differences of those sequences that are arithmetic sequences:

a 10, 11, 12, 13 **b** 20, 17, 14, 11, 8 **c** 1, 2, 4, 8

d $a, 2a, 3a, 4a$ **e** $-9, -6, -3, 0, 3$ **f** $\frac{1}{2}, \frac{1}{3}, \frac{1}{4}, \frac{1}{5}$

2 Find the nth term of the following arithmetic series:

a $1 + 5 + 9 + \dots$ **b** $10 + 12 + 14 + \dots$ **c** $8 + 17 + 26 + 35 + \dots$

d $19 + 16 + 13 + 10 + \dots$ **e** $25 + 21 + 17 + 13 + \dots$

3 Find the given term of the following arithmetic sequences:

a the 20th term of 11, 16, 21, …

b the 12th term of 30, 37, 44, …

c the 8th term of $\frac{1}{2}, 1, 1\frac{1}{2}, 2, 2\frac{1}{2}, \dots$

d the 7th term of 31, 27, 23, 19,…

e the 11th term of $\frac{1}{4}, \frac{1}{2}, \frac{3}{4}, 1, \dots$

4 a What is the nth term of the arithmetic series $3 + 12 + 21 + 30 + \dots$?

b Which term of the series is equal to 138?

5 a What is the nth term of the arithmetic sequence 10, 17, 24, 31, …?

b Which term of the sequence is equal to 164?

6 **a** What is the nth term of the arithmetic series $29 + 23 + 17 + 11 + \dots$?

b Which term of the series is equal to -55?

7 In the following arithmetic series, find:

a the sum of the first 10 terms: $2 + 7 + 12 + \dots$

b the sum of the first 20 terms: $11 + 16 + 21 + \dots$

c the sum of the first 6 terms: $18 + 14 + 10 + 6 + \dots$

d the sum of the first 18 terms: $5 + 4\frac{1}{2} + 4 + 3\frac{1}{2} + 3 + \dots$

8 **a** Find the nth term of the arithmetic series $1 + 5 + 9 + \dots$

b Which term of the series is equal to 41?

c Hence find $1 + 5 + 9 + \dots + 41$.

9 **a** Find the nth term of the arithmetic series $3 + 10 + 17 + \dots$

b Which term of the series is equal to 38?

c Hence find $3 + 10 + 17 + \dots + 38$.

10 Use a method similar to that in question **9** to find:

a $103 + 100 + 97 + \dots + 1$

b $\frac{1}{4} + \frac{1}{2} + \frac{3}{4} + \dots + 2$

c $1020 + 1001 + 982 + \dots + 602$

11 In an arithmetic series the first term is 9 and the 20th term is 104.

a Find the common difference.

b Find the sum of the first twenty terms.

12 In an arithmetic series the common difference is 5 and the seventh term is 41.

a Find the first term of the sequence.

b Find the sum of the first seven terms.

13 In an arithmetic series the third term is 27 and the sixth term is 48.

a Write down two equations involving the first term, a and the common difference, d.

b Hence find a and d.

14 The fourth term of an arithmetic series is 5 and the eleventh term is -23.

a Write down two equations involving the first term, a and the common difference, d.

b Hence find a and d.

c Find also the sum of the first six terms.

15 In an arithmetic series the fifth term is 30 and the ninth term is 18.

a Find the first term and the common difference.

b Show that the sum of the first n terms is $\dfrac{87n - 3n^2}{2}$.

c Hence find the value of n such that the sum of the first n terms is zero.

16 In an arithmetic series the twelfth term is 15 and the tenth term is 9.

a Find the first term and the common difference.

b Show that the sum of the first n terms is $\dfrac{n(3n - 39)}{2}$.

c Hence find the smallest value of n such that the sum of the first n terms is positive.

17 The fifth term of an arithmetic series is 17 and the thirteenth term is 57. Find the common difference, d and the first term, a.

18 If the first term of an arithmetic series is 3 and the one hundredth term is 307 then find the sum of the first 100 terms. (Try to do this without finding the common difference.)

19 A boy invests £1 in the first week of the year, £1.20 the next, £1.40 the next and so on. How much has he invested by the end of the year?

20 Each year for 20 years, Amber will pay money into a savings scheme. In the first year she pays £100 and her payments increase by £50 each year; so she pays £150 in the second year, £200 in the third year and so on.

a How much will Amber's final payment be?

b How much will she pay into the scheme in total over the 20 years?

21 A broadband cable is to be laid under the sea. It is estimated that the first kilometre will take 5 days to lay and that each subsequent kilometre will take 1 day longer than the one before; so the second kilometre will take 6 days, and so on.

a How long will it take to lay the tenth kilometre of cable?

b How long will it take to lay the hundredth kilometre?

c How long will it take to lay cable under a stretch of sea 20 km wide?

22 Show that the sum of the integers from 1 to n is $\frac{1}{2}n(n + 1)$.

23 Evaluate $\displaystyle\sum_{r=1}^{50} 2r + 1$. [Hint: start by writing down the first few terms.]

24 Evaluate

a $\displaystyle\sum_{r=1}^{100} 3r - 1$ **b** $\displaystyle\sum_{r=1}^{70} 4r + 3$ **c** $\displaystyle\sum_{r=11}^{70} 4r + 3$

25 Find the value of n if $\displaystyle\sum_{1}^{2n} 2r + 1 = \sum_{1}^{n} 6r + 4$.

26 The 4th, 5th and 6th terms of an arithmetic series are $2x + 1$, $3x$ and $x + 20$. Find x and show that the first term of the series is -3.

Example 4

The sum of the first n terms of the arithmetic series

$3 + 8 + 13 + \ldots$ is 1010. Find the value of n.

Using $S_n = \frac{n}{2}[2a + (n - 1)d]$, with $a = 3$ and $d = 5$,

we have $S_n = \frac{n}{2}[6 + (n - 1) \times 5]$

$= \frac{n}{2}(5n + 1)$

So $\frac{n}{2}(5n + 1) = 1010$

$n(5n + 1) = 2020$

$5n^2 + n - 2020 = 0$

Factorising, $(n - 20)(5n + 101) = 0$

So $n = 20$. (n cannot be negative)

Example 5

The tenth term of an arithmetic series is 67 and the sum of the first twenty terms is 1280. Find the first term, a, and the common difference, d.

The tenth term is $a + 9d$

so $a + 9d = 67 \ldots$ ①

Using $S_n = \frac{n}{2}[2a + (n - 1)d]$, $S_{20} = \frac{20}{2}(2a + 19d)$

so $10(2a + 19d) = 1280$

or $2a + 19d = 128 \ldots$ ②

Solving the simultaneous equations, we obtain $a = 121$, $d = -6$.

Example 6

The sum of the first n terms of an arithmetic series is $3n^2 + 4n$.

a Find the first two terms and hence the common difference.

b The sum of the first x terms is 340. Find x.

a We know that $S_n = 3n^2 + 4n$.

So $S_1 = (3 \times 1^2) + (4 \times 1)$

$S_1 = 7$

And $S_2 = (3 \times 2^2) + (4 \times 2)$

$S_2 = 20$

Now S_1 is the first term, a.

So $a = 7$

Since $S_2 = 20$, the second term is 13.

Therefore the common difference, $d = 6$.

b We are given that $S_n = 3n^2 + 4n$.

$$\therefore \quad S_x = 3x^2 + 4x$$
$$\text{and} \quad S_x = 340$$
$$\therefore \quad 3x^2 + 4x = 340$$
$$3x^2 + 4x - 340 = 0$$
$$(x - 10)(3x + 34) = 0$$
$$\therefore \quad x = 10 \qquad (x \text{ must be positive})$$

Example 7

Find the sum of the integers between 1 and 100 which are divisible by 6.

The largest two digit number divisible by 6 is 96.

We require the sum of the numbers $6 + 12 + 18 + \ldots + 96$.

We see that 96 is the sixteenth term of an arithmetic series with first term 6 and common difference 6.

So $S_{16} = 6 + 12 + 18 + \ldots + 96$

$= \frac{16}{2}[(2 \times 6) + (16 - 1) \times 6]$, using the formula.

$S_{16} = 8[12 + 90]$

$= 816$

The sum of the integers between 1 and 100 divisible by 6 is 816.

Exercise 4D

1 The sum of the first fifteen terms of an arithmetic sequence is 630, and the sum of the first ten terms of the same arithmetic sequence is 295.

- **a** Write down two equations involving the first term, a and the common difference, d.
- **b** Solve these to find the first term and the common difference.

2 In an arithmetic sequence the sum of the first three terms is 21 and the sum of the fifth and sixth terms is 28.

- **a** Write down two equations involving the first term, a and the common difference, d.
- **b** Solve these to find the first term and the common difference.

3 The eleventh term of an arithmetic sequence is 85, and the sum of the first 11 terms is 550. Find the first term and common difference.

4 **a** Find an expression for the sum of the first n terms of the arithmetic series $5 + 12 + 19 + 26 + \ldots$

- **b** Use the quadratic formula to find how many terms of the series should be added together in order to give a total of more than 1000.

5 The sum of the first n terms of an arithmetic sequence is $3n^2 + 5n$.

a Find the sum of the first two terms.

b Hence write down the first two terms of the sequence.

c Use this to find the common difference.

6 The sum of the first n terms of an arithmetic sequence is $\frac{n(n+3)}{2}$.

a Find the first two terms of the sequence.

b Find also the 50th term of the sequence.

7 a Find a simplified expression for the sum of the first n terms of the arithmetic sequence whose first term is 5 and whose common difference is 3.

b If the sum of the first n terms of this arithmetic sequence is 258, find n (by factorising a quadratic equation) (NB: $516 = 43 \times 12$).

8 a If the sum of the first n terms of an arithmetic sequence is $2n^2 + 9n$, find the first two terms and hence find the common difference.

b Calculate r if the sum of the first r terms is 585.

9 A man has to put up 50 fence pegs in a straight line – each of them is 3 m from the next one. They are initially all lying in a pile. He puts the first peg in at the foot of the pile. He then carries a peg 3 m and puts that one in. He goes back to the pile, collects another peg and walks 6 m to put in the next one. This continues until he has put in each peg, after which he walks back to where he started. How far did he walk to put in the 50 pegs?

10 Aleksy works for a mobile phone company selling phone contracts. In his first month he sells 65 contracts. The phone company uses a model to predict his future sales. This model assumes that he will sell 5 more contracts per month for the next 23 months, so that he will sell 70 contracts in the second month, 75 in the third month and so on.

a Use this model to predict how many contracts he will sell in the 24th month.

b Use this model to predict how many contracts he will sell in total over his first two years with the company.

Billie also works for the same company. She only sells 50 contracts in her first month. The model for future sales predicts that her sales will increase by x contracts per month.

c Find the least value of x required for her to sell more contracts in total than Aleksy over their first two years with the company.

d Comment on the likely accuracy of this model for future sales.

11 A mining company is mining for copper. The cost of excavating to a depth of 50 m is \$1,000. To excavate a further 50 m costs \$250 more than the previous 50 m, so it costs \$2250 in total to excavate to a depth of 100 m.

a How much does it cost to excavate to a depth of 1 km?

b The mining company has a budget of \$1 million. How deep will they be able to excavate?

12 The sum of the first seven terms of an arithmetic sequence is five times the seventh term. If the fourth term is 15, find the first term and the common difference.

13 Find the sum of the integers between 1 and 100 which are divisible by 3.

14 How many terms of the arithmetic sequence $2 + 3\frac{1}{4} + 4\frac{1}{2} + \dots$ are needed to make a total of 204?

15 The first four terms of an arithmetic progression are 2, $a - b$, $2a + b + 7$ and $a - 3b$ respectively, where a and b are constants. Find a and b and hence find the sum of the first 30 terms of the progression.

4.6 Geometric sequences

In a geometric sequence each term is obtained by multiplying the previous term by a constant, r. This number r is called the *common ratio.*

Here are three examples of geometric sequences:

a 2, 6, 18, 54, … $(r = 3)$

b 27, 9, 3, 1 … $(r = \frac{1}{3})$

c 4, −8, 16, −32, … $(r = -2)$

Consider the geometric series 3, 6, 12, 24, …

The terms may be written $3, 3 \times 2, 3 \times 2^2, 3 \times 2^3, \dots$

We see that the nth term is $3 \times 2^{n-1}$

The nth term of a general geometric sequence with first term a and common ratio r is ar^{n-1}.

Example 1

Find an expression for the nth term of the geometric sequence 3, 12, 48, …

The first term a is 3.

The common ratio is $r = \frac{12}{3} = 4$

So the nth term is $3 \times 4^{n-1}$.

Example 2

Find the 25th term of the geometric sequence 5, 10, 20, 40.

The first term is $a = 5$.

The common ratio is $r = \frac{10}{5} = 2$

The 25th term is $5 \times 2^{25-1} = 5 \times 2^{24}$

$= 83{,}886{,}080$

Example 3

The third term of a geometric sequence is 162 and the sixth term is 6. Find the tenth term of the sequence.

Using nth term $= ar^{n-1}$ we have,

$$ar^2 = 162 \qquad ①$$

and $$ar^5 = 6 \qquad ②$$

② ÷ ① $$\frac{ar^5}{ar^2} = \frac{6}{162}$$

$$r^3 = \frac{1}{27}$$

$$r = \frac{1}{3}$$

From ① $$a \times \left(\frac{1}{3}\right)^2 = 162$$

$$a = 1458$$

Now, the tenth term is given by $1458 \times \left(\frac{1}{3}\right)^9 = \frac{2}{27}$

Example 4

The first, fourth and thirteenth terms of an *arithmetic* sequence form the first three terms of a *geometric* sequence. Find the common ratio of the geometric sequence.

The first term of the arithmetic sequence is a, the fourth term is $(a + 3d)$ and the thirteenth term is $(a + 12d)$.

So the first three terms of the geometric sequence are

$$a, (a + 3d), (a + 12d) \ldots$$

Because a geometric sequence has a common ratio, we know that

$$r = \frac{a + 3d}{a} = \frac{a + 12d}{a + 3d}$$

Cross multiplying $$(a + 3d)^2 = a(a + 12d)$$

$$a^2 + 6ad + 9d^2 = a^2 + 12ad$$

$$9d^2 = 6ad$$

$$9d = 6a \qquad (d \neq 0)$$

$$d = \tfrac{2}{3}a$$

Now substitute back into

$$r = \frac{a + 3d}{a}$$

$$= \frac{a + 3\left(\frac{2}{3}a\right)}{a}$$

$$= \frac{a + 2a}{a}$$

$$= \frac{3a}{a}$$

$$= 3$$

Hence, the common ratio of the geometric sequence is 3.

4.7 The sum of a geometric series

The sum of the first n terms is

$$S_n = a + ar + ar^2 + \dots + ar^{n-1}$$

Multiplying by r, $rS_n = ar + ar^2 + \dots + ar^{n-1} + ar^n$

Subtracting, $S_n - rS_n = a - ar^n$

Factorising, $S_n(1 - r) = a(1 - r^n)$

Dividing by $(1 - r)$, $\boldsymbol{S_n = \frac{a(1 - r^n)}{1 - r}}$

This result may also be written as $\boldsymbol{S_n = \frac{a(r^n - 1)}{r - 1}}$

You must understand and be able to reproduce this proof.

Example 1

Find the sum of the first 10 terms of the geometric series $5 + 15 + 45 + 135 + \dots$

The first term, a, is 5 and the common ratio, r, is 3.

So, using the formula $S_n = \frac{a(1 - r^n)}{(1 - r)}$,

we have $S_{10} = \frac{5(1 - 3^{10})}{(1 - 3)}$

$= 147\,620$

Example 2

Find the sum of the first 10 terms of the geometric series $40 + 20 + 10 + 5 + \dots$

The first term, a, is 40 and the common ratio, r, is $\frac{1}{2}$.

So, using the formula $S_n = \dfrac{a(1 - r^n)}{(1 - r)}$,

we have $S_{10} = \dfrac{40\left[1 - \left(\frac{1}{2}\right)^{10}\right]}{1 - \frac{1}{2}}$

$= 79.9$ (to 3 sf)

Example 3

The first term of a geometric series is 8 and its common ratio is r.

a Write down the second and the third terms of the series, in terms of r.

b Given that the sum of the first three terms is 38, find the two possible values of r.

a If the first term is 8, the second term is $8r$ and the third term is $8r^2$.

b We have $8 + 8r + 8r^2 = 38$

rearrange, $8r^2 + 8r - 30 = 0$

divide by 2, $4r^2 + 4r - 15 = 0$

factorise, $(2r - 3)(2r + 5) = 0$

$r = \frac{3}{2}$ or $r = -\frac{5}{2}$.

Example 4

Evaluate $\sum_{r=1}^{10} 3 \times 2^r$

Begin by writing down the first few terms of the sum.

We have $\sum_{r=1}^{10} 3 \times 2^r = 3 \times 2^1 + 3 \times 2^2 + 3 \times 2^3 + \ldots + 3 \times 2^{10}$

So we have the first 10 terms of a geometric series with first term 6 and common ratio 2.

Using the formula, $S_{10} = \dfrac{6 \times (2^{10} - 1)}{2 - 1}$

$= 6(2^{10} - 1)$

$= 6138$

Exercise 4E

1 Find an expression for the nth term of the following geometric sequences:

a 3, 6, 12, 24, …

b 2, 10, 50, 250, …

c 20, 10, 5, 2.5, …

d 2000, 400, 80, 16, …

e $\frac{1}{8}, \frac{1}{4}, \frac{1}{2}, 1, \ldots$

f 4, 12, 36, 108, …

g 5, −15, 45, −135, …

2 The 5th term of a geometric series is 567 and the 6th term is 1701. Find the first term and the common ratio.

3 The 7th term of a geometric series is 70 and the 9th term is 280. Find the first term and the common ratio (given that it is positive).

4 The 11th term of a geometric series is 5 and the 4th term is 640. Find the first term and the common ratio.

5 A geometric sequence has first term 3 and third term 12.

- **a** Find two possible values of the common ratio r.
- **b** Find two possible values of the second term in the sequence.

6 The first three terms in a geometric sequence are x, 12, $x + 45$. Find two possible values for the fourth term in this sequence.

7 The first, second and fourth terms of an arithmetic series form the first three terms of a geometric series. Find the common ratio.

8 The first, sixth and sixteenth terms of an arithmetic series form the first three terms of a geometric sequence. Find the common ratio.

9 The second, fifth and eleventh terms of an arithmetic series are consecutive terms in a geometric series and the seventh term in the arithmetic series is 4.

- **a** Find the first term and common difference.
- **b** Find also the common ratio of the geometric series.

10 Find the following:

- **a** the sum of the first ten terms of the geometric series $1 + 2 + 4 + 8 \ldots$
- **b** the sum of the first seven terms of the geometric series $2 + 6 + 18 + 54 \ldots$
- **c** the sum of the first eight terms of the geometric series $2 + 10 + 50 + 250 \ldots$
- **d** the sum of the first five terms of the geometric series $3 - 12 + 48 - 192 \ldots$

11 Find the following (to 1 dp):

- **a** the sum of the first ten terms of the geometric series $40 + 20 + 10 + 5 \ldots$
- **b** the sum of the first twenty terms of the geometric series $40 + 20 + 10 + 5 \ldots$
- **c** the sum of the first fifteen terms of the geometric series $405 + 135 + 45 + 15 \ldots$
- **d** the sum of the first thirty terms of the geometric series $1280 + 320 + 80 + 20 \ldots$
- **e** the sum of the first twelve terms of the geometric series $100 - 50 + 25 - 12.5 \ldots$

12 A geometric series is such that the first term is 7 and its common ratio is r.

- **a** Write down the second term of the series in terms of r.
- **b** Given that the sum of the first 2 terms is 42, find r.

13 A geometric series is such that the first term is 5 and its common ratio is r.

- **a** Write down the second and third terms of the sequence in terms of r.
- **b** Given that the sum of the first 3 terms is 65, find the two possible values of r.

14 Abbas decides to save some money for a year before he goes to university. He saves £1 in September, £2 in October, £4 in November and his savings continue to follow a geometric sequence until August the following year.

a How much will he save in August?

b How much will he save in total throughout the 12 months?

c Is this a sensible savings scheme?

15 Josh wants to improve his fitness by swimming each week. In his first week he swims 40 m. He sets himself the target of improving his distance by 10% each week.

a How far does he swim in his tenth week?

b How far does he swim in total over the course of the first ten weeks?

16 Phoebe wants to improve her fitness by running. In her first week she runs 3 km. She sets herself the target of improving this distance by 12% each week.

a In which week will she first run over 5 km?

b How many weeks will it take her to run 100 km in total?

17 Batahan starts a new job as an administrator for his local council. His starting salary is £26,000 per year, and he is promised a 1.8% pay rise each year.

a How much will he earn in his eighth year?

b When would his salary first exceed £35,000, according to this model?

c Why might this model not be particularly accurate in predicting the answer in part **b**?

18 An estate agent estimates that the value of property in a certain area will increase by 12% each year. If a house is worth £170,000 in 2018, how much does the estate agent estimate it will be worth in 2025? Would it be sensible to assume that the property definitely will be worth this much?

19 A geometric series is such that the sum of its first two terms is 28 and the sum of its fourth and fifth terms is 756.

a Write down two equations involving a and r.

b Factorise both equations.

c Divide one equation by the other to solve these to find the common ratio and the first term.

20 A geometric series has first term 3 and common ratio 2. If the sum of the first n terms of the sequence is 98,301

a Show the value of 2^n is 32,768.

b Find the value of n, by trial and improvement.

21 A geometric series has first term 2 and common ratio -3. If the sum of the first n terms of the series is 88,574,

a Find the value of $(-3)^n$.

b Explain why n must be odd.

c Find the value of n.

22 A geometric series has common ratio 3. If the sum of the first five terms is 605, find the first term.

23 **a** Find an expression, in terms of n, for the sum of the first n terms of the geometric series $5 + 15 + 45 + \ldots$

b Find the sum of the first 12 terms of the series.

c Find, by trial and improvement, the smallest number of terms whose total is more than 10^8.

24 A geometric series has common ratio 5. If the sum of the first ten terms is 17 089 842, find the first term.

25 Show that there are two possible geometric series in each of which the first term is 8 and the sum of the first three terms is 14. Find the second term in each series.

26 Evaluate the following:

a $\sum_{r=1}^{10} 3^r$ **b** $\sum_{r=1}^{20} 6 \times 2^r$ **c** $\sum_{r=1}^{8} 5 \times (-2)^r$

4.8 The sum to infinity of a convergent geometric series

What determines whether or not the sum of an infinite number of terms can be found? Look again at the formula $S_n = \dfrac{a(1 - r^n)}{(1 - r)}$.

The key part of this formula when we are considering an infinite number of terms is r^n.

If $r = 3$ then r^n gets very large as n gets large.

If $r = \frac{1}{2}$ then r^n tends towards zero as n gets large.

The rule is as follows…

If $-1 < r < 1$ then $r^n \to 0$ as $n \to \infty$, so the sum to infinity of the series is $\boldsymbol{S_\infty = \dfrac{a}{1 - r}}$.

If $r > 1$ or $r < -1$ then the sum to infinity of the series cannot be found.

Example 1

Find the sum to infinity of the geometric series 108, 36, 12, 4, …

The first term, a, is 108 and the common ratio, r, is $\frac{1}{3}$.

So, using the formula $S_\infty = \dfrac{a}{1 - r}$, we have $S = \dfrac{108}{\left(1 - \frac{1}{3}\right)} = 162$.

Example 2

Find the common ratio of a geometric series which has a first term of 12 and a sum to infinity of 15.

Let the common ratio be r.

Using the formula $S_\infty = \frac{a}{1-r}$, we have $\frac{12}{1-r} = 15$.

$$12 = 15 - 15r$$
$$15r = 3$$
$$r = \tfrac{1}{5}$$

The common ratio of the series is $\frac{1}{5}$.

Example 3

Work out $\sum_{r=1}^{\infty} 6 \times \left(\frac{1}{2}\right)^r$

Writing down the first few terms, we have

$$\sum_{r=1}^{\infty} 6 \times \left(\tfrac{1}{2}\right)^r = 6 \times \left(\tfrac{1}{2}\right)^1 + 6 \times \left(\tfrac{1}{2}\right)^2 + 6 \times \left(\tfrac{1}{2}\right)^3 + \ldots$$

This is a geometric series with first term 3 and common ratio $\frac{1}{2}$.
We require the sum to infinity.

$$\sum_{r=1}^{\infty} 6 \times \left(\tfrac{1}{2}\right)^r = \frac{a}{1-r} = \frac{3}{1-\frac{1}{2}}$$
$$= 6$$

Exercise 4F

1 Find the sum to infinity of the geometric series which has:

a first term 5 and common ratio $\frac{1}{2}$

b first term 2 and common ratio $\frac{2}{3}$

c first term 18 and common ratio 0.1

d first term 7 and common ratio $-\frac{3}{4}$

e first term 16 and common ratio $-\frac{3}{5}$

f first term 4 and common ratio $-\frac{3}{7}$

2 A geometric series has first term 5 and its sum to infinity is 15. Find the common ratio.

3 A geometric series has common ratio $\frac{1}{4}$ and its sum to infinity is 8. Find the first term.

4 A geometric series has common ratio $-\frac{3}{4}$ and its sum to infinity is 12. Find the first term.

5 A geometric series has first term 18 and its sum to infinity is 14. Find the common ratio.

6 Find the sum to infinity of the following:

a $20 + 10 + 5 + 2\frac{1}{2} + \ldots$

b $4 - \frac{4}{3} + \frac{4}{9} - \ldots$

c $8 - \frac{24}{5} + \frac{72}{25} - \ldots$

d $5 + \frac{20}{9} + \frac{80}{81} + \ldots$

7 Show that the sum to infinity of the geometric series $3 + \dfrac{9}{4} + \dfrac{27}{16} + \ldots$ and $4 + \dfrac{8}{3} + \dfrac{16}{9} + \ldots$ are equal.

8 A geometric series has a second term of 6 and a sum to infinity of 27. Calculate the possible values of the common ratio and the first term.

9 A and B are the sums to infinity of two geometric series

where $A = 1 + \frac{1}{2} + \frac{1}{4} + \ldots$

and $B = 1 - \frac{1}{2} + \frac{1}{4} - \ldots$

Find the ratio $\dfrac{A}{B}$.

10 P and Q are the sums to infinity of two geometric series where $P = 1 + r + r^2 + \ldots$

and $Q = 1 - r + r^2 + \ldots$

Given that $\dfrac{P}{Q} = x$, find r in terms of x.

11 A geometric series has first term a and common ratio r, where $0 < r < 1$. The difference between the sum to infinity and the sum of the first three terms is one thousandth of the sum to infinity. Find the common ratio.

12 A geometric series has first term a and common ratio x. A second geometric series has first term $2a$ and common ratio y. Given that $x = 3y$ and that the sum to infinity of both series is the same, find x.

13 When a ball is dropped onto a hard surface it always bounces to a height equal to 0.8 of the height from which it was dropped. The ball is initially dropped from a height of 2 m. How far does the ball travel before it stops bouncing?

14 $\displaystyle\sum_{r=1}^{n} 5\left(\frac{2}{3}\right)^r$ represents the sum of the first n terms of a geometric series.

a Find the first term and the common ratio.

b Hence find an expression for $\displaystyle\sum_{r=1}^{n} 5\left(\frac{2}{3}\right)^r$ in terms of n.

c Find the least value of n such that $\displaystyle\sum_{r=1}^{n} 5\left(\frac{2}{3}\right)^r$ is more than 7.

d To what number does this series converge as n tends to infinity?

15 The sum of the first n terms of a sequence is $S_n = 4^n - 1$.

a Calculate $S_4 - S_3$ and explain why this is the fourth term of the series.

b Calculate $S_n - S_{n-1}$.

c By using **b** or by looking at the first few terms of the series, show that the terms in this series form a geometric series and find the first term and common ratio.

16 The sum of a geometric series converges to 20 and its second term is 5. Find the common ratio and the first term.

17 The fifth term of a geometric series is 8, the third term is 4, and the sum of the first ten terms is positive. Find the first term, the common ratio and the *exact* sum of the first ten terms.

18 The sum of the first n terms of a certain sequence is $3n^2 + 10n$ for all values of n.

a Find the nth term by calculating $S_n - S_{n-1}$.

b Hence say what sort of sequence it is.

19 Work out the following. Leave your answers in index form.

a $\sum_{r=1}^{20} 3^r$ **b** $\sum_{r=1}^{30} 4^r$ **c** $\sum_{r=1}^{10} 7 \times 2^r$

20 Work out the following

a $\sum_{r=1}^{\infty} 10 \times \left(\frac{1}{3}\right)^r$ **b** $\sum_{r=1}^{10} 7 \times \left(-\frac{1}{2}\right)^r$

21 Show that the sum $a^6 - a^5b + a^4b^2 - a^3b^3 + a^2b^4 - ab^5 + b^6$ can be written in the form $\frac{a^7 + b^7}{a + b}$.

22 Given that p, q and r are the first three terms of a geometric sequence, show that p^2, q^2 and r^2 form another geometric sequence.

23 A geometric series has first term a and common ratio r where $-1 < r < 1$. The sum to infinity is S. Show that $0 < a < 2S$.

Review Exercise 4G

1 Write down the first four terms of the sequences whose nth terms are given for $n \geqslant 1$:

a $2n + 1$ **b** $3n - 2$ **c** n^2 **d** 10^n

e $\frac{1}{n}$ **f** $n(n + 2)$ **g** $\frac{n}{n + 1}$ **h** $(-1)^n$

2 Find an expression for the nth term of each sequence:

a 4, 8, 12, 16, … **b** $1^2, 2^2, 3^2\ 4^2, \ldots$ **c** 4, 7, 10, 13, …

d $\frac{1}{3}, \frac{2}{4}, \frac{3}{5}, \frac{4}{6}, \ldots$ **e** $1, \frac{1}{2}, \frac{1}{3}, \frac{1}{4}, \ldots$

3 Write down the first four terms of the following sequences:

a $u_{n+1} = u_n + 3, u_1 = 4$ **b** $u_{n+1} = u_n - 5, u_1 = 50$

c $u_{n+1} = \frac{1}{u_n}, u_1 = 3$ **d** $u_{n+1} = \frac{u_n}{2}, u_1 = 64$

e $u_{n+1} = u_n^2, u_1 = 10$ **f** $u_{n+1} = u_n^3, u_1 = 1$

4 Write down the terms in each series and then find their sum:

a $\sum_{r=1}^{4} 3r + 1$ **b** $\sum_{r=0}^{4} r^2$ **c** $\sum_{r=1}^{5} 2r - 1$

d $\sum_{r=2}^{4} r(r-1)$ **e** $\sum_{r=0}^{4} 2^r$ **f** $\sum_{r=1}^{4} 3$

g $\sum_{r=1}^{5} (-1)^r 2r$ **h** $\sum_{r=0}^{3} \frac{r}{r+1}$ **i** $\sum_{r=2}^{4} \frac{1}{r}$

5 Write each series using the Σ notation:

a $3 + 6 + 9 + 12$ **b** $3^2 + 4^2 + 5^2 + 6^2$ **c** $10^1 + 10^2 + 10^3 + 10^4$

d $2 + 4 + 6 + \ldots 100$ **e** $\frac{1}{1^2} + \frac{1}{2^2} + \frac{1}{3^2} + \ldots \frac{1}{10^2}$ **f** $\frac{1}{3} + \frac{1}{4} + \frac{1}{5} + \frac{1}{6}$

6 Write down the term stated for each arithmetic series:

a $3 + 7 + 11 + \ldots$ 10th term **b** $1 + 6 + 11 + \ldots$ 31st term

c $3 + 3.1 + \ldots$ 101st term **d** $40 + 39 + 38 + \ldots$ 20th term

7 Find the sum of the arithmetic series as far as the term given:

a $3 + 7 + \ldots$ 20th term **b** $300 + 295 + \ldots$ 41st term

c $100 + 102 + \ldots$ 1001st term **d** $2 + 12 + \ldots$ nth term

8 The fifth term of an arithmetic series is 17 and the thirteenth term is 57. Find the common difference, d and the first term a.

9 The third term of an arithmetic series is 13 and the tenth term is 48. Find the common difference and the first term.

10 The tenth term of an arithmetic series is 67 and the sum of the first twenty terms is 1280. Find the common difference, d and the first term, a.

11 If the first term of an arithmetic sequence is 3 and the hundredth term is 307, then find the sum of the first 100 terms.

12 A girl invests £5 on the first week of the year, £5.50 the next, £6.00 the next and so on. How much has she invested by the end of the year?

13 Find how many terms of the arithmetic sequence 5, 12, 19, 26 … should be added together in order to give a total of more than 3000.

14 An arithmetic sequence has thirteen terms whose sum is 143. The third term is 5. Find the first term.

15 What is the sum of the integers from 1 to 100, inclusive, which are not divisible by six?

16 An arithmetic progression has first term a and common difference d. Its ninth term is 22 and the sum of its first ten terms is three times the sum of its first five terms. Find the values of a and d.

17 The third term of an arithmetic series is 11 and the common difference is -3.

a Find the first term.

b Find the smallest value of n such that the nth term is negative.

c Find the sum of the first 15 negative terms.

18 The fifth term of an arithmetic series is 3 and the common difference is 7.

a Find the first term.

b Find the sum of the first ten positive terms.

19 Find an expression for the nth term of the geometric sequences.

a 5, 10, 20, 40, … **b** 2, 6, 18, 54, … **c** 100, 50, 25, …

20 Find the sum of the first eight terms of the geometric series $3 + 6 + 12 + \dots$

21 The seventh term of a geometric series is 160 and the ninth term is 640. Find the first term and the common ratio (given that it is positive).

22 Find the common ratio of a geometric series in which the sum of the first two terms is 45 and the first term is 9.

23 Find all the possible values of the common ratio of a geometric series in which the sum of its first three terms is 105 and the first term is 5.

24 The first two terms of a geometric series are x and $x^2 + x$. Find, in terms of x,

a the common ratio of the series.

b an expression for the one-hundredth term of the series.

25 Given that $\sum_{r=1}^{n} 2^r = 2046$, find the value of n.

26 Evaluate, correct to the nearest whole number, $\sum_{r=1}^{200} (0.98)^r$.

27 A metal stake, 100 cm long, is driven into the ground so that at each blow it penetrates 0.9 of the distance penetrated as a result of the previous blow. The stake penetrates 10 cm at the first blow.
Calculate, to the nearest mm, the length of the stake which is above ground after ten blows.

28 The first two terms of a geometric series are $(x + 1)$ and $(x^3 + 2x^2 - x - 2)$.

a Find the common ratio of the series, in terms of x.

b Given that $x = 2$, find the fourth term of the geometric series.

Examination Exercise 4

1 An arithmetic series has first term a and common difference d.
The sum of the first 5 terms of the series is 575.

a Show that $a + 2d = 115$.

b Given also that the 10th term of the series is 87, find the value of d.

c The nth term of the series is u_n. Given that $u_k > 0$ and $u_{k+1} < 0$, find the value of $\sum_{n=1}^{k} u_n$. [AQA, GCE Mathematics, C2, June 2014]

2 An arithmetic series has first term a and common difference d.
The sum of the first 21 terms is 168.

a Show that $a + 10d = 8$.

b The sum of the second term and the third term is 50.
The nth term of the series is u_n.

i Find the value of u_{12}.

ii Find the value of $\sum_{n=4}^{21} u_n$. [AQA, GCE Mathematics, C2, June 2016]

3 Jess started work 20 years ago. In year 1 her annual salary was £17 000.
Her annual salary increased by £1500 each year, so that her annual salary in year 2 was £18 500, in year 3 it was £20 000 and so on, forming an arithmetic sequence. This continued until she reached her maximum annual salary of £32 000 in year k. Her annual salary then remained at £32 000.

a Find the value of the constant k.

b Calculate the total amount that Jess has earned in the 20 years.
[EDEXCEL, GCE Mathematics, C1, June 2015]

4 In the year 2000 a shop sold 150 computers. Each year the shop sold 10 more computers than the year before, so that the shop sold 160 computers in 2001, 170 computers in 2002, and so on forming an arithmetic sequence.

a Show that the shop sold 220 computers in 2007.

b Calculate the total number of computers the shop sold from 2000 to 2013 inclusive.

In the year 2000, the selling price of each computer was £900. The selling price fell by £20 each year, so that in 2001 the selling price was £880, in 2002 the selling price was £860, and so on forming an arithmetic sequence.

c In a particular year, the selling price of each computer in £s was equal to three times the number of computers the shop sold in that year. By forming and solving an equation, find the year in which this occurred.

[EDEXCEL, GCE Mathematics, C1, June 2014]

5 a A sequence $u_1, u_2, u_3, \ldots$ is defined by

$$u_1 = 4 \quad \text{and} \quad u_{n+1} = \frac{2}{u_n} \quad \text{for } n \geqslant 1.$$

i Write down the values of u_2 and u_3.

ii Describe the behaviour of the sequence.

b In an arithmetic progression the ninth term is 18 and the sum of the first nine terms is 72. Find the first term and the common difference.

[OCR, GCE Mathematics, C2, June 2012]

6 On John's 10th birthday he received the first of an annual birthday gift of money from his uncle. This first gift was £60 and on each subsequent birthday the gift was £15 more than the year before. The amounts of these gifts form an arithmetic sequence.

a Show that, immediately after his 12th birthday, the total of these gifts was £225.

b Find the amount that John received from his uncle as a birthday gift on his 18th birthday.

c Find the total of these birthday gifts that John had received from his uncle up to and including his 21st birthday.

When John had received n of these birthday gifts, the total money that he had received from these gifts was £3375.

d Show that $n^2 + 7n = 25 \times 18$

e Find the value of n, when he had received £3375 in total, and so determine John's age at this time. [EDEXCEL, GCE Mathematics, C1, June 2016]

7 A geometric progression has first term 3 and second term -6.

i State the value of the common ratio.

ii Find the value of the eleventh term.

iii Find the sum of the first twenty terms.

[OCR, GCE Mathematics, C2, June 2015]

8 A geometric series has first term a and common ratio $r = \frac{3}{4}$.
The sum of the first 4 terms of this series is 175.

a Show that $a = 64$.

b Find the sum to infinity of the series.

c Find the difference between the 9th and 10th terms of the series.
Give your answer to 3 dp.

[EDEXCEL, GCE Mathematics, C2, June 2016]

9 The first term of an infinite geometric series is 48. The common ratio of the series is 0.6.

a Find the third term of the series.

b Find the sum to infinity of the series.

c The nth term of the series is u_n. Find the value of $\sum_{n=4}^{\infty} u_n$.

[AQA, GCE Mathematics, C2, June 2015]

10 a The first term of a geometric progression is 50 and the common ratio is 0.8. Use logarithms to find the smallest value of k such that the value of the kth term is less than 0.15.

b In a different geometric progression, the second term is -3 and the sum to infinity is 4. Show that there is only one possible value of the common ratio and hence find the first term. [OCR, GCE Mathematics, C2, June 2014]

11 i All the terms of a geometric series are positive. The sum of the first two terms is 34 and the sum to infinity is 162.

Find

a the common ratio,

b the first term.

ii A different geometric series has a first term of 42 and a common ratio of $\frac{6}{7}$. Find the smallest value of n for which the sum of the first n terms of the series exceeds 290. [EDEXCEL, GCE Mathematics, C2, June 2015]

12 The second and third terms of a geometric series are 192 and 144 respectively. For this series, find

a the common ratio,

b the first term,

c the sum to infinity,

d the smallest value of n for which the sum of the first n terms of the series exceeds 1000. [EDEXCEL, GCE Mathematics, C2, June 2011]

13 The nth term of a sequence is u_n.

The sequence is defined by $u_{n+1} = pu_n + q$, where p and q are constants.

The second term of the sequence is 160. The third term of the sequence is 132.

The limit of u_n as n tends to infinity is 20.

a Find the value of p and the value of q.

b Hence find the value of the first term of the sequence.

[AQA, GCE Mathematics, C2, June 2015]

14 i The first three terms of an arithmetic progression are $2x$, $x + 4$ and $2x - 7$ respectively. Find the value of x.

ii The first three terms of another sequence are also $2x$, $x + 4$ and $2x - 7$ respectively.

a Verify that when $x = 8$ the terms form a geometric progression and find the sum to infinity in this case.

b Find the other possible value of x that also gives a geometric progression.

[OCR, GCE Mathematics, C2, Jan 2013]

15 A sequence $u_1, u_2, u_3, \ldots$ is defined by $u_n = 85 - 5n$ for $n \geqslant 1$.

i Write down the values of u_1, u_2 and u_3.

ii Find $\sum_{n=1}^{20} u_n$.

iii Given u_1, u_5 and u_p are, respectively, the first, second and third terms of a geometric progression, find the value of p.

iv Find the sum to infinity of the geometric progression in part **iii**.

[OCR, GCE Mathematics, C2, Jan 2012]

16 An arithmetic progression $u_1, u_2, u_3, \ldots$ is defined by $u_1 = 5$ and $u_{n+1} = u_n + 1.5$ for $n \geqslant 1$.

i Given that $u_k = 140$, find the value of k.

A geometric progression $w_1, w_2, w_3, \ldots$ is defined by $w_n = 120 \times (0.9)^{n-1}$ for $n \geqslant 1$.

ii Find the sum of the first 16 terms of this geometric progression, giving your answer correct to 3 significant figures.

iii Use an algebraic method to find the smallest value of N such that

$$\sum_{n=1}^{N} u_n > \sum_{n=1}^{\infty} w_n.$$

[OCR, GCE Mathematics, C2, June 2016]

17 A sequence of numbers $a_1, a_2, a_3, \ldots$ is defined by

$$a_{n+1} = 5a_n - 3, \quad n \geqslant 1$$

Given that $a_2 = 7$,

a find the value of a_1

b find the value of $\sum_{r=1}^{4} a_r$

[EDEXCEL, GCE Mathematics, C1, June 2014]

18 A sequence $u_1, u_2, u_3, \ldots$ is defined by

$$u_1 = 7 \quad \text{and} \quad u_{n+1} = u_n + 4 \quad \text{for} \quad n \geqslant 1.$$

i Show that $u_{17} = 71$.

ii Show that $\sum_{n=1}^{35} u_n = \sum_{n=36}^{50} u_n$.

[OCR, GCE Mathematics, C2, Jan 2013]

19 A sequence $a_1, a_2, a_3, \ldots$ is defined by

$$a_1 = k,$$
$$a_{n+1} = 5a_n + 3, \quad n \geqslant 1,$$

where k is a positive integer.

a Write down an expression for a_2 in terms of k.

b Show that $a_3 = 25k + 18$.

c i Find $\sum_{r=1}^{4} a_r$ in terms of k, in its simplest form.

ii Show that $\sum_{r=1}^{1} a_r$ is divisible by 6.

[EDEXCEL, GCE Mathematics, C1, June 2011]

20 A sequence $a_1, a_2, a_3, \ldots$ is defined by

$$a_1 = 4,$$
$$a_{n+1} = 5 - ka_n, \quad n \geqslant 1,$$

where k is a constant.

a Write down an expression for a_2 and a_3 in terms of k.

Find

b $\sum_{r=1}^{3} (1 + a_r)$ in terms of k, giving your answer in its simplest form,

c $\sum_{r=1}^{100} (a_{r+1} + ka_r)$

[EDEXCEL, GCE Mathematics, C1, June 2016]

21 i A sequence $U_1, U_2, U_3, \ldots$ is defined by

$$U_{n+2} = 2U_{n+1} - U_n, \quad n \geqslant 1$$
$$U_1 = 4 \text{ and } U_2 = 4$$

Find the value of

a U_3

b $\sum_{n=1}^{20} U_n$

ii Another sequence $V_1, V_2, V_3, \ldots$ is defined by

$$V_{n+2} = 2V_{n+1} - V_n, \quad n \geqslant 1$$
$$V_1 = k \text{ and } V_2 = 2k, \text{ where } k \text{ is a constant}$$

a Find V_3 and V_4 in terms of k.

Given that $\sum_{n=1}^{5} V_n = 165$,

b find the value of k.

[EDEXCEL, GCE Mathematics, C1, June 2015]

Part 5

Binomial expansion

5.1 Binomial expansion for any rational index

In Pure Mathematics Book 1 we saw that if n is a positive integer

$$(a + b)^n = \binom{n}{0}a^n + \binom{n}{1}a^{n-1}b + \binom{n}{2}a^{n-2}b^2 + \ldots + \binom{n}{r}a^{n-r}b^r + \ldots$$

and

$$(1 + x)^n = 1 + nx + \frac{n(n-1)}{1 \times 2}x^2 + \ldots + \frac{n(n-1)\ldots(n-r+1)}{1 \times 2 \times \ldots \times r}x^r + \ldots$$

In both the above cases these expansions were finite, they had $n + 1$ terms.

We are now going on to consider such expansions in cases where n is no longer a positive integer but where n is any rational number, that is any fraction, positive or negative.

If we put $n = -1$ into the expression

$$(1 + x)^n = 1 + nx + \frac{n(n-1)}{1 \times 2}x^2 + \ldots + \frac{n(n-1)\ldots(n-r+1)}{1 \times 2 \times \ldots \times r}x^r + \ldots$$

we get $(1 + x)^{-1} = 1 + (-1)x + \dfrac{(-1) \times (-2)}{1 \times 2}x^2 + \dfrac{(-1) \times (-2) \times (-3)}{1 \times 2 \times 3}x^3 + \ldots$

$$= 1 - x + x^2 - x^3 + \ldots$$

Now we know from work on geometric series that if $|x| < 1$ (that is $-1 < x < 1$) then the sum of the infinite series $1 - x + x^2 - x^3 + \ldots$ is $\dfrac{1}{1 + x} = (1 + x)^{-1}$.

So it follows from the above that

$(1 + x)^n = 1 + nx + \dfrac{n(n-1)}{1 \times 2}x^2 + \ldots + \dfrac{n(n-1)\ldots(n-r+1)}{1 \times 2 \times \ldots \times r}x^r + \ldots$ is true not simply for n being a positive integer but also for $n = -1$ provided that $-1 < x < 1$.

In some of the questions in the last exercise in this section we will show that

$(1 + x)^n = 1 + nx + \dfrac{n(n-1)}{1 \times 2}x^2 + \ldots + \dfrac{n(n-1)\ldots(n-r+1)}{1 \times 2 \times \ldots \times r}x^r + \ldots$ holds for $n = -2$, $n = -3$, $n = \frac{1}{2}$ and other fractional values, provided that $-1 < x < 1$.

It is beyond the scope of this book but it can be proved that

$(1 + x)^n = 1 + nx + \dfrac{n(n-1)}{1 \times 2}x^2 + \ldots + \dfrac{n(n-1)\ldots(n-r+1)}{1 \times 2 \times \ldots \times r}x^r + \ldots$ is true for all rational values of n, provided that $-1 < x < 1$.

So we use the following result:

$$(1+x)^n = 1 + nx + \frac{n(n-1)}{1 \times 2}x^2 + \ldots + \frac{n(n-1)\ldots(n-r+1)}{1 \times 2 \times \ldots \times r}x^r + \ldots$$

$-1 < x < 1$, n is rational.

It follows from the above that the expansion of $(1 + kx)^n$ is valid provided $-1 < kx < 1$, that is provided $-\frac{1}{k} < x < \frac{1}{k}$.

Example 1

Find the first four terms in ascending powers of x in the expansion of $\frac{1}{(1+x)^5}$, where $-1 < x < 1$.

$$\frac{1}{(1+x)^5} = (1+x)^{-5} = 1 + (-5)x + \frac{(-5) \times (-6)}{1 \times 2}x^2 + \frac{(-5) \times (-6) \times (-7)}{1 \times 2 \times 3}x^3 + \ldots$$

So we see that $(1+x)^{-5} = 1 - 5x + 15x^2 - 35x^3 + \ldots$

Example 2

Find the first four terms in ascending powers of x in the expansion of $(1+x)^{\frac{1}{3}}$, where $-1 < x < 1$.

$$(1+x)^{\frac{1}{3}} = 1 + \left(\frac{1}{3}\right)x + \frac{\left(\frac{1}{3}\right) \times \left(\frac{1}{3} - 1\right)}{1 \times 2}x^2 + \frac{\left(\frac{1}{3}\right) \times \left(\frac{1}{3} - 1\right) \times \left(\frac{1}{3} - 2\right)}{1 \times 2 \times 3}x^3 + \ldots$$

So we see that $(1+x)^{\frac{1}{3}} = 1 + \frac{x}{3} - \frac{x^2}{9} + \frac{5x^3}{81} + \ldots$

Example 3

a Find the first four terms in ascending powers of x in the expansion of $(1+2x)^{\frac{5}{2}}$, where this expansion is valid.

b For what values of x is the expansion valid?

a $$(1+2x)^{\frac{5}{2}} = 1 + \left(\frac{5}{2}\right)(2x) + \frac{\left(\frac{5}{2}\right) \times \left(\frac{5}{2} - 1\right)}{1 \times 2}(2x)^2 + \frac{\left(\frac{5}{2}\right) \times \left(\frac{5}{2} - 1\right) \times \left(\frac{5}{2} - 2\right)}{1 \times 2 \times 3}(2x)^3 + \ldots$$

So we see that $(1+2x)^{\frac{5}{2}} = 1 + 5x + \frac{15x^2}{2} + \frac{5x^3}{2} + \ldots$

b The expansion is valid for $|2x| < 1$. That is $-\frac{1}{2} < x < \frac{1}{2}$.

Example 4

Find $\sqrt[3]{1.03}$ to 4 dp.

From Example **2**, $(1+x)^{\frac{1}{3}} = 1 + \frac{x}{3} - \frac{x^2}{9} + \frac{5x^3}{81} + \ldots$ if $-1 < x < 1$.

If we substitute $x = 0.03$ we see that

$$\sqrt[3]{1.03} = (1 + 0.03)^{\frac{1}{3}} = 1 + \frac{0.03}{3} - \frac{(0.03)^2}{9} + \frac{5(0.03)^3}{81} + \dots$$

$$= 1 + 0.01 - 0.0001 + \dots \approx 1.0099 \dots$$

So we see that $\sqrt[3]{1.03} = 1.0099$ (to 4 dp).

Exercise 5A

1 Find the first three terms in ascending powers of x in the following expansions, where $-1 < x < 1$:

a $(1 + x)^{-2}$ **b** $(1 + x)^{-3}$ **c** $(1 + x)^{-6}$

d $(1 + x)^{-10}$ **e** $(1 + x)^{\frac{1}{2}}$ **f** $(1 + x)^{\frac{3}{2}}$

g $(1 + x)^{-\frac{1}{2}}$ **h** $(1 + x)^{-\frac{3}{4}}$ **i** $(1 - x)^{\frac{2}{3}}$

j $(1 - x)^{-\frac{2}{5}}$ **k** $\sqrt{(1 - x)}$ **l** $\dfrac{1}{\sqrt[3]{1 - x}}$

2 Use question **1 a** to find the value of $(1.01)^{-2}$ to 3 dp.

3 Use the expression in question **1 e** to find the value of $\sqrt{1.02}$, correct to 3 dp.

4 Find the limits for x within which the following expressions are valid:

a $(1 + 2x)^{-3}$ **b** $(1 - x)^{-2}$

c $(1 + 5x)^{-4}$ **d** $(1 + 2x)^{-7}$

e $(1 + 2x)^{\frac{1}{2}}$ **f** $(1 + 4x)^{\frac{5}{2}}$

g $(1 - 3x)^{-\frac{1}{2}}$ **h** $(1 - 2x)^{\frac{1}{4}}$

i $\left(1 - \dfrac{x}{3}\right)^{\frac{1}{2}}$ **j** $\left(1 - \dfrac{x}{2}\right)^{-\frac{1}{3}}$

5 Assuming that in each case x lies within the range so that expansion is valid, find the first four terms in the following expansions:

a $(1 + 2x)^{-3}$ **b** $(1 - x)^{-2}$

c $(1 + 5x)^{-4}$ **d** $(1 + 2x)^{-7}$

e $(1 + 2x)^{\frac{1}{2}}$ **f** $(1 + 4x)^{\frac{5}{2}}$

g $(1 - 3x)^{-\frac{1}{2}}$ **h** $(1 - 2x)^{\frac{1}{4}}$

i $\left(1 - \dfrac{x}{3}\right)^{\frac{1}{2}}$ **j** $\left(1 - \dfrac{x}{2}\right)^{-\frac{1}{3}}$

6 Find the x^4 term in the expansion of $(1 + 2x)^{\frac{1}{4}}$ where $-\frac{1}{2} < x < \frac{1}{2}$.

7 Find the x^5 term in the expansion of $(1 - 2x)^{-\frac{3}{4}}$ where $-\frac{1}{2} < x < \frac{1}{2}$.

8 Find the x^3 term in the expansion of $\left(1 - \dfrac{x}{2}\right)^{\frac{2}{5}}$ where $-2 < x < 2$.

9 **a** Expand $(x + 2)^3$.

b Evaluate $(\sqrt{3} + 2)^3$ leaving your answer in the form $a\sqrt{3} + b$.

10 **a** Show that $(x + y)^4 - (x - y)^4 = 8xy(x^2 + y^2)$.

b Find the exact value of $(3 + \sqrt{2})^4 - (3 - \sqrt{2})^4$.

11 Expand $(1 + x)^{\frac{1}{2}}$ up to and including the term in x^3. Hence calculate the value of $\sqrt{1.08}$ correct to 4 dp.

12 The first four terms in the expansion of $(1 - x)^n$ are $1 - 6x + ax^2 + bx^3$. Show that $a = 15$ and find the value of b.

13 Find the first four terms in the expansion of $\left(1 - \frac{1}{x}\right)^{\frac{1}{2}}$ in *descending* powers of x.

By substituting $x = 100$ find a value of $\sqrt{99}$, giving your answer to 5 dp.

14 **a** Find the first three terms in the expansion of $(1 - x)^{\frac{1}{3}}$.

b By letting $x = \frac{1}{1000}$, evaluate $\sqrt[3]{37}$ to 6 dp.

5.2 Expanding $(a + bx)^n$

Example 1

Find the first four terms in ascending powers of x in the expansion of $(4 + x)^{\frac{1}{2}}$, stating clearly the values of x for which this is valid.

We first of all need to write $(4 + x)^{\frac{1}{2}} = \left[4\left(1 + \frac{x}{4}\right)\right]^{\frac{1}{2}} = 4^{\frac{1}{2}}\left(1 + \frac{x}{4}\right)^{\frac{1}{2}} = 2\left(1 + \frac{x}{4}\right)^{\frac{1}{2}}$.

So we see that the expansion is valid if $-1 < \frac{x}{4} < 1$, that is provided $-4 < x < 4$.

$$\left(1 + \frac{x}{4}\right)^{\frac{1}{2}} = 1 + \left(\frac{1}{2}\right)\left(\frac{x}{4}\right) + \frac{\left(\frac{1}{2}\right) \times \left(\frac{1}{2} - 1\right)}{2 \times 1}\left(\frac{x}{4}\right)^2 + \frac{\left(\frac{1}{2}\right) \times \left(\frac{1}{2} - 1\right) \times \left(\frac{1}{2} - 2\right)}{3 \times 2 \times 1}\left(\frac{x}{4}\right)^3 + \ldots$$

$$= 1 + \frac{x}{8} - \frac{x^2}{128} + \frac{x^3}{1024} + \ldots$$

Hence we see that $(4 + x)^{\frac{1}{2}} = 2\left(1 + \frac{x}{4}\right)^{\frac{1}{2}} = 2 + \frac{x}{4} - \frac{x^2}{64} + \frac{x^3}{512} + \ldots$

Example 2

Find the first four terms in ascending powers of x in the expansion of $(2x + 3)^{-1}$, stating clearly the values of x for which this is valid.

$$(2x + 3)^{-1} = \left[3\left(\frac{2x}{3} + 1\right)\right]^{-1} = 3^{-1}\left(1 + \frac{2x}{3}\right)^{-1} = \frac{1}{3}\left(1 + \frac{2x}{3}\right)^{-1}$$

So we see that the expansion is valid if $-1 < \frac{2x}{3} < 1$, that is provided $-\frac{3}{2} < x < \frac{3}{2}$.

$$(2x+3)^{-1} = \frac{1}{3}\left(1+\frac{2x}{3}\right)^{-1}$$

$$= \frac{1}{3}\left[1 + (-1)\left(\frac{2x}{3}\right) + \frac{(-1)(-2)}{2!}\left(\frac{2x}{3}\right)^2 + \frac{(-1)(-2)(-3)}{3!}\left(\frac{2x}{3}\right)^3 + \ldots\right]$$

Hence $(2x+3)^{-1} = \frac{1}{3} - \frac{2x}{9} + \frac{4x^2}{27} - \frac{8x^3}{81} + \ldots$

Exercise 5B

1 Calculate the first three terms (in ascending powers of x) in the expansion of the following, stating also the values of x for which each expansion is valid:

a $(2+x)^{-1}$ **b** $(4-x)^{-3}$ **c** $(3+x)^{-2}$

d $(5+x)^{-4}$ **e** $(4-x)^{\frac{1}{2}}$ **f** $(9-x)^{-\frac{1}{2}}$

g $(8-x)^{\frac{1}{3}}$ **h** $(8+x)^{-\frac{2}{3}}$ **i** $(25+x)^{\frac{5}{2}}$

2 Calculate the first three terms (in ascending powers of x) in the expansion of the following, stating also the values of x for which each expansion is valid:

a $(4+3x)^{\frac{1}{2}}$ **b** $(9-2x)^{-\frac{1}{2}}$ **c** $(8-5x)^{\frac{1}{3}}$

d $(25-7x)^{\frac{3}{2}}$

3 Given that, in each case, x lies within the range so that the expansion is valid, find the exact values of a and b in the following:

a $(4+3x)^{-\frac{1}{2}} = a + bx + \ldots$ **b** $(8+3x)^{\frac{1}{3}} = a + bx + \ldots$

c $(2-7x)^{-\frac{1}{2}} = a + bx + \ldots$ **d** $(27+2x)^{-\frac{1}{3}} = a + bx + \ldots$

4 Find, in ascending powers of x, up to and including the x^3 term, the expansion of $\sqrt{9+4x}$, stating the values of x for which the expansion is valid.

5 **a** Calculate the first three terms (in ascending powers of x) in the expansion of $(1-2x)^{\frac{1}{2}}$ and state the values of x for which the expansion is valid.

b Use this to estimate the value of $\sqrt{0.98}$ correct to 3 significant figures.

6 **a** Expand $(1-3x)^{\frac{1}{5}}$ in ascending powers of x up to and including the term in x^2.

b By substituting $x = \frac{1}{32}$ in your series, find an approximation for $\sqrt[5]{29}$, giving your answer correct to 3 dp.

5.3 Partial fractions and harder questions

Example 1

Find the first three terms in ascending powers of x in the expansion of $\frac{7+5x}{(x+1)(x+2)}$, stating the values of x for which this is valid.

In example 1 of Part 3 we saw that $\dfrac{7+5x}{(x+1)(x+2)} = \dfrac{2}{(x+1)} + \dfrac{3}{(x+2)}$

So we see that

$$\frac{7+5x}{(x+1)(x+2)} = 2(x+1)^{-1} + 3(x+2)^{-1}$$

$$= 2(1+x)^{-1} + 3\left[2\left(1+\frac{x}{2}\right)\right]^{-1}$$

$$= 2(1+x)^{-1} + \frac{3}{2}\left(1+\frac{x}{2}\right)^{-1}$$

The expansion of $(1+x)^{-1}$ is valid if $-1 < x < 1$, and the expansion of $\left(1+\dfrac{x}{2}\right)^{-1}$ is valid if $-2 < x < 2$. It follows that the expansion of $\dfrac{7+5x}{(x+1)(x+2)}$ is valid if $-1 < x < 1$.

Notice that we take the more restricted range of values for x.

So we have $\dfrac{7+5x}{(x+1)(x+2)} = 2(1 - x + x^2 - x^3) + \dfrac{3}{2}\left(1 - \dfrac{x}{2} + \dfrac{x^2}{4} - \dfrac{x^3}{8}\right)$

$$= \frac{7}{2} - \frac{11}{4}x + \frac{19}{8}x^2 - \frac{35}{16}x^3 + \ldots$$

Exercise 5C

1 Express the following in partial fractions and then find the expansion of each one in ascending powers of x, up to and including the term in x^2. State the values of x for which each expansion is valid:

a $\dfrac{9x-26}{(x-3)(x-2)}$

b $\dfrac{3x-4}{(x-1)(x-2)}$

c $\dfrac{8x+11}{(x+1)(x+2)}$

d $\dfrac{7x+15}{(x+2)(x+3)}$

e $\dfrac{3x}{(x-1)(x+2)}$

f $\dfrac{x+7}{(x-1)(x+3)}$

2 **a** Express $\dfrac{x^2-x-1}{(x-2)(x-1)}$ as partial fractions.

b Hence show that $\dfrac{x^2-x-1}{(x-2)(x-1)} \equiv 1 - (1-x)^{-1} - \dfrac{1}{2}\left(1-\dfrac{x}{2}\right)^{-1}$ and use this to find the first four terms in ascending powers of x in the expansion of $\dfrac{x^2-x-1}{(x-2)(x-1)}$.

c State the range of values for x for which the expansion is valid.

3 a Find the first four terms in ascending powers of x in the expansion of $(x + 1)\sqrt{1 - 4x}$.

b State the range of values of x for which the expansion is valid.

4 In the series expansion of $(1 + \lambda x)^n$ the x coefficient is -6 and the x^2 coefficient is 24. Find λ and n.

5 Show that the coefficients of x^2 and x^4 in the series expansion of $(1 - 4x^2)^{\frac{1}{2}}$ are equal.

6 Find, in ascending powers of x, up to and including the x^2 term, the expansion of $\dfrac{(x + 1)}{\sqrt{1 - x}}$, stating the values of x for which the expansion is valid.

7 a Find, in ascending powers of x, up to and including the x^2 term, the expansion of $\sqrt{\dfrac{1 + x}{1 - x}}$, stating the values of x for which the expansion is valid.

b By taking $x = \dfrac{1}{9}$, show that $\sqrt{5} \approx \dfrac{181}{81}$.

8 a Find the constants a and b so that the expansions of $(1 + 2x)^{\frac{1}{2}}$ and $\dfrac{1 + ax}{1 + bx}$, up to and including the term in x^2, are the same.

b Use the above result, with $x = -\dfrac{1}{100}$, to obtain an approximate value for $\sqrt{2}$ in the form $\dfrac{m}{n}$, where m and n are integers.

9 In the series expansion of $\sqrt{(1 + px + qx^2)}$ the x and x^2 coefficients are both equal to 1.

a Show that $p = 2$ and find the value of q.

b Find the x^3 term in the series expansion of $\sqrt{(1 + px + qx^2)}$.

c By solving the inequality $-1 < px + qx^2 < 1$, find the values of x for which this expansion is valid.

Questions **10** to **13** are more difficult.

10 a Find the sum of the series $1 - x + x^2 - x^3 + \ldots + (-1)^n x^n$.

b For which values of x does the sum to infinity exist?

c If x is restricted in the way described in part **b** then find the sum to infinity of $1 - x + x^2 - x^3 + \ldots$

11 a Deduce from question **10** that $(1 - x)^{-1} = 1 + x + x^2 + x^3 + \ldots$ and state the values of x for which this is true.

b Work out $(1 - x)^{-1}(1 - x)^{-1} = (1 + x + x^2 + \ldots)(1 + x + x^2 + \ldots)$ to express $(1 - x)^2$ as an infinite sum of powers of x.

c Use the fact that $\dfrac{\mathrm{d}}{\mathrm{d}x}((1 - x)^n) = -n(1 - x)^{n-1}$ for all values of n and your answer to **b** to find a formula for $(1 - x)^{-3}$ as an infinite sum of powers of x.

d Use the same method as part **c** to find a formula for $(1 - x)^{-4}$ as an infinite sum of powers of x.

12 Show that your answers to **11a** and **d** both agree with the formula

$$(1 + x)^n = 1 + nx + \frac{n(n-1)}{2!}x^2 + \frac{n(n-1)(n-2)}{3!}x^3 + \ldots \text{ for } (-1 < x < 1)$$

13 a If $(1 + x)^{-\frac{1}{2}} = a_0 + a_1x + a_2x^2 + a_3x^3 + \ldots$ then, by considering $(1 + x)^{-\frac{1}{2}}(1 + x)^{-\frac{1}{2}} = (1 + x)^{-1}$ and using the fact that $(1 + x)^{-1} = 1 - x + x^2 - x^3 + \ldots$, find a_0, a_1, a_2 and a_3 (Note: a_0 must be positive) stating the values of x for which the expansions are valid.

b Show that your answers to **a** agree with the formula

$$(1 + x)^n = 1 + nx + \frac{n(n-1)}{2!}x^2 + \frac{n(n-1)(n-2)}{3!}x^3 + \ldots \text{ for } (-1 < x < 1)$$

Review Exercise 5D

1 State the values of x for which each expansion is valid.

a $(2 + 3x)^{-\frac{1}{2}}$ **b** $(5 - 3x)^{\frac{1}{3}}$ **c** $(2 - 7x)^{-\frac{1}{2}}$

d $(9 + 2x)^{-\frac{1}{3}}$ **e** $(3 - 2x)^{-\frac{2}{3}}$ **f** $(5 - 3x)^{-\frac{3}{2}}$

2 Calculate the first three terms (in ascending powers of x) in the expansion of $(8 - 3x)^{\frac{1}{3}}$ and state the values of x for which the expansion is valid.

3 Given that, in each case, x lies within the range so that the expansion is valid, find the values of a and b in the following:

a $(27 - 2x)^{-\frac{2}{3}} = a + bx + \ldots$ **b** $(4 - 3x)^{-\frac{3}{2}} = a + bx + \ldots$

4 a Express $f(x) = \dfrac{1}{(1 + x)(1 - 2x)}$ in partial fractions.

b Find the first three terms in the expansion of $f(x)$ in ascending powers of x.

c State the set of values of x for which the expansion is valid.

5 a Express $\dfrac{7x + 2}{(2x + 1)(x - 1)}$ as partial fractions.

b Hence find the first three terms in ascending powers of x in the expansion of $\dfrac{7x + 2}{(2x + 1)(x - 1)}$.

c State the range of values of x for which the expansion in **b** is valid.

6 a Express $\dfrac{28x}{(3x - 1)(x + 2)}$ as partial fractions.

b Hence show that $\dfrac{28x}{(3x - 1)(x + 2)} \equiv 4\left[\left(1 + \dfrac{x}{2}\right)^{-1} - (1 - 3x)^{-1}\right]$.

c Show that the x^2 coefficient in the expansion of $\dfrac{28x}{(3x - 1)(x + 2)}$ is -35 and find the x^3 coefficient.

d State the range of values of x for which the expansion is valid.

Examination Exercise 5

1 **a** Find the binomial expansion of $(1 + 5x)^{\frac{1}{5}}$ up to and including the term in x^2.

b i Find the binomial expansion of $(8 + 3x)^{-\frac{2}{3}}$ up to and including the term in x^2.

ii Use your expansion from part **b i** to find an estimate for $\sqrt[3]{\frac{1}{81}}$, giving your answer to 4 dp. [AQA, GCE Mathematics, C4, June 2015]

2 **a** Find the binomial expansion of

$$(4 + 5x)^{\frac{1}{2}}, \ |x| < \frac{4}{5}$$

in ascending powers of x, up to and including the term in x^2.
Give each coefficient in its simplest form.

b Find the exact value of $(4 + 5x)^{\frac{1}{2}}$ when $x = \frac{1}{10}$

Give your answer in the form $k\sqrt{2}$, where k is a constant to be determined.

c Substitute $x = \frac{1}{10}$ into your binomial expansion from part **a** and hence find an approximate value for $\sqrt{2}$.

Give your answer in the form $\frac{p}{q}$ where p and q are integers.

[EDEXCEL, GCE Mathematics, C4, June 2015]

3 **a** Find the binomial expansion of

$$\sqrt[3]{(8 - 9x)}, \ |x| < \frac{8}{9}$$

in ascending powers of x, up to and including the term in x^3.
Give each coefficient as a simplified fraction.

b Use your expansion to estimate an approximate value for $\sqrt[3]{7100}$, giving your answer to 4 dp. State the value of x, which you use in your expansion, and show all your working.

[EDEXCEL, GCE Mathematics, C4 1R, June 2013]

4 **i** Expand $\dfrac{1 + x^2}{\sqrt{1 + 4x}}$ in ascending powers of x, up to and including the term in x^3.

ii State the set of values of x for which this expansion is valid.

[OCR, GCE Mathematics, C4, June 2012]

5 **i** Show that $\dfrac{x}{(1 - x)^3} \approx x + 3x^2 + 6x^3$ for small values of x.

ii Use this result, together with a suitable value of x, to obtain a decimal estimate of the value of $\dfrac{100}{729}$.

iii Show that $\dfrac{x}{(1-x)^3} = -\dfrac{1}{x^2}\left(1 - \dfrac{1}{x}\right)^{-3}$. Hence find the first three terms of the binomial expansion of $\dfrac{x}{(1-x)^3}$ in powers of $\dfrac{1}{x}$.

iv Comment on the suitability of substituting the same value of x as used in part **ii** in the expansion in part **iii** to estimate the value of $\dfrac{100}{729}$.

[OCR, GCE Mathematics, C4, June 2013]

6 Given that the binomial expansion of $(1 + kx)^n$ is $1 - 6x + 30x^2 + \ldots$, find the value of n and k. State the set of values of x for which this expansion is valid.

[OCR, GCE Mathematics, C4, June 2016]

7 Given that $\left(1 + \dfrac{x}{p}\right)^q = 1 - x + \dfrac{3}{4}x^2 + \ldots$, find p and q, and state the set of values of x for which the expansion is valid. [MEI, GCE Mathematics, C4, June 2016]

Part 6

Trigonometry 2

6.1 Secant, cosecant and cotangent

In addition to sine, cosine and tangent, it is helpful to define three further trigonometric ratios.

$$\sec x = \frac{1}{\cos x}$$

$$\operatorname{cosec} x = \frac{1}{\sin x}$$

$$\cot x = \frac{1}{\tan x} \left(= \frac{\cos x}{\sin x}\right)$$

Notice that 'sec x' is written for 'secant x' and so on.

To draw the graphs of sec x, cosec x and cot x we refer to the graphs of cos x, sin x and tan x respectively.

Here is the graph of sin x and cosec x for $-360° \leqslant x \leqslant 360°$. Notice that $y = \operatorname{cosec} x$ has vertical asymptotes at all the values of x for which $\sin x = 0$.

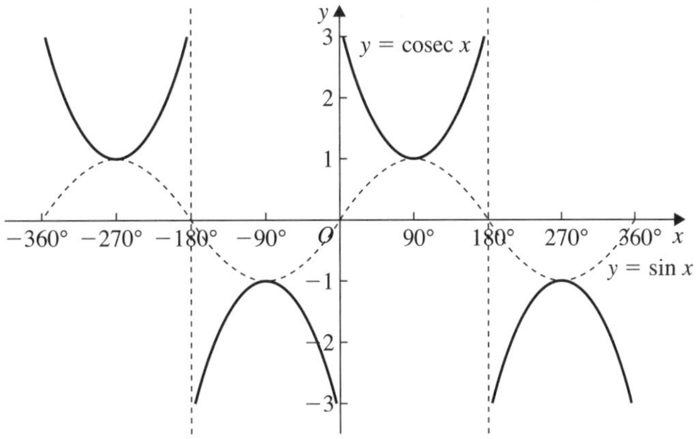

Similarly, the graph of $y = \sec x$ has vertical asymptotes at all the values of x for which $\cos x = 0$.

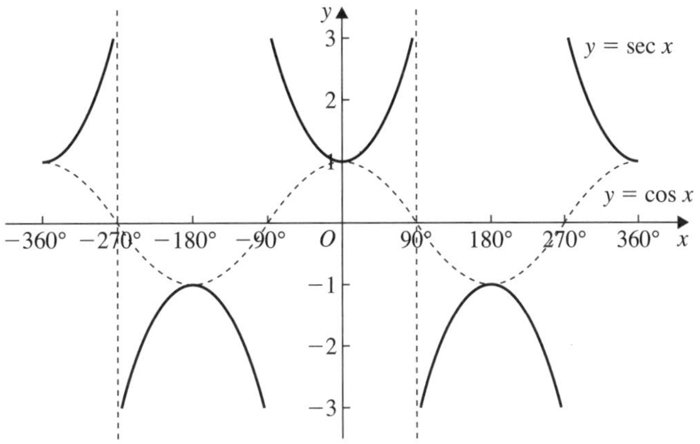

Here is the graph of $\tan x$ and $\cot x$ for $-360 \leqslant x \leqslant 360°$. In this case $y = \cot x$ has vertical asymptotes where $\tan x = 0$, and also $\cot x = 0$ wherever $\tan x$ has vertical asymptotes.

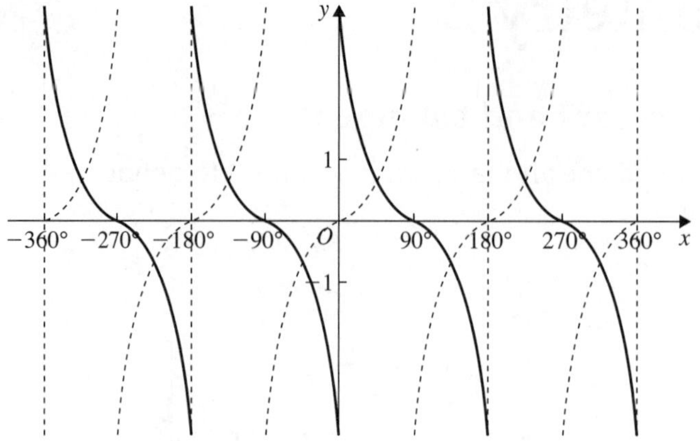

You may wish to learn the graphs of these three new functions, or you can work them out each time from the graphs of $\sin x$, $\cos x$ and $\tan x$, with which you are already very familiar.

Example 1

Evaluate **a** $\sec 60°$ **b** $\cot 40°$

a $\sec 60° = \dfrac{1}{\cos 60°} = \dfrac{1}{\frac{1}{2}} = 2$

b $\cot 40° = \dfrac{1}{\tan 40°} = 1.192$ (3 dp)

Example 2

Sketch the graph of

a $y = \sec 2x$ for $0° \leqslant x \leqslant 360°$

b $y = \operatorname{cosec}\left(\theta - \dfrac{\pi}{2}\right)$ for $-2\pi \leqslant \theta \leqslant 2\pi$

a You can either start with the graph of $y = \sec x$ and perform a stretch with a scale factor $\frac{1}{2}$ in the x-direction, or you can use $\sec 2x = \dfrac{1}{\cos 2x}$.

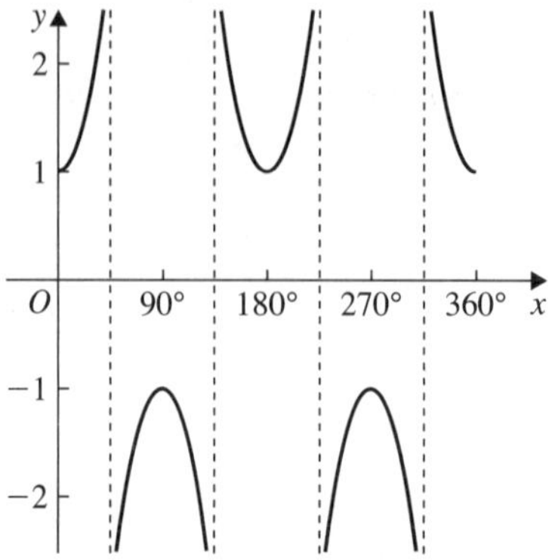

b This is a translation of the graph of $y = \operatorname{cosec}\theta$ by $\frac{\pi}{2}$ in the positive θ-direction,

or you may wish to use $\operatorname{cosec}\left(\theta - \frac{\pi}{2}\right) = \frac{1}{\sin\left(\theta - \frac{\pi}{2}\right)}$.

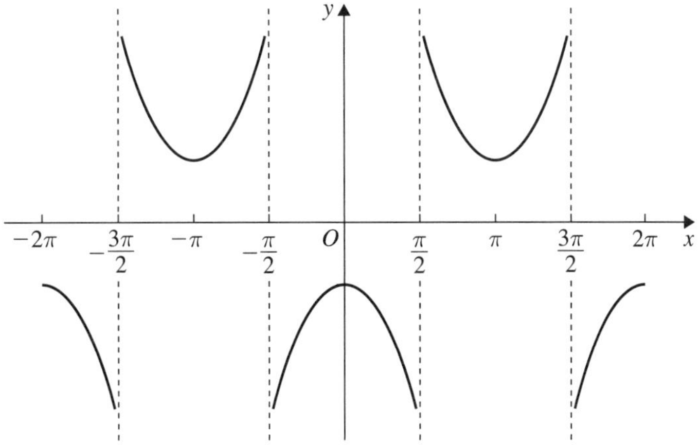

6.2 Solving equations and proving identities

When solving equations involving $\sec\theta$, $\operatorname{cosec}\theta$ or $\cot\theta$, we choose to work with one of the primary ratios, $\cos\theta$, $\sin\theta$ or $\tan\theta$ as appropriate.

Example 3

Solve the equation $\operatorname{cosec}\theta = \sqrt{2}$ for $0 \leqslant \theta \leqslant 360°$.

$$\operatorname{cosec}\theta = \sqrt{2}$$

$$\frac{1}{\sin\theta} = \sqrt{2} \quad \Rightarrow \quad \sin\theta = \frac{1}{\sqrt{2}}$$

$$\theta = 45°, 135°$$

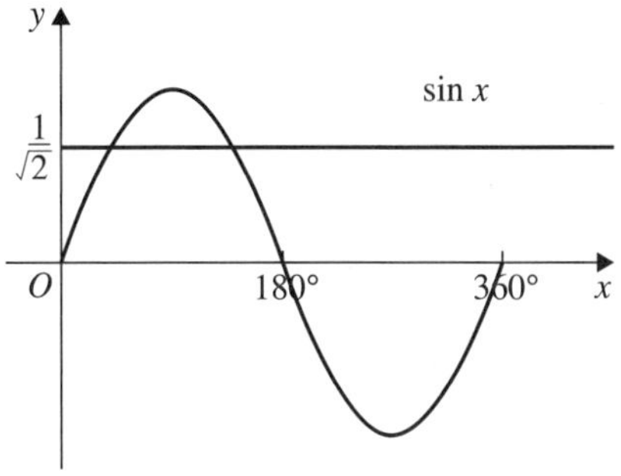

Example 4

Solve the equation $\cot x = \sqrt{3}$ for $0 \leqslant x \leqslant 2\pi$.

$$\cot x = \sqrt{3}$$

$$\frac{1}{\tan x} = \sqrt{3} \quad \Rightarrow \quad \tan x = \frac{1}{\sqrt{3}}$$

From the graph of $y = \tan x$, we obtain

$x = \frac{\pi}{6}$ or $\frac{7\pi}{6}$.

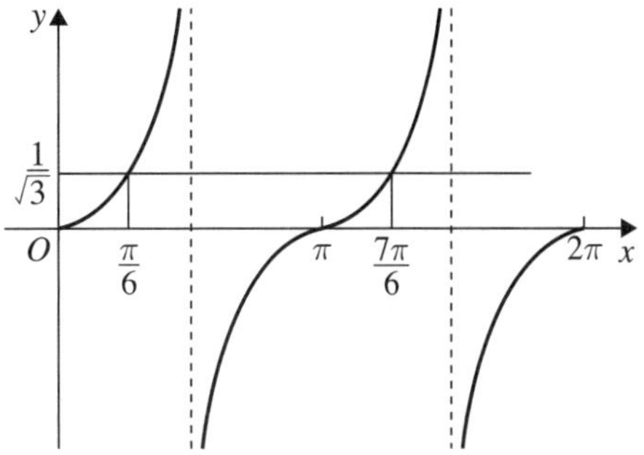

We are already familiar with the identity $\cos^2\theta + \sin^2\theta \equiv 1$.

If we divide both sides by $\cos^2\theta$ we get $\dfrac{\cos^2\theta}{\cos^2\theta} + \dfrac{\sin^2\theta}{\cos^2\theta} \equiv \dfrac{1}{\cos^2\theta}$

and hence we see that:

$$\boxed{1 + \tan^2\theta = \sec^2\theta}$$

If we divide both sides by $\sin^2\theta$ we get $\dfrac{\cos^2\theta}{\sin^2\theta} + \dfrac{\sin^2\theta}{\sin^2\theta} \equiv \dfrac{1}{\sin^2\theta}$

and hence we see that:

$$\boxed{1 + \cot^2\theta \equiv \operatorname{cosec}^2\theta}$$

Example 5

Solve the equation $2\tan^2\theta + 7\sec\theta - 2 = 0$ for $0 \leqslant \theta \leqslant 2\pi$.

Rearrange $\quad 1 + \tan^2\theta = \sec^2\theta$

to give $\quad \tan^2\theta = \sec^2\theta - 1$

then substitute in: $\quad 2(\sec^2\theta - 1) + 7\sec\theta - 2 = 0$

$$2\sec^2\theta + 7\sec\theta - 4 = 0$$

$$(2\sec\theta - 1)(\sec\theta + 4) = 0$$

$$\sec\theta = \tfrac{1}{2} \quad \text{or} \quad \sec\theta = -4$$

Now $\quad \sec\theta = \frac{1}{2} \Rightarrow \dfrac{1}{\cos\theta} = \dfrac{1}{2}$

$\cos\theta = 2 \quad$ no real solutions

and $\quad \sec\theta = -4 \Rightarrow \dfrac{1}{\cos\theta} = -4$

$\cos\theta = -\frac{1}{4}$

$\theta = 1.82, 4.46 \quad$ by use of the graph, or a CAST diagram.

Example 6

Prove the identity $\sec^2\theta - \cos^2\theta = \tan^2\theta + \sin^2\theta$.

When proving a trigonometric identity:

1 Do *not* assume that the identity to be proved, is in fact true.

2 Start with one side, generally the more complicated, and simplify it until you can show that both sides are identical.

3 The identity sign $\equiv$ is sometimes used but normally we use an ordinary '=' sign when proving identities. Remember that an identity is true for *all* values of the variable.

For example $\tan\theta \equiv \dfrac{\sin\theta}{\cos\theta}$ for all values of θ.

Now, consider the left hand side (L.H.S.):

$$\begin{aligned}\text{L.H.S.} &= \sec^2\theta - \cos^2\theta \\ &= (1 + \tan^2\theta) - (1 - \sin^2\theta) \\ &= \tan^2\theta + \sin^2\theta \text{ as required.}\end{aligned}$$

Example 7

Prove the identity $\dfrac{\cos^2\theta}{1 - \sin\theta} = 1 + \sin\theta$.

$$\begin{aligned}\text{L.H.S.} &= \frac{\cos^2\theta}{1 - \sin\theta} = \frac{1 - \sin^2\theta}{1 - \sin\theta} \\ &= \frac{(1 - \sin\theta)(1 + \sin\theta)}{(1 - \sin\theta)} \qquad \text{[Difference of two squares.]} \\ &= 1 + \sin\theta \text{ as required.}\end{aligned}$$

Example 8

Prove the identity $\dfrac{\cos\theta}{1 + \cos\theta} = \cot\theta(\operatorname{cosec}\theta - \cot\theta)$

This time start with the right hand side:

$$\begin{aligned}\text{R.H.S.} &= \frac{\cos\theta}{\sin\theta}\left(\frac{1}{\sin\theta} - \frac{\cos\theta}{\sin\theta}\right) \\ &= \frac{\cos\theta}{\sin\theta}\left(\frac{1 - \cos\theta}{\sin\theta}\right) \\ &= \frac{\cos\theta(1 - \cos\theta)}{\sin^2\theta} \\ &= \frac{\cos\theta(1 - \cos\theta)}{1 - \cos^2\theta} \\ &= \frac{\cos\theta(1 - \cos\theta)}{(1 + \cos\theta)(1 - \cos\theta)} \\ &= \frac{\cos\theta}{1 + \cos\theta} = \text{L.H.S. as required}\end{aligned}$$

As a general rule of thumb, it is easier to start with the more complicated side and simplify it down. It is not always clear whether or not to convert everything to the primary ratios $\sin\theta$ and $\cos\theta$ from the start; you will develop a better feeling for this with practice.

Exercise 6A

1 Evaluate the following. Give answers correct to 3 dp where necessary:

a $\cot 30°$ **b** $\operatorname{cosec} 60°$ **c** $\sec 10°$

d $\operatorname{cosec} 45°$ **e** $\cot 72°$ **f** $\sec^2 30°$

2 Sketch the following graphs:

a $y = \operatorname{cosec}(\theta - 90°)$ for $0° \leqslant \theta \leqslant 360°$

b $y = \cot\left(\theta + \frac{\pi}{2}\right)$ for $0 \leqslant \theta \leqslant 2\pi$

c $y = \operatorname{cosec}(-\theta)$ for $0 \leqslant \theta \leqslant 2\pi$

d $y = 2\sec(\theta + 30°)$ for $0° \leqslant \theta \leqslant 360°$

e $y = \sec 2\theta + 1$ for $-\pi \leqslant \theta \leqslant \pi$

f $y = -\cot 2\theta$ for $-180° \leqslant \theta \leqslant 180°$

g $y = \sec(2\theta - 45°)$ for $0° \leqslant \theta \leqslant 360°$

3 Simplify the expressions:

a $1 + \tan^2 x$ **b** $1 + \tan^2 2x$ **c** $1 - \cos^2 x$

d $\operatorname{cosec} x \tan x$ **e** $\cot\theta(1 - \cos^2\theta)$ **f** $1 + \cot^2\theta$

4 Prove the following identities:

a $(\sin\theta + \cos\theta)^2 - 2\sin\theta\cos\theta = 1$

b $\tan\theta \operatorname{cosec}\theta = \sec\theta$

c $\operatorname{cosec}\theta(1 - \cos\theta)(1 + \cos\theta) = \sin\theta$

d $\cot\theta\sec\theta\tan\theta\sqrt{(1 - \sin^2\theta)} = 1$

e $\dfrac{1}{\sec^2\theta} + \dfrac{1}{\operatorname{cosec}^2\theta} = 1$

f $\sec\theta - \cos\theta = \sin\theta\tan\theta$

g $\sin^2\theta + 2\cos^2\theta = 2 - \sin^2\theta$

h $\tan\theta + \cot\theta = \dfrac{1}{\sin\theta\cos\theta}$

5 Solve the equations for $0° \leqslant x \leqslant 360°$:

a $\sec x = 2$ **b** $\cot x = \sqrt{3}$ **c** $\operatorname{cosec} x = \sqrt{2}$

d $\sec x = 1.2$ **e** $\cot x = 3$ **f** $\operatorname{cosec} x = 1$

6 Prove the identities:

a $\operatorname{cosec}\theta - \sin\theta = \cot\theta\cos\theta$

b $\cos^2\theta - \sin^2\theta = 2\cos^2\theta - 1$

c $\operatorname{cosec}^2\theta + \sec^2\theta = \operatorname{cosec}^2\theta\sec^2\theta$

d $\dfrac{\sin^2\theta}{1 - \cos\theta} = 1 + \cos\theta$

e $\dfrac{\sin\theta}{1 + \sin\theta} = \tan\theta(\sec\theta - \tan\theta)$

f $\operatorname{cosec}^2\theta(\tan^2\theta - \sin^2\theta) = \tan^2\theta$

g $\dfrac{\sec\theta}{\tan\theta + \cot\theta} = \sin\theta$

h $\dfrac{\cos\theta}{\sin\theta + 1} + \dfrac{\sin\theta + 1}{\cos\theta} = 2\sec\theta$

7 Solve the equations:

a $2\cot^2\theta - 3\cot\theta + 1 = 0$ for $0° \leqslant \theta \leqslant 360°$

b $\sec^2\theta - \tan\theta = 1$ for $-180° \leqslant \theta \leqslant 180°$

c $\cot^2\theta - 3\operatorname{cosec}\theta + 3 = 0$ for $0° \leqslant \theta \leqslant 180°$

8 Prove the identities:

a $\sin^4 x - \cos^4 x = \sin^2 x - \cos^2 x$

b $\sec^4 x - \tan^4 x = 1 + 2\tan^2 x$

c $\dfrac{\sin\theta}{1-\cos\theta} + \dfrac{\sin\theta}{1+\cos\theta} = 2\operatorname{cosec}\theta$

d $\dfrac{\cot^2\theta}{1+\cot^2\theta} = \cos^2\theta$

e $\dfrac{1-\tan^2\theta}{1+\tan^2\theta} = 1 - 2\sin^2\theta$

f $\dfrac{2\tan\theta}{1+\tan^2\theta} = 2\sin\theta\cos\theta$

g $\dfrac{\cot\theta + \tan\theta}{\operatorname{cosec}\theta + \sec\theta} = \dfrac{1}{\cos\theta + \sin\theta}$

h $\sin^3 x + \cos^3 x = (\sin x + \cos x)(1 - \sin x\cos x)$

9 Solve the inequality $\operatorname{cosec}\theta < 2$ for values of θ between 0° and 180°.

10 a Simplify the expression $(1 - \sin\theta)(1 + \sin\theta)\sec\theta$.

b Solve the inequality $(1 - \sin\theta)(1 + \sin\theta)\sec\theta > \frac{1}{2}$ for values of θ between $-90°$ and 90°.

11 Solve the equations:

a $\sec 2x = 3$ for $0° \leqslant x \leqslant 360°$

b $3\operatorname{cosec}^2 2x = 4$ for $0° \leqslant x \leqslant 180°$

12 Solve the simultaneous equations

$$\operatorname{cosec} 2x = \sqrt{2}$$
$$\cot(x + y) = \sqrt{3}$$

for values of x and y from 0° to 180°.

6.3 Inverse trigonometric functions (arcsin x, arccos x and arctan x)

We know from the work with functions that only one-to-one functions have inverses. We also know that sin, cos and tan are all many-to-one functions unless we restrict the domain.

By considering the graph of $y = \sin x$ we can see that it is one-to-one if we restrict the domain to $-\dfrac{\pi}{2} \leqslant x \leqslant \dfrac{\pi}{2}$.

If we restrict the domain in this way then there is an inverse, called arcsin. We write $x = \arcsin y$ or $x = \sin^{-1} y$.

The graph of $y = \arcsin x$ is obtained by reflecting $y = \sin x$ about the line $y = x$. We have the following graphs.

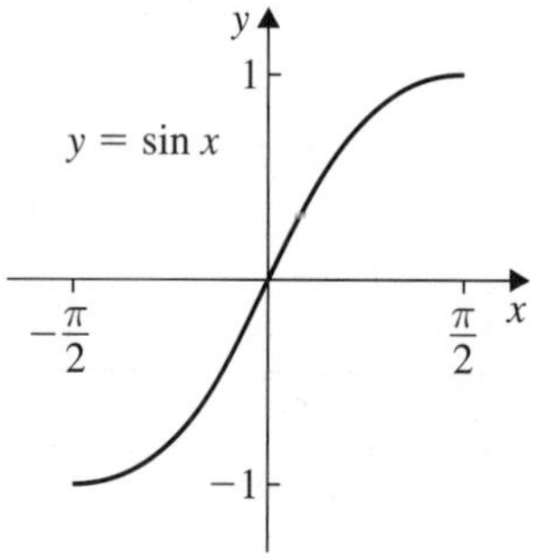

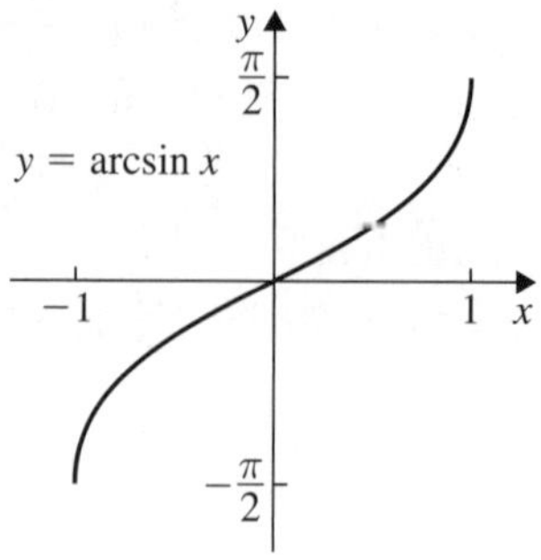

The domain of $y = \arcsin x$ is $-1 \leqslant x \leqslant 1$ and its range is $-\dfrac{\pi}{2} \leqslant \arcsin x \leqslant \dfrac{\pi}{2}$.

By considering the graph of $y = \cos x$ we can see that it is one-to-one if we restrict the domain to $0 \leqslant x \leqslant \pi$.

If we restrict the domain in this way then there is an inverse, called arccos. We write $x = \arccos y$ or $x = \cos^{-1} y$.

The graph of $y = \arccos x$ is obtained by reflecting $y = \cos x$ about the line $y = x$. We have the following graphs.

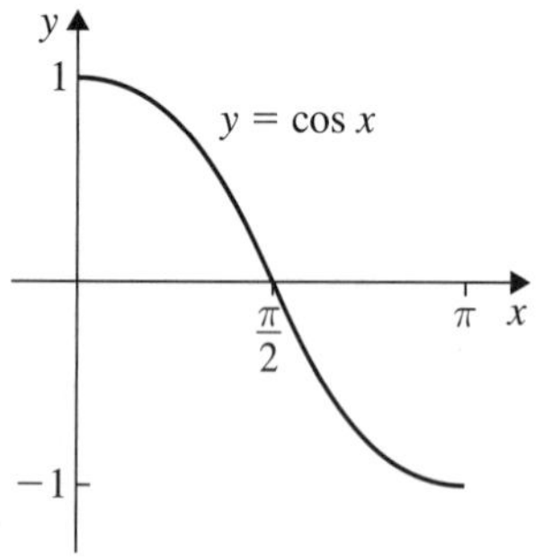

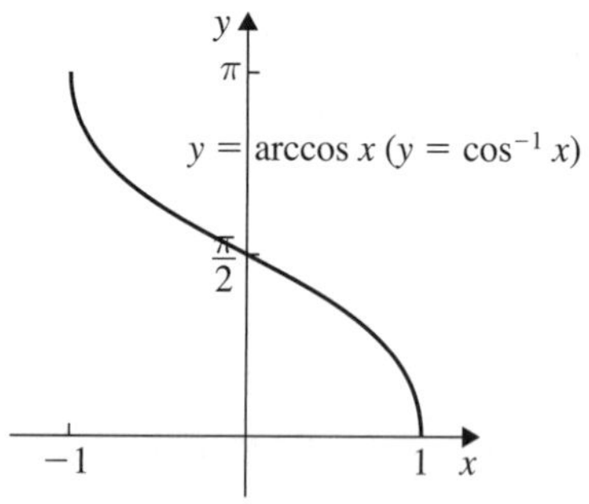

The domain of $y = \arccos x$ is $-1 \leqslant x \leqslant 1$ and its range is $0 \leqslant \arccos x \leqslant \pi$.

By considering the graph of $y = \tan x$ we can see that it is one-to-one if we restrict the domain to $-\dfrac{\pi}{2} < x < \dfrac{\pi}{2}$.

If we restrict the domain in this way then there is an inverse, called arctan. We write $x = \arctan y$.

The graph of $y = \arctan x$ is obtained by reflecting $y = \tan x$ about the line $y = x$. We have the following graphs.

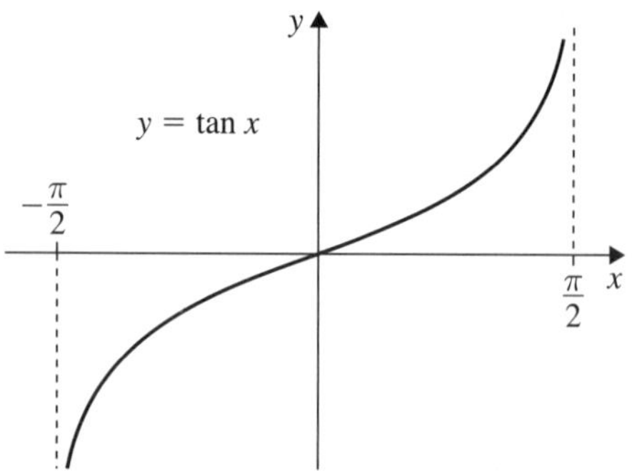

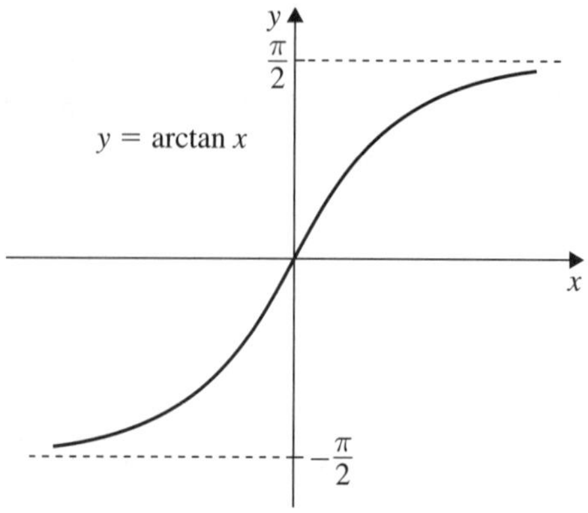

The domain of $y = \arctan x$ is the real numbers and its range is $-\frac{\pi}{2} < \arcsin x < \frac{\pi}{2}$.

Note that an alternative notation for $\arcsin x$, $\arccos x$, $\arctan x$ is $\sin^{-1} x$, $\cos^{-1} x$, $\tan^{-1} x$ respectively.

Example 1

a Find, in degrees, the value of $\arcsin\left(\frac{1}{\sqrt{2}}\right)$.

b Find, in radians in terms of π, the value of $\arctan(-\sqrt{3})$.

a $\arcsin\left(\frac{1}{\sqrt{2}}\right)$ means 'the angle whose sine is $\frac{1}{\sqrt{2}}$'.

We know that $\sin 45° = \frac{1}{\sqrt{2}}$.

$\therefore \quad \arcsin\left(\frac{1}{\sqrt{2}}\right) = 45°$.

b $\arctan(-\sqrt{3})$ means 'the angle whose tan is $-\sqrt{3}$'.

We know that $\tan\left(-\frac{\pi}{3}\right) = -\sqrt{3}$.

$\therefore \quad \arctan(-\sqrt{3}) = -\frac{\pi}{3}$.

Exercise 6B

In Questions **1** and **2** do not use a calculator.

1 Evaluate the following in degrees:

a $\arcsin \frac{1}{2}$ **b** $\arccos 0$ **c** $\arctan 1$

d $\arccos\left(-\frac{1}{2}\right)$ **e** $\arctan\left(-\frac{1}{\sqrt{3}}\right)$ **f** $\arcsin\left(\frac{\sqrt{3}}{2}\right)$

2 Evaluate the following in radians in terms of π:

a $\arctan(-1)$ **b** $\arccos\left(\frac{1}{2}\right)$ **c** $\arcsin\left(\frac{1}{\sqrt{2}}\right)$

d $\arccos(1)$ **e** $\arctan(\sqrt{3})$ **f** $\arcsin(-1)$

3 Sketch the graph of $f(x) = \arcsin x$ for $-1 \leqslant x \leqslant 1$.

4 Sketch the graph of $f(x) = \arccos x$ for $-1 \leqslant x \leqslant 1$.

5 Solve the equations, for $0° \leqslant x \leqslant 360°$.

a $\sin x = \cos\left(\arcsin \frac{1}{2}\right)$

b $\tan x = 2\sin\left(\arccos \frac{\sqrt{3}}{2}\right)$

c $\cos x = \sin\left(\arctan \frac{1}{\sqrt{3}} + \arccos \frac{1}{2}\right)$

6 Simplify the following.

a $\sin\left(\arcsin\frac{1}{2}\right)$

b $\tan\left(\arccos\dfrac{1}{\sqrt{2}}\right) - \sin(\arccos 0)$

c $\cos(\arccos\theta)$

d $3\theta - 2\tan(\arctan\theta)$

6.4 Compound angles; sin, cos and tan of (A ± B)

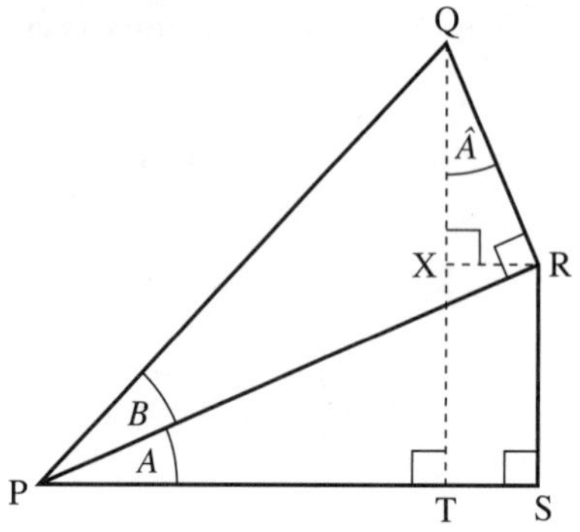

In the diagram $\hat{A} = \text{P}\hat{\text{R}}\text{X}$

$$= 90° - \text{X}\hat{\text{R}}\text{Q}$$
$$= \text{R}\hat{\text{Q}}\text{X} = \hat{A}$$

$$\sin(A + B) = \frac{\text{QT}}{\text{PQ}} = \frac{\text{TX} + \text{XQ}}{\text{PQ}}$$
$$= \frac{\text{TX}}{\text{PQ}} + \frac{\text{XQ}}{\text{PQ}} = \frac{\text{RS}}{\text{PQ}} + \frac{\text{XQ}}{\text{PQ}}$$
$$= \frac{\text{RS}}{\text{PR}} \times \frac{\text{PR}}{\text{PQ}} + \frac{\text{XQ}}{\text{QR}} \times \frac{\text{QR}}{\text{PQ}}$$

$$\mathbf{\sin(A + B) = \sin A\cos B + \cos A\sin B} \qquad ①$$

$$\cos(A + B) = \frac{\text{PT}}{\text{PQ}} = \frac{\text{PS} - \text{TS}}{\text{PQ}} = \frac{\text{PS} - \text{RX}}{\text{PQ}}$$
$$= \frac{\text{PS}}{\text{PR}} \times \frac{\text{PR}}{\text{PQ}} - \frac{\text{RX}}{\text{QR}} \times \frac{\text{QR}}{\text{PQ}}$$

$$\mathbf{\cos(A + B) = \cos A\cos B - \sin A\sin B} \qquad ②$$

By replacing B by $-B$ in ① and ②, we obtain:

$$\sin(A - B) = \sin A\cos(-B) + \cos A\sin(-B)$$
$$\mathbf{\sin(A - B) = \sin A\cos B - \cos A\sin B} \qquad ③$$

and $\cos(A - B) = \cos A\cos(-B) - \sin A\sin(-B)$

$$\mathbf{\cos(A - B) = \cos A\cos B + \sin A\sin B} \qquad ④$$

Finally $\tan(A + B) = \dfrac{\sin(A + B)}{\cos(A + B)} = \dfrac{\sin A\cos B + \cos A\sin B}{\cos A\cos B - \sin A\sin B}$

$$= \frac{\dfrac{\sin A\cos B}{\cos A\cos B} + \dfrac{\cos A\sin B}{\cos A\cos B}}{\dfrac{\cos A\cos B}{\cos A\cos B} - \dfrac{\sin A\sin B}{\cos A\cos B}}$$ [Dividing each term by $\cos A\cos B$]

$$\mathbf{\tan(A + B) = \frac{\tan A + \tan B}{1 - \tan A\tan B}}$$

And similarly $\mathbf{\tan A - B = \dfrac{\tan A - \tan B}{1 + \tan A\tan B}}$

In summary:

$$\sin(A \pm B) \equiv \sin A \cos B \pm \cos A \sin B$$
$$\cos(A \pm B) \equiv \cos A \cos B \mp \sin A \sin B$$
$$\tan(A \pm B) \equiv \frac{\tan A \pm \tan B}{1 \mp \tan A \tan B}$$

These results are called "compound angle formulae" or "addition formulae".

Example 1

Answer 'true' or 'false': $\sin(30° + 30°) = \sin 30° + \sin 30°$.

False!! This is sadly a common error. If you are still not convinced:

$$\sin(30° + 30°) = \sin 60° = \frac{\sqrt{3}}{2}$$

$$\sin 30° + \sin 30° = \tfrac{1}{2} + \tfrac{1}{2} = 1$$

Example 2

Find the exact values of

a $\sin 75°$

b $\tan 15°$

a
$$\begin{aligned}\sin 75° &= \sin(45° + 30°)\\ &= \sin 45° \cos 30° + \cos 45° \sin 30°\\ &= \left(\frac{1}{\sqrt{2}} \times \frac{\sqrt{3}}{2}\right) + \left(\frac{1}{\sqrt{2}} \times \frac{1}{2}\right)\\ &= \frac{\sqrt{3} + 1}{2\sqrt{2}}\\ &= \frac{(\sqrt{3} + 1)\sqrt{2}}{2 \times \sqrt{2} \times \sqrt{2}}\\ &= \frac{\sqrt{6} + \sqrt{2}}{4}\end{aligned}$$

b
$$\begin{aligned}\tan 15° &= \tan(60° - 45°)\\ &= \frac{\tan 60° - \tan 45°}{1 + \tan 60° \tan 45°}\\ &= \frac{\sqrt{3} - 1}{1 + \sqrt{3}}\\ &= \frac{(\sqrt{3} - 1)(1 - \sqrt{3})}{(1 + \sqrt{3})(1 - \sqrt{3})}\\ &= \frac{-4 + 2\sqrt{3}}{1 - 3}\\ &= 2 - \sqrt{3}\end{aligned}$$

Example 3

Given that A and B are acute angles with $\sin A = \frac{3}{5}$ and $\cos B = \frac{12}{13}$, find the exact value of $\cos(A - B)$.

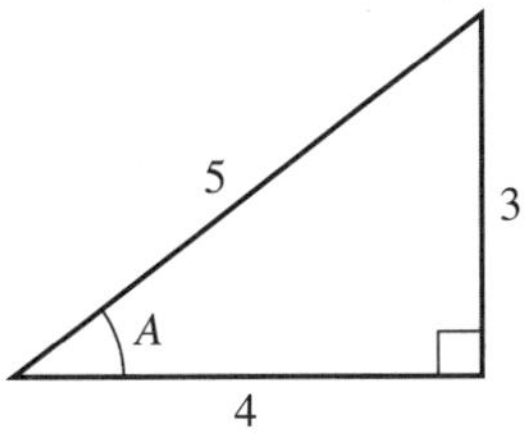

$\sin A = \frac{3}{5}$, $\cos A = \frac{4}{5}$

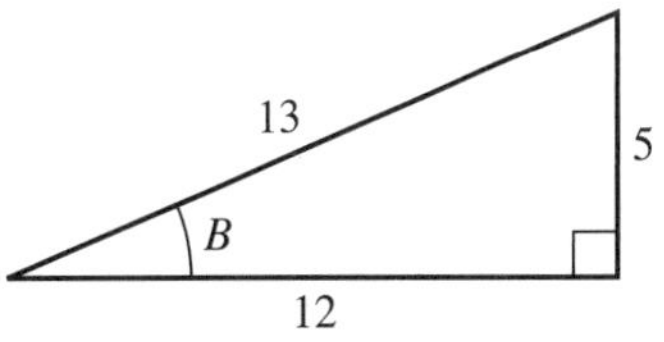

$\cos B = \frac{12}{13}$, $\sin B = \frac{5}{13}$

$$\begin{aligned}\cos(A - B) &= \cos A \cos B + \sin A \sin B\\ &= \tfrac{4}{5} \times \tfrac{12}{13} + \tfrac{3}{5} \times \tfrac{5}{13}\\ &= \tfrac{63}{65}\end{aligned}$$

Example 4

Solve the equation
$\sin\theta\cos 10° + \cos\theta\sin 10° = 0.8$,
for $0 \leqslant \theta \leqslant 360°$.

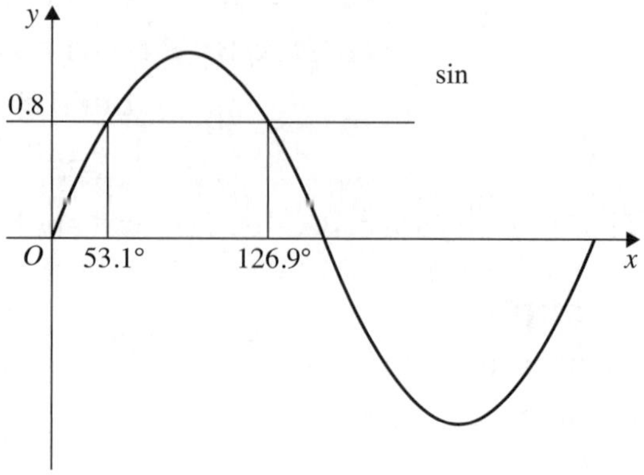

$$\sin\theta\cos 10° + \cos\theta\sin 10° = 0.8$$

which is $\sin(\theta + 10°) = 0.8$

$$\theta + 10° = 53.1° \text{ or } 126.9°$$
$$\theta = 43.1° \text{ or } 116.9°$$

Exercise 6C

1 a Write down the formula for $\sin(A + B)$.
b Evaluate $\sin 80°\cos 10° + \cos 80°\sin 10°$.

2 a Write down the formula for $\cos(A + B)$.
b Evaluate $\cos 50°\cos 40° - \sin 50°\sin 40°$.

3 Answer 'true' or 'false':

a $\tan(A + 45°) = \tan A + 1$

b $\tan(A + 45°) = \dfrac{\tan A + 1}{1 - \tan A}$

4 Simplify the following:

a $\sin\theta\cos 2\theta + \cos\theta\sin 2\theta$

b $\cos 3A\cos A + \sin 3A\sin A$

c $\sin 5x\cos 2x - \cos 5x\sin 2x$

d $\cos B\cos B + \sin B\sin B$

5 Find the exact values of the following (using surds):

a $\sin(60° + 45°)$

b $\sin 105°$

c $\cos 75°$

d $\cos 15°$

e $\tan(-15°)$

6 Given that A and B are acute angles such that $\sin A = \frac{5}{13}$ and $\cos B = \frac{3}{5}$, find the exact values of:

a $\sin(A + B)$

b $\cos(A - B)$

c $\tan(A + B)$

7 Solve the equation $\sin(x + 60°) + \cos(x + 30°) = \frac{1}{2}$ in the range $0° \leqslant x < 360°$.

8 Express the following as single trigonometric expressions:

a $\cos(x + 90°)$

b $\sin(x - 90°)$

c $\sin(x + 180°)$

d $\cos(x - 180°)$

9 Given that $\tan(x + 45°) = 2$, find the value of $\tan x$, without using a calculator.

10 Given that $\tan(A + B) = 3$ and that $\tan B = \frac{1}{2}$, find the exact value of $\tan A$.

11 Solve the equation $\sin(\theta + 45°) = \sqrt{2}\cos\theta$, for $0° \leqslant \theta \leqslant 360°$.

12 Find the greatest value that the following expressions can have and state the value of θ between 0° and 360°, for which these values occur.

a $\sin\theta\cos 40° + \cos\theta\sin 40°$ **b** $\sin\theta\cos 15° - \cos\theta\sin 15°$

13 Prove the following identities:

a $\sin(\theta + 90°) \equiv \cos\theta$ **b** $\sin(A + B) + \sin(A - B) \equiv 2\sin A\cos B$

c $\cos x\cos 2x + \sin x\sin 2x \equiv \cos x$ **d** $\sin 2x\cos x - \cos 2x\sin x \equiv \sin x$

e $\dfrac{\sin(A + B)}{\sin(A - B)} \equiv \dfrac{\tan A + \tan B}{\tan A - \tan B}$ **f** $\tan A + \tan B \equiv \dfrac{\sin(A + B)}{\cos A\cos B}$

g $\sin(A + B)\sin(A - B) \equiv \sin^2 A - \sin^2 B$

14 Using $\tan(x + \alpha)$ for a suitable value of α, express $\dfrac{1 + \tan x}{1 - \tan x}$ as a single trigonometric expression.

15 **a** Find an expression for $\tan 2A$ in terms of $\tan A$.

b Given that $\tan\theta = \frac{4}{3}$ and that θ is acute find the exact value of $\tan\left(\dfrac{\theta}{2}\right)$.

16 If $\sin(x - A) = \cos(x + A)$, show that $\tan x = 1$.

17 Find the exact values of the following:

a $\cot 15°$ (in the form $a + \sqrt{b}$)

b $\sec 75°$ (in the form $\sqrt{a} + \sqrt{b}$)

c $\operatorname{cosec} 105°$ (in the form $\sqrt{a} - \sqrt{b}$)

18 Show that $\operatorname{cosec}(A + B) \equiv \dfrac{\sec A\sec B}{\tan A + \tan B}$.

19 Show that $\cot(A + B) \equiv \dfrac{\cot A\cot B - 1}{\cot A + \cot B}$.

20 Prove that if the sum of A, B and C is 180° then $\dfrac{\tan A + \tan B + \tan C}{\tan A\tan B\tan C} \equiv 1$.

21 Show that $\tan 15° = 2 - \sqrt{3}$.

22 Given $\sin(A + B) = k\sin(A - B)$, show that $\tan A = \dfrac{k + 1}{k - 1}\tan B$.

23 Given that $\tan(A + B) = 1$ and that $\tan A = \frac{1}{2}$, find $\tan B$.

24 **a** Given that $\sin(x + \alpha) = 2\sin(x - \alpha)$ show that $\tan x = 3\tan\alpha$.

b Use the result of part **a** to solve the equation $\sin\left(2y + \dfrac{\pi}{4}\right) = 2\sin\left(2y - \dfrac{\pi}{4}\right)$ for $0 < y < \pi$.

6.5 The double angle formulae

- We know that $\sin(A + B) = \sin A \cos B + \cos A \sin B$.
  Put $B = A$ in this identity.
  $\sin(A + A) = \sin A \cos A + \cos A \sin A$

  or $\boxed{\sin 2A = 2\sin A \cos A}$

- In a similar way we can prove that

  $$\boxed{\cos 2A = \cos^2 A - \sin^2 A}$$

  Using $\sin^2 A + \cos^2 A = 1$, we can show further that

  $$\boxed{\begin{aligned}\cos 2A &= 2\cos^2 A - 1\\ \cos 2A &= 1 - 2\sin^2 A\end{aligned}}$$

- Finally $\boxed{\tan 2A = \dfrac{2\tan A}{1 - \tan^2 A}}$

Example 1

Express more simply

a $2\sin 15° \cos 15°$ **b** $\dfrac{2\tan 60°}{1 - \tan^2 60°}$ **c** $2\cos^2 25° - 1$

a From $2\sin A \cos A = \sin 2A$, we have

$$2\sin 15° \cos 15° = \sin 30°$$
$$= \tfrac{1}{2}$$

b From $\dfrac{2\tan\theta}{1 - \tan^2\theta} = \tan 2\theta$,

$$\frac{2\tan 60°}{1 - \tan^2 60°} = \tan 120°$$
$$= -\sqrt{3}$$

c $2\cos^2 25° - 1 = \cos 50°$

Example 2

You are given that θ is acute and that $\sin\theta = \frac{4}{5}$. Find, without a calculator, the exact values of $\sin 2\theta$ and $\cos 2\theta$.

Draw a right angled triangle and show $\sin\theta = \frac{4}{5}$.

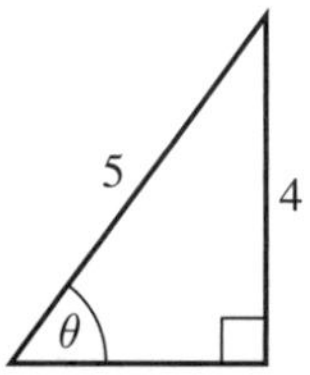

This is a 3, 4, 5 triangle so $\cos\theta = \frac{3}{5}$.

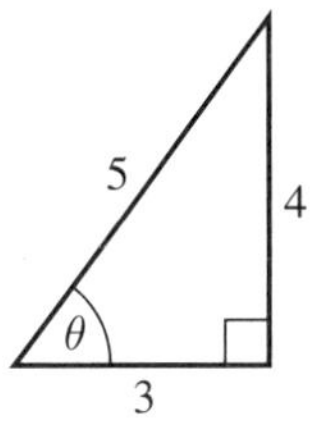

Now $\sin 2\theta = 2\sin\theta\cos\theta$

$$= 2 \times \tfrac{4}{5} \times \tfrac{3}{5}$$

$$= \tfrac{24}{25}$$

And $\cos 2\theta = 2\cos^2\theta - 1$

$$= 2 \times \left(\tfrac{3}{5}\right)^2 - 1$$

$$= -\tfrac{7}{25}$$

Example 3

Solve the equation $\sin 2\theta = \cos\theta$ for $0° \leqslant \theta \leqslant 360°$.

Using $\sin 2\theta = 2\sin\theta\cos\theta$, we have

$$2\sin\theta\cos\theta = \cos\theta \qquad (1)$$

$$2\sin\theta\cos\theta - \cos\theta = 0$$

Factorising, $\cos\theta(2\sin\theta - 1) = 0$

Either $\cos\theta = 0 \Rightarrow \theta = 90°$ or $270°$

Or $2\sin\theta - 1 = 0$

$\sin\theta = \frac{1}{2} \Rightarrow \theta = 30°$ or $150°$

So finally $\theta = 30°, 90°, 150°, 270°$

Notice that in line (1) we did not divide through by $\cos\theta$. If we did that we would lose all the solutions we obtain from $\cos\theta = 0$. The correct method is to factorise as above.

Example 4

Prove the identity $\dfrac{\cos 2A}{\cos A + \sin A} = \cos A - \sin A$

Start with the more complicated side and rearrange it until we obtain the expression on the other side. In this case the more complicated side is the left hand side (L.H.S.).

$$\text{L.H.S.} = \frac{\cos 2A}{\cos A + \sin A}$$

$$= \frac{\cos^2 A - \sin^2 A}{\cos A + \sin A}$$

$$= \frac{(\cos A - \sin A)(\cos A + \sin A)}{\cos A + \sin A} \qquad \text{[Difference of two squares.]}$$

$= \cos A - \sin A$, as required

Example 5

Prove the identity $\cos 3A = 4\cos^3 A - 3\cos A$

Write $\cos 3A = \cos(2A + A)$

$= \cos 2A \cos A - \sin 2A \sin A$

$= (2\cos^2 A - 1)\cos A - (2\sin A \cos A)\sin A$

$= 2\cos^3 A - \cos A - 2\sin^2 A \cos A$

$= 2\cos^3 A - \cos A - 2(1 - \cos^2 A)\cos A$

$= 2\cos^3 A - \cos A - 2\cos A + 2\cos^3 A$

$= 4\cos^3 A - 3\cos A$ as required

EXERCISE 6D

1 Evaluate the following, without using a calculator.

a $2\sin 45° \cos 45°$ **b** $2\cos^2 15° - 1$ **c** $1 - 2\sin^2 30°$ **d** $\dfrac{2\tan 22\frac{1}{2}°}{1 - \tan^2 22\frac{1}{2}°}$

2 Express in a more simple form.

a $2\sin 10° \cos 10°$ **b** $2\cos^2 17° - 1$ **c** $1 - 2\sin^2 35°$ **d** $\dfrac{2\tan 11°}{1 - \tan^2 11°}$

e $\sin\theta\cos\theta$ **f** $\dfrac{\tan 2\theta}{1 - \tan^2 2\theta}$ **g** $\dfrac{\sin 2A}{\cos A}$ **h** $2\sin^2 A + \cos 2A$

3 Find the values of $\sin 2\theta$ and $\cos 2\theta$, given that θ is acute and that $\sin\theta = \frac{3}{5}$.

4 Find the values of $\sin 2\theta$ and $\cos 2\theta$, given that θ is acute and that $\cos\theta = \frac{5}{13}$.

5 Find $\tan 2\theta$ given θ is acute and,

a $\tan\theta = \frac{1}{2}$ **b** $\sin\theta = \frac{3}{5}$

6 Find $\sin x$, if $\cos 2x = \frac{1}{8}$

7 Find $\cos x$, if $\cos 2x = \frac{7}{25}$

8 Find the possible values of $\tan\frac{1}{2}\theta$, if $\tan\theta = \frac{3}{4}$

In Questions **9** to **18** solve the equations, for $0° \leqslant \theta \leqslant 360°$.

9 $\sin 2\theta - \sin\theta = 0$

10 $2\sin 2\theta + \cos\theta = 0$

11 $4\cos 2\theta - 6\cos\theta + 5 = 0$

12 $\sin 2\theta = 2\cos 2\theta$

13 $\cos 2\theta + \sin\theta - 1 = 0$

14 $3\cos 2\theta - \cos\theta + 2 = 0$

15 $\tan 2\theta + \tan\theta = 0$

16 $\sin\theta + \sin\dfrac{\theta}{2} = 0$

17 $\sin\dfrac{\theta}{2} = \sin\theta$

18 $2\cos 2x = 5 - 13\sin x$

19 Prove the identity $2\,\text{cosec}\,2\theta = \sec\theta\,\text{cosec}\,\theta$.

$\left[\text{Hint: Start with 'L.H.S.} = \dfrac{2}{\sin 2\theta}\text{'}\right]$

20 Prove the identity $\tan 2\theta \sec\theta = 2\sin\theta \sec 2\theta$.

$\left[\text{Hint: Start with 'L.H.S.} = \dfrac{\sin 2\theta}{\cos 2\theta} \times \dfrac{1}{\cos\theta}\text{'}\right]$

In Questions **21** to **35** prove the identities.

21 $\dfrac{\cos 2A}{\cos A - \sin A} = \cos A + \sin A$

22 $\dfrac{\sin A}{\sin B} + \dfrac{\cos A}{\cos B} = \dfrac{2\sin(A+B)}{\sin 2B}$

23 $\dfrac{\sin A}{\sin B} - \dfrac{\cos A}{\cos B} = \dfrac{2\sin(A-B)}{\sin 2B}$

24 $\tan A + \cot A = 2\,\text{cosec}\,2A$

25 $\cot A - \tan A = 2\cot 2A$

26 $\dfrac{\sin 2A}{1 + \cos 2A} = \tan A$

27 $\sin 2A = \dfrac{2\tan A}{1 + \tan^2 A}$

28 $\cos 2A = \dfrac{1 - \tan^2 A}{1 + \tan^2 A}$

29 $\sin 3A = 3\sin A - 4\sin^3 A$

30 $\cos 3A = 4\cos^3 A - 3\cos A$

31 $\cot\theta = \dfrac{\sin 2\theta}{1 - \cos 2\theta}$

32 $\cos^4\theta - \sin^4\theta = \cos 2\theta$

33 $\cot 2A + \text{cosec}\,2A = \cot A$

34 $\sin^4\theta + \cos^4\theta = \frac{1}{4}(\cos 4\theta + 3)$

35 $\tan 3\theta = \dfrac{3\tan\theta - \tan^3\theta}{1 - 3\tan^2\theta}$

36 Use the double angle formula for cosine to show that $\cos x = 2\cos^2\left(\dfrac{x}{2}\right) - 1$.

37 Express $\sin x$ in terms of $\sin\left(\dfrac{x}{2}\right)$ and $\cos\left(\dfrac{x}{2}\right)$.

38 Express $\tan x$ in terms of $\tan\left(\dfrac{x}{2}\right)$.

39 **a** Show that $\sin^2\left(\dfrac{x}{2}\right) = \dfrac{1}{2}(1 - \cos x)$.

b Show that $\cos^2\left(\dfrac{x}{2}\right) = \dfrac{1}{2}(1 + \cos x)$.

40 Prove that $\tan 22\frac{1}{2}^\circ = \sqrt{2} - 1$.

41 **a** Show that $\text{cosec}\,2x - \cot 2x = \tan x$

b Hence find the exact value of $\tan 75^\circ$, giving your answer in the form $a + b\sqrt{3}$.

42 Solve the equation $4\tan 2\theta = \cot\theta$, for $0° < \theta < 360°$, giving your answers correct to 1 dp.

43 Express $8\cos^4\theta$ in the form $A\cos 4\theta + B\cos 2\theta + C$, giving the numerical values of the constants A, B and C.

6.6 The form $a\cos\theta + b\sin\theta$

A special technique is used to express $a\cos\theta + b\sin\theta$ in the form $R\cos(\theta - \alpha)$, where α is an acute angle.

We write $a\cos\theta + b\sin\theta = \sqrt{a^2+b^2}\left[\dfrac{a}{\sqrt{a^2+b^2}}\cos\theta + \dfrac{b}{\sqrt{a^2+b^2}}\sin\theta\right]$

Let $\cos\alpha = \dfrac{a}{\sqrt{a^2+b^2}}$

$\sin\alpha = \dfrac{b}{\sqrt{a^2+b^2}}$

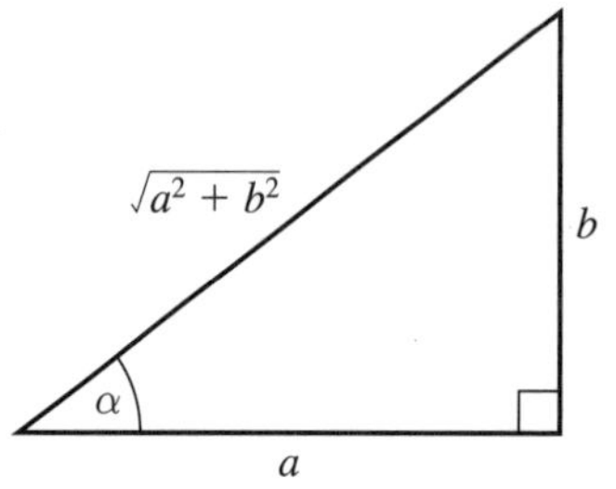

So $a\cos\theta + b\sin\theta = \sqrt{a^2+b^2}\,[\cos\theta\cos\alpha + \sin\theta\sin\alpha]$

$= \sqrt{a^2+b^2}\cos(\theta - \alpha)$

$R = \sqrt{a^2+b^2}$ and the value of α can be obtained from the triangle shown.

The same method, with slight modification, is used for an expression of the form $a\sin\theta - b\cos\theta$ and we can choose to write the expression in the form $R\sin(\theta - \alpha)$ if preferred. The examples below will illustrate the method.

Example 1

Write the expression $f(\theta) = 3\cos\theta + 4\sin\theta$ in the form $R\cos(\theta - \alpha)$.

$$f(\theta) = \sqrt{3^2+4^2}\left[\frac{3}{\sqrt{3^2+4^2}}\cos\theta + \frac{4}{\sqrt{3^2+4^2}}\sin\theta\right]$$

$$= 5\left(\tfrac{3}{5}\cos\theta + \tfrac{4}{5}\sin\theta\right)$$

Let $\cos\alpha = \frac{3}{5}$ and $\sin\alpha = \frac{4}{5}$

So $f(\theta) = 5(\cos\alpha\cos\theta + \sin\alpha\sin\theta)$
$= 5\cos(\theta - \alpha)$

Since $\cos\alpha = \frac{3}{5}$, we have $\alpha = \cos^{-1}\frac{3}{5} = 53.1°$ (to 1 dp)

Finally $f(\theta) = 5\cos(\theta - 53.1°)$

Example 2

a Write $f(\theta) = 2\sin\theta - 3\cos\theta$ in the form $R\sin(\theta - \alpha)$

b Hence write down the largest possible value of $f(\theta)$ and state the smallest positive value of θ for which this value occurs.

a $f(\theta) = 2\sin\theta - 3\cos\theta$

$$= \sqrt{2^2 + (-3)^2}\left[\frac{2}{\sqrt{2^2+3^2}}\sin\theta - \frac{3}{\sqrt{2^2+3^2}}\cos\theta\right]$$

$$= \sqrt{13}\left[\underset{\uparrow \atop \cos\alpha}{\frac{2}{\sqrt{13}}}\sin\theta - \underset{\uparrow \atop \sin\alpha}{\frac{3}{\sqrt{13}}}\cos\theta\right]$$

$f(\theta) = \sqrt{13}\sin(\theta - \alpha)$ where $\alpha = \cos^{-1}\frac{2}{\sqrt{13}} = 56.3°$ (to 1 dp)

$f(\theta) = \sqrt{13}\sin(\theta - 56.3)$

b The largest value for the sine of any angle is 1. The largest value for $f(\theta)$ is therefore $\sqrt{13}$ and this value occurs when $\theta - 56.3 = 90°$, i.e. when $\theta = 146.3$ (correct to 1 dp).

Example 3

Solve the equation $4\sin\theta - \cos\theta = 2$, for $0° \leqslant \theta \leqslant 360°$.

Since this is an *equation*, rather than an expression, we divide each term on both sides by $\sqrt{4^2 + (-1)^2}$.

$$\frac{4}{\sqrt{17}}\sin\theta - \frac{1}{\sqrt{17}}\cos\theta = \frac{2}{\sqrt{17}}$$

Let $\cos\alpha = \frac{4}{\sqrt{17}}$, $\sin\alpha = \frac{1}{\sqrt{17}}$. Then $\alpha = 14.04°$ (2 dp)

We have $\sin\theta\cos\alpha - \cos\theta\sin\alpha = \frac{2}{\sqrt{17}}$

$$\sin(\theta - 14.04°) = \frac{2}{\sqrt{17}}$$

$\theta - 14.04° = 29.02°, 150.98°$

$\theta = 43.1°$ or $165.0°$

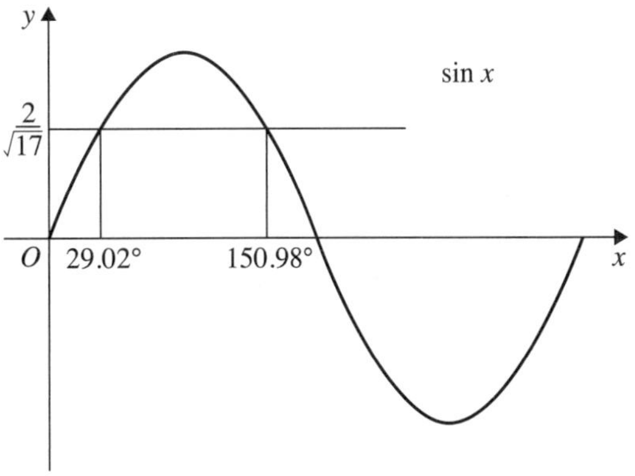

Notice that we chose to work with α correct to 2 dp in the working and then gave the final answer correct to 1 dp.
You can of course retain the value of α in the memory of your calculator.

Example 4

Solve the equation $3\cos\theta + 2\sin\theta = 1$, for $0 \leqslant \theta \leqslant 2\pi$, giving your answers in radians correct to 3 dp.

Divide both sides by $\sqrt{3^2 + 2^2}$.

$$\frac{3}{\sqrt{13}}\cos\theta + \frac{2}{\sqrt{13}}\sin\theta = \frac{1}{\sqrt{13}}$$

Let $\cos\alpha = \frac{3}{\sqrt{13}}$, $\sin\alpha = \frac{2}{\sqrt{13}}$, so $\alpha = \cos^{-1}\frac{3}{\sqrt{13}} = 0.588\,00$ (to 5 dp)

We have $\cos\theta\cos\alpha + \sin\theta\sin\alpha = \frac{1}{\sqrt{13}}$

$$\cos(\theta - 0.588\,00) = \frac{1}{\sqrt{13}}$$

From a calculator $\cos^{-1}\frac{1}{\sqrt{13}} = 1.289\,76$ radians (correct to 5 dp)

$$\theta - 0.588\,00 = 1.289\,76 \text{ or } (2\pi - 1.289\,76)$$
$$\theta - 0.588\,00 = 1.289\,76,\ 4.993\,42$$

$\theta = 1.878$ rad or 5.581 rad (correct to 3 dp).

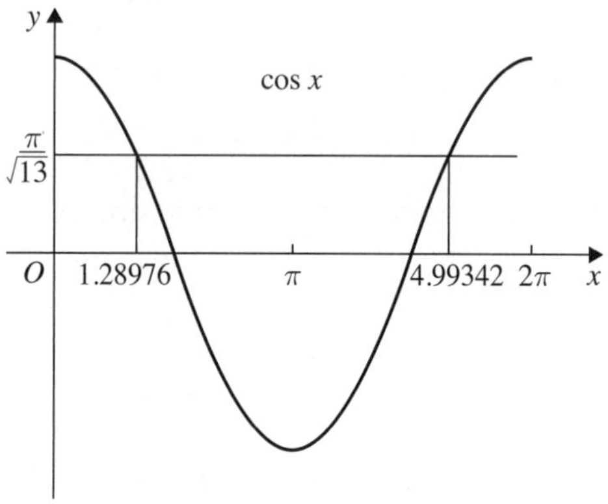

EXERCISE 6E

1 Write each expression in the form $R\cos(\theta - \alpha)$, where $0° < \alpha < 90°$.

a $4\cos\theta + 3\sin\theta$ **b** $5\cos\theta + 12\sin\theta$ **c** $\cos\theta + 2\sin\theta$

2 Find the value of R and α in each of the following:

a $3\sin\theta + 4\cos\theta = R\sin(\theta + \alpha)$ **b** $4\cos\theta - 3\sin\theta = R\cos(\theta + \alpha)$

c $2\cos\theta + \sin\theta = R\cos(\theta - \alpha)$ **d** $8\sin\theta - 15\cos\theta = R\sin(\theta - \alpha)$

e $8\sin\theta + 6\cos\theta = R\sin(\theta + \alpha)$ **f** $\cos\theta - \sin\theta = R\cos(\theta + \alpha)$

3 a Express $f(\theta) = \sin\theta + \sqrt{3}\cos\theta$ in the form $R\sin(\theta + \alpha)$.

b Find the maximum value of $f(\theta)$ and state the smallest positive value of θ that gives this maximum value.

4 Find the maximum value of each expression and state the smallest positive value of θ that gives this value:

a $3\cos\theta + 4\sin\theta$ **b** $5\sin\theta - 12\cos\theta$

c $\cos\theta + \sin\theta$ **d** $8\cos\theta - 15\sin\theta$

5 a Express $4\cos\theta + 3\sin\theta$ in the form $R\cos(\theta - \alpha)$, where $R > 0$ and $0° < \alpha < 90°$.

b Solve the equation $4\cos\theta + 3\sin\theta = 2$, for $0° \leqslant \theta \leqslant 360°$.

6 **a** Express $\sin\theta + \sqrt{8}\cos\theta$ in the form $R\sin(\theta + \alpha)$.

b Solve the equation $\sin\theta + \sqrt{8}\cos\theta = 2$, for $0° \leqslant \theta \leqslant 360°$.

7 Solve the following equations, correct to 1 dp, for $0° \leqslant \theta \leqslant 360°$:

a $8\cos\theta + 15\sin\theta = 8.5$

b $5\sin\theta + 12\cos\theta = 7$

c $\sin\theta + \sqrt{3}\cos\theta = 1$

d $4\sin\theta - 3\cos\theta = 2$

e $4\cos\theta - 6\sin\theta = 5$

f $5\sin\theta - 3\cos\theta = 1$

g $8\sin\theta - 24\cos\theta = 3$

h $5\cos 2x + 2\sin 2x = 3$

8 Solve the equations for $0 < \theta < 2\pi$, giving your answers in radians correct to 2 dp:

a $\cos(\theta - 1.2^c) = \frac{1}{2}$

b $\sin(\theta + 0.4^c) = 0.7$

9 **a** Express $2\cos x + \sqrt{3}\sin x$ in the form $R\cos(x - \alpha)$, where $R > 0$ and $0 < \alpha < \dfrac{\pi}{2}$.

b Find the smallest positive root of the equation $2\cos x + \sqrt{3}\sin x = 2$, giving your answer in radians correct to 2 dp.

10 Solve the equations for $0 \leqslant \theta \leqslant 2\pi$, giving your answers in radians correct to 2 dp:

a $3\sin\theta + \cos\theta = 2$

b $\cos\theta - 2\sin\theta = 1$

c $\cos\theta - \sin\theta = 1$

d $3\sin\theta - 4\cos\theta = 3.5$

11 **a** Express $\sin\theta - 3\cos\theta$ in the form $R\sin(\theta - \alpha)°$, giving the values of R and α.

b Explain why the equation $\sin\theta - 3\cos\theta = 4$ has no solutions.

12 Find the range of values of the constant k for which the equation $\sin\theta + \sqrt{2}\cos\theta = k$, has real solutions for θ.

13 You are given $f(\theta) = (\cos\theta - \sin\theta)(17\cos\theta - 7\sin\theta)$

a Show that $f(\theta)$ may be written in the form $5\cos 2\theta - 12\sin 2\theta + c$, where c is a constant. State the value of c.

b Write $5\cos 2\theta - 12\sin 2\theta$ in the form $R\cos(2\theta + \alpha)$, where $0 < \alpha < \dfrac{\pi}{2}$.

State the value of R and find α in radians correct to 3 dp.

14 **a** Express $3\cos\theta - 4\sin\theta$ in the form $R\cos(\theta + \alpha)$.

b Find the greatest possible value of $\dfrac{2}{(3\cos\theta - 4\sin\theta + 6)}$.

15 **a** Express $f(\theta) = 5\cos\theta + 12\sin\theta$ in the form $R\cos(\theta - \alpha)$.

b Find the smallest possible value of $\dfrac{30}{f(\theta) + 2}$ in the interval $0 \leqslant \theta \leqslant \pi$.

16 **a** Write $8\sin\theta\cos\theta - 6\sin^2\theta$ in the form $R\sin(2\theta + \alpha) + k$.

b Hence solve the equation $8\sin\theta\cos\theta - 6\sin^2\theta = 1$, for $0° < \theta < 180°$.

17 **a** Express $4\cos x + 3\sin x$ in the form $R\cos(x - \alpha)$.

b Find the greatest and least values of $\dfrac{1}{(4\cos x + 3\sin x + 7)}$.

c Find, in radians correct to 3 dp, the solution of the equation $(4\cos x + 3\sin x)^2 = 12.5$, for $0 \leqslant x \leqslant \pi$.

18 The temperature T°C of a shed can be modelled by the equation

$$T = 8 + 3\cos\left(\frac{\pi t}{12}\right) + 7\sin\left(\frac{\pi t}{12}\right), 0 \leqslant t \leqslant 24$$

where t hours is the number of hours after 1200 midday

a Calculate

i the maximum temperature predicted by this model

ii the value of t at which this occurs.

b Calculate, to the nearest minute, the times between which the temperature is predicted to be below 10°C.

19 The height above the ground of a point P on a wind turbine can be modelled by the equation

$$h = 60 - 7\sin(\pi t) - 5\cos(\pi t)$$

where h is measured in metres and t is the time taken in hours.

a Find

i the maximum height

ii the minimum height of P above the ground, and the values of t at which these occur.

b Find the time taken for P to complete one full revolution.

c Find the number of minutes during each revolution that P spends above 64 m.

20 The diagram shows a rectangle OABC such that B has coordinates $(\cos\theta, 2\sin\theta)$ where $0 \leqslant \theta \leqslant \frac{\pi}{2}$.

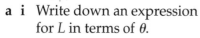

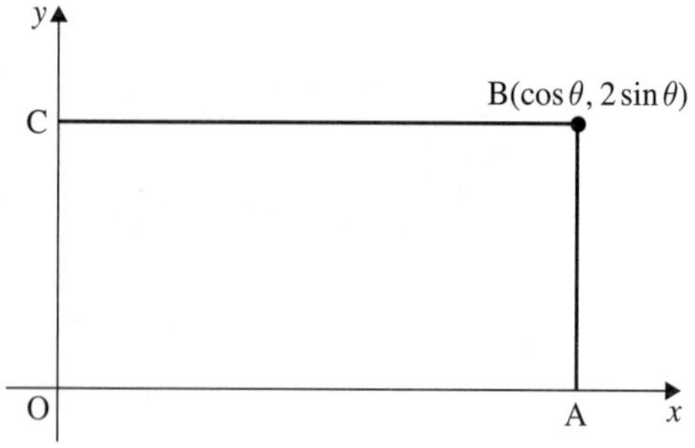

The perimeter of the rectangle has length L.

a **i** Write down an expression for L in terms of θ.

ii Hence form an expression for L in the form $R\sin(\theta + \alpha)$ where $R > 0$ and $0 \leqslant \alpha \leqslant \frac{\pi}{2}$, giving α correct to 3 dp.

b Given that θ varies between 0 and $\frac{\pi}{2}$:

i write down the maximum value of L

ii find the value of θ at which this maximum height occurs.

21 The diagram shows a Ferris wheel at a fairground.

a Given that the wheel takes 20 minutes to complete one revolution, show that the height above the ground, h, of a passenger P can be modelled by the equation

$$h = 9 - 8\cos(18t)$$

where t is the number of minutes after the start of the ride.

b Find how many minutes it takes for the passenger P to first reach a height of 10 m above the ground.

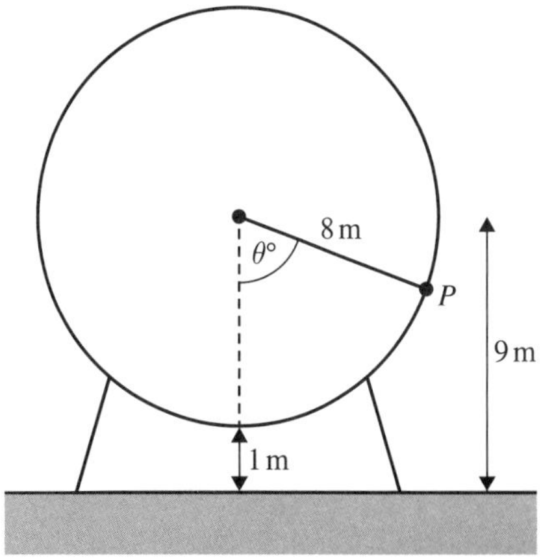

Review Exercise 6F

1 Solve the following trigonometric equations in the given intervals (to 1 dp where necessary):

a $\sin x = \frac{2}{3}$, for $0° \leqslant x \leqslant 360°$

b $\cos x = -\frac{3}{4}$, for $0° \leqslant x \leqslant 360°$

c $\tan x = -0.7$, for $0° \leqslant x \leqslant 360°$

d $\sin x = -\frac{1}{2}$, for $0° \leqslant x \leqslant 360°$

e $\cos x = \frac{1}{2}$, for $0 \leqslant x \leqslant 2\pi$

f $\tan x = 1$, for $-\pi \leqslant x \leqslant \pi$

g $2\sin^2 x = 3\cos x$, for $0° \leqslant x \leqslant 360°$

h $3\tan x = 2\sin x$, for $0° \leqslant x \leqslant 360°$

2 Solve these equations, giving all values of x to the nearest degree in the interval $0° \leqslant x \leqslant 360°$:

a $2\tan^2 x + \sec x - 1 = 0$

b $\operatorname{cosec}^2 x + \cot x - 2 = 0$

3 Find, in terms of π, the solutions of the equation $\tan^4 x - 4\tan^2 x + 3 = 0$, for $0 \leqslant x \leqslant \pi$.

4 Evaluate the following in degrees:

a $\sin^{-1}\frac{1}{\sqrt{2}}$

b $\cos^{-1} 1$

c $\tan^{-1}\sqrt{3}$

5 Evaluate the following in radians, in terms of π:

a $\cos^{-1}\frac{\sqrt{3}}{2}$

b $\tan^{-1}\frac{1}{\sqrt{3}}$

c $\sin^{-1}\frac{1}{2}$

6 Prove the following identities:

a $\operatorname{cosec}\theta\tan\theta \equiv \sec\theta$

b $\operatorname{cosec}\theta - \sin\theta \equiv \cot\theta\cos\theta$

c $(\sin\theta + \operatorname{cosec}\theta)^2 \equiv \sin^2\theta + \cot^2\theta + 3$

d $\sec^2\theta(\cot^2\theta - \cos^2\theta) \equiv \cot^2\theta$

7 Solve the following equations in the range $0° \leqslant \theta \leqslant 360°$:

a $6\sec^2\theta = 5(\tan\theta + 1)$

b $3\cot\theta = 2\sin\theta$

c $\cot\theta + 3\cos\theta = 0$

8 If $\cos A = \frac{4}{5}$, $\cos B = \frac{5}{13}$ and A and B are acute angles, find the value of $\cos(A + B)$.

9 The angle θ is obtuse and $\sin\theta = \frac{4}{5}$.

a Find the value of $\cos\theta$.

b Find the value of $\sin 2\theta$ and $\cos 2\theta$, giving your answers as fractions in their lowest terms.

10 Prove the following identities:

a $\dfrac{\sin 2\theta}{1 + \cos 2\theta} \equiv \tan\theta$

b $\dfrac{1 - \cos 2\theta}{1 + \cos 2\theta} \equiv \tan^2\theta$

c $\dfrac{\sin 2\theta + \sin\theta}{1 + \cos 2\theta + \cos\theta} \equiv \tan\theta$

d $\dfrac{1 - \cos 2\theta + \sin 2\theta}{1 + \cos 2\theta + \sin 2\theta} \equiv \tan\theta$

11 Solve the following equations in the range $0° \leqslant x \leqslant 360°$:

a $\cos 2\theta + \cos\theta = 0$

b $3\sin 2\theta = \sin\theta$

c $2\cos 2\theta = 3\sin\theta$

d $\sin 2\theta = \cos\theta$

e $\cos 2\theta = \cos\theta$

f $2\sin 2\theta = 3\tan\theta$

12 If θ is an acute angle such that $\cos\theta = \frac{3}{5}$ then find the exact values of:

a $\cos 2\theta$ **b** $\sin 2\theta$ **c** $\tan 2\theta$

13 **a** Find the exact values of the following (using surds):

i $\sin 15°$ **ii** $\tan 75°$ **iii** $\cos 105°$

b Hence show that $\sin 15° + \cos 105° = 0$.

14 If θ is an acute angle such that $\cos\theta = \frac{5}{13}$ then find the exact values of:

a $\cos 2\theta$ **b** $\sin\left(\dfrac{\theta}{2}\right)$ **c** $\tan 2\theta$

15 If θ is an acute angle such that $\tan\theta = \frac{3}{4}$ then find the exact value of $\tan\left(\dfrac{\theta}{2}\right)$.

16 Solve the equations in the range $0° \leqslant \theta \leqslant 360°$:

a $\cos 2\theta = \sin\theta$

b $3\tan\theta = \tan 2\theta$

c $\cos 2\theta + \cos\theta + 1 = 0$

d $2\sin\theta = \tan\frac{1}{2}\theta$

e $\tan\theta = 3\tan\frac{1}{2}\theta$

17 Express $\sin 3\theta$ in terms of $\sin\theta$.

18 **a** Express $\cos x - \sin x$ in the form $R\cos(x + \alpha)$, $R > 0$, $0 < \alpha < \dfrac{\pi}{2}$.

State the value of R in surd form and find the exact value of α in radians.

b Hence find the exact solutions in the interval $0 \leqslant x \leqslant 2\pi$ of the equation $\cos x - \sin x = 1$.

c State the maximum value of $\cos x - \sin x$.

19 **a** Express $\sin\theta° + \sqrt{2}\cos\theta°$ in the form $R\sin(\theta + \alpha)°$, where $R > 0$ and $0° < \alpha < 90°$.

b Solve the equation $\sin\theta + \sqrt{2}\cos\theta = 1$, for $0° < \theta < 360°$.

20 **a** Express $f(\theta) = \cos\theta - \sqrt{3}\sin\theta$ in the form $R\cos(\theta + \alpha)$, where $R > 0$ and $0° < \alpha < 90°$.

b Hence find the least value of $\dfrac{1}{[f(\theta)]^2}$.

21 **a** Express $3\cos\theta + 4\sin\theta$ in the form $R\sin(\theta + \alpha)$, where $R > 0$ and $0° < \alpha < 90°$. Give the value of α correct to 1 dp.

b Solve the equation $3\cos\theta + 4\sin\theta = 2$, for $0° < \theta < 360°$, giving each solution to the nearest degree.

22 The depth of water in a harbour varies throughout the day with the tide. The depth d m of the water can be modelled by the equation

$$d = 4 + \cos\left(\frac{\pi t}{6}\right) + 3\sin\left(\frac{\pi t}{6}\right),\ 0 \leqslant t \leqslant 24$$

where t is the number of hours after 0000 midnight.

Find the minimum depth of water in the harbour, and the times at which these low tides occur, giving your answers to the nearest minute.

23 A courier is delivering a package which consists of a smaller rectangular box inside a larger rectangular box, as shown in diagram A. During transit, the smaller box tilts and becomes wedged at an angle, as shown in diagram B.

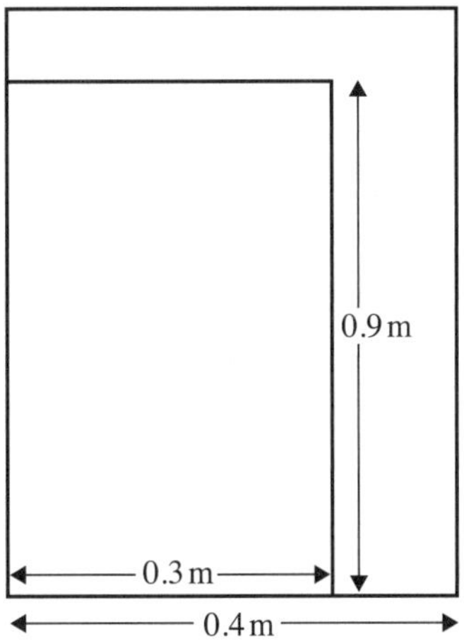

Diagram A

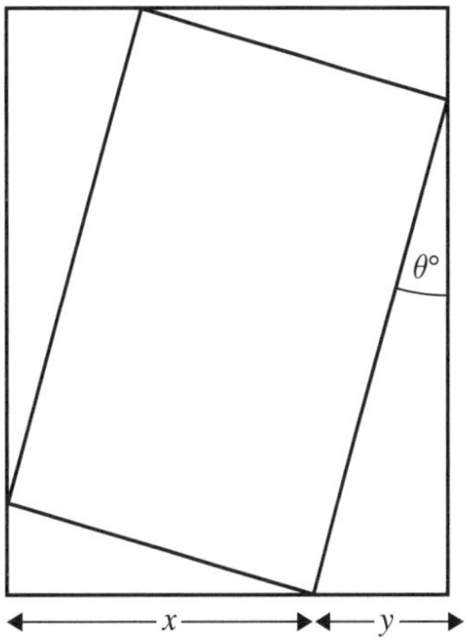

Diagram B

a Find expressions for x and y in terms of θ, and hence show that

$$3\cos\theta + 9\sin\theta = 4$$

b Find the value of θ.

EXAMINATION EXERCISE 6

1 Solve, for $0 \leqslant \theta \leqslant 180°$,

$$2\cot^2 3\theta = 7\operatorname{cosec} 3\theta - 5$$

Give your answers in degrees to 1 decimal place.

[EDEXCEL, GCE Mathematics, C3, Jan 2012]

2 It is given that θ is the acute angle such that $\cot\theta = 4$. Without using a calculator, find the exact value of

i $\tan(\theta + 45°)$,

ii $\operatorname{cosec}\theta$.

[OCR, GCE Mathematics, C3, June 2015]

3 The acute angles α and β are such that

$$2\cot\alpha = 1 \quad \text{and} \quad 24 + \sec^2\beta = 10\tan\beta$$

i State the value of $\tan\alpha$ and determine the value of $\tan\beta$.

ii Hence find the exact value of $\tan(\alpha + \beta)$.

[OCR, GCE Mathematics, C3, Jan 2012]

4 **a** It is given that $\sec x - \tan x = -5$.

i Show that $\sec x + \tan x = -0.2$.

ii Hence find the exact value of $\cos x$.

b Hence solve the equation

$$\sec(2x - 70°) - \tan(2x - 70°) = -5$$

giving all values of x, to one decimal place, in the interval $-90° \leqslant x \leqslant 90°$.

[AQA, GCE Mathematics, C3, June 2016]

5 By first using appropriate identities, solve the equation

$$5\cos 2\theta \operatorname{cosec}\theta = 2$$

for $0° < \theta < 180°$.

[OCR, GCE Mathematics, C3, June 2014]

6 **i** Use an appropriate double angle formula to show that

$$\operatorname{cosec} 2x = \lambda \operatorname{cosec} x \sec x,$$

and state the value of the constant λ.

ii Solve, for $0 \leqslant \theta < 2\pi$, the equation

$$3\sec^2\theta + 3\sec\theta = 2\tan^2\theta$$

You must show all your working. Give your answers in terms of π.

[EDEXCEL, GCE Mathematics, C3 1R, June 2013]

7 **a** Prove that

$$\sec 2A + \tan 2A \equiv \frac{\cos A + \sin A}{\cos A - \sin A}, \quad A \neq \frac{(2n+1)\pi}{4}, \quad n \in \mathbb{Z}$$

b Hence solve, for $0 \leqslant \theta < 2\pi$,

$$\sec 2\theta + \tan 2\theta = \tfrac{1}{2}$$

Give your answers to 3 dp.

[EDEXCEL, GCE Mathematics, C3, June 2015]

8 i Show that $\sin 2\theta(\tan\theta + \cot\theta) \equiv 2$.

ii Hence

a find the exact value of $\tan\frac{1}{12}\pi + \tan\frac{1}{8}\pi + \cot\frac{1}{12}\pi + \cot\frac{1}{8}\pi$,

b solve the equation $\sin 4\theta(\tan\theta + \cot\theta) = 1$ for $0 < \theta < \frac{1}{2}\pi$,

c express $(1 - \cos 2\theta)^2\left(\tan\frac{1}{2}\theta + \cot\frac{1}{2}\theta\right)^3$ in terms of $\sin\theta$.

[OCR, GCE Mathematics, C3, June 2016]

9 By forming and solving a suitable quadratic equation, find the solutions of the equation

$$3\cos 2\theta - 5\cos\theta + 2 = 0$$

in the interval $0° < \theta < 360°$, giving your answers to the nearest $0.1°$.

[AQA, GCE Mathematics, C4, June 2016]

10 a Without using a calculator, find the exact value of

$$(\sin 22.5° + \cos 22.5°)^2$$

You must show each stage of your working.

ii a Show that $\cos 2\theta + \sin\theta = 1$ may be written in the form

$k\sin^2\theta - \sin\theta = 0$, stating the value of k.

b Hence solve, for $0 \leqslant \theta < 360°$, the equation

$$\cos 2\theta + \sin\theta = 1$$

[EDEXCEL, GCE Mathematics, C3, Jan 2013]

11 a Prove that

$$\frac{1}{\sin 2\theta} - \frac{\cos 2\theta}{\sin 2\theta} = \tan\theta, \quad \theta \neq 90n°, \quad n \in \mathbb{Z}$$

b Hence, or otherwise,

i show that $\tan 15° = 2 - \sqrt{3}$,

ii solve, for $0 < x < 360°$,

$$\operatorname{cosec} 4x - \cot 4x = 1$$

[EDEXCEL, GCE Mathematics, C3, June 2011]

12 i Prove that

$$\cos^2(\theta + 45°) - \tfrac{1}{2}(\cos 2\theta - \sin 2\theta) \equiv \sin^2\theta$$

ii Hence solve the equation

$$6\cos^2\left(\tfrac{1}{2}\theta + 45°\right) - 3(\cos\theta - \sin\theta) = 2$$

for $-90° < \theta < 90°$

iii It is given that there are two values of θ, where $-90° < \theta < 90°$, satisfying the equation

$$6\cos^2\left(\tfrac{1}{3}\theta + 45°\right) - 3\left(\cos\tfrac{2}{3}\theta - \sin\tfrac{2}{3}\theta\right) = k$$

where k is a constant. Find the set of possible values of k.

[OCR, GCE Mathematics, C3, Jan 2013]

13 **a** Express $2\cos x - 5\sin x$ in the form $R\cos(x + \alpha)$, where $R > 0$ and $0 < \alpha < \frac{\pi}{2}$, giving your value of α, in radians, to three significant figures.

b **i** Hence find the value of x in the interval $0 < x < 2\pi$ for which $2\cos x - 5\sin x$ has its maximum value. Give your value of x to three significant figures.

ii Use your answer to part **a** to solve the equation $2\cos x - 5\sin x + 1 = 0$ in the interval $0 < x < 2\pi$, giving your solutions to three significant figures.

[AQA, GCE Mathematics, C4, June 2015]

14 **a** Express $2\cos\theta - \sin\theta$ in the form $R\cos(\theta + \alpha)$, where R and α are constants, $R > 0$ and $0 < \alpha < 90°$. Give the exact value of R and give the value of α to 2 dp.

b Hence solve, for $0 \leqslant \theta < 360°$,

$$\frac{2}{2\cos\theta - \sin\theta - 1} = 15$$

Give your answers to 1 dp.

c Use your solutions to parts **a** and **b** to deduce the smallest positive value of θ for which

$$\frac{2}{2\cos\theta + \sin\theta - 1} = 15$$

Give your answer to 1 dp.

[EDEXCEL, GCE Mathematics, C3, June 2016]

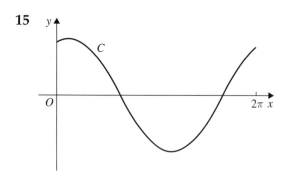

15

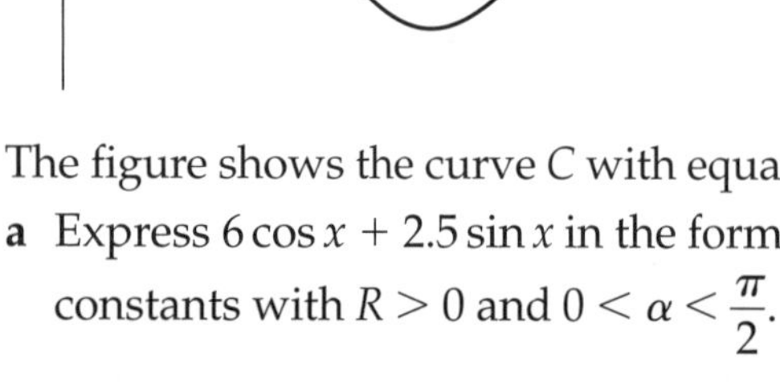

The figure shows the curve C with equation $y = 6\cos x + 2.5\sin x$ for $0 \leqslant x \leqslant 2\pi$

a Express $6\cos x + 2.5\sin x$ in the form $R\cos(x - \alpha)$, where R and α are constants with $R > 0$ and $0 < \alpha < \frac{\pi}{2}$. Give your value of α to 3 dp.

b Find the coordinates of the points on the graph where the curve C crosses the coordinate axes.

A student records the number of hours of daylight each Sunday throughout the year. She starts on the last Sunday in May with a recording of 18 hours, and continues until her final recording 52 weeks later.

She models her results with the continuous function given by

$$H = 12 + 6\cos\frac{2\pi t}{52} + 2.5\sin\frac{2\pi t}{52}, \quad 0 \leqslant t \leqslant 52$$

where H is the number of hours of daylight and t is the number of weeks since her first recording.

Use this function to find

c the maximum and minimum values of H predicted by the model.

d the values for t when $H = 16$ giving your answers to the nearest whole number. [EDEXCEL, GCE Mathematics, C3 1R, June 2014]

16 i Express $3\sin\theta + 4\cos\theta$ in the form $R\sin(\theta + \alpha)$, where $R > 0$ and $0° < \alpha < 90°$.

ii Hence

a solve the equation $3\sin\theta + 4\cos\theta + 1 = 0$, giving all solutions for which $-180° < \theta < 180°$

b find the values of the positive constants k and c such that

$$-37 \leqslant k(3\sin\theta + 4\cos\theta) + c \leqslant 43$$

for all values of θ. [OCR, GCE Mathematics, C3, June 2012]

17 a i Express $3\sin x + 4\cos x$ in the form $R\sin(x + \alpha)$ where $R > 0$ and $0° < \alpha < 90°$, giving your value of α to the nearest $0.1°$.

ii Hence solve the equation $3\sin 2\theta + 4\cos 2\theta = 5$ in the interval $0° < \theta < 360°$, giving your solutions to the nearest $0.1°$.

b i Show that the equation $\tan 2\theta \tan\theta = 2$ can be written as $2\tan^2\theta = 1$.

ii Hence solve the equation $\tan 2\theta \tan\theta = 2$ in the interval $0° \leqslant \theta \leqslant 180°$, giving your solutions to the nearest $0.1°$.

c i Use the Factor Theorem to show that $2x - 1$ is a factor of $8x^3 - 4x + 1$.

ii Show that $4\cos 2\theta\cos\theta + 1$ can be written as $8x^3 - 4x + 1$ where $x = \cos\theta$.

iii Given that $\theta = 72°$ is a solution of $4\cos 2\theta\cos\theta + 1 = 0$, use the results from parts **c i** and **c ii** to show that the exact value of $\cos 72°$ is $\frac{(\sqrt{5} - 1)}{p}$ where p is an integer.

[AQA, GCE Mathematics, C4, June 2014]

18 Solve each of the following equations, giving your answers in exact form.

i $6 \arcsin x - \pi = 0$

ii $\arcsin x = \arccos x$. [MEI, GCE Mathematics, C3, June 2015]

19 **a** Sketch the graph of $y = \cos^{-1} x$, where y is in radians. State the coordinates of the end points of the graph.

b Sketch the graph of $y = \pi - \cos^{-1} x$, where y is in radians. State the coordinates of the end points of the graph.

[AQA, GCE Mathematics, C3, June 2013]

PART 7

Differentiation 1

7.1 Function of a function

Consider the function $y = (x + 3)^7$. Suppose we let $u = x + 3$, so that $y = u^7$. Now y is a function of u and u is a function of x. So y 'is a function of a function' of x.

The Chain Rule

> If y is a function of u and u is a function of x,
> $$\frac{dy}{dx} = \frac{dy}{du} \times \frac{du}{dx}$$

Note that the chain rule is easy to remember because it *appears* that the term du cancels. Remember that cancellation in this context is in fact meaningless.

In the above example $y = (x + 3)^7$ and $u = x + 3$ so that $y = u^7$.

$$\frac{dy}{du} = 7u^6 \quad \text{and} \quad \frac{du}{dx} = 1$$

By the chain rule,

$$\frac{dy}{dx} = \frac{dy}{du} \times \frac{du}{dx} = 7u^6 \times 1$$
$$= 7(x + 3)^6$$

We can also write the chain rule using function notation:

> If $\quad y = f(g(x))$
>
> then $\quad \dfrac{dy}{dx} = f'(g(x))g'(x)$

Example 1

If $y = (4x - 1)^3$, find $\dfrac{dy}{dx}$

Method 1: Let $u = 4x - 1$, so $y = u^3$

$$\frac{du}{dx} = 4 \quad \text{and} \quad \frac{dy}{du} = 3u^2$$

$$\frac{dy}{dx} = \frac{dy}{du} \times \frac{du}{dx} = 3u^2 \times 4$$
$$= 12u^2$$

$$\frac{dy}{dx} = 12(4x - 1)^2$$

Method 2: You may find it quicker to use the function notation form of the chain rule.

$$y = (4x - 1)^3$$

$$\frac{dy}{dx} = 3(4x - 1)^2 \times \frac{d}{dx}(4x - 1)$$

$$= 3(4x - 1)^2 \times 4$$

$$= 12(4x - 1)^2$$

Example 2

Find $\frac{dy}{dx}$ in each case:

a $y = (5x + 1)^4$

$$\frac{dy}{dx} = 4(5x + 1)^3 \times \frac{d}{dx}(5x + 1)$$

$$= 4(5x + 1)^3 \times 5$$

$$= 20(5x + 1)^3$$

b $y = 3(1 + x^2)^7$

$$\frac{dy}{dx} = 3 \times 7(1 + x^2)^6 \times \frac{d}{dx}(1 + x^2)$$

$$= 21(1 + x^2)^6 \times 2x$$

$$= 42x(1 + x^2)^6$$

c $y = \sqrt{2x + 3}$

$$= (2x + 3)^{\frac{1}{2}}$$

$$\frac{dy}{dx} = \frac{1}{2}(2x + 3)^{-\frac{1}{2}} \times \frac{d}{dx}(2x + 3)$$

$$= \tfrac{1}{2}(2x + 3)^{-\frac{1}{2}} \times 2$$

$$= (2x + 3)^{-\frac{1}{2}}$$

d $y = \frac{1}{(3x^3 + 1)^2} = (3x^3 + 1)^{-2}$

$$\frac{dy}{dx} = -2(3x^3 + 1)^{-3} \times \frac{d}{dx}(3x^3 + 1)$$

$$= -2(3x^3 + 1)^{-3} \times 9x^2$$

$$= \frac{-18x^2}{(3x^3 + 1)^3}$$

Exercise 7A

1 Find $\frac{dy}{dx}$:

a $y = (2x + 5)^3$, let $u = 2x + 5$.
b $y = (x^2 + 7)^4$, let $u = x^2 + 7$.

2 Find $\frac{dy}{dx}$.

a $y = (3x - 4)^4$ **b** $y = (8x + 11)^5$ **c** $y = (x^2 - 3)^2$
d $y = (3x^3 + 1)^3$ **e** $y = (1 - 3x)^4$ **f** $y = (3 - x)^{10}$

3 Differentiate the following:

a $y = (1 + 3x)^{-1}$ **b** $y = \frac{1}{(2x + 1)^2}$ **c** $y = \frac{1}{(5x + 2)^3}$

d $y = \frac{3}{(4x - 1)^2}$ **e** $y = \frac{5}{(x^2 + 1)}$ **f** $y = \frac{10}{(1 - x)^4}$

4 **a** If $f(x) = \sqrt{2x^2 - 1}$, show that $f'(x) = \dfrac{2x}{\sqrt{2x^2 - 1}}$.

b Find $f'(2)$.

5 Find $f'(x)$:

a $f(x) = \sqrt{5x^2 + 3}$

b $f(x) = (3x + 1)^{\frac{1}{3}}$

c $f(x) = \dfrac{1}{\sqrt{x^2 - 3}}$

d $f(x) = \dfrac{1}{x^3 + 1}$

e $f(x) = \dfrac{1}{\sqrt{8x + 7}}$

f $f(x) = \dfrac{1}{\sqrt{x} + 2}$

6 Find the equation of the tangent to the curve $y = (x^2 + 1)^4$ at the point (1, 16).

7 Find the equation of the normal to the curve $y = (3x + 1)^{\frac{3}{2}}$ at the point where $x = 5$.

8 For the curve $y = (2 + x^2)^3$, find the coordinates of the point where the gradient is zero.

9 Given $y = (3x + 1)^2 + (3x + 1)^3$, find the value of $\dfrac{dy}{dx}$ at $x = \frac{1}{3}$.

10 Find the equation of the tangent to the curve $y = \sqrt{x^2 + 3}$ at the point (1, 2).

11 Differentiate the following:

a $y = (2\sqrt{x} - 3x)^3$

b $y = \sqrt{1 - \dfrac{1}{x}}$

c $y = \dfrac{2}{x^{\frac{3}{2}} + 2}$

d $y = \left(\dfrac{1}{1 + \sqrt{x}}\right)^2$

e $y = \sqrt{x^2 - \dfrac{1}{x}}$

f $y = 10x^2 + \sqrt{2x - 3}$

12 **a** Find the coordinates of the two stationary points of $y = \dfrac{8}{(x + 1)} + 2x + 1$.

b Show that one is a local maximum and the other is a local minimum.

13 **a** Find the coordinates of the stationary point of $y = \dfrac{32}{(3x + 1)^2} + 3x - 3$.

b Show that this is a local minimum.

7.2 The product rule

Consider the product uv where u and v are functions of x.

$$y = uv \quad ①$$

Let x increase by a small amount δx and let the corresponding increase in u be δu, in v be δv and in y be δy.

So $y + \delta y = (u + \delta u)(v + \delta v)$ ②

② − ① $y + \delta y - y = (u + \delta u)(v + \delta v) - uv$

$$\delta y = u\,\delta v + v\,\delta u + \delta u\,\delta v$$

$$\frac{\delta y}{\delta x} = u\frac{\delta v}{\delta x} + v\frac{\delta u}{\delta x} + \delta u\frac{\delta v}{\delta x}$$

As $\delta x \to 0$, $\frac{\delta y}{\delta x} \to \frac{dy}{dx}$, $\frac{\delta v}{\delta x} \to \frac{dv}{dx}$ and $\frac{\delta u}{\delta x} \to \frac{du}{dx}$.

And as $\delta x \to 0$, δu and δv both tend towards zero.

So if	$y = uv$
then	$\frac{dy}{dx} = u\frac{dv}{dx} + v\frac{du}{dx}$

Or, using function notation:

If	$y = f(x)g(x)$
then	$\frac{dy}{dx} = f(x)g'(x) + g(x)f'(x)$

You only need to remember this result.

Example 1

Find $\frac{dy}{dx}$:

a $y = x(x + 2)^2$ **b** $y = (x + 3)^2(2x + 1)^3$ **c** $y = (2x + 1)^2\sqrt{4x - 3}$

a We have $y = uv$, where $u = x$ and $v = (x + 2)^2$

$\therefore \quad \frac{du}{dx} = 1$ and $\frac{dv}{dx} = 2(x + 2)$

$$\frac{dy}{dx} = u\frac{dv}{dx} + v\frac{du}{dx}$$

$$= x \times 2(x + 2)^1 + (x + 2)^2 \times 1$$

$$= (x + 2)(2x + x + 2)$$

$$= (x + 2)(3x + 2)$$

b $y = (x + 3)^2(2x + 1)^3$

We have $y = uv$, where $u = (x + 3)^2$ and $v = (2x + 1)^3$

$$\frac{dy}{dx} = u\frac{dv}{dx} + v\frac{du}{dx}$$

$$= (x + 3)^2 \times 3(2x + 1)^2 \times 2 + (2x + 1)^3 \times 2(x + 3)^1$$

$$= (x + 3)(2x + 1)^2[6(x + 3) + (2x + 1) \times 2]$$

$$= (x + 3)(2x + 1)^2(10x + 20)$$

$$= 10(x + 3)(2x + 1)^2(x + 2)$$

c $y = (2x + 1)^2\sqrt{4x - 3}$

We have $y = uv$, where $u = (2x + 1)^2$ and $v = (4x - 3)^{\frac{1}{2}}$

$$\frac{dy}{dx} = (2x + 1)^2 \times \frac{1}{2}(4x - 3)^{-\frac{1}{2}} \times 4 + (4x - 3)^{\frac{1}{2}} \times 2(2x + 1)^1 \times 2$$

$$= \frac{(2x + 1)}{(4x - 3)^{\frac{1}{2}}}[2(2x + 1) + (4x - 3) \times 4]$$

$$= \frac{2x + 1}{\sqrt{4x - 3}}[20x - 10]$$

$$= \frac{10(2x + 1)(2x - 1)}{\sqrt{4x - 3}}$$

Exercise 7B

Differentiate the following with respect to x and simplify your answers:

1 $y = x(2x + 1)^2$

2 $y = x^2(3x - 1)^2$

3 $y = x^3(x - 1)^2$

4 $y = (x + 2)^2(x + 3)^2$

5 $y = 2x(1 - x)^3$

6 $y = (4x^3 + 1)(x - 1)^2$

7 $y = 5x(1 + 2x)^4$

8 $y = (3x + 1)^4(x - 3)$

9 $y = (x + 2)x^{\frac{3}{2}}$

10 $y = (4x + 1)^2\sqrt{x}$

11 $y = x^2\sqrt{2x + 1}$

12 $y = x^3\sqrt{4x - 1}$

13 Find the equation of the tangent to the curve $y = 6x\sqrt{x + 8}$ at the point (1, 18).

14 Find the gradient of the curve $y = x^3(x + 1)^2$ at the point (1, 4).

15 Find the x coordinates of the two points where the gradient of the curve $y = \sqrt{x}(x - 2)^2$ is zero.

16 a Find the x coordinates of the turning points of the curve $y = (x + 3)^2(x - 1)$.

b Determine the nature of each turning point.

17 a For the curve $y = (x + 2)(x - 4)^2$, find:

i the points where it meets the axes,

ii the turning points.

b Sketch the curve.

18 The curve $y = x^2(x - 3)$ has a minimum value at the point A.

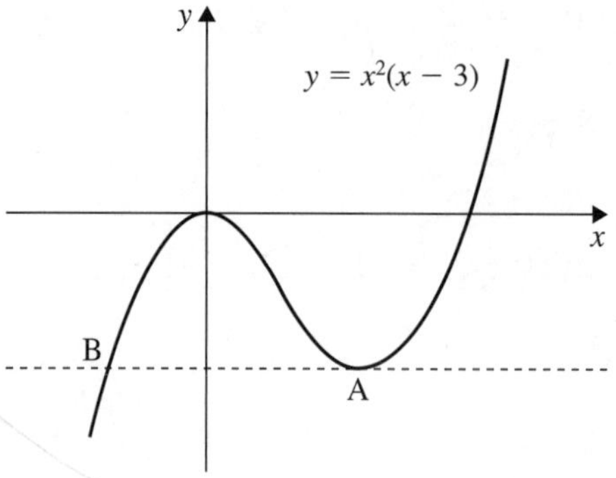

a Find the coordinates of A.

b The tangent to the curve at A meets the curve again at B. Find the coordinates of B.

19 i Given that $y = (x + 1)\sqrt{2x - 1}$, show that $\dfrac{dy}{dx}$ can be written in the form $\dfrac{kx}{\sqrt{2x - 1}}$ and state the value of k.

ii Hence evaluate

$$\int_1^5 \frac{x}{\sqrt{2x - 1}}\,dx$$

7.3 The quotient rule

Consider the function $y = \dfrac{u}{v}$, where u and v are both functions of x.

Write $y = uv^{-1}$ and then differentiate using the product rule.

$$\frac{dy}{dx} = u\frac{d}{dx}(v^{-1}) + v^{-1}\frac{d}{dx}(u)$$

$$= u \times (-1)v^{-2}\frac{dv}{dx} + v^{-1}\frac{du}{dx}$$

$$= -\frac{u}{v^2}\frac{dv}{dx} + \frac{1}{v}\frac{du}{dx}$$

$$= \frac{-u\dfrac{dv}{dx} + v\dfrac{du}{dx}}{v^2}$$

Finally, if $y = \dfrac{u}{v}$

$$\frac{dy}{dx} = \frac{v\dfrac{du}{dz} - u\dfrac{dv}{dx}}{v^2}$$

Or, in function notation:

$$\text{If } y = \frac{f(x)}{g(x)}$$

$$\frac{dy}{dx} = \frac{g(x)f'(x) - f(x)g'(x)}{(g(x))^2}$$

Remember this result or perhaps this verse!
'low D-high minus high D-low over the square of what's below'.

Example 1

Find $\frac{dy}{dx}$ in each case.

a $y = \frac{x^2}{2x + 3}$

This is of the form $y = \frac{u}{v}$, where $u = x^2$ and $v = 2x + 3$.
By the quotient rule,

$$\frac{dy}{dx} = \frac{(2x + 3) \times 2x - x^2 \times 2}{(2x + 3)^2}$$

$$= \frac{4x^2 + 6x - 2x^2}{(2x + 3)^2}$$

$$= \frac{2x^2 + 6x}{(2x + 3)^2} = \frac{2x(x + 3)}{(2x + 3)^2}$$

b $y = \frac{3x^2 - 1}{(2x - 1)^3}$

This is of the form $y = \frac{u}{v}$, where $u = 3x^2 - 1$ and $v = (2x - 1)^3$.

$$\frac{dy}{dx} = 6x \quad \text{and} \quad \frac{dv}{dx} = 3(2x - 1)^2 \times 2$$

$$= 6(2x - 1)^2$$

$$\frac{dy}{dx} = \frac{(2x - 1)^3 \times 6x - (3x^2 - 1) \times 6(2x - 1)^2}{(2x - 1)^6}$$

$$= \frac{(2x - 1)^2[6x(2x - 1) - 6(3x^2 - 1)]}{(2x - 1)^6}$$

$$= \frac{12x^2 - 6x - 18x^2 + 6}{(2x - 1)^4} \qquad \text{(cancel } (2x - 1)^2\text{)}$$

$$= \frac{6 - 6x - 6x^2}{(2x - 1)^4} = \frac{6(1 - x - x^2)}{(2x - 1)^4}$$

Example 2

a Find $\frac{dy}{dx}$ if $y = \frac{x}{\sqrt{2x-1}}, x > \frac{1}{2}$.

b Find any turning points and determine their nature.

a $y = \frac{x}{(2x-1)^{\frac{1}{2}}}$

So $y = \frac{u}{v}$, where $u = x$ and $v = (2x-1)^{\frac{1}{2}}$

Differentiating u and v, $\frac{du}{dx} = 1, \frac{dv}{dx} = \frac{1}{2}(2x-1)^{-\frac{1}{2}} \times 2 = (2x-1)^{-\frac{1}{2}}$

$$\therefore \quad \frac{dy}{dx} = \frac{(2x-1)^{\frac{1}{2}} \times 1 - x \times \frac{1}{(2x-1)^{\frac{1}{2}}}}{(2x-1)}$$

Multiply numerator and denominator by $(2x-1)^{\frac{1}{2}}$.

$$\frac{dy}{dx} = \frac{(2x-1) - x}{(2x-1)^{\frac{3}{2}}}$$

$$\frac{dy}{dx} = \frac{x-1}{(2x-1)^{\frac{3}{2}}}$$

b At turning points $\frac{dy}{dx} = 0 \quad \Rightarrow \quad \frac{x-1}{(2x-1)^{\frac{3}{2}}} = 0$

$$\Rightarrow \quad x = 1$$

When $x = 1, y = \frac{1}{\sqrt{2-1}} = 1$.

There is a turning point at (1, 1).

To determine the nature of the turning point find $\frac{d^2y}{dx^2}$.

$$\frac{d^2y}{dx^2} = \frac{(2x-1)^{\frac{3}{2}} \times 1 - (x-1) \times \frac{3}{2}(2x-1)^{\frac{1}{2}} \times 2}{(2x-1)^3}$$

$$= \frac{(2x-1)^{\frac{1}{2}}[(2x-1) - 3(x-1)]}{(2x-1)^3}$$

$$= \frac{-x+2}{(2x-1)^{\frac{5}{2}}}$$

When $x = 1, \frac{d^2y}{dx^2} = \frac{-1+2}{1} = 1$ which is greater than zero.

This tells us that there is a minimum value at (1, 1).

Here is a sketch of the curve.

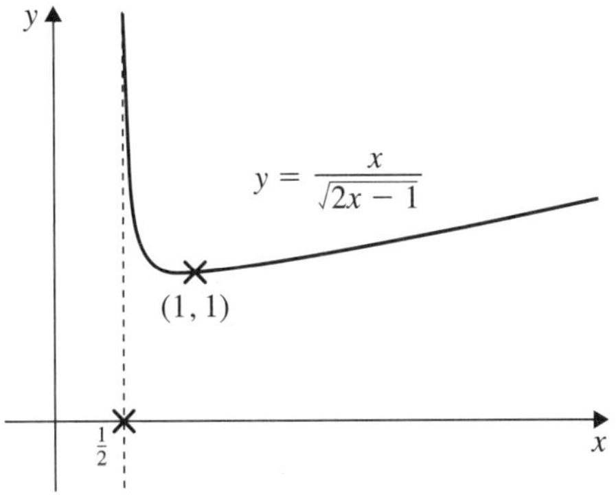

Notice that as $x \to \frac{1}{2}$, $y \to \infty$.

EXERCISE 7C

Find $\frac{dy}{dx}$:

1 $y = \frac{2x}{x+1}$

2 $y = \frac{x+7}{2x-1}$

3 $y = \frac{x^2}{3x+1}$

4 $y = \frac{4x+5}{x^2+1}$

5 $y = \frac{(x+1)^2}{x^2}$

6 $y = \frac{2x+1}{(x+1)^3}$

7 $y = \frac{(3x+2)^2}{(4x+1)^3}$

8 $y = \frac{x^3}{(x-3)^4}$

9 $y = \frac{(3x-4)^3}{(2x+1)^2}$

10 $y = \frac{\sqrt{x+1}}{x}$

11 $y = \frac{x}{\sqrt{(4x+3)}}$

12 $y = \frac{3x+1}{\sqrt{2x-1}}$

13 Find the equation of the tangent to the curve $y = \frac{x^2}{(x+1)^3}$ at the point $(1, \frac{1}{8})$.

14 Find the equation of the tangent to the curve $y = \frac{x+1}{2x-1}$ at the point $(0, -1)$.

15 Find the equation of the normal to the curve $y = \frac{x+4}{x^2+1}$ at the point $(0, 4)$.

16 Find the x coordinate of the point on the curve $y = \frac{2x}{\sqrt{4x-3}}$ where the gradient is zero.

17 Find the coordinates of the turning points of $y = \frac{1-x}{x^2+3}$. Determine their nature.

18 Show that the gradient of the curve $y = \frac{x^3}{\sqrt{x^2+1}}$ is positive for all values of x except $x = 0$.

19 Show that if $y = \frac{x^2}{\sqrt{x+1}}$ then $\frac{dy}{dx} = \frac{x(3x+4)}{2(x+1)\sqrt{x+1}}$.

7.4 Differentiating e^x

In Pure Mathematics Book 1 we stated that when we differentiate the function e^{kx} we obtain ke^{kx}. It is not necessary at this level to understand a proof of this result but we indicate below how we can 'justify' the result by a numerical method.

For a function, f(x), $f'(x) = \lim_{h \to 0}\left(\frac{f(x+h) - f(x)}{h}\right)$.

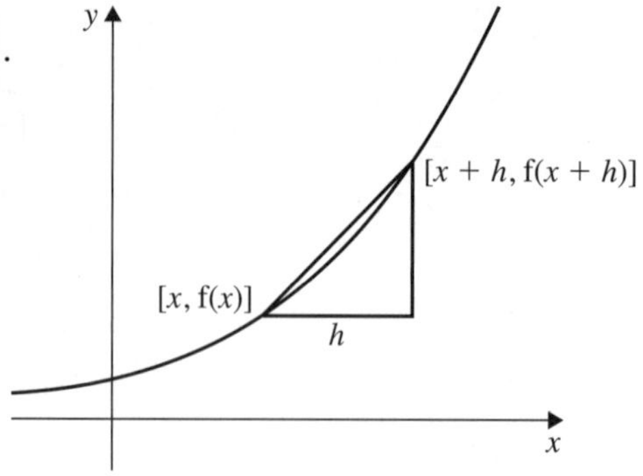

So if $f(x) = a^x$ we see that

$$f'(x) = \lim_{h \to 0}\left(\frac{a^{x+h} - a^x}{h}\right) = \lim_{h \to 0}\left(\frac{a^x.a^h - a^x}{h}\right)$$

$$= a^x \lim_{h \to 0}\left(\frac{a^h - 1}{h}\right)$$

We require the value of a such that $f'(a^x) = a^x$.

We need $\lim_{h \to 0}\left(\frac{a^h - 1}{h}\right) = 1$.

Try $a = 2, h = 0.001$: $\frac{2^{0.001} - 1}{0.001} \approx 0.693$. So $a = 2$ is too small.

Try $a = 3, h = 0.001$: $\frac{3^{0.001} - 1}{0.001} \approx 1.099$. So $a = 3$ is too large.

Try $a = 2.71, h = 0.001$: $\frac{2.71^{0.001} - 1}{0.001} \approx 0.997$. So $a = 2.71$ is too small.

Try $a = 2.72, h = 0.001$: $\frac{2.72^{0.001} - 1}{0.001} \approx 1.001$. So $a = 2.72$ is too large.

When this process is continued we obtain the number 2.718 281 828 correct to 9 dp. Note that this is an *approximate* value for e. The number e is in fact an irrational number which means that it cannot be written in the form $\frac{a}{b}$ where a and b are integers.

A frequently asked question is 'What is e?'

Answer: e is just a *number* which has the unique property that $\frac{d}{dx}(e^x) = e^x$.

If	$y = e^{kx}$
then	$\frac{dy}{dx} = ke^{kx}$

More generally:

If	$y = e^{f(x)}$
	$\frac{dy}{dx} = f'(x)e^{f(x)}$

Differentiating a^{kx}

Let $y = a^{kx}$.

We can write $y = e^{\ln a^{kx}}$

$$= e^{kx \ln a}$$

Now $\frac{dy}{dx} = k \ln a \, (e^{kx \ln a})$

$$= k \ln a \, (e^{\ln a^{kx}})$$

$$= k \ln a \, (a^{kx})$$

> So, if $y = a^{kx}$
>
> $\frac{dy}{dx} = k \ln a (a^{kx})$

You should be able to reproduce this result yourself.

Example 1

Find the gradient of the curve $y = e^x$ at the point $(2, e^2)$.

$$y = e^x$$

$$\frac{dy}{dx} = e^x$$

When $x = 2$, $\frac{dy}{dx} = e^2$.

At the point $(2, e^2)$ the gradient of the curve is e^2.

[As a decimal the gradient is 7.39 correct to 2 dp.]

Example 2

Find $\frac{dy}{dx}$, if $y = e^{3x}$.

$$y = e^{3x}$$

$$\frac{dy}{dx} = 3e^{3x}$$

Example 3

Find $\frac{dy}{dx}$, if $y = 10 \times 2^{3x}$.

$$\frac{dy}{dx} = 10 \times 3 \times \ln 2 \times (2^{3x})$$

$$= 30 \ln 2(2^{3x})$$

Example 4

Find $\frac{dy}{dx}$ in each of the following

a $y = e^{x^2}$

$$\frac{dy}{dx} = \frac{d}{dx}(x^2)\, e^{x^2}$$
$$= 2xe^{x^2}$$

b $y = e^{4x+1}$

$$\frac{dy}{dx} = \frac{d}{dx}(4x + 1)\, e^{4x+1}$$
$$= 4e^{4x+1}$$

Example 5

a Find $\frac{dy}{dx}$ if $y = x^2e^x$

We have $y = uv$, where $u = x^2$, $v = e^x$

$$\frac{dy}{dx} = u\frac{dv}{dx} + v\frac{du}{dx}$$
$$= (x^2e^x) + (e^x \times 2x)$$
$$= xe^x(x + 2)$$

b Find $\frac{dy}{dx}$ if $y = \frac{e^{2x}}{3x + 1}$

We have $y = \frac{u}{v}$, where $u = e^{2x}$ and $v = 3x + 1$.

$$\frac{dy}{dx} = \frac{v\frac{du}{dx} - u\frac{dv}{dx}}{v^2} = \frac{(3x + 1)\, 2e^{2x} - e^{2x} \times 3}{(3x + 1)^2}$$

$$= \frac{e^{2x}(6x + 2 - 3)}{(3x + 1)^2} = \frac{e^{2x}(6x - 1)}{(3x + 1)^2}$$

Example 6

Find the equation of the tangent to the curve $y = x + e^x$ at the point $(1, 1 + e)$.

$$y = x + e^x$$
$$\frac{dy}{dx} = 1 + e^x$$

At $x = 1$, $\frac{dy}{dx} = 1 + e$.

The gradient of the tangent at $x = 1$ is $1 + e$.

The equation of the tangent is $y - (1 + e) = (1 + e)(x - 1)$

$$y - 1 - e = (1 + e)x - 1 - e$$

The equation of the tangent is $y = (1 + e)x$.

Example 7

Find the coordinates of the turning point of the curve $y = xe^{2x}$ and determine its nature.

$$y = xe^{2x}$$

$$\frac{dy}{dx} = x2e^{2x} + e^{2x} \times 1 \quad \text{[product rule]}$$

$$= e^{2x}(2x + 1)$$

At turning points $\quad e^{2x}(2x + 1) = 0$

$$\Rightarrow \quad 2x + 1 = 0 \quad \text{[since } e^{2x} \text{ is never zero]}$$

$$x = -\tfrac{1}{2}$$

When $x = -\frac{1}{2}, y = -\frac{1}{2} \times e^{-1} = -\frac{1}{2e}$

$$\frac{d^2y}{dx^2} = e^{2x} \times 2 + (2x + 1) \times 2e^{2x} \quad \text{[product rule]}$$

$$= 2e^{2x}[1 + 2x + 1]$$

$$= 4e^{2x}(x + 1)$$

When $x = -\frac{1}{2}, \frac{d^2y}{dx^2} = 2e^{-1}$ which is >0.

So there is a minimum point at $\left(-\frac{1}{2}, -\frac{1}{2e}\right)$

Here is a sketch of the curve.

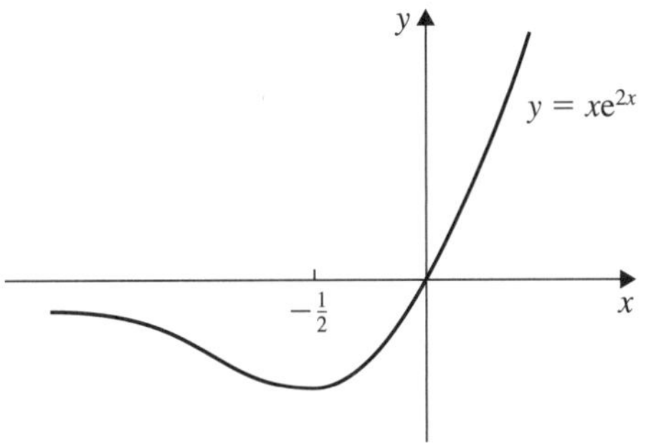

EXERCISE 7D

1 Find $\frac{dy}{dx}$ for each of the following:

a $y = e^x$

b $y = e^{3x}$

c $y = 2e^x$

d $y = e^{x^2}$

e $y = e^{2x+1}$

f $y = e^{-x}$

g $y = 5e^{4x}$

h $y = e^x + e^{2x}$

i $y = x^2 - e^{-x}$

j $y = \frac{1}{e^{2x}}$

k $y = \frac{4}{e^x}$

l $y = e^{x^3} + x^3$

m $y = 5^{4x}$

n $y = 30 \times 2^{10x}$

o $y = \frac{2}{3^{7x}}$

2 Differentiate with respect to x:

a $x\,e^x$ **b** $x^2 e^x$ **c** $2x\,e^{2x}$

d $(x^2 + 1)e^x$ **e** $4x^3 e^{2x}$ **f** $x^2(e^{3x} - x)$

g $\dfrac{e^{3x}}{x}$ **h** $\dfrac{e^x + 1}{x^2}$ **i** $\dfrac{x^2}{e^x}$

j $e^x(1 + x)^3$ **k** $e^{-x}(x^3 + 1)$ **l** $\dfrac{e^{2x}}{1 - e^x}$

3 Find the gradient of each curve at the given point:

a $y = x\,e^x$ at $x = 2$ **b** $y = x\,e^{x-2}$ at $(2, 2)$

c $y = e^x + x^2$ at $(0, 1)$ **d** $y = \dfrac{e^{2x} + 1}{e^{2x} - 1}$ at $x = 1$.

4 Find the equation of the tangent to the curve $y = e^x$ at the point where $x = 2$.

5 Find the equation of the tangent to the curve $y = x\,e^x$ at the point $(0, 0)$.

6 **a** Sketch the curves $y = e^x$ and $y = e^{x-2}$.

b Find the equation of the normal to the curve $y = e^{x-2}$ at the point where the curve meets the y-axis.

c Find the coordinates of the point where the normal meets the x-axis.

7 Find the coordinates of the turning point on the curve $y = x\,e^x$ and show whether it is a maximum or minimum point.

8 Find the coordinates and nature of any turning points on the curve $y = \dfrac{e^x}{x}$.

9 **a** Find the stationary point of the curve $y = e^x + e^{-x}$.

b Show that this is a local minimum.

10 **a** Find the coordinates and nature of any turning points on the curve $y = x^2 e^x$.

b Sketch the curve.

11 Given that $y = e^x + \dfrac{1}{e^x}$, show that $y\dfrac{dy}{dx} = e^{2x} - \dfrac{1}{e^{2x}}$.

12 Given that $y = e^x - e^{-x}$, show that $\left(\dfrac{dy}{dx}\right)^2 = y^2 + 4$.

13 Show that if $y = e^{2x} + e^{-2x}$ then $\dfrac{d^2y}{dx^2} = 4y$.

14 Given that $y = A + B\,e^{-4x}$, where A and B are constants, show that

$$\frac{d^2y}{dx^2} + 4\frac{dy}{dx} = 0.$$

15 Given that $y = e^{2t}(A + Bt)$, where A and B are constants, show that

$$\frac{d^2y}{dt^2} - 4\frac{dy}{dt} + 4y = 0.$$

16 Find the coordinates of the turning point on the curve $y = 2e^{3x} + 8e^{-3x}$, and determine the nature of this turning point.

7.5 Differentiating ln *x*

To find $\frac{d}{dx}(\ln x)$ we use the result $\frac{dy}{dx} = \frac{1}{\left(\frac{dx}{dy}\right)}$.

This result is justified below.

Now if $y = \ln x$, [Remember $\ln x = \log_e x$]

then $x = e^y$ ①

Differentiate with respect to y.

$$\frac{dx}{dy} = e^y$$

$$\frac{dy}{dx} = \frac{1}{\left(\frac{dx}{dy}\right)} = \frac{1}{e^y}$$

$$\therefore \quad \frac{dy}{dx} = \frac{1}{x} \quad \text{[from ①]}$$

So if	$y = \ln x$
	$\frac{dy}{dx} = \frac{1}{x}$

You only need to remember this result.

To show that $\frac{dy}{dx} = \frac{1}{\left(\frac{dx}{dy}\right)}$:

$$\frac{dy}{dx} = \lim_{\delta x \to 0}\left(\frac{\delta y}{\delta x}\right) = \lim_{\delta x \to 0}\left[\frac{1}{\left(\frac{\delta x}{\delta y}\right)}\right] \quad ②$$

Now as $\delta x \to 0$, $\delta y \to 0$ also and so ② becomes

$$\frac{dy}{dx} = \lim_{\delta y \to 0}\left[\frac{1}{\left(\frac{\delta x}{\delta y}\right)}\right]$$

$$\textbf{So } \frac{dy}{dx} = \frac{1}{\left(\frac{dx}{dy}\right)}$$

You only need to remember this result.

Example 1

a Sketch the curve $y = \ln x$.

b Find the gradient of the curve at the point where the curve cuts the x-axis.

a The curve is shown.
Remember that $\ln x$ is defined for $x > 0$ and that the curve cuts the x-axis at $(1, 0)$.

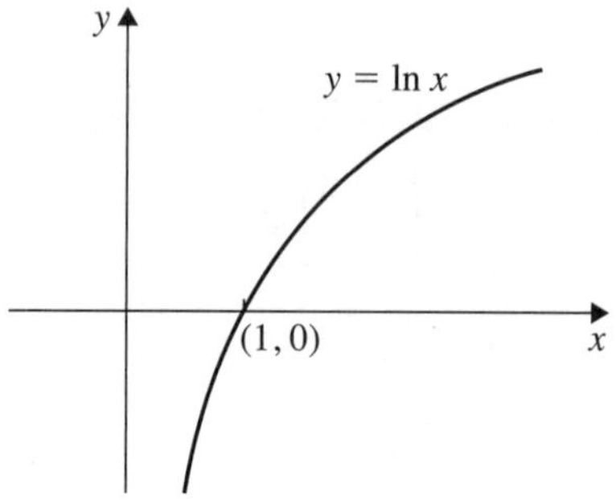

b $y = \ln x$

$$\frac{dy}{dx} = \frac{1}{x}$$

At $x = 1$, $\frac{dy}{dx} = \frac{1}{1} = 1$.

The gradient of the curve is 1 at the point where it cuts the x-axis.

Example 2

Find $\frac{dy}{dx}$ in each of the following:

a $y = \ln 3x^2$

Let $u = 3x^2$

$\therefore \quad y = \ln u$

$$\frac{dy}{dx} = \frac{dy}{du} \times \frac{du}{dx}$$

$$= \frac{1}{u} \times 6x$$

$$\frac{dy}{dx} = \frac{1}{3x^2} \times 6x = \frac{2}{x}$$

b $y = \ln(4x - 1)$

Let $u = 4x - 1$

$\therefore \quad y = \ln u$

$$\frac{dy}{dx} = \frac{dy}{du} \times \frac{du}{dx}$$

$$= \frac{1}{u} \times 4$$

$$= \frac{4}{4x - 1}$$

Notice that in each case we have $y = \ln[f(x)]$

$$\text{and } \frac{dy}{dx} = \frac{1}{f(x)} \times f'(x).$$

This is a quick way of differentiating $\ln[f(x)]$.

Example 3

Find $\frac{dy}{dx}$ in each case.

a $y = (x^2 + 1)\ln 2x$

We have $y = uv$, where $u = x^2 + 1$ and $v = \ln 2x$.

Differentiating, $\frac{du}{dx} = 2x$, $\frac{dv}{dx} = \frac{1}{2x} \times 2 = \frac{1}{x}$.

$$\frac{dy}{dx} = u\frac{dv}{dx} + v\frac{du}{dx}$$

$$= (x^2 + 1)\frac{1}{x} + (\ln 2x)\,2x$$

$$= \frac{x^2 + 1}{x} + 2x\ln 2x$$

b $y = e^x \ln x^2$

We have $y = uv$, where $u = e^x$ and $v = \ln x^2$.

Differentiating, $\frac{du}{dx} = e^x$, $\frac{dv}{dx} = \frac{1}{x^2} \times 2x = \frac{2}{x}$.

$$\frac{dy}{dx} = u\frac{dv}{dx} + v\frac{du}{dx}$$

$$= e^x\frac{2}{x} + (\ln x^2)\,e^x$$

$$= \frac{2e^x}{x} + e^x\ln x^2$$

Exercise 7E

1 Find $\frac{dy}{dx}$ for each of the following:

a $y = \ln 4x$ **b** $y = \ln x^3$ **c** $y = 6\ln x$

d $y = \ln(3x - 1)$ **e** $y = \ln(1 - 2x)$ **f** $y = \ln(x^3 + x)$

g $y = \ln\frac{x+1}{2}$ **h** $y = \ln 4x^2$ **i** $y = 3\ln(x + 2)$

j $y = \ln\frac{1}{x}$ **k** $y = \ln\sqrt{x}$ **l** $y = \ln(x^2 + x - 2)$

2 a Write $\ln\left(\frac{x+4}{x-2}\right)$ as the difference of two logarithms.

b Hence find $\frac{d}{dx}\left[\ln\left(\frac{x+4}{x-2}\right)\right]$

3 Differentiate with respect to x:

a $y = \ln\left(\frac{3x}{x+1}\right)$ **b** $y = \ln\left(\frac{2x+3}{4x-1}\right)$

4 Find $\frac{dy}{dx}$ for each of the following:

a $y = x \ln x$ **b** $y = x^2 \ln x$ **c** $y = x \ln(1 + x)$

d $y = \frac{\ln x}{x}$ **e** $y = \frac{\ln x}{(x+1)^2}$ **f** $y = \frac{x}{\ln x}$

g $y = x^2 + \ln x$ **h** $y = 3\ln x + \frac{1}{x}$ **i** $y = \ln\sqrt{x} + \sqrt{x}$

j $y = \frac{1 + \ln x}{x}$ **k** $y = x^2 \ln(1 + x^2)$ **l** $y = \ln\left(\frac{x+1}{x+2}\right)$

5 If $y = x^2 \ln x$, find $\frac{dy}{dx}$ and $\frac{d^2y}{dx^2}$.

6 Given that $y = \ln(\ln x)$, show that $x \ln x \frac{dy}{dx} = 1$.

7 Given that $y = \ln(1 + e^x)$, find $\frac{dy}{dx}$ and show that $(1 + e^x)\frac{d^2y}{dx^2} = \frac{dy}{dx}$.

8 **a** Sketch the curves $y = \ln x$ and $y = \ln(x + 1)$.

b Find the equation of the tangent to the curve $y = \ln(x + 1)$ at the point $(2, \ln 3)$.

9 Find the equation of the normal to the curve $y = \ln(1 + x^2)$ at the point where $x = 1$.

10 **a** Find the equation of the tangent to the curve $y = \ln(x - 1)$ at the point where the curve meets the x-axis.

b The tangent above meets the x and y axes at the points A and B respectively. Find the area of triangle OAB where O is the origin.

11 The diagram shows the curve $y = \frac{\ln x}{x}$.

The curve crosses the x-axis at A and B is the maximum point on the curve. Find the coordinates of A and B.

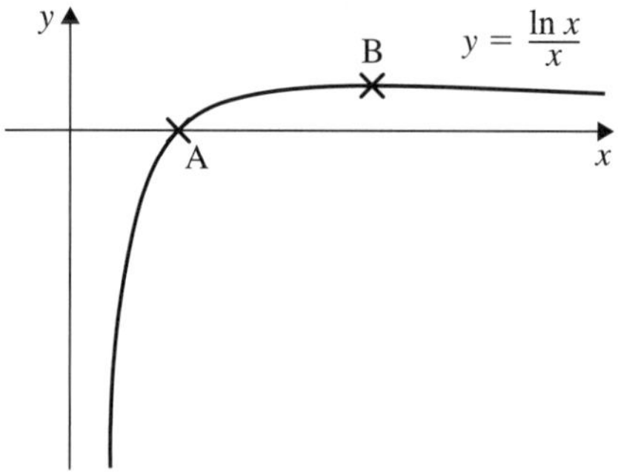

12 Find the coordinates of the point on the curve $y = x \ln x$ where the gradient is zero.

13 Find the x-coordinate of the point on the curve $y = x \ln 2x$ where the gradient is zero.

14 **a** Find the stationary point of the curve $y = \ln(3x - 8) - x - 2$.

b Show that this is a local maximum.

15 a If $y = \ln(f(x))$ then find $\frac{dy}{dx}$ in terms of $f(x)$ and $f'(x)$.

b Hence find $\int \frac{3x^2}{x^3 + 1} dx$.

16 Find the equation of the tangent to the curve $y = e^x \ln x$ at the point where $x = 1$.

17 Find the coordinates of the point on the curve $y = \ln(e^x + x)$ where the gradient of the curve is 1.

7.6 Differentiating sin *x*, cos *x*, tan *x*

When we differentiate the trigonometric functions we must measure angles in *radians*.

Recall from Pure Mathematics Book 1.

$$f'(x) = \lim_{h \to 0} \frac{f(x + h) - f(x)}{h}$$

Now, consider $f(x) = \sin x$

$$f'(x) = \lim_{h \to 0} \frac{\sin(x + h) - \sin x}{h}$$

$$= \lim_{h \to 0} \frac{\sin x \cos h + \cos x \sin h - \sin x}{h} \quad \text{[using } \sin(A + B)\text{]}$$

Now, as h is very small, $\sin h \approx h$ and $\cos h \approx 1 - \frac{1}{2}h^2$ [using small angle approximations]

$$\text{So } f'(x) = \lim_{h \to 0} \frac{(1 - \frac{1}{2}h^2)\sin x + h\cos x - \sin x}{h}$$

$$= \lim_{h \to 0} \frac{\sin x - \frac{1}{2}h^2 \sin x + h\cos x - \sin x}{h}$$

$$= \lim_{h \to 0} (\cos x - \tfrac{1}{2}h \sin x)$$

$$= \cos x$$

So if $y = \sin x$

$$\frac{dy}{dx} = \cos x$$

You must be able to reproduce this result from first principles.

It is left to the reader to obtain the next two results.

If $y = \cos x$

$$\frac{dy}{dx} = -\sin x$$

Hint: follow the same steps as before, but this time use $\cos(A + B) = \cos A \cos B - \sin A \sin B$.

$$\text{If} \quad y = \tan x$$
$$\frac{dy}{dx} = \sec^2 x$$

Hint: write $\tan x$ as $\frac{\sin x}{\cos x}$ then differentiate using the quotient rule.

Remember that the angle x must always be measured in radians. In the rest of this book whenever we use calculus with trigonometric functions, the assumption is made that the angles are given in radians.

Example 1

Find $\frac{dy}{dx}$ in each of the following:

a $y = \cos x$

$$\frac{dy}{dx} = -\sin x$$

b $y = 3\tan x$

$$\frac{dy}{dx} = 3\sec^2 x$$

c $y = 2\sin x + \cos x$

$$\frac{dy}{dx} = 2\cos x - \sin x$$

d $y = \sin 4x$

Let $u = 4x$

So $y = \sin u$

$$\frac{dy}{dx} = \frac{dy}{du} \times \frac{du}{dx}$$
$$= \cos u \times 4$$
$$\frac{dy}{dx} = 4\cos 4x$$

e $y = \cos 3x^2$

Let $u = 3x^2$

So $y = \cos u$

$$\frac{dy}{dx} = \frac{dy}{du} \times \frac{du}{dx}$$
$$= -\sin u \times 6x$$
$$\frac{dy}{dx} = -6x \sin 3x^2$$

In **d** and **e** observe that

$$\frac{d}{dx}[\sin f(x)] = f'(x)\cos f(x)$$
$$\frac{d}{dx}[\cos f(x)] = -f'(x)\sin f(x)$$

and similarly

$$\frac{d}{dx}[\tan f(x)] = f'(x)\sec^2 f(x)$$

We use this as a quick method to avoid the use of the substitution $u = f(x)$.

Example 2

Find $\frac{dy}{dx}$.

a $y = \sin 4x^2$

$$\frac{dy}{dx} = 8x\cos 4x^2$$

b $y = 2\tan 3x$

$$\frac{dy}{dx} = 2 \times 3 \times \sec^2 3x$$
$$= 6\sec^2 3x$$

c $y = \cos\left(\frac{x}{5}\right)$

$$\frac{dy}{dx} = -\frac{1}{5}\sin\left(\frac{x}{5}\right)$$

Example 3

Find $\frac{dy}{dx}$.

a $y = \sin^2 x$

$y = (\sin x)^2$

$\frac{dy}{dx} = 2(\sin x)^1 \times \cos x$

$= 2\sin x \cos x$

[Function of a function]

b $y = \cos^3 4x$

$y = (\cos 4x)^3$

$\frac{dy}{dx} = 3(\cos 4x)^2 \times (-4\sin 4x)$

$= -12\cos^2 4x \sin 4x$

c $y = x^2 \tan 7x$

$\frac{dy}{dx} = x^2 \times 7\sec^2 7x + (\tan 7x) \times 2x$

$= 7x^2 \sec^2 7x + 2x \tan 7x$

d $y = \sqrt{\sin 4x}$

$y = (\sin 4x)^{\frac{1}{2}}$

$\frac{dy}{dx} = \frac{1}{2}(\sin 4x)^{-\frac{1}{2}} \times (\cos 4x) \times 4$

$= 2\frac{\cos 4x}{\sqrt{\sin 4x}}$

Example 4

Find the equation of the tangent to the curve $y = \cos x$ at the point $\left(\frac{\pi}{6}, \frac{\sqrt{3}}{2}\right)$.

$y = \cos x$

$\frac{dy}{dx} = -\sin x$

At $x = \frac{\pi}{6}$, $\frac{dy}{dx} = -\sin\frac{\pi}{6} = -\frac{1}{2}$

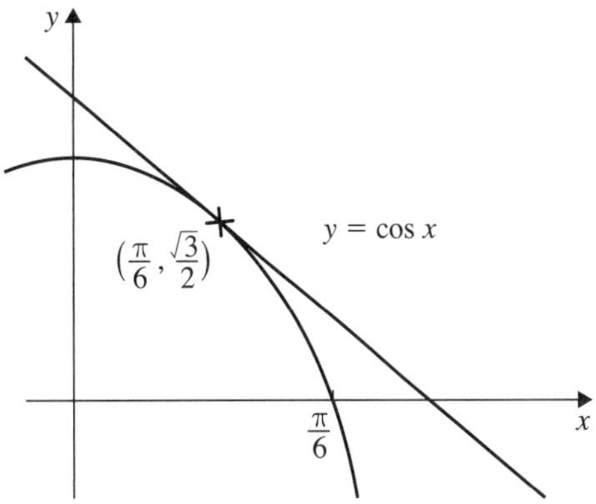

The tangent passes through $\left(\frac{\pi}{6}, \frac{\sqrt{3}}{2}\right)$.

The equation of the tangent is

$y - \frac{\sqrt{3}}{2} = -\frac{1}{2}\left(x - \frac{\pi}{6}\right)$

$2y - \sqrt{3} = -x + \frac{\pi}{6}$

$2y + x = \sqrt{3} + \frac{\pi}{6}$

Exercise 7F

1 Differentiate the following with respect to x:

a $\sin x$ **b** $\cos 3x$ **c** $4\tan x$

d $\sin 6x$ **e** $\cos\frac{3}{2}x$ **f** $5\sin 2x$

g $\tan\frac{1}{2}x$ **h** $10\cos x + \sin x$ **i** $\tan x - \cos x$

j $\sin(x + 1)$ **k** $\tan(2x - 1)$ **l** $-\cos\frac{1}{2}x$

2 Find $\dfrac{dy}{dx}$ in the following:

a $y = (\sin x)^2$ **b** $y = 3(\cos x)^2$ **c** $y = \sin^3 x$

d $y = 2\cos^3 x$ **e** $y = \sqrt{\cos x}$ **f** $y = \cos^2 4x$

g $y = \tan^2 9x$ **h** $y = x + \sqrt{\sin x}$ **i** $y = (\sin 2x)^{\frac{3}{2}}$

3 Differentiate the following with respect to x:

a $x \sin x$ **b** $x \cos 2x$ **c** $x^2 \sin x$

d $\sin x \cos x$ **e** $\dfrac{\cos x}{x}$ **f** $\dfrac{\sin 2x}{x^2}$

g $\dfrac{x}{\sin x}$ **h** $\dfrac{x^3}{\cos x}$ **i** $\dfrac{\cos x}{\sin x}$

4 Prove from first principles that the derivative of $\cos x$ is $-\sin x$.

5 Differentiate $\dfrac{\sin x}{\cos x}$ to show that $\dfrac{d}{dx}(\tan x) = \sec^2 x$.

6 Find the gradient of each curve at the point given:

a $y = 3\sin 2x$ at $\left(\dfrac{\pi}{2}, 0\right)$. **b** $y = 4\sin x - \cos x$ at $(0, -1)$.

c $y = (\cos 2x)^4$ at $\left(\dfrac{\pi}{8}, \dfrac{1}{4}\right)$. **d** $y = x\tan x$ at $\left(\dfrac{\pi}{4}, \dfrac{\pi}{4}\right)$.

7 Given that $y = \cos 2x$, show that $\dfrac{d^2y}{dx^2} = -4y$.

8 Given that $y = \sin x + \cos x$, show that $\dfrac{d^2y}{dx} + y = 0$.

9 Find the equation of the tangent to the curve $y = \tan x$ at the point $\left(\dfrac{\pi}{4}, 1\right)$.

10 Differentiate with respect to x:

a $\sin \pi x$ **b** $\tan 2\pi x$ **c** $\cos(x - \pi)$

d $\cos \dfrac{\pi}{2} x$ **e** $\sin x^2$ **f** $\tan x^3$

g $\sin(2x - \pi)$ **h** $\sin \dfrac{x}{\pi}$ **i** $\sin^2 x^2$

11 Consider the curve $y = \sin x^2$ for $0 \leqslant x \leqslant \dfrac{\pi}{2}$.

Find the x coordinates of the two points on the curve where the gradient is zero.

12 Show that the equation of the tangent to the curve $y = \sin x$ at the point $(\pi, 0)$ is $y + x = \pi$.

13 Find the equation of the normal to the curve $y = x - \cos x$ at the point where $x = \dfrac{\pi}{2}$.

14 Show that, at $x = \frac{\pi}{4}$, $\frac{d}{dx}(\sin^2 x + \cos^3 x) = \frac{2\sqrt{2} - 3}{2\sqrt{2}}$.

15 Find the maximum value of $y = x + \sin 2x$ for $0 < x < \frac{\pi}{2}$.

16 Find the minimum value of $y = \tan x - 8 \sin x$ which is given by a value of x between 0 and $\frac{\pi}{2}$.

17 Show that for $0 < x < \frac{\pi}{2}$, $f(x) = x \sin x + \cos x$ is an increasing function.

18 **a** If $y = \frac{1 + \cot x}{1 - \cot x}$, show that $\frac{dy}{dx} = \frac{2}{\sin 2x - 1}$.

b Find the gradient of the curve at $x = \frac{\pi}{12}$.

19 The tangent to the curve $y = \cos 2x$ at the point where $x = -\frac{\pi}{6}$ meets the y-axis at the point Y.

Find the distance OY where O is the origin.

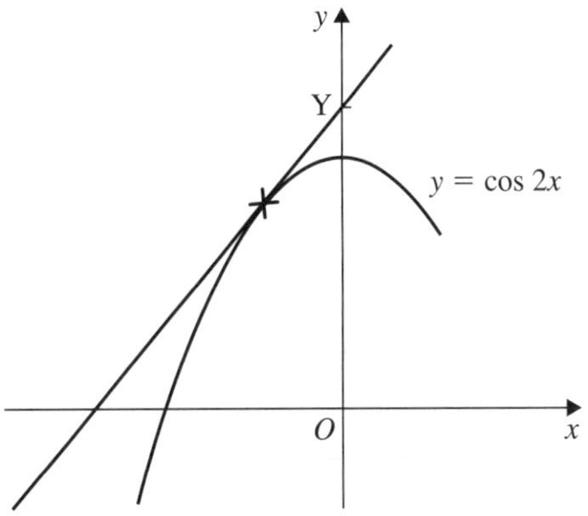

20 Given $f(\theta) = 4 \cos \theta - \sin^2 \theta$, find $f'\left(\frac{\pi}{2}\right)$.

21 Find the coordinates of the stationary points on the curve $y = \sin x + \cos x$ for $0 \leq x \leq 2\pi$.
Determine the nature of each point.

22 **a** If $y = \sin x (\cos x)^2$, find $\frac{dy}{dx}$.

b Find the three values of x between 0 and π radians at which $\frac{dy}{dx} = 0$.

Give your answers as decimals correct to 2 dp.

23 **a** Find the equation of the tangent to the curve $y = \sin x$ at the point where $x = \frac{4\pi}{3}$.

b Find the coordinates of the point where this tangent meets the y-axis.

24 **a** Find the gradient of the curve $y = \sin \pi x$ at the point where $x = 1$.

b Find the equation of the normal to the curve $y = \sin \pi x$ at the point where $x = 1$.

Derivatives of cosec x, cot x and sec x

The derivatives of cosec x, cot x and sec x can be found as follows:

a $y = \operatorname{cosec} x = \dfrac{1}{\sin x} = (\sin x)^{-1}$

$$\frac{dy}{dx} = -(\sin x)^{-2}\cos x$$
$$= -\frac{\cos x}{\sin^2 x}$$
$$= -\frac{1}{\sin x} \times \frac{\cos x}{\sin x}$$
$$= -\operatorname{cosec} x \cot x$$

b $y = \sec x = \dfrac{1}{\cos x} = (\cos x)^{-1}$

$$\frac{dy}{dx} = -(\cos x)^{-2}(-\sin x)$$
$$= \frac{\sin x}{\cos^2 x} = \frac{1}{\cos x} \times \frac{\sin x}{\cos x}$$
$$= \sec x \tan x$$

c $y = \cot x = (\tan x)^{-1}$

$$\frac{dy}{dx} = -(\tan x)^{-2}\sec^2 x$$
$$= -\frac{\cos^2 x}{\sin^2 x} \times \frac{1}{\cos^2 x}$$
$$= -\operatorname{cosec}^2 x$$

In summary:

$$\frac{d}{dx}(\operatorname{cosec} x) = -\operatorname{cosec} x \cot x$$
$$\frac{d}{dx}(\sec x) = \sec x \tan x$$
$$\frac{d}{dx}(\cot x) = -\operatorname{cosec}^2 x$$

Some people learn these results, while others, including the authors of this book, can never remember them and work them out each time!

EXERCISE 7G

1 Differentiate with respect to x:

a cosec x **b** cot x **c** sec $2x$ **d** cot $3x$
e cosec $4x$ **f** $2\cot x$ **g** $\sec(2x+1)$ **h** $x^2 + \sin x + \sec x$

2 Find $\dfrac{dy}{dx}$:

a $y = (\cot x)^2$ **b** $y = (\sec x)^2$ **c** $y = \tan x \sec x$
d $y = \sec^2 3x$ **e** $y = x \sec x$ **f** $y = x^2 \cot 2x$
g $y = \dfrac{\sec x}{x}$ **h** $y = \dfrac{x^2}{\cot x}$ **i** $y = (1 + \sec x)^2$

3 Show that $\dfrac{d}{dx}\left(\dfrac{\tan x}{1 + \sec x}\right) = \dfrac{1}{1 + \cos x}$

4 Given that $y = \cot x$, show that $\dfrac{d^2y}{dx^2} = 2(1 + y^2)y$.

5 If $y = \sqrt{\sec x + \tan x}$, show that $\dfrac{dy}{dx} = \dfrac{1}{2}y \sec x$.

6 Work out $\displaystyle\int \frac{2 + \cos x}{\sin^2 x}\,dx$.

7.7 Differentiating inverse trigonometric functions

We can differentiate inverse trigonometric functions as follows.

Consider $y = \arcsin x$

We can write $x = \sin y$

and so $\dfrac{dx}{dy} = \cos y$

Now, $\sin^2 y + \cos^2 y = 1$

$$x^2 + \cos^2 y = 1$$

$$\cos^2 y = 1 - x^2$$

$$\cos y = \sqrt{1 - x^2}$$

So $\dfrac{dx}{dy} = \sqrt{1 - x^2}$

and finally $\dfrac{dy}{dx} = \dfrac{1}{\sqrt{1 - x^2}}$

Example 1

Find the derivative of $\operatorname{arcsec}(x)$, giving your answer in terms of x.

Let $\operatorname{arcsec}(x) = y$

then $x = \sec(y)$

and $\dfrac{dx}{dy} = \sec(y)\tan(y)$

Now, using $\tan^2(y) + 1 = \sec^2(y)$

we have $\tan^2(y) = \sec^2(y) - 1$

$$= x^2 - 1$$

$$\tan(y) = \sqrt{x^2 - 1}$$

So $\dfrac{dx}{dy} = \sec(y)\tan(y)$

$$= x\sqrt{x^2 - 1}$$

and finally $\dfrac{dy}{dx} = \dfrac{1}{x\sqrt{x^2 - 1}}$

Exercise 7H

1 Show that if $y = \arccos(x)$, then $\dfrac{dy}{dx} = \dfrac{-1}{\sqrt{1 - x^2}}$

2 Show that the derivative of $\arctan(x)$ is $\dfrac{1}{1 + x^2}$

3 Differentiate the following:

a $\arcsin(2x)$ **b** $\arccos(x + 1)$ **c** $\arctan\left(\dfrac{x}{3}\right)$ **d** $\arcsin\left(\dfrac{x + 1}{2}\right)$

e $\arctan(x^2)$ **f** $\operatorname{arccosec}(x)$ **g** $\operatorname{arccot}(x)$ **h** $\arccos(3 - x)$

i $x^3 \arcsin(x)$ **j** $e^{\arccos(x)}$

7.8 Further questions on differentiation

Here is a summary of the results used in this section.

$$\frac{dy}{dx} = \frac{dy}{du} \times \frac{du}{dx} \quad \text{(chain rule)}$$

$$\frac{d}{dx}(uv) = u\frac{dv}{dx} + v\frac{du}{dx} \qquad \frac{d}{dx}\left(\frac{u}{v}\right) = \frac{v\frac{du}{dx} - u\frac{dv}{dx}}{v^2}$$

$$\frac{d}{dx}(e^x) = e^x \qquad \frac{d}{dx}(\ln x) = \frac{1}{x} \qquad \frac{d}{dx}(a^{kx}) = k\ln a(a^{kx})$$

$$\frac{d}{dx}(\sin x) = \cos x \qquad \frac{d}{dx}(\cos x) = -\sin x \qquad \frac{d}{dx}(\tan x) = \sec^2 x$$

$$\frac{dy}{dx} = \frac{1}{\frac{dx}{dy}}$$

In this section you will do questions where more than one of these results may be required.

Example 1

Find $\frac{dy}{dx}$.

a $y = e^x \sin x^2$

$$\frac{dy}{dx} = e^x(\cos x^2)2x + \sin x^2 e^x \quad \text{(product rule)}$$
$$= e^x(2x\cos x^2 + \sin x^2)$$

b $y = e^{2x}\ln(1 + x)$

$$\frac{dy}{dx} = e^{2x} \times \frac{1}{(1 + x)} + \ln(1 + x) \times 2e^{2x} \quad \text{(product rule)}$$
$$= e^{2x}\left[\frac{1}{1 + x} + 2\ln(1 + x)\right]$$

c $y = \frac{\sin 4x}{e^x}$

$$\frac{dy}{dx} = \frac{e^x \times 4\cos 4x - \sin 4x \times e^x}{(e^x)^2} \quad \text{(quotient rule)}$$
$$= \frac{4\cos 4x - \sin 4x}{e^x}$$

Example 2

Find the equation of the tangent to the curve $y = e^x \sin x$ at the point $(\pi, 0)$.

$$y = e^x \sin x$$
$$\frac{dy}{dx} = e^x \cos x + \sin x\, e^x$$
$$= e^x(\cos x + \sin x)$$

At $x = \pi$, $\frac{dy}{dx} = e^{\pi}(\cos \pi + \sin \pi)$

$$= -e^{\pi}$$

Equation of tangent at $(\pi, 0)$ is $y - 0 = -e^{\pi}(x - \pi)$

$$y = e^{\pi}(\pi - x)$$

Example 3

If $x = \sin y$, find $\frac{dy}{dx}$ in terms of x.

$$x = \sin y$$

Differentiate both sides with respect to y.

$$\frac{dx}{dy} = \cos y$$

$$\frac{dy}{dx} = \frac{1}{\frac{dx}{dy}} = \frac{1}{\cos y}$$

Now $\sin^2 y + \cos^2 y = 1$

$$\cos^2 y = 1 - \sin^2 y$$

$$\cos y = \sqrt{1 - \sin^2 y}$$

$$= \sqrt{1 - x^2}$$

$$\therefore \quad \frac{dy}{dx} = \frac{1}{\sqrt{1 - x^2}}$$

Example 4

If $x = \ln 5y$, find $\frac{dy}{dx}$ in terms of x.

$$x = \ln 5y$$

$$e^x = 5y$$

$$y = \tfrac{1}{5}e^x$$

$$\therefore \quad \frac{dy}{dx} = \frac{1}{5}e^x$$

EXERCISE 7I

1 Differentiate the following:

a $\ln x$ **b** $\ln(2x)$ **c** $2\ln(3x)$

d $x + \ln(2x)$ **e** $5e^x + \ln(3x)$ **f** $2e^x + 5\ln x$

2 **a** Find the exact coordinates of the stationary point of the curve $y = \ln x - 3x + 1$.

b Show that this is a local maximum.

3 **a** Find the exact coordinates of the stationary point of the curve $y = \ln(4x) - x - 2$.

b Show that this is a local maximum.

4 **a** Show that the curve $y = \ln(2x) + x^2$ passes through $\left(\frac{1}{2}, \frac{1}{4}\right)$.

b Find the equation of the normal to $y = \ln(2x) + x^2$, at $\left(\frac{1}{2}, \frac{1}{4}\right)$.

5 Find the equation of the tangent to the curve $y = \ln x + x^2 + 3x$ at the point $(1, 4)$.

6 Find $\frac{dy}{dx}$ in the following:

a $y = 5e^x$ **b** $y = 7e^x$ **c** $y = 5e^{4x}$

d $y = \ln(x + 1)$ **e** $y = \frac{4}{e^x}$ **f** $y = (e^{3x} + 1)^2$

g $y = 2e^x + \ln 3x$ **h** $y = \frac{5e^{3x} + 2e^{2x}}{e^{2x}}$ **i** $y = \frac{e^x + 1}{e^x - 1}$

7 If $y = (e^{\frac{x}{2}} + 1)(e^{\frac{x}{2}} - 1)$ then find $\frac{dy}{dx}$.

8 Differentiate the following:

a $y = \ln(x^2)$ **b** $y = \ln(2x^3)$ **c** $y = \ln(\sqrt{x})$

d $y = \ln\left(\frac{1}{x}\right)$ **e** $y = \ln(\sqrt{9x})$ **f** $y = \ln\left(\frac{1}{\sqrt[3]{x}}\right)$

9 Find $\frac{dy}{dx}$ in the following:

a $y = (x + 1)^2$ **b** $y = (2x + 1)^7$ **c** $y = (3x - 5)^8$

d $y = 5(3x - 7)^3$ **e** $y = (4x + 13)^{-3}$ **f** $y = \frac{1}{(5x - 2)^4}$

g $y = (4x + 11)^{\frac{1}{2}}$ **h** $y = \sqrt[3]{(15x - 17)}$ **i** $y = (ax + b)^n$

10 Show that the equation of the tangent to the curve $y = 2e^x$ at the point where $x = \frac{1}{2}$ is $y = \sqrt{e}(2x + 1)$.

11 Find the turning point of the curve $y = x^2 - 2\ln x$, where $x > 0$, and show that this is a local minimum.

12 Find the turning point of the curve $y = x - e^x$ and show that this is a local maximum.

13 Find $\frac{dy}{dx}$ in the following:

a $y = x \ln x$ **b** $y = x^2 e^x$ **c** $y = \sin x \cos x$

d $y = \sqrt{x}e^x$ **e** $y = e^x \tan x$ **f** $y = x \cot x$

g $y = e^x \operatorname{cosec} x$ **h** $y = x^3 \sec x$ **i** $y = x^3 \cos x$

14 If $y = x^n e^x$ then show that $\frac{dy}{dx} = x^{n-1}e^x(x + n)$.

15 Find $\frac{dy}{dx}$ in the following, simplifying and factorising where possible:

a $y = \frac{\ln x}{x}$ **b** $y = \frac{e^x}{x^2}$ **c** $y = \frac{\sec x}{e^x}$

d $y = \frac{\sin x}{\cos x}$ **e** $y = \frac{\cos x}{\sin x}$ **f** $y = \frac{x^2}{e^x}$

g $y = \frac{x + 1}{\sqrt{x}}$ **h** $y = \frac{x^3}{\cos x}$ **i** $y = \frac{\cot x}{x^2}$

16 **a** If $y = \frac{2x + 3}{\sqrt{x}}$ then show that $\frac{dy}{dx} = \frac{2x - 3}{2x\sqrt{x}}$.

b Show that the turning point is at $\left(\frac{3}{2}, 2\sqrt{6}\right)$.

17 The gradient of the curve $y = e^x(ax^2 + bx + c)$ is zero at $x = 1$ and at $x = -2$. The curve passes through the point $(0, -1)$. Find the values of a, b and c.

18 Find $\frac{dy}{dx}$ in the following:

a $y = \sin 2x$ **b** $y = e^{5x}$ **c** $y = e^{\sin x}$

d $y = \cos(x^2)$ **e** $y = e^{\sec x}$ **f** $y = \operatorname{cosec}\left(3x + \frac{\pi}{3}\right)$

g $y = \cot(3x)$ **h** $y = \ln(x^3 + 3)$ **i** $y = \ln(\sin 2x)$

j $y = \ln(\cos x)$ **k** $y = e^{x^3}$ **l** $y = \ln(\sec x)$

m $y = (x^2 + 1)^3$ **n** $y = \sin^3 x$ **o** $y = \tan^3(2x)$

19 If $x = \cos y$, find $\frac{dy}{dx}$. Give your answer in terms of x.

20 If $x = \sin 2y$, find $\frac{dy}{dx}$ in terms of x.

21 Find $\frac{dy}{dx}$, in terms of x:

a $x = \tan y$ **b** $x = \tan 3y$ **c** $x = e^{2y}$

d $x = e^{-y}$ **e** $x = \ln 5y$ **f** $x = \ln y^2$

g $x = \sin\left(2y - \frac{\pi}{6}\right)$

22 **a** Consider $x = y^2$, $y \geqslant 0$. Find $\frac{dy}{dx}$, using $\frac{dy}{dx} = \frac{1}{\frac{dx}{dy}}$.

b Write $y = \sqrt{x}$ and find $\frac{dy}{dx}$. Confirm that your result is the same as that obtained in part **a**.

23 Express $\frac{dy}{dx}$ in terms of $f(x)$ and $f'(x)$:

a $y = f(x)^n$ **b** $y = e^{f(x)}$ **c** $y = \sin(f(x))$

24 **a** If $\log_a x = p$, $\log_e a = q$ and $\log_e x = r$ then write down three equations involving p, q and r without logarithms.

b Hence show that $p = \frac{r}{q}$.

c Hence express $\log_a x$ in terms of $\ln x$ and $\ln a$ and so show that if $y = \log_a x$ where a is a constant then $\frac{dy}{dx} = \frac{1}{x \ln a}$.

Review Exercise 7J

1 Differentiate the following with respect to x:

a $y = (3x - 1)^4$ **b** $y = 5(3x - 4)^3$ **c** $y = (4x + 3)^{-2}$

d $y = \frac{1}{(5x - 1)^3}$ **e** $y = \frac{1}{(2 - 3x)^4}$ **f** $y = (3x + 1)^{\frac{1}{2}}$

2 Differentiate the following with respect to x:

a $y = (x^2 + 3)^4$ **b** $y = (2 - x^3)^5$ **c** $y = (3x^2 + 1)^5$

d $y = (x^2 + x)^4$ **e** $y = \left(1 + \frac{1}{x}\right)^3$ **f** $y = \left(x^2 + \frac{1}{x}\right)^{-3}$

3 Differentiate with respect to x, simplify your results:

a $y = x(x + 1)^3$ **b** $y = (x + 1)(2x - 3)^4$

c $y = (x + 1)^3(x - 1)^2$ **d** $y = x^2(3x - 2)^2$

4 Sketch the curve $y = (x - 1)^2(x + 1)$, showing the coordinates of

a the points where it meets the axes

b the turning points.

5 Find the coordinates of the turning points of the curve $y = (x - 2)(x + 3)^2$. Determine the nature of each turning point.

6 Differentiate with respect to x:

a $\frac{x^2}{x + 1}$ **b** $\frac{\sqrt{x + 1}}{x}$ **c** $\frac{x + 2}{x + 1}$

d $\frac{e^{3x}}{x^2}$ **e** $\frac{3 - 2x}{x^2}$ **f** $\frac{\sin x}{x}$

7 Show that the curve $y = \frac{x^3}{(1 + x^4)^{\frac{1}{2}}}$ has a positive gradient for all values of x except at $x = 0$.

8 Differentiate the following with respect to x:

a $y = e^x$ **b** $y = -3e^x$ **c** $y = \frac{1}{2}e^x$

d $y = 2x^3 - 4e^x$ **e** $y = 3(e^x - x^{\frac{1}{2}})$ **f** $y = \frac{1}{2}(x^{\frac{1}{3}} - \frac{1}{2}e^x)$

9 Differentiate the following with respect to x:

a $y = \ln x$ **b** $y = 4\ln x$ **c** $y = \ln 2x$

d $y = \ln x^2$ **e** $y = \ln x^{\frac{1}{2}}$ **f** $y = \ln\left(\frac{x}{2}\right)$

g $y = \ln\left(\frac{1}{x}\right)$

10 Find the gradient of the following curves at the given points:

a $y = e^x - x$: $x = 2$

b $y = 3e^x - 2x$: $x = 0$

c $y = \ln 2x - \sqrt{x}$: $x = 4$

d $y = x^3 - 3\ln x^2$: $x = 2$

11 Find the equation of the tangent to the following curves at the given point:

a $y = e^x$: $x = 0$

b $y = \ln x$: $x = 1$

c $y = 1 - e^x$: $x = 2$

12 Find the equation of the normal to the following curves at the given point:

a $y = e^x$: $x = 1$

b $y = \ln x^2$: $x = 3$

13 Find the coordinates of the stationary point of the following curves and show whether it is a maximum or a minimum:

a $y = e^x - x$ **b** $y = e^x + e^{-x}$ **c** $y = -x + \ln x$

d $y = 2x^2 - \ln x$ **e** $y = \ln x - 8x + 1$

14 The curve $y = \frac{\ln x}{x}$ cuts the x-axis at A and has a maximum point at B. Find the coordinates of A and B.

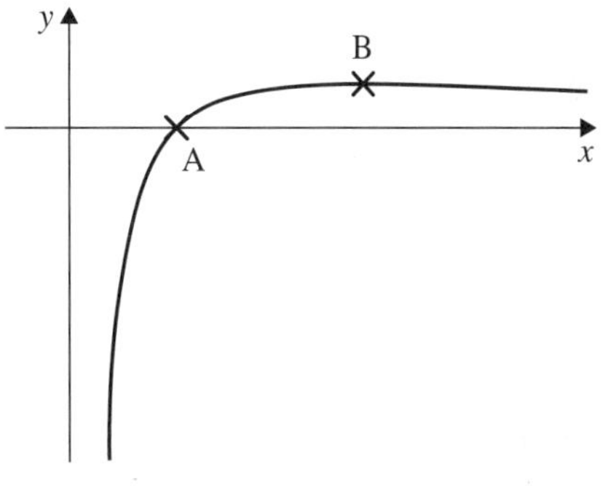

15 If $y = (e^x + 1)^2$, show that $\frac{dy}{dx} = 2e^x(e^x + 1)$.

16 Differentiate the following with respect to x:

a $\sin x + 3$ **b** $2\cos x$ **c** $\sin x + \cos x$

d $2\sin x - 3\cos x$ **e** $\tan x + x^2 + 4$ **f** $3\sin x - \tan x$

17 Find the gradient of the following curves at the given point:

a $y = \sin x$: $x = \frac{\pi}{3}$

b $y = \cos x$: $x = \frac{\pi}{2}$

c $y = \cos x + \sin x \quad : \quad x = \dfrac{\pi}{4}$

d $y = x + \cos x \quad : \quad x = \dfrac{\pi}{6}$

e $y = 3 - \cos 2x \quad : \quad x = \dfrac{\pi}{12}$

18 Find the equation of the tangent to the curve $y = x - \cos x$ where $x = \dfrac{\pi}{2}$.

19 Find the equation of the normal to the curve $y = 2\sin x + \cos x$ where $x = \dfrac{\pi}{2}$.

20 Differentiate the following with respect to x:

a $y = \sin 3x$ **b** $y = \cos 4x$ **c** $y = \tan 5x$

d $y = \sin^2 x$ **e** $y = \tan^4 x$ **f** $y = \sin\left(2x + \dfrac{\pi}{4}\right)$

g $y = \sqrt{\sin x}$ **h** $y = \sin^2 3x$ **i** $y = \cos^3 2x$

21 Differentiate the following with respect to x:

a $y = e^{2x}$ **b** $y = e^{-3x}$ **c** $y = e^{x^2}$

d $y = \dfrac{1}{e^x}$ **e** $y = e^{\sin x}$ **f** $y = \ln(x^2 + 1)$

g $y = \ln(x^3 - 2)$ **h** $y = \ln(x^3 + 2x - 1)$ **i** $y = \ln\left(\dfrac{x^2 + 1}{x - 1}\right)$

j $y = \ln\left(\dfrac{1}{x^2 + 3}\right)$ **k** $y = e^{\ln x}$ **l** $y = e^{\sqrt{x}}$

22 Show that if $y = (e^x + e^{-x})^2$ then $\dfrac{dy}{dx} = 2(e^{2x} - e^{-2x})$.

23 Given that $y = e^x \ln(1 + \sin x)$, find $\dfrac{dy}{dx}$ in terms of x.

24 Differentiate with respect to x:

a $y = x e^x$ **b** $y = x \ln x$ **c** $y = e^x \ln x$

d $y = x \sin x$ **e** $y = x^2 \cos x$ **f** $y = e^x \tan x$

25 The diagram shows a right circular cone of slant height ℓ.

a Show that the volume V of the cone is given by $V = \frac{1}{3}\pi\ell^3 \sin^2\theta \cos\theta$.

b Given that ℓ is constant and that θ varies, find the maximum value of V in terms of ℓ and π.

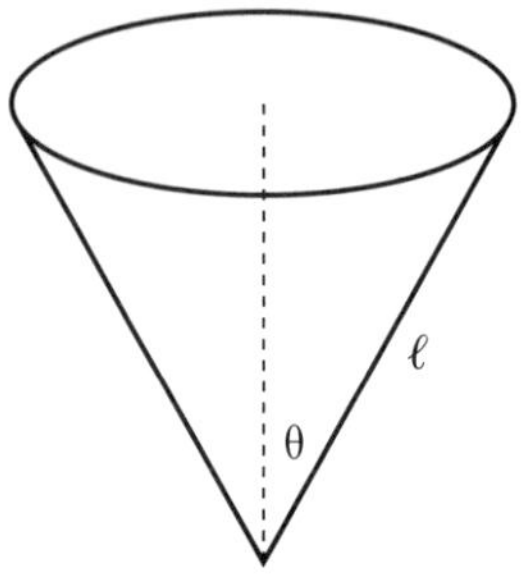

26 Find the coordinates of the points on the curve $y = \sin x \cos^3 x$ where the gradient is zero. Work in the range $0 < x < \pi$.

27 Differentiate the following with respect to x:

a $y = \sin^2 x \cos x$ **b** $y = \ln(2x + 5)$ **c** $y = \sin 2x \cos 3x$

d $y = e^{x^2 + 2}$ **e** $y = (\ln x)^2$ **f** $y = \sin x^2$

28 Find $\frac{dy}{dx}$:

a $y = \sec x$ **b** $y = \operatorname{cosec} x$ **c** $y = \cot x$

29 Find the gradient of the curve $y = \sec 3x$ at the point where $x = \frac{\pi}{9}$.

30 Find the coordinates of the stationary point on the curve $y = 2x - \ln(x^4)$ and determine the nature of this stationary point.

31 Use $\frac{dy}{dx} = \frac{1}{\frac{dx}{dy}}$ to find $\frac{dy}{dx}$ in terms of x for the following:

a $x = \sin y$ **b** $x = e^{3y}$ **c** $x = \ln y$ **d** $x = \ln 2y$

32 Given that $x = y^3 \ln 2y, \quad y > 0$

a Find $\frac{dx}{dy}$

b Use your answer to part **a** to find, in terms of e, the value of $\frac{dy}{dx}$ at $y = e$.

33 Given that $y = \frac{e^x}{x^2 - 3}$, find the x coordinates of the two points on the curve where the gradient is zero.

Examination Exercise 7

1 a i Differentiate $(x^2 + 1)^{\frac{5}{2}}$ with respect to x.

ii Given that $y = e^{2x}(x^2 + 1)^{\frac{5}{2}}$, find the value of $\frac{dy}{dx}$ when $x = 0$.

b A curve has equation $y = \frac{4x - 3}{x^2 + 1}$. Use the quotient rule to find the x-coordinates of the stationary points of the curve.

[AQA, GCE Mathematics, C3, June 2014]

2 i Differentiate with respect to x:

a $y = x^3 \ln 2x$

b $y = (x + \sin 2x)^3$

Given that $x = \cot y$,

ii show that $\dfrac{dy}{dx} = \dfrac{-1}{1 + x^2}$ [EDEXCEL, GCE Mathematics, C3, Jan 2013]

3 **a** Given that $y = (4x + 1)^3 \sin 2x$, find $\dfrac{dy}{dx}$.

b Given that $y = \dfrac{2x^2 + 3}{3x^2 + 4}$, show that $\dfrac{dy}{dx} = \dfrac{px}{(3x^2 + 4)^2}$, where p is a constant.

c Given that $y = \ln\left(\dfrac{2x^2 + 3}{3x^2 + 4}\right)$, find $\dfrac{dy}{dx}$.

[AQA, GCE Mathematics, C3, June 2016]

4 **a** Given that $y = x^4 \tan 2x$, find $\dfrac{dy}{dx}$.

b Find the gradient of the curve with equation $y = \dfrac{x^2}{x - 1}$ at the point where $x = 3$. [AQA, GCE Mathematics, C3, June 2013]

5 For each of the following curves, find the gradient at the point with x-coordinate 2.

i $y = \dfrac{3x}{2x + 1}$

ii $y = \sqrt{4x^2 + 9}$ [OCR, GCE Mathematics, C3, Jan 2013]

6

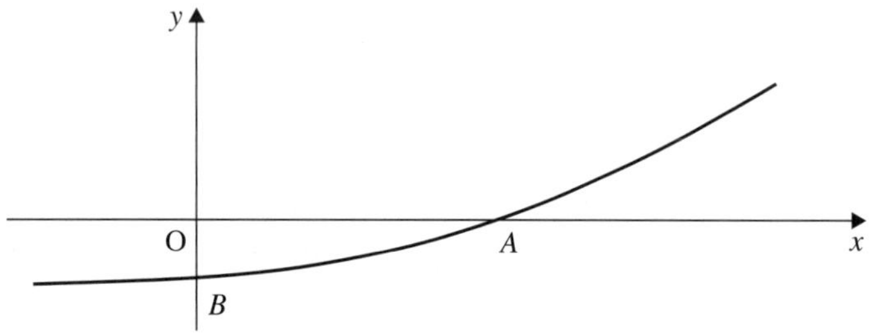

The diagram shows the curve with equation

$$x = (y + 4) \ln (2y + 3).$$

The curve crosses the x-axis at A and the y-axis at B.

i Find an expression for $\dfrac{dx}{dy}$ in terms of y.

ii Find the gradient of the curve at each of the points A and B, giving each answer correct to 2 dp. [OCR, GCE Mathematics, C3, Jan 2013]

7 Given that $y = 4x^2 \ln x$, find the value of $\dfrac{d^2y}{dx^2}$ when $x = e^2$.

[OCR, GCE Mathematics, C3, June 2014]

8 The curve C has equation $y = \mathrm{f}(x)$ where

$$\mathrm{f}(x) = \frac{4x + 1}{x - 2}, \quad x > 2$$

a Show that

$$\mathrm{f}'(x) = \frac{-9}{(x - 2)^2}$$

Given that P is a point on C such that $\mathrm{f}'(x) = -1$,

b find the coordinates of P. [EDEXCEL, GCE Mathematics, C3, June 2014]

9 a Find $\frac{dy}{dx}$ when

$$y = e^{3x} + \ln x$$

b i Given that $u = \frac{\sin x}{1 + \cos x}$, show that $\frac{du}{dx} = \frac{1}{1 + \cos x}$.

ii Hence show that if $y = \ln\left(\frac{\sin x}{1 + \cos x}\right)$, then $\frac{dy}{dx} = \operatorname{cosec} x$.

[AQA, GCE Mathematics, C3, Jan 2013]

10 A curve has equation $y = x^3 \ln x$.

a Find $\frac{dy}{dx}$.

b i Find an equation of the tangent to the curve $y = x^3 \ln x$ at the point on the curve where $x = e$.

ii This tangent intersects the x-axis at the point A. Find the exact value of the x-coordinate of the point A. [AQA, GCE Mathematics, C3, June 2012]

11 Find the equation of the tangent to the curve

$$y = 3x^2(x + 2)^6$$

at the point $(-1, 3)$, giving your answer in the form $y = mx + c$.

[OCR, GCE Mathematics, C3, June 2016]

12 a i Find $\frac{dy}{dx}$ when $y = xe^{2x}$.

ii Find an equation of the tangent to the curve $y = xe^{2x}$ at the point $(1, e^2)$.

b Given that $y = \frac{2 \sin 3x}{1 + \cos 3x}$, use the quotient rule to show that

$$\frac{dy}{dx} = \frac{k}{1 + \cos 3x}$$

where k is an integer. [AQA, GCE Mathematics, C3, June 2011]

13 Find the equation of the normal to the curve $y = \frac{x^2 + 4}{x + 2}$ at the point $(1, \frac{5}{3})$, giving your answer in the form $ax + by + c = 0$, where a, b and c are integers.

[OCR, GCE Mathematics, C3, Jan 2012]

14 A curve has equation $y = 2\ln(2e - x)$.

a Find $\dfrac{dy}{dx}$.

b Find an equation of the normal to the curve $y = 2\ln(2e - x)$ at the point on the curve where $x = e$. [AQA, GCE Mathematics, C3, June 2014]

15 The point P is the point on the curve $x = 2\tan\left(y + \dfrac{\pi}{12}\right)$ with y-coordinate $\dfrac{\pi}{4}$.

Find an equation of the normal to the curve at P.

[EDEXCEL, GCE Mathematics, C3, Jan 2012]

16

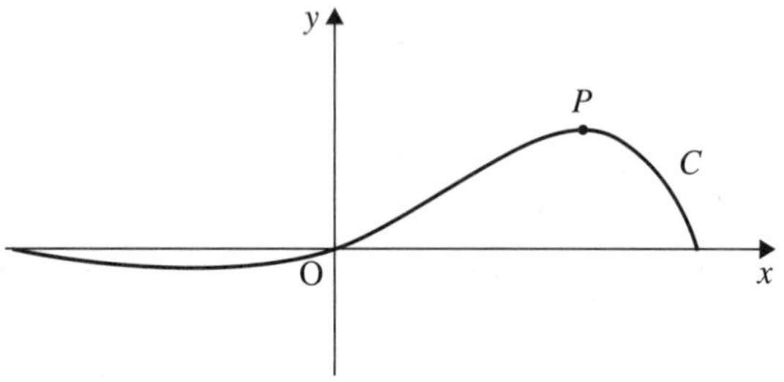

The diagram shows a sketch of the curve C which has equation

$$y = e^{x\sqrt{3}}\sin 3x, \quad -\frac{\pi}{3} \leqslant x \leqslant \frac{\pi}{3}$$

a Find the x-coordinate of the turning point P on C, for which $x > 0$. Give your answer as a multiple of π.

b Find an equation of the normal to C at the point where $x = 0$.

[EDEXCEL, GCE Mathematics, C3, June 2012]

17 **a** Given that $x = \dfrac{\sin y}{\cos y}$, use the quotient rule to show that

$$\frac{dx}{dy} = \sec^2 y$$

b Given that $\tan y = x - 1$, use a trigonometrical identity to show that

$$\sec^2 y = x^2 - 2x + 2$$

c Show that, if $y = \tan^{-1}(x - 1)$, then

$$\frac{dy}{dx} = \frac{1}{x^2 - 2x + 2}$$

d A curve has equation $y = \tan^{-1}(x - 1) - \ln x$.

i Find the value of the x-coordinate of each of the stationary points of the curve.

ii Find $\dfrac{d^2y}{dx^2}$. [AQA, GCE Mathematics, C3, June 2012]

PART 8

Numerical methods

8.1 Finding solutions to equations

We know how to find exact solutions to certain types of equations, for example quadratic equations, but there are many types of equations for which we cannot find exact solutions. For example suppose we want to solve $x^3 + x = 20$. We cannot factorise this and so we are left using trial and error to find the solutions to this equation.

We could rewrite the equation $x^3 + x = 20$ as $x^3 + x - 20 = 0$. If we put $f(x) \equiv x^3 + x - 20$ then we see that we are trying to solve $f(x) = 0$.

We can see that $f(1) = -18$, $f(2) = -10$ and $f(3) = 10$.
From this we can deduce that, since $f(2) < 0$ and $f(3) > 0$ and since $f(x)$ is a **continuous function** there must be a value of x between 2 and 3 for which $f(x) = 0$.

If we had to find x correct to 1 dp we would then need to try more values of x, using a calculator. We would create a table as follows:

x	$f(x)$
2	−10
2.1	−8.639
2.2	−7.152
2.3	−5.533
2.4	−3.776
2.5	−1.875
2.6	0.176
2.7	2.383
2.8	4.752
2.9	7.289
3	10

So we see that $f(2.5) < 0$ and $f(2.6) > 0$ and so we see that a solution to $f(x) = 0$ lies between 2.5 and 2.6.
If we want to know x to 1 dp we need to look at the x value of 2.55. We see that $f(2.55) < 0$. So we see that a solution to $f(x) = 0$ lies between 2.55 and 2.6. It is, therefore, 2.6 (to 1 dp).

It is worth noting that it would have been more efficient for us to have looked at the following values:

x	$f(x)$
2.05	−9.335
2.15	−7.912
2.25	−6.359
2.35	−4.672
2.45	−2.844
2.55	−0.869
2.65	1.26
2.75	3.547
2.85	5.999
2.95	8.622

The reason this is more efficient is that we can see that $f(2.55) < 0$ and $f(2.65) > 0$. So we see that a solution to $f(x) = 0$ lies between 2.55 and 2.65. It is, therefore, 2.6 (to 1 dp).

Note: When we saw that $f(2) = -10$ and $f(3) = 10$ we would have been wrong to have concluded that x must be exactly 2.5.

Example 1

Find the solution (to 1 dp) to the equation $x^3 - x - 100 = 0$.

If we let $f(x) = x^3 - x - 100$ we get the following table:

x	$f(x)$
3	−76
4	−40
5	20

So, since $f(4) < 0$ and $f(5) > 0$ there must be a value of x between 4 and 5 for which $f(x) = 0$. When we try more values between 4 and 5 we get the following:

x	$f(x)$
4.05	−37.6
4.15	−32.7
4.25	−27.5
4.35	−22
4.45	−16.3
4.55	−10.4
4.65	−4.11
4.75	2.422

From this we see that, since $f(4.65) < 0$ and $f(4.75) > 0$ there must be a value of x between 4.65 and 4.75 and so the solution is 4.7 (to 1 dp).

Example 2

Consider the function $f(x) = \frac{1}{x-2} = 0$. Explain why there is **no** solution between $x = 1$ and $x = 3$, despite the fact that $f(1) = -1 < 0$, and $f(3) = 1 > 0$.

If we look at the graph of $y = \frac{1}{x-2}$ it is clear that this function is **not continuous**.

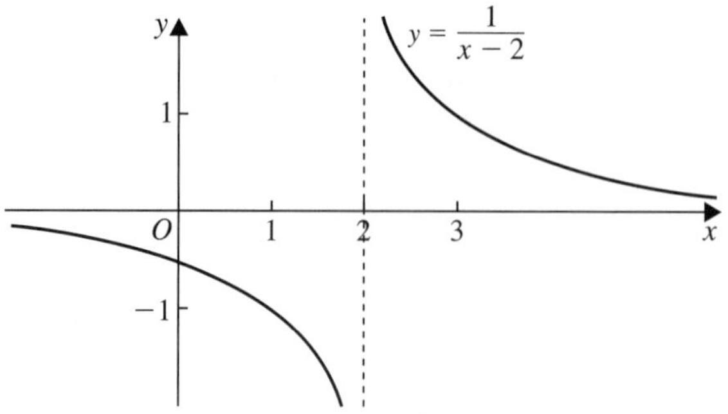

This method of finding solutions by looking for a change of sign is only valid if the function is **continuous**.

EXERCISE 8A

1 a Show that the equation $x^3 - 3x^2 - 5 = 0$ has a root between 3 and 4.
  b Find this root, to 1 dp, by trial and error.

2 a Show that the equation $x^3 - 11x - 21 = 0$ has a root between 4 and 5.
  b Find this root, to 1 dp, by trial and error.

3 The function $f(x) = x^5 - 3x - 1$ is such that there is a root of the equation $f(x) = 0$ between two consecutive negative integers.
  a Find these two integers.
  b Calculate the root to 1 dp.
  c Calculate also the positive root of the equation to 1 dp.

4 a Show by means of a graph that the equation $e^x = 9 - x^2$ has two real roots.
  b Show that one of these roots lies in the interval (1, 2).
  c Calculate this root to 1 dp.
  d Find an interval in the form $(a, a + 1)$ for the other root where a is an integer.

5 a Show graphically that the equation $3\cos x = x^2 + 1$ has exactly one positive real root.
  b Find an interval for this root in the form $\left(\frac{a}{10}, \frac{a+1}{10}\right)$ where a is an integer.
  (Note: Make sure that your calculator is in radians mode.)
  c Calculate this root to 1 dp.

6 a Given that $f(x) = e^{3x}\cos x - 5$, find (to 3 sf) f(1), f(2) and f(3).
  b Hence find an interval for a root of the equation $f(x) = 0$ in the form $(n, n + 1)$ where n is an integer.
  (Note: Make sure that your calculator is in radians mode.)
  c Calculate this root (to 2 dp).

7 a Show graphically that the equation $e^{x-2} = x^3$ has exactly two roots.
  b Find both roots to 1 dp.

8.2 Iteration

In Example 1 we looked to find a solution to $x^3 - x - 100 = 0$. Our only method was trial and error. If we were asked to find the solution to 5 dp it would take a long time, using many different values for x.
Having got one estimate for the solution, we want to have some method of generating a better estimate. We do this using an iterative method.

If we rearrange the equation $x^3 - x - 100 = 0$ we see that $x^3 = x + 100$ and so $x = \sqrt[3]{x + 100}$. So we see that the solution to $x^3 - x - 100 = 0$ is the x-coordinate of the intersection points of $y = x$ and $y = \sqrt[3]{x + 100}$.

Consider the iteration $x_{n+1} = \sqrt[3]{x_n + 100}$. We see that if this converges to a value of say α then we will get to the stage where $x_{n+1} = x_n = \alpha$. Hence we have $\alpha = \sqrt[3]{\alpha + 100}$ and so $\alpha^3 - \alpha - 100 = 0$.

So we see that if the iteration $x_{n+1} = \sqrt[3]{x_n + 100}$ converges to a value then this value is a solution to the equation $x^3 - x - 100 = 0$.

In order to create an iteration for an equation we need to rearrange the equation so that it is written in the form $x = \text{f}(x)$. The iteration formula is then $x_{n+1} = \text{f}(x_n)$.

Example 1

The equation $3^x = 8x$ has a root lying between $x = 0$ and $x = 1$. Use the iteration formula

$$x_{n+1} = \frac{3^{x_n}}{8}, \quad x_0 = 0.2$$

to find this root, correct to 3 dp.

Using the iteration formula $x_{n+1} = \dfrac{3^{x_n}}{8}$

$$x_0 = 0.2$$

$$x_1 = \frac{3^{0.2}}{8} = 0.1557\ldots$$

$$x_2 = \frac{3^{0.1557\ldots}}{8} = 0.148\,32\ldots$$

$$x_3 = \frac{3^{0.14832\ldots}}{8} = 0.147\,12\ldots$$

$$x_4 = \frac{3^{0.14712\ldots}}{8} = 0.146\,92\ldots$$

The solution is $x = 0.147$, correct to 3 dp, as x_3 and x_4 both round to give this value.

Note: you must **not** round at each stage. Instead, you should use the 'store' or 'Ans' function on your calculator.

In this example, each successive iteration got closer to the root from the **same direction**. If we look at a graph of these iterations we can see they form a series of 'steps', often referred to as a **staircase diagram**.

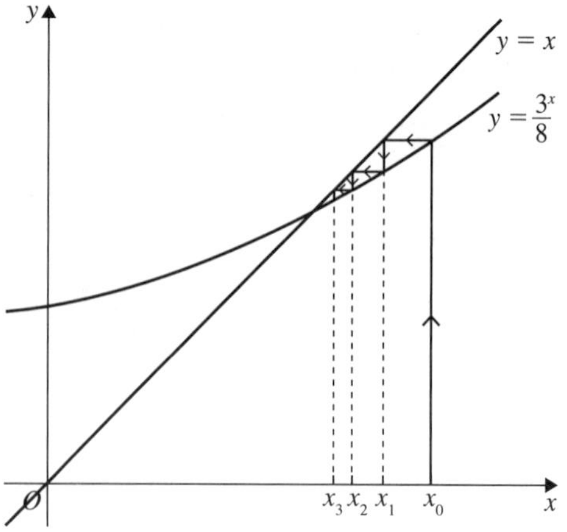

We read up from x_0 to the curve $y = \dfrac{3^x}{8}$ to find x_1 $\left(\text{because } x_1 = \dfrac{3^{x_0}}{8}\right)$.

We can then read up from x_1 to the curve $y = \dfrac{3^x}{8}$ to find x_2 $\left(\text{because } x_2 = \dfrac{3^{x_1}}{8}\right)$ and so on.

This staircase diagram shows graphically how each successive iteration is converging to the root of the equation $x = \dfrac{3^x}{8}$.

Example 2

a Find, correct to 3 dp, the value to which the iterative formula

$x_{n+1} = \dfrac{1}{x_n + 2}$, $x_0 = -1$, converges.

b Find the equation to which the value found in part **a** is a solution.

a $x_0 = -1$

$$x_1 = \frac{1}{-1 + 2} = 1$$

$$x_2 = \frac{1}{1 + 2} = 0.33333\ldots$$

$$x_3 = \frac{1}{0.33333\ldots + 2} = 0.42857\ldots$$

$x_4 = 0.41176\ldots$

$x_5 = 0.41463\ldots$

$x_6 = 0.41414\ldots$

$x_7 = 0.41422\ldots$

As both x_6 and x_7 round to 0.414, the iterative formula converges to 0.414 correct to 3 dp.

b Rearranging the iterative formula:

$$x = \frac{1}{x + 2}$$

$x^2 + 2x = 1$

$x^2 + 2x - 1 = 0$

This is the equation to which the value 0.414 is an approximate solution. In fact, as this is just a quadratic equation, we can use the quadratic formula to obtain an exact solution of $x = -1 + \sqrt{2}$ (= 0.414 to 3 dp).

In this example, each successive iteration alternates being above and below the root to which they are converging. The resulting graph is called a **cobweb diagram**.

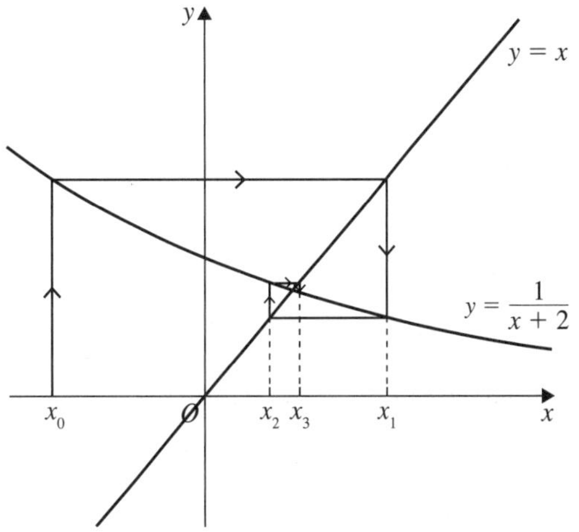

Note: not all iterations or starting values will converge to a root. Consider the equation $x^2 - x - 2 = 0$. This can be rearranged to give the iterative formula

$x_{n+1} = x_n^2 - 2$

If we take $x_0 = 3$

then $x_1 = 7$

$x_2 = 47$

$x_3 = 2207$

These iterations clearly **diverge** from the root.

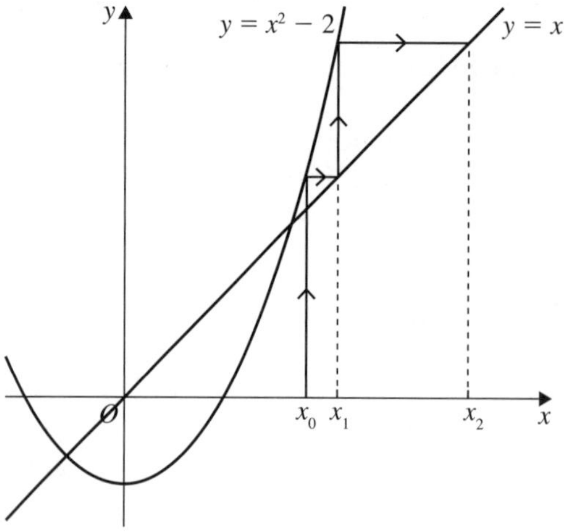

Exercise 8B

1 Find the values to which the following iterative formulae converge. Give answers correct to 3 dp:

a $x_{n+1} = \sqrt[3]{7x_n - 1}$ $\quad x_1 = 5$

b $x_{n+1} = \sqrt[3]{7x_n - 1}$ $\quad x_1 = -4$

c $x_{n+1} = \dfrac{x_n^3 + 1}{7}$ $\quad x_1 = 1$

d $x_{n+1} = \frac{1}{2}\left(x_n + \dfrac{74}{x_n}\right)$ $\quad x_1 = 8$

e $x_{n+1} = \dfrac{3x_n}{4} + \dfrac{5}{x_n^2}$ $\quad x_1 = 3$

f $x_{n+1} = \sin x_n + 1$ $\quad x_1 = 8$

2 Find the equations to which the numbers found in question **1** are solutions.

3 **a** Find the numbers to (3 dp) to which the following iterations converge:

i $x_{n+1} = \dfrac{2 - x_n^2}{3}$ with $x_1 = 1$

ii $x_{n+1} = -\sqrt{1 - 7x_n}$ with $x_1 = -2$

iii $x_{n+1} = \dfrac{2}{x_n + 5}$ with $x_1 = -2$.

b Find the equations to which these numbers are solutions.

c Hence find the *exact* values to which the values in **4 a** are approximations.

4 **a** Show that there is a solution to the equation $f(x) = 0$, where $f(x) = x^3 - 3x + 4$, in the interval $(-2, -3)$.

b Show that the equation $x = \dfrac{2x^3 - 4}{3x^2 - 3}$ can be rewritten as $x^3 - 3x + 4 = 0$.

c Use the iteration $x_{n+1} = \dfrac{2x_n^{\,3} - 4}{3x_n^{\,2} - 3}$ with $x_1 = -2$ to find the solution to 3 dp.

5 **a** Show that there is a solution to the equation $xe^x = 10$ in the interval $(1, 2)$.

b Show also that $xe^x = 10$ can be rearranged to give $x = \ln\left(\dfrac{10}{x}\right)$.

c Use the iteration $x_{n+1} = \ln\left(\dfrac{10}{x_n}\right)$ to find the solution to 1 dp.

6 Suppose the dimensions of a cuboid are $x \times y \times z$, where x is the length, y is the width and z is the height. Suppose also that the volume of the cuboid is $200\,\text{cm}^3$, the surface area is $240\,\text{cm}^3$ and that its length is twice its width.

a Write down three equations involving x, y and z.

b Find y and z in terms of x and hence show that $x^3 - 240x + 1200 = 0$.

c Use the iteration $x_{n+1} = \dfrac{(x_n)^3 + 1200}{240}$ to find x (to 2 dp) given that x is approximately 5 cm.

7 A man invested £1000 into a high interest bank on 1st January 2005. He put £1000 into this account at the beginning of each year – his final payment was on 1st January 2014. He closed the account on 1st January 2015 when it was worth £15,000.

a If the annual rate of interest is $p\%$ and $r = 1 + \dfrac{p}{100}$ then show that $r + r^2 + \ldots + r^{10} = 15$.

b Hence show that $r^{11} - 16r + 15 = 0$

$\left(\text{You may use } a + ar + ar^2 + \ldots + ar^{n-1} = \dfrac{a(r^n - 1)}{(r - 1)}.\right)$

c Use the iteration $r_{n+1} = \sqrt[11]{16r_n - 15}$ to find the annual rate of interest (to 2 sf) given that it is about 8% per year.

8 The graph below shows the number of visitors to a seaside resort from 1st December 2017 to 1st December 2018.

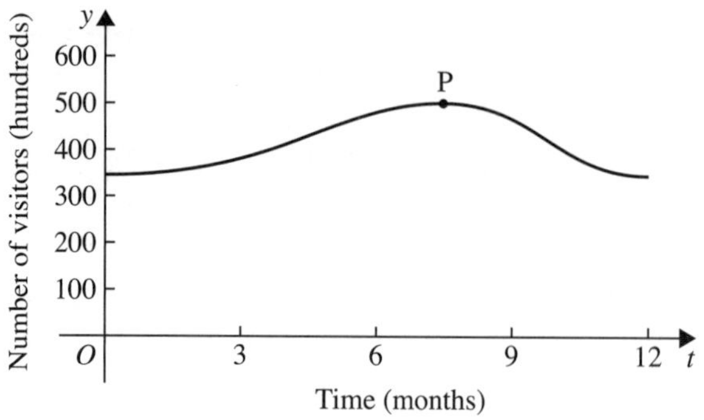

This graph can be modelled by the equation $y = \dfrac{(t-6)^4}{4} - t^2 + 13t + 5$

a Show that the value of t at point P can be found by solving the equation $(t-6)^3 - 2t + 13 = 0$

b Show that the iterative formula

$$t_{n+1} = \frac{(t_n - 6)^3 + 13}{2}$$

can be used to solve this equation.

c Use the iterative formula above to find the value of t correct to 2 dp.

9 The graph opposite shows the speed of a motorcyclist through a section of a road race.

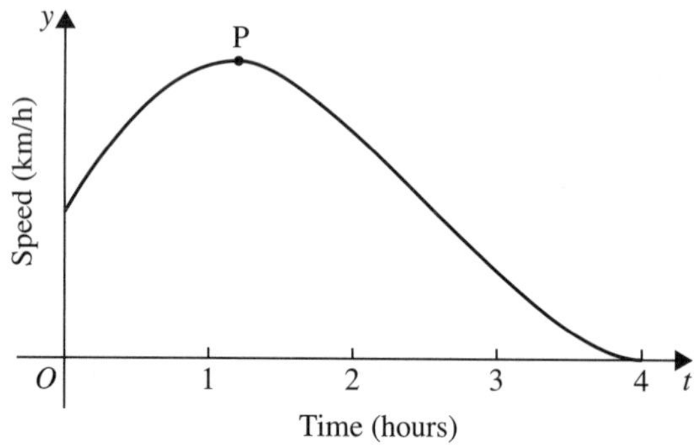

This graph can be modelled by the equation

$$y = -t^4 + 17t^3 - 83t^2 + 79t + 180$$

a Show that the iterative formula

$$t_{n+1} = \frac{-4t_n^{\,3} + 51t_n^{\,2} + 79}{166}$$

can be used to find the value of t at the maximum point P.

b Use the iterative formula above to find the value of t at P correct to 3 dp. Hence find the maximum speed of the motorcyclist through this section of the race.

8.3 The Newton–Raphson method

The Newton–Raphson method of finding the root of an equation uses the tangent to the curve.

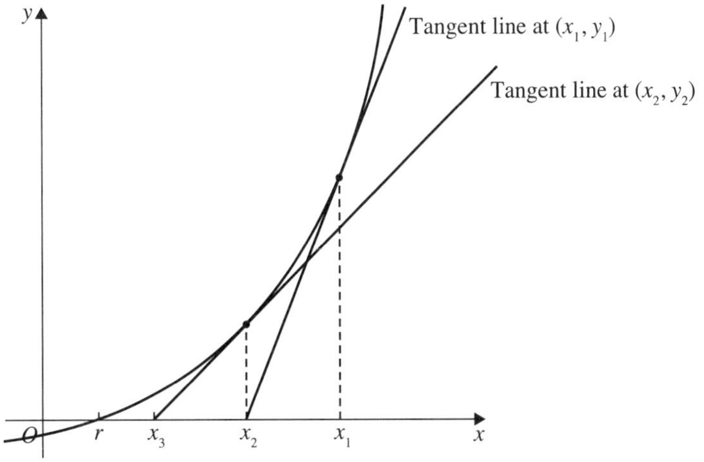

Consider the gradient of the tangent at (x_1, y_1), and in particular, the triangle made by $(x_2, 0)$, $(x_1, 0)$ and (x_1, y_1). We know that the gradient m is given by

$$m = \frac{\text{change in } y}{\text{change in } x}$$

$$= \frac{y_1 - 0}{x_1 - x_2}$$

Given that the gradient at (x_1, y_1) can also be denoted by $f'(x_1)$, and that $y_1 = f(x_1)$, we now have

$$f'(x_1) = \frac{f(x_1)}{x_1 - x_2}$$

This can be rearranged to give

$$x_2 = x_1 - \frac{f(x_1)}{f'(x_1)}$$

Extending this to a general formula gives us the Newton–Raphson formula:

$$x_{n+1} = x_n - \frac{f(x_n)}{f'(x_n)}$$

Example 1

Use the Newton–Raphson method to find the root of the equation $x^3 - 2x - 1 = 0$ in the interval $1 < x < 2$, giving your answer correct to 2 dp.

Let $f(x) = x^3 - 2x - 1$

so $f'(x) = 3x^2 - 2$

Using the bottom of the given interval as our starting value, we have $x_0 = 1$.

So $$x_1 = x_0 - \frac{f(x_0)}{f'(x_0)}$$
$$= 1 - \frac{(1)^3 - 2(1) - 1}{3(1)^2 - 2}$$
$$= 3$$

$$x_2 = x_1 - \frac{f(x_1)}{f'(x_1)}$$
$$= 3 - \frac{(3)^3 - 2(3) - 1}{3(3)^2 - 2}$$
$$= 2.2$$

$$x_3 = x_2 - \frac{f(x_2)}{f'(x_2)}$$
$$= 2.2 - \frac{(2.2)^3 - 2(2.2) - 1}{3(2.2)^2 - 2}$$
$$= 1.7808\ldots$$

$$x_4 = x_3 - \frac{f(x_3)}{f'(x_3)}$$
$$= 1.6363\ldots$$

$$x_5 = 1.6183\ldots$$

$$x_6 = 1.6180\ldots$$

So an approximate solution to the equation $x^3 - 2x - 1 = 0$ in the interval $1 < x < 2$ is 1.62 correct to 2 dp.

Note: you must *not* use rounded values within your calculations. Instead, you should use the memory function or 'Ans' button on your calculator.

EXERCISE 8C

1 $f(x) = x^3 + 5x - 10$

a Find $f'(x)$.

b Use the Newton–Raphson method to find the root of $f(x) = 0$ in the interval $1 < x < 2$, giving your answer correct to 2 dp.

2 Use the Newton–Raphson method to find the root of $x^3 - 7x^2 + 15 = 0$ in the interval $6 < x < 7$, giving your answer correct to 3 dp.

3 Use the Newton–Raphson method to find the root of $2x^3 + x^2 - 3x = 3$ in the interval $1 < x < 2$, giving your answer correct to 3 dp.

4 $f(x) = x^3 - 3x^2 + 1$

a Show that $f(x) = 0$ has a root between 2 and 3.

b Use the Newton–Raphson method to find this root correct to 2 dp. [Note: you will need to take $x_0 = 3$ rather than $x_0 = 2$. Why?]

5 The equation $\cos 2x + \frac{x}{2} - 1 = 0$ has a root in the interval $2 < x < 3$. Use the Newton–Raphson method to find this root correct to four significant figures.

6 Use the Newton–Raphson method to find the root of $\sin(x + 1) + \cos x = 0$ in the vicinity of $x = 1$. Give your answer correct to 3 dp.

7 $f(x) = e^{-x} + \frac{x^2}{2} - 4$

a Use a change of sign method to find an interval in which the root of $f(x) = 0$ lies.

b Use the Newton–Raphson method to calculate this root correct to 3 dp.

8 Find $\sqrt{7}$ correct to 3 dp by using the Newton–Raphson method.
[Hint: let $x = \sqrt{7}$, so $x^2 = 7$, then let $f(x) = x^2 - 7 = 0$]

9 Use the Newton–Raphson method to calculate $\sqrt{17}$ correct to 3 dp.

10 The graph opposite shows the temperature of a beaker of liquid cooling in a freezer.

This cooling process can be modelled by the equation

$$y = 5e^{-(x+1)} - \frac{x+1}{5}$$

Use the Newton–Raphson method to calculate the time at which the liquid freezes, giving your answer correct to 3 dp.

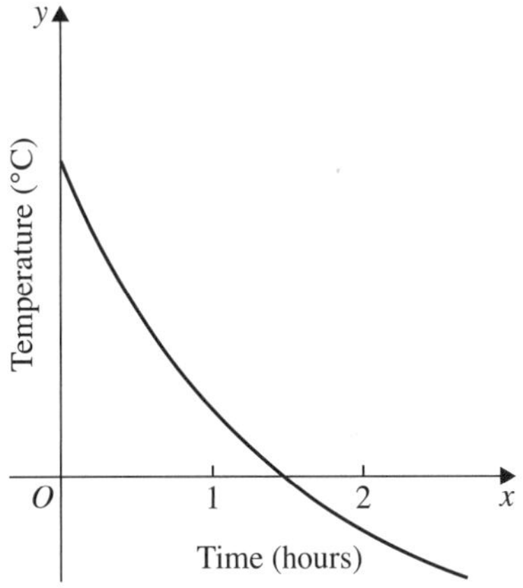

11 A ball is thrown from a window on a gusty day. Its height from the ground can be modelled by the equation $y = \cos x - \frac{x}{4}$, as shown by the graph opposite.

Use the Newton–Raphson method to find how long it takes for the ball to hit the ground, giving your answer correct to 3 dp.

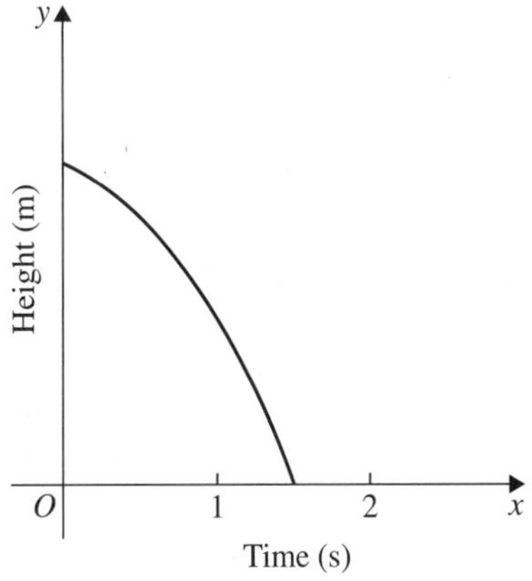

8.4 Numerical integration – the trapezium rule

The trapezium rule

Many functions cannot be integrated exactly. We can obtain an approximate answer by splitting the area under the curve into several trapeziums as illustrated below. When many trapeziums are used (say 100, 1000 ...) a computer can be used to give an answer to a high degree of accuracy.

The trapezium rule in a general case

Consider a curve $y = \mathrm{f}(x)$. The shaded area can be approximated using five trapeziums of width h.

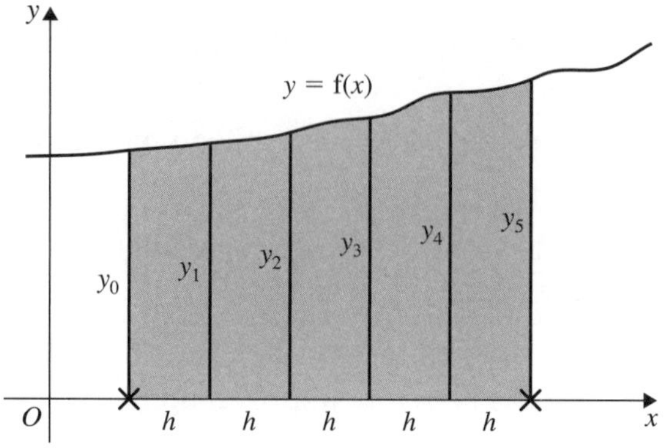

$$\text{Area} \approx \frac{h}{2}(y_0 + y_1) + \frac{h}{2}(y_1 + y_2) + \frac{h}{2}(y_2 + y_3) + \frac{h}{2}(y_3 + y_4) + \frac{h}{2}(y_4 + y_5)$$

$$\approx \frac{h}{2}[y_0 + 2(y_1 + y_2 + y_3 + y_4) + y_5]$$

↑ first ordinate ↑ 'middle' ordinates ↑ last ordinate

This is the trapezium rule, which can shorten the working when several trapeziums are used.

> In general
>
> $$\int_a^b y\,\mathrm{d}x \approx \frac{h}{2}[y_0 + 2(y_1 + y_2 + \ldots + y_{n-1}) + y_n]$$
>
> where $h = \dfrac{b - a}{n}$

Example 1

a Use the trapezium rule with four strips to find an approximate value for the area under the curve $y = \mathrm{e}^{\frac{x}{2}}$ between $x = 0$ and $x = 4$.

b State, with a reason, whether your answer is an overestimate or an underestimate.

a Calculate the values of y at $x = 0, 1, 2, 3, 4$

x	0	1	2	3	4
y	1	1.649	2.718	4.482	7.389

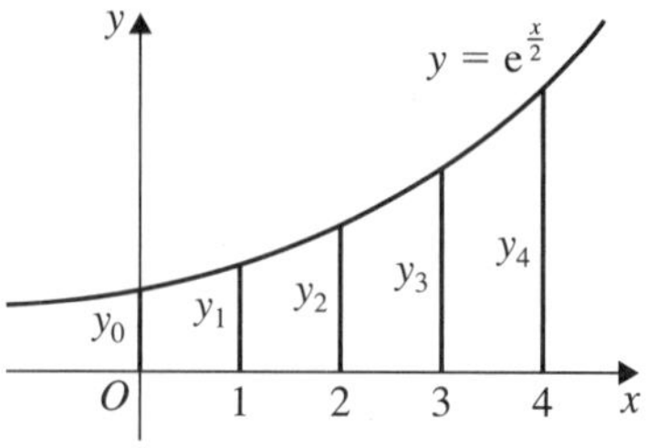

Using the trapezium rule, with $h = 1$,

$$\text{Area} = \tfrac{1}{2}[1 + 2(1.649 + 2.718 + 4.482) + 7.389]$$

$$= 13.0 \quad \text{correct to three significant figures.}$$

b The curvature of the graph $y = e^{\frac{x}{2}}$ is such that the straight lines that make up the tops of the trapeziums are all slightly *above* the actual graph. Therefore, our answer is an *overestimate*.

EXERCISE 8D

1 **a** Find an approximate value for the area under the curve $y = x^2$ between $x = 1$ and $x = 4$. (Divide the area into three trapeziums as shown.)

b State, with a reason, whether your estimate is above or below the actual value for the area.

c Confirm your result by working out $\int_1^4 x^2\,dx$.

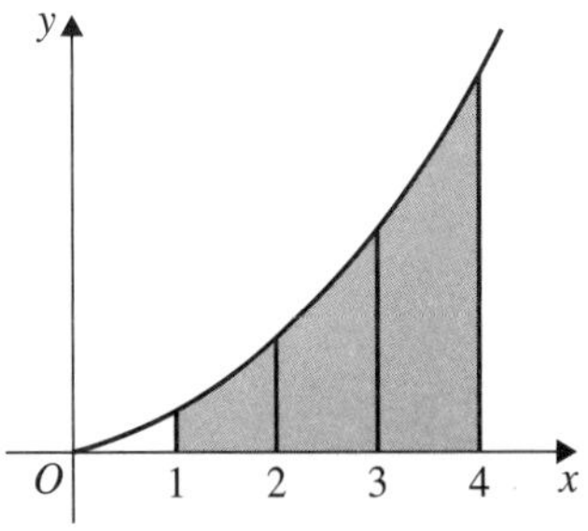

2 Using the trapezium rule, find an approximate value for the following integral, using four equally spaced ordinates.

$$\int_1^4 \frac{4}{x}\,dx.$$

3 Use the trapezium rule, with four trapeziums of width one unit, to evaluate approximately

$$\int_0^4 e^x\,dx.$$

4 Using the number of trapeziums indicated, find an approximate value for

$$\int_0^{\frac{\pi}{2}} \sin x\,dx:$$

a Using three trapeziums, width $\frac{\pi}{6}$.

b Using six trapeziums, width $\frac{\pi}{12}$.

5 Use the trapezium rule, with three trapeziums of equal width, to find an estimate for:

a $\int_0^{0.6} x^2\,dx$ **b** $\int_0^{\frac{\pi}{2}} \ln(1 + \cos x)\,dx$ **c** $\int_0^{\frac{\pi}{2}} \sin^2 x\,dx$

6 Using the trapezium rule with five equally spaced ordinates, find an approximate value for:

a $\int_{-1}^{1} e^{-2x}\,dx$ **b** $\int_{-\frac{\pi}{3}}^{\frac{\pi}{3}} \sec x\,dx$ (in radians) **c** $\int_0^2 (1 + \sin x)\,dx$

7 In the statistics of the Normal Distribution, it can be shown that approximately 95% of the distribution lies within ± 2 standard deviations of the mean.

This is given by the integral

$$\int_{-2}^{2} \frac{1}{\sqrt{2\pi}} e^{-\frac{x^2}{2}}\,dx \approx 0.95$$

Use the trapezium rule with four trapeziums to estimate the value of the integral.

REVIEW EXERCISE 8E

1 Show the following equations have a root in the given interval:

a $e^x - 3x = 0$	$(1, 2)$	
b $x^3 + x - 8 = 0$	$(1, 2)$	
c $2 + 3x - x^4 = 0$	$(1, 2)$	
d $x^2 = 3x - 1$	$(2, 3)$	
e $2x^3 + x^2 + 6x - 1 = 0$	$(0, 1)$	
f $\sin x - \ln x = 0$	$(2, 3)$	[x is in radians.]
g $e^{2x} + 4x - 5 = 0$	$(0, 1)$	
h $x^4 - 2x^2 - 7 = 0$	$(1, 2)$	
i $x^3 - 3x - 1 = 0$	$(-1, 0)$	

2 a Show that the equation $x^3 - x^2 + 5x - 3 = 0$ has a root between $x = 0$ and $x = 1$.

b Using the iterative formula

$$x_{n+1} = -\tfrac{1}{5}(x_n^3 - x_n^2 - 3), \text{ with } x_1 = 0,$$

find the root correct to 3 dp.

3 a Given $f(x) = 3 + 4x - x^4$, show that the equation $f(x) = 0$ has a root between 1 and 2.

b The iterative formula $x_{n+1} = (3 + 4x_n)^{\frac{1}{4}}$ may be used to obtain an approximate root of the equation $f(x) = 0$. Starting with $x_0 = 1.5$, use the formula to find a root of the equation correct to 2 dp.

4 The curve with equation $y = x^3 - 2x^2 - 1 = 0$ intersects the x-axis at the point where $x = \alpha$.

a Show that α lies between 2 and 3.

b Show that the equation $x^3 - 2x^2 - 1 = 0$ can be re-arranged in the form

$$x = 2 + \frac{1}{x^2}$$

c Use the iterative formula $x_{n+1} = 2 + \dfrac{1}{x_n^2}$, with $x_1 = 2$, to find x_4, giving your answer to three significant figures.

In the following questions show that the given equations have a root in the given interval.

Using the given iteration formula and starting value, find the root of the equation to 3 significant figures.

5 $x^3 - x + 3 = 0$ $\qquad -2 < x < -1$

$x_{n+1} = (x_n - 3)^{\frac{1}{3}}$ $\qquad x_0 = -1.5$

6 $x^2 - 5x + 3 = 0$ $\qquad 0 < x < 1$

$x_{n+1} = \dfrac{x_n^2 + 3}{5}$ $\qquad x_0 = 0.5$

7 $x^3 - x^2 - 2 = 0$ $\quad 1 < x < 2$

$x_{n+1} = \sqrt[3]{x_n^2 + 2}$ $\quad x_0 = 1.5$

8 $x^4 - 3x + 1 = 0$ $\quad 1 < x < 2$

$x_{n+1} = (3x_n - 1)^{\frac{1}{4}}$ $\quad x_0 = 1.3$

9 $3x - 2\sin x - 1 = 0$ $\quad 0 < x < 1$ (x in radians)

$x_{n+1} = \dfrac{2\sin x_n + 1}{3}$ $\quad x_0 = 0.8$

10 $e^x - x - 2 = 0$ $\quad -2 < x < -1$

$x_{n+1} = e^{x_n} - 2$ $\quad x_0 = -1.5$

11 $e^x - x^2 - 3 = 0$ $\quad 1 < x < 2$

$x_{n+1} = \ln(x_n^2 + 3)$ $\quad x_0 = 1.8$

12 The equation $x^3 - 3x + 5 = 0$ has a root in the interval $-3 < x < -2$. Use the Newton–Raphson method to find this root correct to four significant figures.

13 Use the Newton–Raphson method to find the root of $x^3 + 2x^2 - 3x + 1 = 0$ in the vicinity of $x = -3$. Give your answer correct to 3 dp.

14 $f(x) = x^4 - 10x$

a Use a change of sign method to find an interval in which a positive root of $f(x) = 0$ lies.

b Use the Newton–Raphson method to calculate this root correct to 2 dp.

15 The equation $x^2 \ln x = 2$ has a root in the interval [1, 2]. Use the Newton–Raphson method to find this root correct to 3 dp.

16 Using the trapezium rule, find an approximate value for the following using four trapeziums in each case.

a $\displaystyle\int_0^4 e^{x^2}\,dx$ $\quad$ **b** $\displaystyle\int_2^6 \ln x\,dx$ $\quad$ **c** $\displaystyle\int_0^{\frac{\pi}{2}} \sin 2x\,dx$

Examination Exercise 8

1 **a** It is given that the curves with equations $y = 6\ln x$ and $y = 8x - x^2 - 3$ intersect at a single point where $x = \alpha$.

i Show that α lies between 5 and 6.

ii Show that the equation $x = 4 + \sqrt{13 - 6\ln x}$ can be rearranged into the form

$$6\ln x + x^2 - 8x + 3 = 0$$

iii Use the iterative formula

$$x_{n+1} = 4 + \sqrt{13 - 6\ln x_n}$$

with $x_1 = 5$ to find the values of x_2 and x_3, giving your answers to 3 dp.

[AQA, GCE Mathematics, C3, June 2015]

2 $\quad \mathrm{f}(x) = 25x^2\mathrm{e}^{2x} - 16, \qquad x \in \mathbb{R}$

a Show that the equation $\mathrm{f}(x) = 0$ can be written as $x = \pm\frac{4}{5}\mathrm{e}^{-x}$.

The equation $\mathrm{f}(x) = 0$ has a root α, where $\alpha = 0.5$ to 1 dp.

b Starting with $x_0 = 0.5$, use the iteration formula

$$x_{n+1} = \tfrac{4}{5}\mathrm{e}^{-x_n}$$

to calculate the values of x_1, x_2 and x_3, giving your answers to 3 dp.

c Give an accurate estimate for α to 2 dp, and justify your answer.

[EDEXCEL, GCE Mathematics, C3, June 2013]

3 The real root of the equation $14 - x^2 = 3\ln x$ is denoted by α.

a Find by calculation the pair of consecutive integers between which α lies.

b Use the iterative formula $x_{n+1} = \sqrt{14 - 3\ln x_n}$, with a suitable starting value, to find α. Show the result of each iteration, and give α correct to 2 dp.

[OCR, GCE Mathematics, C3, June 2012]

4 The curve with equation $y = x^x$, where $x > 0$, intersects the line $y = 5$ at a single point, where $x = \alpha$.

a Show that α lies between 2 and 3.

b Show that the equation $x^x = 5$ can be rearranged into the form

$$x = \mathrm{e}^{\left(\frac{\ln 5}{x}\right)}$$

c Use the iterative formula

$$x_{n+1} = \mathrm{e}^{\left(\frac{\ln 5}{x_n}\right)}$$

with $x_1 = 2$ to find the values of x_2 and x_3, giving your answers to 3 dp.

[AQA, GCE Mathematics, C3, June 2016]

5 $\quad \mathrm{f}(x) = 2\sin(x^2) + x - 2, \quad 0 \leqslant x \leqslant 2\pi$

a Show that $\mathrm{f}(x) = 0$ has a root α between $x = 0.75$ and $x = 0.85$.

The equation $\mathrm{f}(x) = 0$ can be written as $x = [\arcsin(1 - 0.5x)]^{\frac{1}{2}}$.

b Use the iterative formula

$$x_{n+1} = [\arcsin(1 - 0.5x_n)]^{\frac{1}{2}}, \quad x_0 = 0.8$$

to find the values of x_1, x_2 and x_3, giving your answers to 5 dp.

c Show that $\alpha = 0.80157$ is correct to 5 dp.

[EDEXCEL, GCE Mathematics, C3, June 2011]

6 The diagram shows the curve $y = x^4 - 8x$.

i By sketching a second curve on a copy of the diagram, show that the equation

$$x^4 + x^2 - 8x - 9 = 0$$

has two real roots. State the equation of the second curve.

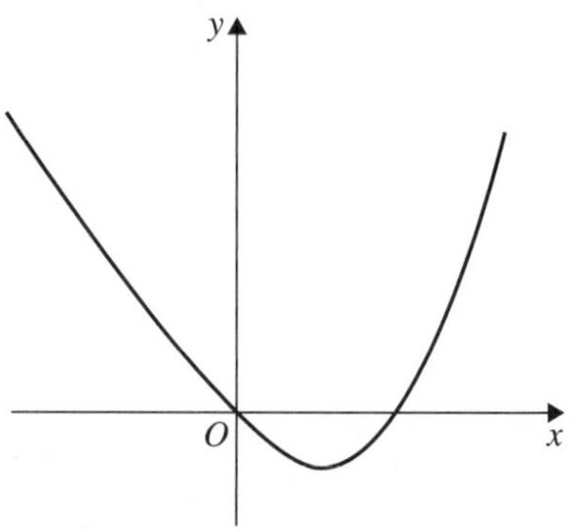

ii The larger root of the equation $x^4 + x^2 - 8x - 9 = 0$ is denoted by α.

a Show by calculation that $2.1 < \alpha < 2.2$.

b Use an iterative process based on the equation

$$x = \sqrt[4]{9 + 8x - x^2},$$

with a suitable starting value, to find α correct to 3 dp.
Give the result of each step of the iterative process.

[OCR, GCE Mathematics, C3, June 2014]

7 $$f(x) = x^3 + 3x^2 + 4x - 12$$

a Show that the equation $f(x) = 0$ can be written as

$$x = \sqrt{\frac{4(3 - x)}{(3 + x)}}, \quad x \neq -3$$

The equation $x^3 + 3x^2 + 4x - 12 = 0$ has a single root which is between 1 and 2.

b Use the iteration formula

$$x_{n+1} = \sqrt{\left(\frac{4(3 - x_n)}{(3 + x_n)}\right)}, \quad n \geqslant 0$$

with $x_0 = 1$ to find, to 2 dp, the value of x_1, x_2 and x_3.

The root of $f(x) = 0$ is α.

c By choosing a suitable interval, prove that $\alpha = 1.272$ to 3 dp.

[EDEXCEL, GCE Mathematics, C3, June 2012]

8 i By sketching the curves $y = \ln x$ and $y = 8 - 2x^2$ on a single diagram, show that the equation

$$\ln x = 8 - 2x^2$$

has exactly one real root.

ii Explain how your diagram shows that the root is between 1 and 2.

iii Use the iterative formula

$$x_{n+1} = \sqrt{4 - \tfrac{1}{2}\ln x_n},$$

with a suitable starting value, to find the root. Show all your working and give the root correct to 3 dp.

iv The curves $y = \ln x$ and $y = 8 - 2x^2$ are each translated by 2 units in the positive x-direction and then stretched by scale factor 4 in the y-direction. Find the coordinates of the point where the new curves intersect, giving each coordinate correct to 2 dp.

[OCR, GCE Mathematics, C3, Jan 2013]

9 a The equation $e^{-x} - 2 + \sqrt{x} = 0$ has a single root, α.
Show that α lies between 3 and 4.

b Use the recurrence relation $x_{n+1} = (2 - e^{-x_n})^2$, with $x_1 = 3.5$, to find x_2 and x_3, giving your answers to 3 dp.

c The diagram overleaf shows parts of the graphs of $y = (2 - e^{-x})^2$ and $y = x$, and a position of x_1.

On the diagram, draw a staircase or cobweb diagram to show how convergence takes place, indicating the positions of x_2 and x_3 on the x-axis.

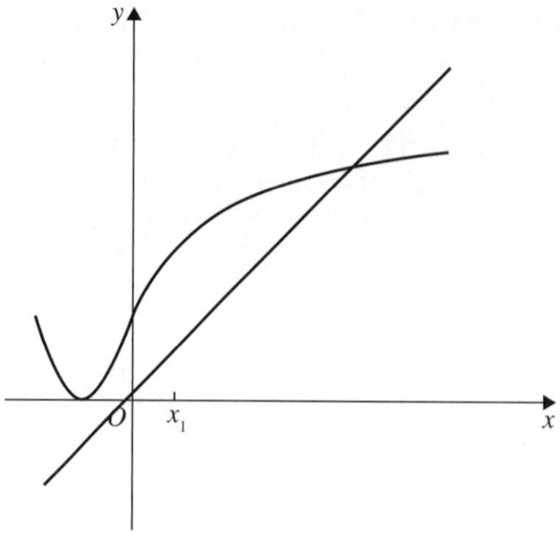

[AQA, GCE Mathematics, C3, June 2013]

10 $$\mathrm{f}(x) = 3x^2 - \frac{11}{x^2}$$

a Write down, to 3 dp, the value of f(1.3) and the value of f(1.4).

The equation $\mathrm{f}(x) = 0$ has a root α between 1.3 and 1.4.

b Taking 1.4 as a first approximation to α, apply the Newton–Raphson procedure once to $\mathrm{f}(x)$ to obtain a second approximation to α, giving your answer to 3 dp. [EDEXCEL, GCE Mathematics, FP1, Jan 2010]

11 a The equation $2x^3 + 5x^2 + 3x - 132\,000 = 0$ has exactly one real root α.

i Show that α lies in the interval $39 < \alpha < 40$.

ii Taking $x_1 = 40$ as a first approximation to α, use the Newton–Raphson method to find a second approximation, x_2, to α. Give your answer to 2 dp. [AQA, GCE Mathematics, FP1, June 2015]

12 Given that α is the only real root of the equation

$$x^3 - x^2 - 6 = 0$$

a show that $2.2 < \alpha < 2.3$

b Taking 2.2 as a first approximation to α, apply the Newton–Raphson procedure once to $\mathrm{f}(x) = x^3 - x^2 - 6$ to obtain a second approximation to α, giving your answer to 3 dp.

[EDEXCEL, GCE Mathematics, FP1, June 2009]

13 The diagram shows part of the curve with equation $y = f(x)$, where

$$f(x) = 1 - x - \sin(x^2).$$

The point A, with x-coordinate p, is a stationary point on the curve.

The equation $f(x) = 0$ has a root α in the interval $0.6 < \alpha < 0.7$.

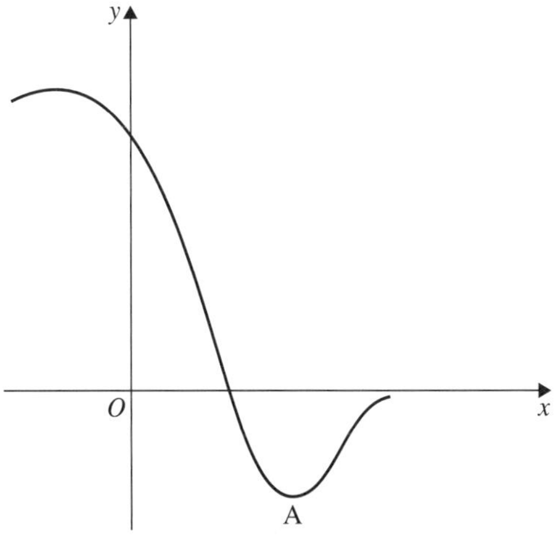

a Explain why $x_0 = p$ is not suitable to use as a first approximation to α when applying the Newton–Raphson procedure to $f(x)$.

b Using $x_0 = 0.6$ as a first approximation to α, apply the Newton–Raphson procedure once to $f(x)$ to find a second approximation to α, giving your answer to 3 dp.

c By considering the change of sign of $f(x)$ over an appropriate interval, show that your answer to part **b** is accurate to 3 dp.

[EDEXCEL, GCE Mathematics, FP1, Jan 2009]

14 It is required to solve the equation $\ln(x - 1) - x + 3 = 0$.

You are given that there are two roots, α and β, where $1.1 < \alpha < 1.2$ and $4.1 < \beta < 4.2$.

i The root β can be found using the iterative formula

$$x_{n+1} = \ln(x_n - 1) + 3.$$

a Using this iterative formula with $x_1 = 4.15$, find β correct to 3 dp. Show all your working.

b Explain with the aid of a sketch why this iterative formula will not converge to α whatever initial value is taken.

ii a Show that the Newton–Raphson iterative formula for this equation can be written in the form

$$x_{n+1} = \frac{3 - 2x_n - (x_n - 1)\ln(x_n - 1)}{2 - x_n}.$$

b Use this formula with $x_1 = 1.2$ to find α correct to 3 dp.

[OCR, GCE Mathematics, FP2, Jan 2013]

15 The diagram shows the curve

$$y = x^3 - x + 1$$

The equation $x^3 - x + 1 = 0$ has one real root, α.

i Taking $x_1 = -1$ as a first approximation to α, use the Newton–Raphson method to find a second approximation, x_2, to α.

ii On the figure, draw a straight line to illustrate the Newton–Raphson method as used in part **i**. Show the points $(x_2, 0)$ and $(\alpha, 0)$ on your diagram.

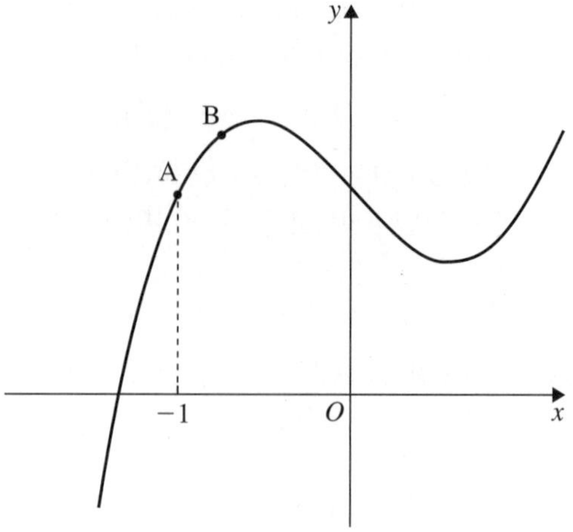

[AQA, GCE Mathematics, FP1, Jan 2008]

16 It is given that the equation $3x^3 + 5x^2 - x - 1 = 0$ has three roots, one of which is positive.

i Show that the Newton–Raphson iterative formula for finding this root can be written

$$x_{n+1} = \frac{6x_n^{\,3} + 5x_n^{\,2} + 1}{9x_n^{\,2} + 10x_n - 1}.$$

ii Apply the iterative formula in part **i** when the initial value is $x_1 = -1$. Describe the behaviour of the iterative sequence.

[OCR, GCE Mathematics, FP2, June 2015]

17 The diagram shows a sketch of part of the curve with equation $y = x^2 \ln x, \quad x \geqslant 1$

The finite region R, shown shaded, is bounded by the curve, the x-axis and the line $x = 2$

The table below shows corresponding values of x and y for $y = x^2 \ln x$

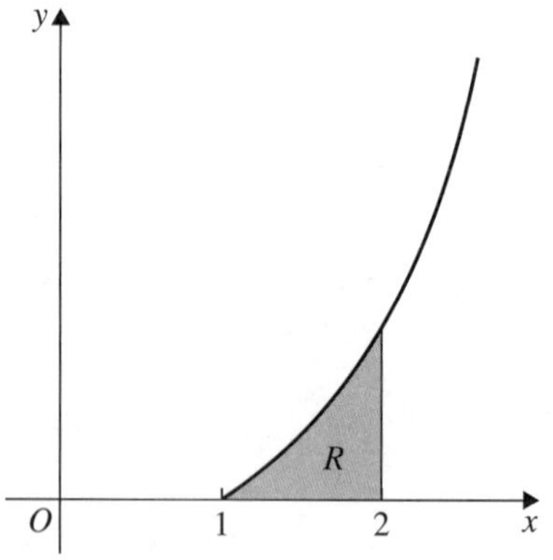

x	1	1.2	1.4	1.6	1.8	2
y	0	0.2625		1.2032	1.9044	2.7726

a Complete the table above, giving the missing value of y to 4 dp.

b Use the trapezium rule with all the values of y in the completed table to obtain an estimate for the area of R, giving your answer to 3 dp.

[EDEXCEL, GCE Mathematics, C4, June 2016]

18 Use the trapezium rule, with 3 strips each of width 2, to estimate the value of

$$\int_5^{11} \frac{8}{x}\,dx.$$

[OCR, GCE Mathematics, C2, June 2013]

19 **i** Use the trapezium rule, with 4 strips each of width 1.5, to estimate the value of

$$\int_4^{10} \sqrt{2x - 1}\, dx,$$

giving your answer correct to 3 significant figures.

ii Explain how the trapezium rule could be used to obtain a more accurate estimate. [OCR, GCE Mathematics, C2, June 2015]

20 **i** Use the trapezium rule, with 2 strips each of width 4, to show that an approximate value of $\int_1^9 4\sqrt{x}\, dx$ is $32 + 16\sqrt{5}$.

ii Use a sketch graph to explain why the actual value of $\int_1^9 4\sqrt{x}\, dx$ is greater than $32 + 16\sqrt{5}$.

iii Use integration to find the exact value of $\int_1^9 4\sqrt{x}\, dx$.

[OCR, GCE Mathematics, C2, June 2012]

21

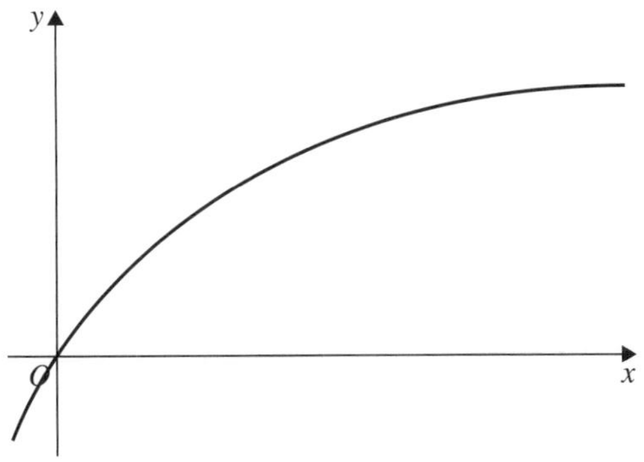

The diagram shows the curve $y = \log_{10}(2x + 1)$.

i Use the trapezium rule with 4 strips each of width 1.5 to find an approximation to the area of the region bounded by the curve, the x-axis and the lines $x = 4$ and $x = 10$. Give your answer correct to 3 significant figures.

ii Explain why this approximation is an under-estimate.

[OCR, GCE Mathematics, C2, Jan 2012]

Part 9

Parametric equations

9.1 Parametric and cartesian form

We are familiar with the idea of writing the equation of a curve in the form $y = f(x)$, where $f(x)$ is a function of x. When we write it in this form we are said to be using the cartesian form of the equation.

We could, however, choose to write the equation in terms of a parameter t.

Consider for example the curve given by $y = (x - 1)^2$.
This curve passes through the points (1, 0), (2, 1) etc.

We could write $y = (x - 1)^2$ by letting $t = x - 1$ and so $y = t^2$. In other words we would say $x = t + 1, y = t^2$.

If $t = 0$ we get $x = 1, y = 0$. So the curve passes through (1, 0).

If $t = 1$ we get $x = 2, y = 1$. So the curve passes through (2, 1).

When we write the curve in the form $x = t + 1, y = t^2$ we are using the parametric form since we are expressing both x and y in terms of the parameter t.

Example 1

A curve has parametric equations $x = t - 2, y = 3t^2, t \in \mathbb{R}$. Find the cartesian equation of this curve, stating its domain and range.

To find the cartesian equation we eliminate the parameter t.

$x = t - 2$ and so $t = x + 2$. From this we see that $y = 3t^2$
$= 3(x + 2)^2$.

So the cartesian form of the curve is $y = 3(x + 2)^2$.

In this example it is easiest to sketch the curve to find the domain and range:

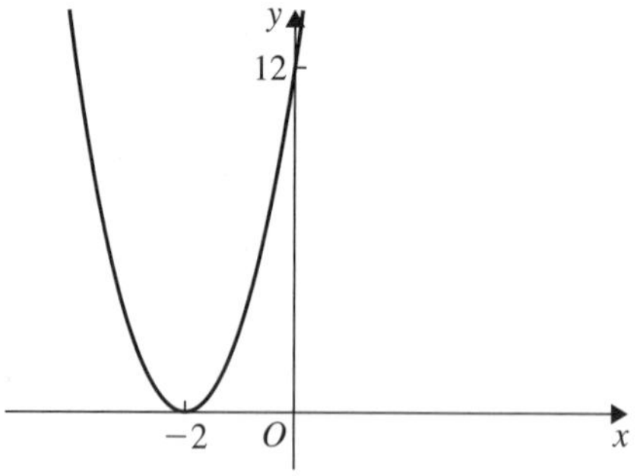

The domain is $x \in \mathbb{R}$, and the range is $y \in \mathbb{R}, y \geqslant 0$.

Example 2

A curve has parametric equations $x = t^3, y = 2t^2 + t, t \in \mathbb{R}$. Find the cartesian equation of this curve, and find its domain and range.

$x = t^3$ and so $t = \sqrt[3]{x}$. From this we see that $y = 2t^2 + t = 2x^{\frac{2}{3}} + x^{\frac{1}{3}}$.

So the cartesian form of the curve is $y = 2x^{\frac{2}{3}} + x^{\frac{1}{3}}$.

This curve is harder to sketch, so in this case it is easier to look at the original parametric equations for x and y to find the domain and range respectively.

Remember: the domain is all the values that x can take, and the range is all the values that y can take.

$$x = t^3, t \in \mathbb{R} \Rightarrow x \in \mathbb{R} \text{ is the domain}$$

$$y = 2t^2 + t, t \in \mathbb{R}$$

$$\frac{dy}{dt} = 4t + 1$$

$$0 = 4t + 1$$

$$-\tfrac{1}{4} = t \Rightarrow y = -\tfrac{1}{8} \text{ is the minimum value of } y.$$

Hence $y \in \mathbb{R}, y \geqslant -\frac{1}{8}$ is the range.

Example 3

A curve has parametric equations $x = 3\sin\theta, y = 2\cos\theta$.
Find the cartesian form of this curve, and its domain and range.

We will use the identity $\sin^2\theta + \cos^2\theta = 1$.

We have $\sin\theta = \dfrac{x}{3}$ and $\cos\theta = \dfrac{y}{2}$

$$\therefore \quad \left(\frac{x}{3}\right)^2 + \left(\frac{y}{2}\right)^2 = 1$$

$$\frac{x^2}{9} + \frac{y^2}{4} = 1$$

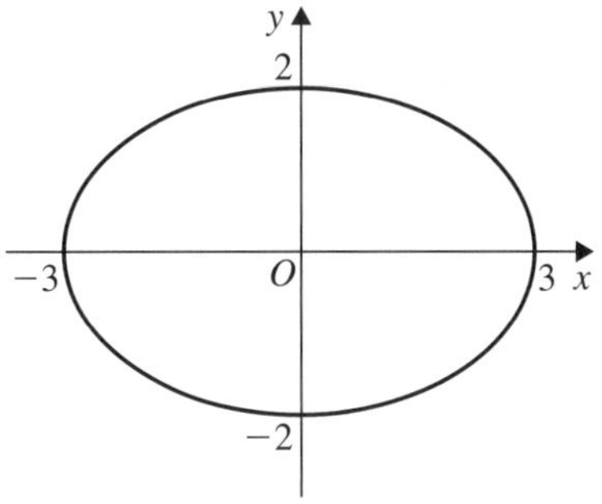

The curve is an ellipse, and its domain is $x \in \mathbb{R}$, $-3 \leqslant x \leqslant 3$ and its range is $y \in \mathbb{R}, -2 \leqslant y \leqslant 2$.

Example 4

Sketch the curve defined by the parametric equations $x = 3t^2, y = t^3, -3 \leqslant t \leqslant 3$.

We can find the corresponding cartesian equation:

$$y = t^3 \Rightarrow \sqrt[3]{y} = t$$

then $x = 3(\sqrt[3]{y})^2$ or $x = 3y^{\frac{2}{3}}$

Note: try to avoid taking even roots as you will lose negative solutions.

but this is not much help with sketching this curve!
In this case we have to resort to a table of values.

t	−3	−2	−1	0	1	2	3
x	27	12	3	0	3	12	27
y	−27	−8	−1	0	1	8	27

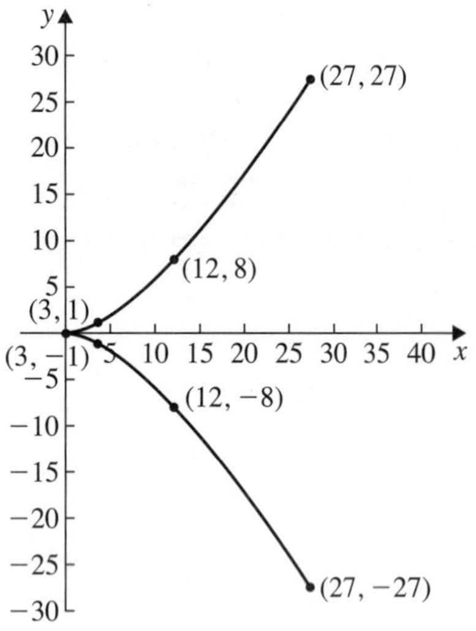

EXERCISE 9A

1 Find the cartesian equations in the following curves, stating the domain and range in each case:

a $x = t + 1,\ y = t^2,\ t \in \mathbb{R}$

b $x = t^2,\ y = t^3,\ t \in \mathbb{R}$

c $x = 3t,\ y = \dfrac{3}{t},\ t \in \mathbb{R},\ t \neq 0$

d $x = 2t,\ y = 8t^3 - 8t,\ t \in \mathbb{R}$

e $x = 2t - 1,\ y = 4t^2 + 1,\ t \in \mathbb{R}$

f $x = t^2,\ y = \dfrac{1}{t},\ t \in \mathbb{R},\ t \neq 0$

g $x = \dfrac{3}{\sqrt{t}},\ y = 2t + 1,\ t \in \mathbb{R},\ t > 0$

h $x = 2\sqrt{t},\ y = 3t^2 + 4,\ t \in \mathbb{R},\ t > 0$

i $x = \dfrac{1}{1 + 3t},\ y = \dfrac{1}{1 - 3t},\ t \in \mathbb{R},\ t \neq \pm\frac{1}{3}$

j $x = t + 2,\ y = 3t^2 + 2t + 1,\ t \in \mathbb{R}$

2 Find y in terms of t in the following curves which have been given in cartesian form:

a $y = x^2 + 1$ $\qquad x = t$

b $x^2 + y^2 = 1$ $\qquad x = \cos t$

c $y = \dfrac{4}{x}$ $\qquad x = 2t$

d $y = \dfrac{x^3 - x}{3}$ $\qquad x = 3t$

3 A curve is given parametrically by $x = t + 1, y = 2t - 1$. Show that the 'curve' is a straight line and sketch the graph.

4 By use of a table of values or otherwise, sketch the following curves:

a $x = 3t,\ y = \dfrac{2}{t},\ -5 \leqslant t \leqslant 5,\ t \neq 0$

b $x = \tan t,\ y = \cos t,\ \dfrac{-3\pi}{8} \leqslant t \leqslant \dfrac{3\pi}{8}$

c $x = 2\sin t,\ y = 3\cos t,\ 0 \leqslant t \leqslant 2\pi$

5 The parametric equations of a curve are $x = \cos t, y = 2\sin t, 0 \leqslant t \leqslant 2\pi$. Find the cartesian equation of the curve, and hence, or otherwise, sketch the curve.

6 a Find the cartesian equation for the curve whose parametric equations are $x = 5\sin t, y = 2\cos t, 0 \leqslant t \leqslant 2\pi$

b Sketch the curve, stating its domain and range.

7 a Find the cartesian equation for the curve $x = \cos^2\theta, y = \sin^2\theta$.

b Sketch the curve, stating its domain and range.

8 Use a formula for $\cos 2\theta$ to obtain the cartesian equation for the curve $x = \cos 2\theta, y = \cos\theta$.

9 a Find the cartesian equation of the curve $x = \sin t, y = \cos 2t$.

b Sketch the curve.

10 The parametric equations of a curve are $x = t^2 + \frac{1}{t}, y = t^2 - \frac{1}{t}$.

Find the cartesian equation of the curve.

11 The diagram shows the curve with parametric equations

$$x = \cos t, y = \tfrac{1}{2}\sin 2t \text{ for } 0 \leqslant t \leqslant 2\pi$$

Show that the cartesian equation of the curve is $y^2 = x^2(1 - x^2)$.

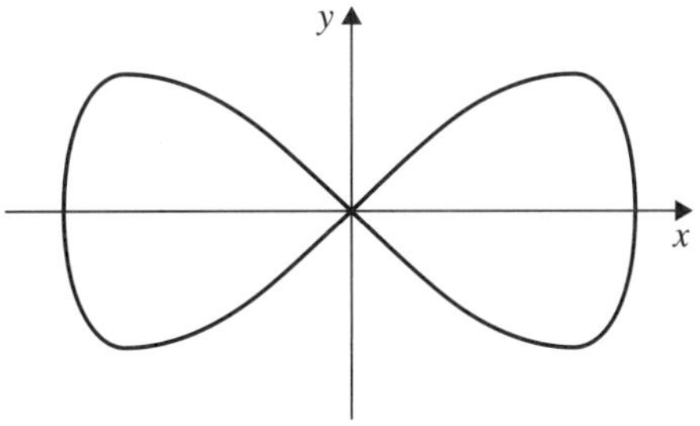

9.2 Parametric differentiation

If x and y are given in terms of t then

$$\frac{dy}{dx} = \frac{dy}{dt} \times \frac{dt}{dx} = \frac{\left(\frac{dy}{dt}\right)}{\left(\frac{dx}{dt}\right)}$$

Remember: $\frac{dt}{dx} = \frac{1}{\left(\frac{dx}{dt}\right)}$

Example 1

A curve is defined by $x = t^2 + 2, y = 3t^3$. Find $\frac{dy}{dx}$ and hence find the gradient of the curve at the point (3, 3).

$$\frac{dx}{dt} = 2t \text{ and } \frac{dy}{dt} = 9t^2 \qquad \therefore \frac{dy}{dx} = \frac{\left(\frac{dy}{dt}\right)}{\left(\frac{dx}{dt}\right)} = \frac{9t^2}{2t} = \frac{9t}{2}$$

At the point (3, 3) we see that $x = t^2 + 2 = 3$ and $y = 3t^3 = 3$. Solving these equations gives $t = 1$.

So at the point (3, 3) the gradient, $\frac{dy}{dx} = 4\frac{1}{2}$.

Example 2

Find the equation of the tangent to the curve given by

$$x = \frac{2}{t}, y = 2t + 1 \text{ at the point } (2, 3)$$

We find the value of t at the point (2, 3).

$$\frac{2}{t} = 2 \text{ and } 2t + 1 = 3 \text{ so } t = 1$$

Differentiating, $\frac{dy}{dt} = 2$ and $\frac{dx}{dt} = -\frac{2}{t^2}$

$$\therefore \quad \frac{dy}{dx} = 2 \times \left(-\frac{t^2}{2}\right) = -t^2$$

When $t = 1$, $\frac{dy}{dx} = -1$

The gradient of the tangent is -1.
The tangent passes through the point (2, 3).
The equation of the tangent is $y - 3 = -1(x - 2)$
or $y + x = 5$

Example 3

Find the coordinates of the stationary point on the curve with equations $x = (t^2 - 3)^2, y = t^2 - 4t$

Differentiating, $\frac{dx}{dt} = 2(t^2 - 3) \times 2t$, $\frac{dy}{dt} = 2t - 4$

$$\frac{dy}{dx} = (2t - 4) \times \frac{1}{4t(t^2 - 3)}$$

At a stationary point $\frac{dy}{dx} = 0$

$$\therefore \quad 2t - 4 = 0$$
$$t = 2$$

When $t = 2$, $x = (2^2 - 3)^2 = 1$
$y = 2^2 - 4 \times 2 = -4$

The stationary point is at the point $(1, -4)$.

Exercise 9B

1 Find $\frac{dy}{dx}$ in terms of t in the following:

a $x = 4t$ and $y = t^2$

b $x = 2\sin t$ and $y = 3\cos t$

2 Find $\frac{dy}{dx}$ in terms of t for the following curves:

a $x = 4t^2,\ y = 8t$

b $x = 5t,\ y = \frac{3}{t}$

c $x = 7\cos t,\ y = 4\sin t$

d $x = 2\sec t,\ y = \tan t$

e $x = e^t,\ y = e^t - e^{-t}$

3 a Show that if $x = \frac{1}{1 + t^3}$ and $y = \frac{t}{1 + t^3}$ then $\frac{dy}{dx} = \frac{2t^3 - 1}{3t^2}$.

b Hence find the equation of the tangent to the curve at the point $\left(\frac{1}{2}, \frac{1}{2}\right)$.

4 a Find the value of t at the point (2, 2) on the curve $x = 1 - t^3, y = 1 + t^2$.

b Hence find the value of $\frac{dy}{dx}$ at (2, 2).

c Use this to find the equation of the normal to the curve at (2, 2).

5 a Show that $\frac{dy}{dx} = \left(\frac{1 - 2t}{1 - t}\right)^2$ on the curve $x = \frac{1 + t}{1 - 2t},\ y = \frac{1 + 2t}{1 - t}$.

b Hence find the equation of the tangent to the curve at the point (1, 1).

c Find also the equation of the normal to the curve at the point $\left(\frac{1}{4}, 0\right)$.

6 A curve is given by $x = t^2 - 4t,\ y = t^3 - 4t^2$.

a Find the points at which the gradient is $\frac{3}{2}$.

b Find the point at which the curve is parallel to the y-axis.

7 a Find $\frac{dy}{dx}$ for the curve $x = 3t^2 + 5,\ y = 2t^3 - 6t$.

b Hence find the stationary points of the curve.

8 Find the stationary points on the curve $x = \frac{1}{1 + t},\ y = \frac{t^2}{1 + t}$.

9 A curve has parametric equations $x = \cos t,\ y = \sin t$.

Find the equation of the tangent to the curve where $t = \frac{\pi}{4}$.

10 A curve has parametric equations $x = t - \cos t,\ y = \sin t$.

Show that the equation of the tangent to the curve, where $t = \pi$, is $x + y = \pi + 1$.

11 The parametric equations of a curve are $x = a\sin\theta,\ y = a\cos^2\theta,\ 0 \leqslant \theta \leqslant \frac{\pi}{2}$.

Find the equation of the normal to the curve at the point where $\theta = \frac{\pi}{6}$.

12 The parametric equations of a curve are

$x = \cos\theta,\ y = 2\sin\theta.$

Find the equation of the normal to the curve at the point $P(\cos\theta, 2\sin\theta)$.

13 A curve has parametric equations $x = \cos t,\ y = \frac{1}{2}\sin 2t$ for $0 \leqslant t \leqslant 2\pi$.

a Find an expression for $\frac{dy}{dx}$ in terms of the parameter t.

b Find the values of t at the points on the curve where the gradient is -1.

14 A curve has equations $x = t - \sin t,\ y = 1 - \cos t$ for $0 \leqslant t \leqslant 2\pi$.
Find the coordinates of the stationary points on the curve.

15 A curve has parametric equations $x = 2 + 3\cos\theta$

$y = 2 + 3\sin\theta$

a Find the cartesian equation of the curve and describe the curve.

b Find the equation of the tangent at the point with parameter $\theta = \frac{\pi}{4}$.

9.3 The area under a curve

In the same way that we use integration to find the area under a curve in cartesian form so we use integration to find the area under a curve given in parametric form.

We know that the area bounded by the curve $y = f(x)$, the x-axis, the lines $x = a$ and $x = b$ is given by $\int_a^b f(x)\,dx$.

If the curve is given parametrically we will have $y = f(t)$ and $x = g(t)$. The lines $x = a$ and $x = b$ will correspond to certain t-values, say t_1 and t_2.

In this case the area bounded is given by $\int_{t=t_1}^{t=t_1} y\,dx = \int_{t=t_1}^{t=t_1} f(t)\frac{dx}{dt}\,dt$.

Example 1

The curve defined by $x = t - 2,\ y = 3t^2$ is shown below. Find the shaded area.

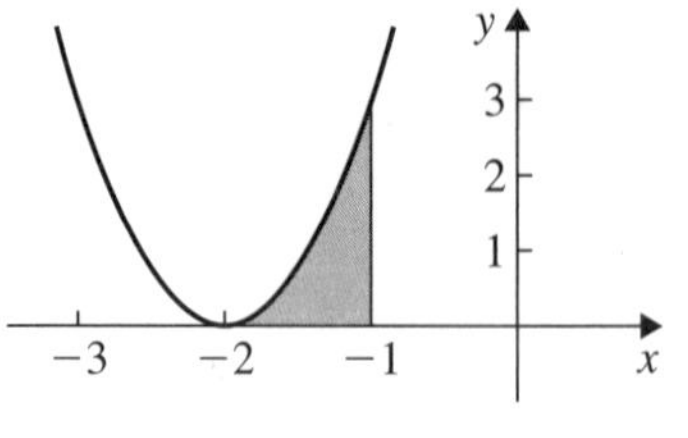

The area is bounded by the values $t = 0$ and $t = 1$. So the area is given by $\int_{t=0}^{t=1} 3t^2\frac{dx}{dt}\,dt$. Now $x = t - 2$ so $\frac{dx}{dt} = 1$. Therefore the area is $\int_{t=0}^{t=1} 3t^2\,dt = [t^3]_0^1 = 1$ square unit.

[Notice that the curve is $y = 3(x + 2)^2$ and so the area is given by $\int_{-2}^{-1} 3(x + 2)^2\,dx$.
We can easily show that the value of this integral is 1 using standard integration.]

Example 2

Find area between the curve defined $x = t^3$ and $y = t^2 - t$, the lines $x = 1$, $x = 8$ and the x-axis.

We can see that when $x = 1$, $t = 1$, when $x = 8$, $t = 2$ and also $\frac{dx}{dt} = 3t^2$.

Therefore the area that we are trying to find is given by $\int y.\frac{dx}{dt}\,dt = \int_1^2 (t^2 - t).3t^2\,dt$

$$\therefore \quad \text{Area} = 3\int_1^2 (t^4 - t^3)\,dt = 3\left[\frac{1}{5}t^5 - \frac{1}{4}t^4\right]_1^2$$

$$= 3\left(\frac{31}{5} - \frac{15}{4}\right) = \frac{147}{20} \text{ square units.}$$

Exercise 9C

1 Find the area enclosed between the following curves, the x-axis and the vertical lines $x = a$ and $x = b$ which correspond to $t = t_1$ and $t = t_2$:

a $x = t - 1$, $\quad y = t^2 \quad t_1 = 1, t_2 = 3$

b $x = t^2$, $\quad y = 2t^3 \quad t_1 = 1, t_2 = 4$

c $x = 5t$, $\quad y = \frac{5}{t} \quad t_1 = 2, t_2 = 6$

2 Find the area enclosed between the following curves, the x-axis and the vertical lines given below:

a $x = t^2 + 1$, $\quad y = 2t\ (t > 0) \quad x = 2, x = 5$

b $x = t + 1$, $\quad y = t^2 \quad x = 1, x = 4$

c $x = 2t^2$, $\quad y = \frac{2}{t}\ (t > 0) \quad x = 2, x = 8$

3 Find the area enclosed between the following curves, the x-axis and the vertical lines given below:

a $x = 3t$, $\quad y = \frac{3}{t} \quad x = 3, x = 12$

b $x = 2t - 1$, $\quad y = 4t^2 + 1 \quad x = 1, x = 7$

c $x = \frac{3}{\sqrt{t}}$, $\quad y = 2t + 1 \quad x = 1.5, x = 3$

d $x = 2\sqrt{t}$, $\quad y = 3t^2 + 4 \quad x = 4, x = 6$

4 The graph shows the curve with parametric equations $x = \theta - \sin\theta$, $y = 1 - \cos\theta$ for $0 \leqslant \theta \leqslant 2\pi$. The curve is called a cycloid.

The area A enclosed by the curve and the x-axis is $\int_0^{2\pi} y \frac{dx}{d\theta} d\theta$.

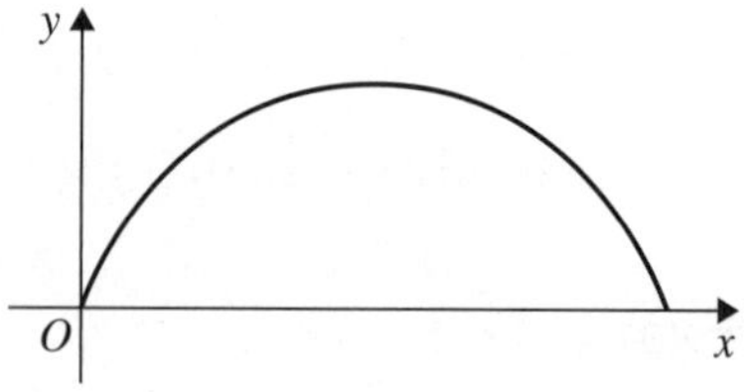

Show that $A = \int_0^{2\pi} (1 - \cos\theta)^2 \, d\theta$ and hence find A, in terms of π.

9.4 Solving coordinate geometry problems using parametric equations

Example 1

A curve C is defined by $x = t - 1$, $y = 5t^2$.

a Find where the curve C intersects the coordinate axes.

b The points $(3, a)$ and $(b, 20)$ lie on C. Find all possible values of a and b.

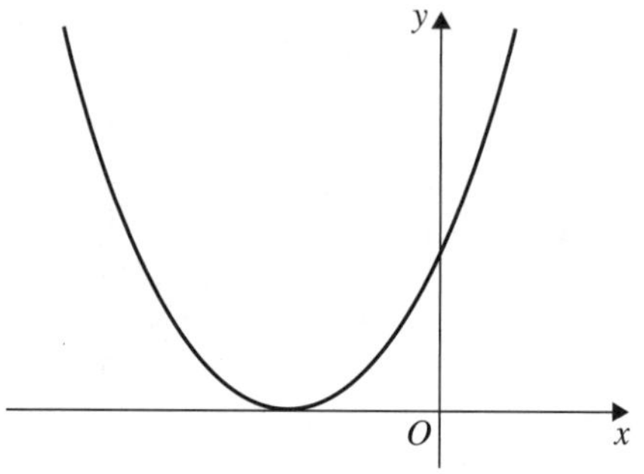

a Any curve intersects the x-axis when $y = 0$.

So $0 = 5t^2$, $t = 0$

Now $t = 0 \Rightarrow x = 0 - 1 = -1$

$\therefore$ C intersects the x-axis at $(-1, 0)$

Any curve intersects the y-axis when $x = 0$.

So $0 = t - 1$, $t = 1$

Now $t = 1 \Rightarrow y = 5(1)^2 = 5$

$\therefore$ C intersects the y-axis at $(0, 5)$

b At the point $(3, a)$ we have $x = 3$.

So $t - 1 = 3$, $t = 4$

Now $t = 4 \Rightarrow y = 5(4)^2 = 80$ $\quad \therefore a = 80$

At the point $(b, 20)$ we have $y = 20$

So $5t^2 = 20$, $t = \pm 2$

Now $t = 2 \Rightarrow x = 2 - 1 = 1$

and $t = -2 \Rightarrow x = -2 - 1 = -3$ $\quad \therefore b = -3$ or 1

Example 2

The line $y = 2x$ intersects the curve defined by $x = 2\sin t$, $y = 5\cos t$, $0 \leqslant t \leqslant 2\pi$, at the points A and B. Find the coordinates of A and B, giving your answers correct to three significant figures.

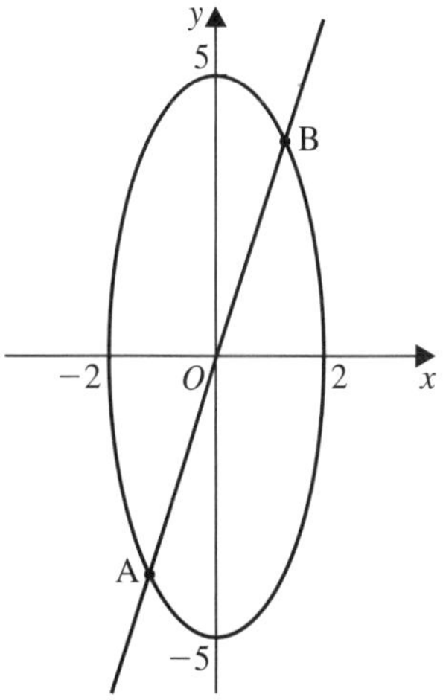

We need to solve the simultaneous equations

$x = 2\sin t$ ①

$y = 5\cos t$ ②

$y = 2x$ ③

Substitute ① and ② into ③:

$$5\cos t = 2(2\sin t)$$

$$5 = 4\tan t,\ t = 0.896\ldots \text{ or } 4.03\ldots$$

Now $t = 0.896\ldots \Rightarrow x = 2\sin(0.896\ldots) = 1.56$

$y = 5\cos(0.896\ldots) = 3.12$

and $t = 4.03\ldots \Rightarrow x = 2\sin(4.03\ldots) = -1.56$

$y = 5\cos(4.03\ldots) = -3.12$

$\therefore\ A = (-1.56, -3.12)$ and $B = (1.56, 3.12)$

Exercise 9D

1 Find where the following curves intersect the x-axis:

a $x = 2t^2,\ y = t - 3$ **b** $x = t + 1,\ y = t^2 - 3$

c $x = 3\sin t,\ y = \cos t$

2 Find where the following curves intersect the y-axis:

a $x = t + 1,\ y = 2t^2$ **b** $x = t - 1,\ y = 3\sqrt{t}$

c $x = t + 1,\ y = e^t$

3 Find where the following curves intersect the coordinate axes:

a $x = 2t,\ y = 3t^3 - 4$ **b** $x = \dfrac{1}{t-2},\ y = (t+1)^2$

c $x = (t-1)^2,\ y = (t-2)^3$ **d** $x = t + 1,\ y = t - 3$

e $x = 2\sin t,\ y = 4\cos t$ **f** $x = 3\cos t,\ y = 2\sin t$

4 Find where the line $y = 16$ intersects the curve with parametric equations $x = t^2,\ y = 2t^3$.

5 Find where the line $x = 1$ intersects the curve with parametric equations $x = 2\sin t,\ y = 5\cos t,\ 0 \leqslant t \leqslant 2\pi$.

6 The curve C is defined by the parametric equations $x = t + 3,\ y = t^2$. The line $y = x + 3$ intersects C at the points A and B. Find the coordinates of A and B.

7 Find the points at which the line $y - x - 5 = 0$ intersects the curve given by the parametric equations $x = \frac{2}{t}$, $y = t - 1$.

8 Show that the line $y = 2x + 1$ is a tangent to the curve with parametric equations $x = t - 1$, $y = t^2$ at the point $(0, 1)$.

9 The curve C has parametric equations $x = 2t - 3$, $y = 2t^2$.

a Find the equation of the normal to C at the point $(-1, 2)$.

b This normal meets C again at point P. Find the coordinates of P.

10 The curve C is given by the parametric equations $x = 2t^2$, $y = 3t - 2$.
The normal to C at the point $(18, 7)$ meets C again at point P.
Find the coordinates of P.

9.5 Modelling with parametric equations

Many situations can be modelled using parametric equations. The parameter t nearly always refers to time.

Example 1

The movement of a car along a motorway can be modelled by the parametric equations $x = t$, $y = 60t$, where x is the time in hours, and y is the distance from the start point in miles.

a Sketch a graph for $0 \leqslant t \leqslant 1.5$.

b Find the distance the car has travelled after 1 hour.

c Find the speed of the car.

a In this simple example it is easiest to substitute $x = t$ into $y = 60t$ to get $y = 60x$.

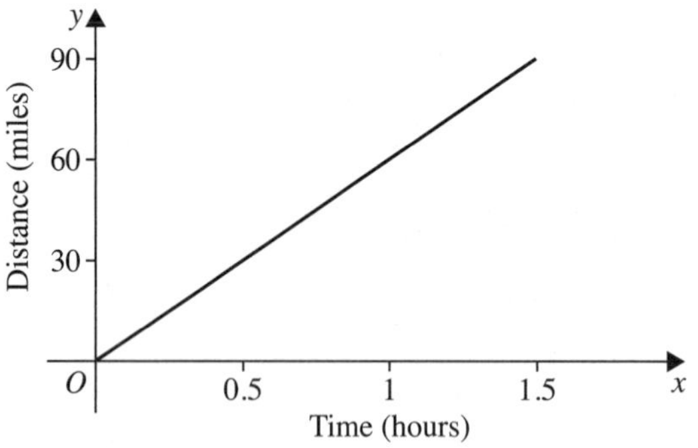

b After 1 hour, $t = 1 \Rightarrow y = 60 \times 1 = 60$ miles.

c The straight line graph shows the car is travelling at a constant speed.
It travels 60 miles in 1 hour, so the speed is 60 mph.

Example 2

The position of a chair lift going up a mountain can be modelled by the parametric equations $x = 2.4t,\ y = 3.2t + 1$, where x is the horizontal displacement and y is the vertical displacement, both measured in metres from the start.

a Find the initial height of the chair from the ground.

b Sketch a graph of the movement of the chair for $0 \leqslant t \leqslant 10$.

c Find the height of the chair after it has travelled 400 m horizontally.

a Initially $t = 0 \Rightarrow y = 3.2 \times 0 + 1 = 1\,\text{m}$.

b We will use a table of values in this case.

t	0	1	2	3	4	5	6	7	8	9	10
x	0	2.4	4.8	7.2	9.6	12	14.4	16.8	19.2	21.6	24
y	1	4.2	7.4	10.6	13.8	17	20.2	23.4	26.6	29.8	33

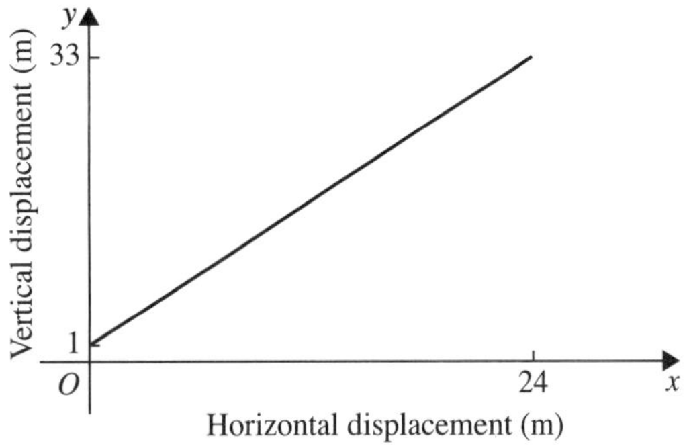

c $x = 400 \Rightarrow 2.4t = 400$

$$t = \frac{500}{3}$$

Now $t = \dfrac{500}{3} \Rightarrow y = 3.2 \times \dfrac{500}{3} + 1 = 534\,\text{m (3 sf)}$

Example 3

A message in a bottle is thrown from a cliff. Its motion as it falls into the sea can be modelled by the parametric equations $x = 2.7t,\ y = -4.9t^2 + 3.1t + 15$, where x is the horizontal displacement and y is the height above sea level, both measured in metres.

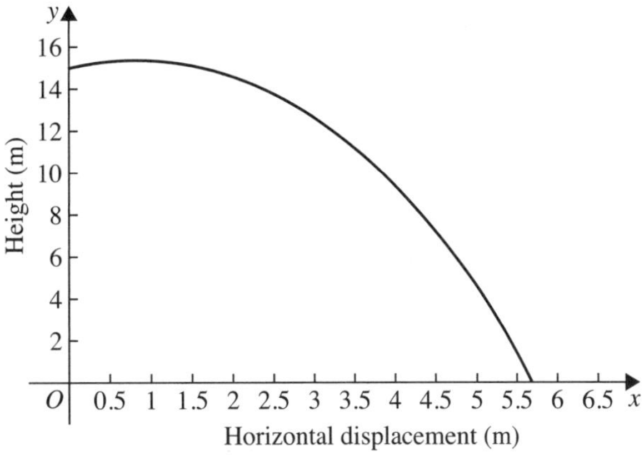

a Find the height of the cliff.

b Find the maximum height of the bottle.

c Find the horizontal displacement when the bottle hits the sea.

a The bottle is initially at the top of the cliff.
$t = 0 \Rightarrow y = -4.9 \times 0^2 + 3.1 \times 0 + 15 = 15\,\text{m}$.

b To find the maximum value of y we differentiate.

$$y = -4.9t^2 + 3.1t + 15$$

$$\frac{dy}{dt} = -9.8t + 3.1$$

Now $\quad -9.8t + 3.1 = 0$

$$t = \frac{31}{98}$$

And $\quad t = \frac{31}{98} \Rightarrow y = -4.9\left(\frac{31}{98}\right)^2 + 3.1\left(\frac{31}{98}\right) + 15$

$$= 15.49\,\text{m} \quad (2\text{ dp})$$

c When the bottle hits the sea $y = 0$

$$0 = -4.9t^2 + 3.1t + 15$$

$$t = \frac{-3.1 \pm \sqrt{3.1^2 - 4(-4.9)(15)}}{2(-4.9)}$$

$(t = -1.46)$ or $t = 2.09\ldots$

Now $t = 2.09\ldots \Rightarrow x = 2.7 \times 2.09\ldots = 5.65\,\text{m}$ (3 sf)

Exercise 9E

1 A van is travelling from Salisbury to London. Its position can be modelled by the parametric equations $x = t,\ y = 120 - 48t$, where x is the time in hours, and y is the distance from London in kilometres.

a How far is Salisbury from London?

b How long does it take for the van to travel to London?

c Sketch a graph to show the van's motion from Salisbury to London.

d Find the speed of the van throughout its journey.

e Is this model likely to be accurate?

2 The motion of a plane taking off from the ground at time t seconds can be modelled by the parametric equations $x = 57.5t,\ y = 17.2t$, where x and y are the horizontal and vertical distance travelled respectively, each measured in metres.

a Sketch a graph showing the position of the plane throughout the first minute after take off.

b Find the height of the plane after it has travelled 200 km horizontally.

c Suggest why the model may have given an unrealistic answer in part **b**.

3 A pebble is thrown from a window. Its position at time t seconds after being thrown can be modelled by the parametric equations $x = 3.5t,\ y = 20 - 4.9t^2$, where x is the horizontal distance travelled and y is the height from the ground, both measured in metres.

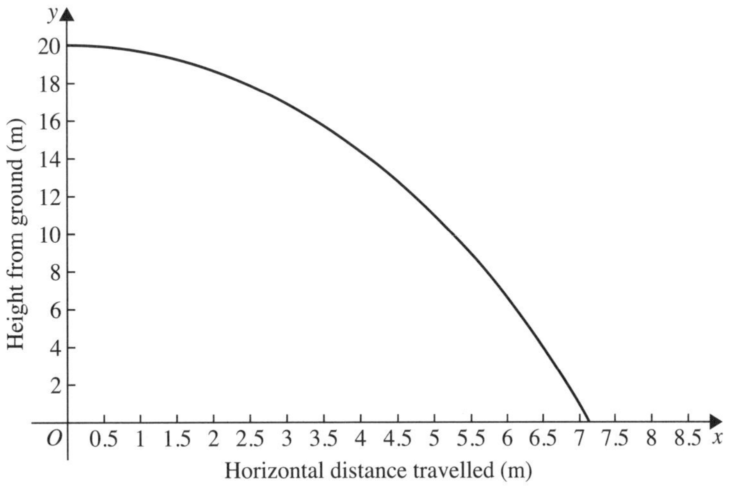

a Find the height of the window from the ground.

b Find the time taken for the pebble to hit the ground.

c Find the total horizontal distance travelled by the pebble.

4 A ball is kicked off the ground. Its position at time t seconds after being kicked can be modelled by the parametric equations $x = 4.3t,\ y = -4.9t^2 + 14.5t$, where x is the horizontal distance travelled and y is the height from the ground, both measured in metres.

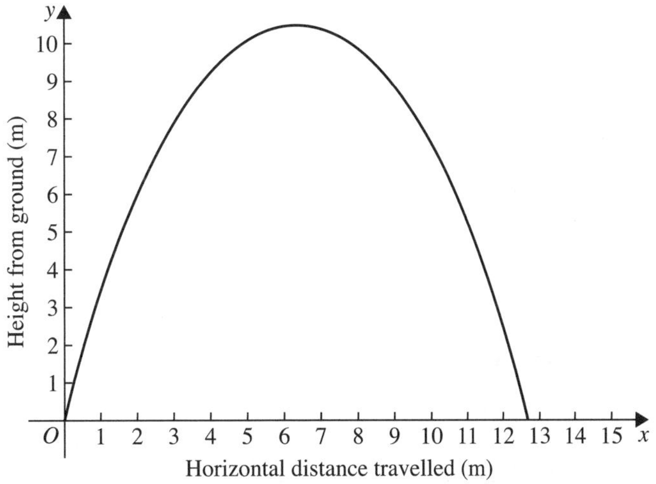

a Find the time taken for the ball to hit the ground again.

b Find the total horizontal distance travelled by the ball.

c Find the maximum height of the ball from the ground.

5 A chair is travelling around a Big Wheel ride. Its position at time t minutes can be modelled by the parametric equations

$x = 40\sin\frac{t}{3} + 40,\ y = 40\cos\frac{t}{3} + 40,$

where x is the horizontal distance of the chair from the edge of the ride and y is the height of the chair from the ground, both measured in metres.

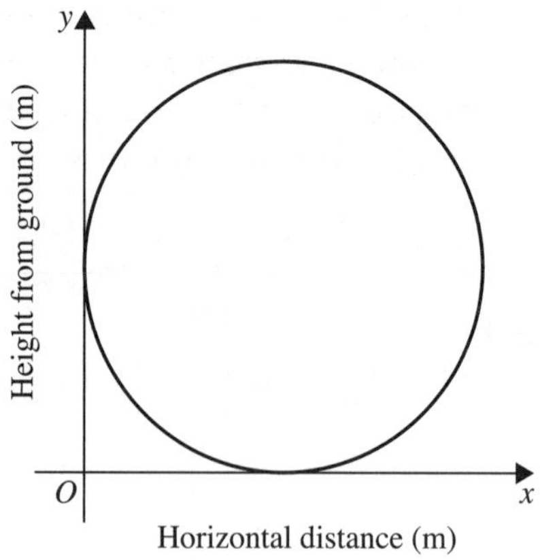

a Show that the cartesian equation of this motion can be written as

$$(x - 40)^2 + (y - 40)^2 = r^2$$

and find the radius of the wheel, r.

b Find the initial position of the chair.

c Find the time taken for the chair to return to this position.

d Find the speed with which the chair is moving in m/s.

6 The position of a go-kart driving round a track, relative to a fixed origin O, at time t minutes, can be modelled by the parametric equations $x = 3\cos\left(\frac{t}{2}\right)$, $y = 5\sin\left(t - \frac{\pi}{6}\right)$ where x and y are both measured in metres.

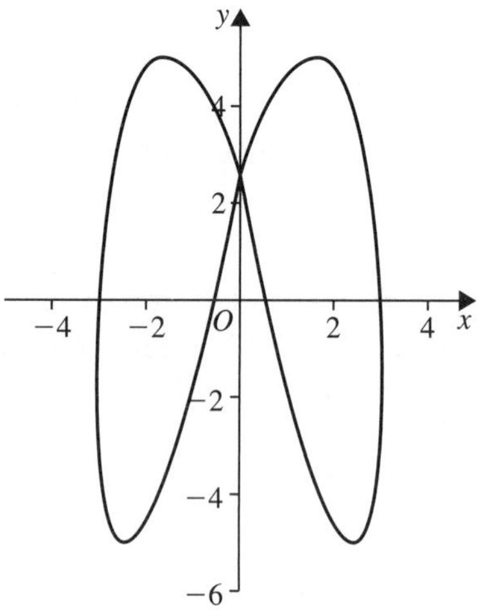

a Find the coordinates of the start/finish point.

b Find the coordinates of the point on the track where a crash could occur. [Hint: use the graph opposite to find the x-coordinate.]

c Find the time taken for the go-kart to complete a full lap of the track. [Hint: both the x and the y coordinates must return to their starting values.

Review Exercise 9F

1 Find the cartesian equation for each curve:

a $x = t + 1,\ y = t^2$

b $x = 3t - 1,\ y = \frac{1}{t}$

c $x = 2t,\ y = \frac{4}{t}$

d $x = \frac{1}{1+t},\ y = \frac{t}{1+t}$

e $x = 5\sin t,\ y = \cos t$

f $x = \cos t,\ y = 2\cos 2t$

2 Show that the cartesian equation of the curve with parametric equations $x = \frac{1}{2}(1 - t^2),\ y = t^3$ is $y^2 = (1 - 2x)^3$.

3 Sketch the following curves, stating their domain and range, and any points where they meet the coordinate axes:

a $x = 3t - 1,\ y = 2t^2 + 1,\ t \in \mathbb{R}$

b $x = t^2,\ y = 2t + 1,\ t \in \mathbb{R}$

c $x = 4\sin t,\ y = 3\cos t,\ 0 \leqslant t \leqslant 2\pi$

4 Find $\frac{dy}{dx}$, in terms of t, for each of the following curves:

a $x = t^2,\ y = t$ **b** $x = \sin t,\ y = \cos t$ **c** $x = t^3,\ y = t^2$

5 Find the turning point of the curve $x = t,\ y = t^2 - 1$.

6 Find the turning points of the curve $x = t,\ y = t^3 - 3t$.

7 Find the equation of the tangent to the following curves at the given point:

a $x = t,\quad y = t^2 \quad$ at $\quad t = -1$

b $x = \cos\theta,\quad y = \sin\theta \quad$ at $\quad \theta = \frac{\pi}{4}$

c $x = t,\quad y = \frac{1}{t} \quad$ at $\quad t = 1$

d $x = 3\cos\theta,\quad y = 4\sin\theta \quad$ at $\quad \theta = \frac{\pi}{3}$

e $x = 4\sin\theta,\quad y = 3\cos 2\theta \quad$ at $\quad \theta = \frac{\pi}{6}$

f $x = \cos 2\theta - 2\cos\theta$, $y = \sin 2\theta - 2\sin\theta \quad$ at $\quad \theta = \frac{\pi}{4}$

8 The curve C is given by the parametric equations $x = 2t + 1,\ y = \frac{1}{t},\ t \neq 0$.

The line $y = x + 1$ intersects the curve C at points A and B. Find the exact coordinates of A and B.

9 The curve C is given by the parametric equations $x = 2t + 3,\ y = t^2 - 1,\ t \in \mathbb{R}$. The normal to the curve C at the point $A\,(7, 3)$ meets C again at point B. Find the coordinates of B.

10 A plane is coming in to land on a runway. Its position at time t seconds after beginning its descent can be modelled by the parametric equations $x = 65t$, $y = -8t + 1500$ where x is the horizontal distance travelled since beginning the descent, and y is the height from the ground, both measured in metres.

a Find the height of the plane when it begins its descent.

b Find the time taken for the plane to land on the ground after beginning its descent.

c Find the horizontal distance of the plane from the runway when it first began its descent.

11 The position of a point P on the wheel of an exercise bike is given by the equations $x = 32.5\sin 8t + 32.5$, $y = 32.5\cos 8t + 32.5$ at time t seconds, where x and y are the horizontal and vertical distance respectively from a fixed origin O, each measured in centimetres.

a Show that P moves in a circle with radius 32.5 cm.

b Find the time taken for P to complete one full revolution of the wheel.

c Find the speed at which P is moving.

12 A dirt bike is moving around a track. Its position at time t minutes can be modelled by the equations $x = 8\cos 4t$, $y = 10\sin\left(2t - \frac{\pi}{3}\right)$.

a Find the coordinates of the start/finish point.

b Find the time taken for the bike to complete one lap of the track.

c Show that a crash could occur at the point $(-4, 0)$.

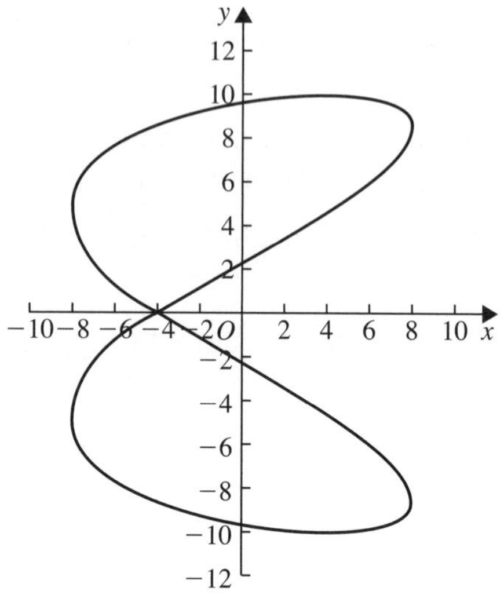

EXAMINATION EXERCISE 9

1

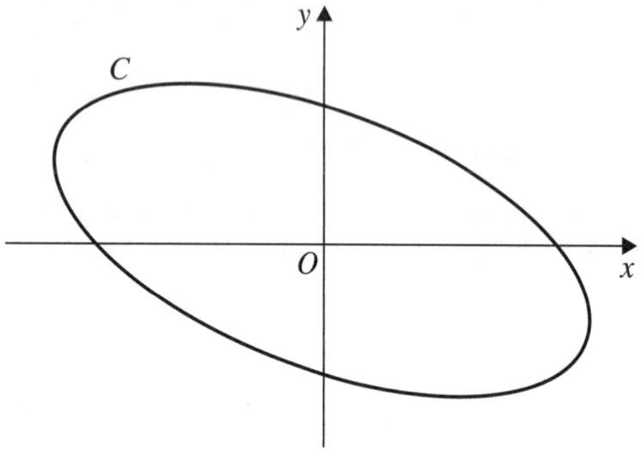

The diagram shows a sketch of the curve C with parametric equations

$$x = 4\cos\left(t + \frac{\pi}{6}\right),\quad y = 2\sin t,\quad 0 \leqslant t \leqslant 2\pi$$

a Show that

$$x + y = 2\sqrt{3}\cos t$$

b Show that a cartesian equation of C is

$$(x + y)^2 + ay^2 = b$$

where a and b are integers to be determined.

[EDEXCEL, GCE Mathematics, C4, June 2014]

2 A curve is defined by the parametric equations

$$x = \sin^2\theta, \ y = 4\sin\theta - \sin^3\theta,$$

where $-\frac{1}{2}\pi \leqslant \theta \leqslant \frac{1}{2}\pi$.

i Show that $\dfrac{dy}{dx} = \dfrac{4 - 3\sin^2\theta}{2\sin\theta}$.

ii Find the coordinates of the point on the curve at which the gradient is 2.

iii Show that the curve has no stationary points.

iv Find a cartesian equation of the curve, giving your answer in the form $y^2 = f(x)$.

[OCR, GCE Mathematics, C4, Jan 2012]

3 A curve has parametric equations $x = \dfrac{1}{t} - 1$ and $y = 2t + \dfrac{1}{t^2}$.

i Find $\dfrac{dy}{dx}$ in terms of t, simplifying your answer.

ii Find the coordinates of the stationary point and, by considering the gradient of the curve on either side of this point, determine its nature.

iii Find the cartesian equation of the curve.

[OCR, GCE Mathematics, C4, June 2013]

4 The diagram shows a sketch of part of the curve C with parametric equations

$$x = 1 - \tfrac{1}{2}t, \ y = 2^t - 1$$

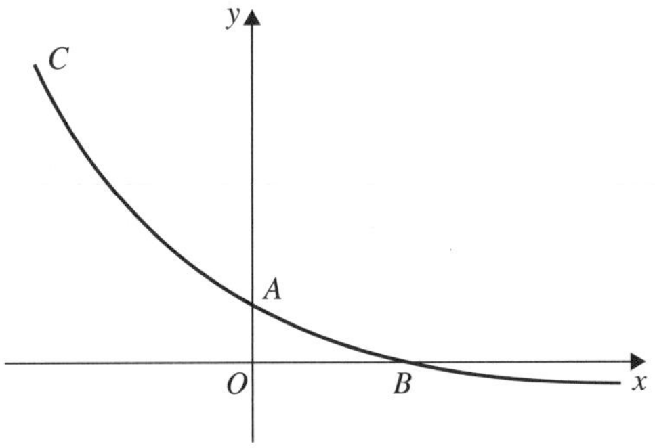

The curve crosses the y-axis at the point A and crosses the x-axis at the point B.

a Show that A has coordinates (0, 3).

b Find the x coordinate of the point B.

c Find an equation of the normal to C at the point A.

[EDEXCEL, GCE Mathematics, C4, Jan 2013]

5 The diagram shows part of the curve with parametric equations

$$x = \tan\theta, \ y = \sin\theta, \ 0 \leqslant \theta \leqslant \frac{\pi}{2}$$

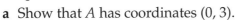

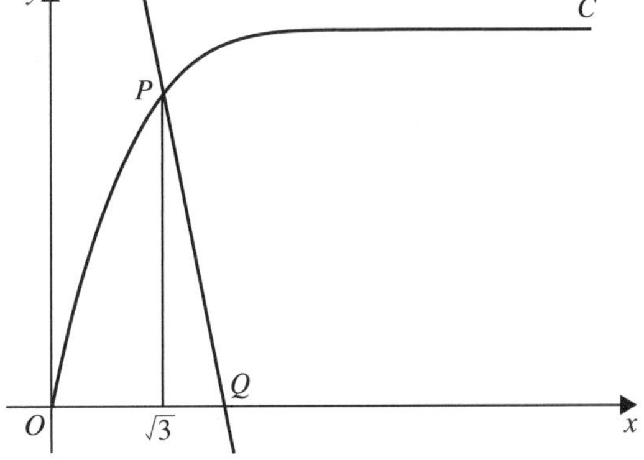

The point P lies on C and has coordinates $\left(\sqrt{3}, \frac{1}{2}\sqrt{3}\right)$.

a Find the value of θ at the point P.

The line l is a normal to C at P. The normal cuts the x-axis at the point Q.

b Show that Q has coordinates $(k\sqrt{3}, 0)$, giving the value of the constant k.

[EDEXCEL, GCE Mathematics, C4, June 2011]

6 The diagram shows a sketch of the curve C with parametric equations

$$x = (\sqrt{3})\sin 2t,\ y = 4\cos^2 t,\ 0 \leqslant t \leqslant \pi$$

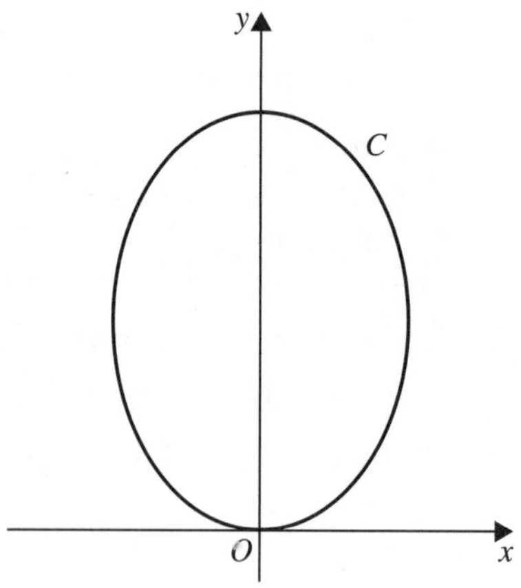

a Show that $\frac{dy}{dx} = k(\sqrt{3})\tan 2t$, where k is a constant to be determined.

b Find an equation of the tangent to C at the point where $t = \frac{\pi}{3}$.

Give your answer in the form $y = ax + b$, where a and b are constants.

c Find a cartesian equation of C.

[EDEXCEL, GCE Mathematics, C4, June 2012]

7 A curve has parametric equations $x = 1 - \cos t,\ y = \sin t \sin 2t$, for $0 \leqslant t \leqslant \pi$.

i Find the coordinates of the points where the curve meets the x-axis.

ii Show that $\frac{dy}{dx} = 2\cos 2t + 2\cos^2 t$. Hence find, in an exact form, the coordinates of the stationary points.

iii Find the cartesian equation of the curve. Give your answer in the form $y = f(x)$, where $f(x)$ is a polynomial.

iv Sketch the curve. [OCR, GCE Mathematics, C4, June 2016]

8 A curve has parametric equations

$$x = 2\sin t,\ y = \cos 2t + 2\sin t$$

for $-\frac{1}{2}\pi \leqslant t \leqslant \frac{1}{2}\pi$.

i Show that $\frac{dy}{dx} = 1 - 2\sin t$ and hence find the coordinates of the stationary point.

ii Find the cartesian equation of the curve.

iii State the set of values that x can take and hence sketch the curve.

[OCR, GCE Mathematics, C4, June 2014]

9 A curve C is defined by the parametric equations

$$x = \frac{4 - e^{2-6t}}{4},\ y = \frac{e^{3t}}{3t},\ t \neq 0$$

a Find the exact value of $\frac{dy}{dx}$ at the point on C where $t = \frac{2}{3}$.

b Show that $x = \frac{4 - e^{2-6t}}{4}$ can be rearranged into the form $e^{3t} = \frac{e}{2\sqrt{(1-x)}}$.

c Hence find the Cartesian equation of C, giving your answer in the form

$$y = \frac{e}{f(x)[1 - \ln(f(x))]}$$

[AQA, GCE Mathematics, C4, June 2016]

PART 10

Differentiation 2

10.1 Using second derivatives

Consider the graph $y = f(x)$.

The first derivative $\frac{dy}{dx}$ tells us the rate of change of the graph.

If $\frac{dy}{dx} > 0$ at a certain point then the gradient is positive at that point, and the graph is increasing.

If $\frac{dy}{dx} < 0$ at a certain point then the gradient is negative at that point, and the graph is decreasing.

The second derivative $\frac{d^2y}{dx^2}$ tells us the rate of change of the gradient.

> If $\frac{d^2y}{dx^2} \geqslant 0$ over a certain interval then the gradient is increasing and the curve is **convex** over that interval.

Consider $y = x^2$

$$\frac{dy}{dx} = 2x$$

$$\frac{d^2y}{dx^2} = 2 > 0$$

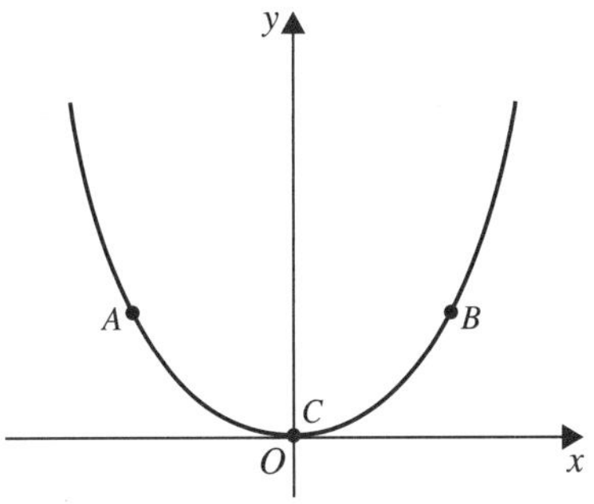

This graph is **convex** for all values of x. At point A the gradient is becoming less negative, at point B the gradient is becoming more positive, and at point C the gradient is switching from negative to positive. At all three points the gradient is **increasing**.

> If $\frac{d^2y}{dx^2} \leqslant 0$ over a certain interval then the gradient is decreasing and the curve is **concave** over that interval.

Consider $y = \ln x$

$$\frac{dy}{dx} = \frac{1}{x}$$

$$\frac{d^2y}{dx^2} = \frac{-1}{x^2}$$

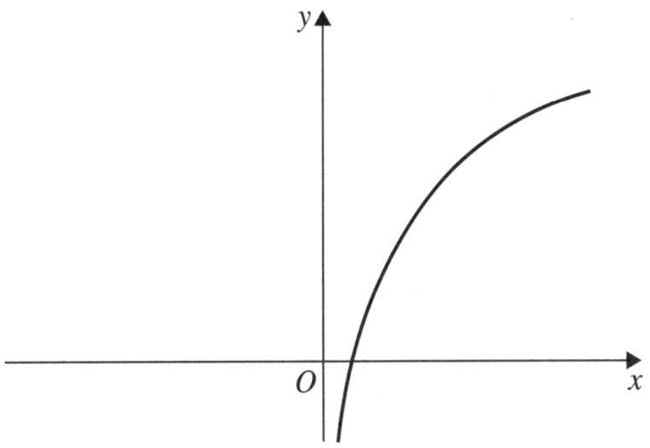

Now $\quad x^2 \geqslant 0 \quad \forall\, x \in \mathbb{R}$

so $\quad \frac{-1}{x^2} \leqslant 0 \quad \forall\, x \in \mathbb{R}$

We can therefore say this graph is **concave** for all values of x.

> Any point where $\frac{d^2y}{dx^2}$ changes sign is called a **point of inflection**.

Note: a point of inflection may also be a stationary point, or it may not.

To find a point of inflection we must find where $\frac{d^2y}{dx^2} = 0$, and also show that $\frac{d^2y}{dx^2}$ has different signs either side of this point.

Example 1

Find the point of inflection on the curve given by $y = x^3 - 8x^2 + 16x$.

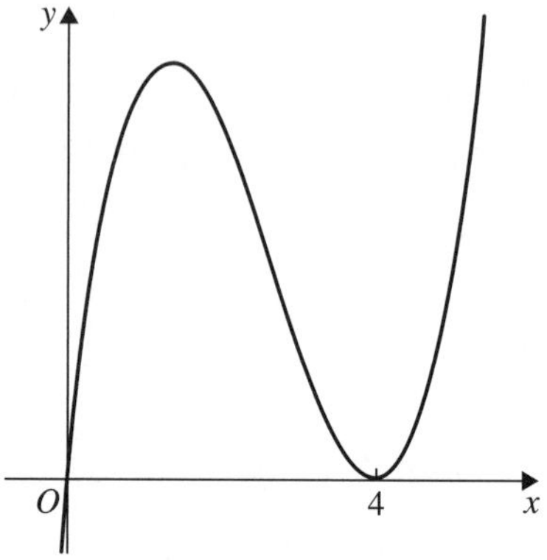

$$\frac{dy}{dx} = 3x^2 - 16x + 16$$

$$\frac{d^2y}{dx^2} = 6x - 16$$

$$6x - 16 = 0$$

$$x = \tfrac{8}{3}, y = \tfrac{128}{27}$$

Now to check either side of this point:

$$x = 2 \Rightarrow \frac{d^2y}{dx^2} = 6(2) - 16 = -4 < 0 \therefore \text{concave}$$

$$x = 3 \Rightarrow \frac{d^2y}{dx^2} = 6(3) - 16 = 2 > 0 \quad \therefore \text{convex}$$

Therefore $\left(\frac{8}{3}, \frac{128}{27}\right)$ is a point of inflection.

Example 2

Find the intervals over which the function $f(x) = x^4 - 8x^3 + 18x^2 - 27$ is **a** convex and **b** concave.

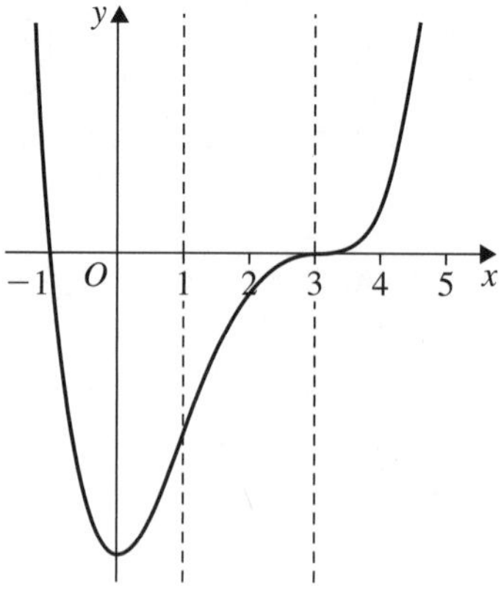

$$f(x) = x^4 - 8x^3 + 18x^2 - 27$$

$$f'(x) = 4x^3 - 24x^2 + 36x$$

$$f''(x) = 12x^2 - 48x + 36$$

$$12x^2 - 48x + 36 = 0$$

$$x^2 - 4x + 3 = 0$$

$$(x - 1)(x - 3) = 0 \quad \Rightarrow \quad x = 1, x = 3$$

Now look at points either side/in between:

x	0	1	2	3	4
$f''(x)$	36	0	−12	0	36

a $f(x)$ is convex for $x \leqslant 1$ and $x \geqslant 3$.

b $f(x)$ is concave for $1 \leqslant x \leqslant 3$.

Exercise 10A

1 At each of the labelled points, state whether the following are positive or negative:

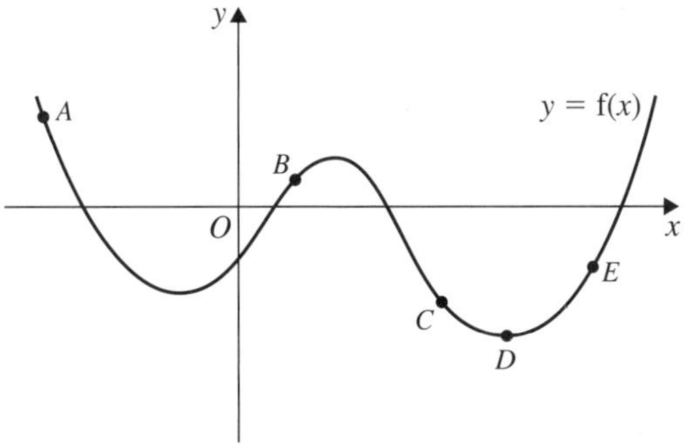

a f(x) **b** f$'(x)$ **c** f$''(x)$

2 Determine the intervals over which the following graphs are convex:

a $y = 3x^2 - 5x + 1$ **b** $y = x^3 - 3x^2 - x + 3$

c $y = x^4 - x^3 - 3x^2 + 5x - 2$ **d** $y = 2e^{-3x} + 5$

3 Determine the intervals over which the following functions are concave:

a $f(x) = x^3 + 5x^2 + 3x - 9$ **b** $f(x) = x^4 + 2x^3 - 3x^2 - 4x + 4$

c $f(x) = \cos x, 0 \leqslant x \leqslant 2\pi$ **d** $f(x) = e^x(2x - 1)$

4 Find the x-coordinates of any points of inflection of the following functions, showing clearly that these points are indeed points of inflection:

a $f(x) = 2x^3 - 4x^2 + x + 6$ **b** $f(x) = x^3 \ln x$

c $f(x) = e^x(x^2 + x + 1)$

5 Show that the curve given by $y = e^x(x^2 - 3x + 5)$ has no points of inflection.

6 The curve C is given by $y = \cos x + 3\sin x, 0 \leqslant x \leqslant 2\pi$.

a Find the coordinates of any stationary points, and determine their nature.

b Find the coordinates of any non-stationary points of inflection, showing clearly that these are indeed points of inflection.

10.2 Implicit functions

In an implicit function the relationship between, say, two variables x and y cannot easily be expressed in the form $y = f(x)$.

Thus $y = x^3 - 3x + 1$ is an explicit function of x but $y^2 + 4xy + 1 = x^3$ is an implicit function. The method of differentiating an implicit function is shown in the examples below.

Example 1

Given $y^2 + 5x = x^2$, find $\frac{dy}{dx}$ in terms of x and y.

Differentiate each term with respect to x.

$$\frac{d}{dx}(y^2) + \frac{d}{dx}(5x) = \frac{d}{dx}(x^2)$$

$$\frac{d}{dy}(y^2)\frac{dy}{dx} + \frac{d}{dx}(5x) = \frac{d}{dx}(x^2)$$

$$2y\frac{dy}{dx} + 5 = 2x$$

$$2y\frac{dy}{dx} = 2x - 5$$

$$\frac{dy}{dx} = \frac{2x-5}{2y}$$

Notice that we obtained $\frac{d}{dx}(y^2)$ using the chain rule.

Example 2

Find $\frac{dy}{dx}$ in terms of x and y: **a** $y^3 + x^2y - x^2 = 0$ **b** $\ln y + x^2 = 3x$

a $$\frac{d}{dx}(y^3) + \frac{d}{dx}(x^2y) - \frac{d}{dx}(x^2) = 0$$

$$\frac{d}{dy}(y^3)\frac{dy}{dx} + \left(x^2\frac{dy}{dx} + y \times 2x\right) - 2x = 0$$ [Use the product rule for the x^2y term.]

$$3y^2\frac{dy}{dx} + x^2\frac{dy}{dx} + 2xy - 2x = 0$$

$$\frac{dy}{dx}(3y^2 + x^2) = 2x - 2xy$$

$$\frac{dy}{dx} = \frac{2x(1-y)}{3y^2 + x^2}$$

b $$\frac{d}{dy}(\ln y)\frac{dy}{dx} + \frac{d}{dx}(x^2) = \frac{d}{dx}(3x)$$

$$\frac{1}{y}\frac{dy}{dx} + 2x = 3$$

$$\frac{1}{y}\frac{dy}{dx} = 3 - 2x$$

$$\frac{dy}{dx} = y(3 - 2x)$$

Example 3

Find the equation of the tangent to the curve $2x^2 - 2xy + y^2 = 5$ at the point $(1, 3)$.

Differentiate with respect to x.

$$4x - \left[2x\frac{dy}{dx} + y \times 2\right] + 2y\frac{dy}{dx} = 0$$

$$4x - 2y + \frac{dy}{dx}(-2x + 2y) = 0$$

$$\frac{dy}{dx} = \frac{2y - 4x}{-2x + 2y}$$

At the point (1, 3), $\frac{dy}{dx} = \frac{2 \times 3 - 4 \times 1}{-2 \times 1 + 2 \times 3} = \frac{2}{4} = \frac{1}{2}$

The tangent passes through the point (1, 3) and has gradient $\frac{1}{2}$.

The equation of the tangent is $\frac{y - 3}{x - 1} = \frac{1}{2}$

$$2y - 6 = x - 1$$
$$2y = x + 5$$

Example 4

Find the coordinates of the stationary points on the curve $x^2 + xy + y^2 = 3$.

Differentiating, $2x + \left(x\frac{dy}{dx} + y \times 1\right) + 2y\frac{dy}{dx} = 0$

$$\frac{dy}{dx}(x + 2y) + 2x + y = 0$$

$$\frac{dy}{dx} = -\frac{(2x + y)}{(x + 2y)}$$

At stationary points $\frac{dy}{dx} = 0$.

$\therefore \quad 2x + y = 0$

$\therefore \quad y = -2x$ ①

Substitute $y = -2x$ in $x^2 + xy + y^2 = 3$.

$$x^2 + x(-2x) + (-2x)^2 = 3$$
$$x^2 - 2x^2 + 4x^2 = 3$$
$$3x^2 = 3$$
$$x^2 = 1$$
$$x = 1 \text{ or } -1$$

From ①, when $x = 1, y = -2$
when $x = -1, y = 2$

The curve has stationary points at $(1, -2)$ and $(-1, 2)$.

[The second derivative will not be used here as the second derivative for implicit functions is not on the syllabus.]

Exercise 10B

1 For each curve find $\frac{dy}{dx}$ in terms of x and y:

a $x^2 + y^2 = 9$

b $xy = 4$

c $x^2 + xy + y^2 = 0$

d $x^2 + y^2 - 6x + 8y = 0$

e $x^2 + 3y^2 - 4y = 0$

f $y^3 = x^2 + 10$

g $3x^3 + 4xy^2 + y^3 = 0$

2 Find $\frac{dy}{dx}$ for the following curves at the points indicated:

a $x^2 + y^2 = 10 \quad (3, 1)$

b $xy = 9 \quad (3, 3)$

c $x^2 + y^2 + 4x = 9 \quad (1, 2)$

d $y^2 = x^3 \quad (4, 8)$

3 The diagram shows a circle with equation $x^2 + y^2 = 8$.

By finding $\frac{dy}{dx}$, calculate the gradient of the tangent to the circle at the point (2, 2).

Using the equation $y - y_1 = m(x - x_1)$, find the equation of the tangent at the point (2, 2).

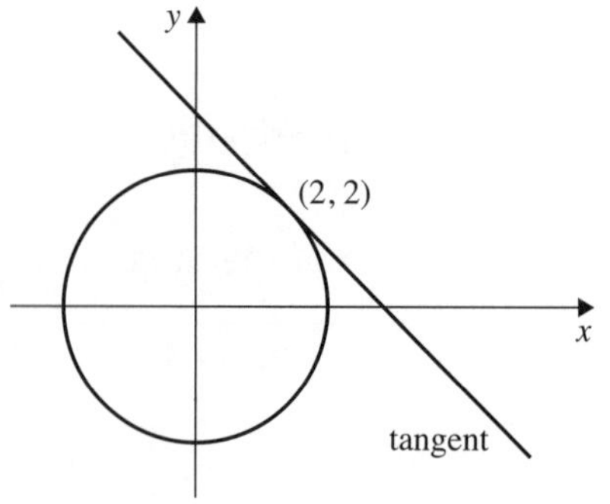

4 Find the equation of the normal to $x^2 + y^2 = 8$ at the point (2, 2).
[Hint: Remember that gradient of tangent × gradient of normal = −1]

5 Find the equation of the tangent to the curve $xy = 4$ at the point (2, 2).

6 Find the equation of the normal to the curve $xy = 4$ at the point (−2, −2).

7 Find the equation of the tangent to the circle $x^2 + y^2 - 2x + 4y = 20$ at the point (4, 2).

8 Find the equation of the normal to the curve $x^2 + xy + y^2 = 3$ at the point (1, 1).

9 For the curve $\ln y + x^2 - x = 0$, show that $\frac{dy}{dx} = y(1 - 2x)$.

10 Find the gradient of each curve at the point given:

a $x^3 + xy + y^3 = 20$ (2, 2)

b $2x^3 - 3x^2y - y^2 = 0$ (−1, −2)

c $\ln y + x^2 = 4$ (2, 1)

d $3\ln y + 2x^3 = 16$ (2, 1)

11 The diagram shows the graph of $xy - x^2 = 4$.

a Show that when $\frac{dy}{dx} = 0$, $y = 2x$.

b Substitute $y = 2x$ into the equation $xy - x^2 = 4$ to find the x coordinates of the two points where the gradient is zero.

c Find the y coordinates of the two turning points.

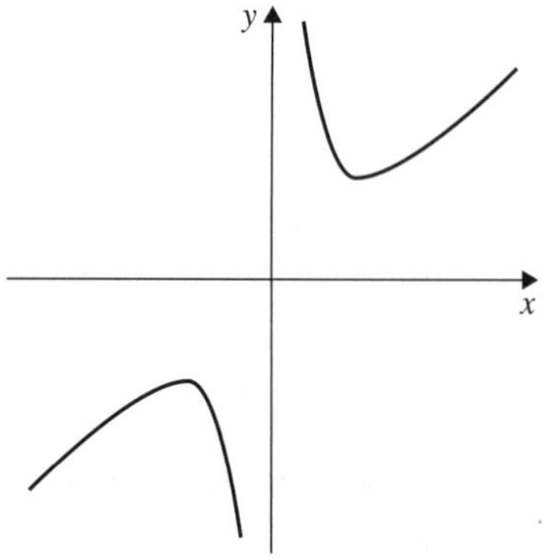

12 Show that the stationary points on the curve $x^2 + 4xy - 2y^2 + 24 = 0$ occur when $x = -2y$. Hence find the stationary points.

13 A curve is defined by the equation $x^2 - 4x - 2xy + 3y^2 - 2 = 0$.

a Find $\frac{dy}{dx}$ in terms of x and y.

b Show that the equation on which the stationary points must lie is $y = x - 2$.

c Show that one of the stationary points is (1, −1) and find the coordinates of the other one.

14 **a** Show that the tangents to the curve $y^2 - 16x - 2y = 47$, at the points (−2, −3) and (13, 17), are perpendicular.

b Find the coordinates of their points of intersection.

15 Calculate $\dfrac{dy}{dx}$ for the following curves at the given points:

a $x^2 - 7xy + y^2 = -29 \quad (2, 3)$

b $xy^2 - 7\sin y + x = 5 \quad (5, 0)$

c $y + x\ln y + x^2 = 5 \quad (2, 1)$

d $e^x y + y^2 = 6 \quad (0, 2)$

e $(x - y)^2 = 4xy - 7 \quad (2, 1)$

16* **a** Given that $x = \cos y$,

i find $\dfrac{dy}{dx}$ in terms of y (by differentiating both sides with respect to x)

ii find $\dfrac{dy}{dx}$ in terms of x (using the fact that $\cos^2 y + \sin^2 y = 1$)

b Use part **a** to find $\dfrac{dy}{dx}$ in terms of x when $y = \cos^{-1} x$.

17* **a** Given that $x = \tan y$,

i find $\dfrac{dy}{dx}$ in terms of y (by differentiating both sides with respect to x)

ii find $\dfrac{dy}{dx}$ in terms of x (using the fact that $1 + \tan^2 y = \sec^2 y$)

b Use part **a** to find $\dfrac{dy}{dx}$ in terms of x when $y = \tan^{-1} x$.

18* Given $y = x^{x^2}$, find $\dfrac{dy}{dx}$ in terms of x.

19* Find $\dfrac{dy}{dx}$ in terms of x and y:

a $e^y = x$

b $e^{xy} = 2$

c $\dfrac{1}{x} + \dfrac{1}{y} = \dfrac{1}{4}$

d $\cos x \sin y = \frac{1}{2}$

e $\sin y + \cos y = x$

10.3 Rates of change

We can differentiate with respect to time to calculate the rate of change of various quantities in real life situations.

Example 1

A substance is decaying exponentially. Its mass, m grams, after t years is given by

$$m = 200e^{-0.04t}$$

a Find the value of t when $m = 50$.

b Find the rate at which the mass is decreasing when $t = 10$.

a When $m = 50$,

$$\begin{aligned} 50 &= 200e^{-0.04t} \\ e^{-0.04t} &= 0.25 \\ -0.04t &= \ln 0.25 = -1.386... \\ t &= 34.7 \text{ years (3 sf)} \end{aligned}$$

b The rate of decrease of the mass is given by $\frac{dm}{dt}$.

$$\frac{dm}{dt} = 200 \times (-0.04) \times e^{-0.04t}$$

When $t = 10$, $\frac{dm}{dt} = 200 \times (-0.04) \times e^{-0.4}$
$= -5.36$ grams/year (3 sf)

The negative sign indicates that the mass is decreasing.

Example 2

The number of microbes N in a culture, after t hours, is given by $N = 50 \times 3^t$.

Find the rate of increase of the number of microbes when $t = 5$ hours.

The rate of increase is given by $\frac{dN}{dt}$.

$$N = 50 \times 3^t$$

$$\frac{dN}{dt} = 50(\ln 3)3^t$$

$t = 5 \Rightarrow \frac{dN}{dt} = 50(\ln 3)3^5 = 13{,}300$ microbes/hour (3 sf)

EXERCISE 10C

1 Find $\frac{dy}{dx}$ in the following:

a $y = 3^x$ **b** $y = 5^{x-1}$ **c** $y = 3(4^x)$

d $y = 2^{x^2}$ **e** $y = e^{-\frac{x^2}{3}}$

2 **a** Find $\frac{d}{dt}(7^t)$ **b** Find $\frac{d}{dt}(4^t)$ **c** Find $\frac{d}{dt}\left(\frac{1}{3^t}\right)$

3 Find $\frac{d\theta}{dt}$ in the following:

a $\theta = 150e^{-\frac{t}{10}}$ **b** $\theta = 100 - e^{-2t}$ **c** $\theta = 10 \times 6^t$

4 At time t minutes the temperature θ°C of a cooling furnace is given by $\theta = 2500e^{-0.9t}$.
Find the rate of decrease of the temperature when $t = 2$.

5 A radioactive substance is decaying exponentially. Its mass, m grams, after t years is given by $m = 300e^{-0.005t}$.

a Find the value of t when $m = 100$.

b Find the rate at which the mass is decreasing when $t = 20$.

6 At time t minutes after being switched on, the temperature of a furnace, θ°C, is given by $\theta = 2000 - 1800e^{-0.1t}$.

a State the value which θ approaches after a long time.

b Find the time taken to reach a temperature of 1500°C.

c Find the rate at which the temperature is increasing when $t = 10$.

7 At time t minutes after being switched on, the temperature of an oven, θ°C, is given by $\theta = 190 - 175e^{-0.08t}$.

a State the value which θ approaches after a long time.

b Find the time taken to reach a temperature of 160°C.

c Find the rate at which the temperature is increasing when $\theta = 50$°C.

10.4 Connected rates of change

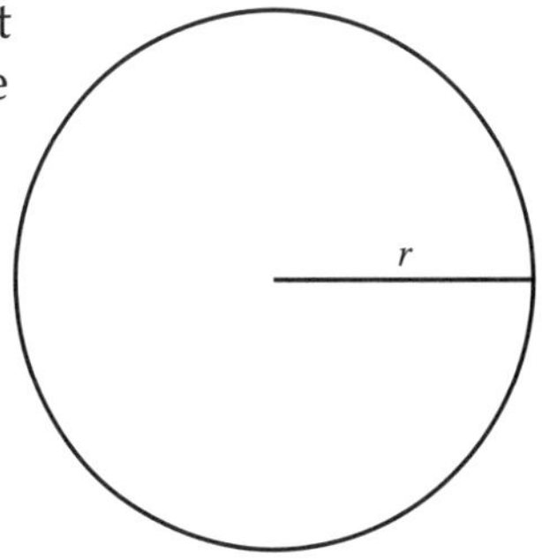

$\frac{dA}{dt} = 10\,\text{cm}^2\,\text{s}^{-1}$

Suppose we are told that the area A of a circle is increasing at a rate of 10 cm² per second. Can we find the rate at which the radius is increasing at the instant when the radius is 4 cm?

We can write $\frac{dA}{dt} = 10$ because $\frac{dA}{dt}$ is the rate of change of the area with respect to time. The question asks us to find $\frac{dr}{dt}$, the rate of change of the radius with respect to time.

The formula connecting A and r is $A = \pi r^2$.
Differentiate with respect to r.

$$\frac{dA}{dr} = 2\pi r, \text{ and when } r = 4, \frac{dA}{dr} = 8\pi.$$

Now $\frac{dA}{dt} = \frac{dA}{dr} \times \frac{dr}{dt}$ ① [Chain rule]

$$\therefore \quad 10 = 8\pi \times \frac{dr}{dt}$$

$$\frac{dr}{dt} = \frac{10}{8\pi} = \frac{5}{4\pi}\,\text{cm}\,\text{s}^{-1}$$

When the radius is 4 cm, the radius is increasing at a rate of $\frac{4}{5\pi}$ cm per second.

In questions on connected rates of change you will always write an equation similar to equation ① above and then use it to find the required rate of change.

Example 1

The side of a square is increasing at a rate of 30 cm s^{-1}. Find the rate at which the area of the square is increasing when the side of the square is 11 cm.

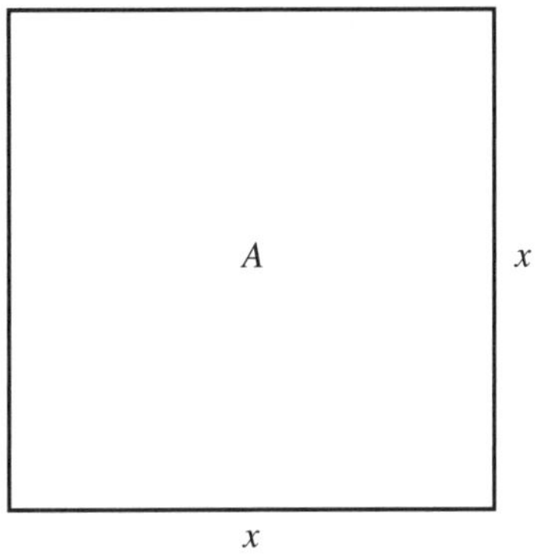

The area A of a square of side x is given by $A = x^2$.

$$\frac{dA}{dx} = 2x, \text{ and when } x = 11, \frac{dA}{dx} = 22.$$

We are given $\frac{dx}{dt} = 30\,\text{cm s}^{-1}$, we have $\frac{dA}{dx} = 22$ and we want to find $\frac{dA}{dt}$.

By the chain rule, $\frac{dA}{dt} = \frac{dA}{dx} \times \frac{dx}{dt}$

$$\frac{dA}{dt} = 22 \times 30 = 660\,\text{cm}^2\,\text{s}^{-1}.$$

The area of the square is increasing at a rate of $660\,\text{cm}^2\,\text{s}^{-1}$.

Example 2

The volume of a sphere is increasing at a rate of $100\,\text{cm}^3\,\text{s}^{-1}$. Find the rate of increase of the radius of the sphere at the instant when the radius is 3 cm.

For a sphere, $V = \frac{4}{3}\pi r^3$

$\frac{dV}{dr} = 4\pi r^2$, and when $r = 3$, $\frac{dV}{dr} = 36\pi$.

We are given $\frac{dV}{dt} = 100$ and we want to find $\frac{dr}{dt}$.

By the chain rule, $\frac{dV}{dt} = \frac{dV}{dr} \times \frac{dr}{dt}$

$$100 = 36\pi \times \frac{dr}{dt}$$

$$\frac{dr}{dt} = \frac{100}{36\pi} = \frac{25}{9\pi}\,\text{cm s}^{-1}.$$

Example 3

A hollow right circular cone, whose height is twice its radius, is held with its vertex downwards and water is poured in at a rate of $5\pi\,\text{cm}^3\,\text{s}^{-1}$. Find the rate of rise of the water level when the depth is 2 cm.

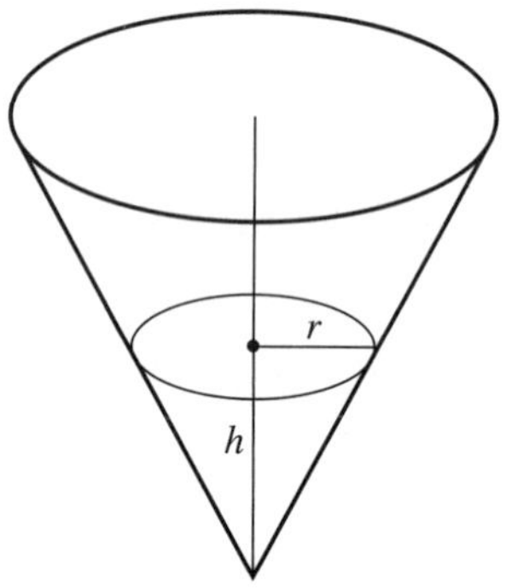

The volume of the water in the cone V when the height is h is given by $V = \frac{1}{3}\pi r^2 h$. We are given that $h = 2r$.

$$\therefore V = \frac{1}{3}\pi\left(\frac{h}{2}\right)^2 h = \frac{1}{12}\pi h^3$$

$\frac{dV}{dh} = \frac{1}{4}\pi h^2$, and when $h = 2$, $\frac{dV}{dh} = \frac{1}{4} \times \pi \times 2^2 = \pi$

We are given $\frac{dV}{dt} = 5\pi\,\text{cm}^3\,\text{s}^{-1}$ and we want to find $\frac{dh}{dt}$.

By the chain rule, $\frac{dV}{dt} = \frac{dV}{dh} \times \frac{dh}{dt}$

$$5\pi = \pi \times \frac{dh}{dt} \quad \Rightarrow \quad \frac{dh}{dt} = 5\,\text{cm s}^{-1}$$

The water level is rising at $5\,\text{cm s}^{-1}$.

Exercise 10D

Give answers to three significant figures where necessary.

1 Given that $y = x^2$ and that x is increasing at a rate of $0.1\,\text{cm s}^{-1}$, find the rate at which y is increasing when $x = 3$ cm.

2 If the radius of a circle increases at a rate of $0.5\,\text{cm}\,\text{s}^{-1}$, find the rate at which the area of the circle increases when the radius is 10 cm.

3 The area of a square is increasing at a rate of $4\,\text{cm}^2\,\text{s}^{-1}$. Find the rate of increase of each side when each side is of length 10 cm.

4 A cube is expanding. Each edge of the cube increases at a rate of $0.01\,\text{cm}\,\text{s}^{-1}$. When the edges of the cube are 8 cm find the rate of increase of

a the volume

b the surface area of the cube.

5 If the radius of a sphere is increasing at $3\,\text{cm}\,\text{s}^{-1}$, find the rate at which the volume is increasing when the radius is 5 cm.

6 The area of a circular ink blot is increasing at a rate of $0.8\,\text{cm}^2\,\text{s}^{-1}$. Find the rate at which the radius is increasing when the radius of the blot is 2 cm.

7 The radius of a sphere is increasing at the rate of $2\,\text{cm}\,\text{s}^{-1}$. Find, in terms of π, the rate of increase of the volume when the radius is 10 cm.

8 The side length of a cube is increasing at the rate of $3\,\text{cm}\,\text{s}^{-1}$. Find the rate of increase of the volume when the length of a side is 5 cm.

9 The volume of a cube is increasing at the rate of $96\,\text{cm}^3\,\text{s}^{-1}$. Find the rate of change of the side of the base when its length is 4 cm.

10 The surface area of a sphere is increasing at the rate of $40\pi\,\text{cm}^2\,\text{s}^{-1}$. Find the rate of change of the radius when its length is 1 cm. [The surface area of a sphere, $S = 4\pi r^2$]

11 A hollow right circular cone, whose height is twice its radius, is held with its vertex downwards and water is poured in at a rate of $4\,\text{cm}^3\,\text{s}^{-1}$.

a Show that when the depth of the water is h the volume in the cone is

$$V = \frac{\pi h^3}{12}.$$

b Find, in terms of π, the rate of rise of the water level when the depth is 2 cm.

12 The empty water container shown is a right prism with AD = 3 m and AC = AB = BC = 1 m. It lies with CF on horizontal ground and with ABDE horizontal.

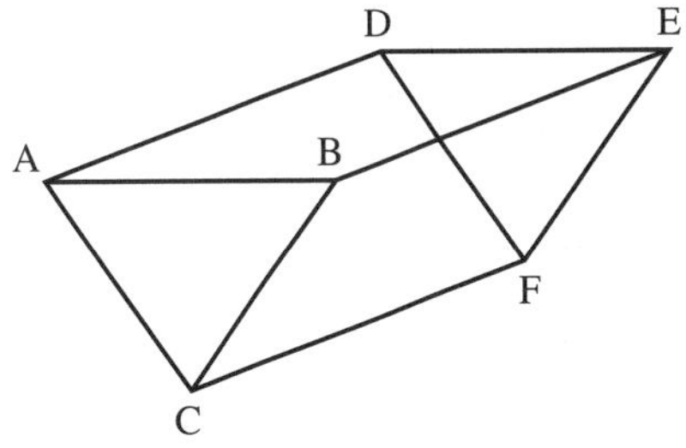

a Show that the volume (in m^3) in the container when the water has height h is $V = \sqrt{3}h^2$.

Water is poured into the container in such a way that the height is rising at $5\sqrt{3}\,\text{cm}\,\text{s}^{-1}$ when the height of the water is 50 cm.

b Find the rate (in $\text{m}^3\,\text{s}^{-1}$) at which the volume of water is increasing at this time.

13 Given that $y^2 = x^3$ and that x is increasing at a rate of 0.5 units per second, find the rate at which y is increasing when $x = 4$ units.

14 A liquid drips onto a surface and forms a circular film of uniform depth 0.1 cm. The liquid drips at a rate of $0.2\,\text{cm}^3\,\text{s}^{-1}$. When the radius of the film is 3 cm, find the rate at which the radius is increasing.

{15* **a** Show that the volume obtained when the part of the curve $y = \sqrt{9 - x^2}$ that is bounded by the x-axis and the line $x = 3 - h$ is rotated about the x-axis is $\frac{\pi h^2}{3}(9 - h)$.

Water is poured at a rate of $18\,\text{cm}^3\,\text{s}^{-1}$ into a hemisphere whose radius is 3 cm.

b Find, in terms of π, the rate of rise of the water level when the water is just about to fill the hemisphere.

Review Exercise 10E

1 Find any points of inflection on the following curves:

a $y = 3x^3 - 2x^2 + x - 1$ **b** $y = \sin 2x + 4\cos 2x,\ 0 \leq x \leq \pi$

2 Find the intervals over which the following functions are **i** convex and **ii** concave.

a $f(x) = x^4 - 5x^2 + 3$ **b** $f(x) = e^{2x}(5x + 3)$

3 Find $\frac{dy}{dx}$ (using implicit differentiation), in terms of x and y:

a $y^2 + y = x$ **b** $y + xy + y^2 = 2$ **c** $x^2 + y^2 = 2$

4 For the following curves express $\frac{dy}{dx}$ in terms of x and y:

a $x^2 + 3y^2 = 7$ **b** $4x^2 - y^3 + 2x + 3y = 0$

c $3x^2 + 4xy - 5y^2 = 20$ **d** $xy^3 + x^3y = x - y$

e $\sin x + 2\cos y = 1$ **f** $x^2y^2 - y = 2$

5 Find the gradient of the curve $x^3 - 2y^3 = 3xy$ at the point (2, 1).

6 A curve is defined by the equation $x^2 + 7xy + 3y^2 = 27$.

a Find $\frac{dy}{dx}$ in terms of x and y.

b Hence find the value of $\frac{dy}{dx}$ at the point (1, 2) on the curve.

7 Find, in the form $ax + by + c = 0$, the equation of the tangent to the curve $x^2 + xy + 4y^2 = 16$ at the point (3, 1).

8 Find, in the form $ax + by + c = 0$, the equation of the normal to the curve $x^2y^2 = x^2 + 5y^2$ at the point $(3, \frac{3}{2})$.

9 **a** For the curve $x^2 + 4y^2 - 4x - 8y + 4 = 0$, express $\frac{dy}{dx}$ in terms of x and y.

b What can you say about the gradient of the curve at the points (2, 2) and (0, 1) on the curve?

10 Show that (−1, 3) and (0, 0) are stationary points on the curve $3x^2 + 2xy - 5y^2 + 16y = 0$.

11 For the curve $\ln y = 3x^2 + 4$, show that $\frac{dy}{dx} = 6xy$.

12 **a** For the curve $3\sin x + 2\cos y = \sqrt{3}$ show that $\frac{dy}{dx} = \frac{3\cos x}{2\sin y}$.

b Find the gradient of the curve at the point $\left(0, \frac{\pi}{6}\right)$.

13 Find the gradient of each curve at the point given:

a $y + x\ln y + x^2 = 10$ at $(3, 1)$

b $e^x y + 2y = 12$ at $(0, 4)$

14 Find $\frac{dy}{dx}$ in terms of x:

a $y = 8^x$ **b** $y = 2 \times 3^x$ **c** $y = 4^{x^2}$

d $y = 4e^{-3x}$ **e** $y = x^x$

15 Show that the gradient of the curve $y = 3^x$ at the point $(1, 3)$ is $\ln 27$.

16 At time t minutes the temperature θ°C of a cooling oven is given by $\theta = 450e^{-0.8t}$.
Find the rate of decrease of the temperature when $t = 10$.

17 The radius of a sphere is increasing at the rate of $1\,\text{cm}\,\text{s}^{-1}$. Find, in terms of π, the rate of increase of the volume when the radius is 5 cm.

18 The side length of a cube is increasing at the rate of $2\,\text{cm}\,\text{s}^{-1}$. Find the rate of increase of the volume when the length of a side is 6 cm.

19 The surface area S of a sphere of radius r is given by the formula $S = 4\pi r^2$. Find the rate of increase of the surface area when $r = 4$ cm, given that the radius increases at $2\,\text{cm}\,\text{s}^{-1}$.

20 The volume of a cube is increasing at the rate of $81\,\text{cm}^3\,\text{s}^{-1}$. Find the rate of change of the side of the base when its length is 3 cm.

21 The surface area of a sphere is increasing at the rate of $2\pi\,\text{cm}^2\,\text{s}^{-1}$. Find the rate of change of the radius when its length is 1 cm.

22 A hollow right circular cone, whose height is three times the radius, is held with its vertex downwards and water is poured in at a rate of $10\,\text{cm}^3\,\text{s}^{-1}$.

a Show that when the depth of the water is h the volume in the cone is $V = \frac{\pi h^3}{27}$.

b Find, in terms of π, the rate of rise of the water level when the depth is 2 cm.

23 When a metal cube is heated, its volume, $V\,\text{cm}^3$, increases at a constant rate of $3.7 \times 10^{-6}\,\text{cm}^3\,\text{s}^{-1}$. Each edge of the cube has length x cm at time t seconds.

a Find $\frac{dx}{dt}$ when $x = 2$.

b Find the rate of increase of the total surface area of the cube in $\text{cm}^2\,\text{s}^{-1}$, when $x = 2$.

24 The area of a circle is increasing at a rate of $6\,\text{cm}^2\,\text{s}^{-1}$. Find the rate of increase of the circumference when the radius is 3 cm.

25 The area and perimeter of the rectangle shown are denoted by A and P respectively. Find $\frac{\mathrm{d}P}{\mathrm{d}t}$, given $\frac{\mathrm{d}A}{\mathrm{d}t} = 16\,\text{cm}^2\,\text{s}^{-1}$ at the instant when $x = 2\,\text{cm}$.

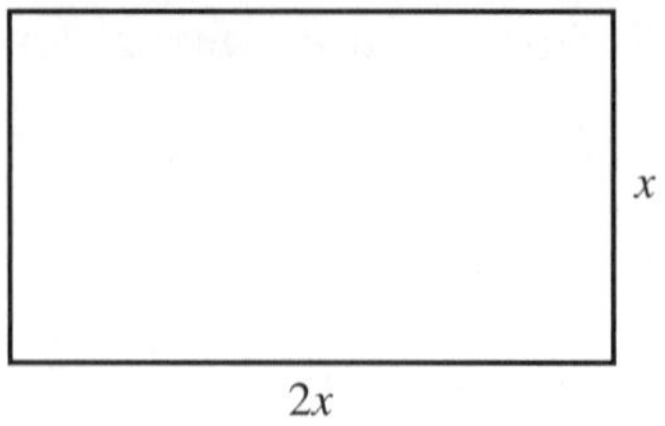

EXAMINATION EXERCISE 10

1 Given that $y \sin 2x + \frac{1}{x} + y^2 = 5$, find an expression for $\frac{\mathrm{d}y}{\mathrm{d}x}$ in terms of x and y.
[OCR, GCE Mathematics, C4, June 2016]

2 A curve has equation $(x + y)^2 = xy^2$. Find the gradient of the curve at the point where $x = 1$. [OCR, GCE Mathematics, C4, June 2015]

3 A curve has equation $y^3 + 2\mathrm{e}^{-3x}y - x = k$, where k is a constant.
The point $P\left(\ln 2, \frac{1}{2}\right)$ lies on this curve.

a Show that the exact value of k is $q - \ln 2$, where q is a rational number.

b Find the gradient of the curve at P. [AQA, GCE Mathematics, C4, June 2015]

4 The equation of a curve is $xy^2 = x^2 + 1$. Find $\frac{\mathrm{d}y}{\mathrm{d}x}$ in terms of x and y, and hence find the coordinates of the stationary points on the curve.
[OCR, GCE Mathematics, C4, Jan 2013]

5 The curve C has the equation $2x + 3y^2 + 3x^2y = 4x^2$.
The point P on the curve has coordinates $(-1, 1)$.

a Find the gradient of the curve at P.

b Hence find the equation of the normal to C at P, giving your answer in the form $ax + by + c = 0$, where a, b and c are integers.
[EDEXCEL, GCE Mathematics, C4, Jan 2012]

6 A curve has equation $\cos 2y + y\mathrm{e}^{3x} = 2\pi$.
The point $A\left(\ln 2, \frac{\pi}{4}\right)$ lies on this curve.

a i Find an expression for $\frac{\mathrm{d}y}{\mathrm{d}x}$.

ii Hence find the exact value of the gradient of the curve at A.

b The normal at A crosses the y-axis at the point B. Find the exact value of the y-coordinate of B. [AQA, GCE Mathematics, C4, June 2014]

7 The equation of a curve C is $(x + 3)(y + 4) = x^2 + y^2$.

i Find $\frac{\mathrm{d}y}{\mathrm{d}x}$ in terms of x and y.

ii The line $2y = x + 3$ meets C at two points. What can be said about the tangents to C at these points? Justify your answer.

iii Find the equation of the tangent at the point $(6, 0)$, giving your answer in the form $ax + by = c$, where a, b and c are integers.

[OCR, GCE Mathematics, C4, Jan 2012]

8 The curve C has equation

$$2x^2y + 2x + 4y - \cos(\pi y) = 17$$

a Use implicit differentiation to find $\dfrac{dy}{dx}$ in terms of x and y.

The point P with coordinates $\left(3, \frac{1}{2}\right)$ lies on C.

The normal to C at P meets the x-axis at the point A.

b Find the x coordinate of A, giving your answer in the form $\dfrac{a\pi + b}{c\pi + d}$, where a, b, c and d are integers to be determined.

[EDEXCEL, GCE Mathematics, C4, June 2016]

9

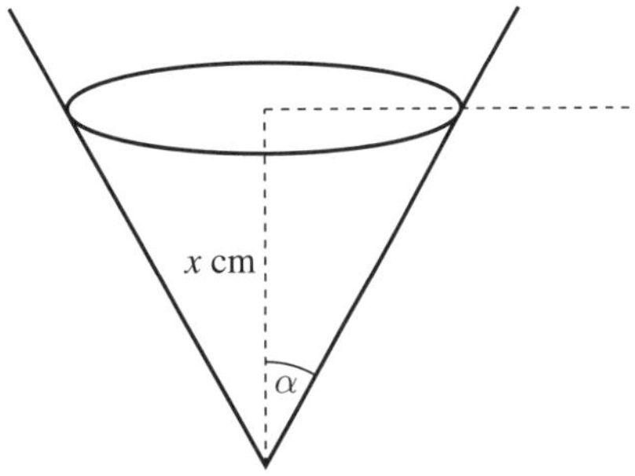

The diagram shows a container in the form of a right circular cone. The angle between the axis and the slant height is α, where $\alpha = \tan^{-1}\left(\frac{1}{2}\right)$. Initially the container is empty, and then liquid is added at the rate of $14\,\text{cm}^3$ per minute. The depth of liquid in the container at time t minutes is $x\,\text{cm}$.

i Show that the volume, $V\,\text{cm}^3$, of liquid in the container when the depth is $x\,\text{cm}$ is given by

$$V = \tfrac{1}{12}\pi x^3.$$

[The volume of a cone is $\frac{1}{3}\pi r^2 h$.]

ii Find the rate at which the depth of the liquid is increasing at the instant when the depth is 8 cm. Give your answer in cm per minute correct to 2 dp.

[OCR, GCE Mathematics, C3, June 2013]

10 At time t seconds the radius of a sphere is r cm, its volume is $V\,\text{cm}^3$ and its surface area is $S\,\text{cm}^2$.

[*You are given that* $V = \frac{4}{3}\pi r^3$ *and that* $S = 4\pi r^2$]

The volume of the sphere is increasing uniformly at a constant rate of $3\,\text{cm}^3\,\text{s}^{-1}$.

a Find $\dfrac{dr}{dt}$ when the radius of the sphere is 4 cm, giving your answer to 3 significant figures.

b Find the rate at which the surface area of the sphere is increasing when the radius is 4 cm.

[EDEXCEL, GCE Mathematics, C4 1R, June 2014]

11 The volume, V cubic metres, of water in a reservoir is given by

$$V = 3(2 + \sqrt{h})^6 - 192,$$

where h metres is the depth of the water. Water is flowing into the reservoir at a constant rate of 150 cubic metres per hour. Find the rate at which the depth of water is increasing at the instant when the depth is 1.4 metres.

[OCR, GCE Mathematics, C3, June 2015]

12

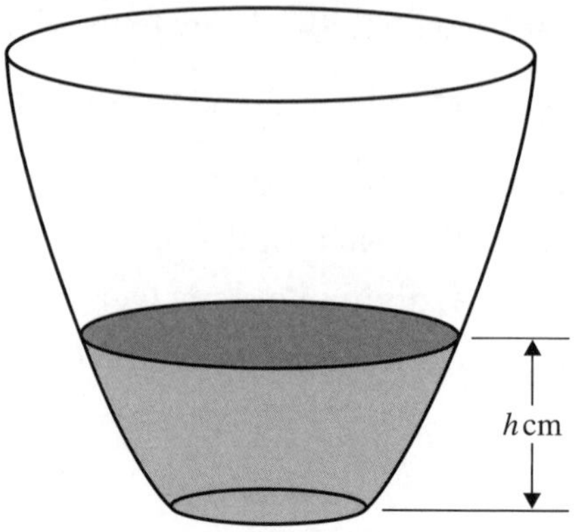

A vase with a circular cross-section is shown above. Water is flowing into the vase. When the depth of the water is h cm, the volume of water V cm^3 is given by

$$V = 4\pi h(h + 4), \quad 0 \leqslant h \leqslant 25$$

Water flows into the vase at a constant rate of $80\pi \, \text{cm}^3 \, \text{s}^{-1}$

Find the rate of change of the depth of the water, in cm s^{-1}, when $h = 6$

[EDEXCEL, GCE Mathematics, C4, June 2014]

13 The volume, V m^3, of liquid in a container is given by

$$V = (3h^2 + 4)^{\frac{3}{2}} - 8,$$

where h m is the depth of the liquid.

i Find the value of $\frac{dV}{dh}$ when $h = 0.6$, giving your answer correct to 2 dp.

ii Liquid is leaking from the container. It is observed that, when the depth of the liquid is 0.6 m, the depth is decreasing at a rate of 0.015 m per hour. Find the rate at which the volume of liquid in the container is decreasing at the instant when the depth is 0.6 m.

[OCR, GCE Mathematics, C3, June 2012]

14

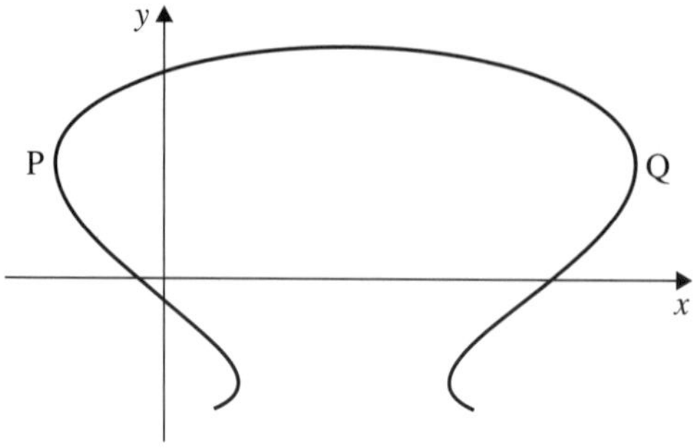

The diagram shows the curve with equation $x^2 + y^3 - 8x - 12y = 4$. At each of the points P and Q the tangent to the curve is parallel to the y-axis. Find the coordinates of P and Q.

[OCR, GCE Mathematics, C4, June 2014]

PART 11

Integration

11.1 Standard functions

In 'Pure Mathematics Book 1' we integrated functions of the form x^n ($n \neq 1$).

We found that $\int x^n \, dx = \dfrac{x^{n+1}}{n+1} + c$

We can now integrate several more functions:

$$e^x \, dx = e^x + c \qquad \int \frac{1}{x} dx = \ln x + c$$

$$\int \sin x \, dx = -\cos x + c \qquad \int \cos x = \sin x + c$$

Earlier in this book we differentiated functions such as $(x + 1)^5$, which is a function of a function. We can now integrate functions such as this.

In general, differentiation is a straight forward procedure but integration can be more difficult if you cannot differentiate standard functions with confidence. The approach to integration is illustrated in the following examples.

Example 1

a $\int (x + 1)^5 \, dx$. We have $\dfrac{d}{dx}(x + 1)^6 = 6(x + 1)^5$.

$\therefore \quad \int (x + 1)^5 \, dx = \frac{1}{6}(x + 1)^6 + c$

b $\int (3x - 1)^4 \, dx$. We have $\dfrac{d}{dx}(3x - 1)^5 = 5(3x - 1)^4 \times 3$.

$\therefore \quad \int (3x - 1)^4 \, dx = \frac{1}{15}(3x - 1)^5 + c$

c $\int \dfrac{1}{(1 + 4x)^2} dx$. We have $\dfrac{d}{dx}(1 + 4x)^{-1} = -1(1 + 4x)^{-2} \times 4$.

$\therefore \quad \int \dfrac{1}{(1 + 4x)^2} dx = -\frac{1}{4}(1 + 4x)^{-1} = -\dfrac{1}{4(1 + 4x)} + c$

Example 2

a $\int 3e^x \, dx = 3e^x + c$

b $\int e^{4x} \, dx$. We have $\dfrac{d}{dx}(e^{4x}) = 4e^{4x}$

$\therefore \quad \int e^{4x} \, dx = \frac{1}{4}e^{4x} + c$

c $\int e^{-2x} \, dx$. We have $\dfrac{d}{dx}(e^{-2x}) = -2e^{-2x}$

$\therefore \quad \int e^{-2x} \, dx = -\frac{1}{2}e^{-2x} + c$

Example 3

a $\int(\sin x + 2\cos x)\,dx = -\cos x + 2\sin x + c$

b $\int \cos 5x\,dx$. We have $\frac{d}{dx}(\sin 5x) = 5\cos 5x$

$\therefore \quad \int \cos 5x\,dx = \frac{1}{5}\sin 5x + c$

c $\int 2\sin(7x-2)$. We have $\frac{d}{dx}[\cos(7x-2)] = -7\sin(7x-2)$

$\therefore \quad \int 2\sin(7x-2)\,dx = -\frac{2}{7}\cos(7x-2) + c$

Example 4

a $\int 3 \times \frac{1}{x}\,dx = 3\ln x + c$

b $\int \frac{1}{2x}\,dx = \frac{1}{2}\int\frac{1}{x}\,dx = \frac{1}{2}\ln x + c$

c $\int \frac{1}{5x-1} = \frac{1}{5}\ln(5x-1) + c$

Example 5

Evaluate the definite integrals.

a $\int_0^{\frac{\pi}{4}} \cos 2x\,dx = \left[\frac{1}{2}\sin 2x\right]_0^{\frac{\pi}{4}} = \frac{1}{2}\left[\sin\left(2 \times \frac{\pi}{4}\right) - \sin 0\right]$

$$= \frac{1}{2}\sin\frac{\pi}{2} - 0 = \frac{1}{2}$$

b $\int_0^1 (1 + e^x + e^{2x})\,dx = \left[x + e^x + \frac{1}{2}e^{2x}\right]_0^1$

$$= 1 + e + \frac{1}{2}e^2 - \left(0 + 1 + \frac{1}{2}\right)$$

$$= e + \frac{1}{2}e^2 - \frac{1}{2}$$

c $\int_2^3 \left(1 + \frac{1}{x}\right)^2 dx = \int_2^3 \left(1 + \frac{2}{x} + \frac{1}{x^2}\right) dx = \int_2^3 \left(1 + \frac{2}{x} + x^{-2}\right) dx$

$$= \left[x + 2\ln x + \frac{x^{-1}}{(-1)}\right]_2^3 = \left[x + 2\ln x - \frac{1}{x}\right]_2^3$$

$$= 3 + 2\ln 3 - \frac{1}{3} - \left(2 + 2\ln 2 - \frac{1}{2}\right)$$

$$= 1\tfrac{1}{6} + 2\ln 3 - 2\ln 2$$

$$= 1\tfrac{1}{6} + 2\ln\tfrac{3}{2}$$

Exercise 11A

1 Integrate with respect to x:

a $(1 + x)^3$ **b** $(x + 4)^6$ **c** $(2x + 1)^4$ **d** $(1 - x)^4$

e $\dfrac{1}{(x + 3)^2}$ **f** $2(3x - 1)^2$ **g** $\dfrac{4}{(x + 1)^3}$ **h** $(5x + 3)^{-2}$

i $7e^x$ **j** $x + 5e^x$ **k** e^{5x} **l** $e^{6x} - 1$

m $3e^{2x}$ **n** $9e^{-x}$ **o** $\dfrac{4}{e^x}$ **p** $\dfrac{1}{e^x} + 2x$

2 Integrate with respect to x:

a $\int \sin x \, dx$ **b** $\int \cos 4x \, dx$ **c** $\int \sin 10x \, dx$

d $2\int \cos 5x \, dx$ **e** $\int \frac{1}{2} \sin 6x \, dx$ **f** $\int (\cos 2x + 2x) \, dx$

g $\int \sin (4x - 1) \, dx$ **h** $\int [x - \cos (x + 1)] \, dx$ **i** $\int \left(2x + \frac{1}{x}\right) dx$

j $\int \left(\cos x + \frac{2}{x}\right) dx$ **k** $\int \frac{1}{4x} \, dx$ **l** $\int \frac{1}{x + 3} \, dx$

m $\int \frac{6}{1 + x} \, dx$ **n** $\int \frac{1}{3x + 2} \, dx$ **o** $\int \left(e^{2x} + \frac{2}{x}\right) dx$

3 **a** Work out $\dfrac{d}{dx}(4x + 1)^{\frac{3}{2}}$. **b** Hence find $\int (4x + 1)^{\frac{1}{2}} dx$.

4 Work out:

a $\dfrac{d}{dx}\sqrt{5x - 2}$ **b** $\int (5x - 2)^{-\frac{1}{2}} dx$

5 Work out the following:

a $\int (6x + 1)^{\frac{1}{3}} dx$ **b** $\int \frac{1}{\sqrt{x + 2}} \, dx$ **c** $\int (1 + 2x)^{\frac{3}{2}} dx$

6 Find the shaded area under the curve $y = e^x$.

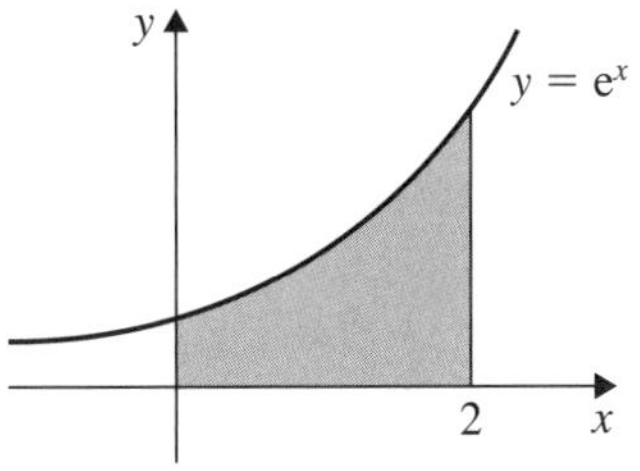

7 Calculate the following indefinite integrals:

a $\int e^{3x+1} \, dx$ **b** $\int 4e^{2x-3} \, dx$ **c** $\int \frac{5}{e^x} \, dx$

$\int (2x+1)^3\,dx$ e $\int \frac{1}{(4x-3)^2}\,dx$ f $\int \frac{e^{2x}+1}{e^x}\,dx$

g $\int \sqrt{2x+1}\,dx$ h $\int \frac{1}{\sqrt{4x+5}}\,dx$ i $\int (e^x+1)^2\,dx$

8 Find $\int y\,dx$ for the following:

a $y = \frac{4}{2x+7}$ b $y = (e^x+1)(e^{-x}+1)$ c $y = \frac{2}{(3x-2)^2}\,dx$

d $y = \sqrt{4x+3}$ e $y = \frac{1}{\sqrt{(8x-1)}}$ f $y = \sqrt[3]{6x+5}$

9 Show that $\frac{x^3+5x+1}{x^2} = x + \frac{5}{x} + \frac{1}{x^2}$.

Hence find $\int \frac{x^3+5x+1}{x^2}\,dx$

10 Find the following indefinite integrals:

a $\int \left(1 - \frac{2}{x}\right)^2 dx$ b $\int \frac{x^2+5x+3}{x^2}\,dx$ c $\int \frac{e^x+1}{2}\,dx$

d $\int \frac{(x-2)(x-3)}{x^2}\,dx$ e $\int \frac{(x-5)(x+5)}{x}\,dx$ f $\int \frac{e^{3x+2}+1}{e^{2x}}\,dx$

11 The curve $y = \sin 4x$ meets the x-axis at $x = 0$ and $x = a$.

a Write down the value of a in radians.

b Find the area enclosed by the curve $y = \sin 4x$ and the x-axis between $x = 0$ and $x = a$.

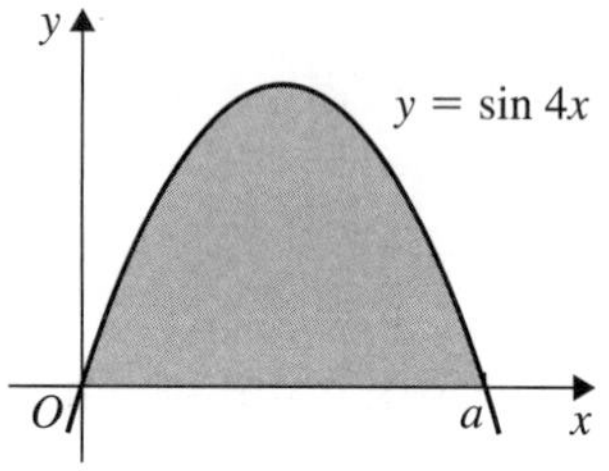

Evaluate:

12 $\int_{\frac{\pi}{6}}^{\frac{\pi}{2}} \cos x\,dx$ **13** $\int_0^1 e^{3x}\,dx$ **14** $\int_2^5 \frac{1}{x}\,dx$

15 $\int_0^{\frac{1}{3}} (3x-1)^3\,dx$ **16** $\int_{\frac{\pi}{6}}^{\frac{\pi}{4}} \sin 2x\,dx$ **17** $\int_{-1}^1 e^{2x+1}\,dx$

18 $\int_2^4 \frac{10}{x}\,dx$ **19** $\int_1^3 \frac{1}{x+3}\,dx$ **20** $\int_0^5 \sqrt{x+4}\,dx$

21 $\int_1^{1.5} \cos(2x-1)\,dx$ **22** $\int_1^3 2x + \frac{1}{2x}\,dx$ **23** $\int_0^{\frac{\pi}{4}} \sec^2 x\,dx$

24 $\int_{\frac{\pi}{6}}^{\frac{\pi}{4}} 3\sec^2 x\,dx$ **25** $\int_1^2 \left(x + \frac{1}{x}\right)^2 dx$ **26** $\int_0^2 \frac{1}{2x+1}\,dx$

27 Show that $5\cos^2 x + 3\sin^2 x - 1 \equiv \cos 2x + 3$

Hence evaluate $\int_0^{\frac{\pi}{4}} (5\cos^2 x + 3\sin^2 x - 1)\,dx$.

28 Evaluate $\int_0^{\frac{\pi}{6}} (\cos 3x + \sin 2x)\,dx$.

29 The sketch shows the curve $y = e^x$ and the lines $x = 1$ and $x = 3$.

Show that the area of the shaded region is $e(e^2 - 2)$.

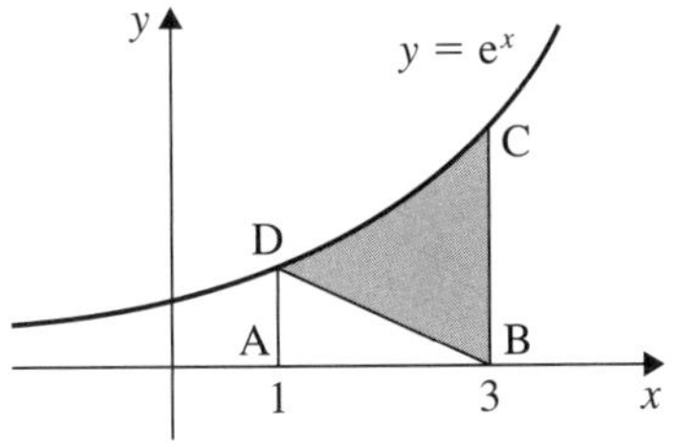

11.2 Integrals of the form $\int \frac{f'(x)}{f(x)}\,dx$

In Part 7 of this book we found that $\frac{d}{dx}[\ln f(x)] = \frac{1}{f(x)} \times f'(x)$.

It follows that $\int \frac{f'(x)}{f(x)}\,dx = \ln f(x) + c$.

The function $\ln x$ is only valid provided $x > 0$ so we need to be able to deal with integrals involving negative values of x.

The area under the curve $y = \frac{1}{x}$ between $x = -1$ and $x = -2$

is equal to the area between $x = 1$ and $x = 2$.

We can write $\int \frac{1}{x}\,dx = \ln|x| + c$ and further that $\int \frac{f'(x)}{f(x)} = \ln|f(x)| + c$

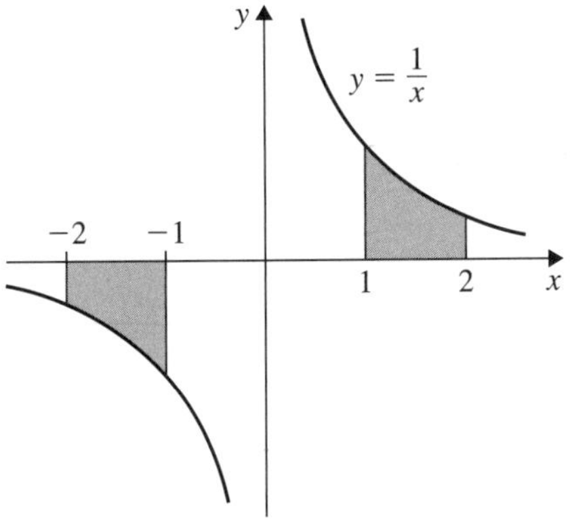

Normally we write the modulus sign only when dealing with definite integrals.

Note that if the interval between the limits a and b of the integral $\int_a^b \frac{1}{x}\,dx$ includes $x = 0$, then the integration is not valid. We cannot integrate across a discontinuity.

Example 1

Integrate the indefinite integrals:

a $\displaystyle\int \frac{2x}{x^2+1}\,dx = \ln(x^2+1) + c$

b $\displaystyle\int \frac{3x^2-1}{x^3-x}\,dx = \ln(x^3-x) + c$

c $\displaystyle\int \frac{\cos x}{\sin x}\,dx = \ln \sin x + c$

d $\displaystyle\int \frac{1}{4x+3} = \frac{1}{4}\int \frac{4}{4x+3} = \frac{1}{4}\ln(4x+3) + c$

e $\displaystyle\int \frac{x}{x^2-7}\,dx = \frac{1}{2}\int \frac{2x}{x^2-7}\,dx$

$\displaystyle= \frac{1}{2}\ln(x^2-7) + c$

f $\displaystyle\int \frac{e^x}{3e^x+11} = \frac{1}{3}\int \frac{3e^x}{3e^x+11}$

$\displaystyle= \frac{1}{3}\ln(3e^x+11) + c$

Example 2

Evaluate the definite integral $\displaystyle\int_1^2 \frac{1}{1-2x}\,dx$.

$$\int_1^2 \frac{1}{1-2x}\,dx = -\frac{1}{2}\int_1^2 \frac{-2}{1-2x}\,dx$$

$$= -\frac{1}{2}\Big[\ln|1-2x|\Big]_1^2$$

We use the modulus function because when $x = 1$ and $x = 2$, $1 - 2x < 0$

$$= -\frac{1}{2}[\ln 3 - \ln 1]$$

[Remember $|-3| = 3$ and $|-1| = 1$.]

$$= -\frac{1}{2}\ln 3$$

Example 3

Find $\int \tan x\,dx$.

$$\int \tan x\,dx = \int \frac{\sin x}{\cos x}\,dx$$

[Remember this method.]

$$= -\int \frac{-\sin x}{\cos x}\,dx$$

$$= -\ln\cos x + c$$

$$= \ln(\cos x)^{-1} + c$$

$$= \ln\sec x + c$$

Exercise 11B

Find the following indefinite integrals:

1 $\displaystyle\int \frac{1}{x+3}\,dx$

2 $\displaystyle\int \frac{2}{2x+1}\,dx$

3 $\displaystyle\int \frac{2x}{x^2+5}\,dx$

4 $\displaystyle\int \frac{3x^2}{x^3+2}\,dx$

5 $\displaystyle\int \frac{1}{4x+1}\,dx$

6 $\displaystyle\int \frac{1}{7x-1}\,dx$

7 $\displaystyle\int \frac{e^x}{e^x + 3}\,dx$ **8** $\displaystyle\int \frac{x}{x^2 + 3}\,dx$ **9** $\displaystyle\int \cot x\,dx$

10 $\displaystyle\int \frac{1}{x+1} + \frac{1}{x-2}\,dx$ **11** $\displaystyle\int \frac{2}{2x+1} + \frac{5}{5x+2}\,dx$ **12** $\displaystyle\int \frac{6}{2x+1} - \frac{1}{x+1}\,dx$

13 Find the area under the curve $y = \dfrac{1}{3x-1}$ between $x = 1$ and $x = 2$.

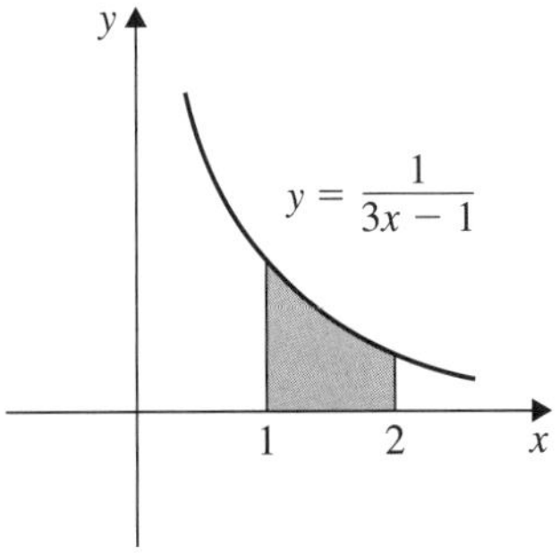

14 Find the exact values of the following definite integrals, leaving your answers in terms of logarithms:

a $\displaystyle\int_1^4 \frac{2}{x}\,dx$ **b** $\displaystyle\int_1^8 \frac{1}{3x}\,dx$ **c** $\displaystyle\int_3^6 \frac{2x+1}{x}\,dx$

d $\displaystyle\int_2^8 \frac{4x-1}{2x}\,dx$ **e** $\displaystyle\int_2^3 \frac{3}{3x-5}\,dx$ **f** $\displaystyle\int_2^4 \frac{2}{x-1}\,dx$

g $\displaystyle\int_1^4 \frac{6}{2x+1} - \frac{3}{3x-2}\,dx$ **h** $\displaystyle\int_2^5 \frac{1}{x+1} - \frac{1}{x-1}\,dx$ **i** $\displaystyle\int_5^{15} \left(\frac{x+1}{x}\right)dx$

j $\displaystyle\int_0^3 \frac{3}{3x+1} + \frac{2}{2x+3}\,dx$ **k** $\displaystyle\int_2^4 \left(\frac{x^2+2x+3}{x}\right)dx$ **l** $\displaystyle\int_1^3 \left(\frac{x^2-4}{x}\right)dx$

15 Obtain the area enclosed by the curve $y = \dfrac{1}{x}$, the x-axis and the lines $x = -2$ and $x = -3$.

16 Evaluate the following, giving your answers correct to 2 dp:

a $\displaystyle\int_{-2}^{0} \frac{1}{x-1}\,dx$ **b** $\displaystyle\int_1^2 \frac{x}{x^2-9}\,dx$ **c** $\displaystyle\int_1^3 \frac{1}{1-4x}\,dx$

17 Find the following:

a $\displaystyle\int \tan x\,dx$ **b** $\displaystyle\int \frac{\cos 2x}{\sin 2x}\,dx$ **c** $\displaystyle\int \frac{\sec^2 x}{\tan x}\,dx$

d $\displaystyle\int \frac{\sin x}{\cos x + 3}\,dx$ **e** $\displaystyle\int \frac{2\sin x\cos x}{\cos 2x}\,dx$ **f** $\displaystyle\int \frac{1}{x\ln x}\,dx$

11.3 Integration by substitution

Some integrals are easier to perform if we change the variable by making a substitution.

Let f(x) be a function of x and let $y = \int f(x)\,dx$

So $\dfrac{dy}{dx} = f(x)$.

If u is a function of x then y is a function of u.

$$\frac{dy}{du} = \frac{dy}{dx} \cdot \frac{dx}{du}$$
$$= f(x)\frac{dx}{du}$$

Integrating with respect to u, $y = \int f(x)\frac{dx}{du}\,du$

or $$\boxed{\int f(x)\,dx = \int f(x)\frac{dx}{du}\,du}$$

So an integral with respect to x is transformed into an integral with respect to u.

We substitute for f(x) and $\dfrac{dx}{du}$ in terms of u.

Example 1

Find $\int x(2x+1)^2\,dx$

Let $u = 2x + 1 \Rightarrow 2x = u - 1$

$$x = \frac{1}{2}u - \frac{1}{2}$$

$$\frac{dx}{du} = \frac{1}{2}$$

$$\int x(2x+1)^2\frac{dx}{du}\,du = \int\left(\frac{u-1}{2}\right)u^2\frac{1}{2}\,du$$

$$= \frac{1}{4}\int u^3 - u^2\,du = \frac{1}{4}\left(\frac{u^4}{4} - \frac{u^3}{3}\right) + c$$

$$= \frac{u^3}{48}(3u-4) + c = \frac{(2x+1)^3}{48}[3(2x+1) - 4] + c$$

$$= \frac{(2x+1)^3}{48}(6x-1) + c$$

Example 2

Find $I = \int x\sqrt{x-1}\,dx$

Let $u = \sqrt{x-1} \Rightarrow x - 1 = u^2$

$$x = u^2 + 1$$

$$\frac{dx}{dx} = 2u$$

$$\therefore \quad I = \int (u^2+1)u \,.\, 2u\,du$$

$$\uparrow x \quad \uparrow \sqrt{x-1} \quad \uparrow \frac{dx}{du}$$

$$= 2\int u^4 + u^2\,du$$

$$= 2\left(\frac{u^5}{5} + \frac{u^3}{3}\right) + c$$

$$= 2\left(\frac{3u^5 + 5u^3}{15}\right) + c$$

$$= \frac{2}{15}(x-1)^{\frac{3}{2}}(3x+2) + c$$

Example 3

Find $I = \int 2x(x^2+1)^2\,dx$

Let $u = x^2 + 1$

$$\frac{du}{dx} = 2x$$

$$\therefore \quad I = \int 2x(x^2+1)^2 \frac{dx}{du}\,dx$$

$$= \int 2x(x^2+1)^2 \frac{1}{2x}\,du$$

$$= \int u^2\,du$$

$$= \frac{u^3}{3} + c$$

$$= \frac{1}{3}(x^2+1)^3 + c$$

Example 4

Evaluate the definite integral $\int_1^2 x(2x-3)^3\,dx$

This is a definite integral and we must remember to change the limits to the corresponding values of the new variable u.

Let $u = 2x - 3 \Rightarrow x = \frac{u+3}{2} \Rightarrow \frac{dx}{du} = \frac{1}{2}$

When $x = 1$, $u = -1$ and when $x = 2$, $u = 1$

$$\therefore \quad \int_1^2 x(2x-3)^3\,dx = \int_{u=-1}^{u=1} x(2x-3)^3 \frac{dx}{du}\,du$$

$$= \int_{-1}^{1} \left(\frac{u+3}{2}\right) u^3 \frac{1}{2}\,du = \frac{1}{4}\int_{-1}^{1} u^4 + 3u^3\,du$$

$$= \frac{1}{4}\left[\frac{u^5}{5} + \frac{3}{4}u^4\right]_{-1}^{1}$$

$$= \frac{1}{4}\left[\frac{1}{5} + \frac{3}{4} - \left(-\frac{1}{5} + \frac{3}{4}\right)\right] = \frac{1}{4}\left[\frac{2}{5}\right] = \frac{1}{10}$$

Example 5

Find $\int \frac{1}{\sqrt{1-x^2}}\,\mathrm{d}x$

In this case we use a non-linear substitution.

Let $x = \sin u$

$\frac{\mathrm{d}x}{\mathrm{d}u} = \cos u$

$$\therefore \quad \int \frac{1}{\sqrt{1-x^2}}\,\mathrm{d}x = \int \frac{1}{\sqrt{1-\sin^2 u}}\,\frac{\mathrm{d}x}{\mathrm{d}u}\,.\,\mathrm{d}u$$

$$= \int \frac{1}{\sqrt{\cos^2 u}} \cos u\,\mathrm{d}u$$

$$= \int 1\,\mathrm{d}u = u + c$$

$$= \sin^{-1} x + c$$

Exercise 11C

1 Find the following integrals, using the given substitutions:

a $\int x(x+2)^2\,\mathrm{d}x$ $\quad u = x + 2$

b $\int x(x-3)^2\,\mathrm{d}x$ $\quad u = x - 3$

c $\int 2x(x+4)^3\,\mathrm{d}x$ $\quad u = x + 4$

d $\int x(x-1)^2\,\mathrm{d}x$ $\quad u = x - 1$

e $\int x\sqrt{x+3}\,\mathrm{d}x$ $\quad u = \sqrt{x+3}$

f $\int \frac{x^2}{\sqrt{x-2}}\,\mathrm{d}x$ $\quad u = x - 2$

2 Find the following indefinite integrals using appropriate substitutions:

a $\int x(x+1)^3\,\mathrm{d}x$

b $\int x(x-1)^5\,\mathrm{d}x$

c $\int x(2x+1)^3\,\mathrm{d}x$

d $\int x\sqrt{(4x-1)}\,\mathrm{d}x$

e $\int \frac{x}{\sqrt{(5x+1)}}\,\mathrm{d}x$

f $\int (x+1)(3x-2)^4\,\mathrm{d}x$

3 Find the following indefinite integrals using the given substitutions:

a $\int 12x(x^2+1)^3\,\mathrm{d}x$ $\quad u = x^2 + 1$

b $\int 18x^2(x^3-3)^2\,\mathrm{d}x$ $\quad u = x^3 - 3$

c $\int \mathrm{e}^x(\mathrm{e}^x-1)^3\,\mathrm{d}x$ $\quad u = \mathrm{e}^x - 1$

d $\int \frac{\mathrm{e}^x}{\sqrt{\mathrm{e}^x+2}}\,\mathrm{d}x$ $\quad u = \mathrm{e}^x + 2$

e $\int \sin^2 x \cos x\,\mathrm{d}x$ $\quad u = \sin x$

f $\int \cos^3 x \sin x\,\mathrm{d}x$ $\quad u = \cos x$

g $\int \tan^3 x \sec^2 x\,\mathrm{d}x$ $\quad u = \tan x$

h $\int \frac{1}{\sqrt{1-x^2}}\,\mathrm{d}x$ $\quad x = \sin u$

4 Find the following definite integrals using appropriate substitutions:

a $\int_0^1 x(x+1)^3\,\mathrm{d}x$

b $\int_3^4 x(x-3)^4\,\mathrm{d}x$

c $\int_3^6 x\sqrt{x-2}\,\mathrm{d}x$

d $\int_0^4 \frac{x}{\sqrt{(2x+1)}}\,\mathrm{d}x$

5 Find the following definite integrals using the given substitutions:

a $\displaystyle\int_0^{\pi} e^{\cos x}\sin x\,dx \qquad u = \cos x$

b $\displaystyle\int_1^3 \frac{x}{\sqrt{x+2}}\,dx \qquad u = x + 2$

c $\displaystyle\int_0^{\frac{\pi}{4}} \frac{\sin x}{\cos x}\,dx \qquad u = \cos x$

d $\displaystyle\int_0^{\frac{\pi}{2}} \sin x \sin 2x\,dx \qquad u = \sin x$

6 Use the substitution $x = \sin\theta$ to show that, for $|x| \leqslant 1$,

$$\int \frac{1}{(1-x^2)^{\frac{3}{2}}}\,dx = \frac{x}{(1-x^2)^{\frac{1}{2}}} + c, \text{ where } c \text{ is an arbitary constant.}$$

7 By making the substitution $x = 2\sin t$, evaluate $\displaystyle\int_0^1 \frac{x^2}{\sqrt{(4-x^2)}}\,dx$.

Give your answer correct to 2 dp. [Hint: see section 11.5]

11.4 Integration by parts

In Part 7 we obtained a formula for differentiating the product of two functions u and v.

$$\frac{d}{dx}(uv) = u\frac{dv}{dx} + v\frac{du}{dx}$$

Integrate both sides of the equation with respect to x.

$$\int \frac{d}{dx}(uv)\,dx = \int u\frac{dv}{dx}\,dx + \int v\frac{du}{dx}\,dx$$

$$uv = \int u\frac{dv}{dx}\,dx + \int v\frac{du}{dx}\,dx$$

or

$$\boxed{\int u\frac{dv}{dx}\,dx = uv - \int v\frac{du}{dx}\,dx}$$

This is the formula for integrating by parts.

Example 1

Find $\int x\,e^{2x}\,dx$

Let $u = x$ and $\dfrac{dv}{dx} = e^{2x}$

Then $\dfrac{du}{dx} = 1$ and $v = \dfrac{1}{2}e^{2x}$

By the formula: $\displaystyle\int u\frac{dv}{dx}\,dx = uv - \int v\frac{du}{dx}\,dx$

$$\int x\,e^{2x}\,dx = x\,.\,\frac{1}{2}e^{2x} - \int \frac{1}{2}e^{2x}\,.\,1\,dx$$

$$= \frac{x}{2}e^{2x} - \frac{1}{4}e^{2x} + c$$

Notice that we had to make a choice in the original integral. We could have chosen $x = u$ or $x = \frac{dv}{dx}$. We chose to let $x = u$ because $\frac{du}{dx} = 1$.

You will learn by experience which substitution to make in different questions. If you find that you have made the wrong choice, abandon the working and start again.

Example 2

Find $I = \int x \ln x \, dx$

Let $u = \ln x$ and $\frac{dv}{dx} = x$. Notice that we could not choose $\frac{dv}{dx} = \ln x$ because it is not easy to integrate $\ln x$.

So $\frac{du}{dx} = \frac{1}{x}$ and $v = \frac{1}{2}x^2$

$$\therefore \quad I = \underset{u}{\underset{\uparrow}{\ln x}} \times \underset{v}{\underset{\uparrow}{\frac{1}{2}x^2}} - \int \underset{v}{\underset{\uparrow}{\frac{1}{2}x^2}} \times \underset{\frac{du}{dx}}{\underset{\uparrow}{\frac{1}{x}}} dx$$

$$I = \frac{1}{2}x^2 \ln x - \frac{1}{2}\int x \, dx$$

$$= \frac{1}{2}x^2 \ln x - \frac{1}{4}x^2 + c$$

Example 3

Find $I = \int \ln x \, dx$.

There is a neat 'trick' involved here.

Write $I = \int 1 \times \ln x \, dx$ and let $u = \ln x$ and $\frac{dv}{dx} = 1$

Then $\frac{du}{dx} = \frac{1}{x}$ and $v = x$

$$\therefore \quad I = \underset{u}{\underset{\uparrow}{(\ln x)}} \times \underset{v}{\underset{\uparrow}{x}} - \int \underset{v}{\underset{\uparrow}{x}} \times \underset{\frac{du}{dx}}{\underset{\uparrow}{\frac{1}{x}}} dx$$

$$= x \ln x - \int 1 \, dx$$

$$= x \ln x - x + c$$

Example 4

Find $I = \int x^2 e^x \, dx$

Let $u = x^2$, $\frac{dv}{dx} = e^x$ so that $\frac{du}{dx} = 2x$ and $v = e^x$

$$\therefore \quad I = x^2 e^x - \int e^x . 2x \, dx$$

Now consider $\int 2x\,e^x\,dx$

Let $u = 2x$, $\dfrac{dv}{dx} = e^x$ so that $\dfrac{du}{dx} = 2$ and $v = e^x$

$$\therefore \quad \int 2x\,e^x\,dx = 2x\,e^x - \int e^x \,.\, 2\,dx$$

$$= 2x\,e^x - 2e^x + c$$

$$\therefore \quad I = x^2 e^x - (2x\,e^x - 2e^x) + c$$

$$= e^x(x^2 - 2x + 2) + c$$

This example shows that in some questions you may have to integrate by parts more than once.

Exercise 11D

1 Use integration by parts to find the following:

a $\int x(1 + x)^2\,dx$ $\quad \left[\text{Let } u = x \text{ and } \dfrac{dv}{dx} = (1 + x)^2\right]$

b $\int x\cos x\,dx$ $\quad \left[\text{Let } u = x \text{ and } \dfrac{dv}{dx} = \cos x\right]$

2 Integrate the following:

a $\int x\,e^x\,dx$ **b** $\int x(1 + x)^3\,dx$ **c** $\int x\,e^{-x}\,dx$

d $\int x\,e^{3x}\,dx$ **e** $\int x\sin x\,dx$ **f** $\int 3x\cos 2x\,dx$

g $\int 2x(x - 1)^3\,dx$ **h** $\int x\sqrt{(x + 1)}\,dx$ **i** $\int x\ln 2x\,dx$

j $\int x^2\ln x\,dx$ **k** $\int \dfrac{\ln x}{x^3}\,dx$ **l** $\int x^2 e^x\,dx$

3 The sketch shows the curve $y = x\,e^{-x}$ and the line $x = 1$. Find the shaded area.

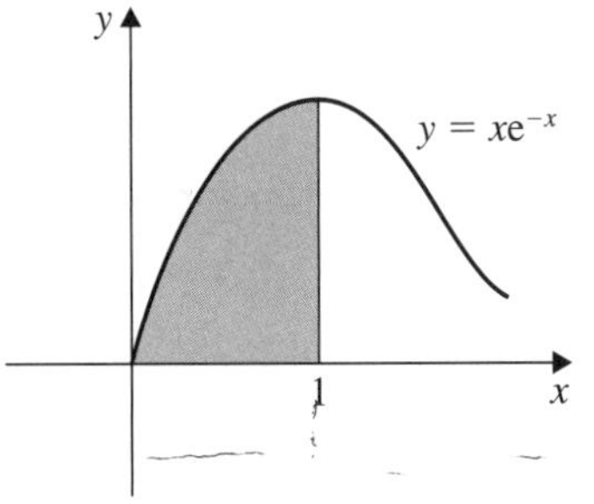

4 Calculate the exact values of the following definite integrals:

a $\int_0^1 xe^{-3x}\,dx$ **b** $\int_0^{\frac{\pi}{4}} x\sin 2x\,dx$

c $\int_0^1 x(2x + 1)^2\,dx$ **d** $\int_3^8 x\sqrt{(x + 1)}\,dx$

e $\int_0^e x^2\ln x\,dx$ **f** $\int_0^{\frac{\pi}{2}} x^2\sin x\,dx$

5 **a** Find the exact value of $\int_0^1 x(2x + 1)^3\,dx$ by using integration by parts.

b Show that you get the same value for $\int_0^1 x(2x + 1)^3\,dx$ by using the method of integration by substitution, with $u = 2x + 1$.

6 **a** Show that $\int 3x(1 + 2x)^4\,dx = \dfrac{(1 + 2x)^5(10x - 1)}{40} + c$.

b Show that $\int \dfrac{x}{e^{2x}}\,dx = \left(\dfrac{2x + 1}{4e^{2x}}\right) + c$.

c Show that $\int \dfrac{4x}{\sqrt{x + 1}}\,dx = \dfrac{8(x - 2)\sqrt{x + 1}}{3} + c$.

7 The curve $y = e^x(1 - x)$ is shown.

a Write down the coordinates of point A and point B where the curve cuts the axes.

b Calculate the area enclosed by the curve and the x and y axes.

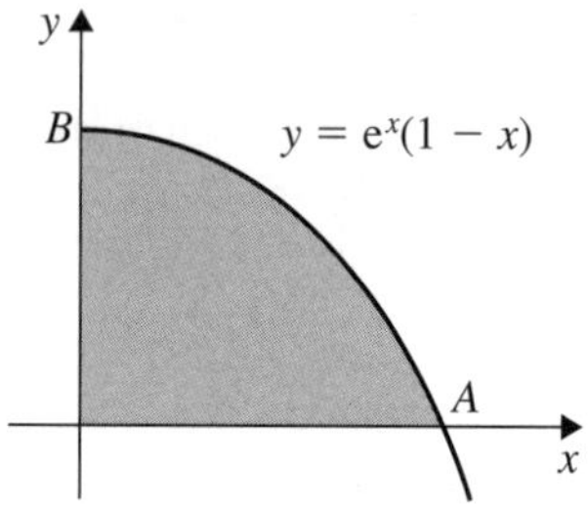

8 **a** Find $\dfrac{d}{dx}(e^{x^2})$.

b By writing $x^3e^{x^2} = \dfrac{x^2}{2}(2xe^{x^2})$, find $\int x^3e^{x^2}\,dx$.

9* **a** Show that $\int e^x \cos x\,dx = e^x \sin x - \int e^x \sin x\,dx$.

b Find a similar expression for $\int e^x \sin x\,dx$.

c Hence find $\int e^x \cos x\,dx$.

10* Find **a** $\int e^{5x} \sin 3x\,dx$

b $\int e^{ax} \sin bx\,dx$

11.5 Using trigonometric identities

Sometimes we use trigonometric identities to transform an integral into a function which can be integrated. The most frequently used formulae are below:

$\cos 2x = 2\cos^2 x - 1$

$\cos 2x = 1 - 2\sin^2 x$

$1 + \tan^2 x = \sec^2 x$

Remember also that $\cos 4x = 2\cos^2 2x - 1$ and so on.

Example 1

Find $I = \int \sin^2 x \, dx$

Rearrange the formula

$$\cos 2x = 1 - 2\sin^2 x$$
$$2\sin^2 x = 1 - \cos 2x$$
$$\sin^2 x = \tfrac{1}{2}(1 - \cos 2x)$$

$$\therefore \quad I = \tfrac{1}{2}\int (1 - \cos 2x) \, dx = \tfrac{1}{2}(x - \tfrac{1}{2}\sin 2x) + c$$
$$= \tfrac{1}{2}x - \tfrac{1}{4}\sin 2x + c$$

Example 2

Find $I = \int \cos^2 4x \, dx$

Rearrange the formula

$$\cos 8x = 2\cos^2 4x - 1$$
$$\cos^2 4x = \tfrac{1}{2}(\cos 8x + 1)$$

$$\therefore \quad I = \tfrac{1}{2}\int (\cos 8x + 1) \, dx = \tfrac{1}{16}\sin 8x + \tfrac{1}{2}x + c$$

Example 3

Find $I = \int \tan^2 x \, dx$

From above $\tan^2 x = \sec^2 x - 1$

$$\therefore \quad I = \int (\sec^2 x - 1) dx$$
$$= \tan x - x + c$$

EXERCISE 11E

1 Integrate with respect to x:

a $\int \sin^2 x \, dx$ **b** $\int \cos^2 x \, dx$ **c** $\int \tan^2 x \, dx$

d $\int \sin^2 3x \, dx$ **e** $\int \cos^2 2x \, dx$ **f** $\int (1 - 2\sin x)^2 \, dx$

g $\int (\cos x + \sec x)^2 \, dx$ **h** $\int \tan^2 2x \, dx$ **i** $\int (1 + \tan x)^2 \, dx$

2 Evaluate the following:

a $\int_0^{\frac{\pi}{4}} \sin^2 x \, dx$ **b** $\int_0^{\frac{\pi}{2}} \cos^2 \tfrac{1}{2}x$ **c** $\int_0^{\frac{\pi}{3}} \tan^2 x \, dx$

d $\int_0^{\frac{\pi}{4}} (1 + 2\cos 2x)^2 \, dx$ **e** $\int_{\frac{\pi}{6}}^{\frac{\pi}{4}} (\sin^2 x + \cos^2 x) \, dx$

11.6 Integration using partial fractions

Example 1

Evaluate $\mathrm{I} = \int_2^3 \frac{12x^2 - 13x + 2}{(2x-1)^2(x-1)}\,\mathrm{d}x$

Using the methods from Part 3 we obtain

$$\frac{12x^2 - 13x + 2}{(2x-1)^2(x-1)} \equiv \frac{4}{2x-1} + \frac{3}{(2x-1)^2} + \frac{1}{x-1}$$

$$\therefore\quad \mathrm{I} = \int_2^3 \frac{4}{2x-1} + \frac{3}{(2x-1)^2} + \frac{1}{x-1}\,\mathrm{d}x$$

$$= \left[2\ln|2x-1| - \frac{3}{2}(2x-1)^{-1} + \ln|x-1|\right]_2^3$$

$$= 2\ln 5 - \frac{3}{2}\times\frac{1}{5} + \ln 2 - \left(2\ln 3 - \frac{3}{2}\times\frac{1}{3} + \ln 1\right)$$

$$= \ln 5^2 + \ln 2 - \ln 3^2 - \frac{3}{10} + \frac{1}{2}$$

$$= \ln\left(\frac{50}{9}\right) + \frac{1}{5}$$

Exercise 11F

1 **a** Express $\dfrac{x}{(1+x)(1+2x)}$ in partial fractions.

b Find $\displaystyle\int \frac{x}{(1+x)(1+2x)}\,\mathrm{d}x$.

2 Using partial fractions, calculate the following indefinite integrals:

a $\displaystyle\int \frac{2}{x^2-1}\,\mathrm{d}x$ **b** $\displaystyle\int \frac{x+6}{x^2+9x+20}\,\mathrm{d}x$ **c** $\displaystyle\int \frac{x+18}{x^2-9x+14}\,\mathrm{d}x$

3 Use partial fractions to show that $\displaystyle\int_0^1 \frac{18-4x-x^2}{(4-3x)(1+x)^2} = \frac{7}{3}\ln 2 + \frac{3}{2}$.

4 The diagram shows the graph of

$y = \dfrac{1}{(x-1)(x-3)}$

The line $y = -\frac{4}{3}$ intersects the curve at points P and Q.

Calculate the area of the shaded region, giving your answer correct to 3 dp.

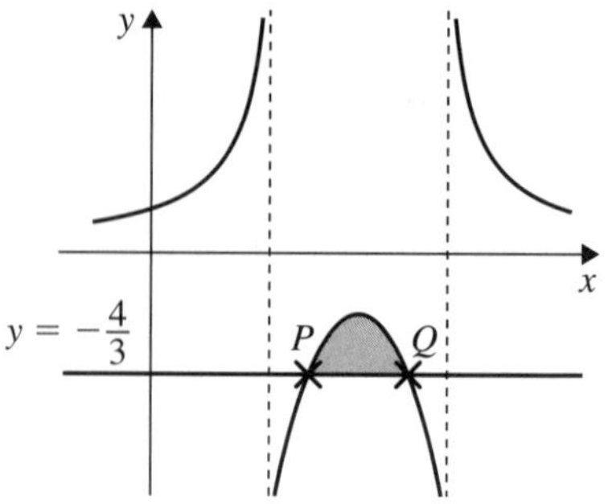

5 **a** Express $\dfrac{8x^2+16x+7}{(x+1)^2(2x+1)}$ in partial fractions.

b Hence show that $\displaystyle\int_0^1 \frac{8x^2+16x+7}{(x+1)^2(2x+1)}\,\mathrm{d}x = \frac{1}{2} + 2\ln 6$

6 **a** Express $\dfrac{6x^3 - 7x^2 + 14x - 7}{(2x-1)(3x-1)}$ in partial fractions.

b Hence show that $\displaystyle\int_1^2 \frac{6x^3 - 7x^2 + 14x - 7}{(2x-1)(3x-1)}\,dx = \frac{7}{6} + \frac{26}{9}\ln\left(\frac{5}{2}\right) - \ln(3)$.

7 Show that $\displaystyle\int_2^3 \frac{2x^3 - 9x^2 + 11x - 9}{(2x-7)(x-1)}\,dx = \frac{5}{2} + \ln\left(\frac{2}{3}\right)$.

8 Show that $\displaystyle\int_2^4 \frac{4x^4 - 28x^3 + 51x^2 - 39x + 1}{(2x-1)^2(x-5)}\,dx = \frac{88}{21} - \frac{3}{2}\ln 3 + \frac{1}{2}\ln 7$

9 $f(x) \equiv x^3 + 6x^2 + 11x + 6$

A root of the equation $f(x) = 0$ is -2.

a Using algebra and showing all your working, factorise $f(x)$ completely.

b Express $\dfrac{2}{f(x)}$ in partial fractions.

c Evaluate $\displaystyle\int_0^1 \frac{2}{f(x)}\,dx$, giving your answer in the form $\ln\left(\frac{a}{b}\right)$ where a and b are integers.

10 Using the substitution $u = e^x$ and partial fractions, show that

$$\int_0^{\ln 2} \frac{1}{1+e^x}\,dx = \ln\left(\frac{4}{3}\right)$$

11.7 Integration methods, summary

One of the main problems in integration is in deciding which of several different methods to use. In this section we will briefly review six main types of integral and provide a large number of mixed questions so that you can practise making decisions about the best method to adopt. Use the exercise sensibly, it is not necessary to do *all* the questions.

Type 1 Standard functions

$\int \cos ax\,dx = \frac{1}{a}\sin ax$ $\qquad$ $\int \sin ax\,dx = -\frac{1}{a}\cos ax$

$\int \sec^2 x\,dx = \tan x$ $\qquad$ $\int e^{ax}\,dx = \frac{1}{a}e^{ax}$ $\qquad$ $\int \frac{1}{x}\,dx = \ln x$

$\int (ax+b)^n\,dx = \frac{1}{a(n+1)}(ax+b)^{n+1}$

Examples

a $\int \sin 3x\,dx = -\frac{1}{3}\cos 3x + c$

b $\int \sec^2 5x = \frac{1}{5}\tan 5x + c$

c $\int e^{7x-1}\,dx = \frac{1}{7}e^{7x-1} + c$

d $\int \frac{1}{3x+1}\,dx = \frac{1}{3}\ln(3x+1) + c$

e $\int (2x-3)^4\,dx = \frac{1}{10}(2x-3)^5 + c$

f $\int (5x-3)^{\frac{1}{2}}\,dx = \frac{2}{15}(5x+3)^{\frac{3}{2}} + c$

Type 2 The form $\int \frac{f'(x)}{f(x)}\,dx = \ln f(x) + c$

Examples

a $\int \frac{2x}{x^2+7}\,dx = \ln(x^2+7) + c$

b $\int \frac{x^2}{x^3-5} = \frac{1}{3}\int \frac{3x^2}{x^3-5} = \frac{1}{3}\ln(x^3-5) + c$

c $\int \frac{\cos x}{\sin x}\,dx = \ln \sin x + c$

d $\int \frac{e^x}{e^x+11}\,dx = \ln(e^x+11) + c$

Type 3 By substitution

$$\int f(x)dx = \int f(x)\frac{dx}{du}\,du$$

Example

$\int x(1+x)^3\,dx$

Let $u = 1 + x$

$\therefore \quad x = u - 1$

$\frac{dx}{du} = 1$

$$\int x(1+x)^3\frac{dx}{du}\,du = \int (u-1)u^3\,du = \frac{u^5}{5} - \frac{u^4}{4} + c$$

$$= \frac{4u^5 - 5u^4}{20} + c$$

$$= \frac{(1+x)^4}{20}[4(1+x) - 5] + c$$

$$= \frac{(1+x)^4}{20}(4x - 1) + c$$

Type 4 Integration by parts

$$\int u\frac{dv}{dx}\,dx = uv - \int v\frac{du}{dx}\,dx$$

Example

$\int x e^x\,dx$ Let $u = x$ and $\frac{dv}{dx} = e^x$

Then $\frac{du}{dx} = 1$ and $v = e^x$

$$\therefore \quad \int x e^x\,dx = x e^x - \int e^x \times 1\,dx$$

(↑ u, ↑ $\frac{dv}{dx}$; ↑ uv; ↑ v; ↑ $\frac{du}{dx}$)

$$= x e^x - e^x + c$$

Type 5 Using trigonometric identities

For $\int \sin^2 x\,dx$ or $\int \cos^2 x\,dx$ use $\cos 2x = 2\cos^2 x - 1$

or $\cos 2x = 1 - 2\sin^2 x$

For $\int \tan^2 x\,dx$ use $1 + \tan^2 x = \sec^2 x$

Examples

a $\int \cos^2 x\,dx = \frac{1}{2}\int (\cos 2x + 1)\,dx = \frac{1}{2}\left(\frac{1}{2}\sin 2x + x\right) + c$

b $\int \tan^2 x\,dx = \int (\sec^2 x - 1)\,dx = \tan x - x + c$

Type 6 Using partial fractions

Example

$$\int \frac{2 + 3x}{(1 + x)(1 + 2x)}\,dx = \int \frac{1}{1 + x} + \frac{1}{1 + 2x}\,dx \qquad \text{(working omitted)}$$

$$= \ln(1 + x) + \frac{1}{2}\ln(1 + 2x) + c$$

EXERCISE 11G

Section A Find the following:

1 $\int (x + 2)^3\,dx$ **2** $\int \cos 3x\,dx$ **3** $\int 4e^x\,dx$

4 $\int \frac{1}{x}\,dx$ **5** $\int \frac{1}{x^2}\,dx$ **6** $\int \frac{2}{x^2 - 1}\,dx$

7 $\int x\cos x\,dx$ **8** $\int \frac{5}{5x - 1}\,dx$ **9** $\int \sec^2 2x\,dx$

10 $\int \frac{2x}{x^2 + a}\,dx$ **11** $\int x(x + 4)^2\,dx$ **12** $\int x\,e^{5x}\,dx$

13 $\int \frac{\cos 3x}{\sin 3x}\,dx$ **14** $\int e^{3x+2}\,dx$ **15** $\int x^3\sqrt{x^4 - 1}\,dx$

16 $\int \frac{5}{x - 7}\,dx$ **17** $\int \frac{5x + 7}{(x^2 + 3x + 2)}\,dx$ **18** $\int \cos^2 x\,dx$

19 $\int x\ln x\,dx$ **20** $\int \frac{x + 1}{x}\,dx$ **21** $\int \frac{1}{1 + x}\,dx$

22 $\int x^2 e^x\,dx$ **23** $\int \sin(3 - 4x)\,dx$ **24** $\int \frac{4}{\cos^2 x}\,dx$

25 $\int (e^x - e^{-x})^2$ **26** $\int \frac{x^2 + 3x + 1}{x}\,dx$ **27** $\int \tan x\,dx$

28 $\int \tan^2 x\,dx$ **29** $\int x(x^2 + 1)^3\,dx$ **30** $\int x\sin 2x\,dx$

31 Integrate by using the given substitution:

a $\int 3x^2 e^{x^3}\,dx$ $\quad u = x^3$

b $\int \cos x\, e^{\sin x}\,dx$ $\quad u = \sin x$

c Show that $\int_0^1 \frac{1}{1+x^2}\,dx = \frac{\pi}{4}$ $\quad$ [Let $x = \tan u$]

d Evaluate $\int_2^{10} \frac{x}{\sqrt{2x+5}}\,dx$ $\quad u^2 = 2x + 5$

32 Find the exact values of the following:

a $\int_0^1 e^x\,dx$

b $\int_0^2 \frac{e^x}{2}\,dx$

c $\int_1^3 \frac{1}{x}\,dx$

d $\int_1^4 \frac{1}{2x}\,dx$

33 Find the exact values of the following:

a $\int_1^3 \frac{x+1}{x}\,dx$

b $\int_1^2 \left(\frac{x+2}{x}\right)^2 dx$

c $\int_3^6 \left(\frac{1}{x}+3\right)^2 dx$

d $\int_1^{e^2} \left(\frac{e}{x+1}\right)^2 dx$

34 Given that $\frac{dy}{dx} = \frac{1}{2x}$ and that $y = 3$ when $x = 1$, find y in terms of x.

35 Given that $\frac{dy}{dx} = \frac{5}{3x}$ and that $y = 2$ when $x = e$, find y in terms of x.

36 Given that $\frac{dy}{dx} = \frac{x^2+1}{3x}$ and that $y = 1$ when $x = 1$, find y in terms of x.

37 Given that $\frac{dy}{dx} = e^x + 1$ and that $y = e$ when $x = 1$, find y in terms of x.

38 a Express $\cos 2x$ in terms of $\sin x$.

b Hence find the exact value of $\int_{\frac{\pi}{4}}^{\frac{\pi}{2}} \sin^2 x\,dx$.

39 a Show that $\tan^2 x + 1 = \sec^2 x$.

b Use this to find $\int_{\frac{\pi}{4}}^{\frac{\pi}{3}} \tan^2 x\,dx$.

40 Find $\int x^2 \sin x\,dx$ by integrating by parts twice.

Section B

1 Calculate the exact values of the following definite integrals:

a $\int_0^{\pi} \sin x \, dx$ b $\int_0^{\frac{\pi}{2}} \cos 2x \, dx$ c $\int_0^{\frac{\pi}{12}} \sin 3x \, dx$

d $\int_0^{\frac{\pi}{3}} \sec^2 x \, dx$ e $\int_0^{1} e^{2x+1} \, dx$ f $\int_0^{\infty} e^{-3x} \, dx$

g $\int_1^{2} (5x-1)^2 \, dx$ h $\int_4^{12} \sqrt{2x+1} \, dx$ i $\int_2^{10} \frac{1}{\sqrt{x-1}} \, dx$

Find the following indefinite integrals:

2 $\int \frac{3}{2x+5} \, dx$ 3 $\int 2x \, e^{x^2} \, dx$ 4 $\int \frac{\cos x}{4+\sin x} \, dx$

5 $\int \frac{3x-6}{x(x-3)} \, dx$ 6 $\int 3x \ln x \, dx$ 7 $\int x(1+x)^{10} \, dx$

8 $\int \ln x \, dx$ 9 $\int 3 e^{-3x} \, dx$ 10 $\int \sin\left(\frac{x}{2}\right) dx$

11 $\int \frac{x}{x+3} \, dx$ 12 $\int \cos x - \tan x \, dx$ 13 $\int \sin^2 2x \, dx$

14 $\int \sqrt{5x+1} \, dx$ 15 $\int \frac{1}{\sqrt{x-4}} \, dx$ 16 $\int 3x(2x-1) \, dx$

Find the exact values of the following indefinite integrals:

17 $\int_0^{1} e^x + e^{-x} \, dx$ 18 $\int_1^{2} (e^x+1)^2 \, dx$ 19 $\int_1^{3} \frac{(e^x+1)}{e^x} \, dx$

20 $\int_1^{3} (3x-2)^2 \, dx$ 21 $\int_0^{1} (5x+1)^3 \, dx$ 22 $\int_{-2}^{3} (4x-3)^4 \, dx$

23 $\int_1^{2} \frac{4}{(2x-1)^3} \, dx$ 24 $\int_0^{\frac{1}{3}} \frac{4}{(3x+2)^2} \, dx$ 25 $\int_{0.8}^{2} \frac{4}{(5x-2)} \, dx$

26 $\int_0^{1} x \, e^{3x} \, dx$ 27 $\int_0^{\pi} x \cos x \, dx$ 28 $\int_1^{2} x \ln x \, dx$

29 $\int_5^{8} x\sqrt{9-x} \, dx$ 30 $\int_1^{4} \frac{2}{x} \, dx$ 31 $\int_{\frac{\pi}{6}}^{\frac{\pi}{2}} \cot x \, dx$

32 a If $u^2 = x + 1$ then show that $2u\frac{du}{dx} = 1$.

b Use the substitution $u^2 = x + 1$ to find $\int_0^{3} \frac{x}{\sqrt{x+1}} \, dx$.

c Show that you get the same value for $\int_0^{3} \frac{x}{\sqrt{x+1}} \, dx$ when you use the substitution $u = x + 1$.

33 Use the substitution $u = \ln x$ to find $\int_1^{e} \frac{\ln x}{x} \, dx$.

34 a Show that $1 + \cot^2 x = \operatorname{cosec}^2 x$.

b Use this to find $\int_{\frac{\pi}{4}}^{\frac{\pi}{3}} \cot^2 x \, dx$.

35 **a** Calculate $\frac{d}{dx}\left((1 - x^2)^{\frac{3}{2}}\right)$ and so find $\int x\sqrt{1 - x^2}\, dx$.

b Calculate $\int x^3\sqrt{1 - x^2}\, dx$ by considering $x^3\sqrt{1 - x^2} = x^2(x\sqrt{1 - x^2})$.

36 Show that $\int_1^5 \frac{6x + 11}{(2x + 3)(x + 2)}\, dx = \ln\frac{1183}{75}$.

37 Use an appropriate trigonometric substitution to show that

$$\int \frac{1}{\sqrt{1 - x^2}}\, dx = \sin^{-1} x + c$$

38 Evaluate $\int_0^{\ln 4} \left(\frac{e^{2x} + e^x}{e^x} - 1\right) dx$

39 Find $\int \sec 2x\, dx$

11.8 The area between two curves

We are already familiar with using integration to find the area under a curve:

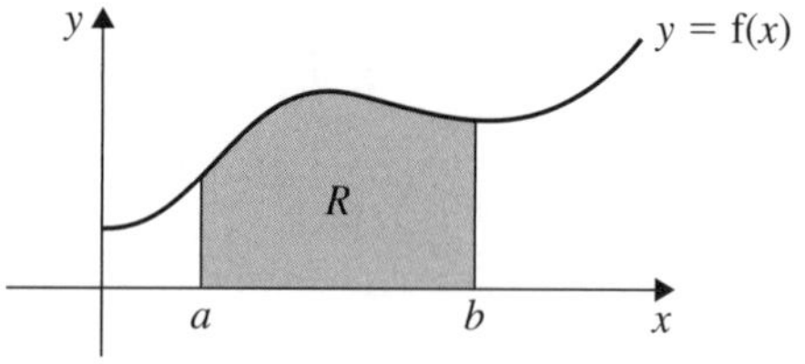

Area of $R = \int_a^b f(x)\, dx$

We can also use integration to find the area between two curves:

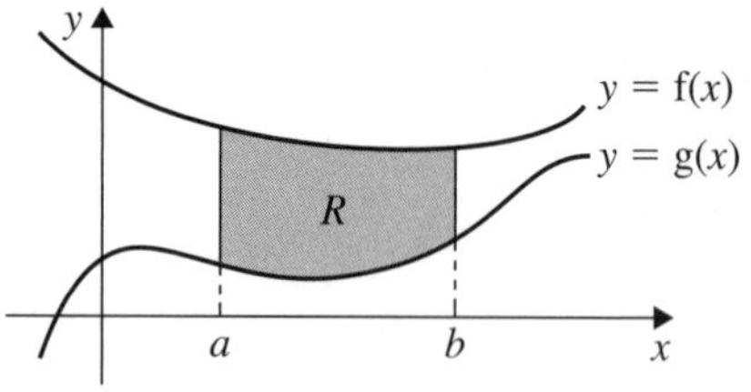

$$\text{Area of } R = \int_a^b f(x)\, dx - \int_a^b g(x)\, dx$$

$$\text{or Area of } R = \int_a^b f(x) - g(x)\, dx$$

Note: If the two curves intersect betwen a and b, then the area would need to be calculated in two sections:

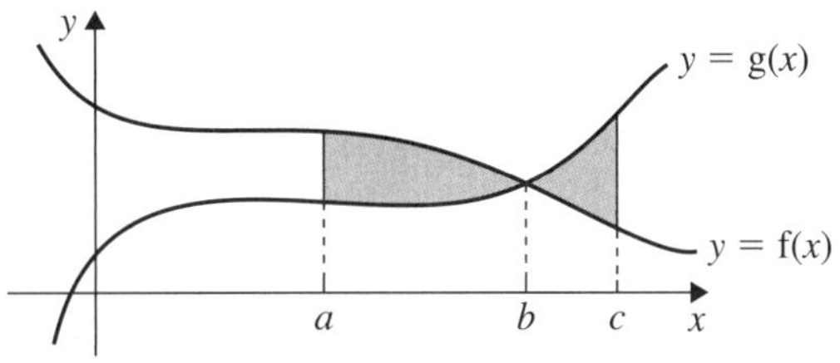

Area $\int_a^b f(x) - g(x)\,dx + \int_b^c g(x) - f(x)\,dx$

Example

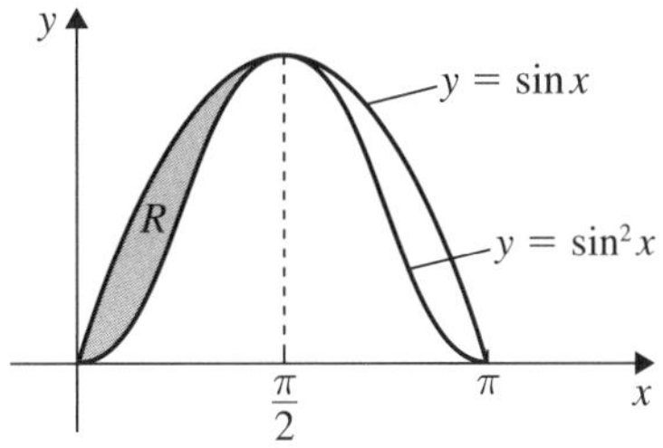

$$\begin{aligned}\text{Area of } R &= \int_0^{\frac{\pi}{2}} \sin x - \sin^2 x\,dx\\ &= \int_0^{\frac{\pi}{2}} \sin x - \frac{1-\cos 2x}{2}\,dx\\ &= \left[-\cos x - \frac{x}{2} + \frac{\sin 2x}{4}\right]_0^{\frac{\pi}{2}}\\ &= \left(0 - \frac{\pi}{4} + 0\right) - (-1 - 0 + 0)\\ &= 1 - \frac{\pi}{4}\end{aligned}$$

Exercise 11H

Find the shaded areas, giving your answers to 3 significant figures where necessary:

1

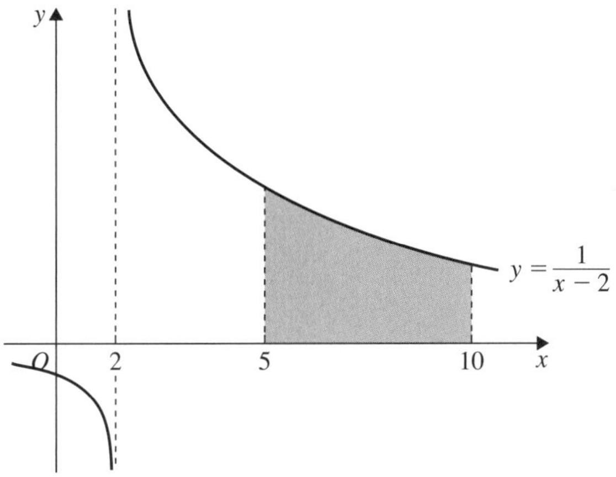

2

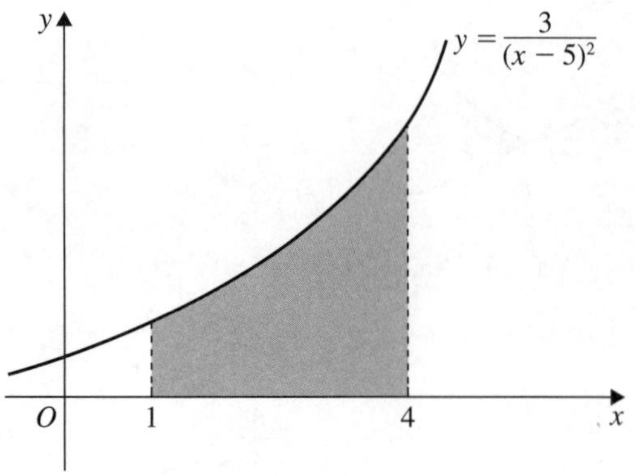

y
$y = \frac{3}{(x-5)^2}$
O
1
4
x

3

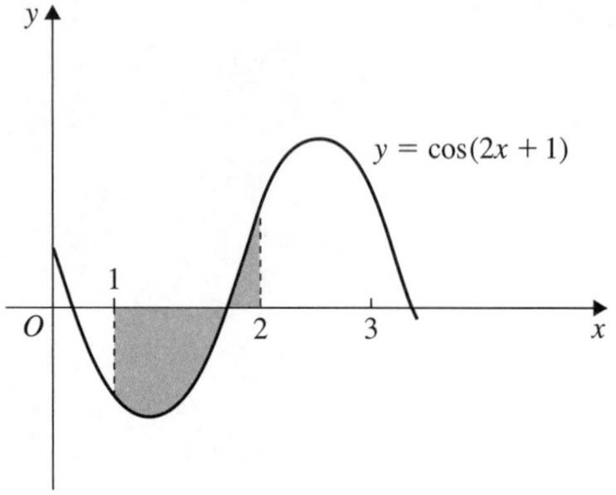

y
$y = \cos(2x + 1)$
1
O
2
3
x

4

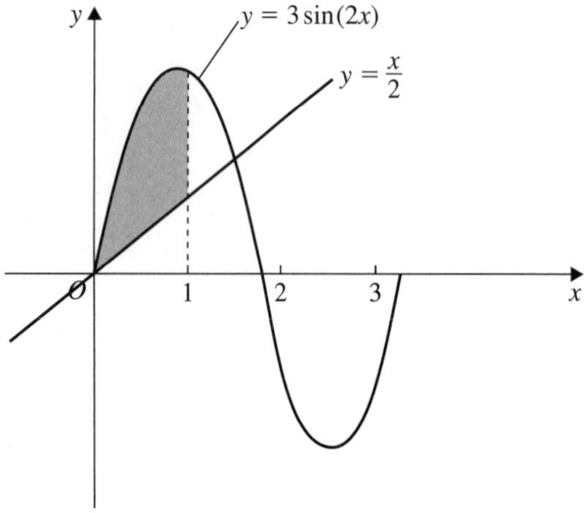

y
$y = 3\sin(2x)$
$y = \frac{x}{2}$
O
1
2
3
x

5

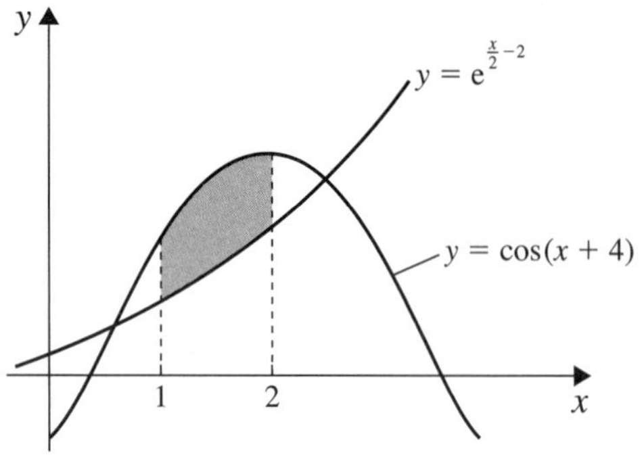

y
$y = e^{\frac{x}{2}-2}$
$y = \cos(x + 4)$
1
2
x

6

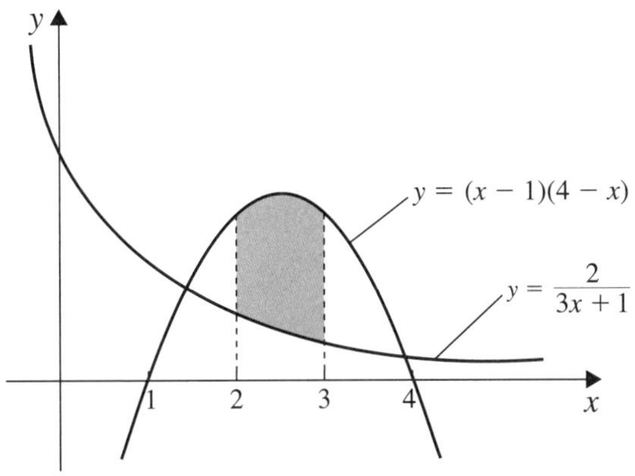

7

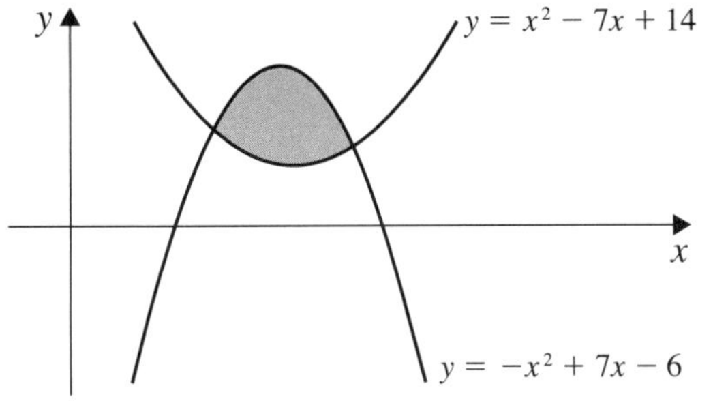

8

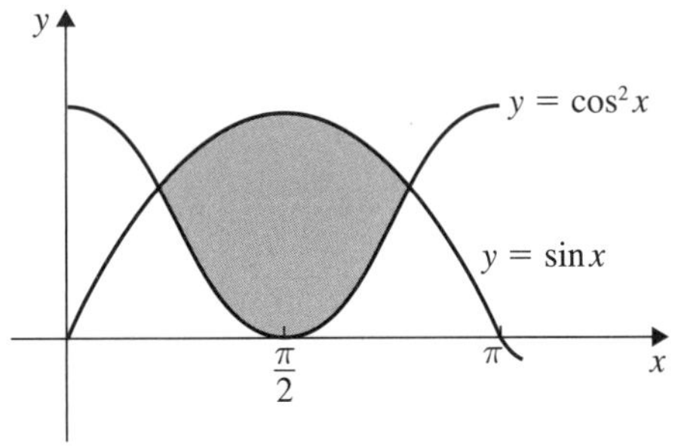

9 **a** Find the x coordinates of the points where the line $y = x - 4$ cuts the curve $y = 1 - \frac{6}{x}$.

b Find the exact area enclosed between the line $y = x - 4$ and the curve $y = 1 - \frac{6}{x}$.

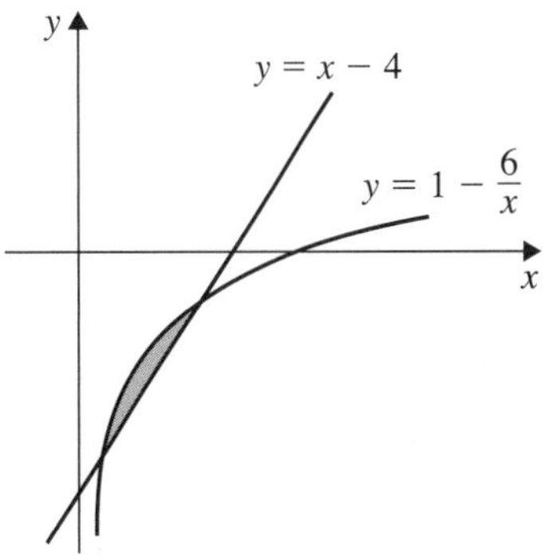

10 Find the exact area enclosed between the curve $y = 4 - \frac{3}{x}$ and the line $y = x$.

11 **a** Draw a sketch of the curve $y = \sqrt{9 - x}$ and the line $y = -\frac{1}{5}x + 3$ for x between 0 and 9.

b Show that where the curve and the line meet, $25(9 - x) = (-x + 15)^2$ and solve this to find the x coordinates of the point of intersection.

c Hence find the exact area enclosed between the curve and the line.

12* **a** Show that the area enclosed between $y = e^{2x} + 1$ and $y = 3e^x - 1$ is $\dfrac{3 - 4\ln 2}{2}$.

b Show that the area enclosed between $y = 2e^{2x}$ and $y = 18(e^x - 2)$ is $27 - 36\ln 2$.

13* **a** Find the exact x coordinates (in terms of logarithms) of the points of intersection of the curves $y = (e^x + 1)^2$ and $y = 10e^x - 11$.

b Hence find the exact area enclosed between the two curves.

11.9 Differential equations

A first order differential equation contains $\dfrac{dy}{dx}$.

Consider the differential equation $\dfrac{dy}{dx} = 2x + 1$.

Integrating both sides with respect to x,

$y = x^2 + x + c$, where c is a constant.

This is the *general solution* of the differential equation.

If we are given that $y = 10$, when $x = 2$

then $10 = 2^2 + 2 + c$

$c = 4$

and $y = x^2 + x + 4$

This is the *particular solution* of the differential equation.

Exercise 11I

1 Find the general solution of each equation:

a $\dfrac{dy}{dx} = \dfrac{x + 1}{x}$ **b** $\dfrac{dy}{dx} = 3x^2 - 1$ **c** $\dfrac{dy}{dx} = e^x - 1$

d $\dfrac{dy}{dx} = \cos x$ **e** $\dfrac{dy}{dx} = \dfrac{e^x + 3}{e^x}$ **f** $\dfrac{dy}{dx} = \dfrac{\cos x}{\sin x}$

2 Solve the following differential equations:

a $\frac{dy}{dx} = (2x + 1)^2$, given that $y = 1$ when $x = 0$.

b $\frac{dy}{dx} = \sqrt{x - 1}$, given that $y = 2$ when $x = 2$.

c $\frac{dy}{dx} = \sin 2x$, given that $y = 1$ when $x = \pi$.

d $\frac{dy}{dx} = \frac{1}{2x - 1}$, given that $y = 1$ when $x = 1$.

Separating the variables

Consider the equation $\frac{dy}{dx} = x^2y$

Write this as $\frac{1}{y}\frac{dy}{dx} = x^2$

Integrating both sides with respect to x,

$$\int \frac{1}{y}\frac{dy}{dx}\,dx = \int x^2\,dx$$

From the work in section 10.3, we can write

$$\int \frac{1}{y}\,dy = \int x^2\,dx$$

$$\therefore\ \ln y = \frac{x^3}{3} + c$$

Until now the symbols dx and dy have no meaning when written on their own. They have generally appeared as $\frac{dy}{dx}$ or perhaps $\int f(x)\,dx$. When solving differential equations it is helpul to think of dx and dy as 'factors' which can be separated and then writing integral signs.

Example 1

Find the general solution of the equation $x\frac{dy}{dx} = 1$

$$x\frac{dy}{dx} = 1$$

Separating the variables, $\int dy = \int \frac{1}{x}\,dx$

Integrating, $\quad y = \ln x + c$

Or you can write $c = \ln A$, where A is a constant,

so that $\quad y = \ln x + \ln A$

$\quad y = \ln Ax$

Example 2

Find the general solution of the equation $x\dfrac{dy}{dx} = y$.

Separating the variables, $\int \frac{1}{y}\,dy = \int \frac{1}{x}\,dx$

$$\ln y = \ln x + c$$

or $\ln y = \ln x + \ln A$

$$\ln y = \ln Ax$$

$$y = Ax.$$

Example 3

Solve the equation $x^2\dfrac{dy}{dx} = y$, given that $y = 1$ when $x = \frac{1}{2}$.

Separating the variables, $\int \frac{1}{y}\,dy = \int \frac{1}{x^2}\,dx$

$$\ln y = -\frac{1}{x} + c$$

When $y = 1, x = \frac{1}{2}$ $\quad \ln 1 = \dfrac{-1}{\frac{1}{2}} + c$

$$0 = -2 + c$$

$$c = 2$$

$$\therefore \ln y = -\frac{1}{x} + 2$$

or $y = e^{2-\frac{1}{x}}$

(This is the *particular* solution of the equation.)

Example 4

Solve the equation $\dfrac{dy}{dx} = y\sin x$, given that $y = 1$ when $x = 0$.

Separating the variables, $\int \frac{1}{y}\,dy = \int \sin x\,dx$

$$\ln y = -\cos x + c$$

When $y = 1, x = 0 \Rightarrow \ln 1 = -\cos 0 + c$

$$0 = -1 + c$$

$$c = 1$$

$$\therefore \ln y = -\cos x + 1$$

$$\ln y = 1 - \cos x$$

$$y = e^{1-\cos x}$$

Exercise 11J

1 Find the general solutions of the following equations:

a $\frac{dy}{dx} = x^2 y$

b $\frac{dy}{dx} = \frac{x}{y}$

c $\frac{dy}{dx} = \frac{y}{x}$

d $x\frac{dy}{dx} = x + 1$

e $2y\frac{dy}{dx} = 3x^2$

f $\frac{dy}{dx} = \frac{e^{4x}}{y}$

g $\frac{dy}{dx} = e^x y^2$

h $\frac{dy}{dx} = \frac{\cos x}{y}$

i $\frac{dy}{dx} = \frac{1}{1 + x}$

j $\frac{dy}{dx} = 2y$

k $\frac{dy}{dx} = 3x^2(3 + y)$

l $x\frac{dy}{dx} = \sec y$

m $\frac{dy}{dx} = 4x\,e^{-y}$

n $\frac{dy}{dx} - 2xy = 0$

o $\frac{dy}{dx} = y^2$

2 Solve the equation $x\frac{dy}{dx} = 2y$, given that $y = 4$ when $x = 1$.

Express y in terms of x.

3 Solve the following differential equations, given the initial conditions:

a $\frac{dx}{dt} = 3x$, given $x = 10$, when $t = 0$

b $\frac{dy}{dt} = -10y$, given $y = 1000$, when $t = 0$

c $\frac{dx}{dt} = x - 5$, given $x = 20$, when $t = 0$

d $-\frac{dy}{dt} = y + 8$, given $y = 10$, when $t = 0$.

4 Solve the following differential equations, giving x or y as a function of t:

a $\frac{dx}{dt} = 5x$, where $x = 100$, when $t = 0$

b $\frac{dy}{dt} = -2y$, where $y = 1000$, when $t = 0$

c $\frac{dx}{dt} = 3x$, where $x = x_0$, when $t = 0$

d $\frac{dy}{dt} = -4y$, where $y = y_0$, when $t = 0$

e $\frac{dx}{dt} = kx$, where $x = x_0$, when $t = 0$

f $-\frac{dy}{dt} = ky$, where $y = y_0$, when $t = 0$.

5 Find the solution of the following differential equations:

a $\dfrac{dy}{dx} = x\,e^{y}$, given that $y = 0$, when $x = 2$

b $\dfrac{dy}{dx} = y \sin x$, given that $y = 1$, when $x = \dfrac{\pi}{2}$

c $\dfrac{dy}{dx} = 2xy + 5x$, given that $y = -1$, when $x = 0$

d $y\dfrac{dy}{dx} = \tan x$, given that $y = 1$, when $x = \dfrac{\pi}{4}$

e $\dfrac{dy}{dx} = \sin x \cos^2 y$, given that $y = \dfrac{\pi}{4}$, when $x = 0$

f $\dfrac{dy}{dx} = xy + x$, given that $y = 1$, when $x = 1$

6 **a** Solve the differential equation

$$\frac{dx}{dt} = \frac{20 - x}{10}$$

given that $x = 5$ at $t = 0$.

b Find the value of t for which $x = 10$, giving your answer to three significant figures.

7 Solve the differential equation $\dfrac{dy}{dx} = y^2 e^{-2x}$, given that $y = 1$ when $x = 0$.

Give your answer in a form expressing y in terms of x.

8 **a** Express $\dfrac{1}{(1 + x)(2 + x)}$ in partial fractions.

b Hence find the solution of the differential equation

$$\frac{dy}{dx} = \frac{y}{(1 + x)(2 + x)},\ x > -1.$$

given that $y = 1$ when $x = 2$.

Express your answer in the form $y = f(x)$.

9 Given x and y are positive, $\dfrac{dy}{dx} + \dfrac{y}{x^2} = 0$ and $y = e$ when $x = 1$, show that the solution may be written in the form $y = e^{\frac{1}{x}}$.

10 Show that the general solution of the differential equation

$(1 + x)(1 + 2x)\dfrac{dy}{dx} = x \tan y$ may be written in the form $\sin y = k\left(\dfrac{1 + x}{\sqrt{1 + 2x}}\right)$.

Formation of differential equations

If the rate of increase of n is proportional to n, $\frac{dn}{dt} = kn$, where k is a positive constant.

If the rate of decrease of n is proportional to n, $\frac{dn}{dt} = -kn$, where k is a positive constant.

Example 1

Set up and then solve a differential equation for a population P whose rate of growth is proportional to P at that time. The initial population is P_0 and the population doubles after 10 years.

$$\frac{dP}{dt} \propto P \Rightarrow \frac{dP}{dt} = kP$$

Separating the variables, $\int \frac{1}{P}\, dP = \int k\, dt$

$$\ln P = kt + c \qquad ①$$

When $t = 0$, $P = P_0$.

$$\ln P_0 = 0 + c$$

$\therefore$ In ①, $\ln P = kt + \ln P_0$

$$\ln P - \ln P_0 = kt$$

$$\ln\left(\frac{P}{P_0}\right) = kt$$

$$\frac{P}{P_0} = e^{kt} \text{ or } P = P_0 e^{kt}$$

Now, when $t = 10$, $P = 2P_0$

$$2P_0 = P_0 e^{k \times 10}$$

$$e^{10k} = 2$$

$$10k = \ln 2$$

$$k = \frac{1}{10}\ln 2 \approx 0.0693 \quad \text{[3 significant figures]}$$

Finally $P = P_0 e^{0.0693t}$

Example 2

At time t minutes the rate of change of temperature of an object as it cools is proportional to the temperature T °C of the object at that time.

a Given that $T = 60$ °C when $t = 0$, show that $T = 60e^{-kt}$ where k is a positive constant.

b Given also that $T = 40$ °C, when $t = 5$ minutes, find the temperature of the object after 20 minutes.

a We have $\frac{dT}{dt} = -kT$

Separating the variables, $\int \frac{1}{T} dT = \int -k\, dt$

$$\ln T = -kt + c \qquad ①$$

When $t = 0, T = 60$

$\therefore \quad \ln 60 = 0 + c \Rightarrow c = \ln 60$

In ①: $\qquad \ln T = -kt + \ln 60$

$$\ln T - \ln 60 = -kt$$

$$\ln\left(\frac{T}{60}\right) = -kt$$

$$\frac{T}{60} = e^{-kt}$$

$$T = 60\, e^{-kt} \qquad ②$$

b When $t = 5, T = 40$

In ②: $\qquad 40 = 60\, e^{-k \times 5}$

$$e^{5k} = \frac{60}{40} = \frac{3}{2}$$

$$5k = \ln\left(\frac{3}{2}\right)$$

$$k = \frac{1}{5}\ln\left(\frac{3}{2}\right) \approx 0.081\,093\ldots$$

To find the temperature after 20 minutes we use $k = 0.081\,093$ and $t = 20$ in equation ②.

$T = 60\, e^{-0.081\,093 \times 20}$

$T = 11.9\,°\text{C}$ (correct to 3 significant figures).

After 20 minutes the temperature of the object is 11.9 °C.

EXERCISE 11K

1 In a sample of radioactive material, the rate of decay (or decrease) of the number N of radioactive nuclei is proportional to the number of radioactive nuclei as shown by the differential equation

$\frac{dN}{dt} = -kN$ where k is a positive constant.

Solve this equation, given that $N = N_0$ at $t = 0$, to show that $N = N_0\, e^{-kt}$.

2 In a biological experiment, the rate of increase in the number of yeast cells, N, is equal to kN, where k is a positive constant. At time $t = 0$, the number of yeast cells $= N_0$.

a Showing all your working, set up a differential equation and solve it to show $N = N_0\, e^{kt}$.

b Sketch a graph to show the relation between N and t.

3 A body moves in a viscous medium, which causes the velocity v to decrease at a rate proportional to the velocity.

a By forming and then solving an appropriate differential equation, show that $v = v_0 e^{-kt}$ where $v = v_0$ when $t = 0$.

b Show the time taken for the body to decrease its speed to $\frac{1}{2}v_0$ is $\frac{1}{k}\ln 2$.

4 The population P of a country is increasing yearly at a rate proportional to the population at that time. Form and solve an appropriate differential equation. Given that the population at the beginning of the year 1960 was 50 million, and at the beginning of 1980 was 60 million, find the values of the constants in your equation.

5 In a biological experiment the rate of increase of the number of bacteria, N, is proportional to the number of bacteria present at time t minutes.

Initially the number of bacteria was 100, and the rate of increase was 5 per minute.

a Set up and solve an appropriate differential equation.

b Find the time for the number of bacteria to increase to 1000.

c Find the number of bacteria after 1 hour.

6 At time t minutes the rate of change of temperature T °C of a body as it cools is proportional to the temperature of the body at that time. The initial temperature of the body was 80 °C.

a Show that $T = 80\,e^{-kt}$, where k is a positive constant.

b Given also that $T = 60$ when $t = 5$, find the time taken for the temperature to fall to 40 °C.

c Find the value of T when $t = 10$.

7 A model to estimate the value V of a car assumes the rate of decrease of V at time t is proportional to V.

a Showing all your working, set up and solve a differential equation to show

$$V = V_0 e^{-kt}$$

where V_0 and k are positive constants. Given that the car cost £10 000 and that its value decreased to £6000 in two years, find

b the value of the car after one year

c the age of the car in years when its value was £1000.

8 The rate at which liquid leaks from a container is proportional to the volume of liquid in the container.

The initial volume of liquid was 20 litres and 5 hours later the volume had fallen to 10 litres. Form a differential equation and solve it to find the time for the volume to fall to 5 litres.

9 Water flows out of a tank such that the depth h metres of water in the tank falls at a rate which is proportional to the square root of h.

a Show that the general solution of the differential equation may be written as $h = (c - kt)^2$ where c and k are constants.

b Given that at time $t = 0$ the depth of water in the tank is 4 m and that 10 minutes later the depth of water has reduced to 1 m, find the time which it takes for the tank to empty.

10 Liquid is poured into a container at a constant rate of $20\,\text{cm}^3\,\text{s}^{-1}$. After t seconds liquid is leaking from the container at a rate of $\frac{v}{10}\,\text{cm}^3\,\text{s}^{-1}$, where $v\,\text{cm}^3$ is the volume of liquid in the container at that time.

a Show that

$$-10\frac{dv}{dt} = v - 200$$

Given that $v = 500$ when $t = 0$

b Find a solution of the differential equation in the form $v = \text{f}(t)$.

c Find the limiting value of v as $t \to \infty$.

Review Exercise 11L

1 Calculate the following indefinite integrals:

a $\int \sin x\,dx$ **b** $\int \cos 2x\,dx$ **c** $\int \sin \frac{x}{4}\,dx$

d $\int \sec^2 x\,dx$ **e** $\int e^{7x}\,dx$ **f** $\int e^{-3x}\,dx$

g $\int \cos(5x + 4)\,dx$ **h** $\int (2x + 3)^3\,dx$ **i** $\int (1 + 4x)^{-2}\,dx$

j $\int \frac{1}{x}\,dx$ **k** $\int \frac{5}{x}\,dx$ **l** $\int \frac{3}{(2x + 9)}\,dx$

m $\int \frac{5}{x - 7}\,dx$ **n** $\int \cos x + \sin x\,dx$ **o** $\int \sqrt{6x - 1}\,dx$

2 Show that $\int_{a-h}^{a} (a^2 - x^2)\,dx = \frac{h^2}{3}(3a - h)$

3 Evaluate the following:

a $\int_{\frac{\pi}{6}}^{\frac{\pi}{4}} \cos 2x\,dx$ **b** $\int_1^3 \frac{1}{x + 1}\,dx$ **c** $\int_0^5 \sqrt{(3x + 1)}\,dx$

4 A curve has equation $y = 6x - e^{3x}$.

a Show that the x-coordinate of the stationary point on the curve is $\frac{1}{3}\ln 2$. Find the corresponding y-coordinate in the form $a \ln 2 + b$ where a and b are integers to be determined.

b Find an expression for $\frac{d^2y}{dx^2}$ and hence determine the nature of the stationary point.

c Show that the area of the region enclosed by the curve, the x-axis and the lines $x = 0$ and $x = 1$ is $\frac{1}{3}(10 - e^3)$.

5 a Find $\int \frac{2}{x+1} + \frac{3}{x+2}\,dx$

b Use part **a** to find $\int \frac{10x+14}{x^2+3x+2}\,dx$

6 Calculate the following, using natural logarithms:

a $\int \frac{3x^2}{x^3+5}\,dx$ b $\int \frac{2x}{4x^2-7}\,dx$ c $\int \frac{e^{2x}}{1+e^{2x}}\,dx$

d $\int \frac{\sin x}{\cos x}\,dx$ e $\int \frac{f'(x)}{f(x)}\,dx$ f $\int \frac{\cos 2x}{2\sin x \cos x}\,dx$

7 Calculate the following definite integrals by using substitution:

a $\int_0^1 x(2x+1)^3\,dx$ $u = 2x + 1$

b $\int_2^3 \frac{2x+1}{(x+1)^3}\,dx$ $u = x + 1$

c $\int_{\frac{1}{3}}^{\frac{2}{3}} (x+1)(3x-1)^2\,dx$ $u = 3x - 1$

d $\int_{\frac{\pi}{2}}^{\pi} \cos x\, e^{\sin x}\,dx$ $u = \sin x$

e $\int_1^5 \frac{3x+1}{\sqrt{(2x-1)}}\,dx$ f $\int_{-1}^1 (x-1)^8 x\,dx$

g $\int_0^2 3x^2 e^{x^3}\,dx$ h $\int_0^1 \frac{x}{(x^2+1)^3}\,dx$

8 Evaluate $\int_0^1 x\sqrt{4-3x^2}\,dx$. Give your answer as a fraction.

9 Find the exact value of $\int_{-1}^2 x\sqrt{x+2}\,dx$

10 Use the substitution $u = \tan x$ to show that

$$\int_0^{\frac{\pi}{6}} \sec^4 x \tan x\,dx = \frac{7}{36}$$

11 Calculate the following indefinite integrals:

a $\int x e^{2x}\,dx$ b $\int x \sin x\,dx$

c $\int 3x \ln x\,dx$ d $\int x^2 \ln x\,dx$

12 Evaluate $\int_0^2 x e^x\,dx$

13 Evaluate $\int_0^2 x e^{x^2}\,dx$

14 Show that $\int_0^{\frac{\pi}{8}} x \sin 2x \, dx = \dfrac{4 - \pi}{16\sqrt{2}}$

15 **a** Express $\cos 2x$ in terms of $\cos x$.

b Use this to show that $\cos^2 x = \frac{1}{2}(1 + \cos 2x)$.

c Hence fnd the exact value of $\int_0^{\frac{\pi}{2}} \cos^2 x \, dx$

16 Find

a $\int \sin^2 x \, dx$

b $\int \tan^2 x \, dx$

17 Solve the differential equations:

a $\dfrac{dy}{dx} = y^{-\frac{1}{2}}$, given $y = 9$ when $x = 4$

b $\dfrac{dy}{dx} = \dfrac{20}{y}$, given $y = 2$ when $x = 0$

c $\dfrac{dy}{dx} = 2xy$, given $y = 1$ when $x = 2$

d $\dfrac{dy}{dx} = xy + x$, given $y = 1$ when $x = 1$

e $x\dfrac{dy}{dx} = x + 1$, given $y = 3$ when $x = 1$

f $y \cos^2 x \dfrac{dy}{dx} = y^2 + 1$, given $y = 2$ when $x = 0$

18 If $\dfrac{dx}{dt} = k(a - x)^2$ and $x = 0$ when $t = 0$, where k is a constant, show that

$t = \dfrac{x}{ka(a - x)}$.

19 The gradient of a curve at any point (x, y) on the curve is directly proportional to the product of x and y.

The curve passes through the point (1, 1) and the gradient at this point is 4.

Form a differential equation and solve this equation to express y in terms of x.

20 During the initial stages some micro-organisms are growing at a rate $\left(\dfrac{dN}{dt}\right)$ proportional to the number (N) of micro-organisms present.

a Set up and solve a differential equation relating $\dfrac{dN}{dt}$ with N.

b Showing all your working show that

$$N = N_0 e^{kt},$$

where N_0 = the number of micro-organisms at $t = 0$ and k is a constant of proportionality.

c Given the number of micro-organisms increases by 50% in 10 hours, find k.

d Find the time for the number of micro-organisms to double.

21 Calculate the exact area enclosed between $y = 15 - \frac{50}{x}$ and $y = x$.

22 Show that $\int x(2x-1)^7\,dx = \frac{(2x-1)^8(16x+1)}{288} + c$

23 Find the following integrals:

a $\int \sec x \tan x\,dx$ **b** $\int -\operatorname{cosec}^2 3x\,dx$ **c** $\int \ln 2x\,dx$

d $\int x^2 \cos x\,dx$ **e** $\int \frac{x-1}{(x+2)^2}\,dx$

Examination Exercise 11

1 Show that $\int_{\sqrt{2}}^{\sqrt{6}} \frac{2}{x}\,dx = \ln 3$.

[OCR, GCE Mathematics, C3, Jan 2012]

2 Find:

i $\int (4-3x)^7\,dx$

ii $\int (4-3x)^{-1}\,dx$

3 Find:

i $\int \left(2 - \frac{1}{x}\right)^2 dx$

ii $\int (4x+1)^{\frac{1}{3}}\,dx$

[OCR, GCE Mathematics, C3, June 2016]

4 **a** Show that $\int_0^4 \frac{18}{\sqrt{6x+1}}\,dx = 24$.

b Find $\int_0^1 (e^x + 2)^2\,dx$, giving your answer in terms of e.

[OCR, GCE Mathematics, C3, June 2012]

5 **a** Given that $\frac{4x^3 - 2x^2 + 16x - 3}{2x^2 - x + 2}$ can be expressed as $Ax + \frac{B(4x-1)}{2x^2 - x + 2}$, find the values of the constants A and B.

b The gradient of a curve is given by

$$\frac{dy}{dx} = \frac{4x^3 - 2x^2 + 16x - 3}{2x^2 - x + 2}$$

The point $(-1, 2)$ lies on the curve. Find the equation of the curve.

[AQA, GCE Mathematics, C4, June 2014]

6 **i** Use the quotient rule to show that the derivative of $\dfrac{\cos x}{\sin x}$ is $\dfrac{-1}{\sin^2 x}$.

ii Show that $\displaystyle\int_{\frac{1}{6}\pi}^{\frac{1}{4}\pi} \frac{\sqrt{1+\cos 2x}}{\sin x \sin 2x}\,dx = \frac{1}{2}(\sqrt{6}-\sqrt{2})$.

[OCR, GCE Mathematics, C4, June 2015]

7 By using integration by parts twice, find

$$\int x^2 \sin 2x\,dx$$

[AQA, GCE Mathematics, C3, June 2014]

8 Find the exact value of $\displaystyle\int_0^1 (x^2+1)e^{2x}\,dx$.

[OCR, GCE Mathematics, C4, Jan 2012]

9 **a** $\displaystyle\int \frac{1}{x^3}\ln x\,dx$

b $\displaystyle\int_1^2 \frac{1}{x^3}\ln x\,dx$

[EDEXCEL, GCE Mathematics, C4, Jan 2013]

10 **a** Use the substitution $x = u^2$, $u > 0$, to show that

$$\int \frac{1}{x(2\sqrt{x}-1)}\,dx = \int \frac{2}{u(2u-1)}\,du$$

b Hence show that

$$\int_1^9 \frac{1}{x(2\sqrt{x}-1)}\,dx = 2\ln\left(\frac{a}{b}\right)$$

where a and b are integers to be determined.

[EDEXCEL, GCE Mathematics, C4, June 2013]

11 Use the substitution $u = 6 - x^2$ to find the value of $\displaystyle\int_1^2 \frac{x^3}{\sqrt{6-x^2}}\,dx$, giving your answer in the form $p\sqrt{5}+q\sqrt{2}$, where p and q are rational numbers.

[AQA, GCE Mathematics, C3, June 2015]

12 Use the substitution $u = x^2 - 2$ to find the value of $\displaystyle\int \frac{6x^3+4x}{\sqrt{x^2-2}}\,dx$.

[OCR, GCE Mathematics, C4, June 2016]

13 Use the substitution $u = 2x + 1$ to evaluate $\displaystyle\int_0^{\frac{1}{2}} \frac{4x-1}{(2x+1)^5}\,dx$.

[OCR, GCE Mathematics, C4, Jan 2013]

14 Use the substitution $u = \cos x$ to find the exact value of

$$\int_0^{\frac{1}{3}\pi} \sin^3 x \cos^2 x\,dx.$$

[OCR, GCE Mathematics, C4, Jan 2012]

15 **a** Express $\dfrac{16x}{(1-3x)(1+x)^2}$ in the form $\dfrac{A}{1-3x}+\dfrac{B}{1+x}+\dfrac{C}{(1+x)^2}$.

b Solve the differential equation

$$\frac{dy}{dx}=\frac{16x\,e^{2y}}{(1-3x)(1+x)^2}$$

where $y=0$ when $x=0$.

Give your answer in the form $f(y)=g(x)$.

[AQA, GCE Mathematics, C4, June 2014]

16 Solve the differential equation

$$e^{2y}\frac{dy}{dx}+\tan x=0,$$

given that $x=0$ when $y=0$. Give your answer in the form $y=f(x)$.

[OCR, GCE Mathematics, C4, June 2012]

17 In an experiment testing solid rocket fuel, some fuel is burned and the waste products are collected. Throughout the experiment the sum of the masses of the unburned fuel and waste products remains constant.

Let x be the mass of waste products, in kg, at a time t minutes after the start of the experiment. It is known that at time t minutes, the rate of increase of the mass of waste products, in kg per minute, is k times the mass of unburned fuel remaining, where k is a positive constant.

The differential equation connecting x and t may be written in the form

$$\frac{dx}{dt}=k(M-x),\text{ where } M \text{ is a constant.}$$

a Explain, in the context of the problem, what $\dfrac{dx}{dt}$ and M represent.

Given that initially the mass of waste products is zero,

b solve the differential equation, expressing x in terms of k, M and t.

Given also that $x=\frac{1}{2}M$ when $t=\ln 4$,

c find the value of x when $t=\ln 9$, expressing x in terms of M, in its simplest form.

[EDEXCEL, GCE Mathematics, C4, 1R, June 2013]

18 A container in the shape of an inverted cone of radius 3 metres and vertical height 4.5 metres is initially filled with liquid fertiliser. This fertiliser is released through a hole in the bottom of the container at a rate of 0.01 m^3 per second. At a time t seconds the fertiliser remaining in the container forms an inverted cone of height h metres.

[The volume of a cone is $V=\frac{1}{3}\pi r^2 h$.]

i Show that $h^2\dfrac{dh}{dt}=-\dfrac{9}{400\pi}$

ii Express h in terms of t.

iii Find the time it takes to empty the container, giving your answer to the nearest minute.

[OCR, GCE Mathematics, C4, June 2014]

19 Water is being heated in a kettle. At time t seconds, the temperature of the water is θ°C.

The rate of increase of the temperature of the water at any time t is modelled by the differential equation.

$$\frac{d\theta}{dt} = \lambda(120 - \theta), \qquad \theta \leqslant 100$$

where λ is a positive constant.

Given that $\theta = 20$ when $t = 0$,

a solve this differential equation to show that

$$\theta = 120 - 100e^{-\lambda t}$$

When the temperature of the water reaches 100 °C, the kettle switches off.

b Given that $\lambda = 0.01$, find the time, to the nearest second, when the kettle switches off.

[EDEXCEL, GCE Mathematics, C4, June 2013]

20 a Express $\dfrac{2}{P(P-2)}$ in partial fractions.

A team of biologists is studying a population of a particular species of animal.

The population is modelled by the differential equation

$$\frac{dP}{dt} = \frac{1}{2}P(P-2)\cos 2t, \quad t \geqslant 0$$

where P is the population in thousands, and t is the time measured in years since the start of the study.

Given that $P = 3$ when $t = 0$,

b solve this differential equation to show that

$$P = \frac{6}{3 - e^{\frac{1}{2}\sin 2t}}$$

c find the time taken for the population to reach 4000 for the first time. Give your answer in years to 3 significant figures.

[EDEXCEL, GCE Mathematics, C4, June 2015]

Part 12

Vectors

12.1 Using coordinates and vectors in three dimensions

In Pure Mathematics Book 1 we looked at using vectors to describe positions and movements in two dimensions. We will now extend these concepts to three dimensions.

When visualising 3D vectors we usually imagine the xy-plane as a flat, horizontal surface, with the z-axis pointing vertically upwards.

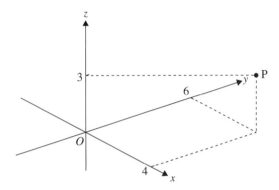

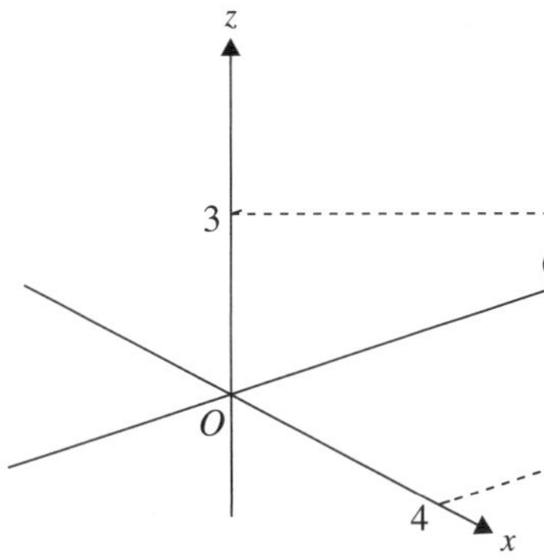

The point P has coordinates (4, 6, 3). You will recall that we use **i** and **j** to denote unit vectors in the positive x and y directions respectively. We now use **k** to denote a unit vector in the positive z direction. So P has position vector

$$\mathbf{p} = \overrightarrow{\mathrm{OP}} = \begin{pmatrix} 4 \\ 6 \\ 3 \end{pmatrix} \quad \text{or} \quad \mathbf{p} = \overrightarrow{\mathrm{OP}} = 4\mathbf{i} + 6\mathbf{j} + 3\mathbf{k}$$

Magnitude of a vector

We used Pythagoras' theorem in two dimensions to calculate the length of a 2D vector. We will now use Pythagoras' theorem in three dimensions to calculate the length of a 3D vector.

> The length l of a vector $x\mathbf{i} + y\mathbf{j} + z\mathbf{k}$ is given by
>
> $$l = \sqrt{x^2 + y^2 + z^2}$$

In the example above, the distance of point P from the origin is given by

$$|\overrightarrow{\mathrm{OP}}| = \sqrt{4^2 + 6^2 + 3^2} = \sqrt{61}$$

Vectors between two points

The vector $\overrightarrow{\mathrm{AB}}$ describes how to get from point A to point B. Many people prefer to think of this as travelling from A back to the origin, and then on to B.

$$\overrightarrow{AB} = \overrightarrow{AO} + \overrightarrow{OB} = \overrightarrow{OB} - \overrightarrow{OA}$$
$$\text{or} \quad \overrightarrow{AB} = \mathbf{b} - \mathbf{a}$$

Distance between two points

To calculate the distance between two points we first need to find the vector between the two points, and then we calculate the magnitude of this vector.

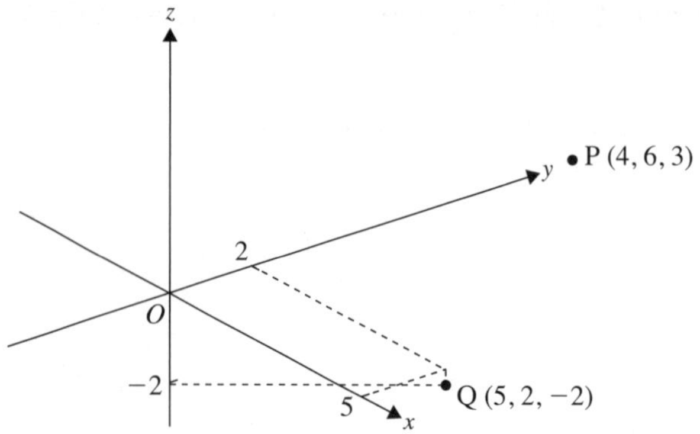

$$\overrightarrow{PQ} = (5-4)\mathbf{i} + (2-6)\mathbf{j} + (-2-3)\mathbf{k}$$
$$= \mathbf{i} - 4\mathbf{j} - 5\mathbf{k}$$
$$|\overrightarrow{PQ}| = \sqrt{1^2 + (-4)^2 + (-5)^2} = \sqrt{42}$$

So the distance between P and Q is $\sqrt{42}$.

In general, for two points $A(x_1, y_1, z_1)$ and $B(x_2, y_2, z_2)$

$$\overrightarrow{AB} = (x_2 - x_1)\mathbf{i} + (y_2 - y_1)\mathbf{j} + (z_2 - z_1)\mathbf{k}$$

and $|\overrightarrow{AB}| = \sqrt{(x_2 - x_1)^2 + (y_2 - y_1)^2 + (z_2 - z_1)^2}$

The angle between a vector and the coordinate axes

We can use basic trigonometry to find the angle θ_x that the vector **a** makes with the x-axis:

$$\cos\theta_x = \frac{x}{|\mathbf{a}|}$$

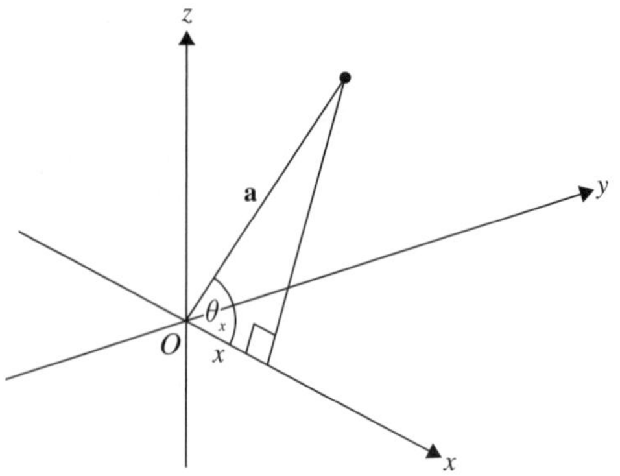

The angle that vector $\mathbf{a} = x\mathbf{i} + y\mathbf{j} + z\mathbf{k}$ makes with the positive

x-axis is given by $\cos\theta_x = \dfrac{x}{|\mathbf{a}|}$

y-axis is given by $\cos\theta_y = \dfrac{y}{|\mathbf{a}|}$

z-axis is given by $\cos\theta_z = \dfrac{z}{|\mathbf{a}|}$

Example 1

The point M has coordinates (1, −5, 3) and the point N has coordinates (2, 3, 1).

Find **a** the position vector $\overrightarrow{OM}$ of M

b the position vector **n** of N

c the vector $\overrightarrow{MN}$

d the distance from M to N.

a $\overrightarrow{OM} = \begin{pmatrix} 1 \\ -5 \\ 3 \end{pmatrix}$

b $\mathbf{n} = \begin{pmatrix} 2 \\ 3 \\ 1 \end{pmatrix}$

c $\overrightarrow{MN} = \begin{pmatrix} 2-1 \\ 3-(-5) \\ 1-3 \end{pmatrix} = \begin{pmatrix} 1 \\ 8 \\ -2 \end{pmatrix}$

d $|\overrightarrow{MN}| = \sqrt{1^2 + 8^2 + (-2)^2} = \sqrt{69}$

Note: it is entirely up to you whether you prefer to use **i**, **j**, **k** notation, or column vectors as above.

Example 2

$\mathbf{a} = -3\mathbf{i} + \mathbf{j} + 2\mathbf{k}$

$\mathbf{b} = 2\mathbf{i} + 2\mathbf{j} - \mathbf{k}$

$\mathbf{c} = x\mathbf{i} + y\mathbf{j} + z\mathbf{k}$

a Calculate **i** $\mathbf{a} + 2\mathbf{b}$

ii $\mathbf{b} - 3\mathbf{a}$

b Given that $\mathbf{a} + \mathbf{c} = \mathbf{i} - 2\mathbf{j} - 7\mathbf{k}$, find the values of x, y and z.

c Find a unit vector parallel to **b**.

We can add and subtract vectors, and multiply them by scalars in the exact same way we did in two dimensions.

a i $\mathbf{a} + 2\mathbf{b} = (-3\mathbf{i} + \mathbf{j} + 2\mathbf{k}) + 2(2\mathbf{i} + 2\mathbf{j} - \mathbf{k})$
$= (-3\mathbf{i} + \mathbf{j} + 2\mathbf{k}) + (4\mathbf{i} + 4\mathbf{j} - 2\mathbf{k})$
$= \mathbf{i} + 5\mathbf{j}$

ii $\mathbf{b} - 3\mathbf{a} = (2\mathbf{i} + 2\mathbf{j} - \mathbf{k}) - 3(-3\mathbf{i} + \mathbf{j} + 2\mathbf{k})$
$= (2\mathbf{i} + 2\mathbf{j} - \mathbf{k}) - (-9\mathbf{i} + 3\mathbf{j} + 6\mathbf{k})$
$= 11\mathbf{i} - \mathbf{j} - 7\mathbf{k}$

b $(-3\mathbf{i} + \mathbf{j} + 2\mathbf{k}) + (x\mathbf{i} + y\mathbf{j} + z\mathbf{k}) = \mathbf{i} - 2\mathbf{j} + 7\mathbf{k}$

$-3 + x = 1, \quad x = 4$

$1 + y = -2, \quad y = -3$

$2 + z = 7, \quad z = 5$

c $|b| = \sqrt{2^2 + 2^2 + (-1)^2} = 3$

So a unit vector parallel to **b** is $\frac{1}{3}(2\mathbf{i} + 2\mathbf{j} - \mathbf{k})$.

Example 3

The point A has coordinates $(4, -2, 3)$ and the point B has coordinates $(2, 5, 1)$. Find the midpoint M of AB.

To reach M we must first travel to A, and then move halfway along the vector from A to B.

i.e. $\overrightarrow{OM} = \overrightarrow{OA} + \frac{1}{2}\overrightarrow{AB}$

$$= \begin{pmatrix} 4 \\ -2 \\ 3 \end{pmatrix} + \frac{1}{2}\begin{pmatrix} 2-4 \\ 5-(-2) \\ 1-3 \end{pmatrix}$$

$$= \begin{pmatrix} 4 \\ -2 \\ 3 \end{pmatrix} + \frac{1}{2}\begin{pmatrix} -2 \\ 7 \\ -2 \end{pmatrix}$$

$$= \begin{pmatrix} 4 \\ -2 \\ 3 \end{pmatrix} + \begin{pmatrix} -1 \\ 3.5 \\ -1 \end{pmatrix}$$

$$= \begin{pmatrix} 3 \\ 1.5 \\ 2 \end{pmatrix}$$

So the coordinates of the midpoint M are $(3, 1.5, 2)$.

Example 4

Find the angle that the vector $\mathbf{a} = 5\mathbf{i} - 2\mathbf{j} + \mathbf{k}$ makes with each of the coordinate axes.

Firstly $|\mathbf{a}| = \sqrt{5^2 + (-2)^2 + (1^2)} = \sqrt{30}$

Now $\theta_x = \cos^{-1}\left(\frac{5}{\sqrt{30}}\right) = 24.1°$ (3 sf)

$\theta_y = \cos^{-1}\left(\frac{-2}{\sqrt{30}}\right) = 111°$ (3 sf)

$\theta_z = \cos^{-1}\left(\frac{1}{\sqrt{30}}\right) = 79.5°$ (3 sf)

Exercise 12A

1 Find the magnitude of the following vectors and hence find a unit vector in their respective directions:

a $4\mathbf{i} + 3\mathbf{j} + 2\mathbf{k}$ **b** $-5\mathbf{i} + 12\mathbf{j} + 3\mathbf{k}$ **c** $7\mathbf{i} - 24\mathbf{j} - 5\mathbf{k}$

2 Find the vector $\overrightarrow{AB}$ between the following pairs of points:

a A(1, 2, 5) B(4, 6, 1)
b A(−3, −1, 2) B(12, 4, −1)
c A(−2, 5, −3) B(3, −1, −3)
d A(3, −2, −2) B(−2, 4, 7)

3 Find the distance between the following pairs of points:

a A(1, 2, 4) B(4, 8, 6)
b A(3, −1, −4) B(11, 3, −3)
c A(2, −1, 3) B(0, 3, −2)
d A(−4, 0, 2) B(1, −1, 3)

4 Find a unit vector in the direction of each of the following vectors:

a $2\mathbf{i} + 2\mathbf{j} + \mathbf{k}$ **b** $4\mathbf{i} - 2\mathbf{j} + 4\mathbf{k}$ **c** $3\mathbf{i} + 6\mathbf{j} - 2\mathbf{k}$ **d** $6\mathbf{i} - 3\mathbf{j} + 6\mathbf{k}$

5 If $3\mathbf{i} + a\mathbf{j} + \mathbf{k}$ is parallel to $6\mathbf{i} + 10\mathbf{j} + b\mathbf{k}$, find the value of a and b.

6 Find a vector that is parallel to $2\mathbf{i} + 6\mathbf{j} + 3\mathbf{k}$ and has magnitude 28 units.

7 Find a vector that is parallel to $4\mathbf{i} - \mathbf{j} - 8\mathbf{k}$ and has magnitude 27 units.

8 Express each of these vectors as a column vector:

a $2\mathbf{i} + 3\mathbf{j} + \mathbf{k}$ **b** $\mathbf{i} - \mathbf{j} + 4\mathbf{k}$ **c** $2\mathbf{j} + \mathbf{k}$
d $-\mathbf{i} + \mathbf{j} + 4\mathbf{k}$ **e** $2\mathbf{j}$ **f** $2\mathbf{i} + 3\mathbf{k}$

9 If $\mathbf{p} = \begin{pmatrix} 2 \\ 3 \\ -1 \end{pmatrix}$, $\mathbf{q} = \begin{pmatrix} 4 \\ 1 \\ -3 \end{pmatrix}$ and $\mathbf{r} = \begin{pmatrix} -2 \\ 2 \\ 2 \end{pmatrix}$, find the number n such that $\mathbf{p} + n\mathbf{q} = \mathbf{r}$.

10 If $\mathbf{m} = 2\mathbf{i} + 7\mathbf{j} + \mathbf{k}$ and $\mathbf{n} = \mathbf{i} + 2\mathbf{j} + 3\mathbf{k}$, find

a $\mathbf{m} + \mathbf{n}$ **b** $|\mathbf{m} + \mathbf{n}|$ **c** $\mathbf{m} - \mathbf{n}$ **d** $2\mathbf{m} - 3\mathbf{n}$

11 If $\mathbf{s} = \begin{pmatrix} 4 \\ 1 \\ 2 \end{pmatrix}$ and $\mathbf{t} = \begin{pmatrix} -1 \\ 2 \\ 3 \end{pmatrix}$, find

a $\mathbf{s} + \mathbf{t}$ **b** $|\mathbf{s} + \mathbf{t}|$ **c** the vector $\mathbf{u}$ such that $\mathbf{s} + \mathbf{u} = \mathbf{t}$

12 If $\mathbf{a} = \begin{pmatrix} -2 \\ -3 \\ 3 \end{pmatrix}$, $\mathbf{b} = \begin{pmatrix} -1 \\ 1 \\ -12 \end{pmatrix}$ and $\mathbf{c} = \begin{pmatrix} -2 \\ 3 \\ 0 \end{pmatrix}$

then find the following:

a $3\mathbf{a}$ **b** $5\mathbf{a} + 2\mathbf{b}$ **c** $2\mathbf{a} - \mathbf{b} + \mathbf{c}$
d the magnitude of $\mathbf{b} + \mathbf{c}$
e a unit vector parallel to $\mathbf{a} + \mathbf{c}$

13 Given $\overrightarrow{OP} = 3\mathbf{i} + 7\mathbf{j} + 5\mathbf{k}$ and $\overrightarrow{OQ} = \mathbf{i} - \mathbf{j} + 2\mathbf{k}$, find

a $\overrightarrow{PQ}$ **b** $\overrightarrow{QP}$

14 Given $\overrightarrow{OS} = \mathbf{i} + 2\mathbf{j} + \mathbf{k}$ and $\overrightarrow{OT} = 3\mathbf{i} + 8\mathbf{j} + \mathbf{k}$, find

a $\overrightarrow{ST}$ **b** $\overrightarrow{SM}$, where M is the midpoint of $\overrightarrow{ST}$
c $\overrightarrow{OM}$

15 If A, B and C are three points with coordinates (1, −2, 3), (4, 2, 7) and (16, 5, 11) respectively, then find the following:

a the vector $\overrightarrow{AB}$

b the distance BC

c the coordinates of the point D such that $\overrightarrow{AD} = 2\overrightarrow{AB}$

d the coordinates of the point E such that $\overrightarrow{AE} = 2\overrightarrow{AC}$

e the ratio of DE : BC

16 Find the angle between:

a the vector $\mathbf{a} = -3\mathbf{i} - 2\mathbf{j} + \mathbf{k}$ and the positive x-axis

b the vector $\mathbf{b} = 4\mathbf{i} + 2\mathbf{j} - 2\mathbf{k}$ and the positive y-axis

c the vector $\mathbf{c} = 3\mathbf{i} + 7\mathbf{j} + 9\mathbf{k}$ and the positive z-axis

17 The points A and B have coordinates (2, −3, 1) and (14, 3, 4) respectively. The point C is such that $\overrightarrow{AC} = 2\overrightarrow{CB}$.

a Find the coordinates of point C.

b Find the angle that the vector $\overrightarrow{OC}$ makes with the positive y-axis.

12.2 Solving geometrical problems using vectors

When solving geometrical problems, it may be useful to remember the following facts.

A triangle is right-angled if and only if its sides satisfy Pythagoras' theorem.

A quadrilateral is:

- a trapezium if one pair of sides are parallel
- a parallelogram if two pairs of sides are parallel, or opposite sides are the same length
- a rhombus if all four sides are the same length
- a rectangle if two pairs of sides are parallel, or opposite sides are the same length, **and** both diagonals are the same length
- a square if all four sides are the same length **and** both diagonals are the same length
- a kite if two pairs of adjacent sides are equal (the diagonals will be perpendicular).

Example 1

Show that the triangle ABC with vertices A(5, 1, 2), B(7, −2, −2) and C(7, 4, −2) is isosceles.

$$AB = \sqrt{(7-5)^2 + (-2-1)^2 + (-2-2)^2} = \sqrt{29}$$

$$AC = \sqrt{(7-5)^2 + (4-1)^2 + (-2-2)^2} = \sqrt{29}$$

AB = AC $\quad\therefore$ ABC is isosceles.

Example 2

Show that the triangle PQR with vertices P(4, 7, 3), Q(4, 2, 3) and R(12, 7, 9) is right-angled, and find its area.

$PQ^2 = (4 - 4)^2 + (2 - 7)^2 + (3 - 3)^2 = 25$
$PR^2 = (12 - 4)^2 + (7 - 7)^2 + (9 - 3)^2 = 100$
$QR^2 = (12 - 4)^2 + (7 - 2)^2 + (9 - 3)^2 = 125$

so $PQ^2 + PR^2 = QR^2$ $\quad \therefore$ PQR is right-angled.

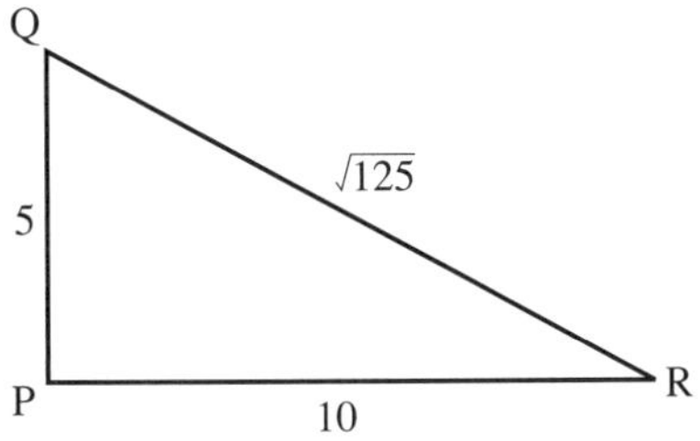

A small sketch can be helpful here.

Area $= \frac{1}{2} \times 10 \times 5 = 25$

Example 3

Determine the nature of the quadrilateral ABCD with vertices at A(6, −1, 5), B(5, 2, 3), C(6, 5, 5) and D(7, 2, 7).

$\overrightarrow{AB} = \begin{pmatrix} -1 \\ 3 \\ -2 \end{pmatrix} \qquad \overrightarrow{DC} = \begin{pmatrix} -1 \\ 3 \\ -2 \end{pmatrix} \qquad \overrightarrow{BC} = \begin{pmatrix} 1 \\ 3 \\ 2 \end{pmatrix} \qquad \overrightarrow{AD} = \begin{pmatrix} 1 \\ 3 \\ 2 \end{pmatrix}$

So $\overrightarrow{AB} = \overrightarrow{DC}$ and $\overrightarrow{BC} = \overrightarrow{AD}$, hence two pairs of equal parallel sides.

Now $AB = BC = CD = DA = \sqrt{14}$, so in fact all four sides are the same length.

Finally, looking at the diagonals, $AC = 6$ but $BD = \sqrt{20}$, so the diagonals are not the same length.

Therefore ABCD is a rhombus.

Example 4

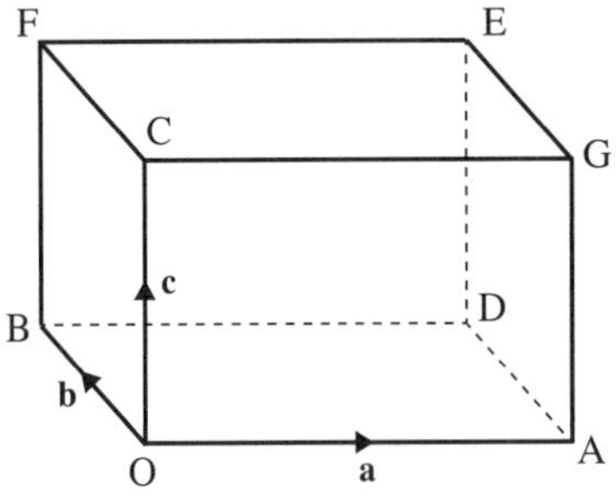

In the cuboid shown opposite, prove that the diagonals OE and BG bisect each other.

Firstly, $\overrightarrow{OE} = \mathbf{a} + \mathbf{b} + \mathbf{c}$

and $\quad \overrightarrow{BG} = \mathbf{a} - \mathbf{b} + \mathbf{c}$

Now, let the point of intersection of the two diagonals be X.

We can reach X from O by travelling some distance along $\overrightarrow{OE}$

i.e. $\overrightarrow{OX} = s\,\overrightarrow{OE}$

$= s(\mathbf{a} + \mathbf{b} + \mathbf{c})$

We can also reach X from O by travelling first to B, and then some distance along $\overrightarrow{BG}$

i.e. $\overrightarrow{OX} = \overrightarrow{OB} + t\,\overrightarrow{BG}$

$\quad = \mathbf{b} + t(\mathbf{a} - \mathbf{b} + \mathbf{c})$

We now have two expressions for $\overrightarrow{OX}$, which must be equal to each other:

$$s(\mathbf{a} + \mathbf{b} + \mathbf{c}) = \mathbf{b} + t(\mathbf{a} - \mathbf{b} + \mathbf{c})$$

Since **a**, **b** and **c** are non-coplanar (they lie in different planes) we can equate coefficients on each side of the equation.

a: $s = t$ ①

b: $s = 1 - t$ ②

Solving ① and ② simultaneously, we get $s = \frac{1}{2}$ and $t = \frac{1}{2}$.

Therefore $\overrightarrow{OX} = \frac{1}{2}\overrightarrow{OE}$, so X is the midpoint of OE.

and $\overrightarrow{BX} = \frac{1}{2}\overrightarrow{BG}$, so X is the midpoint of BG.

Hence the two diagonals OE and BG bisect each other.

Exercise 12B

1 Show that the triangle with vertices A(4, −2, −3), B(9, 0, −4) and C(9, 0, −2) is isosceles.

2 Show that the triangle with vertices P(−1, 5, 2), Q(2, 9, −9) and R(−8, 24, 7) is right-angled, stating where the right-angle is.

3 Show that the quadrilateral ABCD with vertices A(−2, 10, 7), B(−1, 7, 12), C(5, 2, −3) and D(7, −4, 7) is a trapezium.

4 Show that the quadrilateral EFGH with vertices E(5, −1, 4), F(10, 1, 1), G(−4, 2, 7) and H(1, 4, 4) is a parallelogram.

5 Show that the quadrilateral ABCD with vertices A(4, 1, −2), B(6, 0, −4), C(3, 1, −2) and D(6, 2, 0) is a kite.

6 Show that the quadrilateral with vertices at A(2, 1, 3), B(5, 5, −8), C(−5, 20, 8) and D(−2, 24, −3) is a rectangle.

7 The quadrilateral ABCD is a rhombus. Given that the coordinates of A, B and C are (7, 1, 3), (2, 2, 1) and (7, 3, −1) respectively, find the coordinates of D.

8 **a** Show that the points A(3, 0, 1), B(3, 5, 1) and C(6, 5, 5) form an isosceles right-angled triangle.

b Find the coordinates of D such that ABCD is a square, and find the area of this square.

9 ABCDEFGH is a cube with vertices A(1, 2, −1), B(6, 2, −1), C(6, 7, −1), D(1, 7, −1), E(1, 2, 4), F(6, 2, 4), G(6, 7, 4), H(1, 7, 4).

a Find **i** its volume
ii its surface area.

b Verify that the diagonals AG and BH are equal in length.

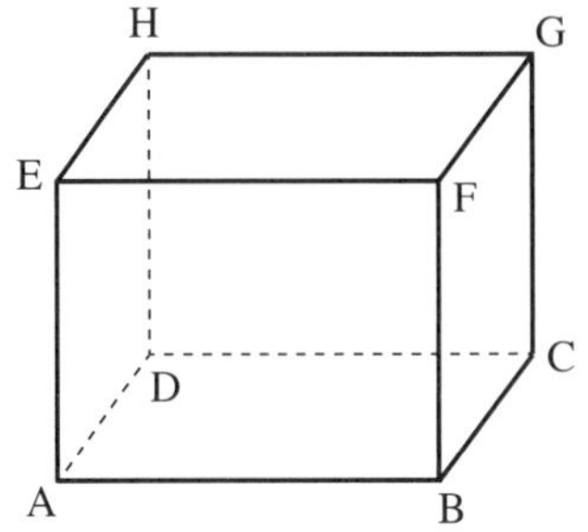

10 Prove that the diagonals of the rectangle shown opposite bisect each other.

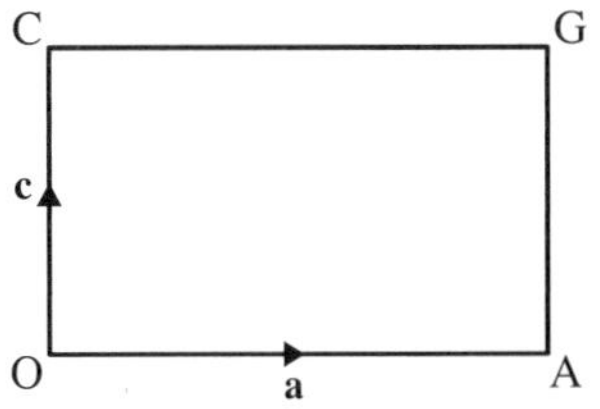

11 Prove that the diagonals OF and AG of the cuboid shown opposite bisect each other.

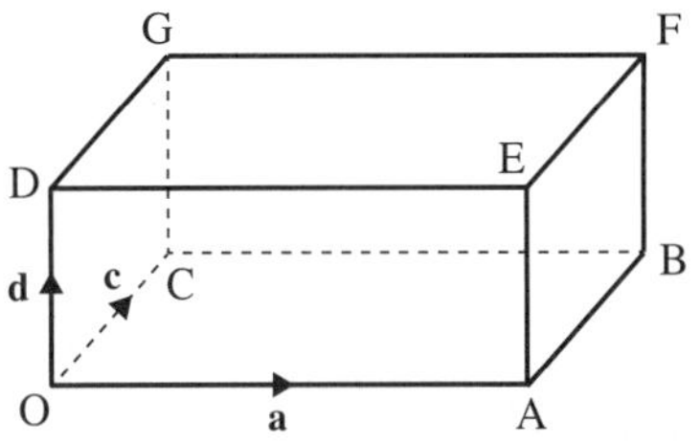

12.3 Applications of vectors to mechanics

Displacement vectors

In mechanics, **r** is generally used as a symbol for displacement and position vectors.

If $\mathbf{r}_A$ and $\mathbf{r}_B$ represent the position vectors of points A and B respectively then the displacement vector $\overrightarrow{AB}$ which gives the position of B relative to A is given by

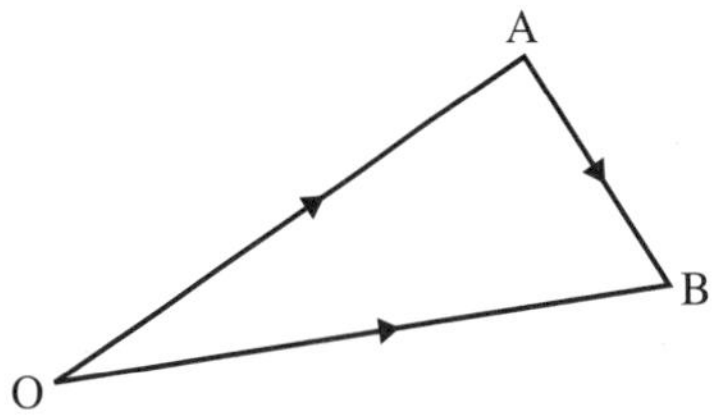

$$\overrightarrow{AB} = \mathbf{r}_B - \mathbf{r}_A$$

For a particle moving with constant velocity **v** and initial position $\mathbf{r}_0$, its position **r** at any time t can be found by using the equation

$$\mathbf{r} = \mathbf{r}_0 + \mathbf{v}t$$

Example 1

A particle with an initial position vector $(3\mathbf{i} + 2\mathbf{j} - \mathbf{k})$ m travels with a velocity $(5\mathbf{i} - 4\mathbf{j} + 2\mathbf{k})$ m s^{-1}. Find:

a the position vector after t seconds

b the position vector after 2 seconds

c the distance moved over 5 seconds.

a At time t, $\mathbf{r} = \mathbf{r}_0 + \mathbf{v}t$
$= (3\mathbf{i} + 2\mathbf{j} - \mathbf{k}) + (5\mathbf{i} - 4\mathbf{j} + 2\mathbf{k})t$

b After 2 seconds, $\mathbf{r} = (3\mathbf{i} + 2\mathbf{j} - \mathbf{k}) + 2(5\mathbf{i} - 4\mathbf{j} + 2\mathbf{k})$
$= (13\mathbf{i} - 6\mathbf{j} + 3\mathbf{k})\,\text{m}$

c The particle moves $(5\mathbf{i} - 4\mathbf{j} + 2\mathbf{k})$ m every second. So over 5 seconds it moves

$$5(5\mathbf{i} - 4\mathbf{j} + 2\mathbf{k}) = (25\mathbf{i} - 20\mathbf{j} + 10\mathbf{k})\,\text{m}$$

The distance moved is therefore

$$\sqrt{25^2 + (-20)^2 + 10^2} = 15\sqrt{5} = 33.5\,\text{m}$$

Example 2

A particle with an initial position vector $(2\mathbf{i} + 5\mathbf{j} + \mathbf{k})$ m travels with speed $27\,\text{m}\,\text{s}^{-1}$ in the direction of the vector $(\mathbf{i} - 8\mathbf{j} + 4\mathbf{k})$. Find the position of the particle after 3 seconds.

Velocity of the particle $\mathbf{v} = s(\mathbf{i} - 8\mathbf{j} + 4\mathbf{k})$

Speed (magnitude of velocity) $|\mathbf{v}| = \sqrt{s^2 + (-8s)^2 + (4s)^2}$
$= \sqrt{81s^2} = 9s$

Hence $9s = 27$
$s = 3$

So velocity $\mathbf{v} = (3\mathbf{i} - 24\mathbf{j} + 12\mathbf{k})\text{m}\,\text{s}^{-1}$

Now, position after 3 seconds, $\mathbf{r} = \mathbf{r}_0 + \mathbf{v}t$
$= (2\mathbf{i} + 5\mathbf{j} + \mathbf{k}) + 3(3\mathbf{i} - 24\mathbf{j} + 12\mathbf{k})$
$= (11\mathbf{i} - 67\mathbf{j} + 37\mathbf{k})\,\text{m}$

The velocity vector

When there is no acceleration and the velocity is constant:

$$\text{velocity} = \frac{\text{change in displacement}}{\text{time}}$$

Example 3

Initially a particle has position vector $(-2\mathbf{i} + 5\mathbf{j} - 3\mathbf{k})$ m and 4 seconds later its position vector is $(6\mathbf{i} - 7\mathbf{j} - \mathbf{k})$ m. Assuming the velocity is constant find:

a the velocity of the particle

b the speed of the particle.

a $\text{velocity} = \dfrac{\text{change in displacement}}{\text{time}}$

$$\mathbf{v} = \frac{(6\mathbf{i} - 7\mathbf{j} - \mathbf{k}) - (-2\mathbf{i} + 5\mathbf{j} - 3\mathbf{k})}{4}$$

$$= \frac{8\mathbf{i} - 12\mathbf{j} + 2\mathbf{k}}{4}$$

$$= (2\mathbf{i} - 3\mathbf{j} + 0.5\mathbf{k})\,\text{m}\,\text{s}^{-1}$$

b speed $= |\mathbf{v}|$

$$= \sqrt{2^2 + (-3)^2 + (0.5)^2} = 3.64\,\text{m}\,\text{s}^{-1}$$

The acceleration vector

When the acceleration is constant:

$$\text{acceleration} = \frac{\text{change in velocity}}{\text{time}}$$

Example 4

A particle moving with constant acceleration has an initial velocity $(2\mathbf{i} - 2\mathbf{j} + 5\mathbf{k})\,\text{m s}^{-1}$ and 3 seconds later its velocity is $(8\mathbf{i} + \mathbf{j} - \mathbf{k})\,\text{m s}^{-1}$. Find the acceleration of the particle.

$$\mathbf{a} = \frac{(8\mathbf{i} + \mathbf{j} - \mathbf{k}) - (2\mathbf{i} - 2\mathbf{j} + 5\mathbf{k})}{3}$$

$$= \frac{6\mathbf{i} + 3\mathbf{j} - 6\mathbf{k}}{3}$$

$$= (2\mathbf{i} + \mathbf{j} - 2\mathbf{k})\,\text{m s}^{-2}$$

Given also that the mass of the particle is 4 kg, find the force acting on the particle.

Recall $\mathbf{F} = m\mathbf{a}$

$$\mathbf{F} = 4(2\mathbf{i} + \mathbf{j} - 2\mathbf{k})$$

$$= (8\mathbf{i} + 4\mathbf{j} - 8\mathbf{k})\,\text{N}$$

We can also solve problems by using the 'suvat' equations that we are already familiar with.

Example 5

A particle P of mass 3 kg is being held in static equilibrium by three forces:

$$\mathbf{F}_1 = (4\mathbf{i} - \mathbf{j} + 2\mathbf{k})\,\text{N}$$

$$\mathbf{F}_2 = (-\mathbf{i} + 3\mathbf{j} + b\mathbf{k})\,\text{N}$$

$$\mathbf{F}_3 = (a\mathbf{i} - 2\mathbf{j} + \mathbf{k})\,\text{N}$$

a Calculate the values of a and b.

b $\mathbf{F}_3$ is now removed. Find the resultant vector of $\mathbf{F}_1$ and $\mathbf{F}_2$.

c Find the acceleration of the particle, giving your answer in vector form.

d Find the distance moved by the particle in the first 10 seconds of motion.

a When a particle is held in static equilibrium the resultant vector is zero.

$$\mathbf{F}_1 + \mathbf{F}_2 + \mathbf{F}_3 = 0\mathbf{i} + 0\mathbf{j} + 0\mathbf{k}$$

i: $4 - 1 + a = 0, \quad a = -3$

k: $2 + b + 1 = 0, \quad b = -3$

b $\mathbf{R} = \mathbf{F}_1 + \mathbf{F}_2$

$$= (4\mathbf{i} - \mathbf{j} + 2\mathbf{k}) + (-\mathbf{i} + 3\mathbf{j} - 3\mathbf{k})$$

$$= (3\mathbf{i} + 2\mathbf{j} - \mathbf{k})\,\text{N}$$

c $\mathbf{F} = m\mathbf{a}$

$$3\mathbf{i} + 2\mathbf{j} - \mathbf{k} = 3\mathbf{a}$$

$$(\mathbf{i} + \tfrac{2}{3}\mathbf{j} - \tfrac{1}{3}\mathbf{k})\,\text{m s}^{-2} = \mathbf{a}$$

d $u = 0$, $a = |\mathbf{a}| = \dfrac{\sqrt{14}}{3}$, $t = 10$, $s = ?$

$$s = ut + \tfrac{1}{2}at^2$$
$$= 0 + \tfrac{1}{2} \times \frac{\sqrt{14}}{3} \times 10^2$$
$$= \frac{50\sqrt{14}}{3} = 62.4\,\text{m}$$

Exercise 12C

1 A particle is initially at the point with position vector $\mathbf{r}_0$. It moves with constant velocity $\mathbf{v}$ and after a time t seconds is at a point with position vector $\mathbf{r}$.

Find $\mathbf{r}$ when:

a $\mathbf{r}_0 = 2\mathbf{i} + \mathbf{j} - \mathbf{k}$, $\quad \mathbf{v} = 3\mathbf{i} + \mathbf{j} + \mathbf{k}$, $\quad t = 2$

b $\mathbf{r}_0 = 3\mathbf{j} + 2\mathbf{k}$, $\quad \mathbf{v} = \mathbf{i} + \mathbf{j} - 3\mathbf{k}$, $\quad t = 3$

c $\mathbf{r}_0 = \mathbf{i} + 2\mathbf{j}$, $\quad \mathbf{v} = \mathbf{i} + 2\mathbf{j} + 5\mathbf{k}$, $\quad t = 4$

d $\mathbf{r}_0 = -2\mathbf{i} + \mathbf{j} - 2\mathbf{k}$, $\quad \mathbf{v} = 3\mathbf{i} + \mathbf{j} + 2\mathbf{k}$, $\quad t = 2$

2 A particle is initially at the point $\mathbf{r}_0$ and t seconds later it is at the point $\mathbf{r}$. Find the velocity vector and the speed of the particle, assuming the velocity is constant, when:

a $\mathbf{r}_0 = 2\mathbf{i}$, $\quad \mathbf{r} = 12\mathbf{i}$, $\quad t = 2$

b $\mathbf{r}_0 = 2\mathbf{j} + \mathbf{k}$, $\quad \mathbf{r} = \mathbf{i} - 10\mathbf{j} - 3\mathbf{k}$, $\quad t = 4$

c $\mathbf{r}_0 = 2\mathbf{i} + \mathbf{j} - 2\mathbf{k}$, $\quad \mathbf{r} = 8\mathbf{i} + 4\mathbf{j} + \mathbf{k}$, $\quad t = 3$

d $\mathbf{r}_0 = -3\mathbf{i} - 5\mathbf{k}$, $\quad \mathbf{r} = -2\mathbf{i} + 5\mathbf{j} + 3\mathbf{k}$, $\quad t = 2$

3 A particle has an initial velocity $\mathbf{u}\,\text{m s}^{-1}$ and after t seconds it has velocity $\mathbf{v}\,\text{m s}^{-1}$. Given that the particle moves with uniform acceleration $\mathbf{a}\,\text{m s}^{-2}$, find $\mathbf{a}$ when:

a $\mathbf{u} = 3\mathbf{i} + 2\mathbf{j} - 3\mathbf{k}$, $\quad \mathbf{v} = 9\mathbf{i} + 6\mathbf{j} + \mathbf{k}$, $\quad t = 2$

b $\mathbf{u} = 6\mathbf{i} + \mathbf{j} - \mathbf{k}$ $\quad \mathbf{v} = 2\mathbf{i} - \mathbf{j} + 3\mathbf{k}$, $\quad t = 2$

c $\mathbf{u} = 4\mathbf{i} - 7\mathbf{k}$, $\quad \mathbf{v} = 8\mathbf{i} + 12\mathbf{j}$, $\quad t = 4$

d $\mathbf{u} = 2\mathbf{j} - \mathbf{k}$, $\quad \mathbf{v} = 9\mathbf{i} + 8\mathbf{j} + 2\mathbf{k}$, $\quad t = 3$

4 A particle has an initial velocity $\mathbf{u}\,\text{m s}^{-1}$. The particle moves with uniform acceleration $\mathbf{a}\,\text{m s}^{-2}$, and after t seconds it has velocity $\mathbf{v}\,\text{m s}^{-1}$.

Find $\mathbf{v}$ when:

a $\mathbf{u} = 2\mathbf{i} + 5\mathbf{j} + 3\mathbf{k}$, $\quad \mathbf{a} = 3\mathbf{i} - \mathbf{j} + \mathbf{k}$, $\quad t = 2$

b $\mathbf{u} = 3\mathbf{j} + 4\mathbf{k}$, $\quad \mathbf{a} = 2\mathbf{i} + \mathbf{j} - 2\mathbf{k}$, $\quad t = 4$

c $\mathbf{u} = \mathbf{i} + \mathbf{j} + 4\mathbf{k}$, $\quad \mathbf{a} = 2\mathbf{i} + 3\mathbf{j} - \mathbf{k}$, $\quad t = 2$

d $\mathbf{u} = \mathbf{i} + 2\mathbf{j} + 5\mathbf{k}$, $\quad \mathbf{a} = 3\mathbf{i} - 2\mathbf{j} + 4\mathbf{k}$, $\quad t = 3$

5 Find in vector form the velocity of a particle moving

a with speed $4\,\text{m s}^{-1}$ parallel to the positive z-axis

b with speed $35\,\text{m s}^{-1}$ parallel to the vector $6\mathbf{i} - 2\mathbf{j} - 3\mathbf{k}$

c with speed $36\,\text{m s}^{-1}$ parallel to the vector $-\mathbf{i} + 4\mathbf{j} + 8\mathbf{k}$

6 A body moves with constant velocity from A to B in 5 seconds, where A and B have position vectors $(2\mathbf{i} - \mathbf{j} + 3\mathbf{k})$ m and $(22\mathbf{i} - 31\mathbf{j} - 2\mathbf{k})$ m respectively. Find the velocity of the body, giving your answer in vector form.

7 A body moves with constant velocity $(2\mathbf{i} - 3\mathbf{j} - 5\mathbf{k})\,\text{m s}^{-1}$ from A to B in 3 seconds. If the position vector of A is $(2\mathbf{i} + 11\mathbf{j} + 4\mathbf{k})$ m, find the position vector of B.

8 A particle moves from A to B where A and B have position vectors $(3\mathbf{i} + 4\mathbf{j} + 7\mathbf{k})$ m and $(23\mathbf{i} + y\mathbf{j} - 3\mathbf{k})$ m respectively. If the velocity is $(4\mathbf{i} - 3\mathbf{j} - z\mathbf{k})\,\text{m s}^{-1}$, find:

a the time taken to go from A to B

b the values of y and z.

9 A body has speed $26\,\text{m s}^{-1}$ and its velocity is $(x\mathbf{i} + 3\mathbf{j} - 4\mathbf{k})\,\text{m s}^{-1}$. Find x given that it is negative.

10 A particle has an initial position vector of $(3\mathbf{i} - 4\mathbf{j} + 2\mathbf{k})$ m. The particle moves with a constant velocity of $(5\mathbf{i} + 2\mathbf{j} + \mathbf{k})\,\text{m s}^{-1}$.

a Find its position vector after 2 seconds.

b Determine whether or not the particle passes through the point with position vector $(38\mathbf{i} + 8\mathbf{j} + 5\mathbf{k})$ m.

11 A particle has a constant velocity of $(5\mathbf{i} + 4\mathbf{j})\,\text{m s}^{-1}$. After 5 seconds it has a position vector of $(21\mathbf{i} + 22\mathbf{j} - 8\mathbf{k})$ m. Find its initial position vector.

12 A body has a constant velocity of $(2\mathbf{i} + 7\mathbf{j} + 5\mathbf{k})\,\text{m s}^{-1}$ and an initial position of $(2\mathbf{i} - 15\mathbf{j} - 10\mathbf{k})$ m. Find its distance from the origin after 3 seconds.

13 Initially a plane P is at a point O and a helicopter H is at a point $(5\mathbf{i} + 10\mathbf{j} + 2\mathbf{k})$ km relative to O, where $\mathbf{i}$ and $\mathbf{j}$ are unit vectors directed East and North respectively, and $\mathbf{k}$ is a unit vector vertically upwards.

The plane P is moving with velocity $(30\mathbf{i} + \mathbf{k})\,\text{km h}^{-1}$ and the helicopter H is moving with velocity $(10\mathbf{i} - 15\mathbf{j} + 2\mathbf{k})\,\text{km h}^{-1}$.

Find the distance of H from P after one hour.

14 A particle P of mass 2 kg is being acted on by two forces

$$\mathbf{F}_1 = (3\mathbf{i} - 5\mathbf{j} + 4\mathbf{k})\,\text{N}$$
$$\mathbf{F}_2 = (-\mathbf{i} + 7\mathbf{j} + 5\mathbf{k})\,\text{N}$$

a Find the resultant force acting on the particle.

b Find the acceleration of the particle, giving your answer in vector form.

c Given that the particle starts from rest, find the distance moved in the first 5 seconds.

15 A particle P of mass 4 kg is being held in static equilibrium by three forces

$$\mathbf{F}_1 = (2\mathbf{i} + 5\mathbf{j} + 3\mathbf{k})\,\text{N}$$
$$\mathbf{F}_2 = (\mathbf{i} - 2\mathbf{j} - 4\mathbf{k})\,\text{N}$$
$$\mathbf{F}_3 = (a\mathbf{i} + b\mathbf{j} + c\mathbf{k})\,\text{N}$$

a Find the values of a, b and c.

The force $\mathbf{F}_3$ is removed and the particle begins to move.

b Find the acceleration of the particle in vector form.

c Find the speed of the particle after 7 seconds.

16 Particle A has an initial position vector $(\mathbf{i} + 6\mathbf{j} + 2\mathbf{k})$ m and is moving with velocity $(-10\mathbf{i} + \mathbf{j} - 2\mathbf{k})$ m s^{-1}. Particle B has an initial position vector $(-19\mathbf{i} + 22\mathbf{j} - 34\mathbf{k})$ m and is moving with velocity $(-5\mathbf{i} - 3\mathbf{j} + 7\mathbf{k})$ m s^{-1}. Show that the two particles will collide, and find the time and position at which the collision occurs.

Review Exercise 12D

1 Find a unit vector in the direction of each of the following vectors:

a $3\mathbf{i} - \mathbf{j} + 5\mathbf{k}$ **b** $-2\mathbf{i} - 7\mathbf{j} + \mathbf{k}$ **c** $\mathbf{i} + 4\mathbf{j} - 3\mathbf{k}$

2 Find a vector that is parallel to $3\mathbf{i} - 12\mathbf{j} - 4\mathbf{k}$ and has magnitude 32.5 units.

3 Find **i** the vector $\overrightarrow{AB}$ **ii** the distance between the following pairs of points:

a A(−2, 1, 4) B(4, −3, −1)

b A(5, −2, 2) B(7, 4, 9)

c A(11, 12, −8) B(−2, 0, −4)

4 If $\mathbf{m} = 3\mathbf{i} + 4\mathbf{j} - 3\mathbf{k}$, $\mathbf{n} = \mathbf{i} - 2\mathbf{j} - \mathbf{k}$ and $\mathbf{p} = 7\mathbf{i} - 4\mathbf{j} - 7\mathbf{k}$, find

a $|\mathbf{m}|$ **b** $|\mathbf{m}| + |\mathbf{n}|$ **c** $|\mathbf{m} + \mathbf{n}|$ **d** $3\mathbf{m} - 2\mathbf{p}$

e the constant s such that $\mathbf{m} + s\mathbf{n} = \mathbf{p}$

5 Given that $\overrightarrow{OA} = -2\mathbf{i} + 3\mathbf{j} + 6\mathbf{k}$ and $\overrightarrow{OB} = \mathbf{i} - \mathbf{j} - 2\mathbf{k}$, find:

a $\overrightarrow{AB}$

b $\overrightarrow{AM}$, where M is the midpoint of $\overrightarrow{AB}$

c $\overrightarrow{OM}$

6 Given that the points A and B have coordinates (−3, 7, 5) and (2, −4, −3) respectively, find the coordinates of the midpoint, M, of AB.

7 Find the angle between:

a the vector $\mathbf{p} = \begin{pmatrix} 5 \\ -2 \\ 1 \end{pmatrix}$ and the positive x-axis

b the vector $\mathbf{q} = \begin{pmatrix} -3 \\ 2 \\ -3 \end{pmatrix}$ and the positive y-axis

c the vector $\mathbf{r} = \begin{pmatrix} 0 \\ 4 \\ -7 \end{pmatrix}$ and the positive z-axis

8 The points A and B have coordinates (4, 3, 5) and (6, −1, −2) respectively. The point C is such that $\overrightarrow{AC} = 3\overrightarrow{AB}$. Find the coordinates of point C.

9 Determine whether the triangle with vertices A(2, 0, 1), B(−3, 1, 1) and C(5, −2, −4) is equilateral, isosceles or scalene.

10 Show that the triangle with vertices P(5, −10, 18), Q(11, −2, −4) and R(−9, 28, 28) is right-angled, and find its area.

11 Determine the nature of each of the following quadrilaterals ABCD (i.e. determine whether they are a square, rectangle, rhombus, parallelogram, trapezium or kite):

a	A(4, −1, 5)	B(4, 4, 5)	C(10, 4, 13)	D(10, −1, 13)
b	A(−1, 2, 0)	B(1, 1, 3)	C(10, −6, 8)	D(4, −3, −1)
c	A(4, −3, 5)	B(3, −4, 7)	C(8, −6, 10)	D(9, −5, 8)

12 Find in vector form the velocity of a particle moving with speed $56\,\mathrm{m\,s^{-1}}$ parallel to the vector $2\mathbf{i} + 3\mathbf{j} - 6\mathbf{k}$.

13 A particle moves with constant velocity from A to B in 6 seconds, where A and B have position vectors $(-\mathbf{i} - 2\mathbf{j} + 4\mathbf{k})$ m and $(11\mathbf{i} - 20\mathbf{j} + 10\mathbf{k})$ m respectively. Find the velocity of the particle, giving your answer in vector form.

14 A particle is moving with constant velocity $(2\mathbf{i} + \mathbf{j} + 3\mathbf{k})\,\mathrm{m\,s^{-1}}$. Given that the particle has an initial position vector of $(5\mathbf{i} - 3\mathbf{j} - 7\mathbf{k})$ m, find its position after 4 seconds.

15 A particle accelerates uniformly over a period of 5 seconds. Given that the initial velocity is $(3\mathbf{i} + \mathbf{j} - 2\mathbf{k})\,\mathrm{m\,s^{-1}}$ and the final velocity is $(8\mathbf{i} - 4\mathbf{j} + 8\mathbf{k})\,\mathrm{m\,s^{-1}}$, find its acceleration vector.

16 A particle accelerates uniformly over 3 seconds with an acceleration of $\mathbf{a} = (7\mathbf{i} + 2\mathbf{j} - 4\mathbf{k})\,\mathrm{m\,s^{-1}}$. Given that its initial velocity is $\mathbf{u} = (6\mathbf{i} - 3\mathbf{j} - 3\mathbf{k})\,\mathrm{m\,s^{-1}}$, find its final speed.

17 A particle P of mass 3 kg is being acted on by two forces

$$\mathbf{F}_1 = (-5\mathbf{i} - 6\mathbf{j} + \mathbf{k})\,\mathrm{N}$$
$$\mathbf{F}_2 = (2\mathbf{i} - 4\mathbf{j} - \mathbf{k})\,\mathrm{N}$$

a Find the acceleration of the particle, giving your answer in vector form.

b Given that the particle starts from rest, find the distance it moves in the first 8 seconds.

18 Particle A has an initial position vector $(-4\mathbf{i} - 16\mathbf{j} + 11\mathbf{k})$ m and is moving with a velocity of $(2\mathbf{i} + \mathbf{j} - 2\mathbf{k})\,\mathrm{m\,s^{-1}}$. Particle B has an initial position vector $(-11\mathbf{i} + 5\mathbf{j} - 10\mathbf{k})$ m and is moving with a velocity of $(3\mathbf{i} - 2\mathbf{j} + \mathbf{k})\,\mathrm{m\,s^{-1}}$. Show that the two particles will collide, and find the time and position at which this collision occurs.

PART 13

Proof by contradiction

In order to prove a statement by contradiction we first start by assuming that the **opposite** is true. We then proceed to show that this assumption leads to a contradiction, and cannot therefore be true. We can then conclude that the original statement must have been true.

Example 1

Prove by contradiction that there exist no integers m and n for which $15m + 10n = 1$.

Start by assuming that there **do** exist integers m and n for which $15m + 10n = 1$.

Now, dividing by 5 $\quad 3m + 2n = \frac{1}{5}$

Since m and n are integers, $3m$ and $2n$ must also be integers, and so $3m + 2n$ must also be an integer.

But $\frac{1}{5}$ is **not** an integer. This therefore contradicts the assumption that m and n are integers and proves the original statement that there are **no** integers m and n for which $15m + 10n = 1$.

Example 2

Prove by contradiction that if n^2 is a multiple of 3 then n must also be a multiple of 3.

Start by assuming that n is **not** a multiple of 3, i.e. $n = 3m + 1$ or $n = 3k + 2$.

If $\quad n = 3m + 1$

then $\quad n^2 = (3m + 1)^2$

$= 9m^2 + 6m + 1$

$= 3(3m^2 + 2m) + 1$ $\quad$ which is **not** a multiple of 3.

If $\quad n = 3k + 2$

then $\quad n^2 = (3k + 2)^2$

$= 9k^2 + 6k + 4$

$= 3(3k^2 + 2k + 1) + 1$ $\quad$ which is also **not** a multiple of 3.

Therefore the assumption that n is **not** a multiple of 3 contradicts the statement that n^2 **is** a multiple of 3.

This proves that the original statement that if n^2 is a multiple of 3 then n must also be a multiple of 3, is true.

Example 3

Prove by contradiction that $\sqrt{3}$ is irrational.

Start by assuming that $\sqrt{3}$ is **rational**. That is, $\sqrt{3} = \frac{a}{b}$ where a and b are integers, and $\frac{a}{b}$ is written in its simplest terms, i.e. there are no common factors between a and b.

Then $\quad 3 = \frac{a^2}{b^2}$

$3b^2 = a^2 \qquad$ so a^2 is a multiple of 3.

We just proved in Example 2 that if a^2 is a multiple of 3, then a must also be a multiple of 3. So we can write $a = 3c$ for some integer c, and therefore $a^2 = 9c^2$.

Now $\quad 3b^2 = 9c^2$

and so $\quad b^2 = 3c^2 \qquad$ so b^2, and therefore also b, are also multiples of 3.

But if both a and b are multiples of 3, this contradicts the assumption that $\frac{a}{b}$ was a fraction written in its simplest terms. This shows that $\sqrt{3}$ **cannot** be written as a fraction, and that it must therefore be irrational.

Example 4

Prove by contradiction that if a is an irrational number and b is a rational number, then $a + b$ must be an irrational number.

Start by assuming that $a + b$ is rational i.e. $a + b = \frac{m}{n}$ for some integers m and n.

We can also write $b = \frac{c}{d}$ for some integers c and d, as b is rational.

Then $\quad a + \frac{c}{d} = \frac{m}{n}$

$$a = \frac{m}{n} - \frac{c}{d}$$

$$= \frac{dm - cn}{dn}$$

Now, if c, d, m and n are all integers, then $dm - cn$ and dn are also integers.

We have therefore shown that a is rational, which contradicts the statement that a is irrational.

We can therefore conclude that the original statement was in fact true.

Example 5

Prove by contradiction that there are infinitely many primes.

Start by assuming that there are **not** infinitely many primes, i.e. there are a finite number, n of primes, which can be listed as

$$p_1, p_2, p_3, \dots p_n$$

Now consider the number

$$N = p_1 \times p_2 \times p_3 \times \dots p_n + 1$$

When we divide N by any of the primes in our list $p_1, p_2, \dots p_n$ we get a remainder of 1. This leaves us with two options. Either N has a prime factor which was not in our original list, or N is itself a new prime which was not in our original list. Both scenarios contradict our assumption that there are a finite number of primes.

We can therefore conclude that the original statement that there are infinitely many primes is true.

Exercise 13A

1 Prove by contradiction that there exist no integers m and n such that

$$28m + 21n = 1$$

2 a Prove by contradiction that there exist no integers a and b such that

$$27a + 36b = 1$$

b Prove by counter example that the statement "there exist no integer values of x and y such that

$$3x + 4y = 1"$$

is **not** true.

3 Prove by contradiction that for any irrational number a and any rational number b, their product ab must be irrational.

4 Prove by contradiction that if n^2 is even, then n must also be even.

5 Prove by contradiction that $\sqrt{2}$ is irrational.

6 Prove by contradiction that there is no greatest even number.

7 Prove by contradiction that there is no greatest odd number.

8 Prove by contradiction that there is no greatest rational number.

9 Prove by contradiction that there is no smallest positive rational number.

10 Prove that the sum of any two odd square numbers cannot itself be a square number.

11 Prove by contradiction that for any positive real numbers x and y, $x + y \geqslant 2\sqrt{xy}$.

Answers

Exercise 1A page 1

1 $\frac{4}{5}$ **2** $4a$ **3** $\frac{1}{3}$ **4** 4

5 $\frac{a}{2b}$ **6** 3 **7** $\frac{a}{2}$ **8** $2b$

9 $\frac{3}{4y}$ **10** $\frac{11y}{12x}$ **11** $\frac{2ya}{3}$ **12** $\frac{4m}{n}$

13 AG, BE, CH, DF

14 $\frac{a}{5b}$ **15** a **16** $\frac{7}{8}$ **17** $\frac{3}{4-x}$

18 $\frac{5+2x}{3}$ **19** $\frac{3x+1}{x}$ **20** $\frac{4+5a}{5}$ **21** $\frac{b}{3+2a}$

22 $\frac{3-x}{2}$ **23** $\frac{2x+1}{y}$ **24** $\frac{2x+5}{2}$ **25** $y+xy$

26 $\frac{5x+4}{3x-2}$ **27** $\frac{1+4a}{b+b^2}$ **28** $\frac{1+2x+2x^2}{x}$

29 $\frac{6n-3m}{2mn}$

30 a False **b** True **c** True **d** False

31 a $(x-3)(x+2)$ **b** $x-3$

32 a $x-4$ **b** $\frac{x-2}{x-1}$ **c** $\frac{x+5}{x+2}$

d $\frac{x}{x+1}$ **e** $\frac{x+4}{2(x-5)}$ **f** $\frac{x+5}{x-2}$

g $\frac{x}{2x-1}$ **h** $\frac{2x+1}{2x+3}$ **i** $\frac{x-1}{3x-4}$

33 $\frac{6x+3}{6x+2}$

34 a $\frac{x^2+1}{x^2}$ **b** $2x^2-1$ **c** $2x-1$

d $12x+1$ **e** $30x-2$ **f** $\frac{1-4x}{2}$

g $\frac{3x^2+1}{x^2+2}$ **h** $\frac{x+2}{x}$ **i** $\frac{x}{2x+3}$

j x^2-1 **k** $\frac{x+2}{x}$ **l** $\frac{x+3}{x+4}$

Exercise 1B page 3

1 a $\frac{3x}{5}$ **b** $\frac{3}{x}$ **c** $\frac{4x}{7}$ **d** $\frac{4}{7x}$

e $\frac{7x}{8}$ **f** $\frac{7}{8x}$ **g** $\frac{5x}{6}$ **h** $\frac{5}{6x}$

2 AF, BH, CD, EG

3 a $\frac{23x}{20}$ **b** $\frac{23}{20x}$ **c** $\frac{x}{12}$

d $\frac{1}{12x}$ **e** $\frac{5x+2}{6}$ **f** $\frac{7x+2}{12}$

4 a $\frac{1-2x}{12}$ **b** $\frac{2x-9}{15}$ **c** $\frac{3x+12}{14}$

5 a $\frac{9x+13}{10}$ **b** $\frac{3x+1}{x(x+1)}$

c $\frac{7x-8}{x(x-2)}$ **d** $\frac{8x+9}{(x-2)(x+3)}$

e $\frac{4x+11}{(x+1)(x+2)}$ **f** $\frac{x^2+4x+6}{2(x+2)}$

Exercise 1C page 4

1 a **2** $\frac{10m}{3}$ **3** $\frac{2y}{3x}$ **4** $\frac{15b}{4a}$

5 $\frac{4}{a^2}$ **6** $\frac{8}{3}$ **7** $\frac{x-1}{x+2}$ **8** $\frac{y^2}{5x}$

9 $\frac{x}{8}$ **10** $3(x+2)$

11 a 6 **b** 4 **c** $2a$

12 AF, BH, CE, DG

13 a $\frac{26}{3}$ **b** $\frac{6q}{p}$ **c** $\frac{2xy}{9}$ **d** $\frac{4}{aq}$

e 25 **f** $\frac{y}{2x}$ **g** $2a$ **h** 1

14 a 1 **b** $\frac{ab^3}{x}$ **c** $\frac{x}{x-1}$ **d** $\frac{z^2}{y}$

15 a $\frac{x}{10}$ **b** $3x$ **c** 11

16 $\frac{1}{4}$

17 $\frac{1}{5}$

Exercise 1D page 7

1 a one-one **b** many-one

c one-one **d** one-one

e many-one **f** many-one

g many-one **h** many-one

i one-one **j** one-one

2 a $f(x) \geqslant 3$ **b** $f(x) \geqslant 2$

c $f(x) \geqslant 1$ **d** $f(x) \geqslant 0$

e $0 \leqslant f(x) \leqslant 1$ **f** $-\frac{9}{4} \leqslant f(x) \leqslant 0$

g $0 \leqslant f(x) \leqslant \frac{25}{4}$ **h** $0 \leqslant f(x) \leqslant 5$

i $0 < f(x) \leqslant 1$ **j** $0 < f(x) \leqslant 1$

3 a $(x+3)^2-5$ **b** $f(x) \geqslant -5$

4 a $f(x) \geqslant 3$ **b** $f(x) \geqslant -50$

c $0 < f(x) \leqslant \frac{1}{2}$ **d** $0 < f(x) \leqslant 1$

Exercise 1E page 10

1 a $4(x+5)$ **b** $4x+5$

c $(4x)^2$ **d** $4x^2$

e x^2+5 **f** $x+10$

g $4(x^2+5)$ **h** $[4(x+5)]^2$

2 a -2.5 **b** $\pm\sqrt{\frac{5}{3}}$

3 a $x \mapsto 2(x-3)$ **b** $x \mapsto 2x-3$
c $x \mapsto x^2-3$ **d** $x \mapsto 4x^2$
e $x \mapsto (4x)$ **f** $x \mapsto (2x)^2-3$
g $x \mapsto (2x-3)^2$

4 a 2 **b** 11 **c** 6
d 2 **e** 1 **f** 64

5 a −3 **b** 2 **c** $1\frac{1}{2}$ **d** 5

6 a $2(3x-1)+1$ **b** $3(2x+1)-1$
c $2x^2+1$ **d** $(3x-1)^2$
e $2(3x-1)^2+1$ **f** $3(2x^2+1)-1$

7 a 11 **b** 9 **c** 11
d 14 **e** 81 **f** −1

8 a 2 **b** 0, 2 **c** $\pm\sqrt{2}$

9 $\dfrac{x+2}{5}$ **10** $\dfrac{x}{5}+2$

11 $\dfrac{x}{6}-2$ **12** $\dfrac{3x-1}{2}$

13 $\dfrac{4x}{3}+1$ **14** $\dfrac{(x+6)/2-4}{3}$

15 $x \mapsto \dfrac{2(x-10)-4}{5}$ **16** $x \mapsto \dfrac{2x-3}{-7}$

17 $x \mapsto \dfrac{12}{3x-5}$ **18** $x \mapsto \dfrac{3x-4}{5}$

19 $x \mapsto \dfrac{4(5x+3)+1}{2}$ **20** $x \mapsto \dfrac{12}{x}$

21 a $x \mapsto \dfrac{x}{3}$ **b** $x \mapsto x+5$ **c** $x \mapsto \dfrac{x-1}{2}$

d $x \mapsto 3(x-5)$ **e** $x \mapsto \dfrac{x}{3}+5$ **f** $x \mapsto \dfrac{x}{3}+5$

22 a $x \mapsto 6x+1$ **b** $x \mapsto \dfrac{2x}{3}+1$ **c** $x \mapsto \dfrac{x-1}{6}$

d $x \mapsto 2x-9$ **e** $x \mapsto \dfrac{x+9}{2}$ **f** $x \mapsto \dfrac{x+9}{2}$

23 a 7 **b** 21 **c** 5
d 5 **e** 2

24 a 1 **b i** $x > -2\frac{1}{2}$ **ii** $x > 5$

25 a $x \mapsto \dfrac{3x-5}{2}$ **b** 2

5 a $\dfrac{8x+10}{x-1}$ **b** $12\frac{1}{2}$
c 10 **d** 10

6 a

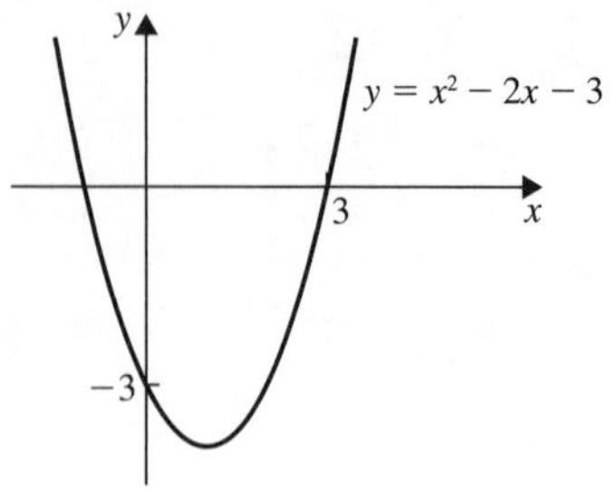

b i $f(x) \geqslant -4$

ii domain $x \geqslant -4$, range $f^{-1}(x) \geqslant 1$

iii

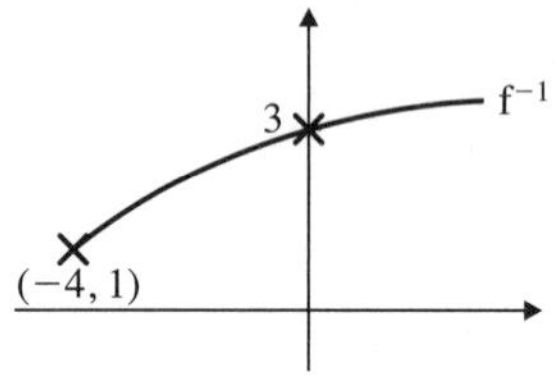

7 a $f^{-1}(x) = \dfrac{1}{2-x}, x \neq 2$

b $x = 1$

8 a domain $x \geqslant 0$, range $f^{-1}(x) \geqslant 2$

b $f^{-1}(x) = 2 + \sqrt{x}$

c $x = 4$

9 a $a = 2$ $b = 0$

b $f^{-1}(x) = x^2 + 2, x \geqslant 0$; $g^{-1}(x) = \dfrac{1}{\sqrt{x}}, x \geqslant 0$

10 $f^{-1}(x) = \dfrac{x-1}{2}$; $g^{-1}(x) = \dfrac{5+3x}{x}, x \neq 0$

11 a $-\infty < x < \infty$ **b** $x \geqslant 0$
c $-90 < x \leqslant 90°$ **d** $x \geqslant 1$
e $x \leqslant -1$ **f** $x \geqslant -4$

EXERCISE 1F PAGE 13

1 a $2-x$ **b** $\dfrac{13}{2x}$ **c** $\dfrac{3-x}{5}$

d $\dfrac{7x+5}{x-2}$ **e** $\dfrac{7x+5}{3-2x}$

2

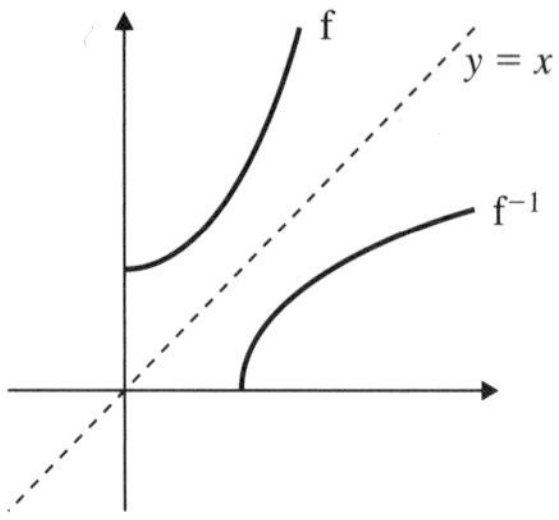

3 a $\dfrac{x+8}{3}, \dfrac{x+22}{3}$ **b** 4, 8

4 a $9x-4, \dfrac{x+1}{3}$ **b** Both are $\dfrac{x+4}{9}$

EXERCISE 1G PAGE 17

1 a

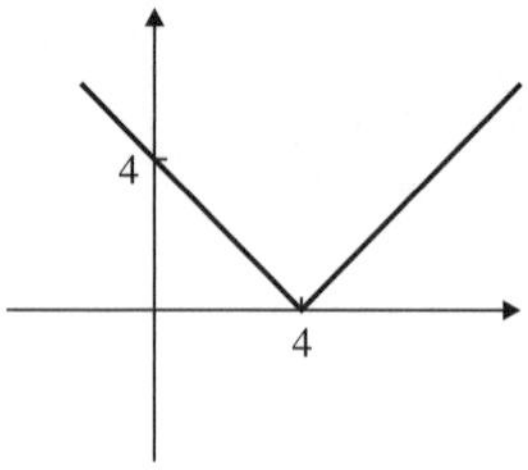

b

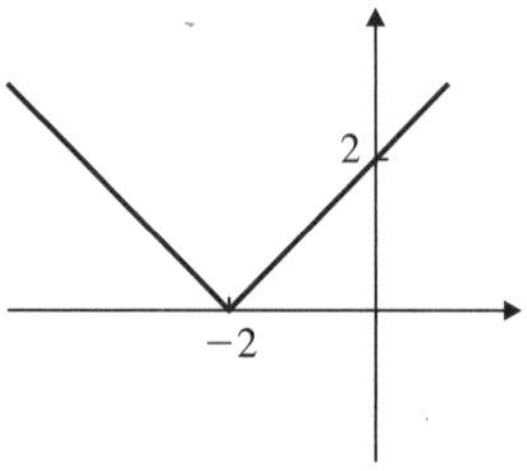

c

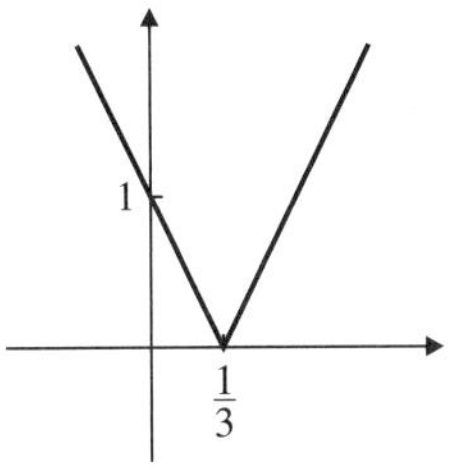

d

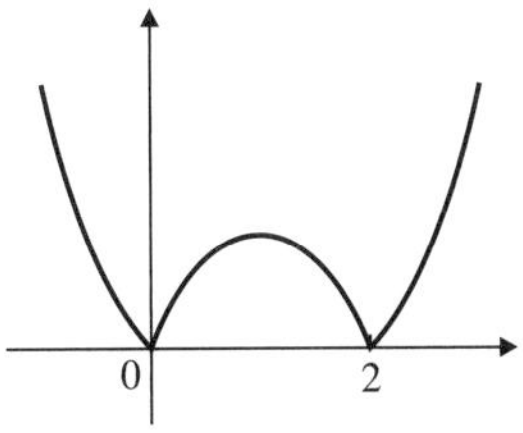

e

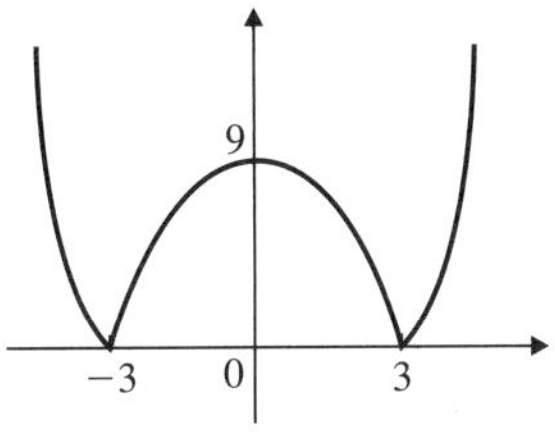

f

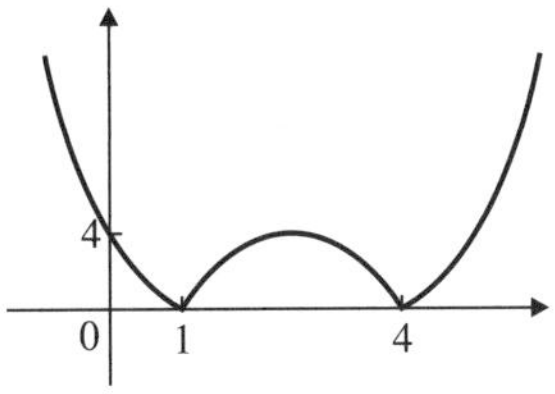

g

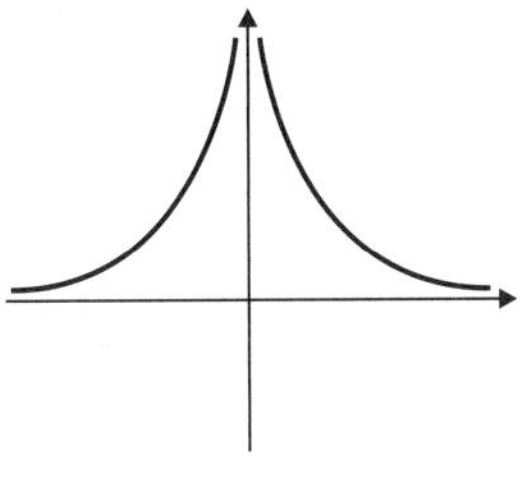

h

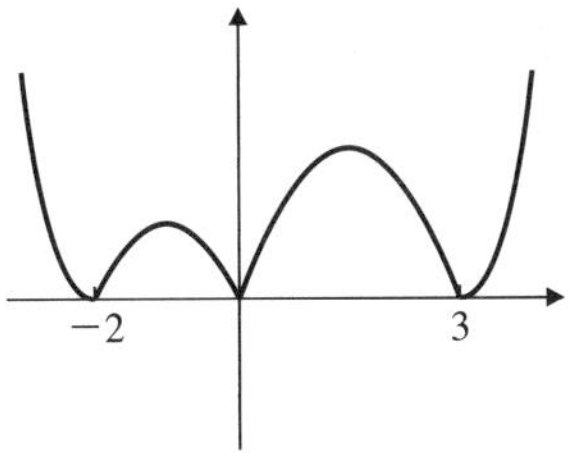

2 a $-3, 7$ **b** $0, 3$
c $-2, 3$ **d** $\pm 1, \pm 3$
e $\pm 5, \pm 7$ **f** $-7, 1$
g $-1, 2$ **h** $\pm \frac{1}{2}$

3 a $x < -1, x > 9$ **b** $-4 < x < 2$
c $x > 2, x < -5$ **d** all x
e $-\frac{14}{3} < x < 6$ **f** $-2 < x < 2$
g $\frac{1}{3} < x < 1$ **h** $x > -1$
i $0 < x < \frac{4}{3}$

4 $4 \pm \sqrt{11}$

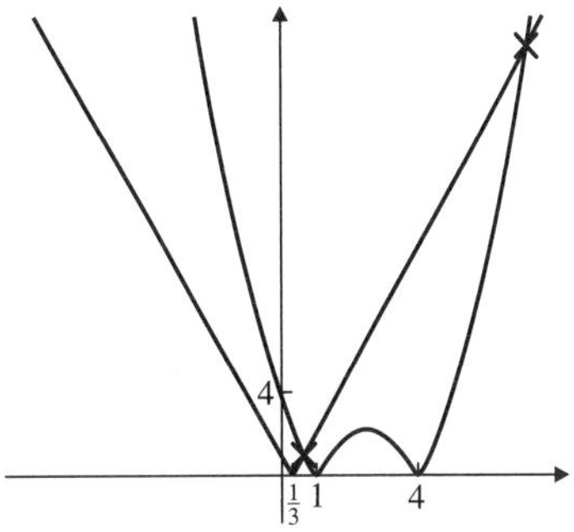

5 a

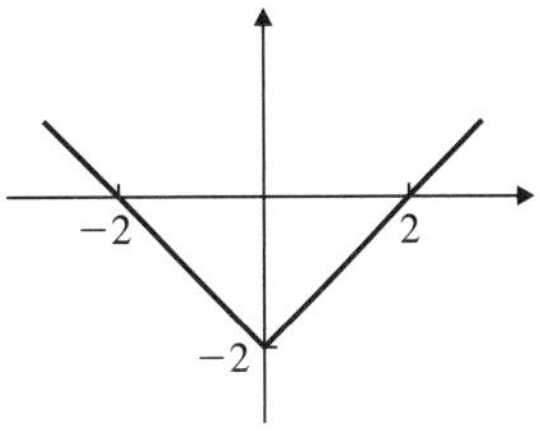

b

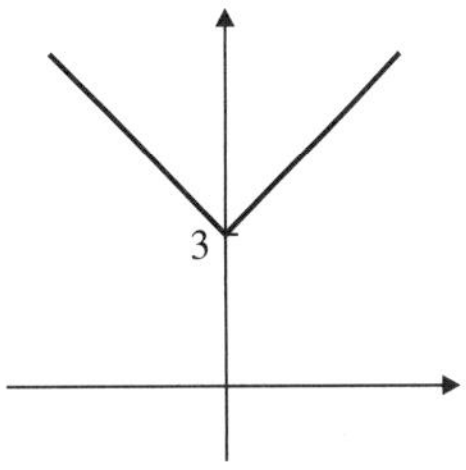

c

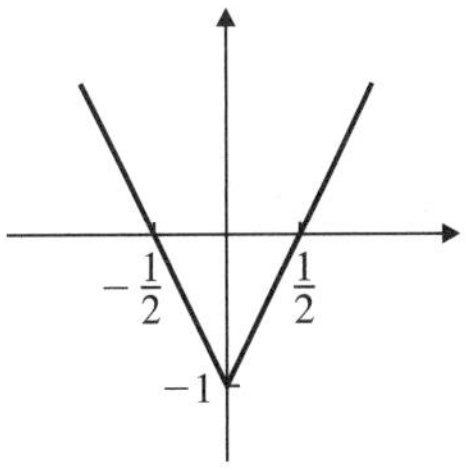

d

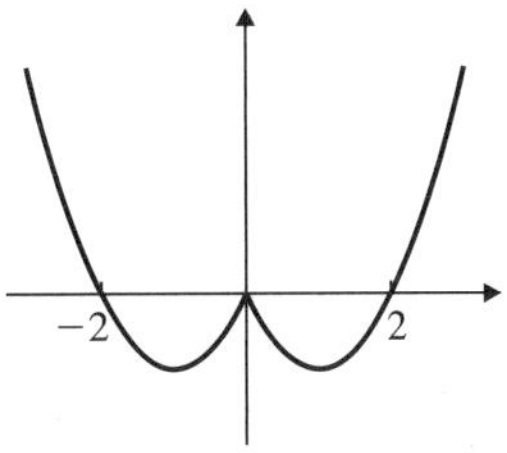

e

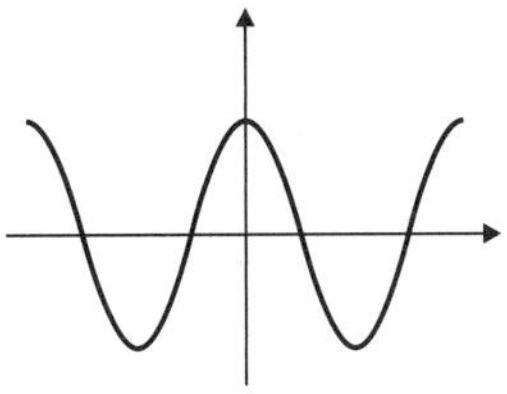

f

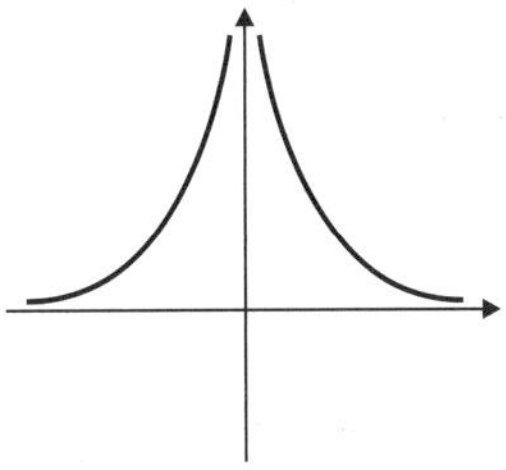

6 a

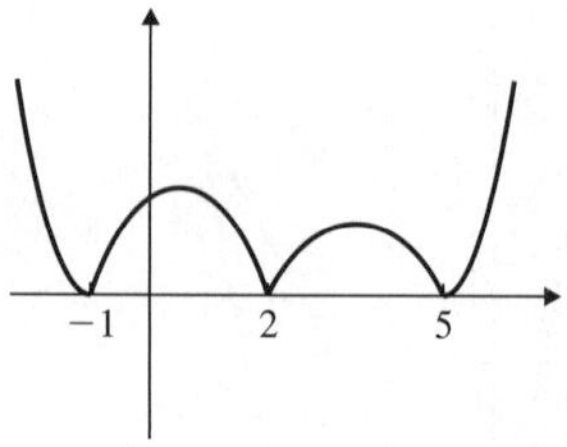

b

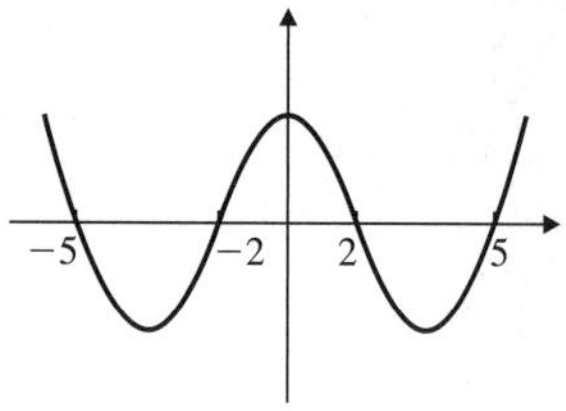

c

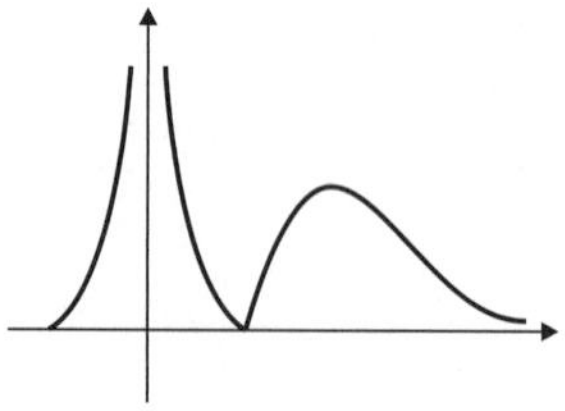

d

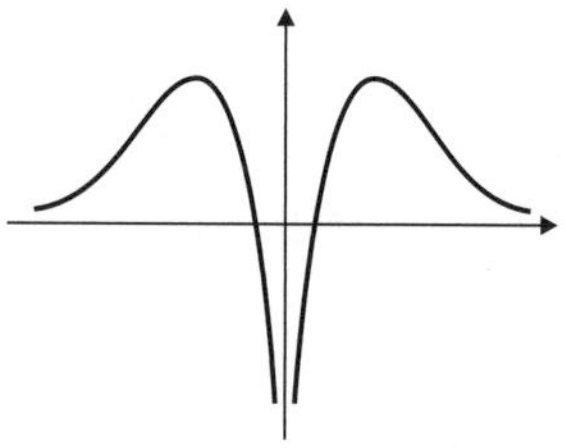

7 a

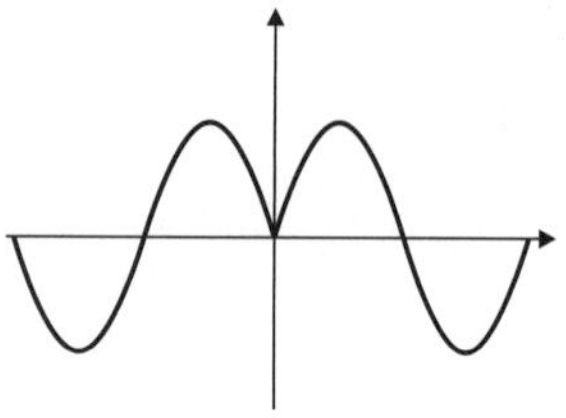

b 4

8 a

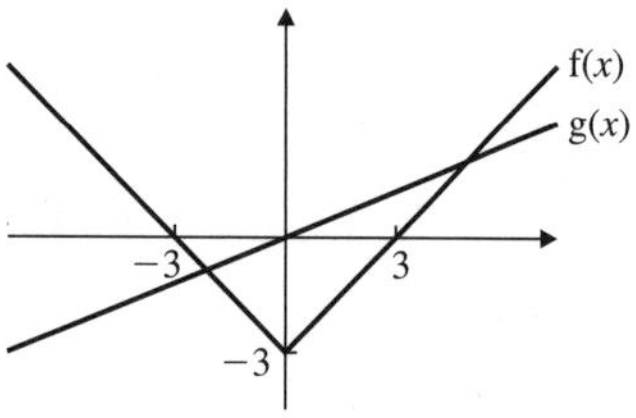

b $x > \frac{9}{2}, x < -\frac{9}{4}$

9 a

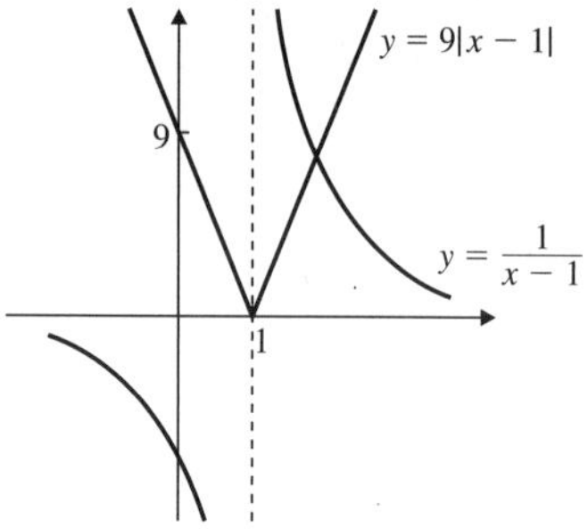

b $x > \frac{4}{3}, x < 1$

10 a i

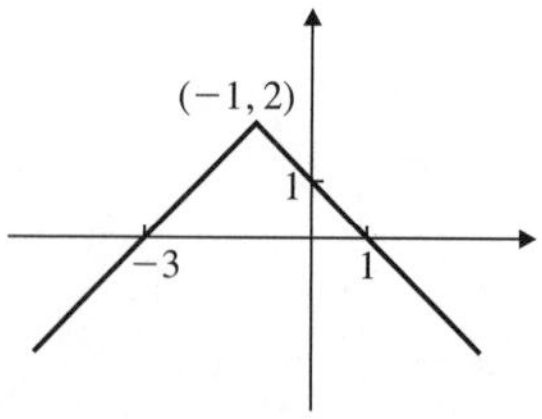

ii

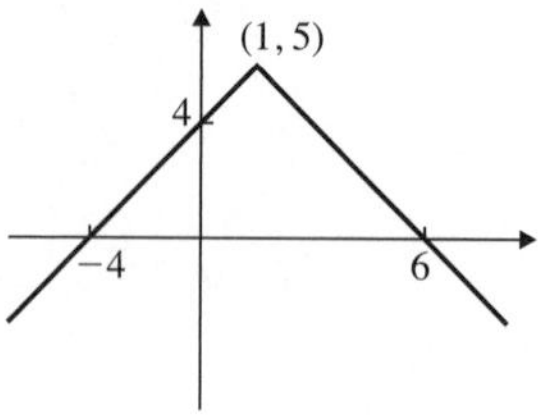

b i range $y \leqslant 2$ **ii** range $y \leqslant 5$

11 a

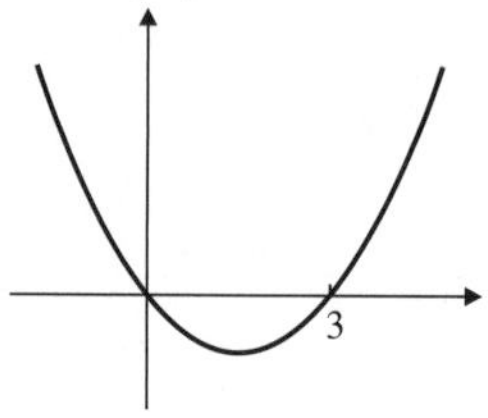

b

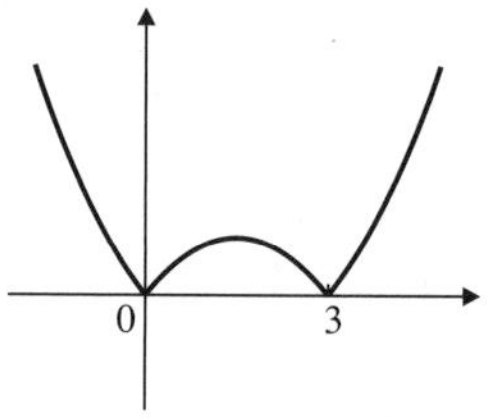

c

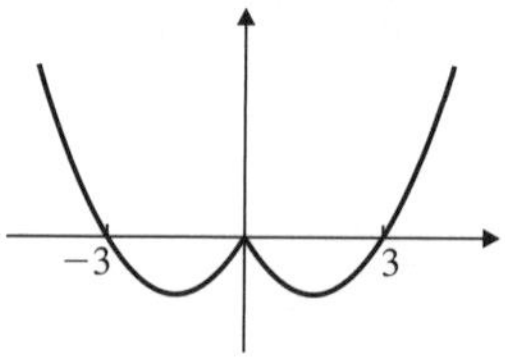

Exercise 1H page 21

1 a

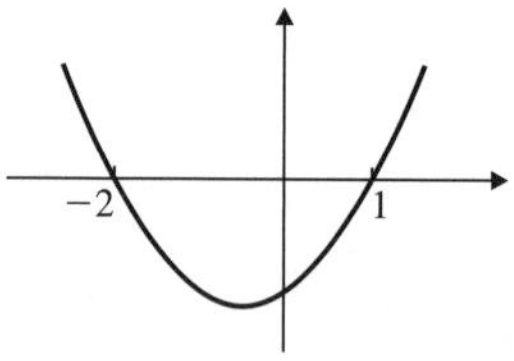

b

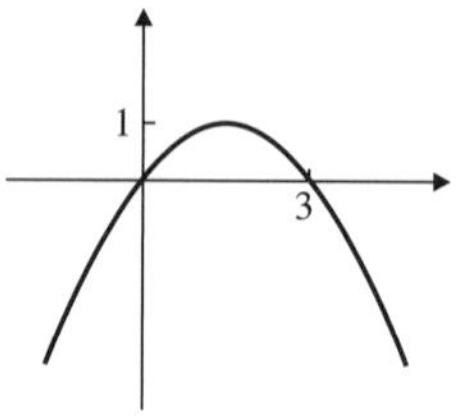

2 a

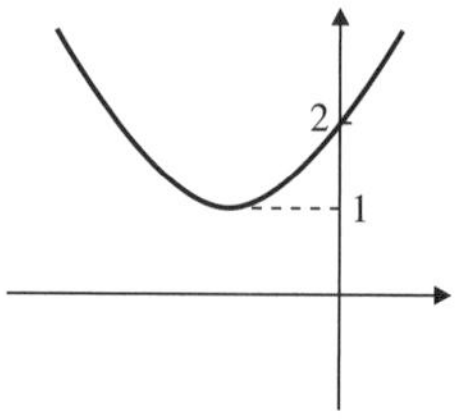

b

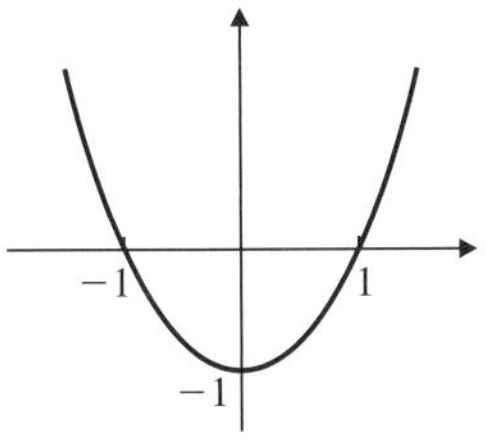

c

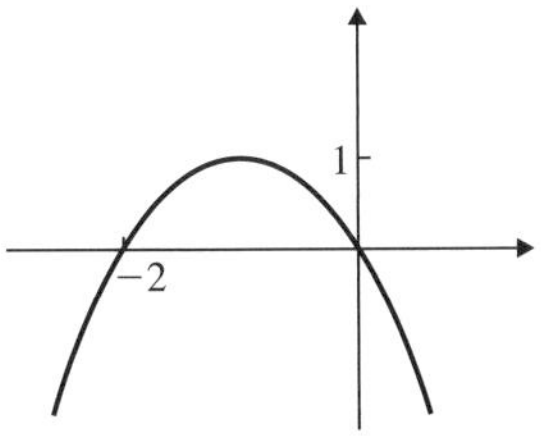

d

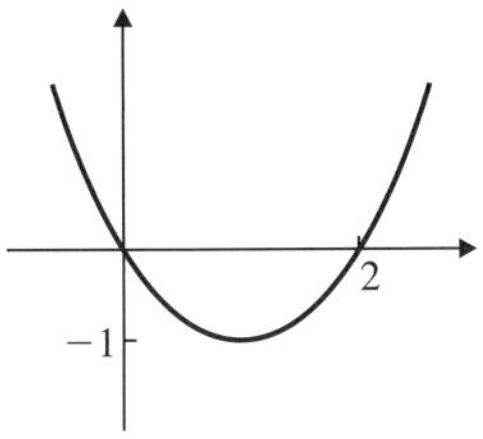

3 a

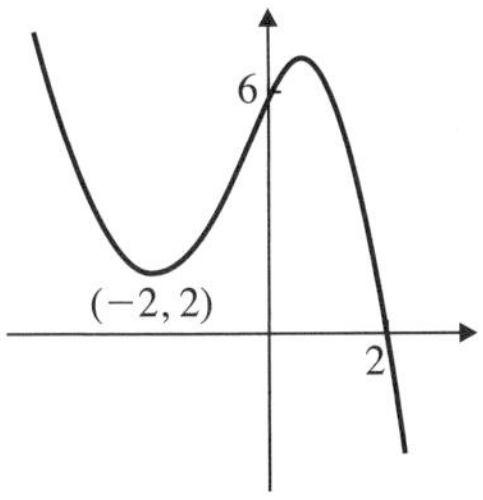

b

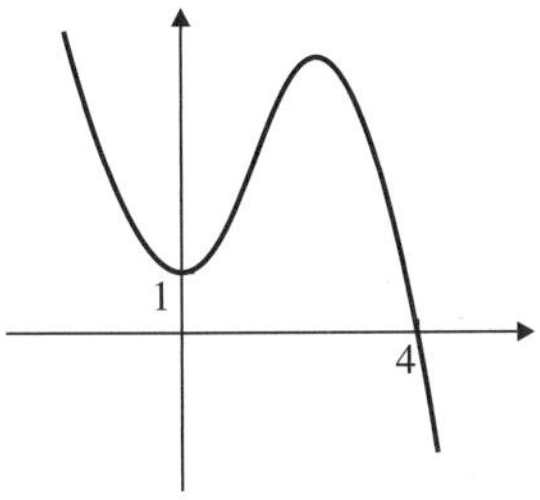

c

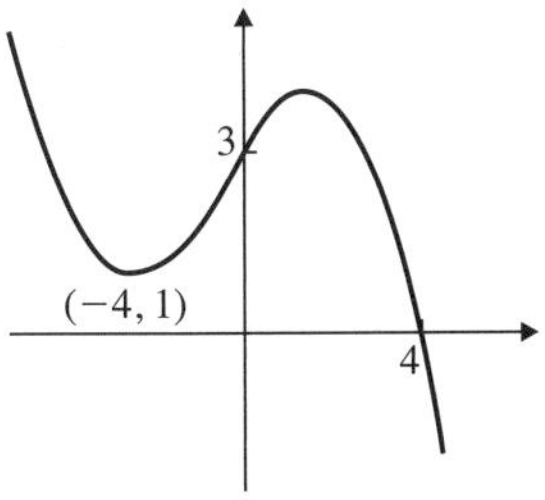

4

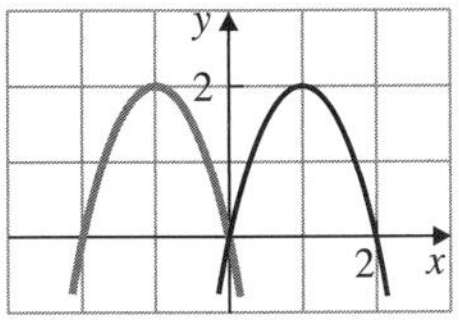

Sketch f(x + 2)

5

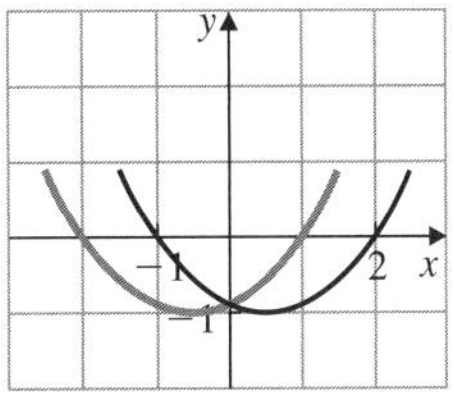

Sketch f($-x$)

6

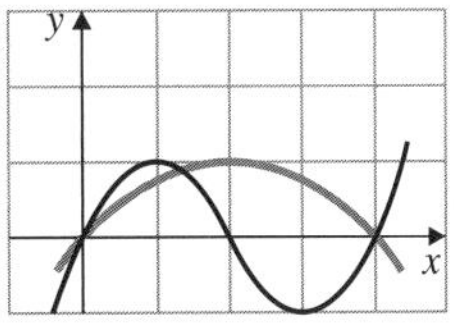

Sketch f($\frac{1}{2}x$)

7

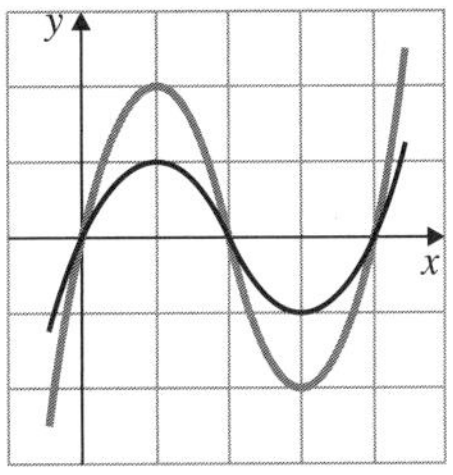

8

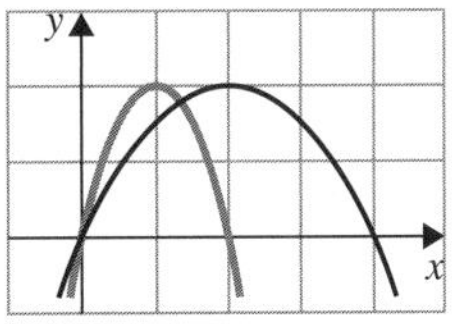

9

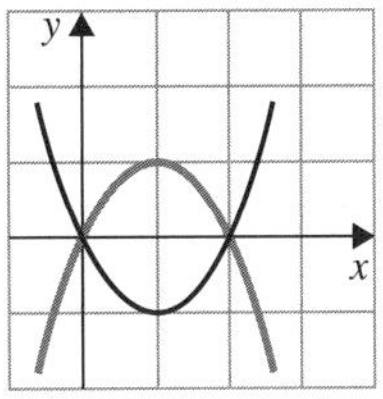

10 a

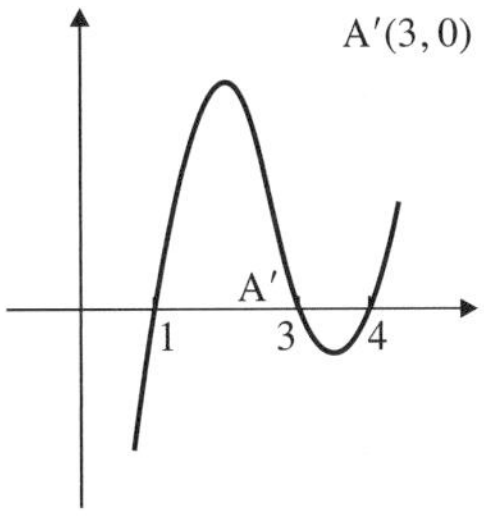

b

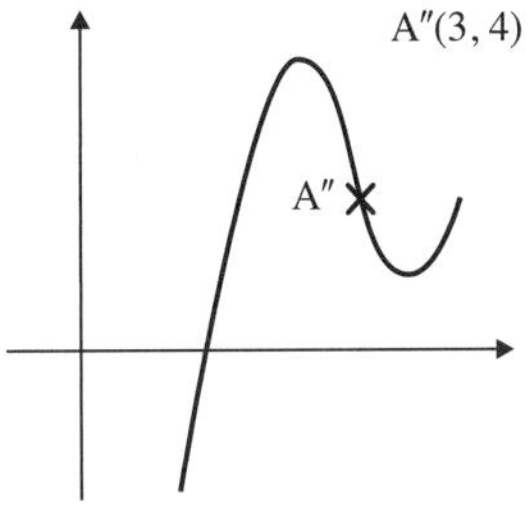

11 a

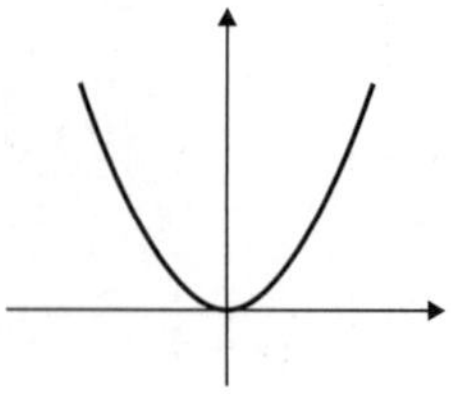

b

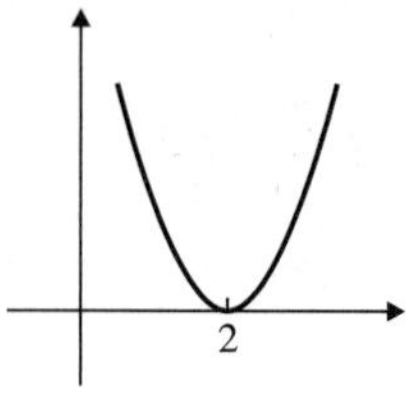

c

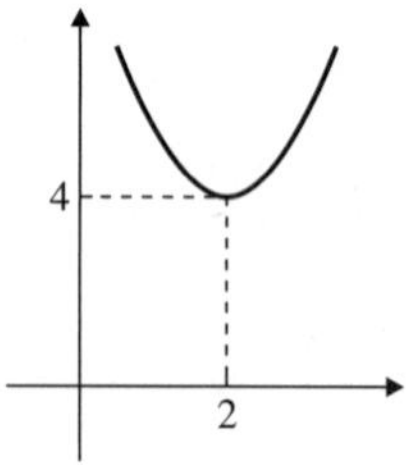

12 a

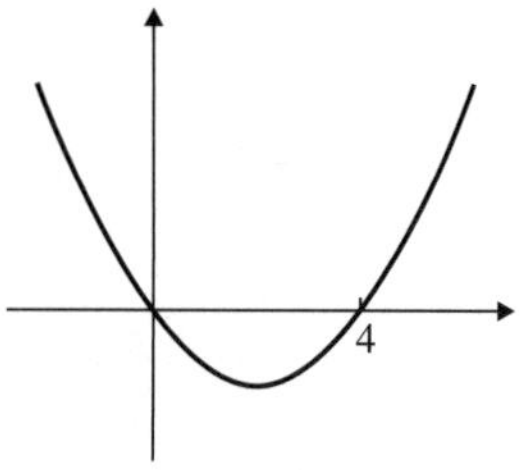

b

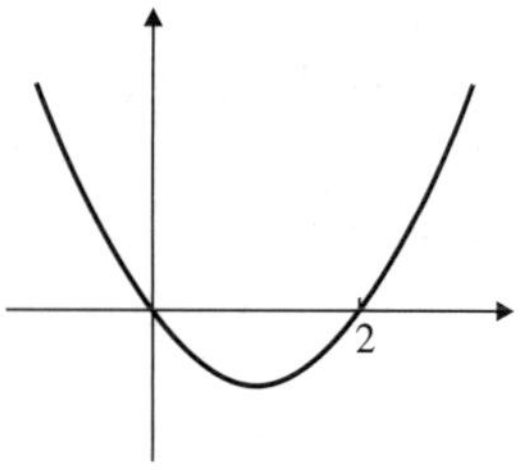

c

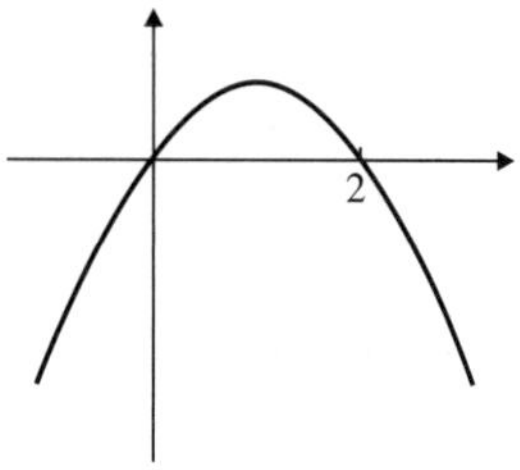

13 a

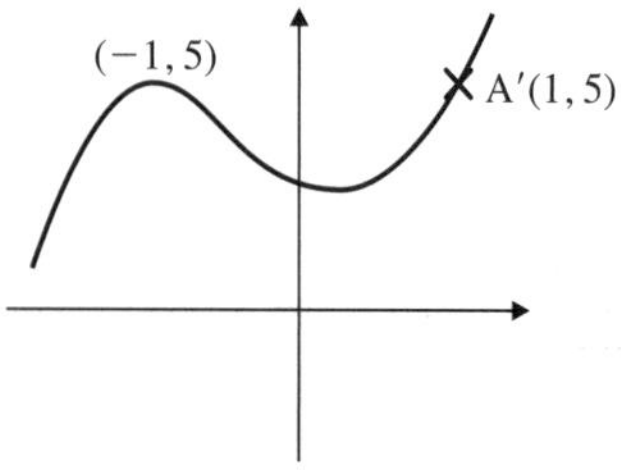

b

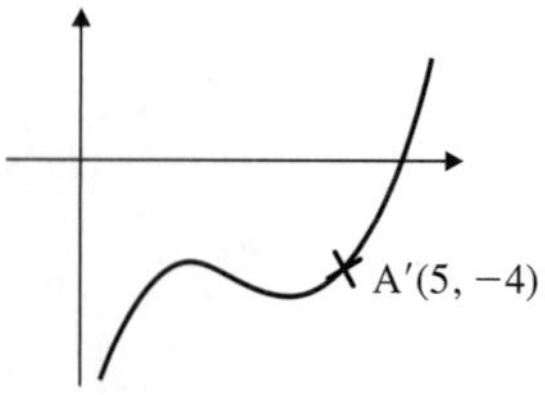

c

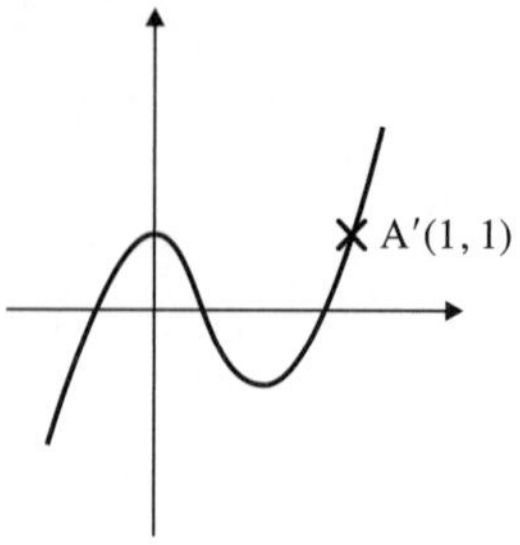

14 a $y = x^3 + 5$
b $y = (x - 2)^3$
c $y = (x - 2)^3 + 5$

15 a

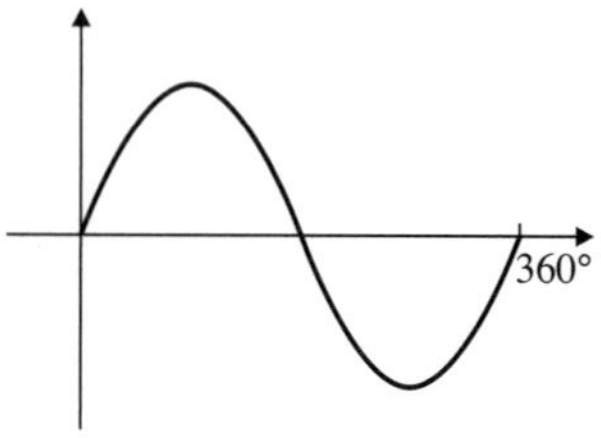

b

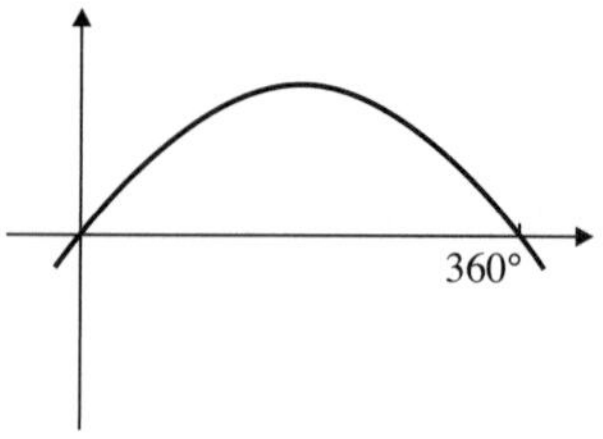

16 a

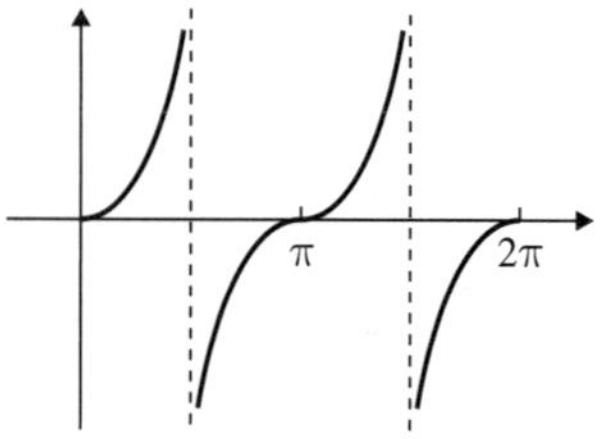

b

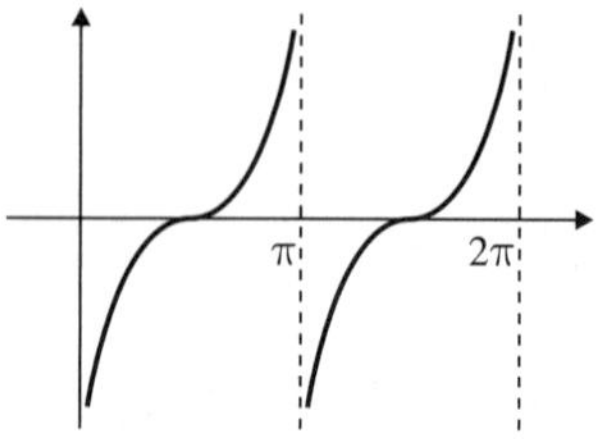

17 Stretch, scale factor 3 parallel to y-axis, Translation $\begin{pmatrix} 0 \\ -4 \end{pmatrix}$

18 Stretch, scale factor 4 parallel to y-axis, Translation $\begin{pmatrix} 0 \\ 9 \end{pmatrix}$

19 a $a = 2, b = 3$

b

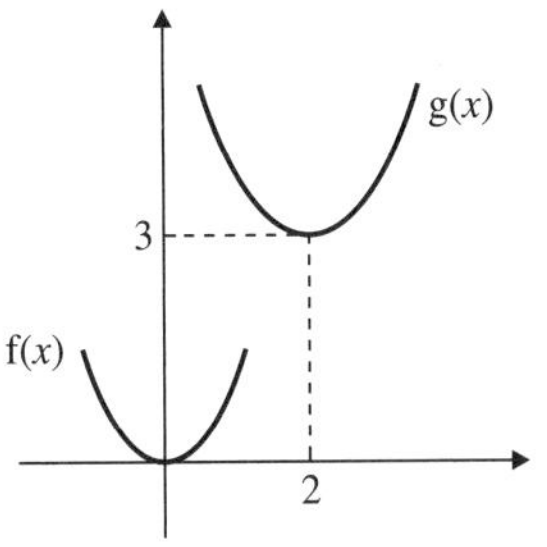

20 a $a = 4, b = 1$

b

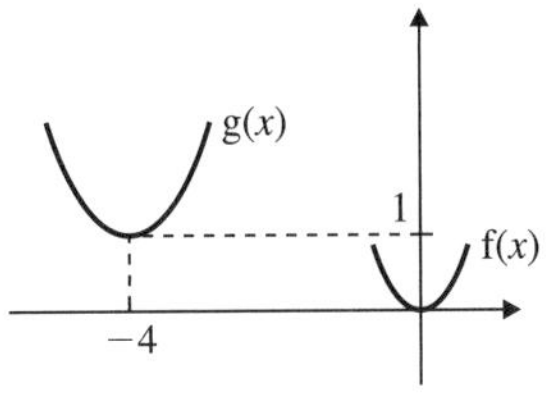

21

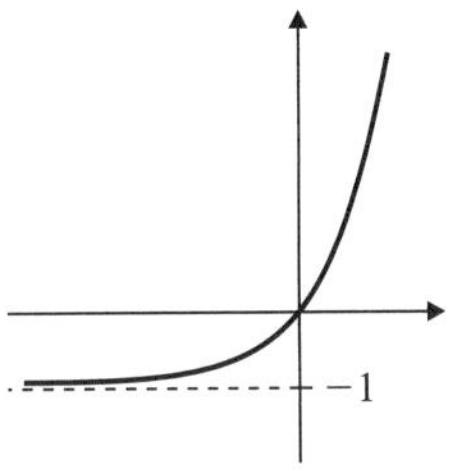

22 a

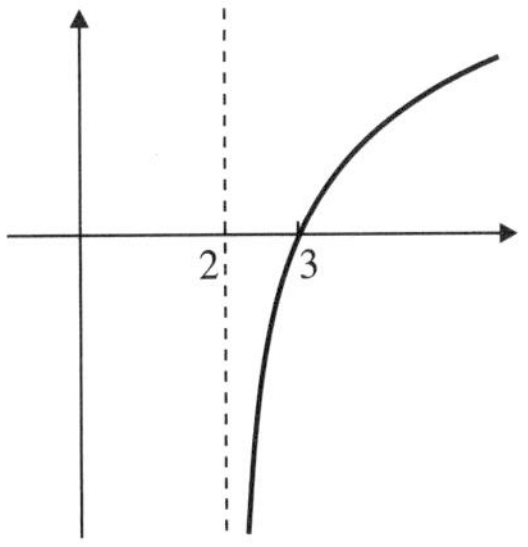

b

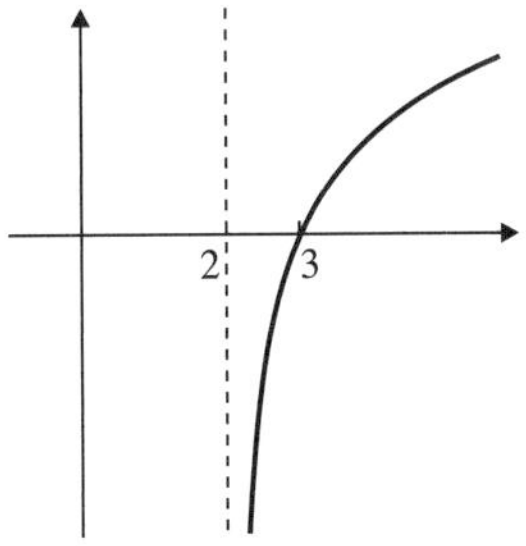

Review Exercise 1I page 24

1 a $\frac{5}{3-x}$ **b** $\frac{x^2}{2}$ **c** $\frac{3x+2}{x}$

d $1 + x$ **e** $\frac{1+4x}{y+y^2}$ **f** $\frac{3x}{2}$

2 $4(x-1)(x+1), \frac{(x-4)}{4(x+1)}$

3 a $\frac{x+2}{x}$ **b** $\frac{x-3}{x+1}$ **c** $\frac{2x-1}{x-4}$

d $\frac{2x^2+1}{x^2}$ **e** $3x^2 - 1$ **f** $\frac{4x^2-1}{x}$

4 a $\frac{8x+5}{6}$ **b** $\frac{4x+1}{x(x+1)}$

c $\frac{x^2+3x-2}{(x+1)(x-1)}$ **d** $\frac{x+4}{12}$

e $-\frac{(3x+5)}{10}$ **f** $\frac{2(x-1)}{x+3}$

5 a $(2x - 1)$ is common factor

b $\frac{3x+1}{x(2x+1)}$

6 a $f(x) \leqslant 1$

b $x = 0, \pm\sqrt{2}$

7 a $\frac{5x+2}{2x+1}$ **b** $\frac{1}{x-2}$

8 a $\frac{3}{4-x}$, not defined for $x = 4$

b 1, 3

9 a $0 \leqslant f(x) < 1$

b $\frac{3}{\sqrt{1-x^2}}$, range $f^{-1}(x) \geqslant 3$, domain $0 \leqslant x < 1$

10 a $g(x) \geqslant 3$ **b** $\frac{3}{2x^2+5}$

c $\frac{3+x}{2x}$ **d** $-1, \frac{3}{2}$

11 a $\frac{2}{2-x^2}$ **b** $\frac{2-x}{x}$ **c** $-2, 1$

12 a $f(x) \geqslant -9$

b domain $x \geqslant -9$, range $f^{-1}(x) \geqslant 2$

c

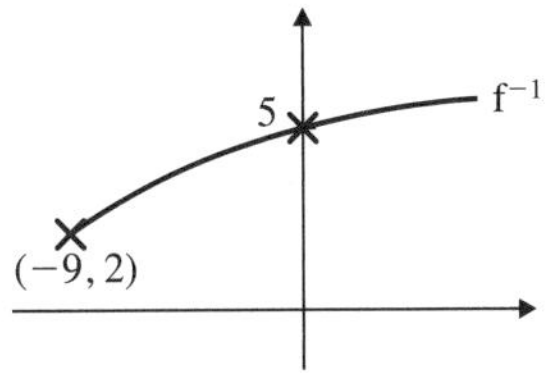

13 a

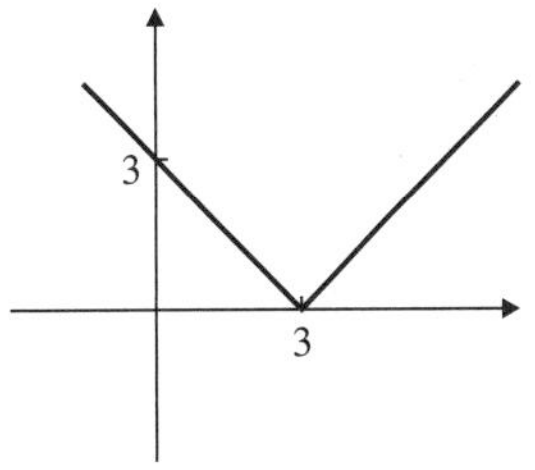

b

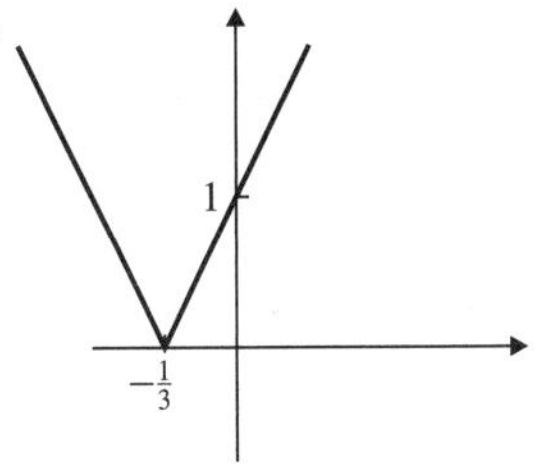

c

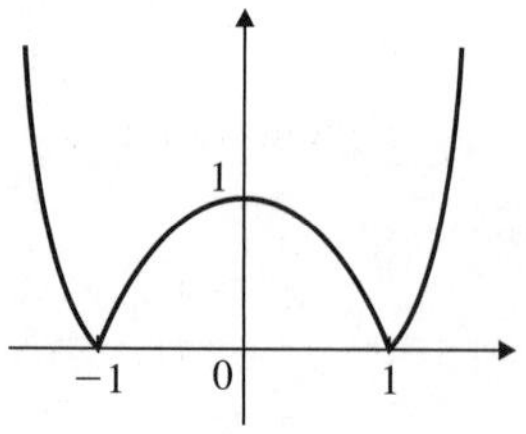

d

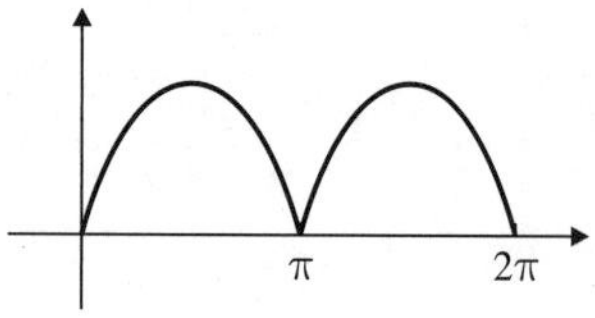

14 a

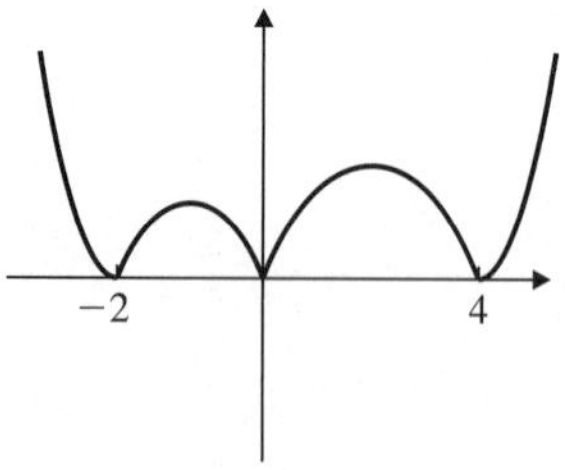

b

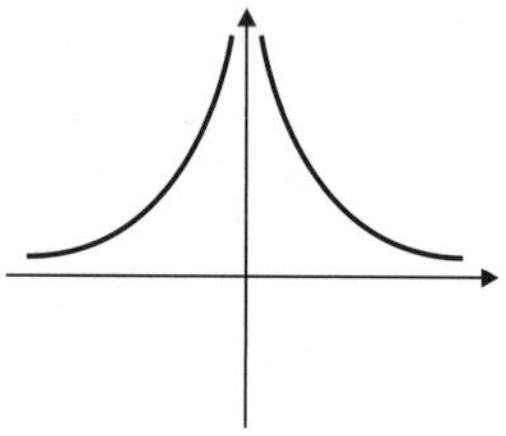

c

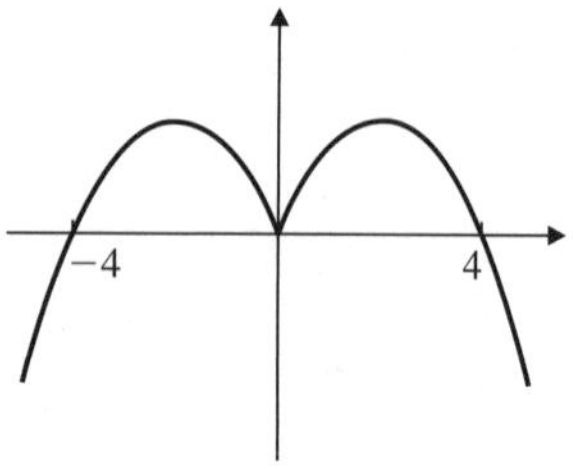

d

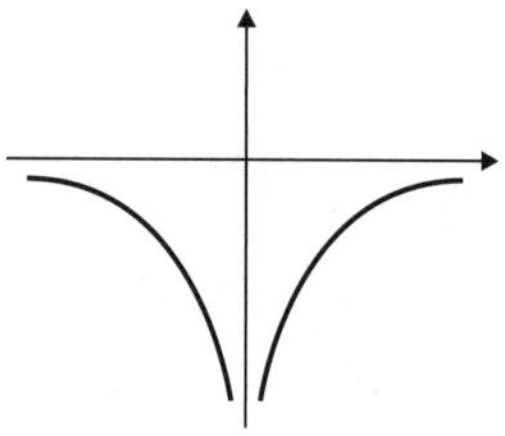

15 a $x > -\frac{1}{2}$ **b** $x < -2, x > 0$

16 a $-4 < x < 6$ **b** $x < 1, x > 2$

17 a

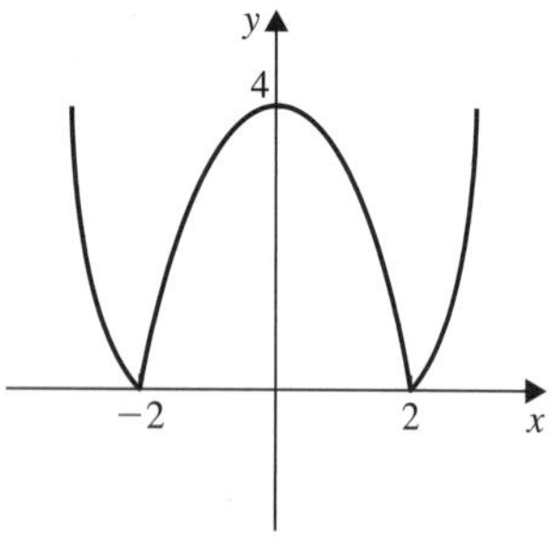

b $x > 3, x < -3$

18

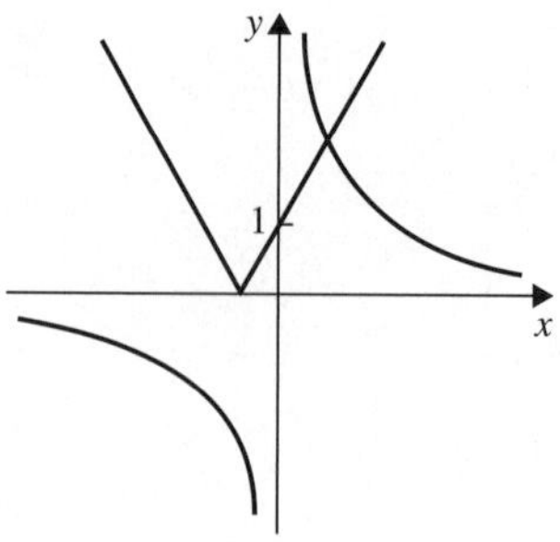

b one solution

19 a

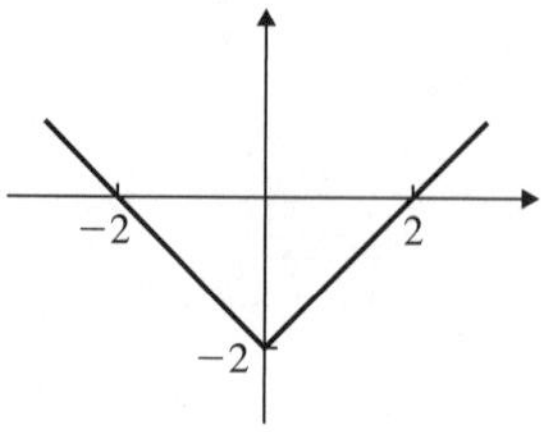

b

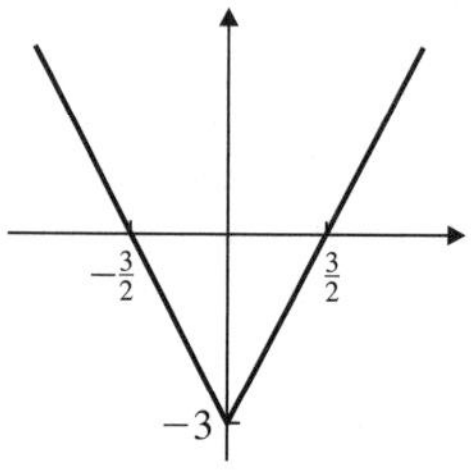

c

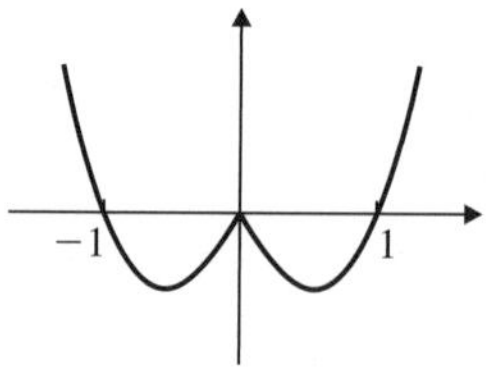

20 a

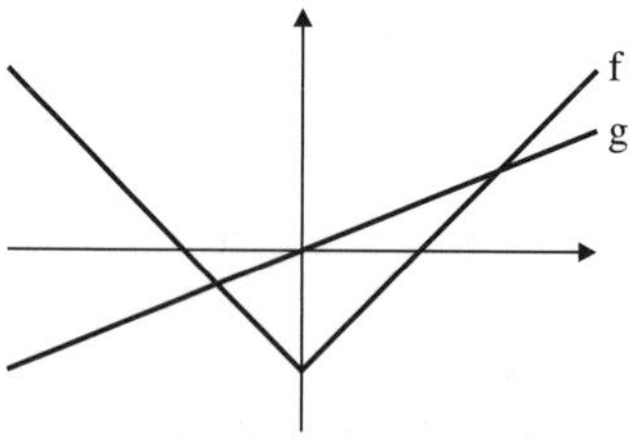

b $x > 10, x < -\frac{10}{3}$

21 a

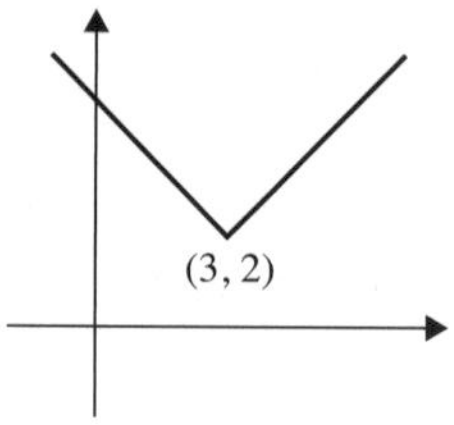

range: $f(x) \geqslant 2$

b $x = 0, 6$ **c** 3

22 a

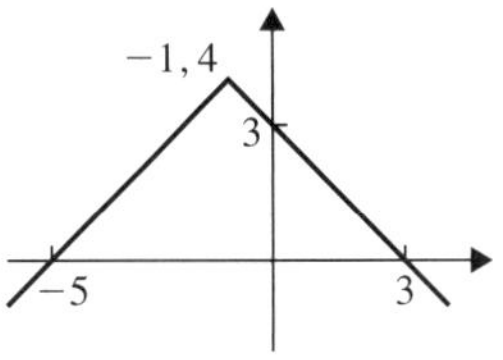

b $f(x) \leqslant 4$

23 a

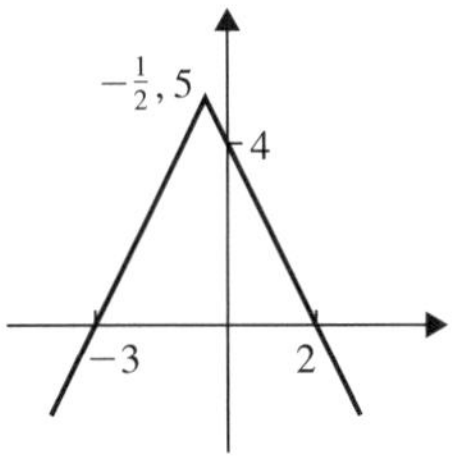

b 2 roots　　**c** $g(x) \leqslant 5$

24 a

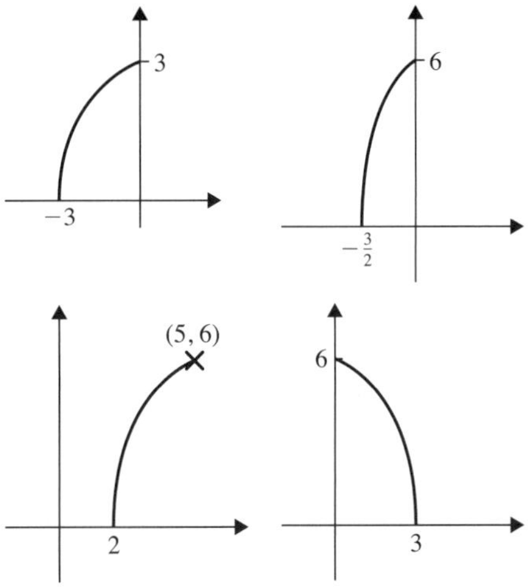

25 a i $(2, -9)$　**ii** $(3, -4)$　**iii** $(3, 9)$
　iv $(1, -9)$　**v** $(-3, -9)$
b $f(x) = (x - 3)^2 - 9$

26 a i $(-1, 5)$　**ii** $(2, -1)$　**iii** $(-2, 5)$
b $1 + 4x - x^2$

27 translation $\begin{pmatrix} 3 \\ 0 \end{pmatrix}$;
stretch scale factor 2 parallel to y-axis;
translation $\begin{pmatrix} 0 \\ -4 \end{pmatrix}$

28 stretch, scale factor $\frac{1}{2}$, parallel to x-axis;
translation $\begin{pmatrix} 0 \\ -1 \end{pmatrix}$

29 stretch, scale factor 2, parallel to x-axis;
translation $\begin{pmatrix} 0 \\ 3 \end{pmatrix}$

30 f: translation $\begin{pmatrix} 4 \\ 0 \end{pmatrix}$,　g: translation $\begin{pmatrix} 0 \\ -3 \end{pmatrix}$

Examination Exercise 1 page 28

1 $\dfrac{1}{x + 4}$

2 i $\dfrac{1}{2 - x}$　**ii** $\dfrac{3}{(x - 1)(x - 4)}$

3 i $\dfrac{11 - x}{(3 - x)(1 + x)}$　**ii** $\dfrac{-1}{1 + x}$

4 i 26, 4　**ii** reflection in $y = x$

5 i -3

6 a $x = 6, x = -5$　**b** $a = 6$

7 a $f(x) < 5$
b i $\frac{1}{3}\ln(5 - x)$　**ii** 4
c $\dfrac{2x - 3}{11 - 6x}$

8 a $0 \leqslant f(x) \leqslant 10$　**b** 3
c $\dfrac{5x - 4}{3 + x}$　**d** 6, 0.4

9 a $f(x) \geqslant -4$　**b** $3 + \sqrt{x + 4}$
c i $|x^2 - 6x - 1|$　**ii** 5, 7

10 $x \leqslant -6, 1 \leqslant x \leqslant 2, x \geqslant 3$

11 $4a, -14a$

12 a

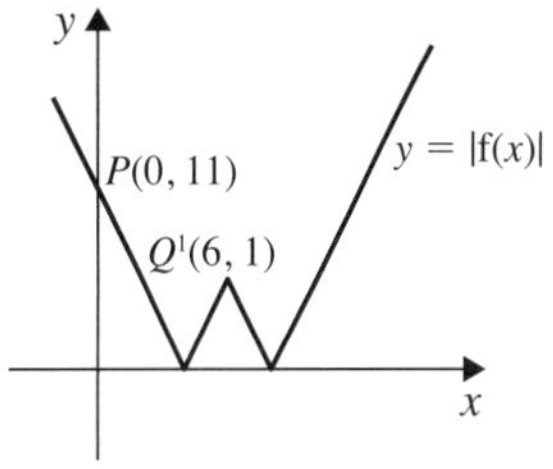

b

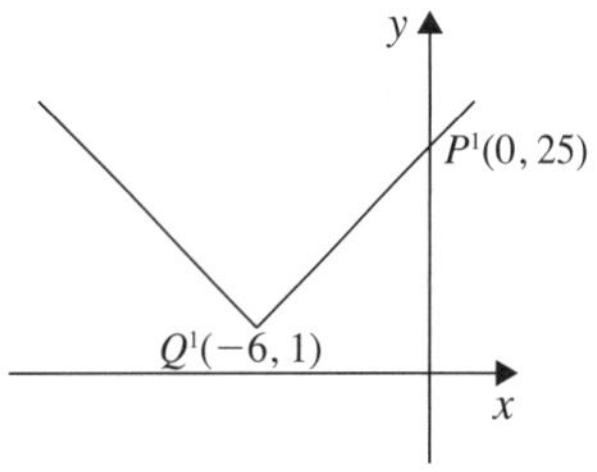

c $a = 2, b = 6$

13 i translation $\begin{pmatrix} -3 \\ 0 \end{pmatrix}$ and stretch s.f. 2 in the y direction
ii $-6 < x < -2$

Exercise 2A page 33

1 a $\frac{2}{3}\pi$　**b** $\frac{3}{2}\pi$　**c** $\frac{3}{4}\pi$
d $\frac{11}{6}\pi$　**e** $\frac{7}{4}\pi$　**f** 4π

2 a 0.698^c　**b** 1.75^c　**c** 0.873^c
d 3.80^c　**e** 1.52^c　**f** 0.0175^c

3 a 225°　**b** 270°　**c** 157.5°
d 115°　**e** 74.5°　**f** 28.6°

4 a $\dfrac{\sqrt{3}}{2}$　**b** 1　**c** $\dfrac{\sqrt{3}}{2}$
d -0.644　**e** -0.942　**f** 2.57

6 a

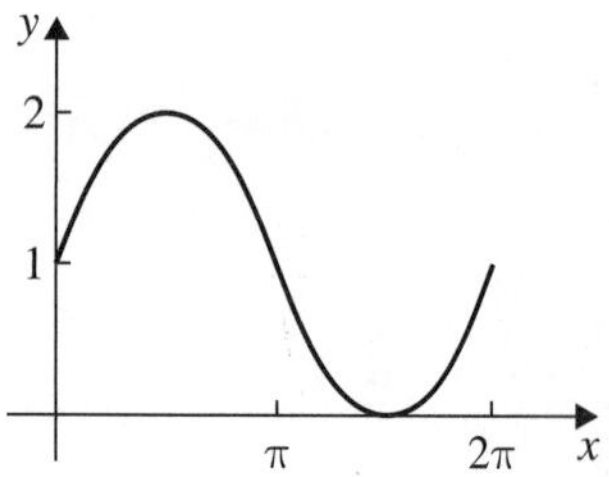

b

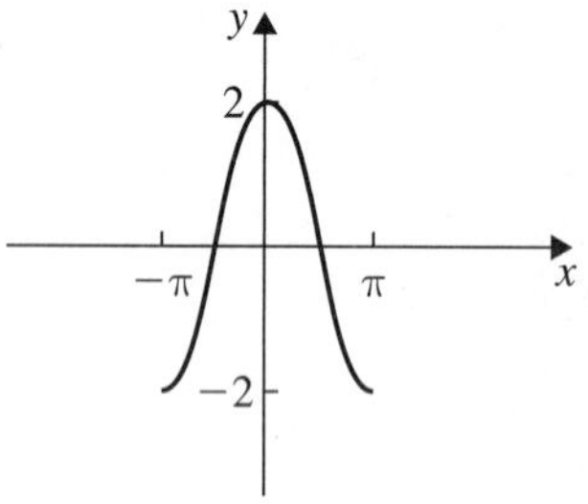

c

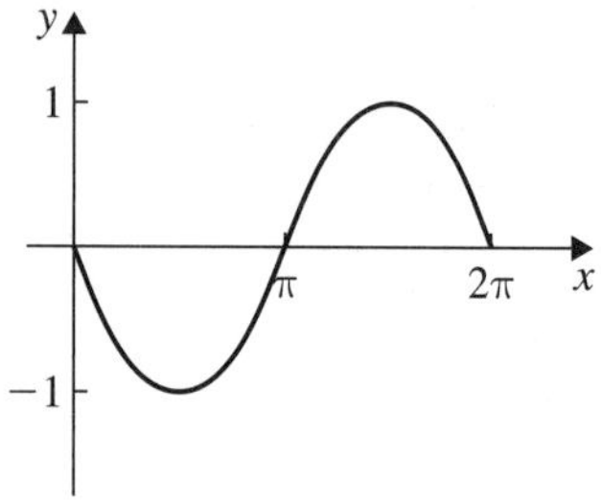

d

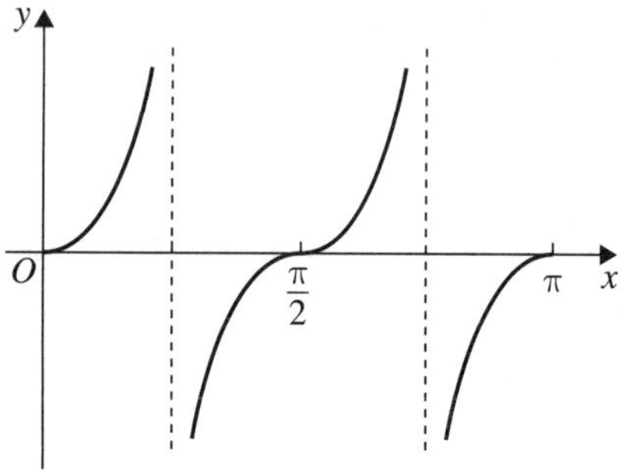

e

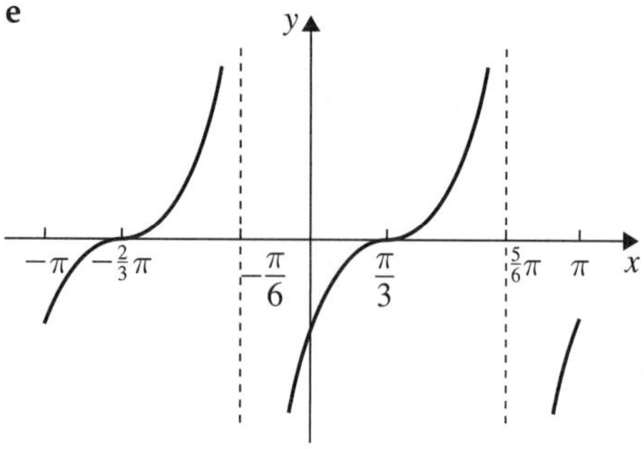

Exercise 2B page 36

1 a 8 cm **b** 40 cm^2
2 a 4 cm **b** 60 cm^2 **c** 0.4 rad
d 6 cm **e** 0.072 m^2
3 a $\frac{2}{9}\pi$ **b** 20.2 m **c** 1.04^c
4 a $\frac{\pi}{3}$ **b** $\frac{5}{18}\pi$
5 a 0.8 rad **b** 10.7 cm **c** 0.8 rad
d 7.98 cm **e** 4 cm
6 a 9 cm **b** $\frac{2^c}{3}$
7 a 20 cm **b** $\frac{3^c}{4}$
8 6.56 cm
9 5π cm (= 15.7 cm)
10 b $\frac{32\pi}{3}$ cm^2 **d** 18.5 cm^2, 37.0 cm^2
e 3.44 cm^2
11 $\frac{2}{3}$ rad
12 a 34.3 cm^2 **b** 24.1 cm^2 **c** 10.2 cm^2
13 a i 50θ **ii** $50\sin\theta$ **iii** $50(\theta - \sin\theta)$
15 b 1.17^c
16 a $12r + 2\pi r + \frac{\pi}{3}r^2$ **c** 7.6 cm
17 a i 8θ **ii** $8\sin\theta$ **iii** $8\theta - 8\sin\theta$
b 1.1^c
18 b $\sqrt{72(1-\cos\theta)} + 60$ **d** 1.6^c
19 $16\left(\frac{2\pi}{3} - \frac{\sqrt{3}}{2}\right)$

Exercise 2C page 44

1 a 0 **b** 0 **c** 0 **d** 0
e 0 **f** −1 **g** −1 **h** 1

2

	0	$\frac{\pi}{6}$	$\frac{\pi}{4}$	$\frac{\pi}{3}$	$\frac{\pi}{2}$
sin	0	$\frac{1}{2}$	$\frac{1}{\sqrt{2}}$	$\frac{\sqrt{3}}{2}$	1
cos	1	$\frac{\sqrt{3}}{2}$	$\frac{1}{\sqrt{2}}$	$\frac{1}{2}$	0
tan	0	$\frac{1}{\sqrt{3}}$	1	$\sqrt{3}$	undefined

3 a $\frac{\sqrt{3}}{2}$ **b** $-\frac{1}{\sqrt{2}}$ **c** −1 **d** $\frac{1}{2}$
4 a 0.589 **b** 0.264 **c** −0.416
d 0.951 **e** 0.451 **f** 0.282
5 $\frac{\pi}{6}, \frac{5\pi}{6}$ **6** $\frac{\pi}{3}, \frac{4\pi}{3}$
7 a $\frac{\pi}{4}, \frac{7\pi}{4}$ **b** $\frac{\pi}{2}$ **c** $\frac{\pi}{6}, \frac{7\pi}{6}$
8 a 0.412, 2.730 **b** 0.708, 2.434
c 1.359, 4.924 **d** 1.107, 4.249
9 a $-\frac{\pi}{6}, \frac{\pi}{6}$ **b** 5.508, 3.917
c 1.039, −2.103 **d** $\frac{2\pi}{3}, \frac{4\pi}{3}, \frac{8\pi}{3}, \frac{10\pi}{3}$
10 a 0.775 or 2.366
11 6.06 cm
12 a $\frac{\pi}{4}, \frac{5\pi}{4}$ **b** $\frac{\pi}{4}, \frac{3\pi}{4}, \frac{5\pi}{4}, \frac{7\pi}{4}$
c 0.491, 2.062, 3.633, 5.204
d 2.319
13 a $\frac{7\pi}{12}, \frac{23\pi}{12}$ **b** $\frac{5\pi}{12}, \frac{11\pi}{12}$

c $\frac{\pi}{2}, \frac{3\pi}{2}$ **d** 1.620, 2.522

14 $\frac{\pi}{3}, \frac{2\pi}{3}$ **15** 0.983

16 $\frac{\pi}{4}, \frac{3\pi}{4}$ **17** $0, \pi, 1.107$

18 0.308, 2.834 **19** $0, \pi, \frac{\pi}{3}$

20 $\frac{\pi}{2}$ **21** $1.107, \frac{3\pi}{4}$ (2.356)

22 $\frac{\pi}{8}, \frac{5\pi}{8}$ **23** $\frac{\pi}{6}, \frac{5\pi}{6}$

24 $\frac{\pi}{2}$ **25** $\frac{\pi}{2}$

Exercise 2D page 47

1 a 0.24740 **b** 0.25 **c** 1.05%
2 13.1%
3 0.294%
5 b 1
6 a 3 **b** 3 **c** 7 **d** 6
7 $x \approx 2, y \approx 9.8$
8 $a \approx 2.1, b \approx 7.7$

Review Exercise 2E page 48

1 a 12.5 **b** 6.68 **c** 14.6
2 1.74 **3** 0.652 **4** 2.41
5 0.683
6 a $6.55\,\text{cm}^2$ **b** $26.6\,\text{cm}^2$
7 $\frac{2\pi}{5}$

8 $\sin\frac{\pi}{4} = \cos\frac{\pi}{4}, \tan\left(-\frac{\pi}{6}\right) = \tan\frac{5\pi}{6},$

$\cos\frac{\pi}{6} = \cos\frac{11\pi}{6} = -\sin\left(-\frac{\pi}{3}\right) = \sin\frac{2\pi}{3},$

$\sin\frac{\pi}{6} = \sin\frac{5\pi}{6}, \tan\frac{\pi}{6} = \tan\left(-\frac{5\pi}{6}\right)$

9 a

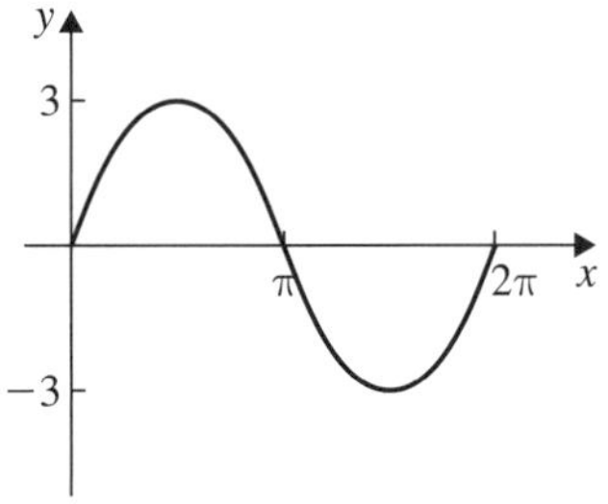

b

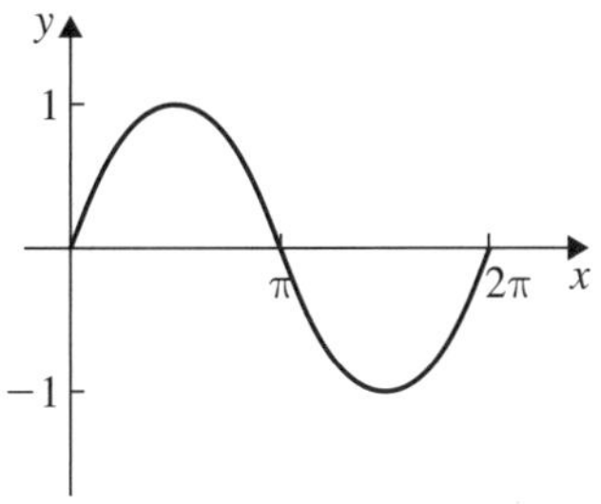

c

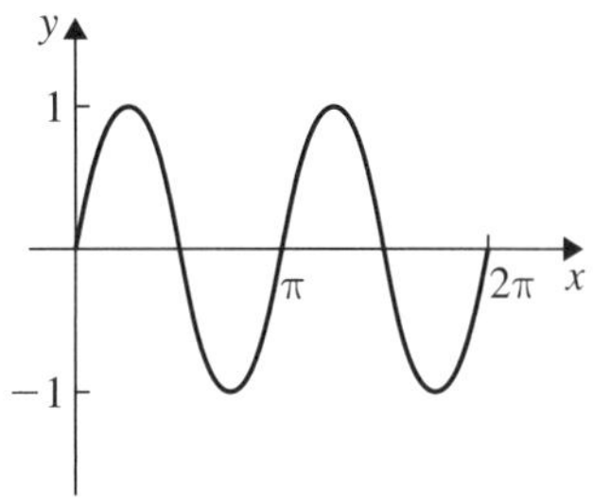

d

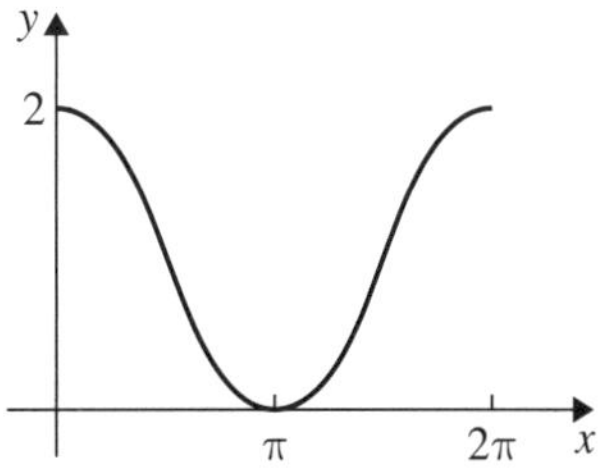

e

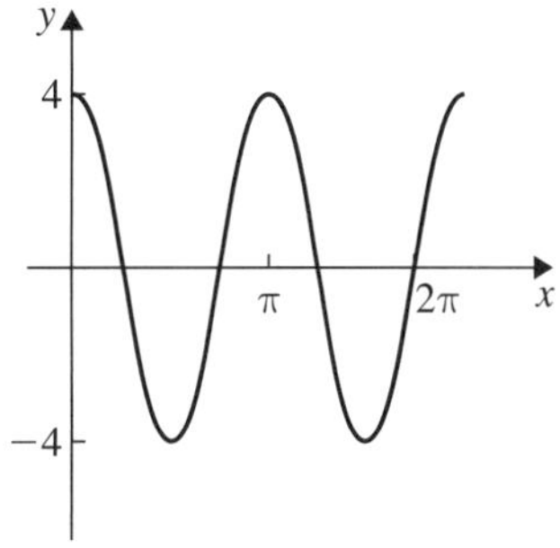

10 b i 2 **ii** 4
11 a 12 cm **b** $14.4\,\text{cm}^2$ **c** 12 cm
d 10^c **e** 2.5^c **f** $r = 2, \theta = 1.5$
g 4 cm
12 $50, 25\pi - 50$
13 a 4.2 cm **b** $1.0\,\text{cm}^2$
14 a $20\sqrt{3}$ **b** 200π **c** $20\sqrt{3}\left(\frac{\pi}{3} + 2\right)$
15 a $r^2\left(\frac{5}{4} - \cos\theta\right)$ **b** 0.634
c $0.68\,\text{cm}^2$
16 a 0.729 **b** $9.11\,\text{cm}^2$
c $11.9\,\text{cm}^2$ **d** 15.6 cm
17 a $\frac{\pi}{3}, \frac{5\pi}{3}$ **b** $-\frac{3\pi}{4}, \frac{\pi}{4}$
c $\frac{\pi}{4}, \frac{7\pi}{4}$ **d** $\frac{\pi}{3}, \frac{2\pi}{3}$
e 3.9, 5.6 **f** 2.4, 3.9
g −0.6, 2.5 **h** $-\frac{\pi}{6}, -\frac{5\pi}{6}$
18 a $\frac{11\pi}{6}, \frac{\pi}{6}$ **b** $\frac{\pi}{2}, \frac{7\pi}{6}$
c $\frac{5\pi}{12}, \frac{13\pi}{12}$ **d** $\frac{\pi}{2}, -\frac{\pi}{2}$
19 $0.85, 2.3, \frac{7\pi}{6}, \frac{11\pi}{6}$
20 a $\frac{\pi}{2}$ **b** $\frac{\pi}{3}, \pi, \frac{5\pi}{3}$
c $\frac{\pi}{6}, \frac{5\pi}{6}, -0.3, -2.8$ **d** $-\frac{2\pi}{3}, \frac{2\pi}{3}, -0.8, 0.8$
e $-\frac{\pi}{6}, -\frac{5\pi}{6}$

21 a $-\frac{11\pi}{12}, -\frac{5\pi}{12}, \frac{\pi}{12}, \frac{7\pi}{12}$

b $\frac{2\pi}{3}, \pi, \frac{5\pi}{3}$ **c** $\frac{\pi}{6}, \frac{\pi}{2}, \frac{7\pi}{6}, \frac{3\pi}{2}$

22 a $\frac{7\pi}{12}, \frac{11\pi}{12}, \frac{19\pi}{12}, \frac{23\pi}{12}$ **b** $\frac{\pi}{6}, \frac{5\pi}{6}, \frac{7\pi}{6}, \frac{11\pi}{6}$

c 0.8, 2.3, $\frac{7\pi}{6}, \frac{11\pi}{6}$ **d** 1.25, 4.39

e 0, π, 2π, 0.46, 3.61

24 a −3 **b** 0

Examination Exercise 2 page 51

1 i $\frac{3\pi}{10}$ **ii** 20.4

2 b 40.9 **c** 96.7

3 i 8π **ii** $48\pi - 36\sqrt{3}$

4 6

5 a 17.5 **b** 0.943 **c** 38.9

6 ii 15.2 **iii** 9.76

7 a 18.8 cm^2 **b** 2 **c** 2π

8 b 19.9 cm^2 **c** 13.8 cm

9 $-\frac{2\pi}{15}, \frac{8\pi}{15}$

10 i 15 **ii** $(2x+1)(2x-3)(x+1)$

iii $\frac{2\pi}{3}, \frac{4\pi}{3}, \pi$

11 $-\pi$, −0.84, 0, 0.84, 0

12 $\frac{\pi}{2}$, 0.85, 2.29

13 a −0.056, 1.8 **b i** $\frac{1}{2}, -\frac{1}{3}$

14 b 1.2, 4.4, 2.0, 5.2

15 $5 + 3\cos\theta$, least value is 2, occurs when $\theta = \pi$

16 i

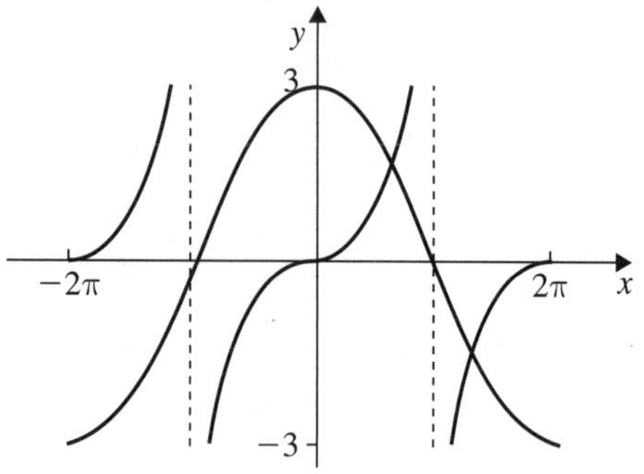

ii 2.02, 4.26

Exercise 3A page 59

1 a $A = 1, B = 2$ **b** $A = 3, B = 2$

c $A = 2, B = 3$ **d** $A = 5, B = 2$

e $A = 7, B = -2$ **f** $A = 4, B = -3$

2 a $\frac{1}{x-3} + \frac{8}{x-2}$ **b** $\frac{1}{x-1} + \frac{2}{x-2}$

c $\frac{3}{x+1} + \frac{5}{x+2}$ **d** $\frac{1}{x+2} + \frac{6}{x+3}$

e $\frac{1}{x-1} + \frac{2}{x+2}$ **f** $\frac{2}{x-1} - \frac{1}{x+3}$

g $-\frac{4}{x} + \frac{5}{x-2}$ **h** $\frac{2}{x} + \frac{3}{x+1}$

3 a $A = 3, B = 1$ **b** $A = 4, B = -3$

c $A = 1, B = 3$ **d** $A = 2, B = 1$

e $A = -2, B = 5$ **f** $A = 7, B = -1$

4 a $\frac{3}{2x-3} + \frac{4}{x-3}$ **b** $\frac{3}{2x+1} + \frac{1}{x-1}$

c $\frac{5}{3x-2} + \frac{2}{3x+4}$ **d** $\frac{1}{2x-1} + \frac{1}{5x-1}$

e $\frac{4}{x+3} + \frac{3}{2x-1}$ **f** $\frac{2}{3x+5} + \frac{3}{2x-3}$

g $\frac{7}{2x-1} - \frac{1}{2x+1}$ **h** $\frac{2}{5x-2} + \frac{9}{5x+2}$

Exercise 3B page 61

1 a $A = 1, B = 3, C = 2$

b $A = 1, B = -1, C = 2$

c $A = 2, B = 3, C = 6$

d $A = 4, B = -1, C = 5$

e $A = 3, B = 2, C = 1$

2 a $\frac{1}{x-2} + \frac{3}{2x+1} + \frac{1}{x+2}$

b $\frac{5}{x-3} + \frac{1}{x+1} + \frac{1}{2x+3}$

c $\frac{2}{x-1} - \frac{4}{x} + \frac{1}{3x-4}$

d $\frac{3}{5x-2} + \frac{1}{4x-1} + \frac{2}{3x-2}$

e $\frac{5}{x-2} + \frac{5}{x-1} - \frac{3}{x+1}$

f $\frac{1}{5x+1} + \frac{2}{4x+3} + \frac{3}{4x-1}$

3 a $\frac{2}{x+3} + \frac{5}{x-2} + \frac{1}{(x-2)^2}$

b $\frac{2}{x-1} - \frac{1}{x+2} - \frac{3}{(x+2)^2}$

c $\frac{3}{2x-1} - \frac{7}{(3x+1)^2} - \frac{1}{(3x+1)}$

d $\frac{2}{3x-2} + \frac{4}{2x-1} + \frac{1}{(2x-1)^2}$

4 a $\frac{1}{x-2} + \frac{2}{(x-2)^2}$ **b** $\frac{1}{2x-1} + \frac{2}{(2x-1)^2}$

c $\frac{5}{x+1} + \frac{4}{(x-1)^2}$ **d** $\frac{3}{x-1} - \frac{1}{(x+3)^2}$

e $\frac{5}{(x+5)^2} + \frac{4}{3x-2}$ **f** $\frac{5}{x} + \frac{3}{x+1} - \frac{7}{x-1}$

g $\frac{7}{2x-1} - \frac{3}{x} - \frac{1}{2x+1}$

h $\frac{2}{x+4} + \frac{1}{(x-1)^2} - \frac{1}{(x-1)}$

Exercise 3C page 65

1 a $1 + \frac{1}{x+3} + \frac{1}{x-2}$

b $3 - \frac{1}{5x+1} + \frac{2}{2x-1}$

c $x + \frac{1}{x-3} + \frac{1}{x-1}$

d $2x + \frac{2}{x-2} + \frac{3}{x-1}$

e $x + 1 + \frac{3}{x+3} + \frac{4}{x+1}$

f $2x + 3 - \frac{2}{x-3} + \frac{5}{x+4}$

g $3x + 2 + \frac{2}{x+1} - \frac{1}{2x-1}$

h $2x - 1 + \frac{4}{2x-3} - \frac{3}{3x-5}$

2 a $3 + \frac{1}{x+1} + \frac{2}{(x-1)^2}$

b $2 - \frac{3}{2x-1} + \frac{4}{3x-2} - \frac{5}{(3x-2)^2}$

c $x + \frac{1}{x-2} + \frac{1}{x-1} + \frac{2}{(x-1)^2}$

d $x + \frac{2}{x+1} + \frac{3}{x-2} + \frac{4}{(x-2)^2}$

3 $\frac{1}{1-2x} - \frac{1}{1-x} + \frac{1}{(1-x)^2}$

Examination Exercise 3 page 66

1 $A = -\frac{5}{2}, B = \frac{9}{2}$

2 $A = 3, B = -1$

3 $A = 4, B = 3, C = 1$

4 $A = -2, B = 3$

5 $\frac{2}{x-2} - \frac{1}{x+1} - \frac{3}{(x-2)^2}$

6 $\frac{4}{x+2} - \frac{3}{x-1} + \frac{2}{(x-1)^2}$

7 $\frac{-50}{x} + \frac{25}{x^2} + \frac{100}{2x+1}$

Exercise 4A page 70

1 a 4, 7, 10, 13 **b** 3, 7, 11, 15
c 1, 4, 9, 16 **d** $1, \frac{1}{2}, \frac{1}{3}, \frac{1}{4}$
e 2, 4, 8, 16 **f** 2, 6, 12, 20
g $\frac{1}{3}, \frac{2}{4}, \frac{3}{5}, \frac{4}{6}$ **h** −1, 1, −1, 1

2 a $5n$ **b** $2n + 1$ **c** $4n - 3$
d n^2 **e** 3^n **f** 10^n
g $\frac{n}{n+1}$ **h** n^3 **i** $\frac{1}{n+1}$

3 a 2, 7, 12, 17, 22 **b** −1, 9, 19, 29, 39
c 1, 7, 1, 7, 1 **d** 2, 4, 16, 256, 65 536
e $2, \frac{1}{2}, 2, \frac{1}{2}, 2$ **f** 0, −2, −8, −26, −80
g $1000, 100, 10, 1, \frac{1}{10}$ **h** $1, 2, 2\frac{1}{2}, \frac{29}{10}, \frac{941}{290}$

4 a $2n + 3$ **b** $14 - 4n$
c $7n - 15$ **d** $12 - 3n$

5 a $u_{n+1} = u_n + 5, u_1 = 7$
b $u_{n+1} = u_n + 3, u_1 = -2$
c $u_{n+1} = u_n - 2, u_1 = 2$
d $u_{n+1} = u_n + \frac{1}{2}, u_1 = 10\frac{1}{2}$

6 a $1, \frac{1}{2}, \frac{1}{3}, \frac{1}{4}, \frac{1}{5}, \frac{1}{6}$ **b** convergent.
c 0

7 a $0, \frac{1}{3}, \frac{2}{4}, \frac{3}{5}$ convergent. **b** 1

8 a $1, \frac{1}{3}, \frac{1}{9}, \frac{1}{27}$; convergent; limit 0
b 5, 9, 13, 17; divergent.
c 2, 5, 10, 17; divergent.
d $\frac{1}{2}, \frac{2}{3}, \frac{3}{4}, \frac{4}{5}$; convergent, limit 1
e −5, 5, −5, 5; periodic.
f 1, 5, 1, 5; periodic.
g $5, \frac{1}{5}, 5, \frac{1}{5}$; periodic.
h $1, 100, \frac{1}{100}, 1\,000\,000$; divergent.
i 2, 12, 2, 12; periodic.
j −2, 4, −8, 16; divergent.

9 1, 2, 3, 5, 8, 13

10 1, 2, 5, 11, 26

11 $3, 5.\dot{3}$, 4.3125, 4.623 188…, 4.514 10…, 4.550 694, 4.538 226…, 4.542 452 7,
a $u = 4.54$

12 $1, 3, 2\frac{2}{3}$, 2.6875, 2.686 046 512, 2.686 147 186
a 2.69

13 a −2.79

14 a 3.30 **b** $x^2 - 3x - 1 = 0$

Exercise 4B page 73

1 a 24 **b** 14 **c** 10
d 38 **e** 30 **f** $2\frac{1}{12}$
g 21 **h** 28 **i** 63
j −6 **k** 35 **l** $\frac{23}{12}$

2 a $\sum_{r=1}^{4} r^2$ **b** $\sum_{r=1}^{4} 3^r$ **c** $\sum_{r=1}^{5} \frac{1}{r}$
d $\sum_{r=1}^{4} 2r$ **e** $\sum_{r=1}^{100} r$ **f** $\sum_{r=1}^{n} r(r+1)$
g $\sum_{r=1}^{100} \frac{r}{r+1}$ **h** $\sum_{r=1}^{6} (-1)^r$ **i** $\sum_{r=1}^{5} 4r + 1$
j $\sum_{r=1}^{5} 5r - 1$ **k** $\sum_{r=1}^{\infty} r^3$ **l** $\sum_{r=1}^{\infty} (-1)^{r+1} 2r$

3 10 **4** 10 000 **5** $\frac{1}{1000}$

Exercise 4C page 76

1 a Yes, 1 **b** Yes, −3 **c** No
d Yes, a **e** Yes, 3 **f** No

2 a $4n - 3$ **b** $2n + 8$ **c** $9n - 1$
d $22 - 3n$ **e** $29 - 4n$

3 a 106 **b** 107 **c** 4
d 7 **e** $\frac{11}{4}$
4 a $9n - 6$ **b** 16th
5 a $7n + 3$ **b** 23rd
6 a $35 - 6n$ **b** 15th
7 a 245 **b** 1170 **c** 48 **d** $13\frac{1}{2}$
8 a $4n - 3$ **b** 11th **c** 231
9 a $7n - 4$ **b** 6th **c** 123
10 a 1820 **b** 9 **c** 18 653
11 a 5 **b** 1130
12 a 11 **b** 182
13 b $a = 13, d = 7$
14 b $a = 17, d = -4$ **c** 42
15 a $a = 42, d = -3$ **c** 29
16 a $a = -18, d = 3$ **c** 14
17 $d = 5, a = -3$
18 15 500 **19** £317.20
20 a £1050 **b** £11 500
21 a 14 days **b** 104 days **c** 290 days
23 2600
24 a 15 050 **b** 10 150 **c** 9900
25 $n = 3$ **26** $x = 7$

Exercise 4D page 80

1 b $a = 7, d = 5$
2 b $a = 5, d = 2$
3 $a = 15, d = 7$
4 b 17
5 a 22 **b** 8, 14 **c** 6
6 a 2, 3 **b** 51
7 a $\frac{n}{2}(3n + 7)$ **b** 12
8 a $a = 11, d = 4$ **b** $r = 5$
9 a 7350 m
10 a 180 **b** 2940 **c** 7
d Unlikely to be able to increase sales month on month indefinitely.
11 a £67 500 **b** 4.3 km
12 $a = 9, d = 2$
13 1683 **14** 17
15 $a = 2, b = -3, S_{30} = 1365$

Exercise 4E page 85

1 a $3 \times 2^{n-1}$ **b** $2 \times 5^{n-1}$
c $20 \times (\frac{1}{2})^{n-1}$ **d** $200 \times (\frac{1}{5})^{n-1}$
e $\frac{1}{8} \times 2^{n-1} (= 2^{n-4})$ **f** $4 \times 3^{n-1}$
g $5 \times (-3)^{n-1}$
2 $a = 7, r = 3$
3 $a = \frac{35}{32}, r = 2$
4 $a = 5120, r = \frac{1}{2}$
5 a ± 2 **b** ± 6
6 $192, \frac{3}{4}$
7 2
8 2
9 a $a = 1, d = \frac{1}{2}$ **b** $r = 2$
10 a 1023 **b** 2186
c 195 312 **d** 615
11 a 79.9 **b** 80.0
c 607.5 **d** 1706.7
e 66.7
12 a $7r$ **b** 5
13 b $-4, 3$
14 a £2048 **b** £4095
c No. The amounts are increasing too much by the end of the year.
15 a 94.3 m **b** 637.5 m
16 a 6th week **b** 15 weeks
17 a £29 458 **b** 18th year
c Unlikely to stay in the same role for 17 years, rate of inflation likely to change.
18 £376 000 (3 sf). No, the market can fluctuate significantly over this time.
19 c $r = 3, a = 7$
20 b 15
21 a $-177\,147$ **c** 11
22 5
23 a $\frac{5}{2}(3^n - 1)$ **b** 1 328 600 **c** 16
24 7
25 $4, -12$
26 a 88 572 **b** 12 582 900 **c** 850

Exercise 4F page 89

1 a 10 **b** 6 **c** 20
d 4 **e** 10 **f** $\frac{14}{5}$
2 $\frac{2}{3}$ **3** 6 **4** 21 **5** $-\frac{2}{7}$
6 a 40 **b** 3 **c** 5 **d** 9
8 $r = \frac{1}{3}, a = 18$ or $r = \frac{2}{3}, a = 9$
9 3 **10** $\frac{x-1}{x+1}$ **11** $\frac{1}{10}$
12 $\frac{3}{5}$ **13** 18 m
14 a $a = \frac{10}{3}, r = \frac{2}{3}$ **b** $10[1 - (\frac{2}{3})^n]$
c 3 **d** 10
15 a 192 **b** $3 \times 4^{n-1}$ **c** $a = 3, r = 4$
16 $r = \frac{1}{2}, a = 10$
17 $a = 2, r = \sqrt{2}, S_{10} = 62(\sqrt{2} + 1)$
18 a $6n + 7$ **b** Arithmetic
19 a $\frac{3}{2}(3^{20} - 1)$ **b** $\frac{4}{3}(4^{30} - 1)$ **c** $14(2^{10} - 1)$
20 a 5 **b** $-2\frac{1}{3}$

Review Exercise 4G page 91

1 a 3, 5, 7, 9 **b** 1, 4, 7, 10
c 1, 4, 9, 16 **d** 10, 100, 1000, 10 000
e $1, \frac{1}{2}, \frac{1}{3}, \frac{1}{4}$ **f** 3, 8, 15, 24
g $\frac{1}{2}, \frac{2}{3}, \frac{3}{4}, \frac{4}{5}$ **h** $-1, 1, -1, 1$
2 a $4n$ **b** n^2 **c** $3n + 1$
d $\frac{n}{n+2}$ **e** $\frac{1}{n}$

3 a 4, 7, 10, 13 b 50, 45, 40, 35
c $3, \frac{1}{3}, 3, \frac{1}{3}$ d 64, 32, 16, 8
e 10, 100, 10 000, 10^8 f 1,1, 1, 1

4 a 34 b 30 c 25
d 20 e 31 f 12
g −6 h $\frac{23}{12}$ i $\frac{13}{12}$

5 a $\sum_{r=1}^{4} 3n$ b $\sum_{r=3}^{6} r^2$ c $\sum_{r=1}^{4} 10^r$
d $\sum_{r=1}^{50} 2n$ e $\sum_{r=1}^{10} r^{-2}$ f $\sum_{r=3}^{6} \frac{1}{r}$

6 a 39 b 151 c 13 d 21
7 a 820 b 8200 c 1 101 100 d $n(5n - 3)$
8 $a = -3, d = 5$ 9 $a = 3, d = 5$
10 $a = 121, d = -6$ 11 15 500
12 £923 13 30
14 2 15 4234
16 $a = 6, d = 2$
17 a 17 b 7 c −330
18 a −25 b 345
19 a $5 \times 2^{n-1}$ b $2 \times 3^{n-1}$ c $100 \times (\frac{1}{2})^{n-1}$
20 765 21 $a = 2\frac{1}{2}, r = 2$
22 $r = 4$ 23 4, −5
24 a $x + 1$ b $x(x + 1)^{99}$
25 10 26 48 27 34.9 cm
28 a $(x^2 + x - 2)$ b 192

Examination Exercise 4 page 94

1 b −4 c 1953
2 b i 6 ii 90
3 a 11 b £557 500
4 b 3010 c 2009
5 a i $\frac{1}{2}, 4$ ii periodic/oscillating
b $a = -2, d = \frac{5}{2}$
6 b 180 c £1710
e $n = 18$, aged 27
7 i −2 ii 3072 iii −1 048 575
8 b 256 c 1.602
9 a 17.28 b 120 c 25.92
10 i $k = 28$ b $r = -\frac{1}{2}, |r| < 1, a = 6$
11 i a $\frac{8}{9}$ b 18 ii 28
12 a 0.75 b 256 c 1024 d 14
13 a $p = \frac{4}{5}, q = 4$ b 195
14 i 7.5 ii 64 iii $-\frac{2}{3}$
15 i 80, 75, 70 ii 650 iii 8 iv 320
16 i 91 ii 978 iii 38
17 a 2 b 198
19 a $5k + 3$ b $156k + 114 = 6(26k + 19)$
20 a $a_2 = 5 - 4k$
$a_3 = 5 - k(5 - 4k)$
b $17 - 9k + 4k^2$
c 500
21 i a 4 b 80
ii a $3k, 4k$ b 11

Exercise 5A page 101

1 a $1 - 2x + 3x^2$ b $1 - 3x + 6x^2$
c $1 - 6x + 21x^2$ d $1 - 10x + 55x^2$
e $1 + \frac{1}{2}x - \frac{1}{8}x^2$ f $1 + \frac{3}{2}x + \frac{3}{8}x^2$
g $1 - \frac{1}{2}x + \frac{3}{8}x^2$ h $1 - \frac{3}{4}x + \frac{21}{32}x^2$
i $1 - \frac{2}{3}x - \frac{1}{9}x^2$ j $1 + \frac{2}{5}x + \frac{7}{25}x^2$
k $1 - \frac{1}{2}x - \frac{1}{8}x^2$ l $1 + \frac{1}{3}x + \frac{2}{9}x^2$
2 0.980
3 1.010
4 a $-\frac{1}{2} < x < \frac{1}{2}$ b $-1 < x < 1$
c $-\frac{1}{5} < x < \frac{1}{5}$ d $-\frac{1}{2} < x < \frac{1}{2}$
e $-\frac{1}{2} < x < \frac{1}{2}$ f $-\frac{1}{4} < x < \frac{1}{4}$
g $-\frac{1}{3} < x < \frac{1}{3}$ h $-\frac{1}{2} < x < \frac{1}{2}$
i $-3 < x < 3$ j $-2 < x < 2$
5 a $1 - 6x + 24x^2 - 80x^3$
b $1 + 2x + 3x^2 + 4x^3$
c $1 - 20x + 250x^2 - 2500x^3$
d $1 - 14x + 112x^2 - 672x^3$
e $1 + x - \frac{1}{2}x^2 + \frac{1}{2}x^3$
f $1 + 10x + 30x^2 + 20x^3$
g $1 + \frac{3}{2}x + \frac{27}{8}x^2 + \frac{135}{16}x^3$
h $1 - \frac{1}{2}x - \frac{3}{8}x^2 - \frac{7}{16}x^3$
i $1 - \frac{x}{6} + \frac{x^2}{72} - \frac{x^3}{432}$
j $1 + \frac{x}{6} + \frac{x^2}{18} + \frac{7x^3}{324}$
6 $-\frac{77}{128}x^4$ 7 $\frac{4389}{256}x^3$ 8 $-\frac{1}{125}x^3$
9 a $x^3 + 6x^2 + 12x + 8$
b $15\sqrt{3} + 26$
10 b $264\sqrt{2}$
11 $1 + \frac{1}{2}x - \frac{1}{8}x^2 + \frac{1}{16}x^3$, 1.0392
12 −20
13 $1 - \frac{1}{2x} - \frac{1}{8x^2} - \frac{1}{16x^3}$, 9.94987
14 a $1 - \frac{x}{3} - \frac{x^2}{9}$ b 3.332222

Exercise 5B page 103

1 a $\frac{1}{2} - \frac{x}{4} + \frac{x^2}{8}$, $|x| < 2$
b $\frac{1}{64}\left(1 + \frac{3x}{4} + \frac{3}{8}x^2\right)$, $|x| < 4$
c $\frac{1}{9}\left(1 - \frac{2}{3}x + \frac{x^2}{3}\right)$, $|x| < 3$
d $\frac{1}{625}\left(1 - \frac{4x}{5} + \frac{2x^2}{5}\right)$, $|x| < 5$
e $2\left(1 - \frac{1}{8}x - \frac{1}{128}x^2\right)$, $|x| < 4$
f $\frac{1}{3}\left(1 + \frac{1}{18}x + \frac{1}{216}x^2\right)$, $|x| < 9$

g $2\left(1 - \frac{1}{24}x - \frac{1}{576}x^2\right),\ |x| < 8$

h $\frac{1}{4}\left(1 - \frac{1}{12}x + \frac{5}{576}x^2\right),\ |x| < 8$

i $5^5\left(1 + \frac{x}{10} + \frac{3x^2}{1000}\right),\ |x| < 25$

2 a $2\left(1 + \frac{3x}{8} - \frac{9x^2}{128}\right),\ |x| < \frac{4}{3}$

b $\frac{1}{3}\left(1 + \frac{x}{9} + \frac{x^2}{54}\right),\ |x| < \frac{9}{2}$

c $2\left(1 - \frac{5x}{24} - \frac{25x^2}{576}\right),\ |x| < \frac{8}{5}$

d $125\left(1 - \frac{21x}{50} + \frac{147}{5000}x^2\right),\ |x| < \frac{25}{7}$

3 a $a = \frac{1}{2}, b = -\frac{3}{16}$ **b** $a = 2, b = \frac{1}{4}$

c $a = \frac{1}{\sqrt{2}}, b = \frac{7}{4\sqrt{2}}$ **d** $a = \frac{1}{3}, b = -\frac{2}{243}$

4 $3 + \frac{2x}{3} - \frac{2x^2}{27} + \frac{4x^3}{243},\ |x| < \frac{9}{4}$

5 a $1 - x - \frac{x^2}{2},\ |x| < \frac{1}{2}$

b 0.990

6 a $1 - \frac{3x}{5} - \frac{18}{25}x^2$ **b** 1.961

Exercise 5C page 104

1 a $-\left(\frac{13}{3} + \frac{19}{9}x + \frac{28}{27}x^2\right),\ |x| < 2$

b $-\left(2 + \frac{3x}{2} + \frac{5x^2}{4}\right),\ |x| < 1$

c $\frac{11}{2} - \frac{17x}{4} + \frac{29x^2}{8},\ |x| < 1$

d $\frac{5}{2} - \frac{11x}{12} + \frac{25x^2}{72},\ |x| < 2$

e $-\frac{3}{2}x - \frac{3}{4}x^2,\ |x| < 1$

f $-\frac{7}{3} - \frac{17x}{9} - \frac{55x^2}{27},\ |x| < 1$

2 a $1 + \frac{1}{x-2} + \frac{1}{x-1}$

b $-\left(\frac{1}{2} + \frac{5x}{4} + \frac{9x^2}{8} + \frac{17x^3}{16}\right)$

c $|x| < 1$

3 a $1 - x - 4x^2 - 6x^3$ **b** $|x| < \frac{1}{4}$

4 $\lambda = 2, n = -3$

5 Both equal -2

6 $1 + \frac{3x}{2} + \frac{7x^2}{8},\ |x| < 1$

7 a $1 + x + \frac{1}{2}x^2,\ |x| < 1$

8 a $a = \frac{3}{2}, b = \frac{1}{2}$ **b** $\frac{1970}{1393}$ or $\frac{1393}{985}$

9 a $q = 3$

b $-x^3$

c $-1 < x < \frac{1}{3}$

10 a $\frac{[1 - (-x)^n]}{1 + x}$ **b** $-1 < x < 1$ **c** $\frac{1}{1 + x}$

11 b $1 + 2x + 3x^2 + 4x^3 + \ldots$

c $1 + 3x + 6x^2 + 10x^3 + \ldots$

d $1 + 4x + 10x^2 + \ldots$

13 a $a_0 = 1, a_1 = -\frac{1}{2}, a_2 = \frac{3}{8}, a_3 = -\frac{5}{16}$

Review Exercise 5D page 106

1 a $|x| < \frac{2}{3}$ **b** $|x| < \frac{5}{3}$ **c** $|x| < \frac{2}{7}$

d $|x| < \frac{9}{2}$ **e** $|x| < \frac{3}{2}$ **f** $|x| < \frac{5}{3}$

2 $2 - \frac{x}{4} - \frac{x^2}{32},\ |x| < \frac{3}{8}$

3 a $a = \frac{1}{9}, b = \frac{4}{729}$ **b** $a = \frac{1}{8}, b = \frac{9}{64}$

4 a $\frac{1}{3(x+1)} + \frac{2}{3(1-2x)}$ **b** $1 + x + 3x^2$

c $|x| < \frac{1}{2}$

5 a $\frac{1}{2x+1} + \frac{3}{x-1}$ **b** $-2 - 5x + x^2$

c $|x| < \frac{1}{2}$

6 a $\frac{4}{3x-1} + \frac{8}{x+2}$ **b** $-108\frac{1}{2}$

c $|x| < \frac{1}{3}$

Examination Exercise 5 page 107

1 a $1 + x - 2x^2$

b i $\frac{1}{4} - \frac{1}{16}x + \frac{5}{256}x^2$ **ii** 0.2313

2 a $2 + \frac{5}{4}x - \frac{25}{64}x^2$ **b** $\frac{3}{2}\sqrt{2}$ **c** $\frac{181}{128}$

3 a $2 - \frac{3}{4}x - \frac{9}{32}x^2 - \frac{45}{256}x^3$

b $x = 0.1, 19.2201$

4 i $1 - 2x + 7x^2 - 22x^3$

ii $|x| < \frac{1}{4}$

5 ii 0.136 **iii** $-\frac{1}{x^2} - \frac{3}{x^3} - \frac{6}{x^4}$

6 $n = -1.5, k = 4$

7 $p = 2, q = -2,\ |x| < 2$

Exercise 6A page 114

1 a $\sqrt{3}$ **b** $\frac{2}{\sqrt{3}}$ **c** 1.015

d $\sqrt{2}$ **e** 0.325 **f** $\frac{4}{3}$

2 a

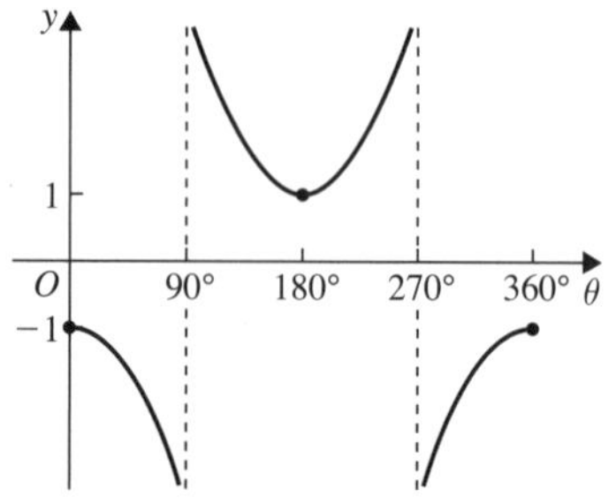

b

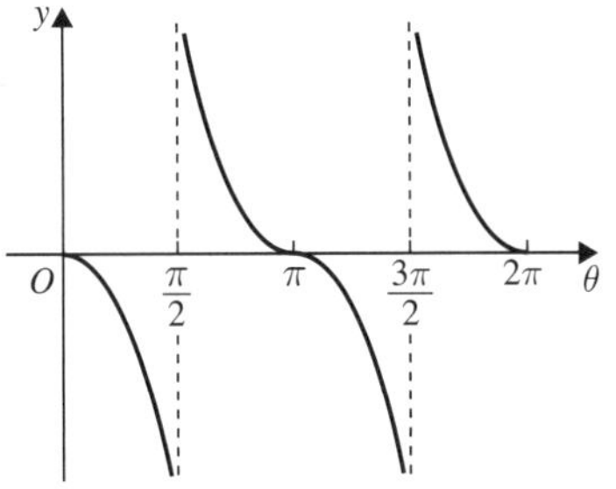

c

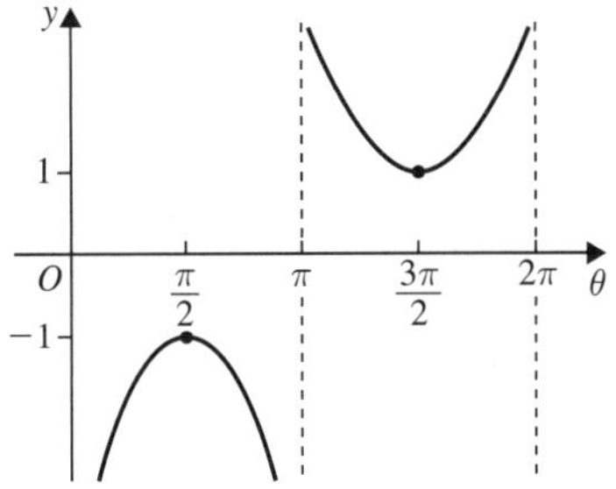

d

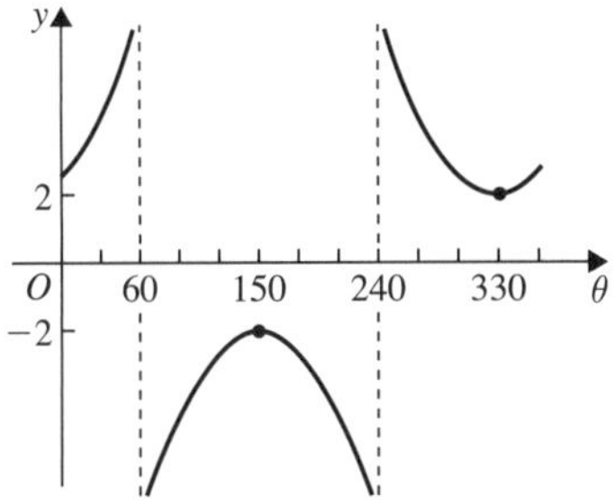

e

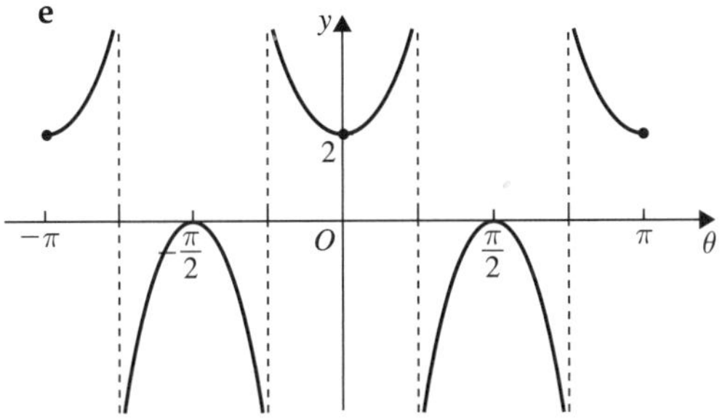

f

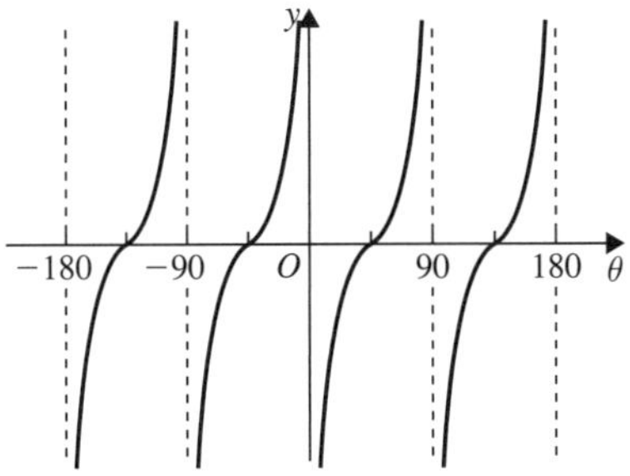

g

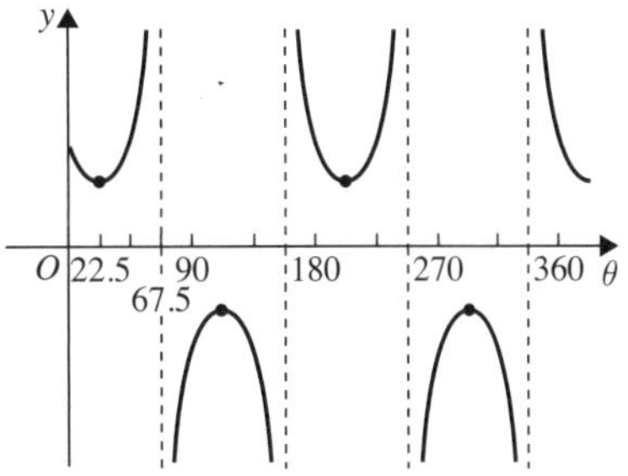

3 a $\sec^2 x$ **b** $\sec^2 2x$ **c** $\sin^2 x$
d $\sec x$ **e** $\sin\theta\cos\theta$ **f** $\operatorname{cosec}^2\theta$

5 a 60°, 300° **b** 30°, 210° **c** 45°, 135°
d 33.6°, 326.4° **e** 18.4°, 198.4° **f** 90°

7 a 45°, 225°, 63.4°, 243.4°
b −180°, 0, 180°, −135°, 45°
c 90°, 30°, 150°

9 $30° < \theta < 150°$

10 a $\cos\theta$ **b** $-60° < \theta < 60°$

11 a 35.3°, 144.7°, 215.3°, 324.7°
b 30°, 60°, 120°, 150°

12 (22.5, 7.5), (67.5, 142.5)

Exercise 6B page 117

1 a 30° **b** 90° **c** 45°
d 120° **e** −30° **f** 60°

2 a $-\frac{\pi}{4}$ **b** $\frac{\pi}{3}$ **c** $\frac{\pi}{4}$
d 0 **e** $\frac{\pi}{3}$ **f** $-\frac{\pi}{2}$

3/4 See text

5 a 60°, 120° **b** 45°, 225° **c** 0, 360°

6 a $\frac{1}{2}$ **b** 0 **c** θ **d** θ

Exercise 6C page 120

1 b 1

2 b 0

3 a False **b** True

4 a $\sin 3\theta$ **b** $\cos 2A$ **c** $\sin 3x$ **d** 1

5 a $\frac{1+\sqrt{3}}{2\sqrt{2}}$ **b** $\frac{1+\sqrt{3}}{2\sqrt{2}}$ **c** $\frac{\sqrt{3}-1}{2\sqrt{2}}$
d $\frac{\sqrt{3}+1}{2\sqrt{2}}$ **e** $\sqrt{3}-2$

6 a $\frac{63}{65}$ **b** $\frac{56}{65}$ **c** $\frac{63}{16}$

7 73.2°, 286.8°

8 a $-\sin x$ **b** $-\cos x$ **c** $-\sin x$ **d** $-\cos x$

9 $\frac{1}{3}$

10 1

11 45°, 225°

12 a 1, $\theta = 50°$ **b** 1, $\theta = 105°$

14 $\tan(x + 45°)$

15 a $\frac{2\tan A}{1-\tan^2 A}$ **b** $\frac{1}{2}$

17 a $2+\sqrt{3}$ **b** $\sqrt{6}+\sqrt{2}$ **c** $\sqrt{6}-\sqrt{2}$

23 $\frac{1}{3}$

24 **b** 0.625, 2.195

Exercise 6D page 124

1 **a** 1 **b** $\frac{\sqrt{3}}{2}$ **c** $\frac{1}{2}$ **d** 1

2 **a** sin 20° **b** cos 34° **c** cos 70° **d** tan 22°
e $\frac{1}{2}\sin 2\theta$ **f** $\frac{1}{2}\tan 4\theta$ **g** $2\sin A$ **h** 1

3 $\sin 2\theta = \frac{24}{25}$, $\cos 2\theta = \frac{7}{25}$

4 $\sin 2\theta = \frac{120}{169}$, $\cos 2\theta = -\frac{119}{169}$

5 **a** $\frac{4}{3}$ **b** $\frac{24}{7}$

6 $\frac{\pm\sqrt{7}}{4}$

7 $\pm\frac{4}{5}$

8 $\frac{1}{3}$ or -3

9 0, 180°, 360°, 60°, 300°

10 90°, 270°, 194.5°, 345.5°

11 60°, 300°, 75.5°, 284.5°

12 31.7°, 121.7°, 211.7°, 301.7°

13 0°, 180°, 360°, 30°, 150°

14 60°, 300°, 109.5°, 250.5°

15 0°, 60°, 120°, 180°, 240°, 300°, 360°

16 0°, 360°, 240°

17 0°, 120°, 360°

18 14.5°, 165.5°

37 $2\sin\frac{x}{2}\cos\frac{x}{2}$

38 $\frac{2\tan\frac{x}{2}}{1-\tan^2\frac{x}{2}}$

41 **b** $2+\sqrt{3}$

42 18.4°, 161,6°, 198.4°, 341.6°

43 $A = 1, B = 4, C = 3$

Exercise 6E page 128

1 **a** $5\cos(\theta - 36.9)°$ **b** $13\cos(\theta - 67.4)°$
c $\sqrt{5}\cos(\theta - 63.4)°$

2 **a** $5\sin(\theta + 53.1)°$ **b** $5\cos(\theta + 36.9)°$
c $\sqrt{5}\cos(\theta - 26.6)°$ **d** $17\sin(\theta - 61.9)°$
e $10\sin(\theta + 36.9)°$ **f** $\sqrt{2}\cos(\theta - 45)°$

3 **a** $2\sin(\theta + 60)°$
b Maximum value = 2 at $\theta = 30°$

4 **a** 5, 53.1° **b** 13, 157.4°
c $\sqrt{2}$, 45° **d** 17, 298.1°

5 **a** $5\cos(\theta - 36.9)°$ **b** 103.3°, 330.5°

6 **a** $3\sin(\theta + 70.53)°$ **b** 67.7°, 331.3°

7 **a** 1.9°, 121.9° **b** 80.0°, 325.2°
c 90°, 330° **d** 60.4°, 193.3°
e 257.6°, 349.8° **f** 40.8°, 201.1°
g 78.4°, 244.8°
h 39.0°, 162.8°, 219.0°, 342.8°

8 **a** 2.25, 0.15 **b** 0.38, 1.97

9 **a** $\sqrt{7}\cos(x - 0.714)$ **b** 1.43

10 **a** 0.36, 2.14 **b** 0, 4.07, 6.28
c 0, 4.71, 6.28 **d** 1.70, 3.29

11 **a** $\sqrt{10}\sin(\theta - 71.6)°$ **b** $\frac{4}{\sqrt{10}} > 1$

12 $-\sqrt{3} \leqslant k \leqslant \sqrt{3}$

13 **a** $c = 12$ **b** $13\cos(2\theta + 1.176)$

14 **a** $5\cos(\theta + 0.93)°$ **b** 2

15 **a** $13\cos(\theta - 1.176)$ **b** 2

16 **a** $5\sin(2\theta + 36.9)° - 3$
b 8.1°, 45.0°

17 **a** $5\cos(x - 0.6435)$
b $\frac{1}{2}, \frac{1}{12}$
c 1.429, 3.000

18 **a** **i** 15.6°C **ii** 4.45
b 2126 and 1128

19 **a** **i** max: $h = 68.6$ m, $t = 1.30$
min: $h = 51.4$ m, $t = 0.30$
b 2 hours
c 41.5 minutes

20 **a** **i** $L = 2\cos\theta + 4\sin\theta$
ii $L = 2\sqrt{5}\sin(\theta + 0.464)$
b **i** $2\sqrt{5}$ **ii** 1.11

21 **a** $0 \leqslant \theta \leqslant 360$ and $0 \leqslant t \leqslant 20 \Rightarrow 0 \leqslant 18t \leqslant 360$
b 5.4 minutes

Review Exercise 6F page 131

1 **a** 41.8°, 138.2° **b** 138.6°, 221.4°
c 145.0°, 325.0° **d** 210°, 330°
e $\frac{\pi}{3}, \frac{5\pi}{3}$ **f** $\frac{\pi}{4}, -\frac{3\pi}{4}$
g 60°, 300° **h** 0°, 180°, 360°

2 **a** 0°, 132°, 228°, 360°
b 58°, 238°, 148°, 328°

3 $\frac{\pi}{4}, \frac{\pi}{3}, \frac{2\pi}{3}, \frac{3\pi}{4}$

4 **a** 45° **b** 0° **c** 60°

5 **a** $\frac{\pi}{6}$ **b** $\frac{\pi}{6}$ **c** $\frac{\pi}{6}$

7 **a** 18.4°, 198.4°, 26.6°, 206.6°
b 60°, 300°
c 90°, 270°, 199.5°, 340.5°

8 $-\frac{16}{65}$

9 **a** $-\frac{3}{5}$
b $\sin 2\theta = -\frac{24}{25}$, $\cos 2\theta = -\frac{7}{25}$

11 **a** 60°, 300°, 180°
b 0, 180°, 360°, 80.4°, 279.6°
c 25.2°, 154.8°
d 90°, 270°, 30°, 150°
e 0, 360°, 120°, 240°
f 0, 180°, 360°, 30°, 330°, 150°, 120°, 210°

12 **a** $-\frac{7}{25}$ **b** $\frac{24}{25}$ **c** $-\frac{24}{7}$

13 **a** **i** $\frac{\sqrt{6}-\sqrt{2}}{4}\left(=\frac{\sqrt{3}-1}{2\sqrt{2}}\right)$
ii $2+\sqrt{3}\left(=\frac{\sqrt{3}+1}{\sqrt{3}-1}\right)$
iii $\frac{\sqrt{2}-\sqrt{6}}{4}\left(=\frac{1-\sqrt{3}}{2\sqrt{2}}\right)$

14 a $-\frac{119}{169}$ b $\frac{2}{13}\sqrt{13}$ c $-\frac{120}{119}$

15 $\frac{1}{3}$

16 a 30°, 150°, 270°
 b 0, 180°, 360°, 30°, 150°, 210°, 330°
 c 90°, 120°, 240°, 270°
 d 0, 120°, 240°, 360°
 e 0, 60°, 300°, 360°

17 $3\sin\theta - 4\sin^3\theta$

18 a $\sqrt{2}\cos\left(x + \frac{\pi}{4}\right)$ b $0, \frac{3\pi}{2}, 2\pi$
 c $\sqrt{2}$

19 a $\sqrt{3}\sin(\theta + 54.74)°$ b 90°, 340.5°

20 a $2\cos(\theta + 60)°$ b $\frac{1}{4}$

21 a $5\sin(\theta + 36.9)°$ b 120°, 347°

22 $d = 0.838$ m, 0823 and 2023

23 a $x = 0.3\cos\theta$, $y = 0.9\sin\theta$
 b 6.5°

Examination Exercise 6 page 134

1 6.5°, 53.5°, 126.5°, 173.5°

2 i $\frac{5}{3}$ ii $\sqrt{17}$

3 i $\tan\alpha = 2$, $\tan\beta = 5$
 ii $-\frac{7}{9}$

4 a ii $-\frac{5}{13}$ b −21.3°

5 37.9°, 142°

6 i $\lambda = \frac{1}{2}$ ii $\frac{2\pi}{3}, \frac{4\pi}{3}, \pi$

7 b 2.820, 5.961

8 ii a $4 + 2\sqrt{2}$ b 0.659 c $32\sin\theta$

9 99.6°, 260.4°

10 i a $1 + \frac{\sqrt{2}}{2}$ ii a $k = 2$
 b 0°, 30°, 150°, 180°

11 b ii 22.5°, 112.5°, 202.5°, 292.5°

12 ii 70.5°, −70.5°
 iii $0 < k < \frac{3}{2}$

13 a $R = \sqrt{29}$, $\alpha = 1.19$
 b i 5.09 ii 0.567, 3.34

14 a $R = \sqrt{5}$, $\alpha = 26.57°$
 b 33.0°, 273.9° c 86.1°

15 a $R = 6.5$, $\alpha = 0.395$
 b (0, 6), (1.97, 0), (5.11, 0)
 c $H_{max} = 18.5$, $H_{min} = 5.5$
 d 11, 48

16 i $R = 5$, $\alpha = 53.1$
 ii a −64.7°, 138°
 b $k = 8$, $c = 3$

17 a i $R = 5$, $\alpha = 53.1$
 ii 18.4°, 198.4°
 b ii 35.3°, 144.7°
 c iii $\cos 72° = \frac{\sqrt{5} - 1}{4}$

18 i 0.5 ii $\frac{\sqrt{2}}{2}$

19 a

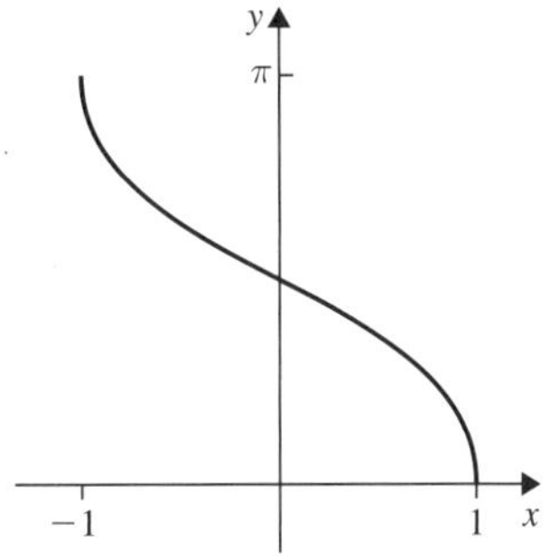

$(-1, \pi)$, $(1, 0)$

b

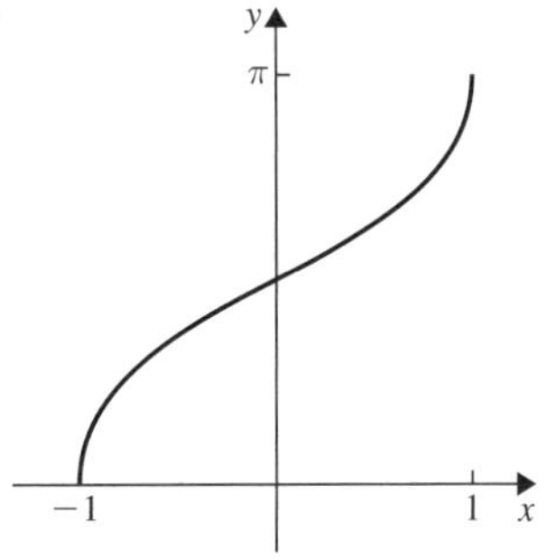

$(-1, 0)$, $(1, \pi)$

Exercise 7A page 140

1 a $6(2x + 5)^2$ b $8x(x^2 + 7)^3$

2 a $12(3x - 4)^3$ b $40(8x + 11)^4$
 c $4x(x^2 - 3)$ d $27x^2(3x^3 + 1)^2$
 e $-12(1 - 3x)^3$ f $-10(3 - x)^9$

3 a $-3(1 + 3x)^{-2}$ b $-4(2x + 1)^{-3}$
 c $-15(5x + 2)^{-4}$ d $-24(4x - 1)^{-3}$
 e $-10x(x^2 + 1)^{-2}$ f $40(1 - x)^{-5}$

4 b $\frac{4}{7}\sqrt{7}$

5 a $\frac{5x}{\sqrt{5x^2 + 3}}$ b $(3x + 1)^{-\frac{2}{3}}$
 c $-x(x^2 - 3)^{-\frac{3}{2}}$ d $-\frac{3x^2}{(x^3 + 1)^2}$
 e $-4(8x + 7)^{-\frac{3}{2}}$ f $-\frac{1}{2\sqrt{x}(\sqrt{x} + 2)^2}$

6 $y = 64x - 48$ 7 $x + 18y - 1157 = 0$

8 (0, 8) 9 48

10 $2y = x + 3$

11 a $3(2\sqrt{x} - 3x)^2\left(\frac{1}{\sqrt{x}} - 3\right)$ b $\frac{1}{2x^2}\left(1 - \frac{1}{x}\right)^{-\frac{1}{2}}$
 c $-3\sqrt{x}(x^{\frac{3}{2}} + 2)^{-2}$ d $-\frac{1}{\sqrt{x}}(1 + \sqrt{x})^{-3}$
 e $\frac{1}{2}\left(x^2 - \frac{1}{x}\right)^{-\frac{1}{2}}\left(2x + \frac{1}{x^2}\right)$ f $20x + (2x - 3)^{-\frac{1}{2}}$

12 a (1, 7) minimum and (−3, −9) maximum

13 a (1, 2)

Exercise 7B page 143

1 $(2x + 1)(6x + 1)$ 2 $2x(3x - 1)(6x - 1)$

3 $x^2(x - 1)(5x - 3)$ 4 $2(x + 2)(x + 3)(2x + 5)$

5 $2(1-x)^2(1-4x)$ **6** $2(x-1)(10x^3-6x^2+1)$
7 $5(1+2x)^3(10x+1)$ **8** $5(3x+1)^3(3x-7)$
9 $\frac{\sqrt{x}}{2}(5x+6)$ **10** $\frac{(4x+1)}{2\sqrt{x}}(20x+1)$

11 $\frac{x}{\sqrt{2x+1}}(5x+2)$ **12** $\frac{x^2}{\sqrt{4x-1}}(14x-3)$
13 $y=19x-1$ **14** 16 **15** $2, \frac{2}{5}$
16 a $-3, -\frac{1}{3}$
b maximum at $x=-3$, minimum at $x=-\frac{1}{3}$
17 a i $(-2, 0), (4, 0), (0, 32)$
ii $(0, 32)$ maximum; $(4, 0)$ minimum
18 a $(2, -4)$ **b** $(-1, -4)$
19 i $k=3$ **ii** $\frac{16}{3}$

Exercise 7C page 147

1 $\frac{2}{(x+1)^2}$ **2** $-\frac{15}{(2x-1)^2}$
3 $\frac{3x^2+2x}{(3x+1)^2}$ **4** $\frac{4-10x-4x^2}{(x^2+1)^2}$
5 $\frac{-2(x+1)}{x^3}$ **6** $\frac{-4x-1}{(x+1)^4}$
7 $\frac{-6(3x+2)(2x+3)}{(4x+1)^4}$ **8** $\frac{-x^3-9x^2}{(x-3)^5}$
9 $\frac{(3x-4)^2(6x+25)}{(2x+1)^3}$ **10** $\frac{-x-2}{2x^2\sqrt{x+1}}$
11 $\frac{2x+3}{(4x+3)^{\frac{3}{2}}}$ **12** $\frac{3x-4}{(2x-1)^{\frac{3}{2}}}$
13 $16y=x+1$ **14** $y=-3x-1$
15 $y=4-x$ **16** $\frac{3}{2}$
17 $(3, -\frac{1}{6})$ minimum, $(-1, \frac{1}{2})$ maximum

Exercise 7D page 151

1 a e^x **b** $3e^{3x}$ **c** $2e^x$
d $2xe^{x^2}$ **e** $2e^{2x+1}$ **f** $-e^{-x}$
g $20e^{4x}$ **h** e^x+2e^{2x} **i** $2x+e^{-x}$
j $-2e^{-2x}$ **k** $-4e^{-x}$ **l** $3x^2e^{x^3}+3x^2$
m $(4\ln 5)5^{4x}$ **n** $(300\ln 2)2^{10x}$ **o** $(-14\ln 3)3^{-7x}$
2 a xe^x+e^x **b** $x^2e^x+2xe^x$
c $2e^{2x}(2x+1)$ **d** $e^x(x^2+2x+1)$
e $4x^2e^{2x}(2x+3)$ **f** $3x^2e^{3x}+2xe^{3x}-3x^2$
g $\frac{e^{3x}}{x^2}(3x-1)$ **h** $\frac{xe^x-2e^x-2}{x^3}$
i $\frac{2x-x^2}{e^x}$ **j** $e^x(1+x)^2(4+x)$
k $e^{-x}(3x^2-x^3-1)$ **l** $\frac{2e^{2x}-e^{3x}}{(1-e^x)^2}$
3 a $3e^2$ **b** 3
c 1 **d** $-\frac{4e^2}{(e^2-1)^2}$
4 $y=e^2(x-1)$
5 $y=x$
6 b $y+e^2x=\frac{1}{e^2}$ **c** $\left(\frac{1}{e^4}, 0\right)$
7 $\left(-1, -\frac{1}{e}\right)$ minimum
8 $(1, e)$ minimum
9 a $(0, 2)$
10 a $(0, 0)$ minimum, $(-2, 4e^{-2})$ maximum
16 $(\frac{1}{3}\ln 2, 8)$ minimum

Exercise 7E page 155

1 a $\frac{1}{x}$ **b** $\frac{3}{x}$ **c** $\frac{6}{x}$
d $\frac{3}{3x-1}$ **e** $\frac{-2}{1-2x}$ **f** $\frac{3x^2+1}{x^3+x}$
g $\frac{1}{x+1}$ **h** $\frac{2}{x}$ **i** $\frac{3}{x+2}$
j $-\frac{1}{x}$ **k** $\frac{1}{2x}$ **l** $\frac{2x+1}{x^2+x-2}$
2 a $\ln(x+4)-\ln(x-2)$ **b** $\frac{1}{x+4}-\frac{1}{x-2}$
3 a $\frac{1}{x}-\frac{1}{x+1}$ **b** $\frac{2}{2x+3}-\frac{4}{4x-1}$
4 a $1+\ln x$ **b** $x+2x\ln x$
c $\frac{x}{1+x}+\ln(1+x)$ **d** $\frac{1-\ln x}{x^2}$
e $\frac{(x+1)-2x\ln x}{x(x+1)^3}$ **f** $\frac{\ln x-1}{(\ln x)^2}$
g $2x+\frac{1}{x}$ **h** $\frac{3}{x}-\frac{1}{x^2}$
i $\frac{1}{2x}+\frac{1}{2\sqrt{x}}$ **j** $-\frac{\ln x}{x^2}$
k $\frac{2x^3}{1+x^2}+2x\ln(1+x^2)$ **l** $\frac{1}{x+1}-\frac{1}{x+2}$
5 $x+2x\ln x, 3+2\ln x$
7 $\frac{e^x}{1+e^x}$
8 b $3y=x+3\ln 3-2$
9 $y=-x+\ln 2+1$
10 a $y=x-2$
b 2 square units
11 $A(1, 0)$ $B\left(e, \frac{1}{e}\right)$
12 $\left(\frac{1}{e}, -\frac{1}{e}\right)$
13 $\frac{1}{2e}$
14 a $(3.67, -4.57)$
15 a $\frac{f'(x)}{f(x)}$ **b** $\ln(x^3+1)$
16 $y=e(x-1)$
17 $[1, \ln(e+1)]$

Exercise 7F page 159

1 a $\cos x$ b $-3\sin 3x$
c $4\sec^2 x$ d $6\cos 6x$
e $-\frac{3}{2}\sin\frac{3}{2}x$ f $10\cos 2x$
g $\frac{1}{2}\sec^2\frac{1}{2}x$ h $-10\sin x + \cos x$
i $\sec^2 x + \sin x$ j $\cos(x+1)$
k $2\sec^2(2x-1)$ l $\frac{1}{2}\sin\frac{1}{2}x$

2 a $2\sin x\cos x$ b $-6\cos x\sin x$
c $3\sin^2 x\cos x$ d $-6\cos^2 x\sin x$
e $-\frac{1}{2}(\cos x)^{-\frac{1}{2}}\sin x$ f $-8\cos 4x\sin 4x$
g $18\tan 9x\sec^2 9x$ h $1 + \dfrac{\cos x}{2\sqrt{\sin x}}$
i $3(\sin 2x)^{\frac{1}{2}}\cos 2x$

3 a $\sin x + x\cos x$ b $\cos 2x - 2x\sin 2x$
c $x^2\cos x + 2x\sin x$ d $\cos^2 x - \sin^2 x$
e $-\left(\dfrac{x\sin x + \cos x}{x^2}\right)$ f $\dfrac{2x\cos 2x - 2\sin 2x}{x^3}$
g $\dfrac{\sin x - x\cos x}{\sin^2 x}$ h $\dfrac{3x^2\cos x + x^3\sin x}{\cos^2 x}$
i $-\dfrac{1}{\sin^2 x} = -\operatorname{cosec}^2 x$

6 a -6 b 4 c -2 d $\dfrac{\pi}{2} + 1$

9 $y = 2x + 1 - \dfrac{\pi}{2}$

10 a $\pi\cos\pi x$ b $2\pi\sec^2 2\pi x$
c $-\sin(x-\pi)$ d $-\dfrac{\pi}{2}\sin\dfrac{\pi}{2}x$
e $2x\cos x^2$ f $3x^2\sec^2 x^3$
g $2\cos(2x-\pi)$ h $\dfrac{1}{\pi}\cos\dfrac{x}{\pi}$
i $4x\sin(x^2)\cos(x^2)$

11 $0, \sqrt{\dfrac{\pi}{2}}$ 13 $2y + x = \dfrac{3\pi}{2}$

15 $\dfrac{\pi}{3} + \dfrac{\sqrt{3}}{2}$ 16 $-3\sqrt{3}$

18 b -4 19 $\dfrac{\pi\sqrt{3} + 3}{6}$

20 -4

21 $\left(\dfrac{\pi}{4}, \sqrt{2}\right)$ maximum $\left(\dfrac{5\pi}{4}, -\sqrt{2}\right)$ minimum

22 a $(\cos x)^3 - 2(\sin x)^2\cos x$
b 0.62 1.57 2.53

23 a $2y + \sqrt{3} = -x + \dfrac{4\pi}{3}$
b $\left(0, \dfrac{4\pi - 3\sqrt{3}}{6}\right)$

24 a $-\pi$ b $y\pi = x - 1$

Exercise 7G page 162

1 a $-\operatorname{cosec} x\cot x$ b $-\operatorname{cosec}^2 x$
c $2\sec 2x\tan 2x$ d $-3\operatorname{cosec}^2 3x$
e $-4\operatorname{cosec} 4x\cot 4x$ f $-2\operatorname{cosec}^2 x$
g $2\sec(2x+1)\tan(2x+1)$
h $2x + \cos x + \sec x\tan x$

2 a $-2\cot x\operatorname{cosec}^2 x$ b $2\sec^2 x\tan x$
c $\sec x\tan^2 x + \sec^3 x$ d $6\sec^2 3x\tan 3x$
e $\sec x(x\tan x + 1)$
f $2x\cot 2x - 2x^2\operatorname{cosec}^2 2x$
g $\dfrac{\sec x(x\tan x - 1)}{x^2}$
h $\dfrac{2x\cot x + x^2\operatorname{cosec}^2 x}{\cot^2 x}$
i $2\sec x\tan x(1 + \sec x)$

6 $-2\cot x - \operatorname{cosec} x + c$

Exercise 7H page 163

1 a $\dfrac{2}{\sqrt{1-(2x)^2}}$ b $\dfrac{-1}{\sqrt{1-(x+1)^2}}$
c $\dfrac{1}{3\left(1 + \left(\frac{x}{3}\right)^2\right)}$ d $\dfrac{1}{2\sqrt{1 - \left(\frac{x+1}{2}\right)^2}}$
e $\dfrac{2x}{1+x^4}$ f $\dfrac{-1}{x\sqrt{x^2-1}}$
g $\dfrac{-1}{1+x^2}$ h $\dfrac{1}{\sqrt{1-(3-x)^2}}$
i $3x^2\arcsin(x) + \dfrac{x^3}{\sqrt{1-x^2}}$ j $\dfrac{-e^{\arccos(x)}}{\sqrt{1-x^2}}$

Exercise 7I page 165

1 a $\dfrac{1}{x}$ b $\dfrac{1}{x}$ c $\dfrac{2}{x}$
d $1 + \dfrac{1}{x}$ e $5e^x + \dfrac{1}{x}$ f $2e^x + \dfrac{5}{x}$

2 a $\left(\frac{1}{3}, \ln\frac{1}{3}\right)$

3 a $(1, \ln 4 - 3)$

4 b $4x + 12y = 5$

5 $y = 6x - 2$

6 a $5e^x$ b $7e^x$ c $20e^{4x}$
d $\dfrac{1}{x+1}$ e $\dfrac{-4}{e^x}$ f $6e^{3x}(e^{3x}+1)$
g $2e^x + \dfrac{1}{x}$ h $5e^x$ i $\dfrac{-2e^x}{(e^x-1)^2}$

7 e^x

8 a $\dfrac{2}{x}$ b $\dfrac{3}{x}$ c $\dfrac{1}{2x}$
d $-\dfrac{1}{x}$ e $\dfrac{1}{2x}$ f $-\dfrac{1}{3x}$

9 a $2(x+1)$ b $14(2x+1)^6$
c $24(3x-5)^7$ d $45(3x-7)^2$
e $-12(4x+3)^{-4}$ f $-20(5x-2)^{-5}$
g $2(4x+11)^{-\frac{1}{2}}$ h $5(15x-17)^{-\frac{2}{3}}$
i $na(ax+b)^{n-1}$

11 $(1, 1)$

12 $(0, -1)$

13 a $1 + \ln x$ b $x^2e^x + 2xe^x$
c $\cos^2 x - \sin^2 x$ d $e^x\left(\sqrt{x} + \dfrac{1}{2\sqrt{x}}\right)$
e $e^x(\sec^2 x + \tan x)$ f $\cot x - x\operatorname{cosec}^2 x$
g $e^x\operatorname{cosec} x(1 - \cot x)$ h $x^2\sec x(x\tan x + 3)$
i $x^2(3\cos x - x\sin x)$

15 **a** $\dfrac{1 - \ln x}{x^2}$ **b** $\dfrac{e^x}{x^3}(x - 2)$

c $\dfrac{\sec x}{e^x}(\tan x - 1)$ **d** $\sec^2 x$

e $-\operatorname{cosec}^2 x$ **f** $\dfrac{x}{e^x}(2 - x)$

g $\dfrac{x - 1}{2x\sqrt{x}}$ **h** $\dfrac{x^2(3\cos x + x\sin x)}{\cos^2 x}$

i $-\dfrac{(x\operatorname{cosec}^2 x + 2\cot x)}{x^3}$

17 $a = 1, b = -1, c = -1$

18 **a** $2\cos 2x$ **b** $5e^{5x}$

c $\cos x\, e^{\sin x}$ **d** $-2x\sin(x^2)$

e $\sec x \tan x\, e^{\sec x}$

f $-3\operatorname{cosec}\left(3x + \dfrac{\pi}{3}\right)\cot\left(3x + \dfrac{\pi}{3}\right)$

g $-3\operatorname{cosec}^2 3x$ **h** $\dfrac{3x^2}{x^3 + 3}$

i $2\cot 2x$ **j** $-\tan x$

k $3x^2 e^{x^3}$ **l** $\tan x$

m $6x(x^2 + 1)^2$ **n** $3\sin^2 x\cos x$

o $6\tan^2(2x)\sec^2 2x$

19 $-\dfrac{1}{\sqrt{1 - x^2}}$ **20** $\dfrac{1}{2\sqrt{1 - x^2}}$

21 **a** $\dfrac{1}{1 + x^2}$ **b** $\dfrac{1}{3(1 + x^2)}$

c $\dfrac{1}{2x}$ **d** $-\dfrac{1}{x}$

e $\dfrac{e^x}{5}$ **f** $\dfrac{e^{\frac{x}{2}}}{2}$

g $\dfrac{1}{2\sqrt{1 - x^2}}$

22 **a** $\dfrac{1}{2\sqrt{x}}$ **b** $\dfrac{1}{2\sqrt{x}}$

23 **a** $n\mathrm{f}(x)^{n-1}\mathrm{f}'(x)$ **b** $\mathrm{f}'(x)e^{\mathrm{f}(x)}$

c $\mathrm{f}'(x)\cos[\mathrm{f}(x)]$

24 **a** $x = a^p, a = e^q, x = e^r$

c $\log_a x = \dfrac{\log_e x}{\log_e a}$

Review Exercise 7J page 168

1 **a** $12(3x - 1)^3$ **b** $45(3x - 4)^2$

c $-8(4x + 3)^{-3}$ **d** $-15(5x - 1)^{-4}$

e $12(2 - 3x)^{-5}$ **f** $\frac{3}{2}(3x + 1)^{-\frac{1}{2}}$

2 **a** $8x(x^2 + 3)^3$ **b** $-15x^2(2 - x^3)^4$

c $30x(3x^2 + 1)^4$ **d** $4(2x + 1)(x^2 + x)^3$

e $-\dfrac{3}{x^2}\left(1 + \dfrac{1}{x}\right)^2$ **f** $-3\left(x^2 + \dfrac{1}{x}\right)^{-4}\left(2x - \dfrac{1}{x^2}\right)$

3 **a** $(x + 1)^2(4x + 1)$ **b** $5(2x - 3)^3(2x + 1)$

c $(x + 1)^2(x - 1)(5x - 1)$ **d** $4x(3x - 2)(3x - 1)$

4

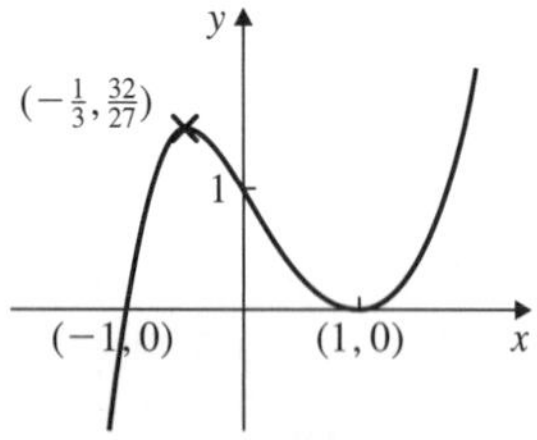

5 **a** $(-3, 0)$ maximum, $\left(\frac{1}{3}, -\frac{500}{27}\right)$ minimum

6 **a** $\dfrac{x^2 + 2x}{(x + 1)^2}$ **b** $\dfrac{-(x + 2)}{2x^2\sqrt{x + 1}}$

c $-\dfrac{1}{(x + 1)^2}$ **d** $\dfrac{e^{3x}}{x^3}(3x - 2)$

e $\dfrac{2x - 6}{x^3}$ **f** $\dfrac{x\cos x - \sin x}{x^2}$

8 **a** e^x **b** $-3e^x$

c $\frac{1}{2}e^x$ **d** $6x^2 - 4e^x$

e $3e^x - \frac{3}{2}x^{-\frac{1}{2}}$ **f** $\frac{1}{6}x^{-\frac{2}{3}} - \frac{1}{4}e^x$

9 **a** $\dfrac{1}{x}$ **b** $\dfrac{4}{x}$ **c** $\dfrac{1}{x}$ **d** $\dfrac{2}{x}$

e $\dfrac{1}{2x}$ **f** $\dfrac{1}{x}$ **g** $-\dfrac{1}{x}$

10 **a** $e^2 - 1$ **b** 1 **c** 0 **d** 9

11 **a** $y = x + 1$ **b** $y = x - 1$

c $y = e^2 + 1 - e^2 x$

12 **a** $ey = 1 + e^2 - x$ **b** $y = \frac{9}{2} + \ln 9 - \frac{3}{2}x$

13 **a** $(0, 1)$ minimum

b $(0, 2)$ minimum

c $(1, -1)$ maximum

d $\left(\frac{1}{2}, \frac{1}{2} + \ln 2\right)$ minimum

e $\left(\frac{1}{8}, \ln\frac{1}{8}\right)$ maximum

14 $A(1, 0)$ $B\left(e, \dfrac{1}{e}\right)$

16 **a** $\cos x$ **b** $-2\sin x$

c $\cos x - \sin x$ **d** $2\cos x + 3\sin x$

e $\sec^2 x + 2x$ **f** $3\cos x - \sec^2 x$

17 **a** $\frac{1}{2}$ **b** -1 **c** 0 **d** $\frac{1}{2}$ **e** 1

18 $y = 2x - \dfrac{\pi}{2}$ **19** $y = x + 2 - \dfrac{\pi}{2}$

20 **a** $3\cos 3x$ **b** $-4\sin 4x$

c $5\sec^2 5x$ **d** $2\sin x\cos x$

e $4\tan^3 x\sec^2 x$ **f** $2\cos\left(2x + \dfrac{\pi}{4}\right)$

g $\dfrac{1}{2}\dfrac{\cos x}{\sqrt{\sin x}}$ **h** $6\sin 3x\cos 3x$

i $-6\cos^2 2x\sin 2x$

21 **a** $2e^{2x}$ **b** $-3e^{-3x}$

c $2x\, e^{x^2}$ **d** $-e^{-x}$

e $\cos x\, e^{\sin x}$ **f** $\dfrac{2x}{x^2 + 1}$

g $\dfrac{3x^2}{x^3 - 2}$ **h** $\dfrac{3x^2 + 2}{x^3 + 2x - 1}$

i $\dfrac{2x}{x^2 + 1} - \dfrac{1}{x - 1}$ **j** $-\left(\dfrac{2x}{x^2 + 3}\right)$

k 1 **l** $\dfrac{1}{2\sqrt{x}}e^{\sqrt{x}}$

23 $\dfrac{e^x\cos x}{(1 + \sin x)} + e^x\ln(1 + \sin x)$

24 **a** $e^x(x + 1)$ **b** $1 + \ln x$

c $e^x\left(\dfrac{1}{x} + \ln x\right)$ **d** $x\cos x + \sin x$

e $-x^2\sin x + 2x\cos x$ **f** $e^x\sec^2 x + e^x\tan x$

25 $\dfrac{2\pi\ell^3\sqrt{3}}{27}$ at $\theta = \tan^{-1}\sqrt{2}$

26 $\left(\dfrac{\pi}{6}, \dfrac{3\sqrt{3}}{16}\right)$ maximum $\left(\dfrac{\pi}{2}, 0\right)$ shoulder

$\left(\dfrac{5\pi}{6}, -\dfrac{3\sqrt{3}}{16}\right)$ minimum

27 a $\sin x\,(2\cos^2 x - \sin^2 x)$

b $\dfrac{2}{2x+5}$

c $2\cos 2x\cos 3x - 3\sin 2x\sin 3x$

d $2x\,e^{x^2+2}$

e $\dfrac{2}{x}\ln x$

f $2x\cos x^2$

28 a $\sec x\tan x$ **b** $-\operatorname{cosec} x\cot x$

c $-\operatorname{cosec}^2 x$

29 $6\sqrt{3}$

30 $(2, 4 - \ln 16)$ minimum

31 a $\dfrac{1}{\sqrt{1-x^2}}$ **b** $\dfrac{1}{3x}$

c e^x **d** $\frac{1}{2}e^x$

32 a $y^2 + 3y^2\ln 2y$ **b** $\dfrac{1}{(4e^2 + 3e^2\ln 2)}$

33 -1 and 3

Examination Exercise 7 page 171

1 a i $5x(x^2+1)^{\frac{3}{2}}$ **ii** 2

b $2, -\frac{1}{2}$

2 i a $3x^2\ln 2x + x^2$

b $3(x + \sin 2x)^2(1 + \cos 2x)$

3 a $2(4x+1)^3\cos 2x + 12\,(4x+1)^2\sin 2x$

b $p = -2$

c $\dfrac{-2x}{(2x^2+3)(3x^2+4)}$

4 a $4x^3\tan 2x + 2x^4\sec^2 2x$

b $\frac{3}{4}$

5 i 0.12 **ii** 1.6

6 i $\ln(2y+3) + \dfrac{2(y+4)}{2y+3}$

ii A: 0.27, B: 0.17

7 28

8 b (5, 7)

9 a $3e^{3x} + \dfrac{1}{x}$

10 a $x^2 + 3x^2\ln x$

b i $y - e^3 = 4e^2(x - e)$

ii $x = \frac{3}{4}e$

11 $y = 12x + 15$

12 a i $2xe^{2x} + e^{2x}$

ii $y - e^2 = 3e^2(x - 1)$

b $k = 6$

13 $27x + 3y - 32 = 0$

14 a $\dfrac{-2}{2e - x}$

b $y = \dfrac{e}{2}x - \dfrac{e^2}{2} + 2$

15 $y - \dfrac{\pi}{4} = -8(x - 2\sqrt{3})$

16 a $\dfrac{2\pi}{9}$ **b** $y = -\frac{1}{3}x$

17 d i $x = 1, 2$

ii $\dfrac{-(2x-2)}{(x^2-2x+2)^2} + \dfrac{1}{x^2}$

iii at $x = 1$, $\dfrac{d^2y}{dx^2} > 0$ $\therefore$ min, and $y = 0$

Exercise 8A page 177

1 b 3.4

2 b 4.0

3 a $-1, -2$ **b** -1.2 **c** 1.4

4 c 1.8 **d** $(-3, -2)$

5 b $a = 9$ **c** 0.9

6 a 5.85, -173, -8030

b (1, 2) **c** 1.52

7 b 0.6, 8.4

Exercise 8B page 180

1 a 2.571 **b** -2.714 **c** 0.143

d 8.602 **e** 2.714 **f** 1.935

2 a $x^3 - 7x + 1 = 0$ **b** $x^3 - 7x + 1 = 0$

c $x^3 - 7x + 1 = 0$ **d** $x^2 - 74 = 0$

e $x^3 - 20 = 0$ **f** $x - \sin x - 1 = 0$

3 a i 0.562 **ii** -7.140 **iii** 0.372

b i $x^2 + 3x - 2 = 0$

ii $x^2 + 7x - 1 = 0$

iii $x^2 + 5x - 2 = 0$

c i $\dfrac{\sqrt{17} - 3}{2}$ **ii** $\dfrac{-7 - \sqrt{53}}{2}$ **iii** $\dfrac{-5 + \sqrt{33}}{2}$

4 a $f(-2) = 2$, $f(-3) = -14$ **c** -2.196

5 c 1.7

6 c 5.82

7 $p = 7.2\%$

8 c 6.61

9 b 0.572 hrs, 201 km/h

Exercise 8C page 184

1 a $3x^2 + 5$ **b** 1.42

2 6.662 **3** 1.378 **4** 2.88

5 2.285 **6** 1.856

7 a (2, 3) **b** 2.807

8 2.646 **9** 4.123 **10** 1.360

11 1.252

Exercise 8D page 187

1 a 21.5 **b** above **c** 21

2 5.83 **3** 58.0

4 a 0.977 **b** 0.994

5 a 0.076 **b** 0.720 **c** 0.785

6 a 3.92 **b** 2.78 **c** 3.39

7 0.937

Review Exercise 8E page 188

2 b 0.629
3 1.78
4 c 2.21
5 −1.67 **6** 0.697 **7** 1.70
8 1.31 **9** 0.821 **10** −1.84
11 1.87 **12** −2.279 **13** −3.080
14 a (2, 3) **b** 2.15 **15** 1.824
16 a 4.5×10^6 **b** 5.3 **c** 0.95

Examination Exercise 8 page 189

1 iii 5.828, 5.557
2 b 0.485, 0.492, 0.489
c 0.49
3 a 3 and 4 **b** 3.24
4 c 2.236, 2.054
5 b 0.80219, 0.80133, 0.80167
6 i $y = 9 - x^2$
ii b $\alpha = 2.156$
7 b 1.41,1.20,1.31
8 iii 1.917 **iv** (3.92, 2.60)
9 b 3.880, 3.918
10 a −1.439, 0.268
b 1.384
11 ii 39.59
12 b 2.219
13 a at a stationary point $f'(x) = 0$
b 0.622
14 i a 4.146
b staircase diagram will always move to upper root
ii b 1.159
15 i $x_2 = -1.5$
16 ii values alternate
17 a $y = 0.6595$ **b** 1.083
18 6.39
19 i 21.4
ii more/narrower strips
20 ii curve is above tops of trapezia
iii $69\frac{1}{3}$
21 i 6.97
ii tops of trapezia are below the curve

Exercise 9A page 198

1 a $y = (x-1)^2,\ x, y \in \mathbb{R},\ y \geqslant 0$
b $y^2 = x^3,\ x, y \in \mathbb{R},\ x \geqslant 0$
c $y = \frac{9}{x},\ x, y \in \mathbb{R},\ x \neq 0,\ y \neq 0$
d $y = x^3 - 4x,\ x, y \in \mathbb{R}$
e $y = x^2 + 2x + 2,\ x, y \in \mathbb{R},\ y \geqslant 1$
f $y^2 = \frac{1}{x},\ x, y \in \mathbb{R},\ x \geqslant 0,\ y \neq 0$
g $y = \frac{18}{x^2} + 1,\ x, y \in \mathbb{R},\ x > 0,\ y > 1$
h $y = \frac{3x^4}{16} + 4,\ x, y \in \mathbb{R},\ x > 0,\ y > 4$
i $y = \frac{x}{2x-1},\ x, y \in \mathbb{R},\ x \neq \frac{1}{2},\ y \neq \frac{1}{2}$
j $y = 3x^2 - 10x + 9,\ x, y \in \mathbb{R},\ y \geqslant \frac{2}{3}$
2 a $y = t^2 + 1$ **b** $y = \sin t$
c $y = \frac{2}{t}$ **d** $y = 9t^3 - t$
3 $y = 2x - 3$
4 a

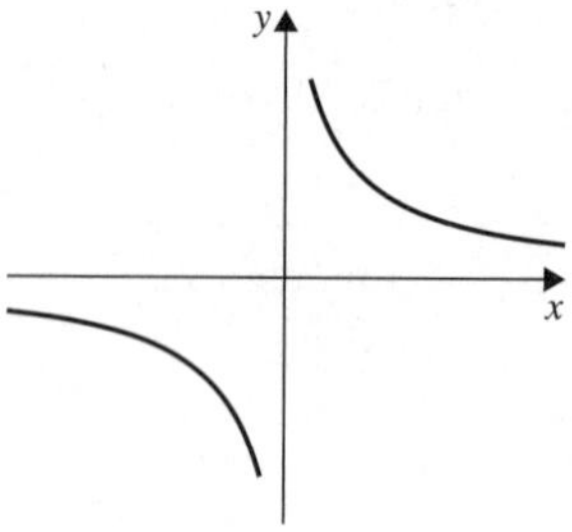

b

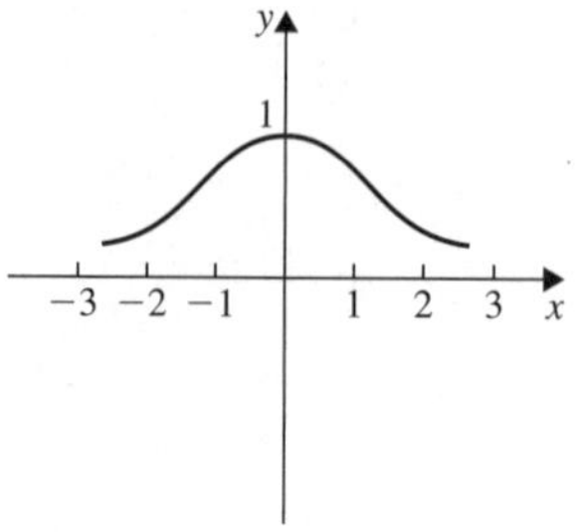

c

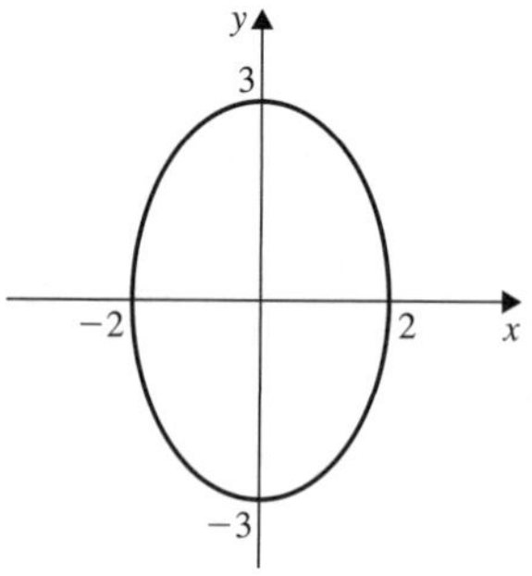

5 a $x^2 + \frac{y^2}{4} = 1$

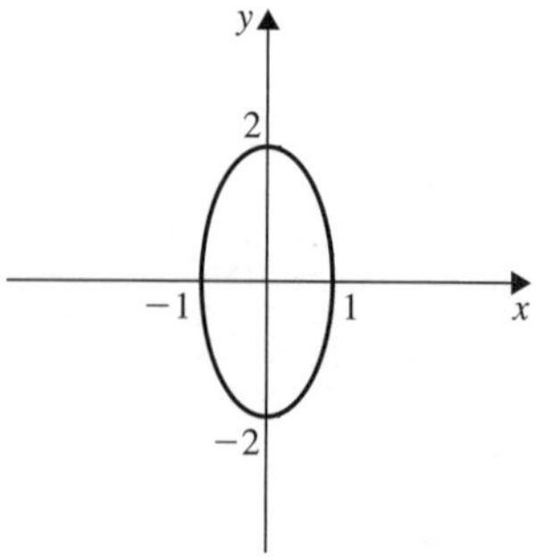

6 a $\frac{x^2}{25} + \frac{y^2}{4} = 1$

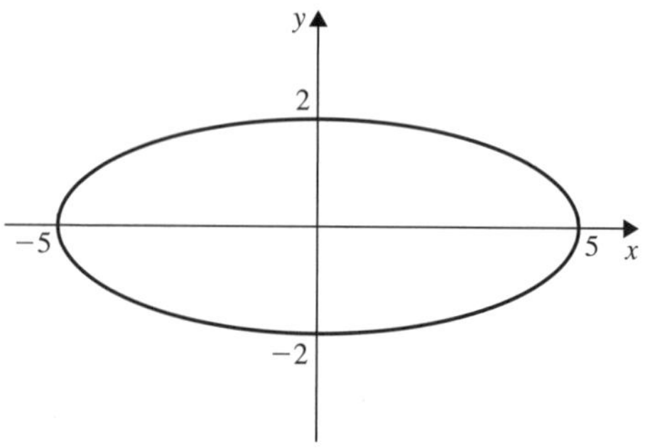

7 a $x + y = 1$

b $0 \leqslant x \leqslant 1, 0 \leqslant y \leqslant 1$

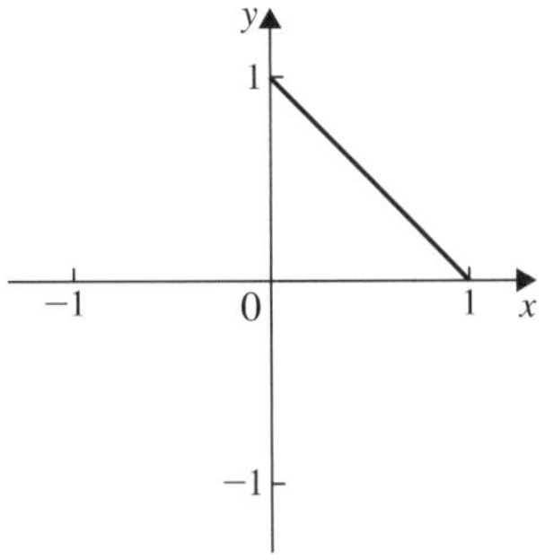

8 $x = 2y^2 - 1$

9 a $y = 1 - 2x^2$

10 $(x + y)(x - y)^2 = 8$

Exercise 9B page 201

1 a $\frac{t}{2}$ **b** $-\frac{3}{2}\tan t$

2 a $\frac{1}{t}$ **b** $-\frac{3}{5t^2}$ **c** $-\frac{4}{7}\cot t$

d $\frac{1}{2\sin t}$ **e** $\frac{e^t + e^{-t}}{e^t}$

3 b $3y = x + 1$

4 a $t = -1$ **b** $\frac{2}{3}$ **c** $2y + 3x = 10$

5 b $y = x$ **c** $16y = -9x + \frac{9}{4}$

6 a $\left(-\frac{20}{9}, -\frac{40}{27}\right), (-3, -9)$ **b** $(-4, -8)$

7 a $\frac{t^2 - 1}{t}$ **b** $(8, -4)$ and $(8, 4)$

8 $(1, 0)$ and $(-1, -4)$

9 $y + x = \sqrt{2}$

11 $4y = 4x + a$

12 $\frac{2y}{\sin\theta} - \frac{x}{\cos\theta} = 3$

13 a $-\frac{\cos 2t}{\sin t}$ **b** $\frac{\pi}{6}, \frac{5\pi}{6}, \frac{3\pi}{2}$

14 $(0, 0), (\pi, 2), (2\pi, 0)$

15 a $(x - 2)^2 + (y - 2)^2 = 9$; circle, centre $(2, 2)$, radius 3

b $x + y = 4 + 3\sqrt{2}$

Exercise 9C page 203

1 a $\frac{26}{3}$ **b** 818.4 **c** $25\ln 3$

2 a $\frac{28}{3}$ **b** 9 **c** 8

3 a $9\ln 4$ **b** 174 **c** $7\frac{1}{2}$ **d** 261.2

4 $A = 3\pi$

Exercise 9D page 205

1 a $(18, 0)$ **b** $(-0.73, 0), (2.73, 0)$

c $(\pm 3, 0)$

2 a $(0, 2)$ **b** $(0, 3)$ **c** $(0, 0.37)$

3 a $(2.2, 0), (0, -4)$ **b** $(-0.33, 0)$

c $(1, 0), (0, -1)$ **d** $(4, 0), (0, -4)$

e $(\pm 2, 0), (0, \pm 4)$ **f** $(\pm 3, 0), (0, \pm 2)$

4 $(4, 16)$

5 $\left(1, \frac{\pm 5\sqrt{3}}{2}\right)$

6 $(1, 4), (6, 9)$

7 $(0.317, 5.32), (-6.32, -1.32)$

9 a $2y + x - 3 = 0$ **b** $(-6, 4.5)$

10 $\left(\frac{729}{32}, -\frac{97}{8}\right)$

Exercise 9E page 208

1 a 120 km **b** 2.5 hrs

c

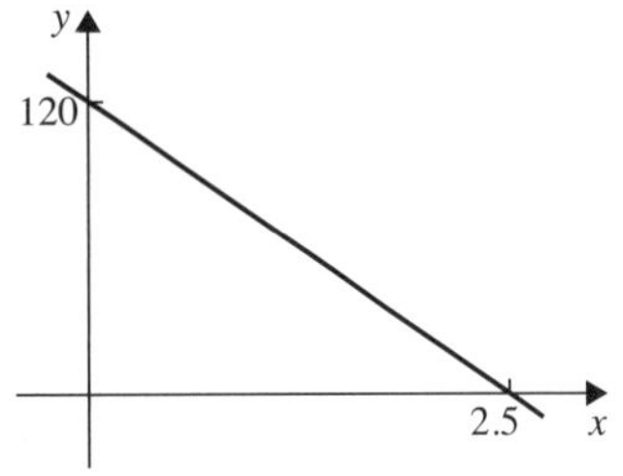

d 48 km/h

e No – constant speed is unlikely throughout the whole journey.

2 a

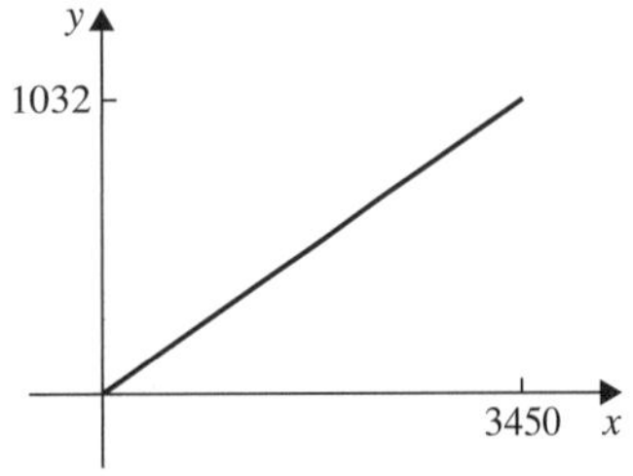

b 59.8 km

c The plane cannot keep climbing indefinitely.

3 a 20 m **b** 2.0 sec **c** 7.07 m

4 a 2.96 sec **b** 12.7 m **c** 10.7 m

5 a $r = 40$ m **b** $(40, 80)$

c $t = 6\pi = 18.8$ mins **d** 0.2 m/s

6 a $(3, -2.5)$ **b** $(0, 2.5)$

c $4\pi = 12.6$ mins

Review Exercise 9F page 210

1 a $y = (x - 1)^2$ **b** $y = \frac{3}{x + 1}$ **c** $xy = 8$

d $y = 1 - x$ **e** $\frac{x^2}{25} + y^2 = 1$ **f** $y = 4x^2 - 2$

3 a

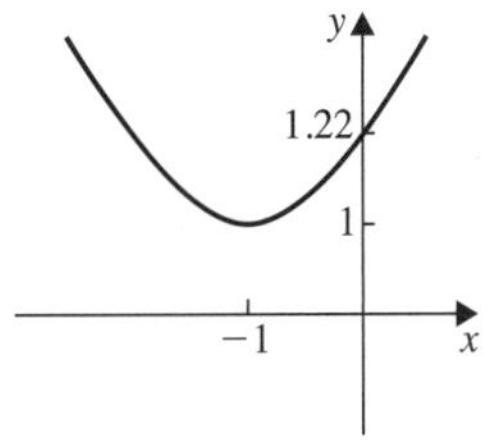

$x, y \in \mathbb{R}, y \geqslant 1$

b

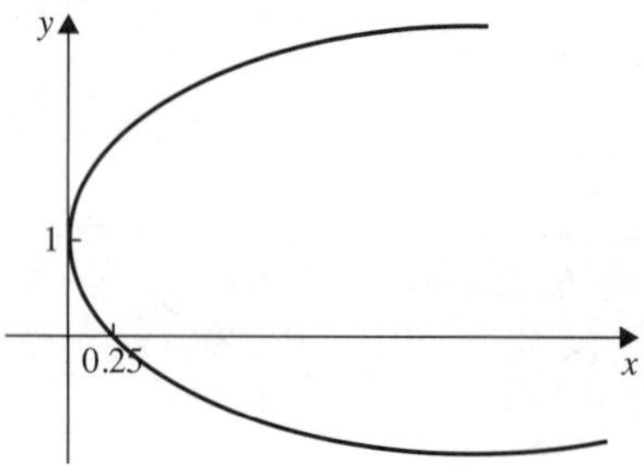

$x, y \in \mathbb{R}, x \geqslant 0$

c

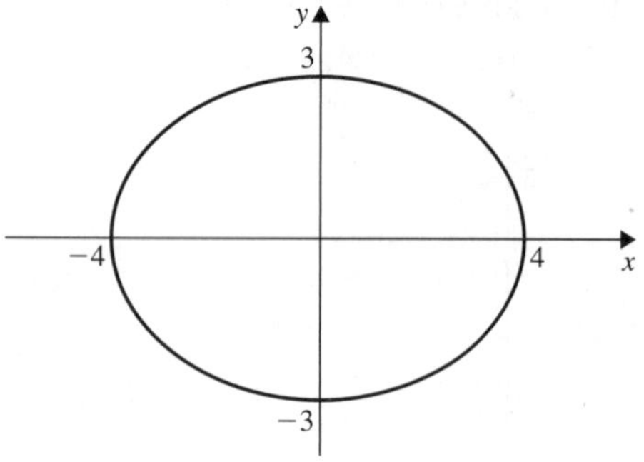

$x, y \in \mathbb{R}, -4 \leqslant x \leqslant 4$
$-3 \leqslant y \leqslant 3$

4 a $\frac{1}{2t}$ **b** $-\tan t$ **c** $\frac{2}{3t}$

5 $(0, -1)$ **6** $(1, -2), (-1, 2)$

7 a $y = -2x - 1$ **b** $y + x = \sqrt{2}$
c $x + y = 2$ **d** $9y = 24\sqrt{3} - 4\sqrt{3}x$
e $2y = 9 - 3x$ **f** $y = x(1 + \sqrt{2}) + 3$

8 $(\sqrt{3}, 1 + \sqrt{3}), (-\sqrt{3}, 1 - \sqrt{3})$

9 $(-3, 8)$

10 a 1500 m **b** 187.5 sec **c** 12.2 km

11 b $\frac{\pi}{4} = 0.79$ sec **c** 2.6 m/s

12 a $(8, -5\sqrt{3})$ **b** $\pi = 3.14$ mins

Examination Exercise 9 page 212

1 b $a = 3, b = 12$

2 ii $\left(\frac{4}{9}, \frac{64}{27}\right)$ **iv** $y^2 = x(4 - x)^2$

3 i $\frac{2}{t} - 2t^2$
ii $(0, 3)$ minimum
iii $y = \frac{2}{x+1} + (x + 1)^2$

4 b $x = 1$ **c** $y = 3 + \frac{1}{8 \ln 2}x$

5 a $\frac{\pi}{3}$ **b** $k = \frac{17}{16}$

6 a $k = -\frac{2}{3}$ **b** $y = 2x - 2$
c $x^2 = 3y\left(1 - \frac{y}{4}\right)$ OR $\frac{x^2}{3} + \frac{(y-2)^2}{4} = 1$

7 i $(0, 0), (1, 0), (2, 0)$
ii $\left(1 + \frac{1}{\sqrt{3}}, \frac{-4}{3\sqrt{3}}\right), \left(1 - \frac{1}{\sqrt{3}}, \frac{4}{3\sqrt{3}}\right)$
iii $y = 2x^3 - 6x^2 + 4x$
iv

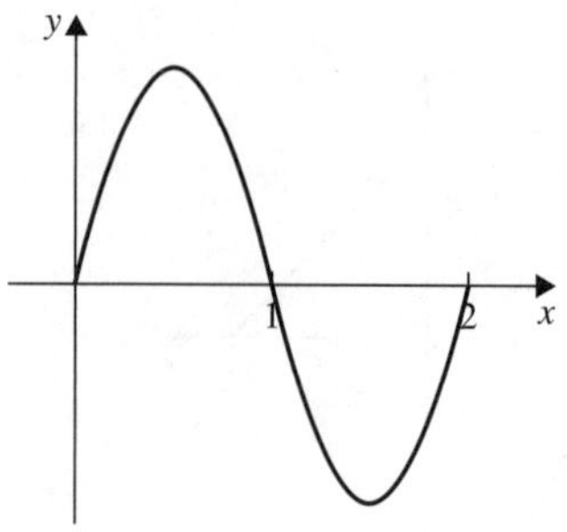

8 i $\left(1, 1\frac{1}{2}\right)$
ii $y = 1 + x - \frac{1}{2}x^2$
iii $-2 \leqslant x \leqslant 2$

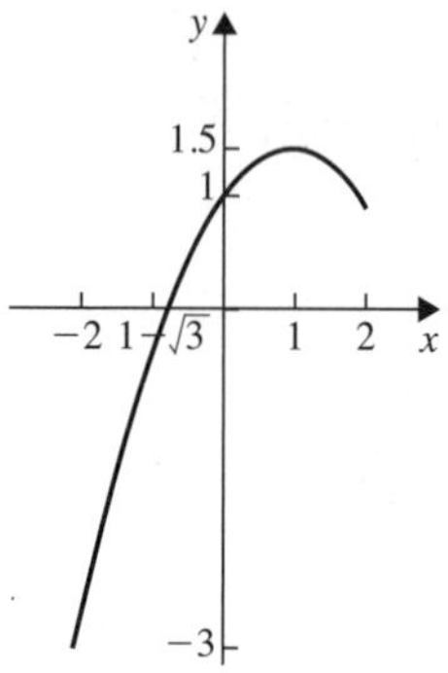

9 a $\frac{1}{2}e^4$ **b** $y = \frac{e}{2\sqrt{1-x}\,(1 - \ln 2\sqrt{1-x})}$

Exercise 10A page 217

1 a A, B positive, C, D, E negative
b B, E positive, A, C negative, D zero
c A, C, D, E positive, B negative

2 a all $x \in \mathbb{R}$ **b** $x \geqslant 1$
c $x \leqslant -\frac{1}{2}, x \geqslant 1$ **d** all $x \in \mathbb{R}$

3 a $x \leqslant -\frac{5}{3}$
b $\frac{-1-\sqrt{3}}{2} \leqslant x \leqslant \frac{-1+\sqrt{3}}{2}$
c $0 \leqslant x \leqslant \frac{\pi}{2}, \frac{3\pi}{2} \leqslant x \leqslant 2\pi$
d $x \leqslant -\frac{3}{2}$

4 a $\frac{2}{3}$ **b** $e^{-\frac{5}{6}}$ **c** $\frac{-5 \pm \sqrt{5}}{2}$

6 a $(1.25, 3.16)$ max
$(4.39, -3.16)$ min
b $(2.82, 0), (5.96, 0)$

Exercise 10B page 219

1 a $-\frac{x}{y}$ **b** $-\frac{y}{x}$ **c** $-\left(\frac{2x+y}{x+2y}\right)$
d $\frac{3-x}{y+4}$ **e** $-\frac{2x}{(6y-4)}$ **f** $\frac{2x}{3y^2}$
g $-\left(\frac{9x^2+4y^2}{8xy+3y^2}\right)$

2 a -3 **b** -1 **c** $-\frac{3}{2}$ **d** 3

3 $x + y = 4$ **4** $y = x$ **5** $x + y = 4$

6 $y = x$ **7** $4y + 3x = 20$ **8** $y = x$

10 a -1 **b** 6 **c** -4 **d** -8

11 b $2, -2$ **c** $(2, 4), (-2, -4)$

12 $(-4, 2), (4, -2)$

13 a $\dfrac{2 - x + y}{3y - x}$ **c** $(5, 3)$

14 $(-7, 7)$

15 a $-\frac{17}{8}$ **b** $\frac{1}{7}$ **c** $-\frac{4}{3}$ **d** $-\frac{2}{5}$ **e** $-\frac{1}{5}$

16 a i $\dfrac{-1}{\sin y}$ **ii** $-\dfrac{1}{\sqrt{1 - x^2}}$ **b** $-\dfrac{1}{\sqrt{1 - x^2}}$

17 a i $\cos^2 y$ **ii** $\dfrac{1}{1 + x^2}$ **b** $\dfrac{1}{1 + x^2}$

18 $x^{x^2}(x + 2x \ln x)$

19 a $\dfrac{1}{x}$ or $\dfrac{1}{e^y}$ **b** $-\dfrac{y}{x}$ **c** $-\dfrac{y^2}{x^2}$

d $\tan x \tan y$ **e** $\dfrac{1}{\cos y - \sin y}$

Exercise 10C page 222

1 a $3^x \ln 3$ **b** $5^{x-1} \ln 5$ **c** $3(4^x) \ln 4$

d $2x(\ln 2)2^{x^2}$ **e** $-\dfrac{2x}{3} e^{-\frac{x^2}{3}}$

2 a $7^t(\ln 7)$ **b** $4^t (\ln 4)$ **c** $-3^{-t} \ln 3$

3 a $-15e^{-\frac{t}{10}}$ **b** $2e^{-2t}$ **c** $6^t (10 \ln 6)$

4 372°C/min

5 a 220 **b** 1.36 g/year

6 a 2000 **b** 12.8 min

c $\dfrac{180}{e}$ (= 66.2°C/min)

7 a 190°C **b** 22.0 min **c** 11.2°C/min

Exercise 10D page 224

1 $0.6\,\text{cm s}^{-1}$ **2** $10\pi\,\text{cm}^2\,\text{s}^{-1}$

3 $0.2\,\text{cm s}^{-1}$

4 a $1.92\,\text{cm}^3\,\text{s}^{-1}$ **b** $0.96\,\text{cm}^2\,\text{s}^{-1}$

5 $300\pi\,\text{cm}^3\,\text{s}^{-1}$ **6** $0.0637\,\text{cm s}^{-1}$

7 $800\pi\,\text{cm}^3\,\text{s}^{-1}$ **8** $225\,\text{cm}^3\,\text{s}^{-1}$

9 $2\,\text{cm s}^{-1}$ **10** $5\,\text{cm s}^{-1}$

11 $\dfrac{4}{\pi}\,\text{cm s}^{-1}$ **12 b** $1500\,\text{cm}^3\,\text{s}^{-1}$

13 $\frac{3}{2}\,\text{units s}^{-1}$ **14** $\dfrac{1}{3\pi}\,\text{cm s}^{-1}$ (≈ 0.106)

15 $\dfrac{2}{\pi}\,\text{cm s}^{-1}$

Review Exercise 10E page 226

1 a $\left(\dfrac{2}{9}, -\dfrac{205}{243}\right)$ **b** $(0.908, 0), (2.48, 0)$

2 a i $x \leqslant -\dfrac{\sqrt{30}}{6}, x \geqslant \dfrac{\sqrt{30}}{6}$

ii $-\dfrac{\sqrt{30}}{6} \leqslant x \leqslant \dfrac{\sqrt{30}}{6}$

b i $x \geqslant -1.6$ **ii** $x \leqslant -1.6$

3 a $\dfrac{1}{2y + 1}$ **b** $-\left(\dfrac{y}{1 + x + 2y}\right)$ **c** $-\dfrac{x}{y}$

4 a $-\dfrac{x}{3y}$ **b** $\dfrac{2 + 8x}{3y^2 - 3}$

c $\dfrac{3x + 2y}{5y - 2x}$ **d** $\dfrac{1 - y^3 - 3x^2y}{1 + 3xy^2 + x^3}$

e $\dfrac{\cos x}{2 \sin y}$ **f** $\dfrac{2xy^2}{1 - 2x^2y}$

5 $\frac{3}{4}$

6 a $-\left(\dfrac{2x + 7y}{7x + 6y}\right)$ **b** $-\dfrac{16}{19}$

7 $7x + 11y - 32 = 0$

8 $16x - 10y - 33 = 0$

9 a $\dfrac{2 - x}{4y - 4}$

b At (2, 2) gradient = 0. At (0, 1) gradient of curve is undefined.

12 b 3

13 a $-\frac{3}{2}$ **b** $-\frac{4}{3}$

14 a $8^x \ln 8$ **b** $(2 \ln 3)3^x$ **c** $(2x \ln 4)4^{x^2}$

d $-12e^{-3x}$ **e** $x^x(1 + \ln x)$

16 0.121°C/min

17 $100\pi\,\text{cm}^3\,\text{s}^{-1}$

18 $216\,\text{cm}^3\,\text{s}^{-1}$

19 $64\pi\,\text{cm}^2\,\text{s}^{-1}$

20 $3\,\text{cm s}^{-1}$

21 $0.25\,\text{cm s}^{-1}$

22 b $\dfrac{45}{2\pi}\,\text{cm s}^{-1}$

23 a $3.08 \times 10^{-7}\,\text{cm s}^{-1}$ **b** $7.4 \times 10^{-6}\,\text{cm}^2\,\text{s}^{-1}$

24 $2\,\text{cm s}^{-1}$

25 $12\,\text{cm s}^{-1}$

Examination Exercise 10 page 228

1 $\dfrac{1 - 2x^2y \cos 2x}{(\sin 2x + 2y)x^2}$

2 $-\frac{3}{8}$

3 a $\frac{1}{4} - \ln 2$ **b** $\frac{11}{8}$

4 $\dfrac{1 - x^{-2}}{2y}$, $(1, \sqrt{2}), (1, -\sqrt{2})$

5 a $-\frac{4}{9}$ **b** $9x - 4y + 13 = 0$

6 a i $\dfrac{-3ye^{3x}}{e^{3x} - 2 \sin 2y}$ **ii** $-\pi$

b $y = \dfrac{\pi}{4} - \dfrac{\ln 2}{\pi}$

7 i $\dfrac{2x - y - 4}{x - 2y + 3}$

ii Denominator is zero ⇒ tangents are parallel to y-axis.

iii $8x - 9y = 48$

8 a $\dfrac{-4xy - 2}{2x^2 + 4 + \pi \sin(\pi y)}$

b $\dfrac{3\pi + 62}{\pi + 22}$

9 ii 0.28 cm/min
10 a 0.0149 cm s^{-1} **b** 1.5 $cm^2 s^{-1}$
11 0.06 m/h
12 1.25 cm s^{-1}
13 i 12.17 **ii** 0.18 m^3/h
14 (10, 2), (−2, 2)

EXERCISE 11A PAGE 233

Integration constants omitted.

1 a $\frac{(1+x)^4}{4}$ **b** $\frac{1}{7}(x+4)^7$
c $\frac{1}{10}(2x+1)^5$ **d** $-\frac{1}{5}(1-x)^5$
e $-\frac{1}{(x+3)}$ **f** $\frac{2}{9}(3x-1)^3$
g $-2(x+1)^{-2}$ **h** $-\frac{1}{5}(5x+3)^{-1}$
i $7e^x$ **j** $\frac{x^2}{2}+5e^x$
k $\frac{1}{5}e^{5x}$ **l** $\frac{e^{6x}}{6}-x$
m $\frac{3}{2}e^{2x}$ **n** $-9e^{-x}$
o $-\frac{4}{e^x}$ **p** $-\frac{1}{e^x}+x^2$

2 a $-\cos x$ **b** $\frac{1}{4}\sin 4x$
c $-\frac{1}{10}\cos 10x$ **e** $\frac{2}{5}\sin 5x$
e $-\frac{1}{12}\cos 6x$ **f** $\frac{1}{2}\sin 2x + x^2$
g $-\frac{1}{4}\cos(4x-1)$ **h** $\frac{x^2}{2}-\sin(x+1)$
i $x^2+\ln x$ **j** $\sin x + 2\ln x$
k $\frac{1}{4}\ln x$ **l** $\ln(x+3)$
m $6\ln(1+x)$ **n** $\frac{1}{3}\ln(3x+2)$
o $\frac{1}{2}e^{2x}+2\ln x$

3 a $6(4x+1)^{\frac{1}{2}}$ **b** $\frac{1}{6}(4x+1)^{\frac{1}{2}}$
4 a $\frac{5}{2}(5x-2)^{-\frac{1}{2}}$ **b** $\frac{2}{5}(5x-2)^{\frac{1}{2}}$
5 a $\frac{1}{8}(6x+1)^{\frac{4}{3}}$ **b** $2(x+2)^{\frac{1}{2}}$
c $\frac{1}{5}(1+2x)^{\frac{5}{2}}$
6 e^2-1
7 a $\frac{1}{3}e^{3x+1}$ **b** $2e^{2x-3}$
c $-\frac{5}{e^x}$ **d** $\frac{1}{8}(2x+1)^4$
e $-\frac{1}{4}(4x-3)^{-1}$ **f** e^x-e^{-x}
g $\frac{1}{3}(2x+1)^{\frac{3}{2}}$ **h** $\frac{1}{2}(4x+5)^{\frac{1}{2}}$
i $\frac{1}{2}e^{2x}+2e^x+x$
8 a $2\ln(2x+7)$ **b** $2x+e^x-e^{-x}$
c $-\frac{2}{3}(3x-2)^{-1}$ **d** $\frac{1}{6}(4x+3)^{\frac{3}{2}}$
e $\frac{1}{4}(8x-1)^{\frac{1}{2}}$ **f** $\frac{1}{8}(6x+5)^{\frac{4}{3}}$
9 $\frac{x^2}{2}+5\ln x-\frac{1}{x}+c$
10 a $x-\frac{4}{x}-4\ln x$ **b** $x+5\ln x-\frac{3}{x}$
c $\frac{1}{2}(e^x+x)$ **d** $x-5\ln x-\frac{6}{x}$
e $\frac{x^2}{2}-25\ln x$ **f** $e^{x+2}-\frac{1}{2}e^{-2x}$
11 a $\frac{\pi}{4}$ **b** $\frac{1}{2}$
12 $\frac{1}{2}$ **13** $\frac{1}{3}(e^3-1)$ **14** $\ln\frac{5}{2}$
15 $-\frac{1}{12}$ **16** $\frac{1}{4}$ **17** $\frac{1}{2}e^3-\frac{1}{2}e^{-1}$
18 $10\ln 2$ **19** $\ln\frac{3}{2}$ **20** $12\frac{2}{3}$
21 $0.0339=\frac{1}{2}(\sin 2^c-\sin 1^c)$ **22** $8+\frac{1}{2}\ln 3$
23 1 **24** $3-\sqrt{3}$ **25** $4\frac{5}{6}$
26 $\frac{1}{2}\ln 5$ **27** $\frac{1}{2}+\frac{3\pi}{4}$ **28** $\frac{7}{12}$
30 a 2, 3 **b** $6\ln\frac{3}{2}-\frac{1}{2}$
31 $4-3\ln 3$
32 b 0, 5 **c** $\frac{1}{6}$
34 a ln 2, ln 6 **b** $16-12\ln 3$

EXERCISE 11B PAGE 236

1 $\ln(x+3)$ **2** $\ln(2x+1)$ **3** $\ln(x^2+5)$
4 $\ln(x^3+2)$ **5** $\frac{1}{4}\ln(4x+1)$ **6** $\frac{1}{7}\ln(7x-1)$
7 $\ln(e^x+3)$ **8** $\frac{1}{2}\ln(x^2+3)$ **9** $\ln(\sin x)$
10 $\ln(x+1)(x-2)$
11 $\ln(2x+1)(5x+2)$
12 $3\ln(2x+1)-\ln(x+1)$
13 $\frac{1}{3}\ln\frac{5}{2}$
14 a $2\ln 4$ **b** $\ln 2$ **c** $6+\ln 2$
d $12-\ln 2$ **e** $\ln 4$ **f** $2\ln 3$
g $\ln\frac{27}{10}$ **h** $-\ln 2$ **i** $10+\ln 3$
j $\ln 30$ **k** $10+3\ln 2$ **l** $4-4\ln 3$
15 $\ln\left(\frac{3}{2}\right)$
16 a −1.10 **b** −0.24 **c** −0.32
17 a $-\ln\cos x$ **b** $\frac{1}{2}\ln\sin 2x$
c $\ln(\tan x)$ **d** $-\ln(\cos x+3)$
e $-\frac{1}{2}\ln\cos 2x$ **f** $\ln(\ln x)$

EXERCISE 11C PAGE 240

1 a $\frac{(x+2)^3(3x-2)}{12}$ **b** $\frac{(x-3)^3(x+1)}{4}$
c $\frac{2}{5}(x+4)^4(x-1)$ **d** $\frac{(x-1)^3}{12}(3x+1)$
e $\frac{2(x+3)^{\frac{3}{2}}}{5}(x-2)$
f $\frac{2(x-2)^{\frac{1}{2}}}{15}(3x^2+8x+32)$
2 a $\frac{(x+1)^4(4x-1)}{20}$, $u=x+1$
b $\frac{(x-1)^6(6x+1)}{42}$, $u=x-1$
c $\frac{(2x+1)^4}{80}(8x-1)$, $u=2x+1$

d $\dfrac{(4x-1)^{\frac{3}{2}}}{60}(6x+1),\ u=4x-1$

e $\frac{2}{75}(5x+1)^{\frac{1}{2}}(5x-2),\ u=5x+1$

f $\dfrac{(3x-2)^5}{54}(3x+4),\ u=3x-2$

3 a $\frac{3}{2}(x^2+1)^4$ b $2(x^3-3)^3$
c $\frac{1}{4}(e^x-1)^4$ d $2(e^x+2)^{\frac{1}{2}}$
e $\frac{1}{3}\sin^3 x$ f $-\frac{1}{4}\cos^4 x$
g $\frac{1}{4}\tan^4 x$ h $\sin^{-1} x$

4 a $\frac{49}{20},\ u=x+1$ b $\frac{23}{30},\ u=x-3$
c $21\frac{11}{15},\ u=x-2$ d $3\frac{1}{3},\ u=2x+1$

5 a $e-\dfrac{1}{e}$ b $2\sqrt{3}-\frac{2}{3}\sqrt{5}$
c $\frac{1}{2}\ln 2$ d $\frac{2}{3}$

7 0.18

Exercise 11D page 243

1 a $\dfrac{x}{3}(1+x)^3-\dfrac{(1+x)^4}{12}$
b $x\sin x+\cos x$

2 a xe^x-e^x b $\dfrac{x}{4}(1+x)^4-\dfrac{(1+x)^5}{20}$
c $-xe^{-x}-e^{-x}$ d $\dfrac{x}{3}e^{3x}-\frac{1}{9}e^{3x}$
e $-x\cos x+\sin x$ f $\dfrac{3x}{2}\sin 2x+\frac{3}{4}\cos 2x$
g $\dfrac{x}{2}(x-1)^4-\frac{1}{10}(x-1)^5$
h $\dfrac{2x}{3}(x+1)^{\frac{3}{2}}-\frac{4}{15}(x+1)^{\frac{5}{2}}$
i $\dfrac{x^2}{2}\ln 2x-\dfrac{x^2}{4}$ j $\dfrac{x^3}{3}\ln x-\dfrac{x^3}{9}$
k $-\dfrac{1}{2x^2}\ln x+\dfrac{1}{4x^2}$ l $e^x(x^2-2x+2)$

3 $1-\dfrac{2}{e}(=0.264)$

4 a $\dfrac{1}{9}-\dfrac{4}{9e^3}$ b $\frac{1}{4}$ c $\frac{17}{6}$
d $71\frac{11}{15}$ e $\dfrac{2e^3}{9}$ f $\pi-2$

5 a $7\frac{1}{10}$

7 a $(1,0),(0,1)$ b $e-2$

8 a $2xe^{x^2}$ b $\dfrac{e^{x^2}}{2}(x^2-1)+c$

9 b $-e^x\cos x+\int e^x\cos x\,dx$
c $\dfrac{e^x}{2}(\sin x+\cos x)$

10 a $\dfrac{1}{34}e^{5x}[-3\cos 3x+5\sin 3x]$
b $\dfrac{e^{ax}}{a^2+b^2}[a\sin bx-b\cos bx]$

Exercise 11E page 245

1 a $\frac{1}{2}x-\frac{1}{4}\sin 2x$ b $\frac{1}{2}x+\frac{1}{4}\sin 2x$
c $\tan x-x$ d $\frac{1}{2}x-\frac{1}{12}\sin 6x$
e $\frac{1}{2}x+\frac{1}{8}\sin 4x$ f $3x+4\cos x-\sin 2x$
g $\frac{5}{2}x+\frac{1}{4}\sin 2x+\tan x$
h $\frac{1}{2}\tan 2x-x$ i $\tan x-2\ln\cos x$

2 a $\dfrac{\pi}{8}-\dfrac{1}{4}$ b $\dfrac{1}{2}+\dfrac{\pi}{4}$ c $\sqrt{3}-\dfrac{\pi}{3}$
d $\dfrac{3\pi}{4}+2$ e $\dfrac{\pi}{12}$

Exercise 11F page 246

1 a $\dfrac{1}{1+x}-\dfrac{1}{1+2x}$
b $\ln(1+x)-\frac{1}{2}\ln(1+2x)$

2 a $\ln(x-1)-\ln(x+1)$
b $2\ln(x+4)-\ln(x+5)$
c $5\ln(x-7)-4\ln(x-2)$

4 0.235

5 a $\dfrac{4}{2x+1}+\dfrac{2}{x+1}+\dfrac{1}{(x+1)^2}$

9 a $(x+1)(x+2)(x+3)$
c $\ln\frac{32}{27}$

Exercise 11G page 249

Section A

1 $\frac{1}{4}(x+2)^4$ 2 $\frac{1}{3}\sin 3x$
3 $4e^x$ 4 $\ln x$
5 $-\dfrac{1}{x}$ 6 $\ln\left(\dfrac{x-1}{x+1}\right)$
7 $x\sin x+\cos x$ 8 $\ln(5x-1)$
9 $\frac{1}{2}\tan 2x$ 10 $\ln(x^2+a)$
11 $\dfrac{(x+4)^3}{12}(3x-4)$ 12 $\dfrac{x}{5}e^{5x}-\dfrac{1}{25}e^{5x}$
13 $\frac{1}{3}\ln\sin 3x$ 14 $\frac{1}{3}e^{3x+2}$
15 $\frac{1}{6}(x^4-1)^{\frac{3}{2}}$ 16 $5\ln(x-7)$
17 $2\ln(x+1)+3\ln(x+2)$
18 $\frac{1}{2}x+\frac{1}{4}\sin 2x$ 19 $\frac{1}{2}x^2\ln x-\frac{1}{4}x^2$
20 $x+\ln x$ 21 $\ln(1+x)$
22 $e^x(x^2-2x+2)$ 23 $\frac{1}{4}\cos(3-4x)$
24 $4\tan x$ 25 $\frac{1}{2}e^{2x}-2x-\frac{1}{2}e^{-2x}$
26 $\dfrac{x^2}{2}+3x+\ln x$ 27 $-\ln\cos x$
28 $\tan x-x$ 29 $\frac{1}{8}(x^2+1)^4$
30 $-\frac{1}{2}x\cos 2x+\frac{1}{4}\sin 2x$
31 a e^{x^3} b $e^{\sin x}$ d $\frac{34}{3}$
32 a $e-1$ b $\frac{1}{2}(e^2-1)$
c $\ln 3$ d $\frac{1}{2}\ln 4$
33 a $2+\ln 3$ b $3+4\ln 2$
c $6\ln 2+27\frac{1}{6}$ d $2e^2+4e-2$

34 $y = \frac{1}{2}\ln x + 3$

35 $y = \frac{1}{3}(5\ln x + 1)$

36 $y = \frac{1}{6}(x^2 + 5 + 2\ln x)$

37 $y = e^x + x - 1$

38 a $\cos 2x = 1 - 2\sin^2 x$ **b** $\frac{\pi}{8} + \frac{1}{4}$

39 b $\sqrt{3} - 1 - \frac{\pi}{12}$

40 $2x\sin x + (2 - x^2)\cos x$

Section B

1 a 2 **b** 0 **c** $\frac{1}{3} - \frac{\sqrt{2}}{6}$

d $\sqrt{3}$ **e** $\frac{e}{2}(e^2 - 1)$ **f** $\frac{1}{3}$

g $44\frac{1}{3}$ **h** $\frac{98}{3}$ **i** 4

2 $\frac{3}{2}\ln(2x + 5)$ **3** e^{x^2}

4 $\ln(4 + \sin x)$ **5** $2\ln x + \ln(x - 3)$

6 $\frac{3}{2}x^2\ln x - \frac{3}{4}x^2$ **7** $\frac{(1 + x)^{11}}{132}(11x - 1)$

8 $x\ln x - x$ **9** $-e^{-3x}$

10 $-2\cos\left(\frac{x}{2}\right)$ **11** $x - 3\ln(x + 3)$

12 $\sin x + \ln\cos x$ **13** $\frac{1}{2}x - \frac{1}{8}\sin 4x$

14 $\frac{2}{15}(5x + 1)^{\frac{3}{2}}$ **15** $2(x - 4)^{\frac{1}{2}}$

16 $2x^3 - \frac{3x^2}{2}$ **17** $e - \frac{1}{e}$

18 $\frac{1}{2}e^4 + \frac{3}{2}e^2 - 2e + 1$ **19** $2 + \frac{1}{e} - \frac{1}{e^3}$

20 38 **21** $64\frac{3}{4}$

22 11005 **23** $\frac{8}{9}$

24 $\frac{2}{9}$ **25** $\frac{4}{5}\ln 4$

26 $\frac{2e^3 + 1}{9}$ **27** -2

28 $2\ln 2 - \frac{3}{4}$ **29** $29.6 = \frac{148}{5}$

30 $2\ln 4$ **31** $\ln 2$

32 b $\frac{8}{3}$ **33** $\frac{1}{2}$

34 b $1 - \frac{\sqrt{3}}{3} - \frac{\pi}{12}$

35 a $-\frac{1}{3}(1 - x^2)^{\frac{3}{2}}$

b $-\frac{x^2}{3}(1 - x^2)^{\frac{3}{2}} - \frac{2}{15}(1 - x^2)^{\frac{5}{2}}$

38 3 **39** $\frac{1}{2}\ln(\sec 2x + \tan 2x)$

Exercise 11H page 253

1 $\ln 8 - \ln 3 = 0.981$ **2** $\frac{9}{4}$

3 0.591 **4** 1.87

5 0.390 **6** 1.93

7 9 **8** 1.15

9 a 2, 3 **b** $\frac{5}{2} + 6\ln\frac{2}{3}$

10 $4 - 3\ln 3$

11 a 0, 5 **b** $\frac{1}{6}u^2$

13 a $\ln 2, \ln 6$ **b** $12\ln 3 - 16$

Exercise 11I page 256

1 a $y = x + \ln x + c$ **b** $y = x^3 - x + c$

c $y = e^x - x + c$ **d** $y = \sin x + c$

e $y = x - 3e^{-x} + c$ **f** $y = \ln(\sin x) + c$

2 a $y = \frac{1}{6}(2x + 1)^3 + \frac{5}{6}$ **b** $y = \frac{2}{3}(x - 1)^{\frac{3}{2}} + \frac{4}{3}$

c $y = \frac{3}{2} - \frac{1}{2}\cos 2x$ **d** $y = \frac{1}{2}\ln(2x - 1) + 1$

Exercise 11J page 259

1 a $\ln y = \frac{x^3}{3} + c$ **b** $y^2 = x^2 + c$

c $y = kx$ **d** $y = x + \ln x + c$

e $y^2 = x^3 + c$ **f** $y^2 = \frac{1}{2}e^{4x} + c$

g $y = -\frac{1}{(e^x + c)}$ **h** $y^2 = 2\sin x + c$

i $y = \ln(1 + x) + c$ **j** $y = e^{2x + c}$

k $y = e^{x^3 + c} - 3$ **l** $\sin y = \ln x + c$

m $y = \ln(2x^2 + c)$ **n** $y = e^{x^2 + c}$

o $y = -\frac{1}{(x + c)}$

2 $y = 4x^2$

3 a $x = 10e^{3t}$ **b** $y = 1000e^{-10t}$

c $x = 15e^t + 5$ **d** $y = 18e^{-t} - 8$

4 a $x = 100e^{5t}$ **b** $y = 1000e^{-2t}$

c $x = x_0 e^{3t}$ **d** $y = y_0 e^{-4t}$

e $x = x_0 e^{kt}$ **f** $y = y_0 e^{-kt}$

5 a $-e^{-y} = \frac{x^2}{2} - 3$ or $y = \ln\left(\frac{2}{6 - x^2}\right)$

b $y = e^{-\cos x}$

c $y = \frac{3e^{x^2} - 5}{2}$

d $y = \sqrt{(1 - \ln 2 - 2\ln\cos x)}$

e $\tan y = 2 - \cos x$

f $y = 2e^{\left(\frac{x^2 - 1}{2}\right)} - 1$

6 a $x = 20 - 15e^{-\frac{t}{10}}$ **b** 4.05

7 $y = \frac{2}{1 + e^{-2x}}$

8 a $\frac{1}{1 + x} - \frac{1}{2 + x}$. **b** $y = \frac{4}{3}\left(\frac{1 + x}{2 + x}\right)$

Exercise 11K page 262

2

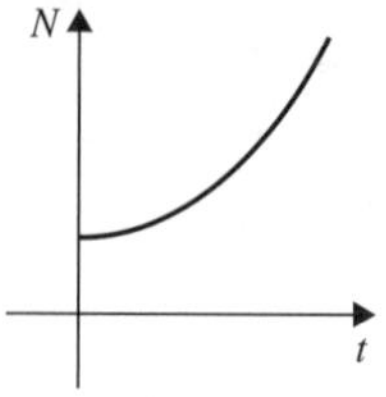

4 $P = 50\,000\,000\, e^{0.00912t}$

5 b 46.1 min **c** $100e^3 \approx 2008$

6 b 12 min **c** 45°C

7 b £7746 **c** 9 years

8 10 hours

9 20 minutes ($c = 2$, $k = \frac{1}{10}$)

10 $V = 300\,e^{-\frac{t}{10}} + 200$ **c** 200 cm^3

Review Exercise 11L page 264

1 a $-\cos x$ **b** $\frac{1}{2}\sin 2x$

c $-4\cos\frac{x}{4}$ **d** $\tan x$

e $\frac{1}{7}e^{7x}$ **f** $-\frac{1}{3}e^{-3x}$

g $\frac{1}{5}\sin(5x+4)$ **h** $\frac{1}{8}(2x+3)^4$

i $-\frac{1}{4}(1+4x)^{-1}$ **j** $\ln x$

k $5\ln x$ **l** $\frac{3}{2}\ln(2x+9)$

m $5\ln(x-7)$ **n** $\sin x - \cos x$

o $\frac{1}{9}(6x-1)^{\frac{3}{2}}$

3 a $\frac{1}{2}-\frac{\sqrt{3}}{4}$ **b** $\ln 2$ **c** 14

4 a $2\ln 2 - 2$ **b** maximum

5 a $2\ln(x+1) + 3\ln(x+2)$

b $4\ln(x+1) + 6\ln(x+2)$

6 a $\ln(x^3+5)$ **b** $\frac{1}{4}\ln(4x^2-7)$

c $\frac{1}{2}\ln(1+e^{2x})$ **d** $-\ln\cos x$

e $\ln f(x)$ **f** $\frac{1}{2}\ln\sin 2x$

7 a $\frac{71}{10}$ **b** $\frac{41}{288}$

c $\frac{19}{108}$ **d** $1-e$

e $18,\ u^2 = 2x-1$ **f** $-\frac{2048}{45},\ u = x-1$

g $e^8-1,\ u = x^3$ **h** $\frac{3}{16},\ u = x^2+1$

8 $\frac{7}{9}$

9 $\frac{46}{15}$

11 a $\frac{x}{2}e^{2x} - \frac{1}{4}e^{2x}$ **b** $\sin x - x\cos x$

c $\frac{3}{2}x^2\ln x - \frac{3}{4}x^2$ **d** $\frac{x^3}{9}(3\ln x - 1)$

12 e^2+1 **13** $\frac{e^4-1}{2}$

15 c $\frac{\pi}{4}$

16 a $\frac{1}{2}x - \frac{1}{4}\sin 2x$ **b** $\tan x - x$

17 a $y = \left[\frac{3}{2}(x+14)\right]^{\frac{2}{3}}$ **b** $y = \sqrt{40x+4}$

c $y = e^{x^2-4}$ **d** $y = 2e^{\frac{1}{2}(x^2-1)} - 1$

e $y = x + \ln x + 2$

f $y = \sqrt{5e^{2\tan x} - 1}$ or $\ln\left(\frac{y^2+1}{5}\right) = 2\tan x$

19 $y = e^{2x^2-2}$

20 c $\frac{1}{10}\ln\left(\frac{3}{2}\right)$ **d** 17.1 hours

21 $\frac{75}{2} - 50\ln 2$

23 a $\sec x$ **b** $\frac{1}{3}\cot 3x$ **c** $x\ln 2x - x$

d $x^2\sin x + 2x\cos x - 2\sin x$

e $\ln(x+2) + \frac{3}{x+2}$

Examination Exercise 11 page 267

2 i $-\frac{1}{24}(4-3x)^8 + c$

ii $-\frac{1}{3}\ln(4-3x) + c$

3 i $4x - 4\ln x - \frac{1}{x} + c$

ii $\frac{3}{16}(4x+1)^{\frac{4}{3}} + c$

4 b $\frac{1}{2}e^2 + 4e - \frac{1}{2}$

5 a $A = 2, B = 3$

b $y = x^2 + 3\ln(2x^2 - x + 2) + 1 - 3\ln 5$

7 $-\frac{1}{2}x^2\cos 2x + \frac{1}{2}x\sin 2x + \frac{1}{4}\cos 2x + c$

8 $\frac{3}{4}e^2 - \frac{3}{4}$

9 a $-\frac{1}{2x^2}\ln x - \frac{1}{4x^2} + c$

b $\frac{3}{16} - \frac{1}{8}\ln 2$

10 a $a = 5, b = 3$

11 $\frac{13}{3}\sqrt{5} - \frac{16}{3}\sqrt{2}$

12 $2(x^2-2)^{\frac{3}{2}} + 16(x^2-2)^{\frac{1}{2}} + c$

13 $-\frac{23}{384}$

14 $\frac{47}{480}$

15 a $A = 1, B = 1, C = -4$

b $-\frac{1}{2}e^{-2y} = -\ln(1-3x) + \ln(1+x) + \frac{4}{1+x} - \frac{9}{2}$

16 $y = \frac{1}{2}\ln(1 - 2\ln|\sec x|)$

17 a $\frac{dx}{dt}$ is the rate of increase of the mass of waste products. M is the initial mass of unburned fuel.

b $x = M(1 - e^{-kt})$

c $x = \frac{2}{3}M$

18 ii $h = \sqrt[3]{\frac{729}{8} - \frac{27t}{400\pi}}$

iii 71 minutes

19 b 161

20 a $\frac{1}{P-2} - \frac{1}{P}$

c 0.473

Exercise 12A page 274

1 a $\sqrt{29}, \frac{1}{\sqrt{29}}(4\mathbf{i} + 3\mathbf{j} + 2\mathbf{k})$

b $\sqrt{178}, \frac{1}{\sqrt{178}}(-5\mathbf{i} + 12\mathbf{j} + 3\mathbf{k})$

c $5\sqrt{26}, \frac{1}{5\sqrt{26}}(7\mathbf{i} - 24\mathbf{j} - 5\mathbf{k})$

2 a $3\mathbf{i} + 4\mathbf{j} - 4\mathbf{k}$ **b** $15\mathbf{i} + 5\mathbf{j} - 3\mathbf{k}$

c $5\mathbf{i} - 6\mathbf{j}$ **d** $-5\mathbf{i} + 6\mathbf{j} + 9\mathbf{k}$

3 a 7 **b** 9 **c** $3\sqrt{5}$ **d** $3\sqrt{3}$

4 a $\frac{1}{3}(2\mathbf{i} + 2\mathbf{j} + \mathbf{k})$ **b** $\frac{1}{6}(4\mathbf{i} - 2\mathbf{j} + 4\mathbf{k})$

c $\frac{1}{7}(3\mathbf{i} + 6\mathbf{j} - 2\mathbf{k})$ **d** $\frac{1}{3}(2\mathbf{i} - \mathbf{j} + 2\mathbf{k})$

5 $a = 5, b = 2$

6 $8\mathbf{i} + 24\mathbf{j} + 12\mathbf{k}$

7 $12\mathbf{i} - 3\mathbf{j} - 24\mathbf{k}$

8 a $\begin{pmatrix}2\\3\\1\end{pmatrix}$ **b** $\begin{pmatrix}1\\-1\\4\end{pmatrix}$ **c** $\begin{pmatrix}0\\2\\1\end{pmatrix}$

d $\begin{pmatrix}-1\\1\\4\end{pmatrix}$ **e** $\begin{pmatrix}0\\2\\0\end{pmatrix}$ **f** $\begin{pmatrix}2\\0\\3\end{pmatrix}$

9 $n = -1$

10 a $3\mathbf{i} + 9\mathbf{j} + 4\mathbf{k}$ **b** $\sqrt{106}$
c $\mathbf{i} + 5\mathbf{j} - 2\mathbf{k}$ **d** $\mathbf{i} + 8\mathbf{j} - 7\mathbf{k}$

11 a $\begin{pmatrix}3\\3\\5\end{pmatrix}$ **b** $\sqrt{43}$ **c** $\begin{pmatrix}-5\\1\\1\end{pmatrix}$

12 a $\begin{pmatrix}-6\\-9\\9\end{pmatrix}$ **b** $\begin{pmatrix}-12\\-13\\-9\end{pmatrix}$ **c** $\begin{pmatrix}-5\\-4\\18\end{pmatrix}$

d 13 **e** $\begin{pmatrix}-0.8\\0\\0.6\end{pmatrix}$

13 a $-2\mathbf{i} - 8\mathbf{j} - 3\mathbf{k}$ **b** $2\mathbf{i} + 8\mathbf{j} + 3\mathbf{k}$

14 a $2\mathbf{i} + 6\mathbf{j}$ **b** $\mathbf{i} + 3\mathbf{j}$
c $2\mathbf{i} + 5\mathbf{j} + \mathbf{k}$

15 a $3\mathbf{i} + 4\mathbf{j} + 4\mathbf{k}$ **b** 13
c (7, 6, 11) **d** (31, 12, 19)
e 2:1

16 a 143° **b** 65.9° **c** 40.2°

17 a (10, 1, 3) **b** 84.5°

Exercise 12B page 278

1 $AB = AC = \sqrt{30}$
2 Right-angle at P
3 $2\overrightarrow{AB} = \overrightarrow{CD}$
4 $\overrightarrow{EF} = \overrightarrow{GH}$ and $\overrightarrow{EG} = \overrightarrow{FH}$
5 $AB = DA = 3$, $BC = CD = \sqrt{14}$
6 $\overrightarrow{AC} = \overrightarrow{BD}$, $\overrightarrow{AB} = \overrightarrow{CD}$, $\overrightarrow{AD} = \overrightarrow{BC} = \sqrt{581}$
7 (12, 2, 1)
8 D(6, 0, 5), Area = 25
9 V = 125, SA = 150

Exercise 12C page 282

1 a $8\mathbf{i} + 3\mathbf{j} + \mathbf{k}$ **b** $3\mathbf{i} + 6\mathbf{j} - 7\mathbf{k}$
c $5\mathbf{i} + 10\mathbf{j} + 20\mathbf{k}$ **d** $4\mathbf{i} + 3\mathbf{j} + 2\mathbf{k}$

2 a $5\mathbf{i}$, 5
b $0.5\mathbf{i} - 3\mathbf{j} - \mathbf{k}, \dfrac{\sqrt{161}}{4}$
c $2\mathbf{i} + \mathbf{j} + \mathbf{k}, \sqrt{6}$
d $0.5\mathbf{i} + 2.5\mathbf{j} + 4\mathbf{k}, \dfrac{3\sqrt{10}}{2}$

3 a $3\mathbf{i} + 2\mathbf{j} + 2\mathbf{k}$ **b** $-2\mathbf{i} - \mathbf{j} + 2\mathbf{k}$
c $\mathbf{i} + 3\mathbf{j} + 1.75\mathbf{k}$ **d** $3\mathbf{i} + 2\mathbf{j} + \mathbf{k}$

4 a $8\mathbf{i} + 3\mathbf{j} + 5\mathbf{k}$ **b** $8\mathbf{i} + 7\mathbf{j} - 4\mathbf{k}$
c $5\mathbf{i} + 7\mathbf{j} + 2\mathbf{k}$ **d** $10\mathbf{i} - 4\mathbf{j} + 17\mathbf{k}$

5 a $4\mathbf{k}$ **b** $30\mathbf{i} - 10\mathbf{j} - 15\mathbf{k}$
c $-4\mathbf{i} + 16\mathbf{j} + 32\mathbf{k}$

6 $4\mathbf{i} - 6\mathbf{j} - \mathbf{k}$
7 $8\mathbf{i} + 2\mathbf{j} - 11\mathbf{k}$
8 a 5 seconds **b** $y = -11, z = 2$
9 $x = -\sqrt{651}$
10 a $13\mathbf{i} + 4\mathbf{k}$ **b** No
11 $-4\mathbf{i} + 2\mathbf{j} - 8\mathbf{k}$
12 $5\sqrt{5}$
13 16.1 km
14 a $2\mathbf{i} + 2\mathbf{j} + 9\mathbf{k}$ **b** $\mathbf{i} + \mathbf{j} + 4.5\mathbf{k}$
c 59.0 m
15 a $a = -3, b = -3, c = 1$
b $0.75\mathbf{i} + 0.75\mathbf{j} - 0.25\mathbf{k}$
c $7.63\,\text{m s}^{-1}$
16 $t = 4\,\text{s}$, $-39\mathbf{i} + 10\mathbf{j} - 6\mathbf{k}$

Review Exercise 12D page 284

1 a $\dfrac{1}{\sqrt{35}}(3\mathbf{i} - \mathbf{j} + 5\mathbf{k})$
b $\dfrac{\sqrt{6}}{18}(-2\mathbf{i} - 7\mathbf{j} + \mathbf{k})$
c $\dfrac{\sqrt{26}}{26}(\mathbf{i} + 4\mathbf{j} - 3\mathbf{k})$

2 $2.5(3\mathbf{i} - 12\mathbf{j} - 4\mathbf{k})$

3 a i $6\mathbf{i} - 4\mathbf{j} - 5\mathbf{k}$ **ii** $\sqrt{77}$
b i $2\mathbf{i} + 6\mathbf{j} + 7\mathbf{k}$ **ii** $\sqrt{89}$
c i $-13\mathbf{i} - 12\mathbf{j} + 4\mathbf{k}$ **ii** $\sqrt{329}$

4 a $\sqrt{34}$ **b** $\sqrt{34} + \sqrt{6} = 8.28$
c 6 **d** $-5\mathbf{i} + 20\mathbf{j} + 5\mathbf{k}$
e $s = 4$

5 a $3\mathbf{i} - 4\mathbf{j} - 8\mathbf{k}$ **b** $1.5\mathbf{i} - 2\mathbf{j} - 4\mathbf{k}$
c $-0.5\mathbf{i} + \mathbf{j} + 2\mathbf{k}$

6 (−0.5, 1.5, 1)
7 a 24.1° **b** 64.8° **c** 150°
8 (10, −9, −16)
9 scalene
10 504
11 a rectangle **b** trapezium
c parallelogram
12 $8(2\mathbf{i} + 3\mathbf{j} - 6\mathbf{k})\,\text{m s}^{-1}$
13 $(2\mathbf{i} - 3\mathbf{j} + \mathbf{k})\,\text{m s}^{-1}$
14 $(13\mathbf{i} + \mathbf{j} + 5\mathbf{k})\,\text{m}$
15 $(\mathbf{i} - \mathbf{j} + 2\mathbf{k})\,\text{m s}^{-2}$
16 $(27\mathbf{i} + 3\mathbf{j} - 15\mathbf{k})\,\text{m s}^{-1}$
17 a $-\mathbf{i} - \frac{10}{3}\mathbf{j}$ **b** 111 m
18 7 seconds, $(10\mathbf{i} - 9\mathbf{j} - 3\mathbf{k})\,\text{m}$

Exercise 13A page 288

1 Assume $\exists\, m, n \in \mathbb{Z}$ s.t. $28m + 21n = 1$.
Then $4m + 3n = \frac{1}{7}$.
But $m, n \in \mathbb{Z} \Rightarrow 4m + 3n \in \mathbb{Z}$, and $\frac{1}{7} \notin \mathbb{Z}$.
This contradicts our assumption that $m, n \in \mathbb{Z}$, and proves that there exist no integers m and n such that $28m + 21n = 1$.

2 a Assume $\exists\, m, n \in \mathbb{Z}$ s.t. $27a + 36b = 1$.
Then $3a + 4b = \frac{1}{9}$.
But $a, b \in \mathbb{Z} \Rightarrow 3a + 4b \in \mathbb{Z}$, and $\frac{1}{9} \notin \mathbb{Z}$.
This contradicts our assumption that $a, b \in \mathbb{Z}$, and proves that there exist no integers a and b such that $27a + 36b = 1$.

b e.g. $x = 7, y = -5$

3 Assume $ab \in \mathbb{Q}$, i.e. $ab = \frac{m}{n}, m, n \in \mathbb{Z}$.

Also, $b = \frac{c}{d}$ as $b \in \mathbb{Q}$.

Then $a\frac{c}{d} = \frac{m}{n}$

$a = \frac{dm}{cn} \Rightarrow a \in \mathbb{Q}$ as $dm, cn \in \mathbb{Z}$.

This contradicts the statement that a is irrational. Therefore the original statement that the product ab is **irrational** must be true.

4 Assume that n is odd, i.e. $n = 2m + 1$.

Then $n^2 = (2m + 1)^2 = 4m^2 + 4m + 1$
$= 2(2m^2 + 2m) + 1$

which is odd.

This contradicts the statement that n^2 is even. Therefore the original statement that if n^2 is even n must also be even must be true.

5 Assume that $\sqrt{2}$ is rational, i.e. $\sqrt{2} = \frac{a}{b}$, $a, b \in \mathbb{Z}$, and that this fraction is written in its simplest terms.

Then $2 = \frac{a^2}{b^2} \Rightarrow 2b^2 = a^2$ i.e. a^2 is even.

If a^2 is even then a must also be even, i.e. $a = 2c, c \in \mathbb{Z}$.

Then $a^2 = 4c^2, 2b^2 = 4c^2, b^2 = 2c^2$ i.e. b^2 is even, and therefore b is also even.

But this contradicts the assumption that $\frac{a}{b}$ was a fraction written in its simplest terms.

Therefore the original statement that $\sqrt{2}$ is irrational is true.

6 Assume there does exist a greatest even number $2n$. Now consider $2n + 2$.

$2n + 2 > 2n$ and also $2n + 2 = 2(n + 1)$ so it is also even. This contradicts our assumption that $2n$ was the greatest even number, and we have therefore proved that there is no greatest even number.

7 Assume that there does exist a greatest odd number $2n + 1$. Now consider $2n + 3$.

$2n + 3 > 2n + 1$ and also $2n + 3 = 2(n + 1) + 1$ so it is also odd. This contradicts our assumption that $2n + 1$ was the greatest odd number, and proves that there is no greatest odd number.

8 Assume that there does exist a greatest rational number $q = \frac{a}{b}, a, b \in \mathbb{Z}$.

Now consider $q + 1 = \frac{a}{b} + 1 = \frac{a + b}{b}$.

$a, b \in \mathbb{Z} \Rightarrow a + b \in \mathbb{Z}$. $\therefore \frac{a + b}{b} \in \mathbb{Q}$ and

$\frac{a + b}{b} > q$. This contradicts the assumption that q was the greatest rational number, and proves that there is no greatest rational number.

9 Assume that there does exist a smallest positive rational number $q = \frac{a}{b}, a + b \in \mathbb{Z}^+$.

Now consider $\frac{a}{b + 1}$. $b \in \mathbb{Z}^+ \Rightarrow b + 1 \in \mathbb{Z}^+$,

so $\frac{a}{b + 1} \in \mathbb{Q}^+$, and $\frac{a}{b + 1} < \frac{a}{b}$.

This contradicts the assumption that q was the smallest positive rational number, and proves that there is no smallest positive rational number.

10 Let a^2 and b^2 be odd, and assume that $a^2 + b^2 = c^2$ for some $c \in \mathbb{Z}$.

Now a^2, b^2 odd $\Rightarrow a, b$ also odd

i.e. $a = 2m + 1$ and $b = 2n + 1$

$a^2 = 4m^2 + 4m + 1$ $b^2 = 4n^2 + 4n + 1$

Then $a^2 + b^2 = 4m^2 + 4m + 1 + 4n^2 + 4n + 1$
$= 2(2m^2 + 2m + 2n^2 + 2n + 1)$
$= c^2$, so c^2 is even.

Now, if c^2 is even then c must also be even, i.e. $c = 2k$ and $c^2 = 4k^2$, so c^2 is in fact a multiple of 4.

But $c^2 = 4m^2 + 4m + 4n^2 + 4n + 2$
$= 4(m^2 + m + n^2 + n) + 2$

which is **not** a multiple of 4.

This contradiction proves that the original statement that the sum of any two odd square numbers cannot itself be a square number must be true.

11 Let $x, y \in \mathbb{Z}^+$. Then $x + y > 0$ and $2\sqrt{xy} > 0$.

Now assume $x + y < 2\sqrt{xy}$. Since both sides of the inequality are positive, we can square each side to get

$$(x + y)^2 < 4xy$$
$$x^2 + 2xy + y^2 < 4xy$$
$$x^2 - 2xy + y^2 < 0$$
$$(x - y)^2 < 0$$

But no square can be negative.

This contradiction shows that $x + y \geqslant 2\sqrt{xy}\ \forall\ x, y \in \mathbb{Z}^+$.

Index